Mastering
Microsoft Office 2003 for Business Professionals

Dr. Wylie Haigh
595-5600
Victoria, B.C.

Mastering™
Microsoft® Office 2003 for Business Professionals

Gini Courter

Annette Marquis

SYBEX®

San Francisco   London

Associate Publisher: Dan Brodnitz

Acquisitions Editor: Ellen L. Dendy

Developmental Editor: Jim Compton

Production Editor: Leslie E.H. Light

Technical Editor: Bill Rodgers

Copyeditor: Linda Stephenson

Compositor: Scott Benoit

Graphic Illustrator: Scott Benoit

Proofreaders: Nancy Riddiough, Laurie O'Connell, Emily Hsuan

Indexer: Lynnzee Elze

Book Designer: Maureen Forys, Happenstance Type-O-Rama

Cover Designer: Design Site

Cover Illustrator/Photographer: Tania Kac, Design Site

Library of Congress Card Number: 2003105192

ISBN: 0-7821-4228-1

Acknowledgments

It CAN BE A bit of a gamble to undertake a large project, knowing the end result depends on the work of so many others. Having worked for eight years now with the wonderful people at Sybex, we no longer see it that way. We continue to be impressed with the skill and dedication of our Sybex team and we are exceedingly fortunate to work with the certainty that they will make sure our final product is no less than great.

Special thanks to Ellen Dendy, our acquisitions editor, who supported us in our desire to focus this book on business users. We wish her well in her new endeavors.

Developmental editor Jim Compton was steady, patient, and, always at the ready to lend a hand when it was needed throughout the erratic course of this project. Production Editor Leslie Light kept us track when no track could even be found. Thanks to you both for hanging in there. We'd also like to thank Pat Coleman and Molly Holzschlag, who stepped in to offer their writing and editing assistance. We couldn't have done it without you! Bill Rogers, our tech editor, reviewed the book for accuracy and made sure we were presenting it like it is. Thanks, Bill, for your input and feedback. Our copy editor, Linda Stephenson, kept our explanations focused and clear.

We also can't say enough about our compositor: Scott Benoit. We write words—he makes them attractive and gets the pages out to the printer on time. We appreciate the incredible job and all the hard work of our entire production team, including the proofreaders and Lynnzee Elze, who created the index.

And finally, we want to thank you, our readers. You are the ones who plow through the pages, try things out, scratch your heads in frustration, and say "Wow" at a moment of discovery. You send us feedback and suggestions. We would not be here without you, and we appreciate your faithfulness and, especially, your diligence.

Contents at a Glance

Contents

Introduction

The Microsoft Office System is the most feature-packed collection of Office products to be released to date. Microsoft Office 2003, the foundation of the Microsoft Office System, has everything you need to produce any kind of print or online document you can conceive. Beyond the traditional word-processing, spreadsheet, and database tools, Office 2003 includes a massive array of collaboration tools, data analysis and reporting tools, and graphic design features that give everyone the ability to create any type of publication and manage any type of data imaginable.

NOTE *In addition to Microsoft Office 2003, the Microsoft Office System includes Microsoft Office Visio 2003, Microsoft Office FrontPage 2003, Microsoft Office OneNote 2003, Microsoft Office InfoPath 2003, Microsoft Office Publisher 2003, and Microsoft Project 2003. The Microsoft Office System also includes XML, Web Services and Visual Studio.Net and complementary server products, Windows Server 2003, SharePoint Portal Server 2003, Microsoft Office Live Communications Server 2003, Microsoft Office Live Meeting, Rights Management Services, and Microsoft Windows Small Business Server 2003. Some of these products are available with specific versions of Microsoft Office and some are sold separately. See Chapter 1 for more about the different editions of Microsoft Office 2003.*

Who This Book Is For

Mastering Microsoft Office 2003 for Business Professionals is specifically written to meet the needs of business people, administrative professionals, and other office staff who work with Office everyday as a means to do their jobs. We need to say at the outset that this book does not cover every feature of Microsoft Office. Instead, we have carefully chosen topics and skills that will help you as a business professional get your work done efficiently and effectively.

We wrote this book for business users who wants to stretch their skills to help them get their jobs done, collaborate with others on a team, manage data, and produce quality documents. We assume that if you are reading this book you have some familiarity with the Office suite or similar applications, so we've kept coverage of the "baby steps" of working in the Windows environment and navigating the Office applications to a minimum.

When we are not writing books, we are training users to put Office to work for them. We train teachers to apply Office in the classroom, administrative professionals to make their employers shine, customer service personnel to help track their interactions with customers, sales managers to take Office on the road with them, and department heads to help run their departments. We have learned that there are a million-and-one ways in which these different types of users need what Office 2003 has to offer. We can't present all of them in the pages that make up this book.

We have chosen to include the features and techniques that we have found to be the most valuable to the widest variety of business people we train. We've included examples and strategies that are taken directly from our work with these good, solid, everyday Office users. To our trainees and, we imagine, to most of the readers of this book, Office 2003 is a tool to help you get your jobs done—it should not be the job itself. We've written this book to help you learn how to use this tool to make your job easier.

Using This Book

This book is designed to serve double duty as both a training manual and an on-the-spot reference. We've presented the topics in a logical sequence based on our experience with training thousands of Office 2003 users.

Throughout the chapters, you'll find sidebars, which are brief, boxed discussions that call your attention to related topics. In general, these sidebars provide additional information about a topic or more detailed explanations of issues presented in the text.

You'll also find Tips, Notes, and Warnings scattered throughout the books to highlight additional useful information. Tips provide you with a shortcut or another way of doing something. Notes give you a little extra information that might help in understanding something. Warnings include the things to watch out for, things that could go wrong, or steps not to take. Warnings are worth heeding!

New! To focus on features introduced or greatly improved in Office 2003, look for the New symbol shown here.

How This Book Is Organized

This book is a collection of ideas. It is not an A–Z guide to working with each of the Microsoft Office 2003 applications. Because we want you to take the tools you need and put them into practice, each chapter focuses on a series of specific tasks—tasks that will help you streamline and organize your work. So let's dig in and see what Mastering Microsoft Office 2003 for Business Users has in store.

What's New and Different?

In Chapter 1, "What's New in Office 2003," you'll get a chance to see many of new and enhanced features in Microsoft Office 2003. From the whole new look for Outlook to the enhanced security features, Office 2003 is filled with new and useful tools. If you want a quick overview to get you started, Chapter 1 will do the trick.

Outlook 2003 wins the prize for the most radical overhaul in this version of Office. Not only does it look different, it is more secure, more powerful, and more functional. Chapter 2, "Digging Out of the E-Mail Avalanche," introduces you the new Outlook interface and gets you moving on the most-used Outlook feature, the Inbox. This chapter focuses on how to manage your e-mail so you can accomplish something in your workday in addition to handing the flood of incoming e-mail messages.

After you get your mail taken care of, it's time to get to your next appointment. Chapter 3, "Taking Control of Your Time and Tasks," makes sure you don't miss an important meeting or a critical deadline; it shows how to schedule meetings with others, use Outlook's new side-by-side calendar feature, and manage recurring tasks.

E-mail and calendars don't mean a thing if you lose track of your important contacts. In Chapter 4, "Unleashing the Power of Outlook Contact Management," you'll enter and organize contacts, add photos of your contacts, and review activities with individual contacts.

Making Visual Impact

Text documents and columns and rows of numbers are just not enough anymore. It seems that unless information is presented with graphics and sound, it's viewed as unimportant. Chapter 5, "Beyond Text: Making an Impression with Multimedia," gives you everything you need to know to add impact to your documents. We'll show you how to incorporate everything from clip art, to digital photos, to your own drawings. You'll learn to create organizational charts and other diagrams and even how to add a music track to your next PowerPoint presentation.

Speaking of PowerPoint, Chapter 6 "Adding Electronic Punch to Your Presentations" and Chapter 7, "Pushing PowerPoint to the Limit," start with the basics and take you through to creating completely custom presentations. Because we still find business users who have never used PowerPoint, we included a step-by-step to creating a presentation. If you are a PowerPoint power user, you may want to skim Chapter 6 and move on to Chapter 7 where we present some of the higher-end features such as custom animation. Power users will be especially interested in PowerPoint's new Package for CD feature.

Collaboration, Communication, and Complex Documents

Collaboration is more than just a buzzword; it's a survival skill in this business environment. With declining resources and increased globalization, businesses that aren't collaborating will not survive the next few years. Learning how to create documents collaboratively is an important new business skill and Office 2003 has a number of tools to help you get there. In Chapter 8, "Collaborating on Documents," you'll learn about tracking revisions and making comments in documents, workbooks, and presentations. You'll also learn how to route documents and send documents for review. Finally, you'll learn how to share your documents online in virtual meetings and in a Windows SharePoint Services site.

After you get your documents into final shape, it's time to distribute them to others. Chapter 9, "Streamlining Mailings and Messaging," focuses on the mail merge features in Office. Whether you are sending e-mail or snail mail, you want to make sure your documents get to the right people at the right addresses. With mail merge, you can sort and filter contact lists from Outlook, Excel, or a variety of other data sources. With the enhanced mail merge features, you can create labels, envelopes, letters, and directories with a few easy steps.

If you are writing a book or a training manual, the everyday tools are just not enough. In Chapter 10, "Taming Complex Publications," you'll create footnotes and endnotes, bookmarks and cross-references, and if you're publishing online documents, you can even insert hyperlinks to help readers navigate through your creation. For really long documents, be sure to check out the section on master documents. You can combine a number of documents to print with consecutive page numbers and consistent headers and footers.

The Web is "where it's at" in the new millennium, and Office 2003 doesn't sell you short. All throughout Office, you'll find ways to make documents web-ready. Chapter 11, "Creating and Modifying Documents for the Web," will show you how to create great-looking web pages in Word and Excel and post PowerPoint presentations to the Web.

If all this talk of collaboration makes you nervous about security, Chapter 12, "Securing and Organizing Documents," should answer all your questions. The new Information Rights Manager gives you total control over individual documents by letting you assign read and change permissions to whomever you choose and keeping out those you don't.

Importing, Exporting, and Working with Numbers and Data

Correctly analyzing numbers and data is essential to any successful business. Chapter 13, "Building Robust and Foolproof Workbooks," is designed for Excel users who want to know the tricks for creating high-quality workbooks. Even if you are an experienced Excel user, you're sure to learn a trick or two in this chapter that will save you time and effort.

If data is more your style, Chapter 14, "Designing and Building Data Sources," will help you discern when you need Access and when your data is better served by leaving it in Excel. Here, you'll learn about Excel's new Create List feature and how to validate your data in both Excel and Access.

If you've ever found yourself opening a document and forgetting to save it under a different name before you make changes to it, you will find Chapter 15, "Creating Templates to Handle Your Repetitive Tasks," a useful addition to your toolbox. Whether it's a form letter or an expense form, with templates you can protect documents that you use over and over again without having to recreate them and without worrying about saving over something you didn't want to lose.

Chapter 16, "Constructing Forms for User Input," takes you through how to create forms in Word, Excel, Outlook, and Access. No matter what application you use, you can create a form that makes it easy for users to enter data and even better yet, assures some consistently in the data they enter. This chapter is essential if you want others to provide you with data.

Goal Seek, Solver, Scenarios, and PivotTables are powerful Excel tools for analyzing and dissecting data that often get ignored because they appear too complicated. Chapter 17, "Dissecting, Importing, and Exporting Data," takes the mystery out of these tools so you can apply them to everyday business problems. You'll also learn how to summarize data with SUMIF and COUNTIF. If your data was created in another application or if you need to send it out in a different format, Excel's importing and exporting features will do the trick for you. This chapter will show you the ins and outs of this business.

Have It Your Way!

Microsoft tries hard to make its applications fit the way you work but some of us are never satisfied. If the default settings just aren't right for you, Chapter 18, "Tweaking Office to Fit the Way You Work," guides you through many of the optional settings you'll want to change to make Office work better for you.

If you still aren't satisfied with an application, perhaps a macro will give you what you need by automating a repetitive task. In Chapter 19, "Using Macros to Do More with Office," will walk you through how to record macros to accomplish a series of tasks at the touch of a button. When you've finished with this chapter, you'll have all kinds of ideas about how to streamline your daily activities.

Isn't it ironic that so many people skipped out on typing class in high school only to find themselves struggling along today with two or three fingers on a keyboard? If you are one of those, the Appendix, "Speech and Handwriting Recognition Tools," may be for you. Although still not perfect, speech and handwriting recognition tools have come a long way. Even if you are a great typist, they are fun to try. You'll learn how to train the speech recognition system and many of the basic commands you need to get going.

Conventions Used in This Book

Throughout this book, you will find references to the Standard and Formatting toolbars. These are the two toolbars most commonly displayed in earlier versions of Office applications, such as the toolbars shown here:

Starting with Office 2000, Microsoft chose to personalize toolbars and menus. By default, you see only one toolbar with the buttons you use most commonly. Menus are collapsed to display only the most recently used commands and, after a pause, uncollapsed to display the commands you haven't used recently. As you work with additional buttons and menu commands, Office adds them to the toolbars and menus, and removes less frequently used buttons and commands.

Buttons displayed on the personalized toolbar still "belong" to either the Standard or Formatting toolbar. In this book, you will see figures and graphics that display the single toolbar option and others that show the traditional two-toolbar display. In either case, the text refers to the native location of the button—that is, the Standard or Formatting toolbar.

We've also included a couple of typographic variations to help you distinguish certain kinds of text: **boldface type** shows any text you would type into Office dialog boxes and `this font` shows file and folder names and any kind of programming instruction, such as URLs, Excel formulas, HTML, or Visual Basic code.

Where to Go from Here

Even when you reach the end of this book, you have not reached the end of learning about Microsoft Office 2003. We highly recommend checking the Microsoft Web site frequently: `www.officeupdate.microsoft.com`. Here you'll find instructional articles, templates, tips, case studies, and a ton of extra material to help you on your way. Like all Microsoft products, Office 2003 will continually evolve. Look in the Office Update and Developers' areas of the Web site for patches, add-ins, graphics, and sample files, as well as the latest news about unique uses for Office 2003 programs.

We'd Love to Hear from You!

We hope this book provides you with the skills you need to master Microsoft Office 2003. We would love to hear what you think. We always enjoy hearing from our readers and are especially interested in hearing about your experiences and accomplishments with Office 2003. You can contact us by writing or e-mailing to:

Gini Courter, Annette Marquis

c/o Sybex, Inc.

1151 Marina Village Parkway

Alameda, CA 94501

E-mail: `authors@triadconsulting.com`

Chapter 1

What's New in Office 2003

IF YOU'VE USED PREVIOUS versions of Office, and your office is upgrading or thinking of upgrading to Office 2003, one of your first concerns is probably, "What's the difference between the newest version and the version I've been using?" The purpose of this chapter is to try to answer that question. We say "try" because the answer depends on which previous version of Office we're talking about.

If you've been using Office 97, you'll find that the differences between it and Office 2003 are major and number in the hundreds. If you've been using Office XP, you'll discover the differences are not extensive and are more on the order of evolutions. Nevertheless, the information in this chapter is intended to point you to areas of change and improvement and give you a running jump as you start to use this latest version of the Office suite of applications.

- ◆ Editions of Office 2003
- ◆ New features that span applications
- ◆ What's new in Word 2003
- ◆ What's new in Excel 2003
- ◆ What's new in PowerPoint 2003
- ◆ What's new in Access 2003
- ◆ What's new in Outlook 2003

Editions of Office 2003

Office 2003 is available in several editions. Which edition you use or purchase depends on your working environment and your business needs.

Professional Edition 2003

This edition of Office 2003 is available in retail stores, can be purchased online, and comes preinstalled on some new computers. It includes the following applications:

- Word 2003
- Excel 2003
- Outlook 2003
- Outlook 2003 with Business Contact Manager
- PowerPoint 2003
- Access 2003
- Publisher 2003

Small Business Edition 2003

This edition of Office 2003 is available in retail stores, can be purchased online, comes preinstalled on some new computers, and is available through volume and academic licensing. It includes all the applications available in the Professional Edition except Access 2003.

NOTE   *For information about licensing, go to* www.microsoft.com/office/preview/choosing/default.asp, *click the Volume-License Editions or Academic-License Editions link, and then click the appropriate Licensing Programs link.*

Professional Enterprise Edition 2003

This edition of Office 2003 is available only through Microsoft volume-licensing programs. It includes all the applications available in the Professional Edition plus InfoPath 2003, the first totally new Office application in a long time. The last was Outlook, introduced in Office 97. You use InfoPath to design and fill out all those forms that have become ubiquitous in today's businesses.

Standard Edition 2003

This edition of Office 2003 is available in retail stores, can be purchased online, and is available through volume-licensing and academic-licensing programs. It includes the following applications:

- Word 2003
- Excel 2003
- Outlook 2003
- PowerPoint 2003

Basic Edition 2003

This edition of Office 2003 is available only as a preinstallation on some new computers. It includes the following applications:

- Word 2003
- Excel 2003
- Outlook 2003

Student and Teacher Edition 2003

This edition of Office 2003 is available only for retail or online purchase. It includes the following applications:

- Word 2003
- Excel 2003
- Outlook 2003
- PowerPoint 2003

Stand-alone Products

In addition, Microsoft makes the following Office 2003 editions available as stand-alone products. In other words, you can purchase the following applications separately:

- Word 2003
- Excel 2003
- Outlook 2003
- PowerPoint 2003
- Access 2003
- FrontPage 2003
- OneNote 2003
- Publisher 2003
- Publisher 2003 with Digital Imaging
- Project Standard 2003
- Project Professional 2003
- Visio Standard 2003
- Visio Professional 2003
- InfoPath 2003
- SharePoint Portal Server 2003

New Features That Span Applications

Many of the new features in Office 2003 are specific to individual applications, and we'll discuss those in detail in the latter sections of this chapter. In this section, let's take a look at new features common to all applications in Office 2003.

New Look and Feel

If you've been using Windows XP, the new colors and the fresh design of the applications in Office 2003 will seem familiar. Not only has Microsoft continued its practice of integrating functionality, it has also integrated the look and the feel, which is evident in a better use of screen space and more efficient ways to move between tasks.

Support for Tablet PCs

Even if you don't own one, you've no doubt seen tablet PCs if you've signed for a UPS package. A tablet PC is a computer that runs Windows XP Tablet PC Edition, and you can write directly on the screen using a tablet pen. You can run Word 2003, PowerPoint 2003, and Excel 2003 on a tablet PC, and if you are using Word 2003 as your e-mail editor, you can run Outlook 2003. Using a tablet pen, you can now compose e-mail messages, make notes on a slide, edit a document, draft slides, and so on—in your own handwriting.

The Research Pane

Often when you are creating or modifying a document, you need to verify information, get additional information, find specific facts, and so on. Nowadays, this is often as simple and quick as connecting to the Internet and your favorite search tool. With Word 2003, Excel 2003, PowerPoint 2003, and Outlook 2003, you can do this research even quicker. Using the new Research Pane, you can access an encyclopedia, a search tool, a dictionary, a thesaurus, a data bank, and on and on without leaving the application.

To display the Research Pane, as shown in Figure 1.1, choose Tools ➤ Research. By default, you can search several thesauruses in several languages and translate between English, French, and Spanish.

FIGURE 1.1

The Research Pane

To add research tools, follow these steps:

1. Click Research Options to open the Research Options dialog box (see Figure 1.2)

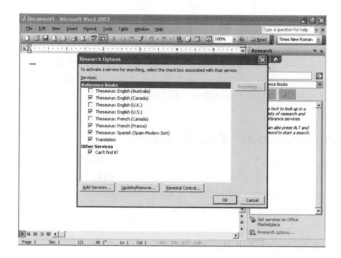

2. Click Add Services to open the Add Services dialog box.

3. In the Address field, enter the URL of the service, and click OK.

4. Click OK again in the Research Options dialog box.

Now, when you want to do research, simply open the Research Pane, enter your criteria in the Search For box, and press Enter.

Windows SharePoint Services

Windows SharePoint Services is a site on which you can create a Document Workspace site and use it to collaborate on documents using Word 2003, Excel 2003, PowerPoint 2003, or Visio 2003. When you open a document locally, the Office application gets updates from the Document Workspace site. You can then decide whether to incorporate those updates. For detailed information about SharePoint Services and how to use it, see Chapter 8, "Collaborating on Documents."

Support for XML

Extracting information from a document that was created for one purpose and using it for another purpose is a necessary task in today's fast-paced business environment. What you are actually doing in this process is separating a document's content from its format. In Word 2003, Excel 2003, and Access 2003, you can do this by saving the document in XML (Extensible Markup Language). Originally developed for the Web, XML is now used for myriad business purposes ranging from page layout applications to messaging systems to business-to-business data exchanges.

Excel 2003, Access 2003, and Word 2003 all contain vast improvements in XML support. However, many of these improvements are available only in Microsoft Office 2003 Professional Edition or the stand-alone version of Word 2003. In the "What's New in Word 2003" section of this chapter, we'll look at how to save Word documents in XML, one of the improvements available in all versions of Word 2003.

Information Rights Management

In Office 2003, Information Rights Management (IRM) is a feature that you can use to protect documents. You can assign levels of access and expiration dates, create permission policies, remove restricted permissions, and so on. For details about how to use this feature to prevent documents of all kinds from falling into unauthorized hands, see Chapter 12, "Securing and Organizing Documents."

What's New in Word 2003

Even if you frequently work in Word all day long, you probably will never use every single feature that Word provides. If you're like most of us, though, you do use certain features repeatedly, and you've even occasionally wished for a feature that wasn't available. Perhaps you'll find it among the new technologies in Word 2003.

Reading Layout View

Increasingly, we get most of our information by reading it on the computer screen—e-mail messages, e-mail attachments, documents of all sorts, web pages, e-books, and so on. A new view in Word 2003 is designed expressly for the purpose of reading on-screen.

Figure 1.3 shows a couple of pages from this book in Reading Layout view. Just above the document window is the Reading Layout toolbar. To view two screens at a time, click the Allow Multiple Pages button. To display a panel of thumbnails of the document screens, click the Thumbnails button.

FIGURE 1.3

A document in
Reading Layout view

The Reading Layout toolbar

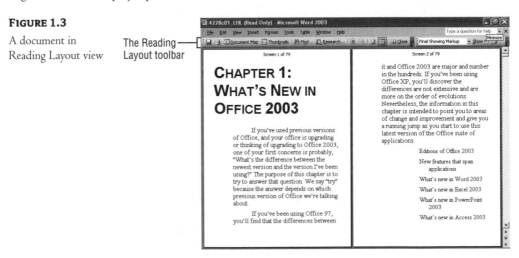

To display an open document in Reading Layout view, you can click the Read button on the Standard toolbar, press Alt+R, or choose View ➢ Reading Layout. The text is displayed in Microsoft ClearType, and you can increase or decrease the font size without changing the font in the original document.

If you want, you can edit a document in Reading Layout view. To track your changes, click the Track Changes button on the Reviewing toolbar.

By default, Word opens a document that you've received as an e-mail attachment in Reading Layout view. If this is not your preference, follow these steps:

1. Choose Tools ➤ Options to open the Options dialog box, and click the General tab.

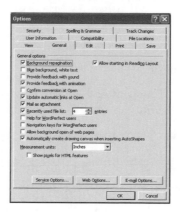

2. Clear the Allow Starting In Reading Layout check box.

3. Click OK.

Compare Documents Side by Side

If your business generates documents that are simultaneously edited, annotated, or changed in any other way by more than one person, it can be useful to display two documents side by side, compare the differences, and edit. You can now do this easily in Word 2003. Follow these steps:

1. Open the documents.

2. Choose Window ➤ Compare Side By Side With. Word display the documents side by side in two separate windows, and displays the Compare Side By Side toolbar:

3. If you want to scroll both documents simultaneously, click the Synchronous Scrolling button. If you want to display the documents in their original positions, click the Reset Window Position button.

4. When you are finished comparing documents, click Close Side By Side on the toolbar.

By default, Track Changes is enabled. Any changes you make in either document are shown in revision marks.

Support for XML

As we mentioned earlier, Office 2003 now has improved support for XML. In this section, we'll look specifically at how to use XML in Word 2003.

When you save a document in XML, you must specify a *schema*. A schema is a set of rules that specifies the type of tags to apply to certain information and defines the structure of the document, such as headings, paragraphs, tables, and so on. In Word, you can save in XML using the Word schema (WordML), or you can attach any other schema. Word then attaches both schemas to the document when you save it as XML.

To save a Word 2003 document in XML, using the WordML schema, simply open the document, choose File ➢ Save As to open the Save As dialog box, choose XML Document from the Save As Type drop-down list box, and click Save.

To save a Word 2003 document in XML, using some other schema, follow these steps:

1. Open the document.

2. Choose Tools ➢ Templates And Add-Ins to open the Templates And Add-Ins dialog box, and click the XML Schema tab:

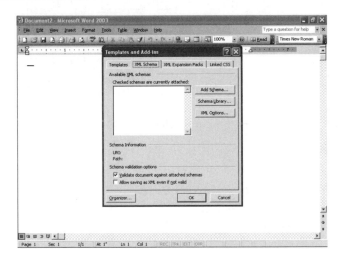

3. Select a schema by clicking either the Add Schema button or the Schema Library button.

4. Click the Validate Document Against Attached Schemas check box if you want Word to validate the document.

5. Click OK.

The XML format is a topic that warrants far more discussion than we have space for here. If you are interested in pursuing the subject of XML in more depth, take a look at *XML Complete* (Sybex, 2001) or visit the XML section of the W3C (World Wide Web Consortium) at www.w3.org/XML.

Enhanced Document Protection

In Chapter 12, you will learn about the many ways that you can now make documents more secure by restricting access, applying passwords, and so on. Here, however, we want to tell you about some new ways that you can protect documents by restricting formatting and allowing only selected editing.

When you restrict formatting, you prevent users of your document from such actions as changing a bulleted list to a numbered list, changing the font, using boldface, and so on. If your business attaches a company style sheet to all documents, you can use this feature to control and enforce the use of these styles.

To restrict formatting, follow these steps:

1. With the document open, choose Tools ➢ Protect Document to open the Protect Document task pane.

2. Click the Limit Formatting To A Selection Of Styles check box, and then click Settings to open the Formatting Restrictions dialog box.

3. In the Checked Styles Are Currently Allowed list, click the check boxes for the styles you want to allow, and clear those that you don't.

4. Click Recommended Minimum if you want to restrict users to only a limited number of recommended choices.

5. If you want Word's AutoFormat features to be retained, click the Allow AutoFormat To Override Formatting Restrictions check box.

6. Click OK.

7. In the Protect Document task pane, click Yes, Start Enforcing Protection to open the Start Enforcing Protection dialog box.

8. To password protect the document, enter a password in the Enter New Password (Optional) text box, and then confirm the password. If you don't want to password protect the document, click Cancel.

9. Click OK.

To specify editing restrictions, follow these steps:

1. With the document open, choose Tools ➢ Protect Document to open the Protect Document task pane.

2. In the Editing Restrictions section, click the Allow Only This Type Of Editing In The Document, and then choose a type from the drop-down list: No Changes (Read Only), Tracked Changes, Comments, Filling In Forms.

3. If you want to apply restrictions to only parts of the document and/or to certain users, select the portion of the document, in the Groups section, click the down-arrow to choose the user(s), click the check box, and then click the down-arrow again to display a submenu. You can then choose from the following:

   ◆ Find Next Region This User Can Edit

   ◆ Show All Regions This User Can Edit

   ◆ Remove All Editing Permissions For This User

4. Click Yes, Start Enforcing Protection.

More International Features

Word 2003 provides better text display in non-English languages, whether you are creating foreign-language documents or using documents in a setting where more than one language is used. In Word's Mail Merge, you'll find improved support for local address formats based on the geographical region of the recipient and a greeting format based on the recipient's gender where gender is required. To work with different languages in your Office programs, you need to first enable the language. You can access the Microsoft Office 2003 Language Settings dialog box by choosing Start ➤ Programs ➤ Microsoft Office ➤ Microsoft Office Tools ➤ Microsoft Office 2003 Language Settings.

What's New in Excel 2003

There were major feature improvements and user interface changes in Excel 2002, so we didn't expect to see many additional enhancements in Excel 2003. We weren't disappointed: Excel 2003 is much like Excel 2002. There are a few new features, though, and at least one—increased functionality for list (database) users—is an incredibly well designed addition.

The Enhanced List Functionality

A new Create List command on the shortcut menu and Data menu quickly turns on the AutoFilter and opens a new List toolbar with additional list commands. The AutoFilter drop-down menus include Sort commands in addition to the familiar filter criteria.

Excel plants a Total Row at the bottom of the list. The Total Row's drop-down arrows create dynamic totals for the list; when the list is filtered, the totals are recalculated to include only the displayed rows. Totals can be hidden and displayed from the new List toolbar. (See Figure 1.4.)

FIGURE 1.4

Excel's new List features work so naturally that you'll wonder why they weren't there in previous versions.

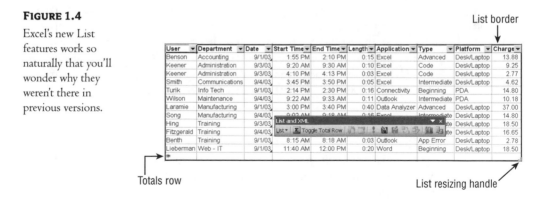

List border

Totals row

List resizing handle

Other toolbar buttons publish the list to a SharePoint Team Services site and fire up the PivotTable Wizard. It's easy to discern Microsoft's goal in designing the list changes in Excel 2003: after defining a section of a worksheet as a list, the user should be able to handle all the common list tasks using a toolbar and the list itself. It was an ambitious goal, and Microsoft pulled it off. For more on the enhanced List feature, see Chapter 14, "Designing and Building Data Sources."

Enhanced Statistical Functions

Aspects of the following statistical functions, including rounding results and precision, have been enhanced:

BINOMDIST	FINV	LOGINV	POISSON	STEYX
CHIINV	FORECAST	LOGNORMDIST	RAND	TINV
CONFIDENCE	GAMMAINV	NEGBINOMDIST	RSQ	TREND
CRITBINOM	GROWTH	NORMDIST	SLOPE	VAR
DSTDEV	HYPGEOMDIST	NORMINV	STDEV	VARA
DSTDEVP	INTERCEPT	NORMSDIST	STDEVA	VARP
DVAR	LINEST	NORMSINV	STDEVP	VARPA
DVARP	LOGEST	PEARSON	STDEVPA	ZTEST

What's New in PowerPoint 2003

If you're in business today, most likely you know about PowerPoint, and you know how to use it. The ability to create and deliver powerful presentation graphics is now an essential computer skill in most corporate environments as well as in educational markets and small-business enterprises. In fact, Power-Point is arguably becoming the worldwide standard for business and technical presentations, including reports to shareholders, marketing plans, promotional schemes, sales projections, meeting guidelines, product specifications, and so on.

As with the other improvements and new features in Office 2003, Microsoft responded to user feed-back by including the following new features in PowerPoint. For information on how to get started with PowerPoint and how to use advanced features in your presentations, see Chapter 6, "Adding Electronic Punch to Your Presentations," and Chapter 7, "Pushing PowerPoint to the Limit."

Package for CD

More often than not, you will create a PowerPoint presentation on one computer and run it from another. For example, you might create a presentation on your home computer and then run it on a computer in the conference room at work. Or you might create a presentation in your office and then run it from your laptop when you're out in the field.

As you probably know if you've used previous versions of PowerPoint, PowerPoint doesn't need to be installed on a computer in order to run a PowerPoint presentation. Thanks to a feature called Pack and Go in previous versions of PowerPoint, you could copy your slides and a viewer to a CD and then run your presentation.

In PowerPoint 2003, Pack and Go has been replaced with Package for CD. Using Package for CD, you can copy slides, supporting files, and linked files to a CD. The updated PowerPoint viewer (see the next section) is also automatically copied to the CD. You can also use Package for CD to create a folder for archiving or for posting to a network.

For details about how to use Package for CD, see Chapter 7.

Updated Viewer

Microsoft says that the most requested new feature in PowerPoint concerned improvements to the viewer. A viewer is a program that displays files in the same way as the program in which the files were created. As mentioned in the previous section, when you use Package for CD to copy a presentation, the viewer is included by default. The updated viewer in PowerPoint runs on any computer that has Windows 98 or later installed and includes the following improvements:

◆ High-fidelity output

◆ Support for graphics, animations, and media

◆ Support for viewing and printing

Improved Media Support

In PowerPoint 2003, you can display a movie in full-screen view. To do so, follow these steps:

1. Right-click the movie, and choose Edit Movie Objects from the shortcut menu to open the Movie Options dialog box.

2. In the Display Options section, click the Zoom To Full Screen check box.

3. Click OK.

Support for Smart Tags

Smart tags first appeared in Office XP in Word, Excel, and Internet Explorer. Microsoft promised to make them more widely available, and you can now use smart tags in PowerPoint 2003.

Using smart tags, you can take actions in PowerPoint that you would typically need to open another application to perform. Text that is underlined with purple dots is a smart tag. Point to the underlined text to display the Smart Tag Actions button (a lowercase *i* in a circle). Click this button to see a list of actions. For example, if a person's name is a smart tag, clicking the Smart Tag Actions button lets you add that person to your Address Book, schedule a meeting with that person, and so on.

To insert smart tags in a presentation, follow these steps:

1. Choose Tools ➤ AutoCorrect Options to open the AutoCorrect dialog box.

2. Click the Smart Tags tab.

3. Click the Label Text With Smart Tags check box, and then choose the type of text you want recognized as a smart tag: a date, a financial symbol, or a person's name.

4. Click OK.

Now when the smart tag finds text that matches the recognizer, it underlines the text with purple dots and enables the associated actions.

The Slide Show Toolbar

When displaying a presentation in Slide Show view, you will notice a new, really subtle toolbar when you point to the lower-left of the screen. This toolbar contains navigation options you can use when running a presentation. The advantages to this new feature of PowerPoint are twofold: it's unobtrusive, and it's handy.

Unless you point to it, this toolbar is not displayed. And even when it is displayed, it's just barely discernible. Consequently, the attention of your audience is drawn to your graphics, not to your slide show tools.

The Slide Show toolbar, not shown here because the effects are too dim to display properly on the printed page, contains the usual Previous and Next buttons as well as two buttons that display menu commands for common tasks. Click the pointer arrow to select a type of pen, the ink color, the highlighter and arrow options, and to erase. Click the slide navigator to navigate between the slides in your presentation.

Save Slide Show Ink Annotations

In some situations, it's useful to be able to add handwritten annotations to your slides while you are presenting them. To do so, select a pen and then use it to add your notes. When you end the presentation, PowerPoint will ask if you want to keep your annotations. If you click Keep, your handwritten annotations are saved along with your slide show.

What's New in Access 2003

Developments in Access 2003 help you create stronger and more robust databases. In this version, you'll find considerable focus on foreseeing and addressing errors, enhancing security, and exchanging data with other sources. Many of the enhancements are designed for high-end users but even database dabblers can find something to help them in their work.

View Dependencies between Objects

Cleaning up a database is an important step in a comprehensive design project. It's inevitable that you'll have database objects, tables, queries, forms, and reports that were created as part of the design process and that are no longer needed in the database. As the database is used, additional objects might be created that will outlive their usefulness. The problem has always been in figuring out whether an object is actually being used somewhere in the database. In Access 2003, that problem has been solved. You can now view relationships between objects to see if an object can be deleted without causing a problem in the database. Figure 1.5 displays the Object Dependencies task pane for the Products table in the North-wind sample database.

NOTE *To access the Northwind sample database in Access, choose Help ➤ Sample Databases ➤ Northwind Sample Database.*

FIGURE 1.5

The Object Dependencies task pane helps you determine how an object is used and whether it can be safely deleted.

To open the Object Dependencies task pane, right-click any table, query, form, or report in the database window and choose Object Dependencies from the shortcut menu.

Automatic Error Checking in User-Interface Objects

When you are creating an Access form or report, it doesn't take much to make a simple error that could result in an afternoon of frustration until you find the problem. In Access 2003, common errors are picked up automatically, and Access gives you information about how to fix them. Automatic error checking is turned on by default. (Of course, you can turn it off if you'd rather go it alone.) Let's say you inadvertently edit a field's text box rather than its label, which destroys the relationship to the field. Error checking immediately identifies the problem and marks the text box with a green error indicator in the top-left corner of the control. To find out what the problem is, select the control. When the Error Checking Options button appears, click the arrow in the button to open a menu, such as the one shown in Figure 1.6. This menu tells you what the problem is—in this case, Invalid Control Property: Control Source—No Such Field In The Field List—gives you options for correcting it and offers additional help. If you are satisfied that the error was intentional, you can also choose to ignore the error.

FIGURE 1.6
The Error Checking menu describes the problem and shows you some possible solutions.

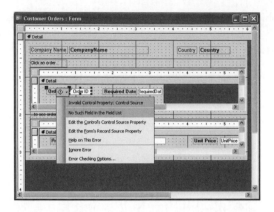

To reset Error Checking Options or to turn the option off completely, choose Error Checking Options from the menu to open the Error Checking Options dialog box.

You can also access these options by choosing Tools ➤ Options and clicking the Error Checking tab of the Options dialog box.

Property Propagation of Table and Query Field Properties

One of the more common problems in working with Access database design is the amount of rework you have to do if you change the properties of a field in a table. Say, for example, you create a database and the accompanying forms and reports that you distribute to several users to test. One of the first complaints is that the unit price fields are not displayed as currency. To fix this, you open each form and each report and change the format of every occurrence of the unit price field. Or, so as not to run into this problem in the future, you open the table that contains the unit price field, change the field's format, and then reinsert the revised field into all the dependent forms and reports. If this experience sounds familiar, you will appreciate Access 2003's ability to propagate changes in field properties to bound controls in forms and reports. Although you still can't propagate changes to field names or field types, you can change a field's description or any of the inherited properties on the General and Lookup tabs and then instruct Access to copy those changes to other objects that use them.

To use the propagation feature, follow these steps:

1. Open a table in Design view.

2. Click to select the field you want to change.

3. Revise the description or change any of the properties on the General or Lookup tabs. If the property you changed is inherited by forms and reports, the Update Options button appears next to the property.

4. Click the Update Options button to access the options.

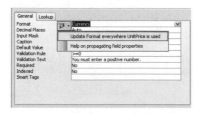

5. Choose the Update option on the menu to open the Update Properties dialog box.

6. Select which objects you would like to update, or, with them all selected, click Yes to update them all. If you change your mind or decide not to update any of them, click No To All or Cancel.

If you would like to know more about inherited properties, click the Update Options button and choose Help On Propagating Field Properties.

Smart Tag Support

Now in Access 2003, support for smart tags will help you add even more power to your databases. You can add smart tags to form controls to allow users easy access to additional actions related to data in a field. For example, in a company name field, a smart tag could let the user check stock information about the company; in a city field, users could check local news or weather information or even make travel arrangements to visit a client. Some predesigned smart tags are available in Access. Other smart tags can be obtained from www.Office.Microsoft.com or from third-party vendors. To add smart tags to a form control, follow these steps:

1. Open a form in Design view.

2. Right-click the control to which you want to add a smart tag and choose Properties to open the Properties dialog box.

3. On the Data tab, click the Smart Tag text box and then click the ellipsis button that opens to the right of the text box.

4. Select the smart tag you want to add and click OK.

That's all there is to it. When you switch the form to Form view, you can distinguish the fields with smart tags by the triangle indicator in the bottom-right corner of the text box. Click the field and then click the Smart Tag Actions button to see the available actions. Figure 1.7 shows an example of a date smart tag.

FIGURE 1.7

Smart tag actions are available by clicking the Smart Tag Actions button on the field.

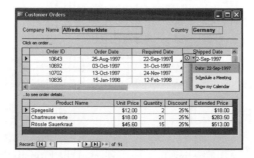

Windows SharePoint Services

Windows SharePoint Services is an exciting new collaboration tool first introduced in Office XP. It's a flexible, customizable website-creation tool designed specifically for use by teams. One of its strengths is the ability to publish lists of data that multiple users need to access. These could be inventory, contacts, products, or any other imaginable lists. In Office 2003, you can import and export lists contained in Access tables and even create dynamic links from SharePoint to a table or query in an Access database. If you'd like to know more about how to use Access with SharePoint, refer to Chapter 8.

Macro Security

Macros have been the carriers for numerous malicious viruses in recent years. Before running a macro in a database, it's important that you are confident the macro is virus-free. In Access 2003, you can set security levels so you are prompted each time you open a database that contains VBA code. You can also block databases that are from untrusted sources. To set security levels in Access, choose Tools ➤ Macro ➤ Security.

If you set the security level to Medium or High, Access 2003 requires your computer to be configured to block unsafe expressions from Microsoft Jet, the database engine that runs Access. After you close the Security dialog box, you are prompted to block unsafe expressions. Click Yes for Access to install the expression blocker. You must then restart Access.

If you are creating databases that contain macro projects, you can sign the projects with a digital certificate. This assures users that the macros are from a trusted source and that they have not been altered in any way. To find out more about digital certificates, see Chapter 12.

Context-Based Help to Make SQL Easier

If you are designing complex queries, a little knowledge of SQL (Structured Query Language) can go a long way in helping you debug a problem or add complicated conditions. Up until now, finding help took a little work. Not anymore. With Access 2003, you can press F1 on any SQL expression in SQL view of a query and get context-sensitive help, as shown in Figure 1.8.

FIGURE 1.8

F1 displays context-sensitive help for any SQL expression.

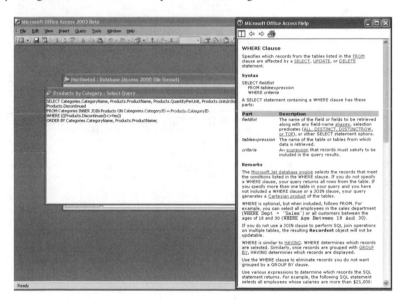

This not only makes it easier for the experienced programmer to get help, but it's a great way to develop your SQL skills.

What's New In Outlook 2003

Outlook 2003 is the Office 2003 application with the most-significant enhancements. Outlook is a personal information manager that has all but replaced those organizer notebooks that were so ubiquitous in office environments a few years ago. It is a scheduler, an address book, a contact manager, a calendar, a task manager, and more.

In this section, we'll briefly describe the new features. See Chapters 2, 3, and 4 for details.

The Navigation and Reading Panes

If you've used previous versions of Outlook, you may be among those users who complained about the organization (or lack thereof) of the Outlook window. In Outlook 2003, you'll find a cleaner and more accessible interface, shown in Figure 1.9. The Outlook bar has been combined with the folder list into the new Navigation Pane. The Navigation Pane takes a little getting used to but in the long run streamlines access to Outlook's folders and views. The Preview pane has morphed into the Reading Pane. The Reading Pane greatly reduces eyestrain while displaying more of each message without having to scroll so much.

FIGURE 1.9

The newly designed Outlook interface

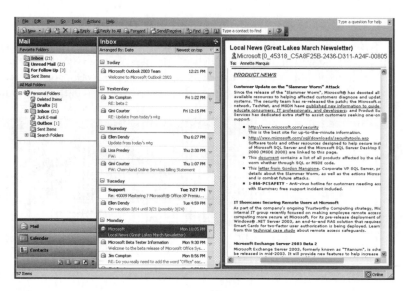

The Go Menu

In the Outlook menu bar, you'll find a new menu—Go. You use the items on this menu or their associated shortcut keys to switch panes in the Navigation Pane.

The Junk E-mail Filter

Although most of us can no longer get along without access to e-mail, we could get along nicely without junk e-mail. The new Junk E-mail Filter in Outlook 2003 won't prevent the activities of determined junk e-mailers, but it will help you deal with these messages.

This filter does not block certain types of messages or messages from particular senders; it does analyze messages in terms of content and time sent and send them directly to a Junk E-mail folder. You can then dispose of them in whatever manner you choose. By default, the filter will identify the most obvious junk. To specify other ways of dealing with junk e-mail, you use the Junk E-mail Options dialog box. For details, see Chapter 2.

Search Folders

Outlook's new Search folders feature is a valuable addition to Outlook's organizational tools. With Search folders, you can set up *virtual folders* that pull messages together that meet certain criteria. Outlook 2003 comes with several default Search folders: Unread Mail, For Follow-Up, and Large Messages. You can create Search folders to display all messages from a particular client, messages from a specific time period, or any other filter criteria of your choosing. You can access Search folders from the Navigation Pane below the Sent Items folder. For more information about Search folders, see Chapter 2.

Open Multiple Calendars Side by Side

Outlook 2003 makes it easy to work with shared calendars. Any calendars you have access to open automatically when you launch Outlook. In addition, calendars of all types are available for side-by-side viewing. You can also view additional calendars that you create and calendars in public folders using the Side-By-Side Calendar view. Figure 1.10 shows two personal calendars and one shared calendar side by side. For details about side-by-side view, see Chapter 3.

FIGURE 1.10

Calendars in side-by-side view

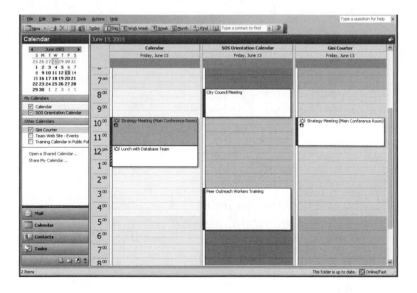

Message Arrangements

A handy way to organize lots of message is to arrange them in groupings. Outlook 2003 comes with 13 preset groupings, called *arrangements:*

Attachments Arranges messages, by received date, into a group that has attachments and a group that has no attachments.

Categories Arranges messages, by received date, into categories.

Conversation Arranges messages by thread (subject matter) and then sorts them according to who replied to whom and when. Particularly helpful when you have many back-and-forths about a particular topic.

Date Arranges messages in chronological order, starting with the most recent. This is the default arrangement.

E-mail Accounts Arranges messages, by received date, into your various e-mail accounts if you have more than one account.

Flag Arranges messages according to the colors of their flags. Any messages not flagged are sorted into a separate group.

Folder Arranges messages, by received date, alphabetically, by folder names.

From Arranges messages, by received date, by names on the From line.

Importance Arranges message, by received date, according to their importance: High, Normal, Low.

Size Arranges messages into the following categories according to size:

- Enormous (more than 5MB)
- Huge (1–5MB)
- Very large (500KB–1MB)
- Large (100–500KB)
- Medium (25–100KB)
- Small (10–25KB)
- Tiny (less than 10KB)

Subject Arranges messages, by received date, alphabetically, by what's in the Subject line.

To Arranges messages, by received date, alphabetically, by the name in the To line.

Type Arranges messages, by received date, according to their type—e-mail messages, meeting requests, task requests, and so on.

Arrangements are available only in Table view. To select an arrangement, click the Arranged By heading, and choose an arrangement.

Quick Flags

When you receive a lot of e-mail, it can be a challenge to separate the information-only messages from the ones that require follow-up. With Outlook 2003, you can quickly assign a flag to any message in the Inbox. For details about how to assign flags, see Chapter 2.

Desktop Alerts

Outlook 2003 includes a new notification option called Desktop Alerts. Desktop Alerts are semi-transparent boxes that appear in the bottom right of your screen notifying you that you have a new message. The Desktop Alert includes the time and date of the message, the name of the sender, and the subject. For more information about Desktop Alerts, see Chapter 2.

The Select Names Dialog Box

When sending an e-mail message, the most direct way to access your address books is to click the To button in the Message window and open the Select Names dialog box (see Figure 1.11). In Outlook 2003, the Select Names dialog box has been redesigned so that more address information is visible without scrolling. If you still have trouble seeing everything, you can resize the dialog box by dragging the border—one of those simple improvements that makes such a difference. You can now more easily distinguish e-mail addresses and fax numbers for a contact.

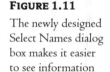

FIGURE 1.11

The newly designed Select Names dialog box makes it easier to see information related to an address.

The Contacts Form Supports Image Files

To us, associating a face with a name is always helpful as we communicate in today's electronic business environment. In Outlook 2003, you can add a digital photo to the information you collect for contacts. To add a picture, open the Contact window (see Figure 1.12), click the Add Contact Picture button, locate and select the photo, and click OK.

FIGURE 1.12

Adding a photo to a contact's information

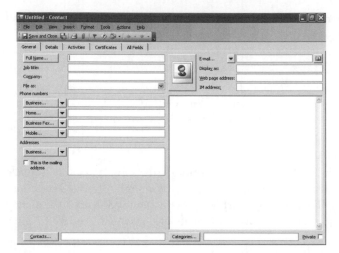

Exchange Enhancements

If you are running Outlook and have an e-mail account on an Exchange server, Microsoft recommends that you use Cached Exchange Mode. In Cached Exchange Mode, you have a copy of your mailbox on your computer that is frequently synchronized with the Exchange server. With this configuration, you can continue to work when your connection to the server is down. Outlook automatically reconnects when the server is back online.

In addition, you can now access your Exchange server remotely through the Internet without using VPN (virtual private network), smart cards, or security tokens. For more information about this and about using Cached Exchange Mode, see the administrator of your Exchange server.

As you may know, writing a book about a new version of any software is a work in progress even after the books are printed and distributed. In this chapter, we've attempted to alert you to the new features in Office 2003, but as you work with the Office applications, you may indeed run across additional enhancements.

Chapter 2

Digging Out of the E-Mail Avalanche

E-MAIL HAS BECOME A way of life for most businesses today and yet many people view e-mail as a curse rather than a blessing. Coping with the volume of mail received, putting up with spam, protecting against viruses, and keeping mail organized are just a few of the additions to the business professional's daily workload. Outlook was first introduced by Microsoft in 1997, the start of the e-mail revolution. Now, six years later, it's evident that e-mail isn't going away anytime soon. In this latest version of Outlook, Microsoft has introduced an entirely new look and feel and incorporated many new features to help alleviate the e-mail avalanche. In this chapter, we'll explore the new Outlook interface and show you how to put the new features to use in managing your own e-mail workload.

◆ Exploring the new Inbox and mail folder views

◆ Using address books

◆ Setting e-mail options

◆ Using signatures

◆ Attaching read and delivery receipts

◆ Inserting Files and Outlook Items into Messages

◆ Organizing and managing mail with Search folders, views, rules, and other tools

It's a Brand New Outlook

New! One of the biggest complaints from users of earlier Outlook versions is the seemingly unorganized Outlook window. Outlook 2003 addresses these concerns with a cleaner and more accessible interface, shown in Figure 2.1. The Outlook bar has been combined with the folder list into the new Navigation Pane. The Navigation Pane takes a little getting used to but in the long run streamlines access to Outlook's folders and views. The Preview pane has morphed into the Reading Pane. The Reading Pane greatly reduces eyestrain while displaying more of each message without having to scroll so much.

FIGURE 2.1

Outlook 2003's new interface streamlines Outlook's folders and their contents.

Reading Pane

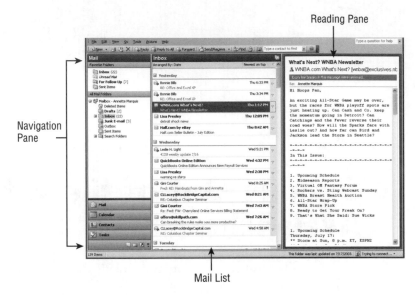

Navigation Pane

Mail List

Using the New Navigation Pane

New! The Navigation Pane helps you move among Outlook's main folders—Mail, Calendar, Contacts, Tasks, and Notes—and gain access to the complete folder list, which includes Microsoft Exchange Public folders. Depending on the folder you are viewing, the Navigation Pane presents you with different options. When Mail is selected, you have access to a default list of four Favorite folders: Inbox, Unread Mail, For Follow-Up, and Sent Mail. All but the For Follow-Up folder show the number of unread messages. For Follow-Up shows the total number of items marked for follow-up (see the section called "Flagging Messages that Require Your Attention" later in this chapter).

Below Favorites is a list with All Mail Folders, which also includes a Current View list of view choices. By default, the All Mail Folder list includes Deleted Items, Drafts, Inbox, Outbox, Sent Items, and a new feature called Search folders (for more about these cool new Search folders see "Creating and Using Search Folders to Simplify Organization" later in this chapter.) Using the Current View list, you can easily switch between folder views by selecting a different view, such as Last Seven Days, to see only messages received in the last week. To display the Current View list, choose View ➤ Arrange By ➤ Show Views in Navigation pane.

At the bottom of the Navigation Pane, you can switch between Outlook's main folders and access Outlook's traditional folder list, shown earlier in Figure 2.1. If the folder you want is not immediately visible on the Navigation Pane, point to the corresponding button at the bottom to select it.

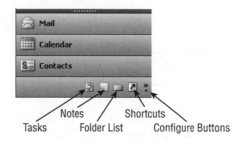

You can choose which buttons will be available and the order in which they will appear by clicking the Configure Buttons button and selecting Navigation Pane Options.

In addition, you can click Shortcuts to open Outlook Today and Microsoft's Outlook Update site. You can also create your own shortcut groups and add your own shortcuts to the list.

NOTE *If you used a previous version of Outlook, you may be wondering how to access your computer and network folders, such as My Computer, in Outlook 2003. We're sorry to report that you can no longer manage your files and folders in Outlook. Microsoft said users found it too confusing. However, you can still do some pretty cool things between Outlook and Windows folders. For example, you can drag and drop a file from a Windows folder to the Inbox to create a message with a document attached. You can also drag and drop a document to Calendar or Tasks to create a shortcut to the document in an appointment or task form. Right-drag the document and choose Copy if you'd like to have a copy instead. If you want to save a message in MSG format, retaining its message properties, you can also drag and drop from Outlook to your Windows folder.*

Reviewing Messages in Your Inbox

New! Unless you are capable of dispensing with every e-mail message as it arrives, chances are messages accumulate in your Inbox. With Outlook 2003's new Smart Dates arrangement, you can readily distinguish today's messages from those that arrived last week or even last month. Smart Date groups separate messages into groups of Today, Yesterday, Last Week, Two Weeks Ago, Last Month, and Older, as shown in Figure 2.2.

FIGURE 2.2

With Smart Date groups, you can easily find mail that arrived sometime last week.

TIP If you like to focus your attention on the present, you might try collapsing all the groups (View ➤ Expand/Collapse Groups ➤ Collapse All Groups) and then clicking the Today expand button to see just today's messages.

You may find that you'd like to see messages without the Smart Date groups. That is accomplished by clicking View ➤ Arrange By ➤ Show in Groups.

Previewing E-Mail in the Reading Pane

New! The Reading Pane, shown earlier in Figure 2.1, appears on the right of the Outlook window and displays significantly more than the retired Preview Pane from previous versions. Microsoft has built in some of the technology it uses in ebook publishing, including ClearType, subpixal positioning, paragraph spacing, and line length, to improve the overall view of the displayed message.

In the Reading Pane, you can click action buttons such as meeting request and voting buttons, navigate to websites using hyperlinks, and activate SmartTags associated with the sender. As a result, you might find that you actually open messages much less frequently, relying instead on the Reading Pane view.

TIP You can adjust the width of the Navigation Pane, the mail list, and the Reading Pane by dragging the border between two panes. You know you've found the right spot when the pointer changes into a double-header resize arrow.

If you find that you don't like the Reading Pane and would rather open each message fully, you can turn the Reading Pane off by clicking View ➤ Reading Pane ➤ Off. Or if you miss the Preview

Pane from previous versions, you can also move the Reading Pane to the bottom by choosing View ➤ Reading Pane ➤ Bottom.

Accessing Blocked Message Content

Junk mail senders are determined to fortify and verify their e-mail mailing lists—this is how their lists become more valuable to other junk mail senders. One way they do this is by attaching a "web beacon" to a message. These web beacons come in the form of inline references to external content, typically pictures or sounds, which your computer retrieves (assuming it is online) when you open the message. This tells the sender that your e-mail address is valid and as a result your address gains value in the world of spam.

New!   Outlook 2003 blocks all external web content and lets you choose if you want to display it. If you decide it's from a trusted site, click the message in the Information bar of the message and choose Download Pictures. You can make this selection from an open message or from the Reading Pane.

NOTE   *Web beacons do not affect file attachments.*

If you don't really care if you are inundated with junk mail, or you'd like to also block content from Trusted and Internet Zones, you can change the External Content Settings by choosing the second option, Change Automatic Download Settings.

Composing and Sending Mail

Composing and sending Outlook e-mail messages is pretty straightforward, but learning a few tricks can give you even more control over what you send. In this section, we'll help you find your way around address books, personal distribution lists, signatures, e-mail options, and document attachments.

ABOUT OUTLOOK PROFILES AND E-MAIL ACCOUNTS

Much of Outlook's work behind the scenes is dictated by the settings in your user profile. A *profile* is a file that contains information about your Outlook configuration. The profile, stored on your local computer, links you to particular e-mail accounts, directories, address books, and folders stored locally, on a local area network, or on the Internet. With Outlook, you can access multiple e-mail accounts, such as a Microsoft Exchange account, a Hotmail account, a personal POP account, and an IMAP account, all in one Outlook profile.

If you work for a company that has a local area network, your network administrator probably already created your Outlook profile on your computer. If you share a computer with others, you should each have your own Outlook profile to keep your Outlook data private and customized to your needs. Talk to your IT department if you need additional Outlook profiles and e-mail accounts on your computer.

Addressing Messages

Addressing a message can be as simple as typing a name in the To text box of an open message form. You don't even have to type the full name or the full e-mail address. When you begin typing a name, two of Outlook's auto features, Auto-Complete and Auto-Resolve, come into play. As you start typing a name in the To text box, Auto-Complete may display a list of possible options based on names or e-mail addresses you've entered before. If one of those options is the one you want, you can select it and press Enter to enter the address automatically. If the name you want does not appear on the list, just keep typing to complete the name yourself.

When you finish typing a name without AutoComplete activating, Outlook tries to AutoResolve the name—that is, find the name in one of your address books (more about address books later in this section). If it finds the name, it fills in the address for you. It might not fill in the address right away, however, and it might not do it at all, so it can be a bit baffling to figure out what's going on. If Outlook cannot resolve the name because the text you entered could refer to more than one name, Outlook underlines the name with a wavy red line like you see when you've misspelled a word. Outlook wants you to make the choice. You can do this by right-clicking the name and choosing the address you want from the list. If this is a new contact, you can choose to Create New Address For the contact from the shortcut menu that opens and then click New Contact to open a new Contact form.

NOTE *The wavy red underline might not appear until you are busy typing your message, so don't panic if you expect it to AutoResolve and it doesn't do it right away.*

If Outlook doesn't AutoResolve and it doesn't mark the name with a wavy red underline, that means it doesn't have a clue to whom you are referring—your address books show no one close to the name you entered. In this case, go ahead and finish your message. When you click Send, Outlook asks you to clarify to whom you are addressing the message. Click New Contact to enter the information into an Outlook Contact form.

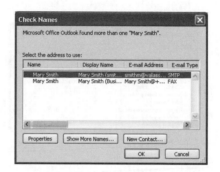

This same screen appears if you forego right-clicking the wavy red underline and click Send without resolving a possible name conflict. In this case, it shows you the list of possible choices, just like you would see if you had right-clicked the name. Click the address you want and click OK to enter the name and send the message.

TIP *If you find AutoComplete and AutoResolve too unnerving to deal with, you can disable either or both of them. From Outlook's main window, choose Tools ➤ Options, click E-mail Options, and then click Advanced E-mail Options. Clear the Automatic Name Checking checkbox to disable AutoResolve and clear the Suggest Names While Completing To, CC, and BCC Fields checkbox to disable AutoComplete.*

USING ADDRESS BOOKS

An address book is a list that, minimally, contains names, e-mail addresses, or fax numbers. You might have only one address book or you might have several of them, depending on the e-mail accounts you have set up in your Outlook profile. The most common address books are described below:

Global Address List An address book stored on a server, such as a Microsoft Exchange Server, for use by members of your organization; sometimes called a *post office address list*. This address book can contain additional books that contain global distribution lists, conference rooms, contacts, users, and public folders.

Outlook Address Book A category of address books that includes Outlook's Contacts folder and potentially any other Contacts folder in your folder set. These address books include only those contacts that have an e-mail address or fax number listed.

NOTE   *If you have installed other mail services or use an Internet Directory Service (Lightweight Delivery Access Protocol, or LDAP), you might also have additional address books.*

When sending an e-mail message, the most direct way to access your address books is to click the To button on a new e-mail message. In Outlook 2003, the Select Names dialog box, which displays your address books, has been redesigned so that more address information is visible without scrolling, as shown in Figure 2.3. If you still have trouble seeing everything, you can now resize the dialog box by dragging the border—one of those simple improvements that makes such a difference.

FIGURE 2.3

The newly designed Select Names dialog box makes it easier to see information related to an address.

If you have more than one address book, begin by choosing an address book from the Show Names From drop-down list in the Select Names dialog box. Follow these steps to add addresses to the messages:

1. When the address book opens, either scroll to the person's name or begin entering the name in the Type Name text box until you find it.

2. With the contact's name selected in the top pane, double-click to place the name in the To box or click the To, Cc, or Bcc button to add the name to the list of recipients. You can also right-click the name and select To, Cc, or Bcc from the Shortcut menu. To select a contiguous list of names, hold Shift while you select them or hold Ctrl to select noncontiguous names before clicking the To, Cc, or Bcc buttons.

3. After you've added all the recipients, click OK to close the Select Names dialog box and return to the message form.

MASTERING TROUBLESHOOTING: MAKING A CONTACTS FOLDER AVAILABLE AS AN ADDRESS BOOK

If you create a new Contacts folder, you have to make it available as an Outlook address book in order to access the e-mail addresses from the Select Name dialog box. Just follow these steps to make the folder available as an Outlook address book:

1. Right-click the new Contacts subfolder and choose Properties from the Shortcut menu.

2. Choose the Outlook Address Book tab of the Properties dialog box.

3. Click the Show This Folder As An E-mail Address Book check box.

4. Enter a different name for the address book, if desired. This is the name that will appear in the Select Names dialog box and other dialog boxes that display the list of address books. Changing the name does not change the folder name—only the name of the address book created from the folder.

5. Click OK to save the changes and close the Properties dialog box.

TIP *To and Cc recipients are listed in the header of the message, while recipients of blind courtesy copies are not. Therefore, recipients of the original message and courtesy copies won't know that the message was also sent to the Bcc recipients, and Bcc recipients won't know what other blind courtesy copies were sent. If you are responsible for sending out an e-mail newsletter or the same message to several competitors, you might consider putting everyone's name in the Bcc box. That way, no one will see who else received the correspondence and you aren't giving away other people's e-mail addresses without their permission. If you want to display the Bcc field without using the Select Names dialog box, click the down-arrow on the Options button on an open message form and choose Bcc. If you are not using Word as your e-mail editor, choose View ➢ Bcc Field from an open message form.*

DETERMINING THE ORDER OF ADDRESS BOOKS

If you find you are always selecting a different address book from the Select Names dialog box, you may want to change the order in which the address books appear. You can also determine the order in which Outlook accesses your address books to locate a name. The order of address books determines which address list or Contacts folder Outlook searches first for an address.

To view or change the order, follow these steps:

1. Choose Tools ➢ Address Book from Outlook's Standard toolbar (outside of a mail message).

2. Choose Tools ➢ Options from the Address Book dialog box's menu.

3. In the Addressing dialog box shown in Figure 2.4, select the address book you would like to show first when you open the Select Names or Address Book dialog boxes from the Show This Address List First drop-down list.

4. Select the folder in which you would like to keep your personal addresses from the Keep Personal Addresses In drop-down list.

5. Click the up- and down-arrows to the right of the open text box to change the order of the address lists in which Outlook checks names before sending mail.

6. If an address book is not appearing in the list of address books shown here, click the Add button to add it to the list.

7. When you have finished setting the order, click OK and then click the Close button on the Address Book dialog box.

FIGURE 2.4

From the Addressing dialog box, you can change the order in which Outlook searches for an e-mail address.

After you've addressed a message, you may want to review message options to request read and delivery receipts, conduct a vote, or adjust security settings. In the next section, we'll show you how.

Setting Message Options

Message options are set for the current message only, not for all new messages, and these options are the same regardless of which text editor you are using (see the "Setting Format Options Including Custom Signatures" section later in this chapter for more about Outlook's text editors, and "Setting General E-mail Options to Simplify Formatting and Message Handling" later in this chapter to learn how to set global options for all messages).

Click the Options button on the toolbar of an open new message form to open the Message Options dialog box, shown in Figure 2.5. Table 2.1 explains each of the message-handling options.

FIGURE 2.5

Message options, like some of those shown here, can be set individually for each message.

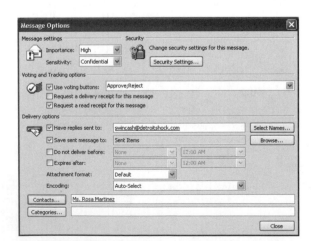

TABLE 2.1: MESSAGE-HANDLING OPTIONS

OPTION	DESCRIPTION
Importance	Alerts the recipient about the importance of the message. Choose from Normal, Low, or High.
Sensitivity	Alerts the recipient about how sensitive the message is. Choose from Normal, Personal, Private, or Confidential.
Security Settings	Encrypts messages and attachments and designates a digital signature to secure the message.
Use Voting Buttons	Enables use of e-mail as a voting tool (see "Using E-mail As a Voting Tool" below).
Tracking Options	Notifies you when the message has been received and/or read; dependent on the capability and settings of the recipient's mailservice.
Have Replies Sent To	Allows you to designate an individual to collect replies to the message.
Save Sent Message To	Indicates which folder you want the sent message stored in; Sent Items is the default.
Do Not Deliver Before	Keeps the message from being delivered before the specified date.
Expires After	Marks the message as unavailable after the specified date.
Attachment Format	Allows you to select among the three major attachment formats: MIME, UUencode, or BINHEX.
Encoding	If you have International Options set on the Mail Format tab of the Options dialog box to designate an encoding option rather than Auto-Select, you can choose a particular encoder here. Otherwise, Auto-Select is the only choice.
Contacts	Relates this message to a contact.
Category	Assigns a category to this message.

A WORD ABOUT READ AND DELIVERY RECEIPTS

When you click that Send button on a really important message, wouldn't it be nice to know when and if the recipient actually reads the message? Some folks think read and delivery receipts are the answer. Delivery receipts are fairly reliable; most e-mail servers accurately reflect that a message has been received by the server. If, however, the recipient's e-mail address is valid but the server can't communicate with the recipient's e-mail client, the message might never be delivered by the recipient's server and you'll still get a receipt confirming delivery. Read receipts are less reliable. Some e-mail clients can't send read receipts, and others send read receipts along with the delivery receipts. Microsoft Exchange Server handles read and delivery receipts very well; however, if your message leaves the Exchange environment, read receipts in particular are less reliable. And even more importantly, in informal surveys done with hundreds of administrative professionals, we consistently find that there are more people offended when they receive messages with read receipts than there are people who actually use them. Add that to the increased load they place on your servers and receipts become a much less attractive option.

Continued on next page

A WORD ABOUT READ AND DELIVERY RECEIPTS *(continued)*

If you still insist on using delivery and read receipts, we recommend setting them for individual messages rather than globally in the E-mail Tracking options. See "Setting Tracking Options" later in this chapter for more about how to set receipts for all messages.

USING E-MAIL AS A VOTING TOOL

Gathering opinions, reaching agreement, and settling on a course of action are all part of working as a team. Outlook has a built-in tool to help generate and then gather responses from groups of e-mail recipients. It then tabulates the results for you, showing you a log of everyone's votes. To activate voting, select the Options tab of an open e-mail message and then click the Use Voting Buttons check box.

You can add your own text to the voting buttons that appear, and you can add additional buttons—put a semicolon between the options or you'll get one big button. If you want to have someone else collect the results, enter their address in the Have Replies Sent To text box. When you've set up the options, click Send to distribute the ballots to the voting list.

NOTE *You will not see the voting buttons on your outgoing message. They only appear on the recipients' messages.*

Recipients respond by clicking one of the voting buttons below the menu bar, as shown in Figure 2.6. Their responses are sent to the Inbox like any other message. When you open the message, you can see the current vote and you can click the Information bar and choose View Voting Responses to open a tracking form where you can view the results, as seen in Figure 2.7.

FIGURE 2.6

Recipients click one of the voting buttons on the message to cast their ballots.

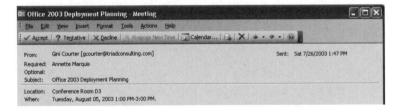

FIGURE 2.7

The Tracking tab of a message with voting options lets you determine the status of the vote.

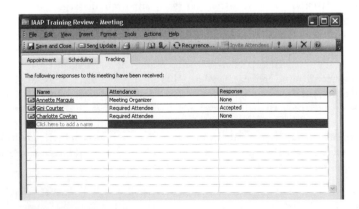

When you have finished setting options for the message, click Close to save the settings and close the Message Options dialog box.

In the next section, we'll review all of Outlook's mail-related options so you can set the ones discussed in this section and other options to apply to all messages.

Setting General E-mail Options to Simplify Formatting and Message Handling

By customizing the way Outlook handles your e-mail, you can gain better control of formatting, simplify mail sending and receiving, control Outlook's behavior as you read messages, and add custom signatures to outgoing mail. As you find yourself spending a lot of time using Outlook e-mail, you might find it worthwhile to review Outlook's e-mail options and set them to accommodate your personal preferences. To access e-mail options, choose Tools ➤ Options from the main Outlook window.

To review the first set of options related to e-mail, click the E-mail Options button on the Preferences tab. These options, shown in Figure 2.8, pertain to message handling—in other words, how do you want Outlook to respond as you process your mail? You can also set your preferences for what content from the original message is included in replies and forwards and how this content is designated.

FIGURE 2.8

With Outlook's Message Handling options, you can set your preferences for how Outlook behaves as you read your mail.

NOTE *If you choose Do Not Include Original Message in replies, it's helpful to include enough information in the reply to remind the recipient about the content of the original message. If you reply with something like, "That's a great idea. Will you take care of that for me?" the recipient might have no choice but to reply back with, "huh?"*

When you are finished setting these options, click the Advanced E-mail Options button. The options available on the Advanced E-mail Options dialog box, shown in Figure 2.9, include options related to saving messages, how you are notified when new messages arrive, and what you'd like to have happen when sending a message.

FIGURE 2.9

Advanced e-mail options give you control over saving messages, new message notification, and options related to sending a message.

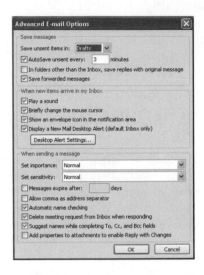

New! Outlook 2003 includes a new notification option called Desktop Alerts. Desktop Alerts are semi-transparent boxes that appear in the bottom right of your screen notifying you that you have a new message. The Desktop Alert includes the time and date of the message, the name of the sender, and the subject. You can change the duration and the level of transparency of Desktop Alerts by clicking the Desktop Alert Settings button.

Setting Tracking Options

When you have finished customizing Desktop Alert and other Advanced Options, click OK to return to the E-mail Options dialog box. Click the Tracking Options button to set options for delivery and read receipts and blank voting and meeting requests. (For more about voting requests, see the "Setting Message Options" section earlier in this chapter. For more about meeting requests, see Chapter 3, "Taking Control of Your Time and Tasks"). Figure 2.10 shows the Tracking Options dialog box. Here you can specify if you want Outlook to notify you if someone is requesting a read or delivery receipt. This gives you the choice rather than refusing all of them or agreeing to all of them. We don't recommend setting this option to Always Send a Response. Many of the spam messages you receive have read and delivery receipts attached to automatically verify your e-mail address. If the spammers can verify that it is an active address and you actually open your message, your address just increased in value to them.

FIGURE 2.10

Use Tracking Options to tell Outlook how to handle delivery and read receipts, blank voting, and meeting requests.

When you are finished setting Tracking Options, click OK to close Tracking Options and OK again to close E-mail Options.

Setting Format Options Including Custom Signatures

The final set of options related to e-mail concern message formatting. With these options, you can choose your preferred text editor, select personalized stationery, and assign custom signatures to your messages. To access Outlook's mail formatting options, click the Mail Format tab on the Options dialog box.

In Outlook 2003, Microsoft Word is the default e-mail editor. If you stick with Word, you have Word's tools at your disposal. You actually compose your e-mail message in a Word document.

If you have a computer with not quite enough memory to support Word as the e-mail editor and you become uncomfortable with the speed hit you are taking, you can decide to use Outlook's built-in text editor. To switch to Outlook's text editor, choose Tools ➢ Options from Outlook's main window and click the Mail Format tab. Clear the Use Microsoft Word To Edit E-mail Messages check box.

TIP   If you like using Word to edit e-mail messages, you might also like using it to read messages. On the Mail Format tab of the Options dialog box, you can also choose to use Word to read messages that you receive in Rich Text format by selecting the Use Microsoft Word To Read Rich-Text Messages option.

In addition to selecting an e-mail editor, you may also choose from one of three e-mail formats: HTML, Rich Text, and Plain Text. For information about changing these options, see the section, "Setting a Message Format," later in this chapter. To learn what these formats have to offer, continue with the next section.

CHOOSING A MESSAGE FORMAT

Outlook 2003 supports three e-mail message formats:

◆ Hypertext Markup Language (HTML) is the default format in Outlook 2003. Your message is created in HTML, the language used to develop pages on the Web. The HTML format supports an incredibly wide range of formatting, including backgrounds, horizontal lines, numbered and bulleted lists, and any other formatting you expect to see on a web page. Most e-mail systems today support HTML.

♦ With Microsoft Outlook Rich Text you can format fonts, align paragraphs, and use bulleted lists in your message. Outlook Rich Text format (RTF) is understood by Microsoft Exchange Client versions 4.0 and higher and all Outlook versions.

♦ Plain text is created using a plain-text font, Courier New, and you can't apply any formatting to the message. Plain text is understood by all e-mail systems.

HTML is the default in Outlook 2003 because it is supported by a large number of e-mail systems. If the recipient's e-mail client only supports plain text, an HTML message appears as plain, unformatted text. With the availability of HTML, RTF messages are, for the most part, a thing of the past.

It's important to remember that while you can compose a message in any of these three formats, the appearance of the message depends on the formats supported by the recipient's e-mail software. Before you spend a long time formatting a message, you might want to check if the person receiving it will be able to see the formatting.

NOTE   When you reply to a message, Outlook automatically uses the original message's format for the reply.

What format to choose and exactly what tools are available for you to use depends on which of the two e-mail editors you are using to compose your message. Table 2.2 shows what tools to expect with each text editor in each available format.

TABLE 2.2: OUTLOOK EDITORS AND FORMATS

TEXT EDITOR	MESSAGE FORMAT	AVAILABLE TOOLS
Word	HTML, Rich Text	Text formatting, numbering, bullets, alignment, horizontal lines, borders and shading, backgrounds, HTML styles, clip art, pictures, drawings, WordArt, hyperlinks, linked objects, linked themes, columns, and tables. You also have access to AutoCorrect, Auto-Text, Spelling and Grammar, and other language tools. Almost anything you can create in Word, you can create in this format.
Word	Plain Text	No formatting tools available—understood by all e-mail systems.
Outlook	HTML	Text formatting, numbering, bullets, alignment, horizontal lines, backgrounds, Spelling, hyperlinks, and HTML styles.
Outlook	Rich Text	Text formatting, numbering, bullets, and alignment. Only supported by Exchange and Outlook clients.
Outlook	Plain Text	No formatting tools available—understood by all e-mail systems.

SETTING A MESSAGE FORMAT

You can set a message format for all messages, and you can choose a different format for a particular message. To set the default message format, follow these steps:

1. Choose Tools ➤ Options from the Outlook menu to open the Options dialog box.

2. Select the Mail Format tab, shown in Figure 2.11.

3. Choose the format you want to use from the Compose In This Message Format drop-down list.

4. To set specific options related to Internet mail, click the Internet Format button to open the dialog box shown in Figure 2.12.

5. Clear the check box under HTML options if you would prefer to include hyperlinks in your messages rather than actual image files.

6. Choose your preferred format when you send Outlook Rich Text messages to Internet recipients from the Outlook Rich Text Formats drop-down list. Unless all Internet recipients are running Outlook, chances are they will not be able to see Rich Text formatting. Converting to HTML format is probably the best choice.

7. If you plan to use plain text, set your line wrapping preference and check the check box under Plain Text Options.

8. Click OK to close the Internet Format dialog box and OK again to close the Options dialog box.

WARNING   *As with any options, unless you are absolutely clear about why you are changing a Mail Format option, we recommend leaving them as they are. You could create unnecessary headaches if you change an option without knowing all of its implications.*

To choose a different format—HTML, Rich Text, or Plain Text—for an individual message, choose the desired format from the Message Format drop-down list on the E-mail toolbar in an open message form.

FIGURE 2.11

Choose an e-mail editor and set message format options in the Options dialog box.

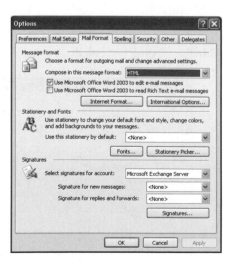

FIGURE 2.12

When sending mail across the Internet, you can set additional options about how messages are handled.

USING STATIONERY

If you use an HTML editor, you can personalize your e-mail messages by choosing HTML stationery, a scheme that includes a font and a background color or picture. To select stationery, select HTML as your e-mail editor on the Mail Format tab in the Options dialog box (Tools ➢ Options from Outlook's main menu). Then choose a stationery pattern from the Use This Stationery By Default drop-down list.

To see what the various stationery patterns look like, click the Stationery Picker button on the Mail Format tab of the dialog box to open the Stationary Picker dialog box. Each stationery choice includes fonts and a background picture or color. Click OK when you've made your selection.

TIP *Rather than setting a default stationery for all your messages, you can choose stationery when you want it by choosing Actions ➢ New Mail Message Using. Most-recently-used stationery appears at the top of the list. If you want to try something different, click More Stationery to open the Select A Stationery dialog box.*

If you'd like to create your own stationery, click the New button and either start with a blank stationery, base your stationery on a template, or base it on a file. You can then click Next to choose fonts and create a background with pictures and colors.

NOTE *If you choose a stationery that includes an image at the top, such as Citrus Punch, don't be surprised if recipients don't read your messages. In most e-mail preview windows the image might be all they see and that's not enough to inspire them to open the message for more.*

DESIGNING CUSTOM SIGNATURES

A *custom signature* is text you add to the end of a message to provide any information you want all of the recipients of your e-mail to know, such as your contact data, confidentiality information, or advertisements for your products. As long as you don't overdo it, a custom signature is a great way to keep your company's message in front of your clients.

Setting Signatures for Different Accounts

With Outlook 2003, you can create multiple custom signatures and select the signature you want to use with each message you send. This lets you create a formal signature for business messages, a specific message for clients, and a friendlier signature for messages to friends and family.

To create a custom signature, follow these steps:

1. Choose Tools ➢ Options from the Outlook menu to open the Options dialog box.

2. On the Mail Format tab, click the Signatures button to open the Create Signature dialog box.

3. Click New and enter a name for the signature.

4. You can choose to start with a blank signature or base this new signature on any existing signatures or on an existing file. Make a choice of how you want to create the new signature and click Next to open the Edit Signature dialog box shown in Figure 2.13.

FIGURE 2.13

Design a custom signature in the Edit Signature dialog box.

5. In the Signature Text box, enter or edit the text you want to include in your signature.

6. Click the Font and Paragraph buttons to select font, alignment, and bullets.

7. Click the Clear button if you want to start over.

8. If you want to apply additional HTML formatting and images, click the Advanced Edit button to launch an HTML editor, such as FrontPage, if it is available. (You can also insert hyperlinks and images if you create or edit the signature in the E-mail Options dialog box, discussed below.)

9. The vCard Options allow you to include your contact information as a "virtual business card" in the signature. Recipients who use Outlook or contact management software that supports the vCard standard can drag or copy the attached vCard to add you to their list of contacts. Select a vCard from the list of available options or click the New vCard From Contact button to create a vCard.

10. When you've finished entering and formatting the text for your custom signature, click Finish to return to the Create Signature dialog box and OK to return to the Options dialog box.

The signature you just created is automatically set as the default, appearing in the text area of every new message. You can choose another default signature (or None) from the drop-down list on the Mail Format tab of the Options dialog box. You can also choose a different default signature for replies and forwards and you can select a specific signature to use with a specific e-mail account.

TIP   Before creating a new signature, create an Outlook contact that includes your business information and excludes private information (for example, your home phone number) that you wouldn't routinely provide to customers or vendors. You can then select this contact to send as a vCard with your messages in the Edit Signature dialog box.

Creating a Custom Signature inside a Word E-mail Message

When you create e-mail signatures from the E-mail Options dialog box within a Word e-mail message, you have a few additional options available, such as inserting hyperlinks and objects. To create signatures using these tools, follow these steps:

1. Create a new e-mail message.

2. Open the E-mail Options dialog box by clicking the drop-down arrow on the Options button and choosing E-mail Signature.

3. Enter a name for the signature.

4. Click in the open text box under Create Your E-mail Signature and enter the text you want to include.

5. Select the text to apply different fonts, font styles, alignments, and font colors.

6. Click the Insert Picture button to insert an image file.

7. Click the Insert Hyperlink button to include a hyperlink to a website, a document, or another e-mail message in your signature.

8. When you have finished creating your signature, click Add to add it to the list of available signatures.

9. If Word prompts you, say Yes if you would like to make this signature the default e-mail signature on new messages or select it from the Signature For New Messages and Signature For Replies And Forwards drop-down lists. Choose the most commonly used signature for the default.

10. To create additional signatures, click New and repeat steps 2–9.

TIP If you would like to create a hyperlink using an image in your signature, select the image before clicking the Insert Hyperlink button.

Selecting a Custom Signature

Regardless of how you create it, if you use Microsoft Word as your e-mail editor, you must choose a default signature to have access to any of your signatures. You can always delete or edit a signature in an individual message. However, if you don't make one signature the default, you can't access any of them. When a signature has been inserted into a message, you can choose a different signature by right-clicking the signature in the e-mail message and making another choice from the menu that opens.

If you are using Outlook's text editor instead of Word, choose Insert ➤ Signature and select a signature from the menu; if the custom signature you want to use isn't displayed on the menu, choose More to open the Signature dialog box. Select a signature and then click OK to add the signature to the message.

You are now ready to attach any supporting documents, files, or Outlook items to the message before sending it.

Inserting Files and Items into Messages

E-mail has quickly become one of the most common ways of exchanging documents in business today. With high-speed Internet connections, sending large files such as PowerPoint presentations and digital photographs is a snap. It doesn't matter which e-mail editor or message format you use; you can attach Outlook items and any other type of file to messages in any format. You can insert a copy of the file or item, the text of the file or item, or a hyperlink to the file.

NOTE A file refers exclusively to a document or object created outside of Outlook, such as a Word document, a graphic, or an Excel workbook. Something created within Outlook, such as an e-mail message or a task, is referred to as an item. See the section, "Inserting Outlook Items into an E-mail Message," later in this chapter.

Inserting a Copy of a File

To insert a file into a message, follow these steps:

1. Choose Insert ➤ File from the menu inside an open message or click the Insert File button on the message toolbar to open the Insert File dialog box.

2. Locate the file as you would any document you want to open.

3. When you find the file, click the Insert button. The Insert File dialog box closes, and Outlook inserts an icon representing the file in a new text box labeled Attach in the message header.

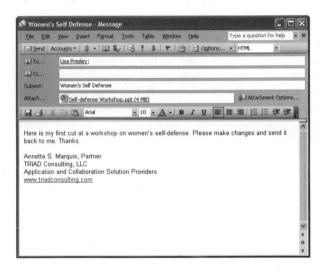

> **WARNING** *By default, Outlook 2003 blocks attachment files (such as* `.bat`, `.exe`, `.vbs`, *and* `.js`) *that can contain viruses. If you insert one of these file types, you are prompted whether or not you really want to send a potentially unsafe attachment. If you say Yes, Outlook will allow you to send the attachment. See Chapter 12, "Securing and Organizing Documents," for more about Outlook's e-mail security features.*

New!   If you are using Windows SharePoint Services, you can attach a document in Outlook 2003 as a Live Attachment rather than a copy. This live attachment is available on a shared document workspace. Click the Attachment Options buttons next to the Attach text box in an open message to open the Attachments Options pane from which you can create a live attachment. If you are interested in learning more about live attachments and Windows SharePoint Services, see Chapter 8, "Collaborating on Documents."

Inserting the Text of a File

If the recipient does not have an application to open the attached file, you can insert the contents of a text-based file as text. For example, rather than attaching a Word document, you can insert the Word document as text. As long as the recipient's e-mail system supports HTML messages, the document retains all of its formatting. You cannot, however, insert a graphic as text. To insert a file as text, follow steps 1–3 described earlier to insert a copy of a file. In step 4,

4. When you find the file, click the drop-down arrow on the Insert button to open the Insert menu. Choose Insert As Text. The Insert File dialog box closes, and Outlook inserts the text of the document in the body of the e-mail message.

Inserting a Hyperlink to a File

If the person (or people) you want to send a file to has access to a shared network drive or web server, you can insert a file shortcut as a hyperlink, rather than attaching a copy of the document. This not only saves server and mailbox space, it allows you to work on the same file rather than having multiple copies floating around. To make this work, you must first move the file to a shared location and verify that the recipient has appropriate access to the file location. Then you can insert a hyperlink into an e-mail message so that the recipient can locate the correct file. To insert a hyperlink using Word as your e-mail editor, follow these steps:

1. In an open e-mail message form, click in the e-mail body where we want the hyperlink to appear or select text in the e-mail body we want the hyperlink to apply to.

2. Choose Insert ➢ Hyperlink from the menu to open the Insert Hyperlink dialog box, shown in Figure 2.14.

FIGURE 2.14

Use the Insert Hyperlink dialog box to insert hyperlinks in your e-mail signatures and messages.

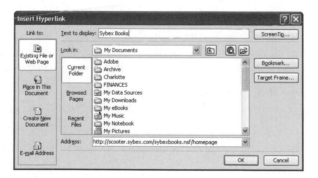

3. Decide if you want to create a link to a web page, a document on a shared drive, a specific place in a document, or an e-mail address:

   ◆ To create a web link, click the Browse The Web button to launch your browser so you can navigate to the site you want. When you get there, click the mail message in the Windows Taskbar to bring it forward. Outlook fills in the Text To Display and the Address for you. Edit the Text To Display text box as desired and click OK to create the hyperlink. You can also click Browsed Pages to locate a recently visited website or click the down-arrow on the Address text box to select a site from the History.

   ◆ To create a link to a document on a shared network drive, navigate to the folder that contains the document and select it from the list. Outlook fills in the Text To Display and the Address for you. Edit the Text To Display text box as desired and click OK to create the hyperlink.

◆ To create a link to an e-mail address so the recipient can send an e-mail to this address (generally this would be to an address other than yours), click the E-mail Address button on the Places bar. Enter the E-mail Address you want to use, a Subject if you want the message to contain a specific subject, and the Text To Display in the signature. Click OK to add the e-mail address link to the signature.

4. Close the Insert Hyperlink dialog box to return to the mail message and insert the link.

TIP   If you know the web address, you can type it into the e-mail message. Outlook automatically converts the text to a hyperlink. You can also type an e-mail address directly to create an e-mail link. However, you cannot use this option to insert a link to file location.

Inserting Outlook Items into an E-mail Message

You can easily exchange Outlook contacts with a colleague who also uses Outlook by inserting the items as attachments. Follow these steps to attach Outlook items to messages:

1. Create a new e-mail message.

2. In a Word message, click the drop-down arrow on the Insert button and choose Item. In an Outlook message, choose Insert ➢ Item from the menu.

3. Select the folder that contains the item you want to insert in the Look In text box.

4. Select the item from the Items list. You can click any of the column headers to sort by that column; click it again to sort in reverse order. If you are inserting a contact, you can click the first contact in the list and start typing the contact's name to locate the contact you want.

5. If you want to insert more than one item of the same type from a list, you can shift-click all contiguous items or Ctrl-click each separate item until you have selected all the items you want.

6. If you are using Outlook as your editor, you can choose to insert the item as text rather than as an attachment. Select Text Only from the Insert As options.

7. Click OK to insert the items.

TIP   If you use Word as your e-mail editor, you cannot insert an Outlook item as text in Outlook 2003. You can, however, get around this obstacle so you can send the contents of Outlook items to people who do not run Outlook. And you can do it without changing your default editor. Before creating a new message, choose Actions ➢ New Mail Message Using ➢ Microsoft Office Outlook (HTML). Follow the steps above to insert the item as text. The next message you create, you'll be back to using Word.

Sending Your Message

You've addressed your message, selected an e-mail editor, added and formatted text, added a custom signature, inserted attachments, and now you're ready to send your message to the recipients. Click the Send button and it's on its way. If you have more than one e-mail account, you can choose the account you want to use to send the message by clicking the Accounts buttons and making your selection. If you're not quite ready to send the message, click the Save button. Outlook saves the message in the Drafts folder. In the next section, we'll show you a number of useful ways to manage incoming mail.

Finding, Organizing, and Storing Messages

One of the most persistent challenges facing the networked business is presented by the proliferation of electronic mail. Learn how to organize your mail and you'll be more efficient and maintain your sanity in the process.

Organizing Using the Ways To Organize Inbox Pane

Outlook makes it painless to organize and manage your Inbox, and all the tools you need are in one place—the Ways To Organize Inbox pane. Choose Tools ➢ Organize to open the pane at the top of the Inbox, shown in Figure 2.15. Using the pane, you can create folders for message management, create rules to color-code your message or automatically move messages for you, change Inbox views, or open Rules and Alerts to create more-complex rules to control the messages you receive.

FIGURE 2.15

With the Ways To Organize Inbox pane, all your message management tools are right at your fingertips.

The Ways To Organize Inbox pane has three tabs: Using Folders, Using Colors, and Using View. You can use the Ways To Organize pane to organize any of your mail folders, and similar options are available for all Outlook folder types, including Calendar and Contacts.

USING FOLDERS

You can use the Using Folders tab of the Ways To Organize Inbox pane, shown earlier in Figure 2.15, to move selected messages out of your Inbox and into different folders. This is a great way to unclutter your Inbox and still keep important messages handy. Hold Ctrl and select the messages you want to move. Then select a folder from the Move Message drop-down list; if the folder you want is not there (or not created yet), choose Other Folder at the bottom of the list. This opens the Select Folder dialog box where you can browse mailbox and public folders or create a new folder.

NOTE   Moving messages to different folders within Outlook does nothing to reduce the size of your mailbox because your mailbox includes all of your Outlook folders. If you are getting those dreaded messages from the System Administrator that your mailbox is getting full, your options are to trim it down by deleting unnecessary items, archiving older items, or exporting less active items to a personal folder file. You can use Outlook 2003's Mailbox Cleanup tool on the Tools menu to help you through these options.

Creating Simple Rules to Automatically Move Messages

Rules take the headache out of managing your Inbox by letting Outlook handle much of your mail automatically. In the Using Folders tab, shown earlier in Figure 2.15, you create rules by example. If you want all messages from Karla Browning to be automatically placed in a specific mail folder, select a message from Karla in the Inbox or any other mail folder. Then choose either From or Sent To in the Create A Rule drop-down list to indicate which type of messages should be moved. If you don't have a message from this recipient in any of your mail folders, enter the person's name or e-mail address in the text box. Use the Into drop-down list to select the folder where you want the messages to/from this person moved; then click the Create button to create the new rule. The rule is applied to all new messages you send or receive and you may choose to run the rule immediately on existing mail.

You'll know it worked because it says Done next to the Create button.

NOTE You can create even more complex rules to handle mail messages. Outlook's Rules and Alerts feature, available from the Tools menu, makes mail handling almost effortless. You'll find a thorough discussion of Rules and Alerts and some of Outlook's higher-level organizational tools in Chapter 12.

Using Colors to Organize Messages

Message information (sender, subject, and so on) is displayed in the Windows text color by default; this is the color you get when you choose the Automatic color in any Windows application. The Using Colors tab, shown in Figure 2.16, lets you apply any of 15 colors to message descriptions based on who sent the message, to whom it was sent, and whether you are the only recipient.

FIGURE 2.16

Automatically apply colors to easily distinguish messages from each other.

To set the color based on the sender or recipient:

1. Choose a message from the sender or addressed to the recipient in the list view.

2. In the Color Messages drop-down lists, choose From or Sent To and a color you wish to apply.

3. Click the Apply Color button to create the color rule.

4. To distinguish messages sent only to you from those sent to multiple recipients, choose a color in the Show Messages Sent Only To Me drop-down list, and click the Turn On button to apply this rule.

TIP Coloring messages sent only to you lets you quickly locate messages that most likely require your attention.

You can create a new Automatic Formatting rule by following these steps:

1. Open the Ways To Organize Inbox pane by clicking Tools ➢ Organize.

2. Click the Using Colors tab in the Ways To Organize Inbox pane.

3. Click the Automatic Formatting button at the top-right of the Ways To Organize Inbox pane.

4. Click the Add button in the Automatic Formatting dialog box, shown in Figure 2.17, to create a rule that Outlook temporarily names *Untitled*.

5. Type a descriptive name for the rule.

6. Click the Font button and choose a font, font color, and other font options you want to apply to the messages.

7. Click the Condition button to open the Filter dialog box. In the three tabs of the dialog box, set the filter conditions (for more about using conditions, see the "Creating Custom Search Folder Criteria" section later in this chapter).

8. Click OK to create the condition.

FIGURE 2.17

You can set automatic formatting options based on a variety of conditions.

SELECTING VIEWS

Views determine how your data is displayed. The Inbox primarily uses table views (columns and rows) to display Inbox items. However, the sort order, how the data is grouped, which fields are visible, and how it is filtered can be changed by choosing a different view. You can select predefined and custom views from the Using Views tab of the Ways To Organize Inbox pane, shown in Figure 2.18.

FIGURE 2.18

Views determine how data is displayed.

You can change the fields, sort order, grouping, filters, settings, and formatting of the current view by clicking the Customize Current View button in the top-right of the Using Views tab. You can learn more about creating custom views in Chapter 4, "Unleashing the Power of Outlook Contact Management."

TIP   In Outlook 2003, you can also change views from the Navigation Pane. Choose View ➤ Arrange By ➤ Show Views in Navigation Pane and scroll to the bottom of the All Mail Folders list to see the list of choices.

Filing Junk Mail Where It Belongs

Businesses have used direct mailing (via snail mail) to market to individuals and companies for years. What marketing companies call direct mailing, others call "junk mail." Junk mail delivered to your electronic mailbox—also known as *spam*—can be just as annoying as its paper-based cousin. With Outlook 2003, you can automatically move junk mail messages to the Junk E-mail folder (or have it permanently deleted if you prefer, so you don't waste your time with them).

To set the rules to manage junk e-mail, click Actions ➤ Junk E-mail ➤ Junk E-mail Options. This opens the Junk E-mail Options dialog box shown in Figure 3.19. The default setting is Low, which moves the most obvious junk e-mail to the Junk E-mail folder. If you would prefer to catch more, you can up the setting to High (no middle ground here, folks). At the High setting, most junk e-mail should be caught but it might also snag some of your real mail. If you choose this setting, be sure to check your Junk E-mail folder regularly to see if anything you want has ended up there.

FIGURE 2.19

Use the Junk E-mail Options dialog box to automatically move junk e-mail to the Junk E-mail folder.

Trusted Lists Only gives you total control over what is treated as junk and what is not. You can create a Trusted Senders list to make sure that mail from these senders, including anyone in your Contacts folders, is not classified as junk (although some of it may actually be). To create a Trusted Senders list, click the Trusted Senders tab. You can individually add e-mail addresses or domain names or, if you have one, you can import a text file that contains trusted e-mail addresses or domain names. By leaving the Always Trust E-mail From My Contacts check box selected, you can avoid adding all of your contacts to the list individually.

A lot of junk mail is sent to "undisclosed recipients" or some other address that makes you wonder how it ever got to you. If you are pretty confident that you rarely receive junk through a particular e-mail account or domain, you can list it in the Trusted Recipients list so no mail to that address or domain is ever treated as junk mail. Click the Trusted Recipients tab to add names and domains to the list.

Finally, if you know specific e-mail addresses or domain names that are junk, you can add them to the Junk Senders list. Outlook always treats any mail from the addresses or domains on this list as junk.

When you are finished with the Junk E-mail Options dialog box, click OK to save the new settings.

ASSIGNING JUNK OR TRUSTED STATUS TO AN INDIVIDUAL MESSAGE

After you have specified the level of protection you want, you don't have to reopen the Junk E-mail Options dialog box again unless you want to make a change or remove an address or domain from the list. As you run across mail from junk or trusted senders, you can add them to the appropriate list by right-clicking and choosing Junk E-mail and then Add to Junk Senders List, Add to Trusted Senders List, Add to Trusted Recipients List, or Junk E-mail Options to reopen the dialog box.

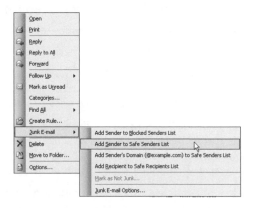

NOTE *Assigning Junk E-mail status to a message does not automatically move it to the Junk E-mail folder. You can drag it there if you want or you can just delete it.*

If a message has already been placed in the Junk E-mail folder, Outlooks assumes it is junk but it does not automatically add the address to the Junk E-mail Senders list. You still have to right-click the message to assure that future mailings from that address or domain get handled appropriately.

RECLAIMING JUNK MAIL

If you find a message in the Junk E-mail folder that isn't junk (or maybe it's mail from your ex that you treated as junk last week but now you've had a change of heart), you can reclaim the message and put it back into its rightful place in the Inbox. To do this, right-click the message, choose Junk E-mail ➢ Mark as Not Junk, or click the Not Junk button on the Standard toolbar. Outlook opens the Mark As Not Junk Dialog box.

Here you can choose to always trust mail from this sender and always trust mail sent to the specific recipient. Check the appropriate check boxes to indicate your choice(s). As soon as you click OK, the message is moved back to the Inbox and the addresses you checked are added to the Trusted Senders or Recipients list.

MASTERING THE OPPORTUNITIES: REDUCING THE AMOUNT OF JUNK MAIL YOU RECEIVE

Reducing the amount of junk mail you receive requires constant vigilance. Here are a few things you can do to begin tackling the problem:

◆ Avoid giving out your primary e-mail address. Create a second e-mail account and use that when required to give an address. If you'd like, you can create an Outlook rule to move mail Through The Specific Account to a separate folder (see more about rules in Chapter 10, "Taming Complex Publications").

◆ Consider altering your e-mail address slightly when posting messages to websites and newsgroups. For example, change your address from amarquis@train2k.com to amarquisNOJUNK@train2K.com. Users are generally smart enough to remove the NOJUNK but search programs scanning for addresses are not (if users are not, you may not want to be hearing from them anyway).

◆ Avoid replying to junk e-mail even if you are requesting to be removed from the list. Senders often ask you to do this as a way to verify your address. They have no intention of removing your name—why would they? It just increased in value.

◆ Use junk e-mail filters. Outlook recognizes junk mail and adult content mail by filtering message content. Outlook filters messages, searching for phrases commonly used in direct marketing messages and adult content messages. For junk mail, phrases include: "cards accepted," "extra income," "money-back guarantee," and "100% satisfied." With adult content mail, Outlook searches for phrases like "over 18," "adults only," "adult web," and "xxx" in the Subject line.

It's worth knowing how Outlook and other programs with content filters determine which messages may be junk mail or have adult content. If you include phrases like "We're brainstorming ways to generate extra income" or "There must be over 18 ways to complete this analysis" in a piece of regular business correspondence, don't be surprised if your recipient never reads the message. Outlook may filter it out just because it includes keywords such as "extra income" and "over 18." At the same time, Outlook may let in spam messages because they don't meet the predefined criteria. The spammer is always looking for ways to beat the system and at this point they have very little to lose. All it takes is for a few people out of thousands to buy a product they are promoting to more than recoup their costs.

Outlook 2003 offers a couple of new ways to make it easier to find your most important messages—Flagging and Search Folders. We'll cover these next.

Flagging Messages that Require Your Attention

New! When you receive a lot of e-mail, it can be a challenge to separate the information-only messages from the ones that require follow-up. With Outlook 2003, you can quickly assign a flag to any message in the Inbox. To apply the default red flag, click the flag icon to the right of the message.

To mark the item complete, click the flag icon again and Outlook replaces it with a check mark. To assign a different color flag, clear a flag, change the default color, set the default flag, or set a reminder, right-click to open the Shortcut menu.

Click Add Reminder on the short-cut ment to open the Flag for Follow-up dialog box, shown in Figure 2.20. You can choose the purpose of the flag from the Flag To drop-down list and the color of the flag from the Flag Type drop-down list. Select the date and time you would like to be reminded of this message from the two Due By drop-down lists. Click OK to set the reminder.

FIGURE 2.20

Use the Flag for Follow-up dialog box to add a reminder to a flagged message.

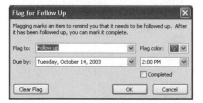

When the time comes, the Reminder Window opens with the reminder.

Creating and Using Search Folders to Simplify Organization

New! Outlook's new Search folders feature is a valuable addition to Outlook's organization tools. With Search folders, you can set up *virtual folders* that pull messages together that meet certain criteria. Outlook 2003 comes with several default Search folders: Unread Mail, For Follow-Up, and Large Messages. You can create Search folders to display all messages from a particular client, messages from a specific time period, or any other filter criteria of your choosing. You can access Search folders from the Navigation Pane below the Sent Items folder.

NOTE *Virtual folders act like regular folders. However, the messages displayed in virtual folders are actually stored in other folders in your Inbox so you are storing only one copy of the message.*

To create a new Search folder follow these steps:

1. Right-click Search Folders in the All Mail Folders section of the Navigation Pane when Mail is selected and in the Folder list when that is visible.

2. Choose Create New Search Folder or choose File ➢ New ➢ Search Folder to open the New Search Folder dialog box shown in Figure 2.21.

3. Choose the type of Search folder you would like to create from the four available categories: Reading Mail, People and Lists, Organizing Mail, and Custom (see more about creating Custom Search folders later in this section). Some of the folders may require additional information. For example, if you choose Mail From Specific People, you must click the Choose button to select the people from the Select Names dialog box.

4. If you have more than one mailbox, click the list for Search Mail In and select the desired mailbox.

5. When you have made the appropriate selections, click OK to create the Search folder.

The new Search folder is visible by clicking the Expand button in front of Search Folders in the Navigation Pane.

FIGURE 2.21

Use the New Search Folder dialog box to create your own Search folders.

If you want to combine a number of criteria, such as mail sent from your supervisor marked as important, you need to create a Custom Search folder. To create a Custom Search folder, follow these steps:

1. Right-click Search Folders in the All Mail Folders section of the Navigation Pane when Mail is selected and in the folder list when that is visible.

2. Choose Create New Search Folder or choose File ➢ New ➢ Search Folder to open the New Search Folder dialog box shown in Figure 2.21.

3. Scroll to the bottom of the list and choose Create a Custom Search Folder. Click the Choose button.

4. Enter a name for the Search folder in the Custom Search Folder dialog box.

5. Click the Browse button to specify the folder or folders you want included in the search—you may want to exclude Deleted Items and Junk E-mail, for example. Clear the Mailbox check box and select the folder or folders you want to include. You can include all the folders in the Inbox by selecting it and leaving the Search subfolders check box selected. Click OK to accept the settings.

6. Click the Criteria button to open the Search Folder Criteria dialog box. The Search Folder Criteria dialog box has three tabs: Messages, More Choices, and Advanced. See the "Creating Custom Search Folder Criteria" section later in this chapter for more information about setting custom criteria. Select the criteria you want to apply and click OK to save the criteria.

7. Click OK on the Custom Search Folder dialog box to create the new Search folder.

Anytime you want to see the contents of the new Search folder, select it in the Search Folders list in All Mail Folders in the Navigation Pane. To help you create specific Search folder criteria, we'll include a more detailed discussion in the next section.

CREATING CUSTOM SEARCH FOLDER CRITERIA

On the first tab of the Search Folder Criteria dialog box, shown in Figure 2.22, you can enter criteria to display messages based on specific words, to or from specific people, and defined time frames. Table 2.3 summarizes the available criteria you can choose.

TABLE 2.3: CRITERIA BY ITEM TYPE

CRITERION	ITEM TYPE	USED TO FILTER
Search for the Words	All	Text in fields and logical field groupings: name fields, address fields, subject field, and message body
From	Address	Contacts with the selected e-mail addresses
Sent To	Address	Contacts with the selected e-mail addresses
Where I Am	Address	The Sent To field: Where I Am the Only Person On The To Line, On The To Line With Other People, On The Cc Line With Other People
Time	Mail	Messages received, sent, due, created, expiring in a selected time frame, or modified in the time frame indicated

FIGURE 2.22

On the first tab of the Search Folder Criteria dialog box, you can select criteria related to search words, people, or timeframes.

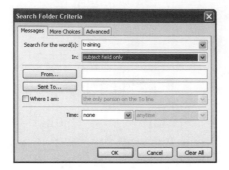

On the More Choices tab of the Search Folder Criteria dialog box, shown in Figure 2.23, you can specify criteria for these options:

Categories	must include all the categories you select (if more than one)
Only items that are	read or unread
Only items with	attachments or no attachments
Whose importance is	normal, low, high
Only Items Which	relates to flags of various colors and flagged messages
Size (in kilobytes)	is greater than, less than, approximately equal to, or between

FIGURE 2.23

Enter criteria on the More Choices tab to further refine your filter.

Use the Advanced tab of the Search Folder Criteria dialog box, shown in Figure 2.24, to create field-specific criteria.

FIGURE 2.24

Use the Advanced page to create filters you can't build in the first two pages.

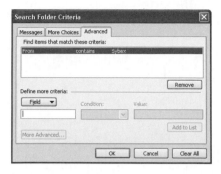

You create an advanced filter by building criteria one at a time and adding them to the Find Items That Match These Criteria list. To create a criterion, click the Field button to open the menu of field lists. Move the mouse pointer to the list that contains the field you want to create a criterion for, and Outlook opens the field list so you can select the field. For example, let's say you'd like to create a Search folder to view e-mail marked as Confidential. You would select Frequently-Used Fields from the Field list and choose Sensitivity.

In the Condition drop-down list, select a condition, and then select the value for the condition in the Value text box. The Condition and Values drop-down lists apply specifically to the field you choose. In this example, the Condition drop-down list includes Equals, Not Equal To, Exists, Does Not Exist. The Value drop-down list includes the choices: Normal, Personal, Private, Confidential.

When all the required parts of the condition are in place, Outlook enables the Add to List button. Click the button to move the condition to the Condition list. Create additional conditions until you've created all the conditions for your filter.

Removing a Condition

To remove a condition from the Advanced tab, select the condition and click the Remove button. This doesn't affect the conditions on the other two tabs of the Filter dialog box. To remove all the conditions from the filter and start again, click the Clear All button at the bottom of the Filter dialog box.

WARNING   When you create Search folder criteria, the items displayed in the Search folder must meet all the criteria you enter. For example, if you create the Advanced criteria to display messages marked confidential and choose Messages Received in the Last Seven Days on the Messages tab, the Search folder will display only messages marked confidential in the last seven days. Confidential messages received last month and messages marked Normal received yesterday will not be displayed in the view.

Search folders simplify organization because no matter where you've stored a message, you can easily locate it and others like it with a well-crafted Search folder.

Digging your way out of the e-mail avalanche may take some effort but as you can see from this chapter, planning ahead can make the work a lot easier. Take a few minutes to review your e-mail frustrations and needs and then make junk mail handling, rules, and search folders do some of the digging for you.

Chapter 3

Taking Control of Your Time and Tasks

NEXT TO E-MAIL, OUTLOOK'S Calendar is the most popular of Outlook's functions. No matter what you do for a living, chances are you spend a fair amount of time making appointments and scheduling meetings. Outlook makes it possible to keep track of your appointments and maybe save a little of your sanity along the way. To stretch Calendar to its limits, you need to be working on a Microsoft Exchange Server. However, even a stand-alone user can reap the benefits of more-efficient time scheduling offered by Outlook.

If you're already a list keeper, you'll find that Outlook takes the To Do list to a new dimension by adding the ability to track progress, assign tasks to other people (our personal favorite), set reminders for tasks, schedule time to complete tasks, and evaluate the progress you are making. Even if making lists is not your favorite pastime, it's hard to ignore the power of Outlook Tasks. In this chapter we'll help you get the most out of Outlook's Calendar and Tasks folders.

- ◆ Setting appointment options
- ◆ Color-coding calendar appointments
- ◆ Scheduling meetings
- ◆ Viewing calendars side-by-side
- ◆ Creating a group schedule
- ◆ Printing calendars to meet your needs
- ◆ Creating one-time and recurring tasks
- ◆ Delegating tasks

Managing Your Time and Your Life

Making appointments, checking dates, and scheduling meetings seems to be all there is to life some days. It's not hard to go home at the end of the day and believe that all you did was rearrange things on the calendar. If that sounds familiar, then this section is for you. We can't guarantee it will give you more time, but maybe you'll feel more on top of that onerous schedule.

Navigating Through Time

If you've ever spent time in an office supply store deciding which of the varied calendar styles to purchase for next year's appointments, then you'll appreciate Outlook's ability to switch calendar views. It doesn't matter it you prefer a day-at-a glance, a week-at-a-glance, or a whole month, you can choose to see your schedule that way in Outlook. Click the Day, Work Week, Week, or Month button on the Standard toolbar to see the calendar displayed for the designated time period. Figure 3.1 shows the typical Day view of the Calendar.

FIGURE 3.1

The typical day view of the Calendar

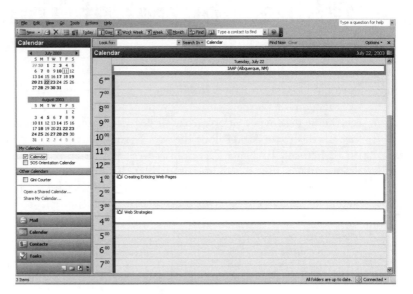

The fastest way to move around to different dates in the Calendar is to make proficient use of the Date Navigator. The Date Navigator, located at the top of the Navigation Pane in Day/Week/Month view, not only shows you the monthly calendar but also lets you select days to view in the calendar itself.

TIP By default, only one month is visible in the Date Navigator in a standard 800 x 600 screen resolution. But depending on your screen size and resolution, you may be able to change it to view several months at a time. Point to the border that separates the Navigation Pane and the Calendar and when the pointer changes to a resize arrow, drag to the right. At a high screen resolution, you might be able to fit three or more months across the screen. You may also find that you can drag the border above the folder buttons at the bottom of the Navigation bar to make another row of months visible. This typically works only if the screen size and resolution is above 1024 x 768.

Click any date in the Date Navigator and that date becomes visible in the Calendar. Use the shortcuts in Table 3.1 to select other dates.

TABLE 3.1: SELECTING DATES IN THE DATE NAVIGATOR

TO SELECT	ACTION
A different month	Click the left and right arrows next to the month headings.
An entire week	Move the pointer to the left side of the Date Navigator. The pointer points toward the Date Navigator. Click the mouse to select the week.
Multiple weeks	Point to the first week and drag.
Nonconsecutive days	Click one day and hold the Ctrl key down on the keyboard before selecting the next day.

To move quickly to a different month, click the month name and select another month from the list. If the month you want is not immediately visible among the months displayed, move the mouse pointer off of the list (below the list to move into the future and above the list to view the past) and continue dragging until you see the month you want. Move the mouse pointer back into the list and select the desired month.

Moving the mouse pointer farther away from the list increases the speed of the scroll. To slow down the scroll rate, move the mouse pointer closer to the list. To move to a previous month, position the mouse pointer above the list.

Any time you want to move quickly back to the current date, click the Today button on the Standard toolbar.

TIP   *If you've used Calendar in a previous Outlook version, you might have trouble adjusting to the Date Navigator on the left of the screen and, even more importantly, the absence of the old TaskPad. If you are suffering from either of these conditions, fear no more—help is a drag away. Just point to the thin border to the right of the vertical scroll bar and, when the pointer changes to a resize arrow, drag to the left. The Date Navigator switches to the right and the TaskPad becomes visible. Display as many months as you want (depending on the screen size) horizontally across the screen. To display more vertically, point to the top of the TaskPad and drag down.*

Appointment Basics

Scheduling an appointment is as easy as clicking in the appointment slot in the Day view and entering the information. After you have finished the entry, point to the lower border of the appointment slot and, with the two-headed arrow pointer, drag to identify the end time of the appointment. Drop the blue line just above the desired end time as shown here:

To change the start time of the appointment, drag the blue line above the appointment slot. If you want to maintain the length of the appointment but alter the start and end times, point to the blue line on the left side of the appointment and, with the four-headed arrow, drag the entire appointment to a new time. As you begin dragging, the four-headed arrow changes shape to a pointer with a move box.

TIP   *The default time increment is 30 minutes. If you routinely schedule 15 or even 10 minute appointments, right-click the time scale and choose a different time increment.*

To change the appointment to a different day, drag the appointment with the four-headed arrow to the new date in the Date Navigator.

NOTE   To change the date of an appointment by dragging to a new date, the new date must be displayed in the Date Navigator. If the desired month is not visible, make it visible before you start dragging or double-click the appointment to open the Appointment form and change the date there.

ENTERING AN APPOINTMENT IN THE APPOINTMENT FORM

When you want to enter more details about an appointment, double-click the appointment to open the Appointment form shown in Figure 3.2. In addition to the Subject and Start and End times, the Appointment form allows you to enter a location, to set a reminder, color code, and to enter other notes about the appointment.

FIGURE 3.2

The Calendar's Appointment form

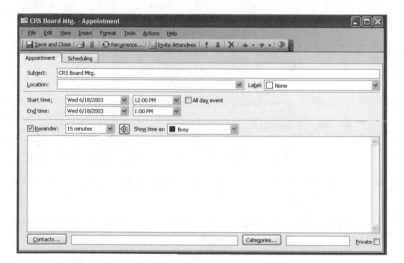

To set the start and end times in an Appointment form, click the down arrow to the right of the first Start Time and End Time fields. The arrow to the right of the second field opens a list of times but you can enter any time period by entering it manually. Be careful to select the correct AM or PM time, or you might be expecting to have lunch some day at midnight.

MANAGING REMINDERS

One of the biggest advantages of using an electronic calendar is that it can automatically remind you when it's time to go to your appointments. The default reminder is set for 15 minutes prior to a scheduled appointment, but from the drop-down list you can select any time from 0 minutes to up to two weeks or you can type any reminder time in the text box. To turn off the reminder, click the check box to the left of the Reminder field.

At the scheduled time, the reminder appears as a small dialog box in whatever application is running at the time (as long as Outlook is running in the background). Outlook 2003 uses a single window for all reminders, whether they're for appointments, events, or tasks. Figure 3.3 shows a reminder window with two appointments and one task.

FIGURE 3.3

Outlook 2003 lets you handle reminders more efficiently by allowing you to deal with them all at once.

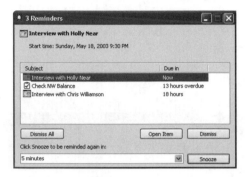

When Outlook displays the Reminder window, choose one of the following options:

◆ Click Dismiss to dismiss the selected reminder, in which case Outlook assumes you are on your way to the appointment (or have tackled the task) and won't bother you again. You can also hold Ctrl to select multiple reminders you want to dismiss.

◆ Click Dismiss All to dismiss all displayed reminders. Outlook won't remind you about these items again.

◆ Select an item and click Snooze to be reminded again in a designated amount of time. To use this option, choose the desired time interval from the Click Snooze To Be Reminded Again In drop-down list and then click the Snooze button.

TIP *You can hold Ctrl or Shift to select multiple items for snoozing.*

◆ Select one or more items and click the Open Item button to open the Appointment or Task form so you can review it and make changes if you wish.

When the Reminder dialog box opens, clicking anywhere outside the dialog box moves the dialog box to the Windows Taskbar. You can then open it at any time to respond to the reminder.

Choosing the Reminder Sound

By default, an appointment reminder is accompanied by a sound called `Reminder.wav`. You have the option of disabling the sound or changing the sound file it plays. Click the speaker icon in the open Appointment form to access the Reminder Sound options.

Clear the Play This Sound check box if you'd prefer your reminders appear on the screen silently. If you would like to hear a sound but would prefer a different sound file, click the Browse button to locate the file you would like to use (perhaps something like Carole King's *It's Too Late?*). Double-click the file-name, and it appears in the Play This Sound text box. Click OK to apply the selected sound file.

TIP   If you change the sound file within a task, it is only in effect for that specific reminder. To change the default sound file for all Reminders, go to Tools ➤ Options ➤ Other ➤ Advanced Options ➤ Reminder Options and choose a new file. Sound files, or wave files, are designated by a .wav *extension. If you have time on your hands, you can use Windows Sound Recorder to record your own reminder message or sound that plays when it is time to do a task.*

SETTING THE FREE/BUSY STATUS

The Show Time As drop-down list on an appointment form is more important than it looks. The setting in this text box determines how your time will be displayed to others who want to schedule appointments with you. This is called your Free/Busy Status. Unless you give someone permission to see the details of your calendar (note that you need to be connected to an Exchange Server to grant such permission), your free/busy status is all they see when they try to schedule a meeting with you.

You have four free/busy options for each appointment:

Busy   is the default option. It is designated by a dark blue color and it means that you are not available. You are typically not available unless there is an emergency (see Out of the Office for more about Busy).

Free   is designated by white and means that although you have something on your calendar you are still available for appointments.

Tentative   is designated by blue and white stripes and means that you could be busy but the meeting has not yet been confirmed.

Out of the Office   is designated by dark purple and is the most ambiguous of the four. We recommend that you come to an agreement in your office about what it means in regard to your availability. It generally means you are not available but it's unclear if you are working or lying on a beach somewhere. In some offices, Out of the Office is used to mean totally unavailable, on vacation, out of there. In these offices, Busy is used to indicate any work activities even if you are at a conference in Las Vegas but theoretically still on company time. Other offices use Out of the Office to mean you might still be working but not at your usual location. If an emergency meeting comes up, you could possibly rearrange things to be there. We have found it helpful to clarify the definition and ask everyone to use it the same way.

SCHEDULING RECURRING APPOINTMENTS

You probably have appointments that occur on a regular basis—for example, a weekly staff meeting, a daily project review meeting, or a monthly district sales meeting. With Outlook's Calendar, you can set up a meeting once and make it automatically recur in your calendar.

To set up a recurring appointment, open the appointment form and enter the data for the first occurrence of the appointment. When you have entered the first appointment, click the Recurrence button on the Standard toolbar within the Appointment form. This opens the Appointment Recurrence dialog box, shown in Figure 3.4.

FIGURE 3.4

Appointment
Recurrence
dialog box

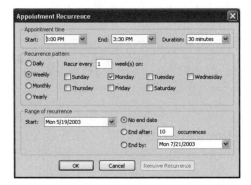

Here you can set the Recurrence Pattern and the Range Of Recurrence. To set the Recurrence Pattern, indicate whether the appointment will occur Daily, Weekly, Monthly, or Yearly. If the appointment will occur every three days, choose Daily; every two months, choose Monthly; and so on. Each of the four options gives you different choices for defining the actual pattern.

Daily   Choose between Every N Days or Every Weekday.

Weekly   Indicate how often the appointment will occur: every week (1), every other week (2), every third week (3), and so on. This is the best option if the appointment will occur every six weeks or every eight weeks (because some months have more than four weeks). Then mark on which day(s) of the week the appointment will occur.

Monthly   Choose between specifying which date of each *N* month(s) or indicating the first, second, third, fourth, or last day of every *N* month(s); for example, the last Friday of every month or the third Thursday of every second month. You could also indicate the first weekday or the last weekend day of the month.

Yearly   Indicate a specific date in a specific month (every May 5), or mark the first, second, third, fourth, or last day of a specific month (the first Friday in May).

Sometimes you have to be creative to figure out how often the appointment will occur. For example, if the appointment will occur two times a year on March 31 and September 31, do you use Monthly or Yearly? Because these dates are six months apart, you could use Monthly and indicate the last day of every six months (as long as the Start date was set to one of the two dates).

However, if this appointment is not so evenly spaced—May 31 and August 31 for example—you can't use Recurrence. Instead you will have to create two appointments: one for the May date every year, and one for the August date every year.

DEFINING THE RANGE OF RECURRENCE

The Range Of Recurrence refers to when the first appointment will occur and how long the appointment will continue.

You have your choice of the following:

No End Date   The appointment continues into eternity (or until you tell it to stop).

End After *N* Occurrences   You only need to schedule the appointment a specific number of times, and then you are finished with it.

End By   You only have to schedule this appointment until a certain date and then you are free.

Once you have set the Range Of Recurrence, click OK to return to the Appointment form. Click Save And Close to save the appointment and return to the Outlook window.

EDITING APPOINTMENT RECURRENCE

To make changes to the recurrence pattern or range that you set, open the appointment. Any time you open a recurring appointment, you are asked if you want to open the series or just the occurrence. To change every instance of the appointment, choose Series. Click the Recurrence Pattern button on the open Appointment form, make your changes, and then click Save And Close again. You can also edit the Subject of the appointment, but any changes you make affect only future occurrences of the appointment.

To delete the recurrence pattern without deleting the appointment, open the appointment, choose to open the series, click the Recurrence button, and click the Remove Recurrence button on the bottom of the Appointment Recurrence dialog box. Close the Appointment Recurrence dialog box and Save And Close the task. The appointment still appears on the calendar, but it is now there for one time only.

SCHEDULING EVENTS

An event is an appointment that has no start or end time, such as a holiday, anniversary, or any other day that you want to note. To schedule an event, open an Appointment form, enter the subject and date information, and then click the All Day Event check box. This removes the Start Time and End Time fields from the Appointment form. You can set a reminder for an event and set a Recurrence Pattern just as you would for any other appointment.

TIP   To automatically open an Event form, double-click in the gray area at the top of the Calendar in Day, Work Week, and Week views.

Outlook assumes that an event does not occupy your time and therefore shows your time as Free. You might want to change this, however. For example, if the event you are entering is your vacation, you could set the Show Time As field to Out Of The Office.

Because there are no times associated with an event, events are displayed differently than regular appointments in the Information Viewer. In the Day view, an event appears at the top of the day's schedule. In the Week and Month views, events are displayed in bordered boxes, such as those shown in Figure 3.5.

FIGURE 3.5

In Month view, you can easily distinguish events by the borders around them.

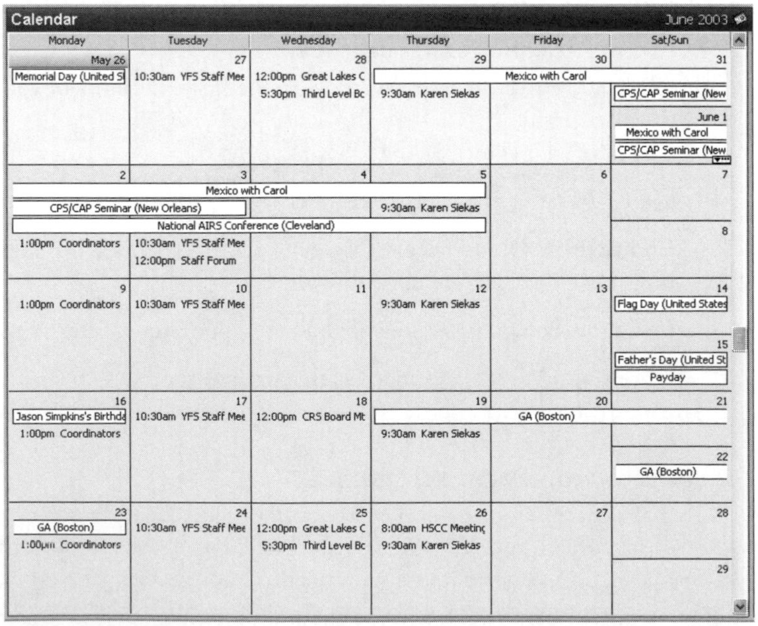

Scheduling a Multiple-Day Event

Multiple-day events are scheduled activities that have no set start and end times and span several days. To enter such an event, open the Appointment form and set the start and end dates to coincide with the actual dates of the event.

Color-Coding Appointments for Quick Reference

If you typically display your calendar in Day/Week/Month view, you'll love Outlook 2003's color-coding feature for appointments and events. You can choose from 10 colors, and each color comes with a label such as Business, Important, Needs Preparation, Phone Call, and more. Naturally, you can edit these labels to fit your own business and personal needs.

There are two ways to color-code calendar items: manually or automatically, using rules. If you create a rule to assign a color automatically, every calendar item you create that meets the criteria for the rule is colored, with no additional effort on your part. This can be a great way to see at a glance all the meetings related to a particular project. Before you decide which method to use, keep the following in mind:

- Manual coloring always takes precedence over coloring applied by rules. So if you've applied manual coloring to a calendar item, you cannot format it with automatic coloring.

- If you've given another person access to your calendar through a public folder or other means, only manually assigned colors are visible. Automatic coloring is only visible to the person who applied it.

- You must be in Day/Week/Month view to see any coloring.

Before you apply calendar coloring, you should modify the list of labels so they reflect your own business practices. To do so, click the Calendar Coloring button on the Standard toolbar and choose Edit Labels. The Edit Calendar Labels dialog box opens as shown in Figure 3.6. Simply select the text of the label you wish to change and overtype it with your own text. Click OK when you're finished editing labels.

FIGURE 3.6

Modify the default color labels to make the most of Outlook 2003's new calendar coloring feature.

To assign a color manually, do any of the following:

- Select an appointment or event in the Day, Week, or Month view. Click the Calendar Coloring button on the Standard toolbar and choose one of the colors from the list.

◆ Right-click a calendar item and choose Label; then click the color you'd like to use.

◆ Double-click a calendar item to open the Appointment, Meeting, or Event form. Click the Label drop-down list and choose a color from there.

To create a rule to assign a color automatically, follow these steps:

1. Right-click a calendar item and click Automatic Formatting, or click the Calendar Coloring button on the Standard toolbar and choose Automatic Formatting. In either case, the Automatic Formatting dialog box opens.

2. Click Add to create a rule, and then type a name for the rule in the Name field.

3. Click the Condition button to establish criteria for the rule.

NOTE   You'll find a thorough discussion of creating rules and setting conditions in Chapter 9, "Streamlining Mailings and Messaging."

4. Select a label from the Label drop-down list and click OK to apply the rule.

Remove calendar coloring by selecting the appointment and changing the color label to None. This works even if the coloring you have applied is the result of a rule.

To delete all coloring associated with a rule, delete the rule. Right-click an appointment and choose Automatic Formatting from the shortcut menu. Select the rule and click the Delete button inside the Automatic Formatting dialog box.

Setting Up Your Work Day and Other Options

Because people work very different schedules these days, Outlook has included a number of options that let you define the days you work, the hours that you want to display in your calendar, and on which day your work week starts. To change the Calendar options, choose Tools ➢ Options on the menu. Click the Calendar Options button on the Preferences tab of the Options dialog box to open the dialog box shown in Figure 3.7.

FIGURE 3.7

Calendar Options let you customize Calendar to fit your needs.

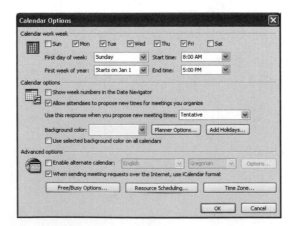

Set the Calendar options as follows:

Calendar Work Week Options

- ◆ Check the boxes for the days of the week to designate the days that make up your workweek. Set the start and end times of your typical day using the Start Time and End Time fields.

- ◆ To keep your calendar in line with your staff schedules, you might want to indicate that your calendar starts on the first four-day week or first full week of the year rather than January 1. Make this selection from the First Week Of Year drop-down list.

Calendar Options

- ◆ Enable the Show Week Numbers In The Date Navigator check box if you need to know what week (1–52) you are in for planning purposes.

- ◆ If you want others to have the flexibility of suggesting alternative times for meetings you organize, enable that check box. (For more on the meeting planner, see the "Scheduling Meetings" section later in this chapter.)

- ◆ Choose a default response for times when you propose alternative meeting times. Click the drop-down arrow next to Use This Response When You Propose New Meeting Times and choose from the list.

- ◆ Click the Background Color drop-down arrow to designate a different color for your calendar's background in Day and Work Week, Week, and Month views.

- ◆ In Outlook 2003, you can display lunar calendar information and make appointments based on that calendar; turn on the Enable Alternate Calendar feature and choose the calendar you'd like to use.

- ◆ Click the Planner Options button to choose certain behaviors for the Meeting Planner (discussed later in this chapter).

- ◆ Click the Add Holidays button to add a variety of religious and national holidays to your calendar (see the "Remembering Holidays" sidebar).

Advanced Options

- ◆ Select When Sending Meeting Requests Over The Internet, Use iCalendar Format to convert appointment items into a format that can be used by people who don't run Outlook.

- ◆ Click the Free/Busy Options button to control how far in advance your free/busy information will be available for others on your Exchange Server and how frequently it will update information with the server. If you want to share your free/busy information with others over the

Internet, you can enter the URL where your information is available. See "Checking Others' Schedules First" later in this chapter for more about free/busy information.

◆ Click the Resource Scheduling button to set options for scheduling resources such as meeting rooms, AV equipment, and the like.

◆ Click the Time Zone button to adjust the time zone you are in and set a second time zone to view simultaneously—an invaluable option if you schedule meetings in one time zone that you plan to attend in another.

REMEMBERING HOLIDAYS

You can add national and religious holidays to your calendar, including Christian, Jewish, and Islamic holidays. Choose Tools ➤ Options and on the Preferences tab click the Calendar Options button. In the Calendar Options dialog box, click the Add Holidays button.

While it only takes a few clicks to add all the Yemeni holidays to your calendar, if you decide you really don't care about holidays in Yemen, it takes a little more effort to remove them from the calendar. You can delete them one by one for each of the three years of holidays Outlook adds, or you can delete all the holidays as a group and then add back in the ones you want. To quickly delete all the holidays in your calendar, choose View ➤ Arrange By ➤ Current View ➤ By Category. All the holidays are in the Holiday category. Select the Holiday group heading and press Delete. Switch back to Day/Week/Month view by choosing View ➤ Arrange By ➤ Current View ➤ Day/Week/Month.

TIP   Outlook imports holidays into the main calendar folder only, so attempting to add holidays to a calendar subfolder or public folder just results in duplicate holidays being added to your main calendar. To have holidays appear in calendar subfolders, move or copy them to the subfolder after first adding them to the main folder. To do this, switch to By Categories view in the main calendar folder. Right-drag the holiday group to the subfolder and choose either Move or Copy from the shortcut menu that appears.

Scheduling Meetings

If you've ever worked in an office that holds lots of meetings, then you know firsthand the inordinate amount of time that is spent scheduling and rescheduling meetings. Some office studies have found that nearly 30 percent of secretarial time is spent scheduling meetings for managers and administrators. Group scheduling tools are one of the fastest-growing software markets today. Companies all over the globe are recognizing the need to simplify the process of scheduling meetings. Outlook is ready to address this challenge, as the Calendar module offers extensive tools for workgroup scheduling.

PLANNING A MEETING WITH OTHERS

Outlook 2003 offers several ways to invite others to attend a meeting. The simplest way is to click the down arrow on the New button and choose Meeting Request from the list of choices. This opens the Meeting e-mail message form, shown in Figure 3.8.

FIGURE 3.8

A meeting request message form

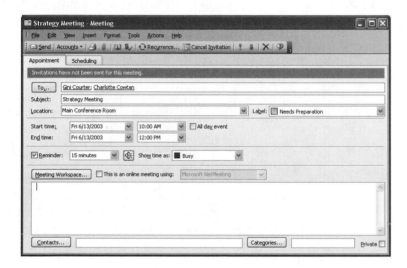

You'll see some differences between the Meeting form and the standard e-mail message form. First, notice the message informing you that invitations for this meeting have not yet been sent. Of course, you already knew that, but you can always find the status of an invitation here even after you send it. Second, in addition to the To and Subject fields, there is a Location field for you to identify where the meeting will take place. The other fields on the Meeting form are similar to a typical Appointment form.

To create a meeting request, follow these steps:

1. Click the down arrow on the New button and choose Meeting Request.

2. Click the To button to open the Select Attendees And Resources dialog box.

3. Double-click the names of those people whose attendance at the meeting is required.

4. If a person's attendance is optional, click their name and click the Optional button.

5. If your Microsoft Exchange administrator set up meeting rooms and other resources, select the resource you want to assign to the meeting and click the Resources button.

6. Click OK to close the Select Attendees And Resources dialog box and return to the Meeting form.

7. Enter the Subject and Location.

8. Fill in the Start Time, End Time, Reminder, and Show Time As fields just as you would for any other appointment.

9. If the meeting is going to be regularly scheduled, you can click the Recurrence button and set up the Recurrence pattern (see "Scheduling Recurring Appointments" earlier in the chapter).

10. If you want to set up a Windows SharePoint Services Meeting Workspace for the meeting, click the Meeting Workspace button and create the workspace or link to an already established meeting workspace.

TIP *Windows SharePoint Services Meeting Workspace is one of the most exciting things to happen to meetings since the introduction of the white board. If you want to learn more about Meeting Workspaces and Windows SharePoint Services, be sure to check out Chapter 8, "Collaborating on Documents." You'll be glad you did.*

11. If this meeting will be held online using Microsoft NetMeeting, Windows Media Services, or Microsoft Exchange Conferencing, click the This Is An Online Meeting Using checkbox to activate additional options related to online meetings. Here you can set the type of meeting, the Directory Server that will host the meeting, whether you want NetMeeting to start automatically with reminder, the organizer's e-mail address, and any Office document that you want available at the meeting.

12. Click the Send button to send out the meeting requests.

NOTE *Outlook automatically creates meeting and task requests in rich-text format, regardless of the default format you have set.*

RESPONDING TO A MEETING REQUEST

Each person you invite to the meeting receives an e-mail message labeled *Meeting Request*. When they open the message, they see the information about the meeting. After they've decided whether they can attend, they can click one of the Accept, Decline, or Tentative buttons at the top of the Meeting form. If they would prefer to meet at another time they can click the Propose New Meeting Time button. Users who choose this option can even see free/busy information of other invitees if their information is available on the Exchange Server or posted in some other location. To view your own calendar while you consider accepting an appointment, click the Calendar button—this opens your calendar in a separate window.

NOTE *In Outlook 2003, you can respond to meeting requests directly from the Reading Pane without even opening the message.*

After an attendee clicks one of these response buttons, Outlook generates an e-mail message back to you, the meeting request originator, indicating whether this person can attend or, if the attendee clicked Propose New Meeting Time, an alternate meeting time and/or date. If the person accepted the meeting request, it's automatically placed on their calendar. In addition, all of the responses are automatically tabulated, so there is no need to keep a manual count. It really couldn't be easier. To see a list of attendees and their responses to date, all you have to do is open the appointment in your calendar and click the Tracking tab, shown in Figure 3.9.

FIGURE 3.9

The Tracking tab of the Meeting form shows responses to date after a meeting request has been sent out.

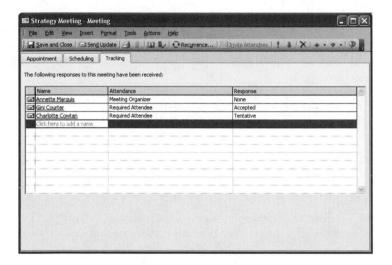

If, after seeing who has accepted your invitation, you decide to invite other people to this meeting, click the Click Here To Add A Name box in the Tracking tab of the Meeting form and enter another name. When you've finished adding new people, click Send Update and then choose to send a meeting request to added or deleted attendees only or to all attendees.

That's all there is to it. Never again will you have to make 25 phone calls to get four people to attend a meeting. Now you'll actually have time to get some real work done.

CHECKING OTHERS' SCHEDULES FIRST

Even the steps outlined above for requesting a meeting could backfire if you find that the majority of the people you need at your meeting can't attend at the time you requested. It might be easier to check individual schedules first and schedule the meeting at a time when all of your key people can attend. A lot of people get nervous when you talk about making their schedules available for others to see. Outlook has found the best of both worlds. It allows you to look at the individual's *free/busy* information; you can see when an individual is free, busy, out of the office, or tentatively scheduled. You cannot, however, see what they are doing or how they are spending their time (unless they have given you permission to do so). This seems to relieve most people's anxiety about Big Brother looking over their shoulder and still allows for the greatest success in scheduling meetings with the first request.

To check to see when someone is available to meet, open a new or existing Meeting form and select the Scheduling tab. The Scheduling tab, shown in Figure 3.10, lists all attendees in the left column. When you first open this page, Outlook automatically goes out to the network to gather the most current free/busy information. The grid on the right side of the page shows each individual's free/busy status.

NOTE *When you click the Scheduling tab, Outlook immediately searches the network for your meeting invitees. If these folks aren't on your network, Outlook invites you to join the Microsoft Office Internet Free/Busy Service. This free service allows people to post their free/busy information on the Web so others can check when they are available. You can click Join to sign up yourself, but you must ask your meeting invitees to do the same or you still won't be able to see their free/busy information.*

An individual's free time is not marked in the grid. If they are out of the office, a maroon bar extends across the time that they will be gone. If they are busy, you see a blue bar, and if they are tentatively scheduled, you see a striped blue bar.

Point to any horizontal bar to see a screen tip with details of any appointment you have permission to view. If you find these screen tips annoying, turn them off by choosing Tools ➤ Options ➤ Calendar Options. Click the Planner Options button on the Preferences tab and disable the Show Popup Calendar Details check box.

The white vertical bar represents the duration of the meeting. The green border on the left indicates the start time, and the brown border represents the end time of the meeting, as shown in Figure 3.10.

FIGURE 3.10

The Scheduling tab of the Meeting form shows free/busy information.

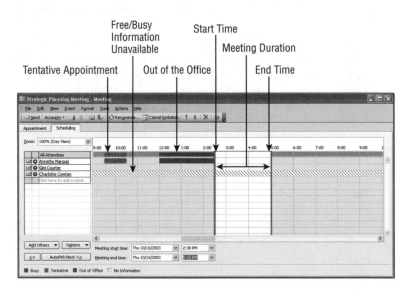

The key to working with the Scheduling grid is to start by manually setting your preferred meeting time in the Meeting Start Time and Meeting End Time text boxes. Even if the desired attendees are not available at this time, this sets a beginning date and the duration of the meeting. Click the AutoPick Next button to locate the first time when all attendees are available. Notice that the Meeting Start Time and Meeting End Time text boxes change to correspond to the time indicated by the grid. If the first time that everyone is available is not agreeable to you, continue clicking AutoPick Next until you find a good time.

If, at any point, you decide to invite others to the meeting, click the Add Others button on the Scheduling tab. Click the Options button to access the following four options:

Show Only Working Hours   Shows only work hours in the calendar

Choose Show Calendar Details   Displays the details of free/busy time, but only if the selected attendees have given you permission to do so

TIP   If you'd like this option on by default, minimize this scheduling window and choose Tools ➢ Options ➢ Calendar Options. Click the Planner Options button on the Preferences tab and enable the Show Calendar Details In The Grid check box.

AutoPick   Determines whose schedules must be free for AutoPick to select an available time slot

Refresh Free/Busy   Forces Outlook to update the free/busy information

As soon as you find an agreeable time for everyone you want to invite, return to the Appointment tab (if you wish) to verify that the start and end times have been adjusted accordingly. Then send the attendees' e-mail message. Now you can be pretty confident that the attendees will accept the meeting request.

TIP   Typically, Outlook refreshes free/busy information every 15 minutes (that's the default Calendar option setting). If you are concerned that one of your invitees might be scheduling something at the same time, click the Option button on the Scheduling tab of the Appointment form and choose Update Free/Busy information. This gives you the most current data available.

CANCELING A MEETING

Suppose you need to cancel a meeting that you arranged. Don't despair, you still don't have to make a slew of phone calls. Open the meeting in your calendar and choose Actions ➢ Cancel Meeting. You then have the option to send a cancellation message to all attendees indicating that the meeting has been canceled, or you can choose to delete the meeting without sending a cancellation. (Only use this option when you want everyone to show up and wonder where you are!) If you choose to send a message, you are even given an opportunity to explain why you are canceling the meeting. You can then follow it up with another invitation to the meeting at the new date and time. What used to take hours is now handled in just a few minutes. Everybody's notified, everyone's calendar is updated, and no one had to be interrupted from their work to make it happen.

New!

Managing Schedules for a Group

If you need to share your calendar with other people on the Microsoft Exchange Server, you can assign folder permissions to let them have direct access to any of your Outlook folders. You can grant them a number of different levels of permission, including giving them full rights to schedule appointments and respond to meeting requests as if they were you. If you want a little more control, you can set a person up as a delegate. As a delegate the person can access your calendar (or other Outlook folders) but they can only send messages on your behalf. No one is fooled into thinking it is actually you. Both are effective ways of sharing your calendar with someone else. Chapter 12, "Securing and Organizing Documents," describes how to assign permissions and set up delegates. Outlook 2003 makes it easy to work with shared calendars. Any calendars you have access to are open automatically when you launch Outlook, saving you the tedium of having to reopen them every day. In addition, it makes calendars of all types available for side-by-side viewing. You can also view additional calendars that you create and calendars in public folders using the side-by-side calendar view. Figure 3.11 shows two personal and one shared calendar side-by-side.

FIGURE 3.11

Viewing calendars side-by-side lets you manage multiple calendars at a single glance.

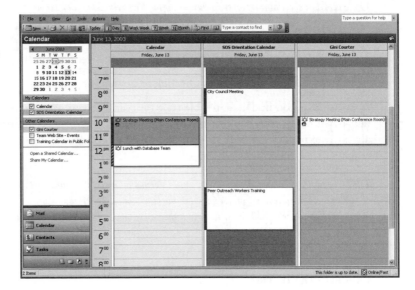

To open a second calendar that you created or a shared calendar, select the check box in front of the folder name in the Navigation Pane. If you would like to make a calendar in Public folders available for side-by-side viewing and add it to the list of Other Calendars on the Navigation Pane, follow these steps:

1. Click the Folder list button at the bottom of the Navigation Pane.

2. Navigate to the public calendar and right-click to open the shortcut menu.

3. Click Add in the new Add To Favorites dialog box.

4. Click the Calendar button in the Navigation Pane to see the list of available calendars. The public calendar should appear in the list. Select the calendar to display it.

5. Click any other calendars you want to display side-by-side.

NOTE   *If other calendars were open when you selected the public calendar, you might have to deselect it and reselect to display it next to the public calendar.*

New! ## Scheduling Multiple Meetings with the Same People

In many businesses, meetings are scheduled with the same groups of people over and over again.

If this is true in your organization, a nifty feature in Outlook 2003 called Group Schedules could save you from having to select the same names over and over again when you want to schedule them for a meeting or even just see what they are up to on a given day. With this tool, you can create and save a group schedule that you can open whenever you need to.

To set up a group schedule, follow these steps:

1. Switch to Outlook's Calendar and click the View Group Schedules button on the Standard toolbar.

2. Click the New button in the Group Schedules dialog box to create a new group schedule.

3. Enter a name for the new group schedule and click OK.

4. Select the names of the people you want to include in the group on the Group Schedules time grid. You can do this by clicking in the Group Members column and entering the names. To add names from the address book, click the Add Others button and choose Add From Address Book.

5. After you've added the names, click the Save And Close button.

Outlook closes the Group Schedules dialog box along with the time grid. To view the group schedule you created, click the View Group Schedules button. Select the group you created and click Open. To see details about anyone's schedule, point to the time slot and a screen tip appears with the rest of the appointment information (see Figure 3.12).

NOTE   *To see the details of someone's schedule, you must have at least Reviewers permissions to that person's calendar. If you have questions about how to set up permissions, see Chapter 12 for the complete story.*

FIGURE 3.12

Point to any time slot to see the details of someone's calendar.

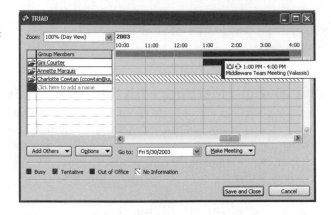

You can use the Group Schedules tool to schedule an appointment with the members of the group. Select any time on the time grid—drag to create a longer appointment—and open the Make Meeting menu to select from the available options.

If you'd rather see only working hours in the time grid or you don't care about seeing appointment details, click the Options button on the Group Schedules time grid and toggle either option.

TIP   *If you prefer, you can see calendar details right in the grid rather than in a popup that appears when you point to an item. To change this option, choose Tools ➢ Options from the main Outlook window. Click Calendar Options on the Preferences tab and then the Planner Options button. Select the Show Calendar Details in the Grid check box for either the Meeting Planner or Group Schedule section or both. Because some details will be lost in the grid display, you might want to leave the Show Popup Calendar Details check boxes checked also.*

Printing Calendars

Before you print your calendar, you can decide what style you want to use. By default, the view that is visible on your screen is the view that prints. For example, if you are in Day view, you'll print all your appointments for that day.

If you are more particular about your calendar's layout, choose File ➤ Page Setup to have a world of options available to you. Before a dialog box even opens, you are presented with a list of choices.

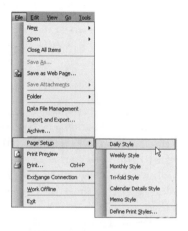

Choose the primary layout that you want for your calendar. The Page Setup options you see depend on the style you choose. Figure 3.13 shows the Format options for the Weekly Style.

FIGURE 3.13

Page Setup options for the Weekly Style

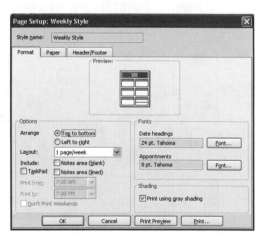

The first tab of the Page Setup dialog box gives you Format options. Here you can enable various check boxes to indicate what sections you would like to appear on the calendar page. You can even include an area for those handwritten notes. At any point in the Page Setup process, you can click the Print Preview button to see how your printed document will appear. If you are satisfied, click the Print button—if it needs more work, click Page Setup and you're brought right back there.

The Paper tab of the Page Setup dialog box is especially critical if you plan to print your calendar on something other than the North American standard 8.5"×11" paper, such as the European standard A4. You can set the paper type, size, dimensions, orientation, and margins, and you can identify what tray of the printer the paper is in.

TIP   If you are using a planner from the big three—Day-Timer, DayRunner, or FranklinCovey—take special note of the Page Size list. Your planner is probably listed, so you'll be able to select an exact match.

HEADERS AND FOOTERS

The Header/Footer tab of the Page Setup dialog box closely resembles Excel's dialog box for defining headers and footers (see Chapter 13, "Building Robust and Foolproof Workbooks"). If you're familiar with Excel—or headers and footers in any application, for that matter—this will be a snap.

A *header* appears on the top of every page of your document—in this case, the calendar. A *footer* appears on the bottom of every page. Typically, you'll find the title and subtitle in the header. By default, Outlook includes the User Name (that's generally you), the Page Number, and the Date Printed in the footer. However, you can put any information anywhere you want it.

The header and footer sections are each divided into three subsections: left, center, and right. Click in any of the six text boxes to enter text in that section. Outlook provides you with placeholders for five variable fields that you can insert in either the header or the footer.

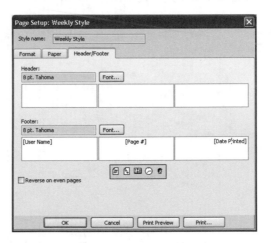

Page Number   Inserts the actual page number of the document

Total Pages   Can be combined with the page number placeholder to create expressions like "Page 1 of 4" (Page [*Page #*] of [*Total Pages*])

Date Printed   Displays the date the calendar was printed, regardless of the date period shown in the calendar

Time Printed   Displays the actual time the calendar was printed

User Name   Displays the name of the user currently logged in to Outlook

To insert a placeholder, click in the section of the header or footer where you want the placeholder to appear, and then click the placeholder button.

TIP   If you're printing a calendar in booklet form, you may want to reverse the header and footer on opposite pages by clicking the Reverse On Even Pages check box on the Header/Footer tab of the Page Setup dialog box. For example, if the date printed appears on the right side on odd pages, it would appear on the left on even pages. This gives your document a more professional appearance.

When you have finished setting up the Page Setup options, click the Print button to print your calendar.

CREATING YOUR OWN CALENDAR STYLE

To save time and use a consistent format for your calendar from week to week, you can define a Page Setup style to use every time you print your calendar. Follow the steps below to define your own print style that will appear in the Page Setup menu list:

1. Choose File ➢ Page Setup ➢ Define Print Styles.

2. Choose to edit an existing style or to create a new style by copying an existing style.

3. If you choose to copy an existing style, enter a name for the new style in the Style Name text box at the top of the Page Setup dialog box.

4. Create your custom style using the Page Setup options.

5. Click OK to save your changes.

6. Select your newly created style from the Page Setup menu.

To delete a custom style, choose File ➢ Page Setup ➢ Define Print Styles, select the style you want to delete, and click Delete. (You'll need to confirm the deletion.)

TIP   If you are editing an existing style, the original style will no longer be available. However, you can reset the original style by choosing Define Print Styles from the Page Setup menu, selecting the style, and clicking the Reset button.

Meeting Deadlines for Yourself and Others

Keeping track of the myriad things you have to do can be a daunting task. Outlook can help with that process by keeping your to-do list for you, giving you gentle reminders when something is due and even delegating tasks to others.

Creating a Task

To create a task, begin by clicking the Tasks button on the Navigation Pane. The default view in Tasks is the Simple List view, shown in Figure 3.14. The Simple List view, organized by logical dates, has four columns:

Icon   An icon that changes if a task is assigned to someone else or was assigned by someone else

Complete   A check box indicating whether the task has been completed

Subject   A descriptive name for the task

Due Date   The date on which you expect or need to complete the task

FIGURE 3.14

The Simple List view of Tasks

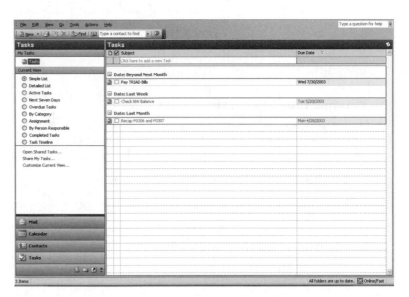

You can enter a task directly by clicking in the Click Here To Add A New Task text box. The row turns blue, and the box that is active for editing is white. Type a subject in the Subject field. It's helpful if you make the subject descriptive but not too long—less than 30 characters is best so you can read it all in the column.

NOTE   *You must be in Simple List or Detailed List view to have the Click Here To Add A New Task text box.*

After you type a subject, press Tab to move to the Due Date field (Shift+Tab moves you back to Subject); the text box turns white.

Because Outlook recognizes natural-language dates using its AutoDate feature, you have multiple options for entering dates in this field. Just about anything you type into the field that remotely resembles a date is converted into a standard date format (Wed 8/18/01). You could type **8-18-01; aug 18; three weeks from now; week from today; tomorrow; one month from next wed**. All are legitimate dates in Outlook (of course, they wouldn't all return the same date). Go ahead and try it—it's fun to see what AutoDate's limits are. Of course, you can also select a date by clicking the down arrow.

NOTE   *You can use AutoDates wherever date fields are available in Outlook.*

Click anywhere in the Task list to move the task into the list. Where the task appears in the list depends on how the list is currently sorted. Enter additional tasks the same way.

ENTERING DETAILS ABOUT A TASK

To take advantage of the powerful features built into Outlook, you need to add more information about the task than just the subject and due date. The most direct way to do this is to enter the data in a Task form. You can open the form for any existing task by double-clicking the task in the list. To open a blank Task form, click the New button on the Standard toolbar (if Tasks is the active module); or click the down arrow to the right of the New button to open the New menu, and choose Task from the list.

The Task form, shown in Figure 3.15, is composed of two tabs: Task and Details. The Task tab focuses on a description of the task (see the section "Completing a Task" later in this chapter for more information about the Details tab). Enter the subject in the Subject text box, and press Tab to move to the Due Date field. Click the Down arrow to choose a date from the calendar, or enter a date in the text box. If the task is not scheduled to start right away, enter a Start Date to indicate when it should be started.

FIGURE 3.15

The Task form

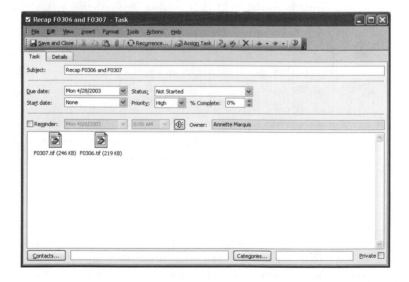

SETTING REMINDERS

If you've entered a due date, Outlook automatically activates the Reminder check box. However, you don't have to enter a due date to use this feature. Click the Reminder check box to activate a reminder that will be displayed at a specified date and time.

The Time drop-down list has a choice for every half hour around the clock, so be careful to select the correct AM or PM time. There's nothing like setting a reminder for 12 hours after something was supposed to be completed! You can also type an entry in this box if you need a reminder at a different time interval.

When the reminder time arrives, a reminder window appears in whatever application you're using at the time. However, in order to see the reminders you've set, Outlook must be running (although it can be minimized). If it's not running, you won't see the reminder(s) until the next time you launch Outlook. Task Reminders work pretty much like calendar reminders. See the "Managing Reminders" section earlier in this chapter to learn about options for handling reminders when they appear.

UPDATING TASK STATUS

When you enter a task, Outlook assumes you haven't started working on the task yet. To help you manage your tasks and assess the status of certain projects, you have four other Status options in addition to Not Started available to you. Click the Status down arrow on the Task tab of the Task form to open the list of choices.

In Progress   If a task is in progress, you might also want to indicate the percentage that is complete in the % Complete text box. Use the spin box to change the percentage, or type the actual percentage directly in the box.

Completed   In addition to marking a task complete, you might also want to complete some additional fields on the Details tab. See "Completing a Task" later in this chapter.

Waiting On Someone Else   It's helpful to set a reminder to yourself to contact this person if you don't hear from them in a reasonable amount of time.

Deferred   You may want to change the start and end dates so this task doesn't show up on your list of active tasks.

SETTING PRIORITIES

By setting a priority level for a task, you can be sure that your most important tasks receive most of your attention. The default priority is set at Normal. You have additional options of High and Low. High priority items are designated by a red exclamation point in the the Task List, and Low priority items are designated by a blue downward-pointing arrow.

OWNING A TASK

The Task Owner is the person who creates the task, or the person to whom the task is currently assigned. When you create a task, you are the owner by default. To give up ownership, however, all you have to do is assign the task to someone else. As soon as that person accepts the task, they officially become the new owner. To learn how to assign tasks to someone else, see "Delegating Tasks" later in this chapter.

Assigning Categories to Manage a Project

Categories are user-defined values that help to organize your data throughout Outlook. Chapter 4, "Unleashing the Power of Outlook Contact Management," provides a thorough discussion of how to create new categories and delete undesired categories. You have the same list of categories available to you as you have in Contacts or any of the other Outlook modules.

Categories can pull related tasks together, making it possible to view the tasks connected with a particular project. Just click the Categories button and assign each task to the same category from the Categories dialog box. When you return to the Task list, you can sort by category, group all the tasks in the same category together, or even filter out just those tasks related to a single category (see Chapter 2, "Digging Out of the E-Mail Avalanche" for more about creating custom views). Figure 3.16 is an example of a Task list grouped by category.

FIGURE 3.16

Task list grouped by category

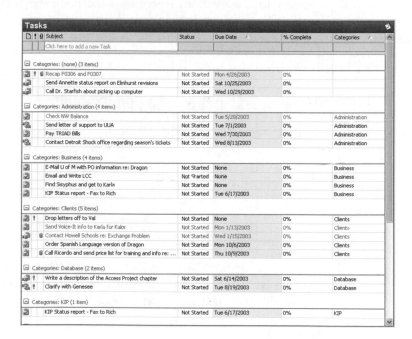

TIP *To assign several tasks to the same category, activate the Organize Pane by choosing Tools ➤ Organize. Select all the tasks you want to assign to the same category (hold Ctrl while you click each task), select the Category from the Add Tasks Selected Below To drop-down list, and click Add. If the category you want doesn't exist, create it first by entering its name in the Create A New Category Called text box.*

Making a Task Private

If your Outlook folders are shared on a network, there may be times when you don't want others to see information about a task. Click the Private check box on the lower-right corner of the Task form to keep this task from being visible to others to whom you have given permission to access your Tasks folder.

NOTE   *The Appointment form also has a Private check box so someone who can view your calendar cannot see what you are doing at a particular time. They will see that you are busy but the details do not display.*

Setting Up Recurring Tasks

A *recurring task* is a task that you must complete on a regular basis—such as a monthly report, a weekly agenda, a quarterly tax submission. Anything that you have to do periodically qualifies. In Outlook you can enter the task once, and then set a pattern for it to recur on your Task list. Outlook doesn't care if you've completed this month's report; when the time comes for next month's, it adds another copy of the task with a new due date to your list.

Recurring tasks work much the same way as recurring appointments discussed earlier in the chapter. Click the Recurrence button on an open task form to set up the recurrence pattern using the Task Recurrence dialog box shown in Figure 3.17.

FIGURE 3.17

Use the Task Recurrence dialog box to set the parameters for a recurring task.

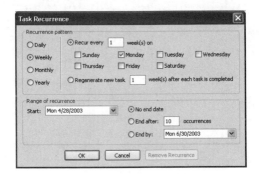

Recurring tasks can be set up in the same way as recurring appointments described earlier in this chapter. The only difference is that you don't have to enter Start and End times or Duration.

Delegating Tasks

If you work as a member of a team, or if you have people reporting to you, there are times when you may want to create a task for someone else to do. As long as the other person is running Outlook and you both have access to e-mail, you can assign tasks to each other (yes, that's right; they can assign tasks to you too).

To assign a task to someone else, create the task as you normally would, add task Recurrence, if appropriate, and click the Assign Task button on the Standard toolbar of the Task form. This opens a message form with the task included, as shown in Figure 3.18.

FIGURE 3.18

Assigning a task to someone else

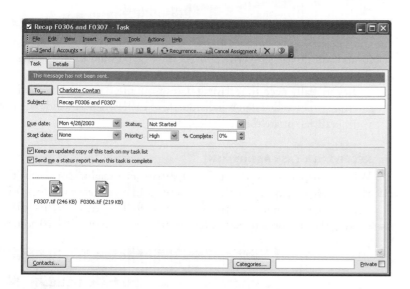

Enter the person's e-mail address, or click the To button and choose the name from your address lists. You have two options related to this assignment.

Keep An Updated Copy Of This Task On My Task List   Even though you have assigned the task to someone else, you might still want to know how the task is going. Every time the new owner of the task revises the task in any way, a message is sent to you indicating that the task was updated. As soon as you open the message, the task is automatically revised in your Task list. When you close the task, the message is removed from your Inbox. This option is not available if the task is recurring. Although you can assign a task to anyone who runs Outlook, if the person is not on your network, you will not receive automatic updates when that person makes revisions to the task.

Send Me A Status Report When This Task Is Complete   When the new owner marks the task as complete, you receive an automatic status report message informing you that the task is complete. This status report message remains in your Inbox until you move it or dispose of it.

If you would like to send a message along with the task assignment, enter the text in the message box. Click Send to transfer the message to your Outbox.

ASSIGNING A TASK TO MORE THAN ONE PERSON

It's possible to assign the same task to more than one person, but if you do, you cannot keep an updated copy of the task in your Task list. To assign an existing task to an additional person, open the task, click the Details tab, and click the Create Unassigned Copy button.

When you make a second task assignment, you are warned that you will become the owner again (the person you originally assigned the task to took over ownership of the task when they accepted it) and will no longer receive updates (unless you want to write them to yourself). Click OK to create the copy and assign the task.

If you really need to receive updates from more than one person about the task, create the task multiple times and assign it individually to each person. Include the person's name in the Subject so you can differentiate the multiple tasks.

RECEIVING A TASK ASSIGNMENT

When someone sends you a task, you receive an e-mail message with the words "Task Request" in the Subject. We would suggest that you delete it immediately so it doesn't infect your workday. But if you feel you must open it, you can choose to accept the task or decline the task (see, there is still hope) by clicking the appropriate button on the message form or in the Reading Pane.

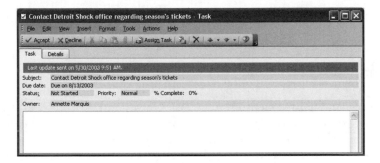

If you click Accept, the task is automatically added to your Task list, and you become the owner of the task. If you click Decline, the person who sent you the task retains ownership. Either way, the person who originated the task is sent a message indicating your response. When you click Send, you are given the option of editing the response before sending it, or sending it without editing. If you want to explain why you're declining your boss's request, click Edit The Response Before Sending and enter your explanation in the message.

Even after you accept a task, you can change your mind and decline the task. Just open the task and choose Decline Task from the Actions menu.

Passing the Task Along

If you receive a task from someone, it's possible for you to accept the task assignment and then turn around and assign the task to someone else (commonly referred to as passing the buck). When you accept the task, you become the owner of the task, and changes and updates you make are returned to the task's originator. When you reassign a task to someone else, that person becomes the owner and future updates are returned to you *and* the originator of the task. To reassign a task:

1. Open the e-mail message that contains the original task request, and click the Accept button to accept the task (if you have not already done so). This sends a Task Update to the originator indicating that you have accepted the task. You are now the owner of the task.

2. Open the task in your Task list and click the Assign Task button. Make sure the Keep An Updated Copy Of The Task On My Task List and the Send Me A Status Report When The Task Is Complete options are both checked so you won't lose track of the task.

3. Enter the e-mail address of the person you want to assign the task to, and click Send to send the Task Request to them. They are now the temporary owner of the task. When they accept the task, they become the task's owner.

4. When you receive a task update from the new owner, the originator also gets a message from you.

By following this process, you keep the task's originator informed, and you have someone else doing the work—not bad work, if you can get it!

Sending Status Reports

Even though Outlook does a great job of keeping a task's originator informed about the status of a task, you might need to incorporate more detail into a report than Outlook generates automatically. If you want to send a manual status report, click Actions ➤ Send Status Report from the Standard toolbar of the open task. Type in (or copy and paste) your status report. Click Send to send an update to the task's originator.

ASSIGNING TASKS IN A TEAM

A practical application of using the Tasks feature on a team is to designate a "task-taker" at each team meeting. This person's responsibility is to maintain the list of things people agreed to do during the meeting and to record the date each task is due. At the end of the meeting, the task-taker returns to their workstation and records the tasks in Outlook, being careful to assign them to the appropriate individual. Because the task-taker is not responsible in any way for completing the tasks, they turn off the task-tracking features. As a result, shortly after returning from the meeting, all the meeting participants have the things they agreed to do recorded for them in their task lists. It makes it a lot harder to forget that you agreed to something and also verifies that everyone left the meeting with the same understanding of the next steps.

Outlook's Tasks feature can also be used to monitor tasks assigned to team members through Microsoft Project. Microsoft Project's TeamAssign feature can directly access Outlook Tasks. When a project team member updates a TeamAssign task, Outlook can update the Project file with information about the task's status, including Actual Work (time spent on the task recorded on a timeline). For more information about using tasks in formal project management, we recommend *Mastering Microsoft Project 2002* (Sybex, 2002), brought to you by your authors and Michael Miller.

Creating Tasks from Other Outlook Items

Outlook's power comes from the incredible ease with which all of the components work together to make your life easier. How many times have you received an e-mail message asking you to do something? Unless you print the message and put it in the stack of papers on your desk and hope you run across it before it needs to get done, you might find yourself forgetting it was even asked of you. Outlook changes all that. The next time you receive an e-mail message asking you to do something, all you have to do is drag the message onto the Task button on the Navigation Pane.

Outlook automatically opens a Task form for you with the information already in it, including the actual contents of the e-mail message.

All you have to do is add Due Dates, assign the task to a category, and add any other details you want—and your reminder is all set. (You will, however, have to actually do the task yourself.)

You can use this trick to create Outlook tasks with any other Outlook item, such as a Journal entry, a Calendar item, or a Note. You can also use it to create Calendar or Note items from e-mail.

Completing a Task

When you've finally completed a task, there is nothing more satisfying than checking it off your list. Outlook wouldn't want you to miss out on this pleasure, so it has incorporated a check box into the Simple List view. To mark a task complete, just click the check box in the Status column.

A completed task is crossed off the list. If the view you are using, such as Active Tasks view, does not include completed items, the item is actually removed from the list altogether. To complete a task in Active Tasks view, change the Status to Completed or change the % Complete to 100%. Of course, you can always see it by switching to a view such as Simple List view, which shows all tasks. If you mistakenly check off a task as complete, just switch to Simple List view and clear the check box.

If you are interested in tracking more information about a completed task, you might want to open the task and click the Details tab of the Tasks form. It has several fields, shown in Figure 3.19, that are designed to be filled in when the task is completed.

FIGURE 3.19

You can track additional information about a completed task on the Details tab of the Task form.

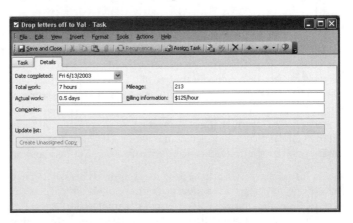

On this tab, you can record the date the task was completed, the planned number of hours (Outlook will translate to days), the actual number of hours, and other billing information you might want to track, such as the number of miles traveled on the job. If you have to submit an expense or billing statement at the end of the month, this is a great way to track the information you need.

Chapter 4

Unleashing the Power of Outlook Contact Management

AS THE OLD ADAGE goes, "It's not what you know but who you know that counts." Outlook's Contacts folder is the place to record all of that critical data about who you know. You can record names and addresses, telephone numbers, e-mail addresses, web page addresses, and other information pertinent to the people with whom you communicate. And it doesn't stop there. After you enter a contact, you can send them a letter, write them an e-mail, schedule meetings and appointments with them, record tasks and journal entries related to them, and even find a map to their house. In this chapter, you'll learn all about entering contact data and how you can use Outlook to communicate with your contacts.

- ◆ Creating contacts
- ◆ Entering address information
- ◆ Entering telephone numbers
- ◆ Entering e-mail, web, and IM addresses
- ◆ Associating contacts and categories
- ◆ Entering additional contact details
- ◆ Viewing activities
- ◆ Saving and deleting contacts
- ◆ Viewing contacts
- ◆ Communicating with your contacts

Creating a Contact

In Outlook, a *contact* is an individual or organization you need to maintain data about. The information can be basic, such as a name and phone number, or more detailed, to include anniversary and birthday information, nicknames, and digital IDs. If you've been tracking contacts manually in a day planner or address book, you have some work ahead of you before Contacts can be fully functional. If you have addresses in any electronic format—an Excel worksheet, contact manager software such as ACT or ECCO, an e-mail program like Eudora or Outlook Express 2003, or a database like Microsoft Access—you don't have to spend time reentering the data. Outlook can import data from a variety of sources.

NOTE   *In Chapter 14, "Designing and Building Data Sources," you can learn more about importing and exporting Outlook data.*

While Outlook is robust enough to manage your business and professional contacts, don't forget to take time to add personal contacts like friends and family members so all your important names, e-mail addresses, phone numbers, and addresses are in one place.

To enter contact data, you can open a blank Contact form in several ways:

- If you're going to be entering a number of contacts, click the Contacts icon in the Outlook Navigation Pane to open the **Contacts** folder. This makes it easier to create subsequent contacts and see the contacts that you've created.

- From within the **Contacts** folder, choose File ➢ New ➢ Contact from the menu.

- From within the **Contacts** folder, click the New Contact button on the toolbar.

- If you're working in another folder (for example, **Calendar**), choose File ➢ New ➢ Contact from the menu—you'll just need to look a bit farther down the menu selections to find Contact. The same list is attached to the toolbar; click the New Item button's drop-down arrow and select Contact from the menu.

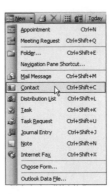

- If your hands are already on the keyboard, there's no need to grab the mouse: press Ctrl+Shift and the letter C.

The Contact form is a multipage form, with tabs labeled General, Details, Activities, Certificates, and All Fields. The form opens with the General tab displayed, where you can enter all the kinds of information you usually store in an address or telephone book. In Outlook 2003, you can even add a charming photograph like the one of one of your authors in Figure 4.1.

FIGURE 4.1

Use Outlook Contact forms to collect and manage information about business and personal contacts.

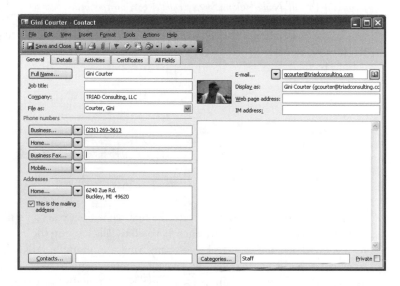

Entering Names, Job Titles, and Companies

To enter a contact's name, begin by entering the contact's name in the first text box on the General tab of the Contact form, next to the Full Name button. If you just want to enter the contact's first and last names, that's fine, but you can also include their title, middle name (or initial), and suffix. For example, **Mary Smith, M.D.; Mary Smith**; and **Smith, III, Mr. Richard M**. are all acceptable ways of entering names.

When you've finished typing the contact's name, press Enter or Tab to move to the next field. Outlook parses (separates) the name into parts for storing it. If Outlook can't determine how to separate the parts of the name, or if the name you entered is incomplete (perhaps you entered only a first name in the Full Name field), the Check Full Name dialog box, shown in Figure 4.2, opens so you can verify that Outlook is storing the name correctly.

FIGURE 4.2

The Check Full Name dialog box appears when Outlook can't verify how a name should be stored.

 If you are not sure how Outlook will parse a name, you can edit these fields manually by clicking the Full Name button to open the Check Full Names dialog box.

TIP *To instruct Outlook not to check incomplete or unclear names, clear the Show This Again When Name Is Incomplete Or Unclear check box in the Check Full Name dialog box before clicking OK. To turn checking back on, open a Contact form, click the Full Name button to open the dialog box, turn the option back on, and then click OK.*

On the General tab of the Contact form, enter the contact's job title and Company. In the File As field, either select an entry from the drop-down list or type a new entry to indicate how the contact should be filed.

If you choose to file contacts with the first name first, you can still sort them by last name, so it's really a matter of personal preference. If you'll usually look up the company rather than the individual, it's a good idea to file contacts by company name. For example, ABC Graphics assigned Jim as the sales representative to your account, but it might be more useful to file the contact as *ABC Graphics (Jim)* than as just *Jim*—particularly if Jim is the fifth sales representative you've had assigned this quarter.

You aren't limited to the choices on the File As drop-down list. Select the text in the File As text box, and then enter the File As text you'd like to use. This allows you to enter formal names for contacts, but store them using their commonly used name. For example, you can enter **Dr. Elizabeth Mitchell** as the contact name, but file your friend as *Mitchell, Beth*.

Entering Contact Telephone Numbers

This is truly the age of connectivity. Although three mail addresses are sufficient for nearly everyone you know, it isn't unusual to have five, six, or more telephone numbers to contact one person: home phones, work phones, home and work fax numbers, mobile phones, ISDN numbers, and pager numbers. With Outlook, you can enter up to nineteen different telephone numbers for a contact and display four numbers "at a glance" on the Contact form, as shown in Figure 4.3.

FIGURE 4.3

The Contact form displays four of the nineteen phone numbers you can enter for a contact.

When you create a new contact, the four default phone number descriptions Outlook displays are Business, Home, Business Fax, and Mobile. To enter a telephone number for one of those four descriptions, click in or tab to the appropriate text box on the General tab of the Contact form and type in the telephone number. You don't need to enter parentheses around the area code or add hyphens or spaces—just enter the digits in the telephone number and Outlook will take care of the formatting for you. If you enter a seven-digit telephone number, Outlook assumes the phone number is local and adds your area code to the number.

WARNING   *If you include letters in your telephone numbers (like 1-800-CALLME), you won't be able to use Outlook's automated dialing program to call this contact.*

Because Outlook only displays four numbers at a time, the numbers displayed in the four text boxes may not be the numbers you use most frequently. That's not a problem—just open the menu next to each text box and, from the menu, select the types you want to display.

ENTERING COUNTRY CODES FOR INTERNATIONAL CALLS

To see the details of a phone number and set the country code for an international number, double-click the phone number to open the Check Phone Number dialog box. Select the country from the Country/Region drop-down list, and Outlook automatically inserts the country code into the number. Click OK to display the country code in the phone number text box.

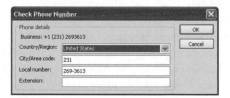

Entering Contact Addresses

Outlook allows you to store three addresses—Business, Home, and Other—for your contact and to designate one of the three as the address you want to use as the contact's primary address. To choose the type of address you want to enter, click the drop-down arrow in the address section, and select the address type from the list. The address type is displayed to the left of the arrow.

To enter an address, click in the Address text box on the General tab of the Contact form and type the address as you would write it on an envelope. Type the street address on the first or first and second lines, pressing Enter to move down a line. Type the city, state or province, country, and zip code or postal code on the last line. If you don't enter a country, Outlook uses the Windows default country.

NOTE   *The Windows default country is set in the Windows Control Panel under Regional Settings (Windows 98), Regional Options (Windows 2000) or Regional and Language Options (Windows 2003).*

When you press Tab to move to the next field, Outlook checks the address just as it did the contact name. If the address is unclear or incomplete, the Check Address dialog box opens, as shown in Figure 4.4. Make sure the information for each field is correct, and then click OK to close the dialog box.

FIGURE 4.4

The Check Address dialog box opens to allow you to verify an incomplete or unclear address.

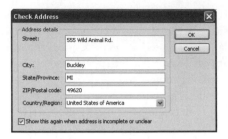

In Outlook, the primary address for a contact is called the *mailing address.* The mailing address is the address displayed in most views and is the address used when you merge a Word main document with your Outlook contacts. By default, the first address you enter for a contact is set as the mailing address. To change the address used as the mailing address, make sure the address you want to use (Home, Business, or Other) is displayed in the Address text box; then click the This Is The Mailing Address check box to make the displayed address the mailing address.

ADDING A PHOTOGRAPH

As digital photography has become more affordable, people have fallen in love with it. Why pay high prices and wait hours or even days to get film developed, when you can have good quality photos available instantly with a digital camera? Outlook has incorporated digital photos into Outlook in a practical and invaluable way. In Outlook 2003, you can add a person's photo to their Outlook contact. What a great way to jog your memory about someone you've recently met. All you have to do is take a bunch of photos at the next social gathering or meeting you attend, and you never have to forget a name again.

To add a photo to a contact, just click the Add Picture button, locate the photo you want to add, and click OK. It's that simple. If you later find one that is more flattering, right-click the picture and choose Change Picture. If you get tired of looking at a photo, right-click and choose Remove Picture.

ENTERING E-MAIL ADDRESSES

You can enter up to three e-mail addresses for a contact. The e-mail addresses, on the General tab of the Contact form, are labeled E-mail, E-mail 2, and E-mail 3, rather than "Business" and "Home" like mail addresses and telephone numbers.

To enter an e-mail address, enter the entire address, including the user name and the domain name. When you move out of the e-mail address text box, Outlook analyzes the address you entered to ensure that it resembles a valid e-mail address. Outlook does *not* check to make sure that the address is the correct e-mail address for this contact or that the address exists. Outlook just looks for a user name, the @ symbol, and a domain name. If all the parts aren't there, Outlook opens the Check Names dialog box. If you cancel the dialog box, Outlook lets you keep the incomplete e-mail address even though it is not usable. Be sure to correct the address before continuing.

Viewing Display Names

When you enter an e-mail address, Outlook automatically creates a display name and inserts it into the Display As text box.

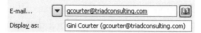

This is the name that appears on an e-mail message form addressed to this person. If you want to change the display name, just type anything you'd like to see in the Display As text box.

Entering an E-Mail Address from the Global Address List

If you are working on a Microsoft Exchange Server, your network administrator has already set up a Global Address List that includes everyone who has a mailbox on the network. In some organizations, complete contact data such as address and company information is entered when the mailbox is created. However, it is more typical to create the mailbox with nothing more than the person's name and e-mail address. In these cases, you may want to create a contact for people within your company so you can add more complete information, home phone numbers, birth dates, and all that other good stuff.

To enter contact information for someone who is in your company's Global Address List or some other address book, click the Address Book button next to the e-mail text box on the General tab of the Contact form to open the Select Name dialog box, shown in Figure 4.5. Select the address you want from the list and click OK. This automatically enters the person's internal e-mail address in the text box.

NOTE   *If Global Address List is not displayed in the Show Names From The drop-down list, you might have to select it.*

FIGURE 4.5

If the contact is already in the Global Address List or other address list, such as the Recipients List, select their name to enter their internal e-mail address.

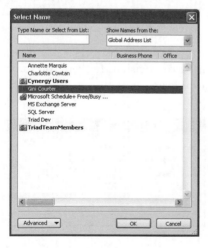

Choosing a Format for Messages to a Contact

The default format for messages created in Outlook 2003 is HTML created with Microsoft Word. If you are certain that this person's mail system does not support HTML messages (most up-to-date mail programs do), you can choose either plain text or rich text as an alternate format.

All versions of Outlook support a file format called *Rich Text format (RTF)*. With RTF, you can format an e-mail message as you would a Word document, using boldface, italicized text, and different fonts and font colors to provide emphasis in the message. If you're using Outlook on a server at work, your colleagues running Outlook on the network will be able to open RTF messages and see your text in all its formatted glory.

NOTE   *If your contact's e-mail service doesn't support RTF, the formatting of the message can make it harder to decipher the actual text of the message because it inserts funny codes. At best, the formatting doesn't appear, and you've spent time formatting for no good reason. RTF is really an outdated format and we generally don't recommend using it.*

To change the message format, right-click an e-mail address or double-click the e-mail address on the General tab of a Contact form and choose Properties. This opens the E-mail Properties dialog box.

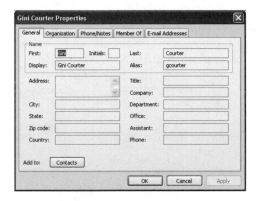

The default Internet Format is Let Outlook Decide The Best Sending Format. If you are uncomfortable letting software make decisions for you, you can choose plain text or Outlook Rich Text format from the drop-down list.

If you make a different selection, click OK to save the change or Cancel to close the dialog box without making a change.

Entering Web Information

To assign an Internet URL to a contact, enter the address in the Web Page Address text box in the Contact form. When you enter a World Wide Web URL in the Web Page Address text box, you don't need to enter the protocol (`http`). Enter the resource name (for example, `www.disney.com`), and when you leave the text box, Outlook automatically adds `http://` to the beginning of the URL. However, if you're entering an address for another type of protocol, such as gopher, telnet, or FTP, you must enter the entire URL, including the protocol and the resource. If you don't, Outlook still adds `http://` to the beginning of the URL, and it will be incorrect.

To visit the user's website, simply point to the URL and the mouse pointer changes to the familiar browser-link hand shape. Click the link to launch your default browser and load the web page.

ENTERING AN INSTANT MESSAGING ADDRESS

The popularity of sending instant messages to others across the Internet has grown so dramatically that Microsoft incorporated the feature into Microsoft Exchange 2000 for use within a corporate setting. With instant messaging (IM), you can have a conversation with someone without ever picking up the telephone or waiting for an e-mail response. Because a contact's IM address sometimes varies from their e-mail address, you can enter their instant messaging address in the IM Address text box below the Web Address text box on the General tab of the Contact form.

If you are not on an Exchange Server or if you want to exchange messages with someone who is not on your network, you can still activate instant messaging as long as you have an Internet connection. Connect to the Internet, choose Options from the Outlook Tools menu (not from within a Contact form), and click the Other tab. Enable the Person Names Smart Tag and the Display Messenger Status in the From Field check boxes.

Entering Contact Comments

The large text box at the bottom of the General tab of the Contact form is an open area for comments about the contact: anything from quick phrases to eloquent paragraphs. For example, an excellent use of the comments box is to record directions or even a map to a contact's home or business. To get a map, click the Display Map of Address button on the toolbar of the Contact form and copy it into the notes area. The next time you have to visit there, just click the Print button and you have their critical phone numbers, address, and directions on one piece of paper. If you sync Outlook with a PDA, the comments also sync (as long as they are not too long), and you have everything you need in one place.

Associating Contacts with Other Contacts

Often, contacts become contacts because someone you already know introduces you. If you would like to associate one contact with another to track referrals, organize families, or just record who introduced you, you can enter a contact in the Contacts text box. Click the Contact button at the bottom of the General tab of the Contacts form to open the Select Contacts dialog box shown in Figure 4.6.

FIGURE 4.6

You can associate
a contact with one
or more other
contacts to
demonstrate
relationships
between them.

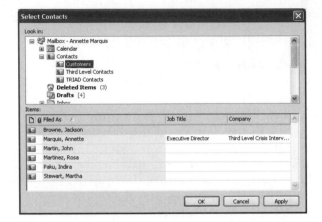

Select one or more contacts from the list. Hold Ctrl while clicking to select more than one associated contact. After you click OK, Outlook displays the associated contacts with links to their contact data. Double-click a name to open its corresponding Outlook form.

Grouping Contacts with Categories

Categories are a way to organize Outlook items based on groupings you set. Outlook comes with a predefined set of categories you can use or, to make the most of categories, you can create your own. To assign categories to a contact, click the Categories button at the bottom of the General tab of the Contact form or, if the contact isn't open, just right-click the Contact and select Categories from the shortcut menu. This opens the Categories dialog box in Figure 4.7.

FIGURE 4.7

Assign categories to
contacts in the Cate-
gories dialog box.

Click to select any of the categories listed. You can assign several categories to a single contact. Be aware, however, that some PDAs accept only a single category assignment. Click OK to assign the categories.

MASTERING THE OPPORTUNITIES: CREATING CUSTOM CATEGORIES

Categories are one of the most powerful features available in Outlook 2003 for organizing and viewing your data. Categories let you decide what individual Outlook items have in common. Although Outlook comes with a predefined list of categories, we recommend that you dump it and create your own list that has meaning to you. The same Categories list crosses over all Outlook items, so you can create categories that tie data together across Outlook folders. Let's say you are in charge of planning a large conference for your organization. By creating a category for the conference, you can assign the category to contacts, tasks, calendar items, and even e-mail related to the conference. You can then use Outlook's Advanced Find (Tools ➢ Find ➢ Advanced Find) to search for all the items in your mailbox related to the conference. You can also use By Category views in the individual Outlook folders to see all the tasks related to the conference, all the appointments, and so on. By using Categories in this way, you can turn Outlook into a simple project management tool to organize all your project-related data.

To access Categories, open any new Outlook item and click the Categories button at the bottom of the item form—if you open a Mail item, choose View ➢ Options to find the Categories button. This opens the Categories dialog box. Click the Master Category List button at the bottom of the dialog box.

To clean out all or most of the items in the list, select the first item and scroll to the bottom of the list. Hold Shift and select the last item in the list. If you would prefer to keep some of the categories in the list, hold down Ctrl and deselect the ones you want to keep. When you are ready, click the Delete button.

To add a new category to the list, type it in the New Category box and click Add to List. If you want to add several new categories, type each one, separated by a semi-colon in the New Category box, and click Add to List. Click OK to close the Master Category List. If you want to assign any of your new categories to the open item, click the check box in front of the category. You can assign more than one category to an item, but we suggest that you limit it to no more than two or three. For one thing, some PDAs can handle only one category at a time, and, in addition, By Category views repeat the item for each category it is assigned to.

If you decide you would like to restore the Master Category list to the original default list, open the Master Category List and click Reset.

To assign several Outlook items to the same category, select any Outlook folder and click Tools ➢ Organize. Select the contacts you want to categorize and click Using Categories to add selected contacts to a category.

To assign categories to e-mail, you must open the message and choose View ➢ Options. To assign categories to Notes, right-click the note and choose Categories or open the note, click the Note icon, and choose Categories from the menu.

MAKING A CONTACT PRIVATE

If you're using Outlook on a network, you can give others permission to access your Contacts folder. However, you might have some contacts—your therapist or fortune-teller, for example—that you prefer to keep private. In the bottom-right corner of the General tab of the Contact form, there's a check box marked Private. By enabling the Private setting, you prevent other users from seeing this contact, even if they have access to your Contacts folder.

Adding Details

On the Details tab of the Contact form, shown in Figure 4.8, you can record less-frequently used information about your contacts. Remember that you can sort and filter your contacts on these fields, so try to use standard entries. If, for example, you want to be able to find all the vice presidents in your Contacts folder, make sure you enter **Vice President** in the Manager's Name field the same way for each contact.

FIGURE 4.8

Use the Details tab to record other information about your contact.

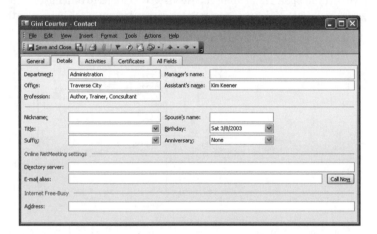

The Birthday and Anniversary fields have drop-down arrows that open a calendar. You can type dates directly in these fields, or you can select a date from the calendar. Click the arrow and the calendar opens, displaying the current month.

ENTERING NETMEETING ADDRESSES

Microsoft NetMeeting is Internet-based collaboration software included with Outlook and Microsoft Exchange Server. With NetMeeting, you can work with one or more contacts "face to face" over the Internet, using video and audio as you would in a video conference call.

NOTE   Some additional hardware is required to support NetMeeting's high-end video and audio functions.

You can use NetMeeting to send files directly to a meeting attendee, have open chat sessions for brainstorming ideas about projects, diagram ideas on a Net whiteboard, and work with other attendees in real time in shared applications.

NetMeetings are held on an Internet Locator Server (ILS), which must be set up by a network administrator; each meeting participant must log on to the server, which maintains a list of users so that other participants can find out who is available for a meeting. On the Details tab, you can enter two NetMeeting settings. Enter the ILS used for meetings with the contact in the Directory Server text box and the contact's E-mail Alias (usually their e-mail address).

ACCESSING YOUR CONTACT'S SCHEDULE ON THE INTERNET

Free/Busy refers to the times that a user is available (for meetings, including NetMeetings) or unavailable, according to their Outlook calendar. With Outlook, you can publish your free/busy times in three different ways: in Exchange Server on your local area network, to the Microsoft Free/Busy server, or over the Internet using the iCalendar standard. With Exchange Server, the only people who can see your free/busy times are colleagues who can log on to your network. By publishing your free/busy times on an Internet server, you make the schedule of free time available to people outside your network.

Before users can access your free/busy schedule stored on a server, FTP site, or web page, you need to tell them where the file that contains the schedule is located. If your contact has given you the URL for their free/busy schedule, enter it in the Internet Free/Busy text box on the Details tab of the Contact form.

NOTE   *For more information on Internet Free/Busy, see Chapter 3, "Taking Control of Your Time and Tasks."*

Tracking Activities

The Activities tab of the Contact form, shown in Figure 4.9, displays a table of both automatic and manual entries related to the contact. The default view of the Activities tab shows the icon to designate the type of entry, the subject of the item, and the Outlook folder in which it resides.

FIGURE 4.9

On the Activities tab of the Contact form, you can see all the entries related to the contact.

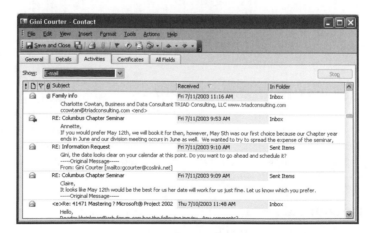

Also, by default, AutoPreview mode is turned on. The first three lines of the note in each message entry are displayed. It's easy to know if the preview shows all the text in the note, including signatures, because the end of the note is marked <end>. If the note is longer than the preview and ends in the middle of a word, the preview ends with ellipses (...). To turn AutoPreview off, right-click anywhere in the Activities window (except on an entry) and select AutoPreview from the short-cut menu.

To see the entire entry, double-click the entry to open it.

SORTING AND GROUPING ACTIVITIES

As with any Outlook view, you can click the heading of a column to sort the entries by the value in the column. For example, to arrange the entries by subject, click the Subject column heading.

To group items by a field, even if the field is not currently displayed, right-click in any open area of the Activities list (you might have to scroll down to the bottom) and choose Group By from the shortcut menu. Choose to group the data by a field that has repetitive entries, such as the In Folder field. Figure 4.10 shows data grouped by In Folder. Click the plus symbol in front of a group to expand the items in that group and click the minus symbol to collapse it again.

To remove grouping, right-click and choose Group By again from the shortcut menu. Click Clear All and OK to remove all grouping.

FIGURE 4.10

Grouping organizes your data so you can find just what you are looking for.

Viewing Certificate Information

A *certificate*, or *Digital ID*, is used to verify the identity of the person who sent an e-mail message. Digital IDs have two parts: a *private key*, stored on the owner's computer, and a *public key* that others use to send messages to the owner and verify the authenticity of messages from the owner. The Certificates tab of the Contact form shows Digital IDs that you've added for this contact. You can view the properties of the ID and choose which ID should be used as the default for sending encrypted messages to this contact.

Viewing All Fields

In the Contact form's All Fields tab, you can display groups of fields in a table format. The default display on this tab is User Defined Fields. Unless you or someone else has customized your Outlook forms and added fields, there won't be any fields displayed—but don't assume that this page is totally useless. Choose Personal Fields, for example, from the Select From drop-down list to have access to fields, shown in Figure 4.11, that are not displayed on any of the Contact form tabs, such as Children,

Gender, and Hobbies. You can enter data directly into these fields and store them with the rest of the contact data.

FIGURE 4.11

The All Fields tab displays fields that are not available on any of the Contact form's tabs.

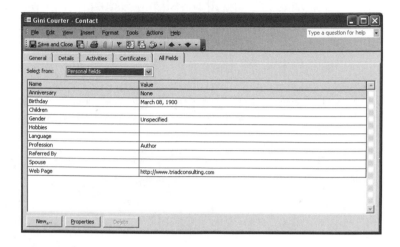

Saving a Contact

 When you've finished entering information in the Contact form, click the Save And Close button, or choose File ➢ Save or Save And New (if you want to create another new contact) to save this contact's information and close the form.

 If you're going to be entering another contact immediately, it's faster to click the Save And New button, or choose File ➢ Save And New to save the current contact and open a blank form.

ADDING A NEW CONTACT FROM THE SAME COMPANY

Once you begin entering contacts, you'll often have several contacts from the same organization. The contacts have the same business address and the same or similar e-mail addresses and business telephone numbers. Outlook lets you create a contact based on an existing contact, so you don't have to enter the business information again. When you've finished entering the first contact, choose Actions ➢ New Contact From Same Company either from the menu in the open Contacts form or from the Outlook menu if the contact is closed. (If the contact is closed, select the contact first.) A new contact form is created and the business information from the previous contact is copied over to the new form. Add the new contact's personal information and edit the business information as required.

Deleting a Contact

To delete a contact, select the contact and choose Edit ➢ Delete from the menu, right-click and choose Delete from the shortcut menu, or press Ctrl+D. To delete an open contact, choose File ➢ Delete. In any case, you are not prompted to confirm the deletion. However, if you immediately notice that you've deleted a contact erroneously, you can choose Undo Delete from the Edit menu to restore the contact or drag it back to Contacts from the Deleted Items folder.

Finding Contact Information When You Need It

When you need to find a contact in a hurry, don't worry about opening the `Contacts` folder and scrolling through a long list of entries. From any folder, click the Find A Contact text box on the Standard toolbar and enter the contact you need to open.

You don't even have to type their full name. Enter a first or last name and if Outlook finds more than one contact with the same name, it shows you a list of possible hits.

Double-click to open the contact you want to see.

Searching Using Find and Advanced Find

Whether you want to find a contact or an e-mail message, you can use Find and Advanced Find to search for what you are looking for. We'll show you the features using Contacts but you can apply the same techniques to find any Outlook items.

When you don't remember a contact's first or last name, you can search for other known information about the contact by clicking the Find button on the Standard toolbar to open the Search Pane at the top of the list.

If you're looking for a contact, enter all or part of their name, company name, or address in the Look For text box. By default, Outlook searches all text in each contact, including comments. To limit your search to just key fields and speed up your search, click the Options button at the far-right end of the Search Pane and unselect Search All Text In The Message.

Click the Find Now button to find all the contacts based on the text you entered in the Look For text box. When you find the contact you're looking for, just double-click it to open the Contact form.

USING ADVANCED FIND

If you can't find the contact you're looking for in the Search Pane, or if you're looking for contacts based on multiple criteria, such as all contacts from Michigan who are salespeople, consider using Advanced Find. Click Advanced Find on the Options menu to open the Advanced Find dialog box.

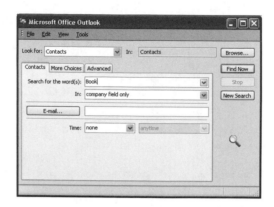

The Advanced Find dialog box works pretty much like the Search Folder Criteria dialog box described in Chapter 2, "Digging Out of the E-Mail Avalanche." In the Advanced Find dialog box, you can select the type of item—Contacts, Tasks, and so on—and click the Browse button to select the folder you'd like to search. If you are searching Contacts, you can enter the name or other text you want to search for in the Search For The Word(s) text box on the Contacts tab. Open the In drop-down list and select the category of field you want to search, such as Name Fields Only, Address Fields Only, and so on. Choose Frequently Used Text Fields for the broadest search. Using the Time options, you can search for contacts that were created or modified within a particular timeframe. For example, you can find contacts you created today or modified in the last seven days.

Flip to the More Choices tab, and you can find contacts by categories. On the Advanced tab of the Advanced Find dialog box you can enter multiple specific search criteria based on the values in fields. To enter a search criterion, click the Field button to open a menu of Outlook field types. Choose a type (for example, All Contact Fields), and then select the field from the menu.

From the Condition text box, choose the appropriate operator. The operators in the list depend on the type of data that will be in the field you selected. For example, with text fields, you'll choose between Contains, Is (Exactly), Doesn't Contain, Is Empty, and Is Not Empty. In the Value text box, enter the value you want to find (or not find). You don't have to enter a Value for Is Empty and Is Not Empty fields. When you're finished building the search criteria, click the Add To List button to add it to the Find Items list. Figure 4.12 shows an example like the one described earlier, contacts from Michigan who are in sales.

FIGURE 4.12

Use the Advanced tab to find contacts based on one or more specific fields.

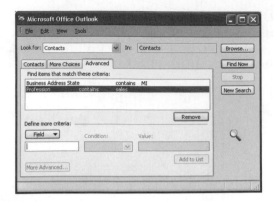

When you've entered all the advanced criteria you need to conduct your search, click Find Now to find the contacts that match all the criteria you entered.

WARNING *You can enter search criteria on more than one tab and find, for example, contacts created in the last seven days in the Business category. If you change your mind about a specific criterion, however, be certain you delete it or you will unwittingly be changing your search criteria.*

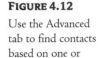

If you're finished with one search and want to search for other contacts, click the New Search button to clear the criteria you entered from all three tabs of the dialog box. If you have existing search criteria, Outlook displays a confirmation message before it clears the search. Click OK to clear the current search.

When you're finished with Advanced Find, choose File ➤ Close or click the Close button on the dialog box title bar to close Advanced Find and return to Contacts. To close the Search Pane, click the Close button at the top of the pane or click the Find button again on the Standard toolbar.

Using Predefined Views to View Contacts

Views improve efficiency by making the data you need visible when you need it. Switching between views gives you a different perspective on your data and helps you capitalize on the powerful grouping features. Views also provide you with a valuable reporting tool. By creating custom views that are sorted, grouped, and filtered to extract the data you need, you can create time logs, calendars, project reports, schedules, company directories, correspondence logs, and a whole host of other management reports. When you use views effectively, raw data is translated into priceless information. In this section, we'll walk you through using predefined views in Outlook and then move on to see the true power of Outlook by creating custom views. Again, we'll use Contacts as the example for the Views feature; however, predefined and custom views can help you organize your data in any Outlook folder.

The Contacts folder has seven predefined views: Address Cards, Detailed Address Cards, Phone List, By Category, By Company, By Location, and By Follow-up Flag. In Outlook 2003, these views are readily accessible on the Navigation Pane, shown in Figure 4.13.

FIGURE 4.13

The newly designed Outlook brings predefined views to the forefront.

The Address Cards view, shown in Figure 4.14, is the default view in Contacts. It displays basic information about the contact: File As name, mailing address, e-mail address, and telephone numbers. Detailed Address Cards view displays additional data, including full name, job title, company name, and categories. Card views have a handy feature: an index on the right side that lets you quickly go to Contacts by the File By name. Clicking the *S*, for example, takes you to contacts whose File By name begins with the letter *S*. Many users choose either Address Cards or Detailed Address Cards as their default view for Contacts.

FIGURE 4.14

Address Cards view works just like an electronic version of a Rolodex.

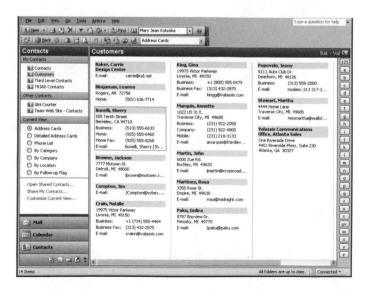

To learn all about applying and creating even more views for Contacts and printing directories of your contacts, keep reading.

Creating Custom Views

As you've seen while working in the various Outlook modules, views define how you see your Outlook data. There are five types of views available in Outlook:

Table view   The default view in Tasks, this shows data in columns and rows.

Timeline view   Used in Journal to see when Activities occurred, this displays data across a timeline.

Card view   This displays Contact data in an address-card format.

Day/Week/Month view   Used with Calendar, this shows a Date Navigator and Day, Work Week, Week, and Month buttons to display data.

Icon view   The default view in Notes, this displays a small or large icon for each Outlook item. If you would like to create a new view, you have three options:

◆   Modify an existing view.

◆   Copy an existing view and modify the copy, leaving the original unchanged.

◆   Create a new view from scratch.

To modify an existing view, follow these steps:

1. Click Customize Current View on the Navigation Pane or choose View ➤ Arrange By ➤ Current View ➤ Customize Current View to open the dialog box shown in Figure 4.15.

NOTE   *If the Current View list is not visible on the Navigation Pane, choose Views ➤ Arrange By ➤ Show Views in Navigation Pane to activate it.*

2. Click the Fields button to add or remove fields from the view.

3. Change the grouping of the data by clicking the Group By button (only available if you are customizing a table or timeline view).

4. Click the Sort button to set the fields you want to sort by.

5. Define criteria for records to display by clicking the Filter button (to learn more about creating criteria, refer to Chapter 2).

6. Change display settings and fonts under the Other Settings button.

7. Click the Automatic Formatting button to apply special formatting rules to items, such as applying bold to unread items in the Inbox.

8. Click Format Columns To change how the data in columns is displayed, for example, to display a long date.

9. Click the Reset view button if you want to restore the predefined view to its original settings.

10. Click OK to apply the customized view.

FIGURE 4.15

Customize existing views by changing fields, grouping, sorting, filters, fonts, and formatting.

Making a copy of an existing view, or creating a new view from scratch, is essentially the same as modifying an existing view, but there are a couple of extra steps involved. To copy an existing view, follow these steps:

1. Switch to the folder for which you want the new view.

2. Choose View ➢ Arrange By ➢ Current View ➢ Define Views to open the Custom View Organizer dialog box shown in Figure 4.16.

3. To copy an existing view for modification, select the view from the list, click Copy, and enter a name for the new view.

    To create an entirely new view, click New, enter a name for the view, and select the type of view.

    With either option, if you are on an Exchange Server network, indicate whether you want this view visible to everyone in this folder, visible only to you in this folder, or available in all Contacts folders. (The In All Contacts Folders choice is available even if you are not on an Exchange Server so you can create a view that you can use in additional Contacts folders you create.)

4. Click OK and follow steps 2–9 in the procedure outlined earlier for modifying an existing view.

5. Click Apply View to make the new view the current view for this folder, or click Close to add the view to the list of available views but not apply it at this time.

TIP   If you modify one of the default views and later decide to return it to its original state, choose View ➢ Arrange By ➢ Current View ➢ Define Views, select the view, and click Reset.

To delete a custom view, switch to the module that contains the view you want to delete. Choose View ➢ Arrange By ➢ Current View ➢ Define Views, select the view you want to delete, and click the Delete button.

FIGURE 4.16

In the Define Views dialog box you can create a new view, make a copy of an existing view, or modify an existing view.

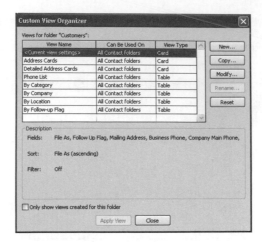

Printing Phone Lists and Directories

If you've ever been asked to create an employee directory for your organization, you know the potential pitfalls. Someone (probably you) has to enter data, choose a layout for the directory, format all the data, and add headings. By the time you send the directory to your printer, you've invested a lot of time in design issues. Outlook includes a number of printing options that will help you quickly and easily create directories, phone lists, and other print resources that formerly took hours or days to create.

Printing in Outlook is dependent on the view you are using. Before you print, select the view that most closely resembles the printed output you want. Add or remove fields from the view, move fields, sort the data into the order you want, and (in table views) adjust column widths. The closer to your finished product you can get, the easier it is to get the results you want.

When you choose File ➤ Page Setup from the Outlook menu, you are presented with a list of styles to choose from. The available styles depend on the current view, so before you print, select the view that most closely resembles the printed output you want. For a simple employee telephone list, switch to Phone List view and choose the table view from the Page Setup menu. For complete names and addresses, choose a Card view. Table 4.1 identifies the Contact views and their corresponding print styles.

TABLE 4.1: PAGE SETUP STYLES

STYLE	TYPE OF VIEW	DEFAULT PRINTED OUTPUT
Table	Table	A list of contacts in columns and rows. Only available when you are in a table view such as Phone List view.
Card	Card	A two-column listing of names and contact information.
Small Booklet	Card	A multiple-section listing of names and contact information prepared for two-sided printing.

Continued on next page

TABLE 4.1: PAGE SETUP STYLES *(continued)*

STYLE	TYPE OF VIEW	DEFAULT PRINTED OUTPUT
Medium Booklet	Card	A two-column listing of names and contact information prepared for two-sided printing.
Memo	Table, Card	Data for the selected contact(s), with your name at the top of each entry.
Phone Directory	Table, Card	A two-column listing of names and phone numbers, with a heading for each letter of the alphabet (very slick).

The Page Setup dialog box using the Medium Booklet style, shown in Figure 4.17, has three tabs: Format, Paper, and Header/Footer. In the Format tab, choose the format options you would like to apply to the style:

Sections To have each letter of the alphabet begin on a new page, choose Start On A New Page. For continuous presentation, choose Immediately Follow Each Other.

Number Of Columns As you increase the number of columns, Outlook decreases the font size.

Blank Forms At End This option allows space for users to add new entries in the correct section in the printed directory.

Contact Index On Side This check box will generate an index, like the index used in Address Card view, with the section's letters highlighted.

Headings For Each Letter This feature gives you a highlighted letter at the beginning of each alphabetic section.

Fonts These lists offer you choices of fonts for the letter headings and body.

Shading This check box enables or disables gray shading in the letter tabs, letter headings, and contact names.

FIGURE 4.17

Use the Page Setup dialog box to design your printed Contacts directory.

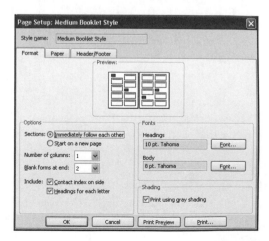

After you make a change, you can click the Print Preview button to see how the change affects your printed output. Click anywhere in the preview to zoom in on the detail; click again to zoom out. To close Print Preview and return to the Page Setup dialog box, choose Page Setup. If you click Close, you close both Print Preview *and* Page Setup.

On the Paper tab of the Page Setup dialog box, choose the settings that describe the dimensions and orientation of the paper you're going to use.

On the Header/Footer tab, you can create a header and footer that contain text and document information. Headers and footers appear on each page of the finished product. If you're creating a 1/4-page booklet, a header appears four times on the printed sheet, so it is at the top of each page after it is folded.

The header and footer each have a left-aligned section, a centered section, and a right-aligned section. To include text in the header or footer, just click in the section and begin typing. Use the five buttons on the toolbar below the header and footer sections to include the page number, total number of pages, date printed, time printed, and user name in the header or footer.

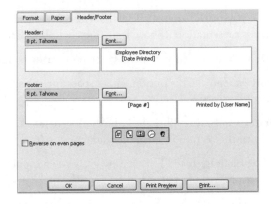

When you've finished setting print options, click the Print button to open the Print dialog box. Select a printer from the Name list, the number of pages to print, and the number of copies. Click the OK button to send the job to the printer.

TIP   If you want to print a booklet with two-sided pages and you have a one-sided printer, choose Odd in the Number Of Pages drop-down list and print all the odd-numbered pages first. Turn the sheets over and reinsert them into the printer. Choose Even to print the rest of the pages. Outlook is smart enough to order the pages with appropriate page numbers so they can be folded into a booklet when they're all printed.

The printing process is the same in all the Outlook modules. Begin by selecting a view that supports the output you want. Preview the output in Print Preview. Change views, if necessary, and then adjust the Page Setup options to further define the final output. Finally, send the job to the printer, and think about how easy this was.

Dialing a Contact

You don't need a lot of fancy hardware to use Outlook's phone dialing features. As long as you have a telephone connected to the line your modem uses, you can place telephone calls from Outlook. You don't need a fast modem to make telephone calls—your voice is simply routed from one port in the modem to the other. Outlook's telephone dialing program is called *AutoDialer*. You must be in the Contacts folder to use AutoDialer.

You can begin by selecting the contact you want to call. Then click the AutoDialer drop-down arrow to open the menu of all the telephone numbers for the contact. Choose a number from the list, and the New Call dialog box opens.

The contact's name appears in the Contact text box, and the phone number you select is in the Number text box. You can click the arrow in the Number box to see other numbers.

If you know your contact's telephone number, or have it in your telephone's speed dial listing, you can dial the number in the time it takes to use AutoDialer. One of the reasons AutoDialer is popular is because of the check box that appears under the number. One simple click and Outlook opens a Journal Entry form for the contact while you place the call.

Click the Start Call button to have Outlook dial the number. If the Create New Journal Entry check box is enabled, a new Journal Entry form opens automatically. The New Call dialog box is still open (and remains open during the call). The Call Status reads *Connected*, and the End Call button is enabled. Pick up (or turn on) the telephone receiver to begin speaking.

When you've completed your call, click the End Call button and hang up the phone to close the connection (you might have to move the Journal Entry form out of the way to see the New Call dialog box). Outlook automatically pauses the timer in the Journal item, and it enters the total time for the call in the Duration control. If you'd like to make some notes about the call, enter them in the open Notes area in the Journal item. You should also change the subject to describe the contents of the telephone call and assign a category if you wish. When you've finished entering information in the Journal form, click the Save And Close button to close the Journal entry.

Creating a Letter to a Contact

To write a letter to a contact (the traditional snail-mail variety), select the contact and choose Actions ➤ New Letter To Contact. This starts the Microsoft Word Letter Wizard. Information available in the Contact form is filled in for you. When you complete the additional information in the Letter Wizard, Outlook passes control over to Word so you can write your letter. Complete the letter as you would any Word document. Close or minimize Word to return to Outlook.

Mail Merging Contacts with Word Documents

If you want to create labels, letters, envelopes, or a customized directory of Outlook names and addresses, we generally recommend starting with Word's Mail Merge wizard and selecting Outlook Contacts as a data source—it is easier to follow with much more help along the way.

NOTE *Word's mail merge features were completely revamped in Office XP so if you jumped to Outlook 2003 from an earlier version you'll want to take a look at Chapter 9, "Streamlining Mailings and Messaging," where the new Mail Merge wizard is discussed in detail.*

However, if you long for Word's old Mail Merge Helper and like to create merge documents using the Mail Merge toolbar, you can access mail merge from within Outlook (you may think this is stupid, but we know people who still miss WordPerfect 5.1 for DOS). To access the mail merge features in Outlook, switch to Contacts, then follow these steps to initiate a mail merge:

1. Create a Contacts view, including the fields you want to merge and any filters you want to apply to the data (View ➤ Arrange By ➤ Current View ➤ Customize Current View). If you don't want to merge all of the visible contacts, select the contacts you want using Ctrl+Click.

2. Choose Tools ➤ Mail Merge to open the new Outlook Mail Merge Contacts dialog box, shown in Figure 4.18.

3. Check whether you want to merge all the contacts or the selected contacts.

4. Check if you want to merge all contact fields or only the fields in the view you selected—with over a hundred contact fields, it is generally better to choose the fields you want, as described in step 1, to make the list more usable.

5. Identify if you want to create a new Word main document or if you have an existing Word document you want to use as the main document.

6. To save a copy of the contacts you include in the merge, check Permanent File and enter a file-name and location or click Browse to select a location and enter a filename.

7. Choose the document type—letters, labels, envelopes, or catalog—and indicate whether you want to merge to a new document, a printer, or e-mail.

8. Click OK to launch Word and open the main document. You can now add merge fields and finish the merge in Word.

FIGURE 4.18

Initiate Word's mail merge features from within Outlook.

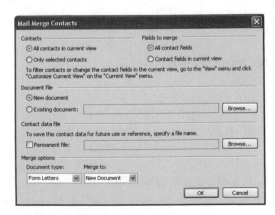

The next steps to completing the merge vary depending on which document you choose to create. With envelopes and labels, Word tells you how to proceed.

After you click OK to the instructional message, the Mail Merge Helper opens for you to set up the labels or envelopes.

If you plan to create form letters or a catalog, a blank Word document opens with the Mail Merge toolbar activated, shown in Figure 4.19.

FIGURE 4.19

The Mail Merge toolbar has all the tools you need to create a form letter or directory mail merge document.

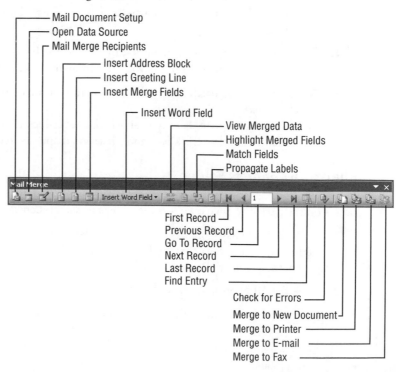

If this process is a little overwhelming, you can still access the Mail Merge wizard by choosing Tools ➤ Letters and Mailings ➤ Mail Merge. It opens on Step 3 and you can follow along to complete the merge (refer to Chapter 9 for help in moving through the wizard).

Sharing Department or Workgroup Contacts

What's the point of re-creating contacts that someone else in your department or workgroup has already entered? Why not share the contacts instead? Outlook offers several ways you can share contacts with others, from e-mailing individual contacts to sharing entire Contact folders.

E-Mailing a Contact

If you want to share a few contacts with someone, even someone who is not on your network, you can send the contacts as attachments to an e-mail message. If the person you are sending to is an Outlook user, you can forward the contact as an Outlook item. If the recipient is not an Outlook user, you can forward the contact as a vCard, the Internet standard for contact data exchange.

To forward a single contact, follow these steps:

1. Open the contact you want to forward or select the contact or contacts you want to forward.

2. Choose Actions ➤ Forward if the recipient has Outlook, or Forward as vCard if the recipient does not have Outlook. Outlook opens an e-mail message and attaches the contact(s).

3. To attach additional contacts to an open message, choose Insert ➤ Item or, if you use Word as your e-mail editor, click the down-arrow on the Insert button on the message toolbar and choose Item.

4. Click the Contacts folder in the Look In Pane of the Insert Item dialog box. Scroll through and select the contact or contacts you want to insert. Click OK to attach the contact.

5. When you've attached all the contacts you want to send, complete the e-mail message form and click Send.

If you receive a message with a contact attached, double-click to open the contact. If you decide to add it to your Contacts folder, click Save and Close and it appears in Contacts—that's all there is to it.

Sharing a *Contacts* Folder

If you work in a Microsoft Exchange Server environment, you can share your Contacts folders with others on the Exchange Server. Follow these steps to share a Contacts folder:

1. Click the Share My Contacts link on the Navigation Pane. If you want to share other Contacts folders, right-click the Contacts folder and select Properties. This opens the Permissions tab of the Contacts folder's Properties dialog box.

2. Click the Add button to open the Add Users dialog box.

3. Double-click the names of the users you want to give permission to open the folder.

4. Click OK to add the users.

5. Select the permission level you would like to assign from the Permission Level drop-down list (for more about Permissions, refer to Chapter 12, "Organizing and Securing Documents") and click OK.

After you grant permissions, it's helpful to e-mail the person or people to which you granted them and tell them about it. Outlook does not do this automatically, so if you don't tell them, no one will know. After you've told them that they can view your Contacts folder, all they have to do is follow these steps:

1. Click Contacts to open the Contacts Navigation Pane and click the Open Shared Contacts link. You can also click File ➤ Open ➤ Other User's Folder and select Contacts from the Folder Type list.

2. Enter the name of the owner of the Contacts folder in the Open Shared Contacts dialog box or click the Name button to select the name.

3. Click OK to close the dialog box(es).

4. The folder appears in the Other Contacts section of the Outlook bar. When you want to open it, click it as you would any other folder. The folder stays open until you select another folder.

The exciting thing about this Outlook 2003 enhancement is that the folder remains available until you choose to hide it from the Other Contacts list (right-click and choose Remove from Other Contacts). No more need to house the shared Contacts folder in Public folders where it might languish unattended; no more concern about having to edit a contact in more than one place (Personal and Public folders); no more concerns about whether you can hot-sync to a handheld PC. One person in a department can assume responsibility for updating and maintaining a shared Contacts folder and everyone can have easy access to it.

Creating Contacts from Other Sources

New! Office 2003 offers a number of ways to create contacts without having to start from scratch. Any time you receive an e-mail or instant message from someone, you can easily capture their information for future use. Look for the Name menu icon.

Wherever you see it, you have a number of options for things you can do with the name from sending that person a message to creating a new contact. Click the Name menu icon to open the Name menu. The options that appear vary depending on where you see the icon, but in most cases you will find options such those shown in Figure 4.20, including opening and creating a contact.

FIGURE 4.20

Use the Name menu
to take actions
related to a name.

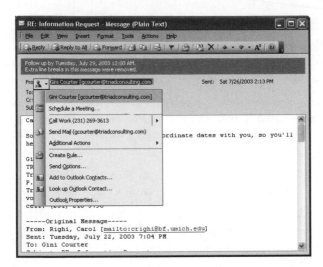

To create a contact using the Name menu, click Create A Contact. Outlook opens a new contact form and inserts as much information as is available. This may include the Full Name, E-Mail, Display As, or IM Address.

The key to having the contact information you need at your fingertips is to capture the contact the first time you see it rather than waiting until you need to call or e-mail them again. It will not only save time but will give you greater control over your contacts and better tracking of your activities.

Chapter 5

Beyond Text: Making an Impression with Multimedia

THE OLD SAYING "A picture is worth a thousand words" is true—pictures, or graphics, can really enhance your message. Pictures add visual interest to a document and often make it more inviting. In some documents, such as newsletters, graphics have come to be an expected ingredient. Graphics can illustrate a concept, prove a point, or simply make your document look more interesting. Graphics can consist of clip art, line art, text, scanned images, or photos. You can use existing images stored in a file or create your own graphic objects.

Graphics tools are available everywhere you look in Office 2003. If you have even the smallest creative bone in your body, there is a tool for you.

To keep track of all your images, Office includes Microsoft's Clip Organizer, which serves as a central catalog for all your media files, and the new Microsoft Picture Manager for managing and editing digital photos.

In this chapter, we'll show you how to make the most of these tools, including Clip Organizer, Microsoft Picture Manager, Microsoft Draw, AutoShapes, WordArt, and the Diagram Gallery. So hold on and watch for that creativity to seep out.

Office 2003 has two tools that you can use to chart numeric data: Excel and Microsoft Graph. If you don't know anything about creating charts and need to choose a tool to learn, choose Excel (refer to Chapter 13, "Building Robust and Foolproof Workbooks"), which has a full-featured charting tool. Because we recommend using Excel to create charts, we will not cover Microsoft Graph directly. However, if you are not an Excel user, you can access Microsoft Graph by choosing Insert ➤ Picture ➤ Chart.

- ◆ Adding illustrations from Clip Organizer

- ◆ Managing your clip collection

- ◆ Inserting photos and scanned images

- ◆ Using the Picture toolbar to enhance images

- ◆ Adding graphical lines and bullets

◆ Using Microsoft Draw

◆ Converting text to graphics with WordArt

◆ Creating diagrams

◆ Using images as PowerPoint slide backgrounds

◆ Adding video and audio to PowerPoint presentations

Organizing Your Clips with Microsoft Clip Organizer

Microsoft Clip Organizer, shared by all of the Office applications, contains a broad selection of clips, including pictures, sounds, and motion clips. You can browse the clips by category (referred to as *collections*) or, if you prefer, search for the clips you want using keywords. In addition, you can add clips from your own collection or download additional clips directly from Microsoft's online clip gallery, the new Clip Art and Media website. Clip Organizer is a great place to catalog and manage all of the graphics, sound files, and animated graphics files you have stored anywhere on your system.

In Office 2003, the Clip Art task pane, shown in Figure 5.1, offers options for searching or organizing clips. You can quickly access clips online, or look at tips for finding the perfect clip.

FIGURE 5.1

Use the Clip Art task pane to search for clips in your collection or in Microsoft's online clip gallery.

NOTE *Not all of the clips visible in Clip Organizer are installed in a typical Office installation. When you insert a clip that is not installed, you may be prompted to insert the Office 2003 CD that contains the clip.*

To access clip art, click Insert ➤ Picture ➤ Clip Art or click the Insert Clip Art button on the Drawing toolbar. The Insert Clip Art task pane opens on the right of the window.

Searching for the Clip You Want

Microsoft assumes you are too busy to spend time going through hundreds of images to find the one you want. So rather than relying on luck to find the perfect graphic, you can use the task pane for immediate access to Clip Organizer's built-in Search feature. Search saves time, frustration, and that inevitable feeling of hopelessness that comes from browsing through the vast clip collection. To search for a specific type of clip, follow these steps:

1. Enter a keyword or two in the Search For text box. (See Table 5.1 for tips on what to enter.)

2. Choose which collection(s) you wish to search by selecting from the Search In drop-down list.

3. Choose the type of file you're looking for—clip art, photograph, movie, or sound—in the Results Should Be list.

4. Click the Go button to display clips that meet your criteria. Figure 5.2 shows results of an Office Collections keyword search on "computer."

TABLE 5.1: CLIP ART SEARCH TIPS

SEARCH FOR	RESULTS TO EXPECT
A particular word: *school*	Clips that are cataloged with *school* as a keyword
Multiple words separated by commas: *school, teacher*	Clips that have one or both of the keywords you typed
Multiple words without quotes or commas: *school teacher*	Clips that have both keywords you typed
Filenames with wildcards: *sc*.jpg*	Media clips with filenames such as `school.jpg` and `scooter.jpg`

FIGURE 5.2

The task pane displays search results.

Scroll through the search results to find the clip(s) you want to use. To see more clips at once, drag the border between the task pane and the vertical scroll bar to the left to expand the task pane.

When you move the mouse over a clip, a drop-down indicator, called the Clip Options button, appears on its right border. Click it to see a shortcut menu with options for things you can do to that clip.

To insert a clip, position the insertion point in the document where you want the image and click the image. (You can also choose Insert from the shortcut menu if you've displayed it.) Presto! A copy of the image now appears in the document. It may not be where you want it but you can adjust its position, size, and text-wrapping properties. See the "Adding Art to Enhance Documents" section later in this chapter for more about how to do this.

Finding Similar Clips

When you've found the perfect clip, you can instruct Clip Organizer to find additional clips that share a similar design style with the first one. Click the clip's drop-down menu and choose Find Similar Style. The results may have nothing in common with the content of the original clip, but you can use this feature when you want to incorporate a consistent look throughout your document.

Exploring Your Clip Collection

If you want to view your entire clip collection, click the Organize Clips link at the bottom of the task pane. Using the new Microsoft Clip Organizer's Explorer interface, shown in Figure 5.3, you can now browse your stored clips and reorganize clips using the file management tools you already know, such as cut, copy, paste, and drag-and-drop.

FIGURE 5.3

Microsoft Clip
Organizer's Explorer
interface lets you
preview your clips
and use file
management tools
to organize them
into collections.

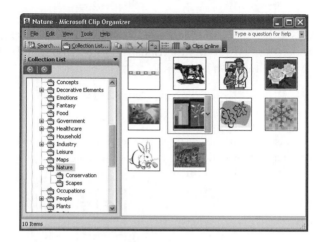

NOTE *The first time you open Clip Organizer, you are prompted to catalog your media files. You'll have better luck searching for clips if you let Office do this, and it only takes a few minutes. When Clip Organizer catalogs your media files, it looks for specific file extensions such as* `.jpg` *and* `.gif`*. This includes media files that were installed with various software programs. So don't be surprised to find an image from a game or other application in the catalog. However, you can exclude entire directories if you want to leave out certain images.*

Rather than folders, Clip Organizer displays collections. You can create new collections and move and copy clips into existing collections. Clip Organizer automatically creates two collections in the My Collections folder. These are:

Favorites   Your most frequently used clips, such as your company's logo or other similar clips.

Unclassified Clips   Clips that you have not added to other collections. Included in this collection are clips that Clip Organizer identifies when it reviews your system to look for media clips.

In addition, Clip Organizer creates folders of Office Collections and Web Collections. Office Collections holds the media clips that come with Office. Click the Expand button (plus symbol) in front of Office Collections to see the list of included collections.

The Web Collections folder lets you access media clips from Microsoft's online clip gallery, Design Gallery Live. You must be connected to the Internet to access the clips in Web Collections. Expand the folder and then select a collection just like you did in the Office Collections folder. The only difference is that the clips that appear are from an ever-changing collection on the Web.

TIP *Microsoft Clip Organizer is a freestanding application you can also launch directly from the Programs menu. Look for a folder called Microsoft Office Tools in the Microsoft Office folder and launch it from there. You can organize your clips, import clips from other sources, search and browse the clips, and insert clips into applications that are not part of the Office suite.*

BROWSING THE COLLECTIONS

Some collections have subcollections that you can also access by clicking the Expand button in front of them. You know when a collection contains clips because thumbnails of the clips appear in the right pane, as shown earlier in Figure 5.3.

TIP   If you'd prefer to see a list of the media files, choose View ➤ List. Choose View ➤ Details to see the Name, Size, Type, Caption, Keywords, and Date.

In Thumbnails view, you can distinguish sound files by the speaker icon and file name that appear in place of an image. Movie files, or animations, are designated by the yellow star in the bottom-right corner.

NOTE   Animated graphics are only animated when displayed in a Web browser or viewed in a PowerPoint slide show (or when previewed in the Clip Organizer). They do not move when inserted into Word documents unless you preview the page in a browser. Refer to Chapter 11, "Creating and Modifying Documents for the Web," to learn more about using animated graphics.

ORGANIZING THE CLIPS YOU FIND

After you find the perfect clips, you can save future searching time by adding them to the Favorites collection or to another collection of your choice. For either option, point to the clip and click the Clip Options button to open the shortcut menu. Choose Copy To Collection or, if it's a clip that is not part of the original Clip Organizer, choose Move To Collection. This opens the Copy To Collection dialog box shown in Figure 5.4. Choose Favorites or select another collection from the list. After you choose the collection you want, click OK to add the clip to that category and close the dialog box.

FIGURE 5.4

You can copy media clips to other collections using the Copy To Collection dialog box.

TIP   Press and hold Ctrl to select multiple clips you want to move or copy to a collection. To select contiguous clips, press and hold Shift to select the first and last clip you want to move or copy.

Creating a New Collection

If you would like to create a new collection, open the Copy To Collection dialog box (see previous section) and click the New button, or click any of the collections in the My Collections folder and choose File ➤ New Collection. This opens the New Collection dialog box. Enter the name of the new collection and select the folder you would like it to be a part of. When you click OK, the new collection appears in the list. In this example, we created a Logos collection in the Favorites folder.

NOTE   You can't create a new collection in the Office Collections or Web Collections folders. You must select a folder in My Collections before attempting to create a new collection.

Assigning Keywords to Clips

To make it easier to find clips, clips can be assigned *keywords*, which are used by Clip Organizer's Search tool to locate the clips you are searching for. The media files that come with Office already have keywords assigned and Clip Organizer assigns some keywords to local files when it does its initial search. With a little investment on your part, you can use keywords to find all the clips you want. Figure 5.5 shows a piece of clip art and the accompanying keywords that will help you find this clip.

FIGURE 5.5

Having a variety of keywords makes it easier to find the clips you are looking for.

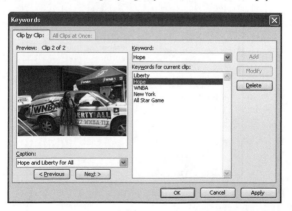

You can add additional keywords and delete existing keywords from any of the clips in My Collections. To add, delete, or modify keywords of individual clips, follow these steps:

1. Point to the clip you want to change.

2. Click the Clip Options button and chose Edit Keywords from the shortcut menu. This opens the Keyword dialog box, such as the one shown in Figure 5.5 above.

3. To edit the keywords of each clip individually, use the Clip By Clip tab.

4. To delete a keyword, select the keyword you want to delete and click the Delete button.

5. To add a keyword, click in the Keyword text box and select the existing text if necessary. Enter the new keyword or, if it's a keyword you've added previously, select it from the drop-down list. Click the Add button.

6. To modify a keyword, select the keyword, make the editing changes you want to make in the Keyword textbox, and click the Modify button.

7. Click the Next button to edit the keywords of the next clip or click OK to apply the changes and close the dialog box.

To add, delete, or modify keywords of a group of clips, select the clips you want to edit: to select multiple clips, hold Ctrl and click each clip; to select multiple contiguous clips, click the first clip and hold Shift while you click the last clip. Then follow steps 2–7 above, selecting the All Clips At Once tab, shown in Figure 5.6, to make your edits.

TIP   If you are editing clips in My Collections, you might also want to add a caption to the clip. The caption appears when you point to the thumbnail of the clip in Clip Organizer. If a clip does not have a caption, the file name, size, and file type appear when you point to the thumbnail. To add a caption, right-click the thumbnail and choose Edit Keywords. Enter the caption in the Caption text box of the Clip By Clip tab and click OK. Also remember to edit keywords if you've added clips to Clip Organizer (see the section "Improving Your Clip Collection" later in this chapter) or have copied clips to a new collection for use in a specific project.

FIGURE 5.6

Use the All Clips At Once tab to add, delete, or modify keywords for multiple clips.

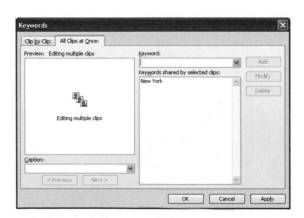

NOTE   *You can add and delete keywords from a clip in the Office Collections and Web Collections folders only if you've previously copied the clip to My Collections.*

MASTERING THE OPPORTUNITIES: ORGANIZING CLIPS ACCORDING TO YOUR OWN PROJECTS

One of the best ways to gain control of your clips is to create your own collections and keywords and organize the clips according to the projects you're working on. Let's say, for example, you produce a monthly newsletter for your department or organization. You can create a collection for the newsletter and copy all the design clips that designate special sections of the newsletter to this collection. To make it even easier, you can add custom keywords and captions to help you quickly find all the clips you need through a keyword search. While you are at it, you may also want to create collections to organize photographs of your company's products, your company logos, and photos of key employees to use as the needs arise. (See "Importing Clips into Clip Organizer" later in this chapter to add your own photos to Clip Organizer.) As you are preparing for the next issue, continue to organize the artwork as you go along. When you are ready to produce the newsletter, all the art you need is right at your fingertips.

Improving Your Clip Collection

The Clip Organizer is not at all limited by the clips that come with Microsoft Office. If you really want to make it useful, add all the photographs, clip art, sound files, and motion clips you have available to you, even if they come with their own cataloging software. Having access to all the clips you need in one place not only makes layout more convenient but also improves the overall quality of your work by offering you the greatest number of choices. You can add clips you already have in your collection, and you can download clips directly from Microsoft's Design Gallery Live as you need them.

IMPORTING CLIPS INTO CLIP ORGANIZER

When you import clips into Clip Organizer, you have three options for how you handle the import process. To access any of these options, choose File ➤ Add Clips To Organizer. From here, you can choose one of the following methods:

Automatically   Searches your hard drive for graphic, sound, and motion files and adds them to Clip Organizer for you. The clips are added to a collection called Unclassified Clips. Keep in mind that when you choose this option, Clip Organizer might even add clips used by applications and websites that you've accessed.

On My Own   Adds clips you select to Clip Organizer. Click the Add To button on the Add Clips To Organizer dialog box to specify which collection to add the clips to.

From Scanner Or Camera   Imports clips directly from an installed scanner or camera. If the scanner or camera you plan to use does not appear in the Device drop-down list, make sure the device is properly installed and working.

Removing Clips from Clip Organizer

In both the Automatically and On My Own options, Clip Organizer creates a shortcut to the clip files but does not change their file locations. If you delete a clip from Clip Organizer, the file is still available in its original location.

To delete a clip from Clip Organizer, select Delete From Clip Organizer from the Clip Options shortcut menu or click the Delete From Clip Organizer button on Clip Organizer toolbar. This option deletes the clip from all Clip Organizer collections it is in.

To delete a clip from a specific collection, choose Delete From [*Collection Name*] from the Clip Options shortcut menu.

Accessing Shared Clip Organizer Catalogs

If your company's system administrator has created shared Clip Organizer catalogs and made them available on the server, you can add them to your Clip Organizer by clicking File ➤ Add Clips To Organizer ➤ On My Own and choosing Shared Catalogs (*.mgc) from the Files Of Type drop-down list in the Pictures—Add Clips To Catalogs dialog box. Locate the shared catalog and click Add to include the catalog in your Clip Organizer.

NOTE *To access the clips in a shared catalog, you have to be logged on to the network and have access to the file location where they are stored.*

FINDING NEW CLIPS ON MICROSOFT OFFICE ONLINE

Microsoft has made sure that you have all the clips you need by posting a special website just for Clip Organizer users that is filled with over 100,000 graphic images and sounds, including clip art, photographs, sound clips, and motion files. The site is updated regularly and always has featured clips based on the season or upcoming holidays.

To access Microsoft Office Online Clip Art and Media website, click the Clips Online button on the Clip Organizer toolbar or the Clip Art on Office Online link from the Insert Clip Art task pane.

On the Microsoft Office Online Clip Art and Media website, you can browse by category or search for keywords. Searching is the best way to find what you are looking for quickly. To search, follow these steps:

1. Enter a search term in the Search For text box at the top-right of the page (see Figure 5.7). To get the best results, be as descriptive as possible and don't be afraid to try a couple of different searches. For example, if you wanted clips of women basketball players, a search for *women basketball players* would give you the most accurate results. *Basketball* is more general and would give you balls, nets, and male and female players, and *women*, being more general yet, would return clips of women in all kinds of settings.

2. Choose the type of results you want from the drop-down list: All Media Types, Clip Art, Photos, Animations, or Sounds. (You can also choose Entire Web Site to view templates and other documents using the same search terms.)

FIGURE 5.7

Microsoft's Clip Art and Media website is a great place to find clip art, photos, sounds, and motion clips.

When you get results, use the page controls in the top-right corner of the navigation bar to see additional pages of clips.

TIP   *If you access Microsoft Office Online Clip Art and Media website from a fast Internet connection, you may want to increase the number and the size of the clips that display on a page. Click the Options link in the top navigation bar of the home page and change the thumbnail and preview size settings. If you notice too much degradation in speed, go back to Options and click Reset.*

To collect clips you want to download in the Selection Basket, click the check box under the clip. The Selection Basket on the left side of the screen is updated.

If you want all the visible clips, click the Select All link. As you add clips to the download, you will notice the counter in the Selection Basket increases. When you are ready to download the files, click the Download *x* Item link or click Preview Basket to see the clips before downloading them. When you are ready, click Download Now and choose Open from the File Download dialog box.

The clips are downloaded and categorized in the Downloaded Clips Collection in Clip Organizer. You can copy or move the new clips to other collections as desired.

NOTE   *If Microsoft Clip Organizer is not running when you download the clip, you can find your new clips by clicking the Downloaded Clips category the next time you launch Clip Organizer.*

TIP   *The Microsoft Clip Organizer maintains a database of the clips, captions, collections, keywords, and other properties. Proper maintenance of this catalog, especially if you have added or deleted clips from the catalog, makes it run faster and with fewer problems. On a routine basis, you can compact the catalog and repair any corrupted data by choosing Tools ➤ Compact from the Clip Organizer menu.*

Gaining Control of Digital Photos with Microsoft Picture Manager

New!   The world of photography has taken a giant leap in the last couple of years with the introduction of affordable digital cameras. If you don't have one of your own, chances are you know someone who does. Many offices have added digital cameras to their lists of standard equipment. In response to the unique demands of digital photos, Microsoft has added a new application to the Office family, Microsoft Picture Manager. With Microsoft Picture Manager, you can view thumbnails, filmstrips, and full-size versions of photos and apply some basic editing tools such as redeye removal, rotating, and brightness and contrast adjustment. You can also resize, crop, and compress photos for maximum portability and flexibility.

Locating and Managing Your Photo Collections

To launch Microsoft Picture Manager, select it from the Microsoft Office ➤ Microsoft Office Tools folder on the Programs menu. If you already have photos in the My Pictures folder, click the picture shortcut to display them. Figure 5.8 shows a thumbnail view of photos located in one Picture Shortcut.

Editing Photos

Microsoft Picture Manager offers a number of picture correction tools, including Brightness and Contrast, Color, Crop, Rotate & Flip, Red Eye Removal, and Resize. Select a picture or hold Ctrl and select multiple photos for editing and click the Edit Pictures link on the Getting Started task pane to open the Edit Pictures task pane, shown in Figure 5.9.

FIGURE 5.8

With Microsoft Picture Manager you can organize, edit, and share digital photos.

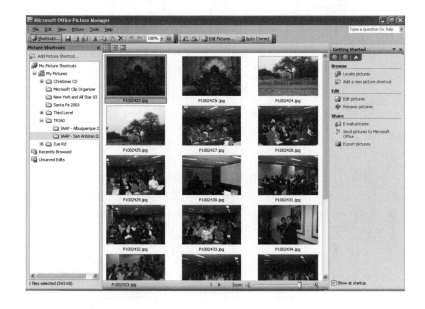

NOTE   If the task pane isn't visible, click the Edit menu and choose Edit Pictures.

FIGURE 5.9

Apply some basic photo editing to improve digital photos using the Edit Pictures task pane.

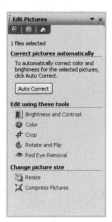

Each of the editing tools contains a number of options, depending on the selection you make. If you're uncertain what changes to make, click the Auto Correct button to auto-correct color and brightness. If you want to try some manual adjustments, select one of the editing tools. If you don't like an adjustment, click the Undo button on the Standard toolbar to reverse the correction. Click the Back to Edit Pictures link or the Back button on the task pane to return to the Edit Pictures task pane.

When you make changes, Picture Manager adds the picture to a collection called Unsaved Edits. You can choose to resave over the existing picture by clicking the Save button or, if you want, preserve the original by clicking Use File ➢ Save As to save the edited version using a different name. If you get cold feet and want to discard all the edits you have made, right-click the Unsaved Edits folder and choose Discard All Changes.

NOTE   *Using Save As does not remove the original file from the Unsaved Edits folder. If you are satisfied with the changes and have saved the edited version using Save As, you can safely discard the original from the Unsaved Edits folder.*

Sharing Photos and Other Images

Sharing photos or any kind of image is a snap with Microsoft Picture Manager. Click any picture or press Ctrl and select a group of pictures and click File ➢ Send To ➢ Mail Recipient As Attachment. This opens the E-mail task pane.

You can send the photos as attachments or you can display them in the body of the message as previews. If you choose the preview option, you can select Thumbnail, Postcard, or Large Postcard from the Preview Size drop-down list. You can also choose to display multiple photos in a table view or in a column (one per line) by setting the Preview Layout option. Click Create Message to open an Outlook message form where you can create your message as you normally would.

Changing Image Size

If you have tried using photos in Word or other documents, you have probably experienced the frustration of dealing with an image that is too large or too small for the intended application, or an e-mail that takes forever to download because someone attached a photo of their new baby. With Picture Manager you can use the Export feature to resize images to the exact pixel size you want and Compress to reduce file size for e-mail and web documents.

With Export you can choose from six image sizes, including:

◆ Original Size

◆ Document Large (1024×768 pixels)

◆ Document Small (800×600 pixels)

◆ Web Large (640×480 pixels)

◆ Web Small (448×336 pixels)

◆ E-mail Large (314×235 pixels)

Follow these steps to export and resize an image or group of images:

1. Select the image or images you want to export.

2. Click the Down arrow on the task pane header and choose Export.

3. Enter the location where you want to export the picture in the Export Select Files To text box. Click Browse to choose a location from the Browse dialog box.

4. Keep the same file name or select the file name and enter a new one in the Export With This File Name text box. If you have selected more than one image, you can enter a common file name and click Rename to set up automatic numbering of the images. Click Return to Export to continue setting up the export.

5. Choose a File Format from the Export With This File Format drop-down list.

6. Choose a size from the Export Using This Size drop-down list.

7. Click OK to export the image or images.

COMPRESSING

If the image file you want to use loads too slowly when you place it in a document, you can use Picture Manager's Compress feature to reduce the actual file size. You will experience some changes in image quality but that's more than made up for by the ease of viewing the document. To compress a picture, follow these steps:

1. Select the image or images you want to compress.

2. Click the Down arrow on the task pane header and choose Compress.

3. Choose Documents, Web Pages, or E-mail Messages from the Compress For option group.

4. Click OK to compress the image or images.

Whether you need to do some basic image editing or you need to compress images for faster viewing, Picture Manager is a useful addition to the Microsoft Office System. In this next section, we'll switch from editing and organizing to working with images in documents.

Adding Art to Enhance Documents

Finding and organizing the perfect clips and pictures is more than half the battle. Positioning them in your document so they enhance rather than detract from your message is the rest. Word makes it easy to work with pictures, but knowing a few tricks will give you full control of how your clips appear in your documents.

When you insert a picture into a Word document, the bottom of the picture is aligned with the text at the location of the insertion point. This default text-wrapping style, In Line With Text, is rather limiting—you can only move the clip as if you were moving a block of text, one character or one line of text at a time.

For more flexibility with how the clip integrates with the text, and with how easily you can move it around the document, choose a different text-wrapping option by clicking the Text Wrapping button on the Picture toolbar. You can access these options from the Picture toolbar that opens automatically when you select a picture (for details about all of the tools on the Picture toolbar, see the section "Modifying Pictures with the Picture Toolbar" later in this chapter).

You can also access text-wrapping options if you right-click the clip and choose Format Picture, or click the Format Picture button on the Picture toolbar, and then click the Layout tab of the Format Picture dialog box, shown in Figure 5.10.

FIGURE 5.10

Display the Layout tab in the Format Picture dialog box to change the layout of the selected picture.

When you change the clip's layout to Square, Tight, Behind Text, or In Front Of Text, you can adjust the horizontal alignment of the clip using the Horizontal Alignment options on the Layout tab of the Format Picture dialog box. Choose Other if you want to reposition the picture by dragging it with your mouse. Click OK to save the new layout changes.

NOTE *Choosing any of the Alignment options does not restrict your ability to reposition a picture.*

You can now reposition the picture by dragging it with the four-headed arrow pointer to a different location on the page while retaining the new text-wrapping style you set for the picture.

TIP   If you would prefer to change the default Word uses to insert pictures, In Line With Text, choose Tools ➤ Options and select a different option from the Insert/Paste Pictures As drop-down list on the Edit tab.

Resizing Clip Art

When you click a picture (or any object) to select it, eight handles appear around the outside: four at the corners and one on each side. When you point to any one of these handles, the pointer changes to a two-headed resize arrow. Drag any handle to resize the object in the desired direction. Drag one of the corner handles if you want to resize the object while maintaining the object's original proportions.

NOTE   As long as you resize a picture using a corner handle, Office 2003 automatically maintains the picture's original proportions. To turn this feature off, clear the Lock Aspect Ratio check box on the Size tab in the Format Picture dialog box (right-click the picture and choose Format Picture). You can still maintain proportions even with this option turned off by holding Shift while dragging a corner handle.

Gaining Control of Positioning and Wrapping

When you need more precise positioning of your graphics and want better control of how text wraps around the picture, click the Advanced button on the Layout tab of the Format Picture dialog box (right-click a picture and choose Format Picture).

Use the Picture Position tab, shown in Figure 5.11, to set the Horizontal and Vertical position relative to the Alignment (Left, Center, Right) or the Absolute Position. For Horizontal position, you can also choose Book Layout (position of left and right margins on opposite pages).

NOTE   There are no options in the Picture Position tab of "Advanced Layout" if In Line With Text is selected in the Layout tab.

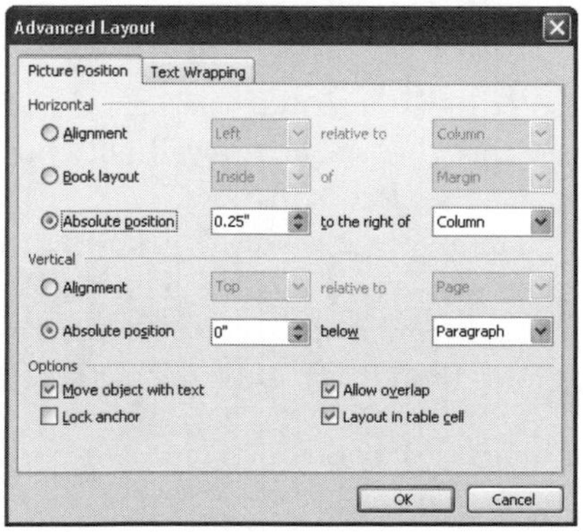

FIGURE 5.11

The Picture Position tab of the Advanced Layout dialog box lets you control the exact positioning of a picture.

The Picture Position tab also gives you these options:

Move Object With Text   Clear this check box to position the picture on the page so it does not move, even if the paragraph it is located in moves.

Lock Anchor   Click this check box so you can move a picture while anchoring it to a particular paragraph so that it always stays in the same relative position to that paragraph.

Allow Overlap   Click this check box to allow two pictures with the same text wrapping to overlap each other.

Layout in Table Cell   Allows a picture to be positioned in the cell of a table.

If you are not satisfied with how close the text is to the picture, click the Text Wrapping tab of the Advanced Layout dialog box, shown in Figure 5.12, to change the Distance From Text properties to increase or decrease the distance.

FIGURE 5.12

Use the Text Wrapping tab in the Advanced Layout dialog box to change how text wraps around a picture.

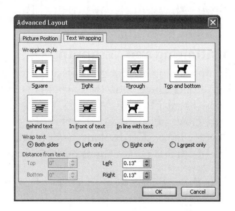

NOTE   *The options that appear for the Distance From Text properties depend on the Wrapping style selected*

The Text Wrapping tab also provides options if you want the text to wrap only on one side of the picture or the other. To indicate this, choose Left Only, Right Only, or Largest Only. To wrap text on the left and right sides of the picture, select Both Sides.

For another option and even more-precise control of how text wraps around the picture, choose Edit Wrap Points by clicking the Text Wrapping button on the Picture toolbar and selecting Edit Wrap Points. This adds numerous points in the picture, as you can see in Figure 5.13. Drag any one of the points to push the text away from that part of the picture.

NOTE   *Many of the settings you learned about in this section in relation to pictures, such as the options on the Picture toolbar and the Format Picture dialog box, can be applied to any object you insert into a Word document regardless of the source application—Excel charts, Microsoft Draw objects, WordArt objects, and so on. If the Picture toolbar does not appear automatically when you select an object, right-click any visible toolbar and choose Picture to activate it.*

FIGURE 5.13

To change how closely text wraps around a picture, you can drag individual points to move the text further away.

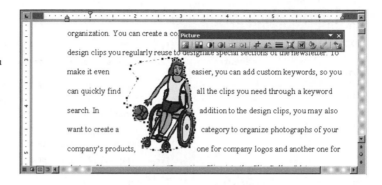

ROTATING IMAGES

At the top of each picture you insert into a document is a green-filled circle above the center handle. This is the Free Rotate tool and it allows you to rotate the picture in any direction. When you point to the tool, the pointer changes to a circular arrow. When you click the arrow, the pointer changes to four circular arrows. Drag the pointer to rotate the image.

NOTE *If the Free Rotate tool is not available, you may need to change the wrapping style to something other than Inline With Text.*

Modifying Pictures with the Picture Toolbar

Although Word does not have the features of photo-editing software such as Microsoft Photo Editor or a third-party image-editing package such as Adobe PhotoShop, you still have some basic editing options available to you within Word. When you want to change a picture by adjusting the contrast or brightness, setting the transparency, or cropping it, the Picture toolbar may just have the tools you need. Table 5.2 describes the buttons you can find on the Picture toolbar.

TABLE 5.2: THE PICTURE TOOLBAR BUTTONS

BUTTON	NAME	USE
	Insert Picture	Inserts a picture from a file.
	Color	Determines the appearance of the picture: Automatic (applies the most appropriate format, usually the defaults); Grayscale (converts each color to a shade of gray); Black & White (changes each color to black or white, converting the image to line art); or washout (changes the picture to a bright, low-contrast format that can be placed behind document text).
	More Contrast	Increases color intensity.
	Less Contrast	Decreases color intensity.
	More Brightness	Adds white to lighten the colors.
	Less Brightness	Adds black to darken the colors.
	Crop	Trims rectangular areas from the image.
	Rotate Left	Rotates the picture 90 degrees to the left with each click.
	Line Style	Formats the border that surrounds the picture.
	Compress Pictures	Reduces the file size of graphics by reducing the resolution of the picture for Web/Screen and Print uses, compressing the picture by applying compression to high-color pictures (may result in a loss of quality), and deleting cropped areas of a picture.
	Text Wrapping	Determines the way document text wraps around the picture.
	Format Picture/Object	Displays the Picture tab in the Format Picture/Object dialog box so you can change the format to exact specifications.
	Set Transparent Color	Used like an eyedropper to make areas of JPEG pictures transparent. Used extensively in Web design.
	Reset Picture	Returns the picture to its original format.

NOTE   *The Crop and Set Transparent Color buttons are used with areas of the picture. All other buttons affect the entire picture.*

Incorporating Photos and Scanned Images into Your Work

In addition to using Clip Organizer as a source of art, you can insert pictures into your document from any file you can access. You can also format pictures inserted from a file by using the buttons on the Picture toolbar. To insert a picture that isn't in Clip Organizer, position the insertion point where you want the picture to appear and follow these steps:

1. Click Insert ➤ Picture ➤ From File, or display the Picture toolbar and click the Insert Picture button to open the Insert Picture dialog box, shown in Figure 5.14.

2. Select the name of the file that contains the picture.

3. Click the Insert button to insert the selected picture into your document.

FIGURE 5.14

You can insert pictures into your documents from a variety of sources using the Insert Picture dialog box.

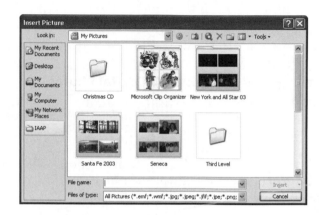

MASTERING THE OPPORTUNITIES: ADDING GRAPHICAL LINES, BULLETS, AND PAGE BORDERS

Adding clip art and photographs isn't the only way to add flair to a Word document. Word 2003 has features that allow you to insert graphical lines and bullets in place of the standard lines and bullet characters and to decorate your pages with graphical page borders. These finishing touches make your documents more interesting and more noticeable and after all, isn't that the point?

To insert a graphical line, follow these steps:

1. Position the insertion point where you want the line to appear.

2. Choose Format ➤ Borders And Shading.

3. Click the Horizontal Line button at the bottom of the Borders tab of the Borders And Shading dialog box. This launches the Horizontal Lines dialog box that searches your clip collections.

4. When you have selected a line, click OK to insert it into your document.

You can format the line by right-clicking it and choosing Format Horizontal Line.

To use graphical bullets in a bulleted list, follow these steps:

1. Select the list you want to bullet, or position the insertion point where you want the first bullet to appear.

2. Choose Format ➤ Bullets And Numbering.

3. Select the Bulleted tab in the Bullets and Numbering dialog box.

Continued on next page

MASTERING THE OPPORTUNITIES: ADDING GRAPHICAL LINES, BULLETS, AND PAGE BORDERS *(continued)*

4. Click any bullet other than None and click Customize.

5. Click the Picture button to see the Picture bullet dialog box with all the picture bullets from your clip collections.

6. When you have selected a bullet, click OK to insert it into your document.

To add an artsy page border, choose Format ➤ Borders And Shading. Click the Page Borders tab and select a border from the Art drop-down list.

Inserting Scanned Graphics and Digital Photos

With today's digital cameras, scanners, and endless CDs filled with photos and clip art, it's pretty easy to capture just the right images for your documents. It may take a little legwork, but if it's out there, there is a way to turn it into a digital image. Office has built-in tools to accept images directly from scanners and digital cameras.

To import images from a digital camera, scanner, or other TWAIN device, first make sure the device is connected to your computer and the software for the device is installed through Windows. Then, follow these steps:

1. Set up the picture in the scanning device.

2. Choose Insert ➤ Picture ➤ From Scanner Or Camera.

3. Select the device you want use from the Device drop-down list.

4. Choose the resolution you want—Web Quality or Print Quality—depending on how you plan to use the picture.

5. Click Insert or, if you are using a scanner and want to change the image settings, choose Custom Insert. If the Insert button is unavailable because your scanner doesn't support automatic scanning, you must choose Custom Insert.

You can modify, reposition, and resize scanned images and digital photos just like any other images.

TIP   If you are scanning text-based documents, you can use Microsoft Document Imaging to scan the document and then use OCR (Optical Character Recognition) to turn the scanned image into editable text. Microsoft Document Imaging is available from the Microsoft Office Tools group in the Microsoft Office group on the Programs menu. OCR is an Install on Demand feature and is available from the Recognize Text Using OCR on the Tools menu in Microsoft Document Imaging.

Creating Your Own Drawings and Diagrams with Microsoft Draw

If you want to design your own graphic objects, Microsoft Draw has a bundle of tools for you to use. You can unleash your creativity or just have fun drawing your own graphics using the drawing tools on Office 2003's Drawing toolbar. Drawing is available in Word, Excel, and PowerPoint, and the drawing tools are available in the Access Toolbox. You use the same methods to create a drawing with the drawing tools, no matter which application you are using.

NOTE *You can also create a drawing in Word, Excel, or PowerPoint and paste it into an Access form or report or into another document.*

The Drawing toolbar is displayed by default in PowerPoint. To display it in Word or Excel, use either of these methods:

◆ Click the Drawing button on the Standard toolbar.

◆ Right-click any toolbar or choose View ➤ Toolbars, and then select Drawing in the toolbar list.

When you display the Drawing toolbar using the Drawing button, your Word document automatically switches to Print Layout view if it is not already in that view. The Drawing toolbar includes two broad categories of menus and buttons. The first set, beginning with the AutoShapes drop-down list button and ending with the Insert Picture button, is used to create drawing objects. The remaining buttons on either side of this set are used to format existing objects.

Working with the Drawing Canvas

Although the Drawing toolbar is shared by Word, Excel, and PowerPoint, Word 2003 offers an additional tool to help you create professional-looking drawings. With the *Drawing Canvas*, you can create drawings in which multiple objects maintain their position in relation to each other. You can easily adjust the size of the Drawing Canvas to fit any size drawing you create. You can also format the Drawing Canvas itself by adding colors, lines, and fills, by changing the size of the drawing area, and by adjusting the layout in relation to text on the page. The biggest advantage you'll find using the Drawing Canvas is that you can easily copy and paste your drawing into other documents and other applications. Let's say you need a flowchart to appear in a Word document and a PowerPoint presentation. Create it once using the Drawing Canvas, and you can use it over and over again. To activate the Drawing Canvas and the Drawing Canvas toolbar, shown in Figure 5.15, just click any object tool, such as Rectangle, Arrow, or Oval, on the Drawing toolbar.

FIGURE 5.15

The Drawing Canvas adjusts to fit any size drawing and keeps drawing objects together.

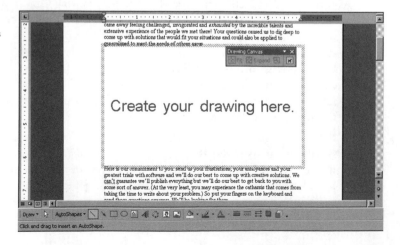

You can add any number of different objects, such as lines, ovals, rectangles, AutoShapes, and WordArt to the Drawing Canvas and then resize and reposition them in the *canvas*, or drawing area. When you move the Drawing Canvas, all of the objects contained within it move together as if they were a single object.

CIRCUMVENTING THE DRAWING CANVAS

If all you want is a simple line or other single object, using the Drawing Canvas may seem like overkill. To create an object without using the Drawing Canvas, click the object button you want on the Drawing toolbar. When the Drawing Canvas appears in your document, press the Esc key to dispose of it. You can then drag to create the object without the added overhead of the Drawing Canvas.

TIP   If you'd like to avoid the Drawing Canvas altogether, you can change the default option. Click Tools > Options and clear the Automatically Create Drawing Canvas When Creating AutoShapes checkbox on the General tab.

RESIZING THE DRAWING CANVAS

If you decide to use the Drawing Canvas, you have several options for resizing it to fit your drawing. The easiest method is to drag the handles in the corners or at the sides, as shown here:

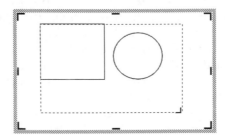

As soon as you add more than one object to the Drawing Canvas, you can click the Fit button on the Drawing Canvas toolbar to shrink the canvas to the exact size of the objects it contains—the edges of the canvas touch the edges of the objects. Click the Expand button if you want to create a larger drawing area. Each click expands the drawing in even increments.

The most precise method of adjusting the size of the Drawing Canvas is to right-click anywhere within its borders and choose Format Drawing Canvas. Click the Size tab and enter the desired height and width in the appropriate text boxes. You can also scale the drawing by entering percentage values in the Scale Height and Width text boxes.

ADDING AND DELETING OBJECTS

To add an object such as an oval or rectangle or even a picture or clip art to an existing Drawing Canvas, click anywhere in the Drawing Canvas to select it and then click the object button. If you skip this step, Word creates a new Drawing Canvas just for the new object.

To delete an object from the Drawing Canvas, click the object and press Delete.

KEEPING THINGS IN PROPORTION

If you drag the handles of the Drawing Canvas, you'll notice that the height and width of the object stay in proportion. You will also find that when you enter a height on the Size tab of the Format Drawing Canvas dialog box, the width also changes. The relationship between the height and width of an object is called the *aspect ratio*. The Lock Aspect Ratio property is turned on by default so you don't end up with drawings that become hopelessly out of proportion through wanton resizing. If you are feeling frisky and want to have more freedom over the height and width of the Drawing Canvas, clear the Lock Aspect Ratio check box in the Format Drawing Canvas dialog box before adjusting its size.

TIP   Office can convert existing Microsoft Draw Server OLE objects into built-in Drawing Canvasses. Right-click the Draw object and choose Convert.

Inserting AutoShapes

Whether or not you plan to use the Drawing Canvas in Word, when you click the AutoShapes button in any application, a drop-down menu appears with a list of AutoShape categories. AutoShapes comprises numerous drawing tools: lines; basic shapes such as triangles, cylinders, hearts, and braces; block arrows; flowchart symbols; and many more. Choose the More AutoShapes option to see even more options on the Clip Art task pane.

The easiest way to insert AutoShapes into your document is to display the AutoShapes toolbar, click the category that contains the shape you want, and then click the shape to select it. Use either of the following methods to display the AutoShapes toolbar:

◆   Click the AutoShapes button on the Drawing toolbar, point to the top of the toolbar, and drag it to make it float.

◆   Choose Insert ➢ Picture ➢ AutoShapes.

To insert an AutoShape in your document (other than a Curve, Freeform, or Scribble line, discussed below):

1.   Click the AutoShapes drop-down list button on the Drawing toolbar, and then highlight a category to display its menu of AutoShapes. Alternatively, display the AutoShapes toolbar and click the button of the category you want to use.

2.   Click an AutoShape, position the insertion point where you want to place the AutoShape, and then click in your document to insert it.

When you click to insert the selected AutoShape, it is created in its default size (with the exception of Line, Arrow, and Double-Arrow on the Line menu—you have to draw these). If you want to create a custom size, first select an AutoShape, position the insertion point in your document (notice that the mouse pointer appears as a crosshair), then drag diagonally from the top-left to the bottom-right to draw an AutoShape in your required size. If you've already inserted the AutoShape, you can drag one of the AutoShape's corner *handles*, the small circles that surround a selected AutoShape, to increase or decrease its size proportionally.

If you intend to add many AutoShapes in the same category, you can drag the title bar at the top of the menu and place the menu in the document as a floating toolbar. For example, when creating a flowchart, you can drag that menu's title bar so the AutoShapes on it are easily available while you work, as shown in Figure 5.16.

FIGURE 5.16

Drag the AutoShape category menu's title bar to create a floating toolbar, making it easier for you to quickly insert shapes in your document.

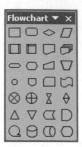

Callout AutoShapes are text boxes used for annotating other objects or elements. When you insert a callout in your document, the insertion point automatically appears inside the callout. To place text in any closed AutoShape except those created using the Lines category, right-click the AutoShape and choose Add Text in the shortcut menu. When you do, the insertion point appears in the object, and the Text Box toolbar appears. (See the explanation on using text boxes in the "Adding Line Art Objects" section later in this chapter.)

Curve, Freeform, and *Scribble* objects are AutoShape line objects that consist of multiple line segments you create individually. The line segments are extremely small in Curve and Scribble objects; in fact, they are so small that the lines appear to be curved. You can easily see the various line segments in a Freeform object. To create a Curve, Freeform, or Scribble AutoShape, follow these steps:

1. Click the AutoShapes drop-down list button and highlight Lines to display its menu of AutoShapes.

2. In the menu, click Curve, Freeform, or Scribble.

3. Position the mouse pointer where you want to begin the line, and then click to start it. Move your mouse to a different location and click again to form the first segment of the line. Continue until the line appears as you want, and then release the mouse button or, with the Curve or Freeform tool, double-click to form the end of the line.

If your object is a closed Freeform, double-click near the beginning of the line to close it. Alternatively, right-click the selected Freeform, and then choose Close Curve in the shortcut menu that appears.

Creating Flowcharts

Almost anyone involved in business today has been asked at one time or another to create a flowchart. Even if you don't know what all the different shapes mean, a basic flowchart is a great way to analyze the steps of a process. AutoShapes provides all the tools you need to create professional-looking flowcharts with minimal effort.

NOTE *To learn the names of the different flow-chart shapes, point to any one of them on the Flowchart menu to see the name displayed in a screen tip.*

To create a flowchart you need two objects: *shapes,* and *lines* to connect the shapes. With AutoShapes, you can create the flowchart shapes and then use Connectors to connect the shapes. After two shapes are connected, they retain their connection when moved. Figure 5.17 shows a simple flowchart using Connectors.

FIGURE 5.17

To design a flowchart, create shapes using the Flowchart shapes and then use Connectors to join them all together.

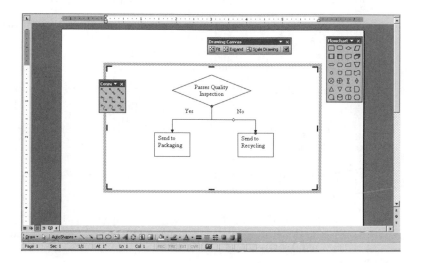

To create a flowchart, follow these steps:

1. Select the first Flowchart shape you want to use from the AutoShapes ➤ Flowchart menu. Click in your document or within a Drawing Canvas to create the shape.

2. Right-click and choose Add Text to place the shape in Edit mode so you can enter text into the shape. Resize as necessary.

3. Create a second flowchart object and position it appropriately. Add text and resize as necessary.

4. Select a Connector from the Connectors menu on the AutoShapes menu.

5. Move the pointer into the first flowchart object. Blue handles appear on the sides of the object.

6. Click the handle you want to connect and drag toward the second object. When blue handles appear on the second object, drag the line to connect to the side you want.

7. Repeat steps 1–6 until you have completed your flowchart.

Adding Line Art Objects

Line art objects include AutoShapes, lines, arrows, rectangles, ovals, and text boxes. You can easily insert any of these objects in your document by using the appropriate tool on the Drawing toolbar. To draw a line or arrow, follow these steps:

1. Click the Line button or the Arrow button on the Drawing toolbar. (Press the Esc key if you do not want to use the Drawing Canvas in Word.) If you plan to draw several lines or arrows, you can double-click the button to keep it turned on.

2. Move the pointer, which now appears as a crosshair, to the position where you want the line to begin.

3. Hold down the left mouse button and drag to draw the line.

4. Release the button to create the line. If you double-clicked the button to turn it on, click the Line or Arrow button to turn it off again.

When you use the Arrow tool, an arrowhead appears at the end of the line where you released the mouse button.

TIP   If you want a line or arrow that is absolutely horizontal or vertical in relation to the page, hold down the Shift key while dragging.

The Line and other object buttons work like the Format Painter button: When you have more than one object to draw, begin by double-clicking its button. The button stays pressed, allowing you to draw more objects, until you click any other drawing object's button. If you don't want to draw any more objects, just click the button that is depressed on the Drawing toolbar to change your mouse pointer back into an I-beam. To draw a rectangle or oval, follow these steps:

1. Click the Rectangle or Oval button. Dismiss the drawing canvas, if you prefer, by pressing Esc.

2. Move the pointer, which now appears as a crosshair, to the top-left corner or edge of the object you want to draw.

3. Hold down the left mouse button and drag down and to the right to draw the object.

4. Release the button to create the rectangle or oval and turn off the Drawing tool.

TIP   To create an exact circle or square, hold down Shift while dragging.

Because both the rectangle and oval are closed objects, you can add text in them just as you can in the closed AutoShapes. Right-click the object, and then choose Add Text in the shortcut menu to position the insertion point inside the object and display the Text Box toolbar.

TIP   If you need a series of identical objects, create one object, copy it, and then paste as many copies of that object as necessary in the locations you want.

CREATING AND APPLYING TEXT BOXES

Use the Text Box tool to create text that floats on a layer above standard document text. Draw the text box as you would a rectangle. When you release the mouse button, the text box is active—an insertion point appears in it, and a lined border appears around it. You can type the text you want in the active text box.

You can also create a text box around existing text. For example, if you are creating a newsletter, it may be easier to type the text and then change the way it is laid out. Text boxes are particularly useful in documents that contain graphics, because they allow you to move text to any position, including within the margins. To create a text box around existing text:

1. Select the text you want to place in a text box.

2. Click the Text Box button on the Drawing toolbar.

When you create a text box this way, the text box is selected—a shaded border with handles appears around the text box, but the insertion point is not in it. When the text box is selected, you can drag it to a different location on the page. You can also use the handles surrounding the selected text box to change its size. This is important, because text boxes do not automatically conform to the size of their contents—in other words, they don't grow as you add text or shrink when you delete text. However, if you would prefer to let Word do the work for you, you can change the text box options. To access this option, select the AutoShape, right-click and choose Format Text Box (or Format AutoShape). Make sure the Resize AutoShape to Fit Text checkbox on the Text Box tab is checked.

To activate a text box when you want to edit or format the text, just click inside the text box to place the insertion point in it. You can then select the text and apply formatting to it using the options and buttons on the Formatting toolbar and the commands on the Format menu.

To delete a text box, select it and press Delete. When you delete a text box, all the text in it is also deleted.

The Text Box toolbar, shown in Figure 5.18, appears when you draw or select a text box in your document.

FIGURE 5.18

Use the Text Box toolbar to create links between text boxes.

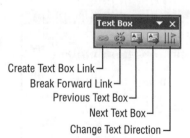

Use the buttons on the toolbar to perform the following actions:

♦ Activate or select a text box, click the Create Text Box Link button on the Text Box toolbar, and then click an empty text box to link the two text boxes in your document. Any text that does not fit in the first text box automatically flows into the next linked text box. For example, your company newsletter may contain a story that is continued on another page. If you place the beginning of the story in a text box, you can link it to the text box that contains the rest of the story.

◆ Create and store the text for linked text boxes in a separate file and make any formatting and editing changes there. Then copy the text into the first text box. Text that will not fit is automatically poured into the next linked text box.

◆ Activate the text box that contains the link (the one that was selected or active when you created the link), and then click the Break Forward Link button to break a link between two text boxes.

◆ Click the Previous Text Box button or the Next Text Box button to select the previous or next linked text box. This is helpful because you can see where each linked text box falls in line.

◆ Click the Change Text Direction button to rotate all the text in the active text box. You can click the button three times to toggle through different settings. You can use rotated text in a text box to provide visual interest in a document.

You can delete a linked text box without deleting its contents. The contents spill into the other linked text boxes. You may need to resize those text boxes to accommodate the additional text.

Designing WordArt

WordArt is used to create a graphic object from text. You can use WordArt to create text logos, emphasize titles, and add excitement to a document. For example, you can create a vibrantly colored title page for a proposal or report. To create WordArt:

1. Place the insertion point where you want the graphic and click the Insert WordArt button on the Drawing toolbar to open the WordArt Gallery dialog box, shown in Figure 5.19. Alternatively, choose Insert ➢ Picture ➢ WordArt to open the WordArt Gallery dialog box.

FIGURE 5.19

You can choose a style for your text graphic in the WordArt Gallery dialog box.

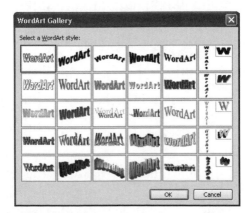

2. Click the style you want for your text graphic in the Select A WordArt Style area.

3. Click OK to display the Edit WordArt Text dialog box, shown in Figure 5.20.

4. Type the text in the Text area of the dialog box.

5. If necessary, apply the following formatting to the text in the Text area:

◆ Select a different font in the Font drop-down list.

◆ Select a different font size in the Size drop-down list.

◆ Click the Bold and/or Italic button to apply that formatting.

6. Click OK to place the WordArt object in your document and open the floating WordArt toolbar.

FIGURE 5.20

Type the text for your WordArt graphic in the Edit WordArt text box.

When the WordArt object is placed in your document, the object is selected and the small, square sizing handles appear around it. The WordArt toolbar is only displayed when a WordArt object is selected in your document. You can use the buttons on the WordArt toolbar to edit and apply formatting to your WordArt object. The toolbar buttons are described in Table 5.3.

NOTE   To deselect an object, just click anywhere in the document. Deselected objects appear just as they will when the document is printed.

TABLE 5.3: WORDART TOOLBAR BUTTONS

BUTTON	NAME	USE
	Insert WordArt	Displays the WordArt Gallery dialog box to create a new WordArt object.
Edit Text...	Edit Text	Displays the Edit WordArt Text dialog box to edit text.
	WordArt Gallery	Opens the WordArt Gallery dialog box to change the WordArt style.
	Format WordArt	Opens the Format WordArt dialog box so you can format colors, size, position, and wrap properties.

Continued on next page

BUTTON	NAME	USE
TABLE 5.3: WORDART TOOLBAR BUTTONS *(continued)*		
	WordArt Shape	Opens a shape menu so you can select the basic shape into which the text will be poured.
	Text Wrapping	Displays a menu so you can select how text wraps around the WordArt object.
	WordArt Same Letter Heights	Makes all letters the same height, irrespective of case. Click again to reverse the action.
	WordArt Vertical Text	Changes the WordArt orientation from horizontal to vertical. Click again to reverse.
	WordArt Alignment	Opens an alignment menu with standard options and unique WordArt options.
	WordArt Character Spacing	Opens an adjustment menu so you can change space between characters.

Formatting Objects

Even though you can create some pretty cool shapes with the tools on the Drawing toolbar, they may not be quite what you need without a little formatting. After you create the objects you want, you can add color, lines, fills, and shadows and even make them 3-D. Most of the formatting tools you need are available on the Drawing toolbar. If you want even more options, right-click any object and choose Format [*Object Type*].

FILLING AND COLORING LINES AND OBJECTS

To select a single object, just click the object. To select multiple objects, either hold down Shift while clicking each object or click the Select Objects tool on the Drawing toolbar and drag a rectangle around the objects you want to select. Use the following tools to format a selected object:

Fill Color   Displays a palette of colors. If you want an object without any color, choose No Fill. You can drag the Fill Color palette onto your screen as a floating menu, which is useful if you want to apply different fill colors to several objects. You can also choose More Fill Colors on the menu to create a custom color and Fill Effect to apply a gradient, texture, pattern, or a picture as the fill for an object.

Line Color   Displays the Line Color palette. Choose a color to apply to the lines in and around the selected object. Like the Fill Color palette, the Line Color palette can be dragged onto your document so it becomes a floating menu. You can create a custom color for the line or apply a pattern to it for different effects.

Font Color   Displays the Font Color palette. Choose a color for the text in a selected object such as a text box or callout. Drag the Font Color palette to make it a floating menu. You can use it to create custom colors to apply to the text in selected objects.

TIP   Click the Fill Color, Line Color, or Font Color button to apply its current color to a selected object.

Line Style   Displays a menu that contains various line styles. Click the style you want for the lines in and around a selected object. Alternatively, select More Lines from the menu to open the Format AutoShape dialog box and display the Colors And Lines tab. You can change the line style, color, and weight as well as many other attributes of the selected object.

NOTE   The Format Text Box dialog box, which appears when you double-click the border of a text box, contains options similar to those of the Format AutoShape dialog box. Each dialog box allows you to change the fill color, line style, line weight, size, scale, and text wrapping style for a selected object. The Format Text Box dialog box also allows you to change the text box's internal margins and convert it to a frame. If the text box is a callout, you can also change the style of the callout.

Dash Style   Displays a menu of dashed line styles. Click one of the styles to apply that style to all of the lines in the selected object. You can change the weight of the line by selecting it in the Line Style menu. To change the lines back to a solid line, select that style in the Dash Style menu.

Arrow Style   Displays a menu of arrow styles. Select the style to apply to the ends of the selected line. You can choose an arrowhead or one of various other line terminators. If the combination of line endings you want isn't in the menu, choose More Arrows to display the Format AutoShape dialog box, set a beginning and ending style for the line, and then click OK. Arrow styles can be applied only to lines, arrows, and open AutoShapes.

FORMATTING OBJECTS USING THE DRAW MENU

The Draw menu, which appears when you click the Draw button on the Drawing toolbar, also contains some commands that allow you to change the appearance of a selected object. These commands include the following:

Text Wrapping   Lets you select how you want the regular document text to appear in relation to the selected object.

Edit Points (on the Text Wrapping menu)   Changes the appearance of a Curve, Freeform, or Scribble AutoShape. When you use this command, each position in which you clicked your mouse while drawing the AutoShape appears with a small, black move handle. Drag the handle to change its position, thereby changing the appearance of the AutoShape.

Change AutoShape   Replaces the current AutoShape with a different one. When you do, the AutoShapes menu appears. Choose the category that contains the AutoShape, and then choose the replacement. Any text in the AutoShape remains in the new shape.

NOTE   You cannot use the Change AutoShape command to change the shape of a Line AutoShape. Instead, you must use the Edit Points command and drag the endpoints to different positions. Alternatively, you can delete a Line AutoShape and insert an AutoShape in a different category.

Set AutoShape Defaults   Defaults Inserts subsequent AutoShapes of the kind selected with the same formatting applied. Every new AutoShape of that type will appear in the same size, color, and so on, until you specify a different default.

Special Shadow and 3-D Effects

Shadow and 3-D effects are designed to give a selected drawing object apparent depth. You cannot apply both shadow and 3-D formatting to an object. If you apply a 3-D effect to a shadowed object, the shadow is removed. If you apply a shadow to an object that has 3-D formatting, the 3-D effect is removed. Any drawing object can have either a shadow or a 3-D effect applied to it.

 Click the Shadow button to display a menu of various shadow styles, and then click the style you want for the selected object. To change the format of the shadow, click the Shadow button again, and then choose Shadow Settings to display the Shadow Settings toolbar. The toolbar buttons and their uses are described in Table 5.4.

TABLE 5.4: The Shadow Settings Toolbar Buttons

Button	Name	Use
	Shadow On/Off	Displays or removes the object's shadow
	Nudge Shadow Up	Pushes the shadow up
	Nudge Shadow Down	Pushes the shadow down
	Nudge Shadow Left	Pushes the shadow to the left
	Nudge Shadow Right	Pushes the shadow to the right
	Shadow Color	Displays a palette so you can select the color for the shadow

To choose the 3-D effect to apply to a selected object, click the 3-D button on the Drawing toolbar, and then click the option you want in the menu that appears. To change the formatting applied to the 3-D effect, click the 3-D button again, and then choose 3-D Settings to display the 3-D Settings toolbar. Table 5.5 shows how to use the buttons on the toolbar to quickly change the format of the 3-D effect.

TABLE 5.5: The 3-D Settings Toolbar Buttons

Button	Name	Use
	3-D On/Off	Hides or displays the 3-D effect applied to the object
	Tilt Down	Tilts the 3-D effect toward the object
	Tilt Up	Tilts the 3-D effect away from the object
	Tilt Left	Rotates the 3-D effect to the left
	Tilt Right	Rotates the 3-D effect to the right
	Depth	Allows you to select or specify a different depth for the 3-D effect
	Direction	Allows you to select a direction the 3-D effect points to and to specify whether the direction is Perspective (extends all sides of the effect to a single point) or Parallel (extends all sides of the effect parallel to one another)

Continued on next page

TABLE 5.5: THE 3-D SETTINGS TOOLBAR BUTTONS *(continued)*

BUTTON	NAME	USE
	Lighting	Adjusts the position and intensity of the "light" shining on the 3-D effect to present a different appearance
	Surface	Allows you to select the appearance of the composition of the 3-D effect
	3-D Color	Displays a palette so you can select the color for the 3-D effect

ARRANGING OBJECTS

The Draw menu on the Drawing toolbar includes other options for manipulating objects. For example, you can change the position of a selected object on the page, display a grid to help you position an object precisely, and even group objects in order to move or edit them simultaneously.

Drawing objects are placed in separate layers on top of the text in a document, in the order in which they were created. To move objects from layer to layer:

1. Select the object you want to reposition.

2. Click the Draw button and choose Order to display the Order menu. If necessary, drag the menu by its title bar to display the Order toolbar.

3. Choose one of the following options to change the order of the selected drawing object:

   ◆ Choose Bring To Front to place the selection above (on the top layer of) other graphic objects. Choose Send To Back to place the selection below (on the bottom layer of) other graphic objects.

   ◆ Choose Bring Forward or Send Backward to move the selected object one layer at a time.

   ◆ Choose Send Behind Text to place a selected object behind (below) the text layer of your document. Choose Bring In Front Of Text to place selected objects in front of the text layer (these options are not available if you use the drawing canvas).

TIP   Use the Send Behind Text command to create a watermark for a single page. Place the watermark in a header or footer (View ➤ Header And Footer) to have it appear on every page of a document. The graphic does not have to be confined to the header or footer area.

If you're doing detailed work, consider turning on a grid of invisible horizontal and vertical lines to help you precisely align various objects in the drawing. The grid works by automatically pulling each object you draw into alignment with the nearest intersection of gridlines. You can display the gridlines and adjust the distance between them to help you as you draw. To turn on the grid:

1. Click the Draw button on the Drawing toolbar.

2. Choose Grid to display the Drawing Grid dialog box shown in Figure 5.21, choose the appropriate options (described below) to define the specifications for the grid, and then click OK. The options include the following:

Snap Objects To Grid   Toggles the grid on and off.

Snap Objects To Other Objects   Aligns drawing objects with both the horizontal and vertical edges of other drawing objects when selected.

Horizontal Spacing   Specifies the distance between the horizontal gridlines.

Vertical Spacing   Specifies the distance between the vertical gridlines.

Horizontal Origin and Vertical Origin   Specifies the beginning point for the gridlines, relative to the edges of the page. Alternatively, check the Use Margins box to specify the margins as the beginning point for the gridlines.

Display Gridlines On Screen   Toggles the gridlines display on and off. Check the Vertical Every box, and then adjust the value in the Vertical Every and Horizontal Every text boxes to a number greater than zero to display both sets of gridlines.

To save the gridline settings you specified so they become the default, click the Default button and choose Yes in the message box that appears asking if you want to change the default gridline settings. The default gridline settings are stored in the Normal template and are used until you change them again.

FIGURE 5.21

You can set options to display a grid to help you align objects within a drawing.

There are several other ways to adjust the positions of selected objects in a drawing. Click the Draw button on the Drawing toolbar and then choose from the following:

Nudge   Pushes the selection incrementally Up, Down, Left, or Right

Align Or Distribute   Sets alignment options relative to the page, the Drawing Canvas, or other objects

Rotate Or Flip   Changes the orientation or direction of an object

NOTE   *If one object is selected, click Relative To Page on the Align Or Distribute toolbar to make the alignment buttons available. Relative To Page aligns the selection in relation to the edge of the page. When multiple objects are selected, turn off Relative To Page if you want the objects aligned in relation to each other. Then choose one of the alignment options to specify the alignment you want use.*

GROUPING AND UNGROUPING OBJECTS

When your drawing is complete, you can group all the drawing objects so that they are treated as a single object. When you group objects, you can select all of the objects by selecting any one object in the group. Any formatting you apply is applied to every object in the group. For example, if you have selected a group of AutoShapes and you choose to apply a shadow, the shadow appears on each object in the group.

You can also use the Nudge, Align Or Distribute, and Rotate Or Flip commands to manipulate the position of the group, or you can simply drag the group to a new location on the page to move every object in the group. To combine several objects into a group:

1. Hold down Shift while you click each object to select it.

2. Click the Draw button on the Drawing toolbar and choose Group.

The handles on the selected objects are replaced with one set of handles that can be used to size or move the entire object.

If you want to move, resize, format, or delete an individual element in a group, you can ungroup the grouped object, thereby changing the group back into separate objects. Each object can then be edited independently of the group. To ungroup a grouped object:

1. Click the group to select it.

2. Click the Draw button on the Drawing toolbar and choose Ungroup. Alternatively, right-click the group and choose Grouping ➢ Ungroup.

TIP   *Clip art images can be composed of a group of objects. To change the appearance of a clip art object, ungroup it and then edit individual objects as necessary. Office may tell you that it first needs to convert the object to a Microsoft Drawing object. Tell it OK, and you can then manipulate the object any way you want.*

When you have finished editing, regroup the objects so you can move or size the entire image. To regroup an ungrouped set of objects:

1. Select any object that was previously in the group.

2. Click the Draw button on the Drawing toolbar and choose Regroup. Alternatively, right-click the object and choose Grouping ➢ Regroup.

NOTE   *Although objects created in a Drawing Canvas move as if they are grouped, they are independent objects and cannot be resized together without grouping them first.*

Constructing Diagrams and Organizational Charts

Microsoft Org Chart has been available as an add-in application for many versions of Office. Starting with Office 2003, you can create organizational charts as a built-in feature of Office. In addition, you can create other types of diagrams such as Cycle and Venn diagrams.

To create a diagram, click the Insert Diagram Or Organizational Chart button on the Drawing toolbar. This opens the Diagram Gallery from which you can choose a diagram type. Table 5.6 shows the types of diagrams you can choose and how you can use them.

TABLE 5.6: TYPES OF DIAGRAMS

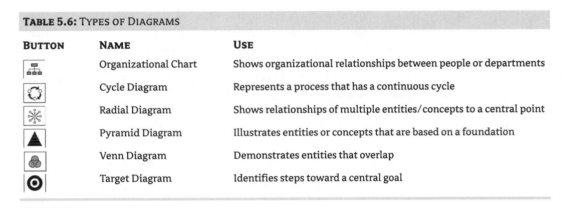

BUTTON	NAME	USE
	Organizational Chart	Shows organizational relationships between people or departments
	Cycle Diagram	Represents a process that has a continuous cycle
	Radial Diagram	Shows relationships of multiple entities/concepts to a central point
	Pyramid Diagram	Illustrates entities or concepts that are based on a foundation
	Venn Diagram	Demonstrates entities that overlap
	Target Diagram	Identifies steps toward a central goal

CREATING AN ORGANIZATIONAL CHART

When you select the Organizational Chart from the Diagram Gallery, Office creates an organizational chart object with four boxes: one manager and three subordinates, as shown in Figure 5.22. You can add additional boxes, delete boxes, and reposition boxes to fit your specific needs.

FIGURE 5.22

An org chart object gives you a head start on creating your organizational chart.

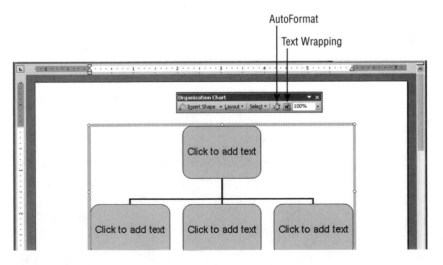

Click in any of the boxes to enter up to two lines of text. To add additional boxes, select the boxes to which the new box is related and choose Insert Shape from the Organizational Chart toolbar. If you click the Down arrow to the right of the Insert Shape button, you can choose to add a subordinate, co-worker, or assistant. To delete a box, click the border of the box to select it and press Delete.

NOTE *If you work in a company that has a nontraditional organizational structure—for example, shared leadership, a partnership, or another less hierarchical structure—you have to be creative to represent your structure with this tool. You cannot position an additional box at the top level. In this case, you might want to use the top level to represent your overall company, board, or maybe even your customers. Another option is to create your organizational chart using AutoShapes and Connectors (see the sections "Inserting AutoShapes" and "Creating Flowcharts" earlier in the chapter).*

CHANGING THE LAYOUT OF THE ORG CHART

The Layout button on the Organizational Chart toolbar gives you options to change the layout of your chart from the standard horizontal configuration to one that is more vertical. To change the layout, select the manager shape at the top of the section you want to alter and then select Both Hanging, Left Hanging, and Right Hanging from the Layout drop-down menu.

You can also change the size of the org chart object by choosing Fit Organizational Chart To Contents, Expand Organizational Chart, or Resize Organizational Chart from the Layout menu. To have Office automatically rearrange and resize the org chart to fit the object frame, choose AutoLayout from the Layout menu.

SELECTING SECTIONS OF THE ORG CHART

As charts become more complex, it becomes harder to select individual sections that you want to move or alter in some way. You can use the Select button on the Organizational Chart toolbar to do your selecting for you. Select the first box in a section you want to select and then choose from the following:

Level   Selects all the boxes on the same level

Branch   Selects all subordinates or assistants in the branch

All Assistants   Selects the assistants in the branch you select

All Connecting Lines   Selects all connecting lines in the chart

APPLYING STYLES FROM THE STYLE GALLERY

To make your org chart stand out, click the AutoFormat button on the Organizational Chart toolbar. This opens the Style Gallery shown in Figure 5.23. From here, you can choose a style for your chart that affects the box shape and style, colors, fills, and lines.

FIGURE 5.23

Choose a style from the Style Gallery to AutoFormat your organizational chart.

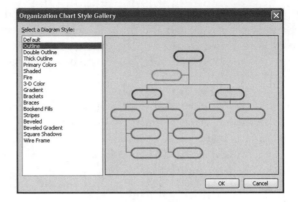

WRAPPING TEXT

After you complete an organizational chart and want to position it within a report or larger document, you might become concerned with how the text wraps around the object. You can change the text wrapping by clicking the Text Wrapping button on the Organizational Chart toolbar.

CREATING CONCEPTUAL DIAGRAMS

The other five types of diagrams available from the Diagram Gallery when you click the Insert Diagram Or Organizational Chart button on the Drawing toolbar can be used interchangeably to represent a process or related concepts. Select the type of diagram that most closely resembles the message you want to communicate. See Table 5.6 earlier to review the types of diagrams and how they can be used.

The Diagram toolbar, shown in Figure 5.24, is similar to the Organizational Chart toolbar with only a couple of exceptions.

FIGURE 5.24

Use the Diagram toolbar to add elements and format the diagram.

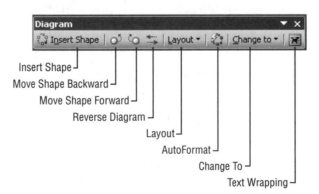

In addition to working with the Insert Shape, Layout, AutoFormat, and Text Wrapping buttons, you can use Move Shape Backward, Move Shape Forward, and Reverse Diagram buttons to change the level or position of a particular shape. You can also use the Change To button to convert a diagram from one type to another—for example, if you created a Pyramid diagram but now feel a Venn diagram would better communicate your message.

Taking PowerPoint to the Next Level

PowerPoint is a graphical tool by design. It appeals to the various learning styles of a typical audience by combining the spoken word with text and images. Although we cover PowerPoint in more detail in Chapter 6, "Adding Electronic Punch to your Presentations," and Chapter 7, "Pushing PowerPoint To the Limit," this chapter wouldn't be complete without a look at a couple of ways you can make your PowerPoint presentations stand out from the crowd. First, we'll look at how you can turn your own digital photographs into powerful PowerPoint slide backgrounds. Then, we'll show you how to add music and narration to presentations that have to stand on their own. These tools take PowerPoint out of the mundane and into the exceptional.

Creating Custom PowerPoint Backgrounds from Your Photos

If your job includes sitting through a lot of PowerPoint presentations, you probably know all the design templates by heart. Nothing can make a presentation more boring than seeing the same old templates over and over again. When you choose to apply a design template, the template includes, among other things, the color scheme and background color. Often, the background is more than just a solid color. It may have a shaded effect, a pattern, or a texture. A picture or graphic object may be part of the background. All these characteristics—shading, patterns, textures, and objects—form the background of the slide. Text and objects that you place on the slide are positioned on top of the background.

Rather than relying on backgrounds supplied by Microsoft, you can create PowerPoint backgrounds using your own digital photos. A background should be subtle enough to sit behind text and not overpower it and yet distinct enough to set your presentation apart. Look around you and try to find something that could fill the bill. Look for an unusual pattern or design, like the one that may be on the floor in the entrance to your corporate headquarters or on the side of the building. Or set up a photo with the special items, scenery, or people you want to include. The possibilities are endless.

NOTE *If a photo has a lot of background colors, you might want to change the font color on the Slide Master to a color with greater contrast so it is visible through the background.*

To use a picture as a slide background, do the following:

1. Choose Format ➤ Background from Normal or Slide Sorter view or right-click a slide (outside of any text boxes or objects). Choose Background from the Shortcut menu.

2. Open the Fill drop-down list and choose Fill Effects.

3. Select the Picture tab of the Fill Effects dialog box.

4. Click the Select Picture button to open the Select Picture dialog box.

5. Locate the picture you wish to use and click Insert. Click OK to close the Fill Effects dialog box.

6. Preview the new pattern and click Apply or Apply To All.

TIP   An easy way to build immediate rapport with your audience is to include pictures that are meaningful to them. When you use an image of a customer's building as the background to a presentation, it's a powerful way to say, "We visited your manufacturing facility." When you're collecting information for a proposal, use a digital camera to take photos of client sites for use in project and sales presentations (however, don't include images of people unless you have obtained their written permission). If you don't have a digital camera with good resolution, you can take 35mm photos and scan them on a high-resolution scanner.

Orchestrating the Soundtrack

In addition to (or instead of) the WAV files that you attach to transitions or include with animation, there are two other audio elements worth considering: CD tracks and narration. Assuming your computer has a CD drive, it's easy to use one or more sequential tracks from a CD as a soundtrack for your presentation. Add a microphone, and you can create narration for the entire presentation or add spoken comments to specific slides.

WARNING   If you won't be present when viewers use your presentation (in a kiosk or on a website), you won't know when viewers have special needs. If critical content is included only in the narration, note that hearing-impaired and deaf viewers—as well as web users whose computers don't have sound cards—won't have access to the content. In a web presentation, you can display notes. For a kiosk presentation, make sure narrated content is handled redundantly in slide text.

ADDING CD TRACKS

Although you don't need to have the CD you want to use in the CD drive to insert a track, you must close any other applications (such as the Deluxe CD player) that take exclusive control of your CD drive so that PowerPoint can access the CD drive. To insert a CD track, switch to Normal view and do the following:

1. Choose Insert ➢ Movies And Sounds ➢ Play CD Audio Track to open the Movie And Sound Options dialog box.

2. Select the starting and ending track(s) and times.

3. Enable the Loop Until Stopped check box if you want the selection to play continuously until you stop the show.

4. Click OK.

5. Indicate whether you'd like the sound icon hidden during slide shows.

6. In Normal or Slide Show view, double-click the CD icon on the slide to hear the audio track.

NOTE *If you add multiple CD tracks, the icons for them appear on top of each other so they are difficult to distinguish. You can click and drag them to separate them.*

WHO OWNS THE MUSIC?

PowerPoint makes it easy to add a CD track or two to your presentation. So why don't more of the presentations you see include a bit of Bette, a few Cranberries, or a slice of Shania?

Broadly speaking, there are two kinds of music ownership: copyrighted music and music in the public domain. Music copyrights can always be renewed. If you use copyrighted music in a public performance, you need to compensate the copyright holder, so if you plug in your MIDI keyboard and record *Happy Birthday (to You)* for a public presentation, you owe a fee to the descendants of the two women who wrote it a century ago. On the other hand, "The Confutatus" from Mozart's *Requiem* is in the public domain, although it may be less suitable for a presentation at your boss's birthday bash.

Not all recordings of Mozart's music are in the public domain. If you intend to use a track directly from a commercial CD in a presentation for a conference, there are other permissions to obtain from the music publisher. Obtaining permission from these media mega-companies is a long process and often ends with a "No." They expect royalties as well as assurances that you'll use their music in an acceptable context, although nonprofit organizations may have better luck.

Most public performances of music in the U.S. are licensed through one of three organizations: ASCAP, BMI, or SESAC. All three are member organizations for songwriters/composers and music publishers. Three is the key here because it generally takes about three months to obtain permission to use a piece of music. (This shows signs of improvement; BMI recently partnered with LicenseMusic.com to create a web-based process for locating and using music written by BMI members.) You'll need to know both the name of the song and the name of the songwriter to determine which of the three organizations to contact for permission to use the music. For more information on using music that is not in the public domain, visit these websites:

◆ www.ascap.com

◆ www.bmi.com

◆ www.sesac.com

So, where can you quickly obtain music for your presentation? The Web, of course. Fire up any Internet search engine and search for royalty-free music to find dozens of sites where you can download or purchase sound files and CDs.

RECORDING AUDIO COMMENTS

Plug in your microphone, lower the ambient noise level in the room (in a home office this means to mute the TV, make the dog stop barking, and give each of the kids a Popsicle), and follow these steps to add a verbal comment to a slide:

1. Display the slide in Normal view.

2. Choose Insert ➤ Movies And Sound ➤ Record Sound to open the Record Sound dialog box.

3. Enter a name for the sound file.

4. Click the Record button (the reddish dot).

5. Talk.

6. When you are finished, click Stop (the blue rectangle).

7. Click OK to save the file.

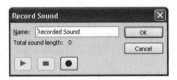

Right-click the sound icon on the slide and choose Custom Animation to animate your recorded comment. In the Custom Animation task pane, recorded sound files are listed as Media. To delete a voice comment from a slide, select the icon and then press Delete.

TIP   If you haven't recorded sound recently, it's a good idea to check your microphone level before recording. Choose Slide Show ➤ Record Narration and click the Set Microphone Level button.

RECORDING NARRATION

Narration—spoken audio that elaborates the content of the slides in a presentation—is used in kiosks, web presentations, and instructional presentations, but it has other uses. Make an audio recording of your presentation, attach it as narration, and you have an easy answer to the question: "What did I miss?"

Narration overrides all other sounds in a presentation, so if you add narration to a presentation that has CD audio, animation sounds, or audio comments, only the narration plays. To mix narration and other sounds, record sound files for individual slides.

To record narration for your presentation, select Slide 1 and choose Slide Show ➤ Record Narration from the menu to open the Record Narration dialog box, shown in Figure 5.25. PowerPoint checks the current drive for space for a sound file and displays the results as disk space and recording time.

FIGURE 5.25

The Record Narration dialog box indicates storage available for your sound file.

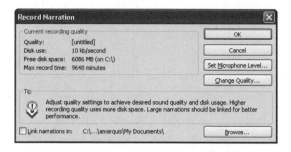

The narration's storage requirements depend on two factors: recording quality and time. Higher quality requires more storage space. If there isn't enough room (enough minutes) on the selected drive for the narration, you have two options:

◆ Click the Browse button and select another location.

◆ Lower the sound quality.

To change the sound quality, click the Change Quality button to open the Sound Selection dialog box.

Choose a quality setting from the Name drop-down list. CD Quality is the best, Telephone the worst. To further tweak the quality, select a group of attributes from the Attributes drop-down list. If you choose attributes, you can save the selection by clicking the Save As button. This is a good idea if you'll be adding narration to more than one presentation for the same audience. Click OK to close the Sound Selection dialog box.

TIP *If your presentation file is large or the narration is going to be long or high quality, enable the Link Narrations dialog box to store each slide's narration as a separate file linked to the presentation.*

Click the Set Microphone Level button in the Record Narration dialog box to make sure that your microphone is plugged in and delivers adequate sound for your presentation.

Click OK to start recording the narration. Move through the presentation, speaking your narration and advancing slides. At the end of the presentation, PowerPoint displays this message box.

Choose Save to save the slide timings—the length of time between each click of the mouse—with the narration. To save the narration only, choose Don't Save.

A sound icon appears in the bottom-right corner of every slide to indicate that the slide includes narration. Delete a slide's narration by deleting the icon.

TIP *When you insert an audio comment with the Record Sound dialog box, the Sound icon is placed in the center of the slide. You can move the icon anywhere on the slide. We'd suggest not moving it to the lower-left corner (or lower-right, depending on the template) because the menu icon resides there.*

To record (or rerecord) narration for part of a presentation, select the slide that you want to begin recording on. Choose Slide Show ➤ Record Narration. When you arrive at the slide that immediately follows the last slide you want to record narration for, press Esc to stop recording.

The narration begins automatically when the slide show starts. To view the presentation without its narration, choose Slide Show ➤ Set Up Show from the menu to open the Set Up Show dialog box. Enable the Show Without Narration check box and click OK; then choose View ➤ Slide Show, or click the Slide Show button, to start the slide show.

Narration adds another dimension to your presentations and may be just the thing when you want a audience to see and hear your presentation even if you are not around.

Chapter 6

Adding Electronic Punch to Your Presentations

FIVE YEARS AGO, IT was still common to watch presenters fumble with overhead projection transparencies, using a piece of cardboard to help the audience track the progress of the presentation. Today, although you still see some fumbling, PowerPoint presentations are the norm in sales meetings, planning sessions, college lectures, and even elementary classrooms. But don't be fooled. Just because presenters use PowerPoint to display slides during their presentations doesn't mean the presentations will be worthy of your attention. A poorly designed and boring PowerPoint presentation can actually detract from a presentation. However, a well constructed and well delivered PowerPoint presentation can turn a mediocre presentation into a better one and a good presentation into a memorable one.

PowerPoint 2003 helps you create dynamic electronic slide shows, including presentations that run automatically. With PowerPoint 2003's enhanced web features, publishing a presentation to the Internet has never been easier. And if you use an overhead transparency projector, PowerPoint 2003 will help you create vivid, full-color transparencies and audience handouts.

NOTE *If you are interested in publishing a presentation to the Web, check out Chapter 11, "Creating and Modifying Documents for the Web."*

Even if you are a dynamite Word or Excel user, you might view PowerPoint as some foreign country you're not sure you want to visit. Unless your job requires you to stand up regularly in front of an audience, you might not have seen its value. However, PowerPoint is not just for presentations anymore. Sure, you can fashion a great presentation for your departmental staff meeting, but you can also put together an electronic album of digital photos taken at your regional sales conference, or publish training material on your company's website. Whatever your task, if it involves sharing information, PowerPoint lets you quickly grab your audience's attention and deliver your message in a most memorable way!

In this chapter, we'll cover the fundamentals of PowerPoint, from creating a basic presentation to customizing and refining a presentation's design. So if you are new to PowerPoint or if you need more practice with the basics, this is the place to start. If you are an experienced PowerPoint user and want to zero in on the more advanced features, you may want to scan this chapter and then dive into Chapter 7, "Pushing PowerPoint to the Limit," where we'll show you how to move beyond the ordinary and into the exciting world of animation, video, and sound.

◆ Adding content to a presentation

◆ Importing content from Word

◆ Working with tables in PowerPoint

◆ Applying design templates and color schemes

◆ Using the Slide Master

◆ Formatting and checking text

Preparing a Presentation

Every PowerPoint presentation is assembled from the same basic elements—slides containing text or pictures, displayed on a graphic background. Sound, video, and animation can take a presentation to the next level. Simple presentations can be completed in a few minutes' time, while high-impact ones can take days. Once you learn the fundamentals, PowerPoint is pretty straightforward—what you put into it is what you get out of it. Add more impact and you'll make more impact. Keep it mundane and your audience will most likely experience it as mundane. Although every presentation takes on its own unique flavor and has its own requirements, most of time you'll follow these steps as you create your masterpiece:

1. Plan the presentation and gather materials you'll want to include. Who is the audience? What do you want to communicate? What is the presentation's tone? Lighthearted? Somber? Bright? These are all questions you'll want to answer before you get started. The answers will help you develop the content and choose the right design elements.

2. Enter and edit text on slides. Rearrange the slides as necessary to create the presentation's flow.

3. Apply a presentation design. Modify the design if necessary. The design establishes the color palette, the fonts, bullet characters, and background. Be sure it helps to communicate your message and not detract from it or, worse yet, contradict it.

4. Format individual slides if needed. Some slides, such as those with exceptionally sparse or dense text, might require special formatting.

5. Add objects, such as clip art, charts, and pictures, to the presentation. Use clip art sparingly in a professional presentation—use photographs instead. Make sure photos are crisp and clear so your audience doesn't have to squint to see them.

6. Apply and modify transitions and animation effects. Transitions determine how slides move from one to the next. Animation effects determine how text and objects appear on the slide,

in terms of order and movement. Transitions and animation effects are powerful tools. Think about your choices to make sure they are consistent with your message and mood.

7. Add links to help you navigate live presentations when you might have reason to jump around.

8. Add sounds and video as appropriate. A little sound can go a long way in a live presentation, so use it prudently. Add music or other narration to kiosk (self-running) presentations.

9. Create audience materials and speaker notes. People like handouts. Create them with care because, sad to say, the handouts may be all they remember about your presentation.

10. Rehearse and add slide timings to a kiosk presentation. We rarely recommend adding timings to live presentations unless you are presenting from a script from which you never waver. But we always recommend rehearsing—and rehearsing and rehearsing. If you don't know what you are going to say, your audience will never know what you said.

11. Present the presentation. Breathe deeply, smile when appropriate, and act confident (even if you are shaking in your boots).

You don't have to work through all the steps sequentially. With PowerPoint, you can create and modify a few slides, adding objects, animation, and speaker notes, and then insert more slides. This chapter will take you through the first four steps and Chapter 7 will cover steps 5 through 12. So let's get started.

Getting Started with PowerPoint

Launch PowerPoint and choose New from the File menu on the Standard toolbar. The task pane displays New Presentation options:

NOTE   *You can display the New Presentations task pane at any time by choosing View ➤ Toolbars ➤ Task Pane. Click the Other Task Panes drop-down list at the top of the task pane and choose New Presentation.*

You can open an existing presentation or create a new presentation. If you choose to create a new presentation, you can start it from scratch, use a design template, or ask PowerPoint to guide you through using the AutoContent wizard. You can also create a presentation full of your fabulous digital photos using PowerPoint's Photo Album creation tool. We'll first show you how to create a presentation from a blank slide and then show you the other methods.

NOTE *PowerPoint displays the toolbars on one row, by default. Click the drop-down arrow at the end of the toolbar to see more buttons, or choose Show Buttons On Two Rows to see all buttons on both toolbars at once.*

Starting from a Blank Presentation

PowerPoint automatically opens with a blank slide and it also provides a blank slide when you click Blank Presentation on the New Presentation task pane. Either way, you are all set to create your first slide. The default for the first slide is the Title Slide layout, shown in Figure 6.1. At the right of this window is the Slide Layout task pane, which displays thumbnail images for a number of Slide Layout options.

FIGURE 6.1

Beginning a new PowerPoint presentation

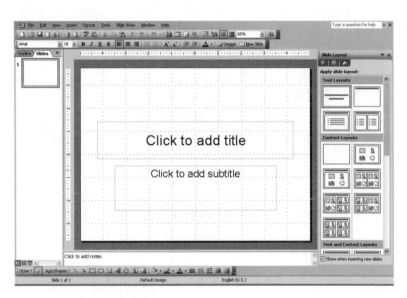

Most slides include two text boxes, one for the title and one for the body text. You can insert, edit, move, and delete text directly on the slide. When you click in the title or body, a frame appears around the text box. To add text to a slide, place your insertion point at the desired location in the text box.

When you have finished adding the text for the title slide, click the New Slide button on the Formatting toolbar to create the second slide. You'll see a new blank slide, along with the Slide Layout task pane.

TIP *If the Slide Layout task pane doesn't open when you click the New Slide button, choose View ➤ Toolbars ➤ Task Pane. Click the Other Task Panes drop-down list at the top of the task pane and choose Slide Layout. Enable the Show When Inserting New Slides check box beneath the slide layout thumbnails to have the task pane open each time you insert a new slide; disable the check box if you'd prefer the task pane didn't open.*

Selecting Slide Layouts

Slide layouts allow you to arrange objects in different ways on slides. Layouts contain placeholders for text, tables, charts, and other graphics you might wish to include in a presentation. When you begin a new presentation, PowerPoint assigns default layouts based on where you are in the presentation. You've already seen the Title slide; the Title And Text Layout is the default for slides after the Title slide.

Pointing to any thumbnail in the Slide Layout task pane displays a description of the layout's placeholders. Notice that the Slide Layout task pane has a scroll bar; scroll down to view other layouts you might want to use, including a blank slide with no placeholders. This particular slide layout is useful if you want to insert a full-screen photo or other picture.

The task pane displays slide layouts in four categories:

Text Layouts Choose a text layout if all you need is a title slide or a title and some form of bulleted list.

WARNING *If you use the Text Tool button on the Drawing toolbar to add text to a slide, the text does not appear in your presentation's outline. The Text Tool button creates a text box object, not slide text. Use an appropriate text layout to insert text in a slide.*

Content Layouts These layouts are for slides that include organization charts and other types of illustrative diagrams as well as tables, charts, video clips, pictures, and clip art. Choose the content layout that best meets your needs for relative size and number of objects to be included.

Text and Content Layouts Choose one of these to create a slide with bulleted text and one or more of the objects included under "Content Layouts."

Other Layouts These include placeholders for specific object types. For example, you can choose bulleted text with a media clip, or title and table. For more about specialized layouts, see the section "Using Specialized Slide Layouts" later in this chapter.

Applying a Layout to Multiple Slides

Some people prefer to create a presentation by entering all of the slide titles and then adding content later as they work on individual slides. This gives you a top-level outline of your presentation without getting immersed in the details. If this is your work style, you will probably not want to make layout decisions until you have decided on the content.

In PowerPoint 2003, you can apply layouts to multiple slides at once:

1. Display the presentation in Normal view and choose the Slides tab of the Outline pane on the left side of the screen.

2. On the Slides tab, click the first slide you want to select. Hold Ctrl to select additional noncontiguous slides; to select additional contiguous slides, hold Shift and click the last slide you want to select.

3. If it is not already visible, display the Slide Layout options in the task pane. (Click View ➤ Task Pane, and then click the drop-down arrow at the top of the pane and choose Slide Layout.)

4. Click the drop-down arrow on the layout you want to use for the selected slides.

5. Choose Apply To Selected Slides from the drop-down menu, as shown in Figure 6.2.

FIGURE 6.2

Use the drop-down menu to apply the layout to selected slides. You can also reapply a layout to a slide you've altered or create a new slide with the selected layout.

TIP   If you've changed the location or size of placeholders, or if you've changed fonts on a slide and wish to return to the slide's original layout and font settings, select the slide and click the drop-down arrow on the layout you're using. Choose Reapply Layout.

Continue adding slides one by one to build your presentation. You can quickly insert a new slide with the layout you want by clicking the drop-down arrow on your chosen layout and choosing Insert New Slide.

To change the layout of an existing slide, display it in Normal view and choose a different slide layout from the task pane. If you'd like to continue creating your presentation, skip to the "Switching Slide Views" section later in this chapter. If you'd prefer to explore the other ways of creating a presentation, keep reading on.

Creating a Presentation from a Design Template

Use a design template to provide a consistent design and mood for your presentation. When you choose the design template option, PowerPoint displays design templates in the Slide Design task pane, as shown in Figure 6.3.

FIGURE 6.3

Click a design template to apply it to all slides.

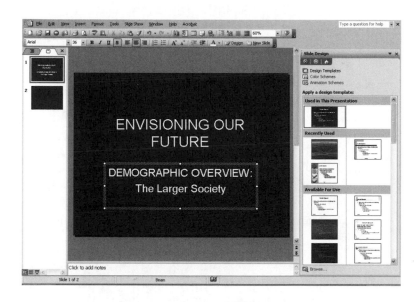

Pointing to a template reveals a screen tip showing the template's file name and a drop-down menu arrow at the right of the template thumbnail.

To enlarge the size of the template thumbnails, choose Show Large Previews from any template's drop-down menu. To view more templates at once, resize the task pane by dragging its left border to the left.

Scroll through the templates until you find one you like.

When you find a design template you like, click the thumbnail image to apply it to all slides in the presentation (Figure 6.3) or use the drop-down menu to apply it to selected slides. It's important to keep in mind that the design template becomes a significant part of your presentation. It needs to be consistent with the message you are trying to communicate. Although the template Ocean may be pleasant to look at, it might not be the best one to use if you are presenting a budget that is in a sea of red ink. On the other hand, Fireworks may be just the ticket to launch an exciting new initiative. Think about your message and, after picking a design, double-check to make sure it says what you need it to say.

NOTE   In the early days of PowerPoint, a presentation could have only one design. Now, you can apply a different design to every slide if you want to—of course, your audience may go crazy, but that may be your intention.

To change the design of the entire presentation, click the drop-down arrow on the slide design you want to apply and click Apply To All Slides.

ACCESSING OTHER DESIGN TEMPLATES

If you have a design template stored in another location—perhaps a template created by your company—you can access it by clicking the Browse button displayed at the bottom of the Slide Design task pane when Design Templates is selected; this will open the Apply Design Templates dialog box. The dialog box opens to the `Templates` folder by default. Open the folder of your choice from the Templates folder, or use the Look In control pane to access templates stored in other locations. Figure 6.4 shows a preview of the Crayons template in the Presentation Designs folder.

FIGURE 6.4

Click the Browse button to open the Apply Design Template dialog box and increase your template choices.

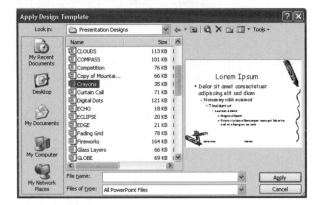

Searching for Designs on the Web

You are not limited to presentation designs that come with PowerPoint. Microsoft is regularly posting new design templates to its website, and third-party vendors often create designs they will sell to you for a modest price. To access the Microsoft website, scroll to the bottom of the design templates in the Slide Design task pane and click Design Templates On Microsoft.com. You'll be whisked off to the Microsoft website (of course, you first need an internet connection), where you can search for other designs to download. To locate third-party designs, fire up your favorite search engine and search for PowerPoint templates—you'll find more than enough to keep you satisfied.

Using the AutoContent Wizard to Design a Presentation for You

The AutoContent wizard is helpful for PowerPoint users who want help in developing content and/or structuring and formatting a presentation. AutoContent templates include formats, transitions, and, in some templates, animation. All you need to do is enter text and you have a usable presentation.

NOTE *Don't think the AutoContent wizard is for wimps. We regularly use the AutoContent wizard to create quick, out-of-the-box presentations. If you don't have much time, this may be the most efficient way to get a presentation up and running.*

The AutoContent wizard works like any of the other wizards in Office. You move through a series of steps that help you design your presentation. In each step, choose Next to advance or Back to return to a previous step.

1. Choose From AutoContent Wizard from the New Presentation task pane and click OK to start the wizard. The first step explains the wizard. Click Next.

2. Choose the presentation type that most closely matches your topic. You can scroll through all the presentation types or narrow your choices by selecting a category from the button list. In Figure 6.5, below, we chose Brainstorming Session from the General category. Click Next.

NOTE *The presentation we chose, "Brainstorming Session," is not installed in the default installation of Office 2003, so you may be prompted to install it.*

FIGURE 6.5

Choose a presentation type from the one of the category lists.

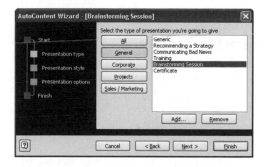

3. Select a style for your presentation (on screen, web, overhead transparencies, or 35mm slides). If you are creating an online presentation, refer to Chapter 11 for more on PowerPoint's dynamic web-publishing features.

   The choice you make here does not prohibit you from switching to another style later, but does limit the options displayed in the AutoContent Wizard. Click Next.

4. Enter the presentation title you want to appear on the first slide. Also, enter information you want included on every slide, such as the current date or a company, department, and/or project name. Click Next.

5. Click Finish. The AutoContent wizard closes and the presentation opens in Outline view, as shown in Figure 6.6. The outline, on the left, contains text suggested by the AutoContent wizard. The first slide is on the right of the screen. The smaller pane at the bottom of the window allows you to add speaker notes for this slide.

FIGURE 6.6

The AutoContent wizard closes and the presentation opens.

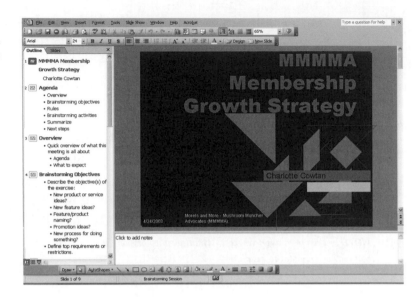

Creating a Presentation Using Existing Content

If you have a presentation that contains content similar to the one you are creating, you can base a new presentation on the existing one or you can import specific slides that you want to use. You can also base a presentation on content in a Word outline. In this section, we'll show you how to accomplish all of these.

CREATING A NEW PRESENTATION FROM A COPY

To create a copy of an existing presentation, choose File ➤ New Presentation ➤ From Existing Presentation to open the dialog box shown in Figure 6.7. Choose the existing presentation you want from the file list and click Create New to create a copy of presentation—your original presentation will be unharmed as you change the copy to suit your needs.

FIGURE 6.7

Select the existing presentation you want to use and click Create New.

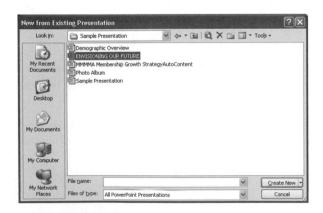

IMPORTING INDIVIDUAL SLIDES FROM AN EXISTING PRESENTATION

To insert one or more slides from an existing presentation into a new presentation, choose Insert ➤ Slides From Files to open the Slide Finder dialog box. Click the Browse button to find and select the presentation containing the slides you want to insert in your new presentation.

Imported slides take on the new presentation's design template by default. If you want slides to retain their original format, check the Keep Source Formatting box at the lower left of the Slide Finder, as shown in Figure 6.8. Select the slide or slides you want imported and click insert.

It is not necessary to select slides if you want to import all of the slides in the existing presentation. Simply click Insert All.

FIGURE 6.8

Use the Slide Finder to select slides from another presentation.

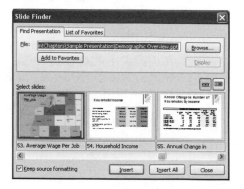

TIP   *If you frequently use slides from a particular presentation, open the presentation in the Slide Finder and click Add To Favorites. Confirm your decision in the message box. In the future, you can access this presentation by clicking the List Of Favorites tab rather than using the browse feature.*

USING WORD OUTLINE CONTENT

You can also import a Word outline to create a PowerPoint presentation. The outline is inserted into the active presentation, so if you have just started, you can use the outline as the entire presentation. You can also use an outline as additional content in a partially completed presentation. If you choose to insert an outline into an existing presentation, each first-level heading becomes a new slide. To do this, follow these steps:

1. In any view, select the slide you want the inserted outline to follow.

2. Choose Insert ➤ Slides From Outline to open the Insert Slides dialog box.

3. Select the Word file you want to insert. In some cases, PowerPoint may prompt you to install the necessary converters. Do so and continue.

4. Click Insert.

TIP   When you insert a Word outline, the complete document appears as part of your presentation. If you only want part of the outline, delete the extra slides after importing. If you have a rather lengthy outline from which you only need a few slides, consider copying those sections to a new Word document and importing from there.

If you are already working in Word, you can create a presentation from the active document by choosing File ➤ Send To ➤ Microsoft PowerPoint from the Word menu.

Creating a Photo Album Presentation from Digital Photos

New!   As digital photography is overtaking the photography market, it's more and more common to see photo-rich presentations. What better way to greet clients as they assemble for a sales presentation than a photo-album slide show of your latest visit to their corporate headquarters? As trainers, we regularly snap photos of training participants and run a photo-album slide show set to music during breaks and at lunch. People love to see themselves on the big screen even if they act embarrassed at being caught in an unflattering pose. If we are training at a conference in an interesting location, we may take photos of the sites around the area so people get a sense of where they are. It's amazing how many people ask us to post those presentations on the Web so they can show their families and co-workers all the stuff they didn't get to see while they diligently attended the conference. PowerPoint 2003 makes it easier than ever to create a photo album from your digital photographs.

Choose Photo Album from the New Presentation task pane or choose Insert ➤ Picture ➤ New Photo Album from the main menu, to open the Photo Album dialog box shown in Figure 6.9. Indicate the location of the photos you want to import: File/Disk or Scanner/Camera. Browse to the location of the desired pictures and use Shift and Ctrl to select them. Click Insert to return to the Photo Album dialog box.

FIGURE 6.9

After choosing your photos, click Insert to return to the Photo Album dialog box.

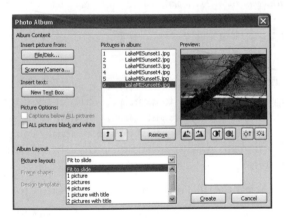

Choose the layout you want for the photo album and click Create. PowerPoint opens with the default title slide followed by your photos in your chosen layout.

Use the Photo Album dialog box (Format ➤ Photo Album) to modify your photo album whenever you want. You can add more photos, change format, add text, rotate photos, adjust the brightness and/or contrast, or create black-and-white photos.

Switching Slide Views

One of the keys to working comfortably and efficiently in PowerPoint is understanding views. The term *view* refers to how you look at and work on your presentation. Knowing when and how to use a specific view separates the PowerPoint masters from the average users. Normal view, Slide Sorter view, and Slide Show view are the views used most frequently, so we'll focus on those first and then introduce you to Master Slide views.

Three view buttons appear at the left end of the horizontal scroll bar.

The Normal view button is on the left; the Slide Sorter view button is in the middle; and the Slide Show view button is on the right.

You can change the view by clicking the appropriate view button at the bottom-left of the PowerPoint window or by choosing the view name from the View menu.

NOTE *When you switch from one view to another, the current slide remains current, regardless of view. For example, if you are on the fifth slide in Normal view and switch to Slide Sorter view, you will find the fifth slide selected. Clicking the Slide Show (From Current Slide) button begins the Slide Show with the fifth slide.*

WHICH VIEW SHOULD YOU USE?

As you work in PowerPoint, you will discover that adjusting the view makes it easier to carry out certain types of formatting and editing. Similarly, you will find that certain types of editing are possible *only* in a specific view.

In the early stages of your presentation's development, you'll probably want to work in Normal view. Normal view provides you with the most editing flexibility and allows you to see text from multiple slides at one time: a bird's eye view of your presentation. Normal view lets you edit text on the outline or on the slide, and the slide display is large enough to easily place objects and apply animation. In Normal view, you can enlarge the Outline pane to focus on text rather than objects (see the section "Working in the Outline Pane") or entire slides. Alternatively, you can make the outline smaller and enlarge the Slide pane to focus on the appearance of each slide. Use Normal view when you want to position objects on a slide in relation to text.

Use Slide Sorter view to focus on entire slides, their order, and how they appear during the presentation.

Use Slide Show view to see how your presentation will look when you eventually show it.

In general, choose Normal view to edit or insert text on slides, to insert objects, and for animation (see Chapter 7 for more information on objects and animation). Choose Slide Sorter view to change the order of slides or to apply slide transitions (see Chapter 7 for more information on transitions). Use Slide Show view to preview (and to practice) your presentation.

Normal View

Normal view is a *tri-pane view* that allows you to see three different aspects of your presentation within one window—it's the view we've been working in so far. As Figure 6.10 shows, Normal view includes a large Slide pane, an Outline pane on the left of the screen, and a pane for notes at the bottom. The sections of the tri-pane window are resizable, so you can enlarge whatever pane you are working on.

FIGURE 6.10

Normal view includes a Slide pane, an Outline pane, and a Notes pane.

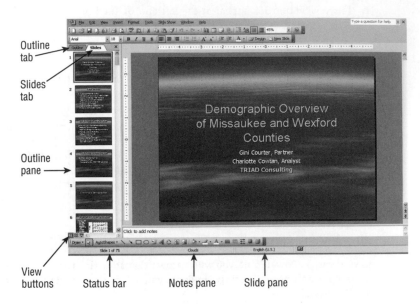

To resize a pane, point to any of the pane dividers. Your mouse pointer changes to the Resize tool. Drag to move the pane divider to the desired location.

You might find that the content no longer fits a resized pane. You will need to change the Zoom for these panes:

Click the area that needs its contents resized (Outline tab, Slides tab, or Slide pane).

Click the Zoom box arrow on the Standard toolbar to open the Zoom box drop-down menu, and choose or type in the magnification you want.

TIP   *Choose Fit from the Zoom menu for the slide pane to have slides automatically resized.*

TIP   *If you accidentally close the left pane, which displays the outline and slide miniatures, you can bring it back by clicking View ➤ Normal (Restore Panes).*

MOVING BETWEEN SLIDES IN NORMAL VIEW

There are several different ways to move between slides in Normal view:

◆ Click anywhere in the outline or on any slide in the left pane to view the full-size slide in the Slide pane.

◆ Use the vertical scroll bar to move forward and backward through your slides.

◆ Use the PgUp and PgDn keys to browse slides. As you drag the vertical scroll bar, a screen tip with slide number and title appears in the Slide pane.

◆ Click the double up-arrow and double down-arrow buttons located at the bottom of the vertical scroll bar to move to the next or the previous slide.

Working in the Notes Pane

The Notes pane below the slide provides an area for private notes. Notes are not visible to the audience in an electronic presentation. They are not visible in online or NetMeeting presentations unless you choose to display them. You can use this feature to keep track of other information about particular slides as you create the presentation. For example, there may be data that need to be verified or alternative information you may add to the slide.

The Notes pane provides a perfect place to put a reminder about when to distribute a handout or tell a specific joke. You can even put the entire text of your verbal presentation in the Notes pane and then print the notes so you can refer to them when you give the presentation. See Chapter 7 for more information about printing notes.

To add notes in Normal view, click anywhere in the Notes pane and type.

TIP   *If the Notes pane is not visible, point to the window divider directly above the Drawing toolbar or Status bar if the Drawing toolbar is turned on. Click and drag upward to resize the Notes pane.*

Working in the Outline Pane

The Outline pane in Normal view has two tabs: Outline and Slides. The Slides tab displays slide miniatures in the left pane and icons on the tabs at the top of the pane, as shown in Figure 6.10. The Outline tab displays slide text in the left pane, as shown in Figure 6.11. Choose the Outline tab to work with text in the Outline pane.

FIGURE 6.11

Use the Outline tab to focus on the text of a presentation.

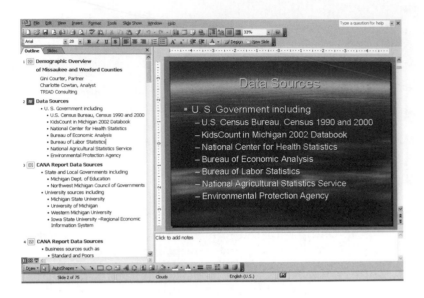

ENTERING AND EDITING TEXT

Working in a PowerPoint outline is similar to using Outline view in Word. As you type in the outline, press Enter at the end of a line to move to a new line. The new line is on the same outline level as the previous line. If you are at the end of a bulleted point when you press Enter, the next line starts with a bullet at the same level as the previous one. If you position the insertion point at the end of a slide's title and press Enter, PowerPoint inserts a new slide.

Promoting and Demoting Text Levels

The Outlining toolbar is not visible by default in PowerPoint 2003. You must turn it on by clicking View ➤ Toolbars ➤ Outlining or right-clicking an existing toolbar and selecting Outlining. If you have not previously moved it, the Outlining toolbar displays vertically to the left of the Outline pane.

To promote text to a higher level, place the insertion point at the beginning of the text you want promoted and either press Shift+Tab or click the Promote button on the Outlining toolbar.

To demote text to a lower level, place the insertion point at the beginning of the text you want demoted and either press Tab or click the Demote button.

NOTE   You may also promote and demote bulleted points by dragging them horizontally. As you drag the bulleted point, a vertical line appears in the outline. Drag this line to the right to demote the text or to the left to promote the text.

Text Font Size

In the PowerPoint Outline pane, font size does not change for different levels of text. You must look at the Slide pane to see how text will look in the actual presentation. PowerPoint 2003's default setting automatically adjusts font size according to the number of items contained on a slide, the available space in the text box, and the level at which the text is placed. This means that the text size for any given text level may vary from slide to slide.

If you do not want font size to vary between slides, you must disable the Autofit Body Text option: choose Tools ➤ AutoCorrect Options to open the AutoCorrect dialog box. Choose the AutoFormat As You Type tab and disable the Autofit Body Text To Placeholder check box, as shown in Figure 6.12. Click OK. Note the similar option for title text. Disable it also if you want the Title text font size to be the same on all slides.

FIGURE 6.12

To keep a constant font size across all slides, you must disable Autofit Body Text.

 Clicking the New Slide button on the PowerPoint toolbar or choosing Insert ➤ New Slide inserts a new slide following the currently active slide (the slide where the insertion point is resting). The insertion point automatically moves into position for the new slide title.

NOTE *If your insertion point is resting immediately in front of the title text when you insert a new slide, the new slide appears above, rather than below, the active slide.*

Selecting Text, Lines, and Slides

Many of the methods used to select text in Word and Excel work in PowerPoint as well. Double-click a word to select it. To select a block of text, click at the beginning and Shift+click at the end. To select an entire point, click the bullet or icon in front of the text or triple-click anywhere within a point.

If you select a first-level point that has second-level points underneath it, the second-level points are also selected. Click and drag to select only the main point. Similarly, selecting the title using any method other than dragging selects the entire slide.

 You can expand and collapse sections of the outline by using the Expand and Collapse buttons on the Outlining toolbar or by right-clicking and choosing Expand or Collapse from the short-cut menu.

 To collapse or expand multiple slides, select them and then right-click anywhere in the selection. Choose Expand or Collapse from the shortcut menu. You can also use the Expand All and Collapse All buttons to expand or collapse the entire outline.

Checking Spelling

PowerPoint includes the same spelling features as Word. AutoSpell automatically underlines misspelled words that you enter. Right-click an underlined word to see suggested correct spellings. Click the Spelling button on the Standard toolbar to check the spelling for an entire presentation.

Inserting, Deleting, and Moving Points and Slides

Part of the process of creating a presentation often involves rearranging the content. Perhaps you originally think it's a good idea to discuss the successes of a project before focusing on the failures. However, when you get the presentation's content all written you realize that by the time you get to the end, the successes are too overshadowed by the problems. It doesn't take much to mix up the slides a little more so successes and failures appear more evenly matched. As you move the mouse over a bullet or slide icon in the Outline pane, the pointer shape changes to a four-headed arrow, the tool for moving text and objects.

To move a point (and all the sub points beneath it) on the Outline tab, drag the bullet preceding that point.

To move an entire slide, click a slide icon, as shown in Figure 6.13, then drag and drop it and the related text to the desired location.

WARNING   *When you use drag-and-drop to rearrange slides or points, be sure to move the mouse vertically. Horizontal dragging causes the selected text to change levels.*

FIGURE 6.13

To move an entire slide, click the slide icon to the right of the slide number.

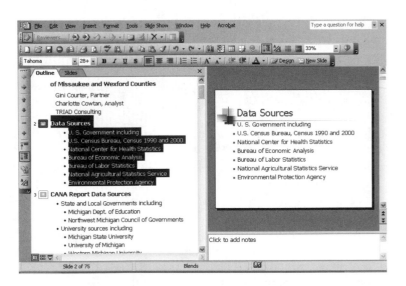

Traditional cut, copy, and paste methods also work in PowerPoint 2003.

PowerPoint supports Smart Cut and Paste, which removes extra spaces when you delete text and inserts extra spaces when you paste from the Clipboard.

TIP   When there are options for formatting pasted text, PowerPoint 2003 displays the Paste Options button with the same choices you saw in Word 2003. Disable Paste Options by clicking Tools ➤ Options ➤ Edit and clearing the Show Paste Options check box.

Delete slides, points, or subpoints as you would in a Word document: select the text and press the Delete key.

Working in the Slide Pane

When your focus is on the outline alone, there is a tendency to put too much on one slide, causing some lines of text to run off the bottom of the slide. It is important to keep one eye on the Slide pane so you can quickly make necessary text adjustments. However, remember that the Slide pane allows you to do much more than view your text outline in a presentation format.

Earlier in this chapter, you saw how you can use the Slide pane in Normal view to insert, edit, move, and delete text directly on the slide. In fact, you might find this method of inserting text easier than working in the Outline pane. You can work with only one slide at a time, but Normal view gives you a better feel for how the slide will actually look in a completed presentation.

Most slides include two text boxes, one for the title and one for the body text. When you click in the title or body, a frame appears around the text box. You can point to the frame and drag the text box to another location on the slide. Be careful, though, with moving text boxes too freely. Part of the professional appearance of a PowerPoint presentation comes from the built-in consistency in formatting and layout. Too much customizing on your part can easily destroy that uniformity.

To add text to a slide, place your insertion point at the desired location in the text box. Promote or demote points and subpoints just as you would in Outline view, selecting the text first and either using the Promote or Demote buttons on the Outlining toolbar, or pressing Tab or Shift+Tab. To format the text in the box, select the text by clicking or dragging as you would in the outline and then change formats using the Formatting toolbar or Format menu.

USING SPECIALIZED SLIDE LAYOUTS

Specialized slide layouts help you create slides with tables and graphic images. You can even combine charts, texts, and graphics all on one slide using the multiple object slide layouts.

Table Slides

When you need to display information in parallel columns, select a Table Slide layout. The enhanced Tables features in PowerPoint 2003 incorporate most of the powerful table tools from Word. You can customize the table by specifying the number of columns and rows, and by inserting and deleting text, applying borders, applying shading, changing fonts and alignment, resizing columns and rows, and modifying your table in dozens of ways.

1. Display the Slide Layout task pane.

2. Insert a new slide with a table placeholder.

3. Activate the Title text box and enter a slide title.

4. Double-click the icon to start a new table. The Insert Table dialog box opens.

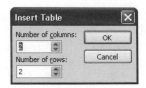

5. Use the spin boxes to indicate the number of columns and rows for your table, or select and overtype the default numbers.

6. Click OK. PowerPoint displays the empty grid.

7. If not visible, turn on the floating Tables And Borders toolbar (View ➤ Toolbars ➤ Tables And Borders).

8. The first tool on the Tables And Borders toolbar is the pencil, which is used to draw new rows or columns and to split cells. You can drag the pencil vertically, horizontally, or diagonally.

9. Click the pencil tool to "put it away." Your mouse pointer becomes an I-beam again for selecting cells and typing text.

10. Use the other options on the Tables And Borders toolbar to apply formatting changes to borders, shading, and alignment.

NOTE   *It isn't required for a slide to have a table placeholder before you can insert a table. Using the Table And Borders toolbar, you can insert a table into an existing slide at any time.*

Multi-object Slides

The slide layouts in the task pane allow you to vary the arrangement of objects on your slides, including placeholders for tables, charts, graphics, text frames, and other objects.

Although you can place charts, clip art, media clips, and other objects on any slide, placeholders provide shortcuts for the objects you include most often. Since placeholders provide frames for objects, they minimize time and energy spent resizing objects. Using a layout with placeholders for multiple objects helps create a balanced, uncrowded look. The result is more-professional-looking slides.

To insert an object into a placeholder, simply click its icon. PowerPoint launches the appropriate application or dialog box to create and insert the object you need.

NOTE   *For an extensive look at working with clip art and other media objects, refer to Chapter 5, "Beyond Text: Making an Impression with Multimedia."*

Slide Sorter View

Slide Sorter view lets you see many slides at once, as shown in Figure 6.14. The number of slides shown depends on the zoom setting, your monitor size, and screen resolution. If you wish to see more or fewer slides, you can adjust the zoom higher or lower or seize this opportunity to request a larger monitor from the appropriate person in your organization.

FIGURE 6.14

Slide Sorter view allows you to see many slides at once.

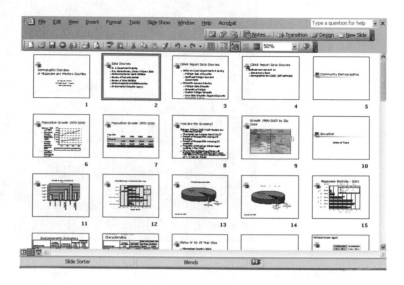

WORKING IN SLIDE SORTER VIEW

Slide Sorter is the best view for judging the overall flow and visual impact of the presentation. You can use drag-and-drop to distribute slides with graphic objects quickly and evenly among those that are text-only. (You may want to return to the outline to confirm that the text flows logically from slide to slide.)

To select slides, use Shift+click to select multiple contiguous slides or use Ctrl+click to select multiple noncontiguous slides. A selected slide has a dark border around it, like slide 2 in Figure 6.14.

To move a selected slide, drag the slide toward its new location. A gray vertical line will appear. Drag to move the line and the selected slide to the new location.

To copy a slide, hold Ctrl while dragging; release Ctrl after dropping the slide in place.

To delete slides, select the slide(s) and then press Delete.

To add notes to a slide, select the slide for which you wish to record notes, and click the Notes button on the Slide Sorter toolbar.

TIP   *Double-click any slide in Slide Sorter view to display it in Normal view.*

TIP   *In Slide Sorter view, the text on a slide is often not legible. To display the title in a readable format, hold Alt and click the slide. When you release the mouse button, the slide miniature returns to normal.*

Slide Show View

Click the Slide Show button for a full-screen view of the current slide, as shown in Figure 6.15.

FIGURE 6.15
Click the Slide
Show button for a
full-screen view.

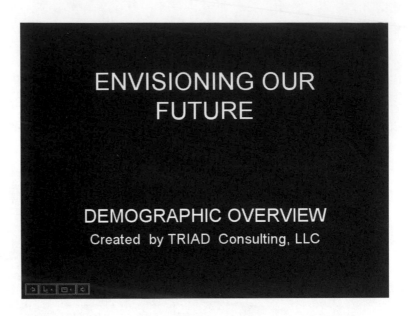

Click the mouse and press Enter or press Page Down to move from one slide to the next; if a slide has multiple lines of text, you might have to click once for each line. After the last slide, PowerPoint returns to the previous view. Press Esc or right-click and choose End Show if you want to exit Slide Show view before the last slide.

To add notes in Slide Show view, right-click the slide and choose Screen ➤ Speaker Notes from the shortcut menu. The Speaker Notes dialog box opens. Enter your notes and click OK. Text you enter is visible in the Notes pane of Normal view. To display the notes in Slide Show view, right-click on the slide and choose Screen ➤ Speaker Notes to reopen the dialog box.

Working with the Slide Masters

Every design includes one or more *Slide Masters* that identify the position of the text and graphic objects, the style of the fonts, the footer elements, and the background for all slides. Most designs include a separate Title Master as well. Templates from earlier versions of PowerPoint usually have only one master.

To display the Master Slide view, as in Figure 6.16, choose View ➤ Master ➤ Slide Master, or hold Shift and click the Normal View button. The Master Title slide and the Slide Master toolbar appear in the Slide pane. Thumbnails of all of the presentation Slide and Title Masters appear in the pane at the left (see Figure 6.16). Note the gray lines connecting Title and Slide Master pairs. Point to any master to see a tip with the name of the master design and the number(s) of the slide(s) based on that master.

FIGURE 6.16

Hold Shift and click the Normal View button to display the Master slide and the Slide Master toolbar.

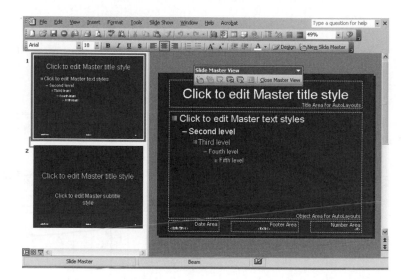

NOTE *Since PowerPoint 2003 allows you to apply different design templates to different slides within a presentation, you may find yourself managing several master slides. For each design you use, there are generally two masters. For a long presentation with three different templates, you may find yourself working with six masters!*

Modifying Master Slides

Every slide in a presentation is based on a Master slide or Master title. Changes made to the Master change all slides that are based on it. For example, if you want a graphic object (a company logo, perhaps) to appear on every slide, place it on the master rather than inserting it on each slide.

To make changes to a Master slide, follow these steps:

1. Open Slide Master view (choose View ➤ Master ➤ Slide Master).

2. Select the text box, placeholder, or object you want to modify.

   A. To change text font, color, size, or style, use the buttons on the Formatting toolbar or choose Format ➤ Font.

   B. To change bullet characters, select the level of bullet you wish to change and choose Format ➤ Bullets And Numbering from the menu. In Office 2003, the Bullets And Numbering feature is nearly identical in Word and PowerPoint.

C. To move or delete placeholders, including graphic objects and text boxes, select the placeholder or object and move or delete in your usual manner.

D. To insert logos or other graphics you want to appear on every slide, choose Insert ➤ Picture.

E. To add or edit slide footers, refer to the "Adding Slide Footers" section later in this chapter.

3. To return to Normal view, click the Close Master View button on the Master view toolbar.

NOTE   When you insert a new master, the design appears in the Used In This Presentation category of the Slide Design task pane. You can easily apply the design to any new slides when you are working in Normal view.

USING THE SLIDE MASTER VIEW TOOLBAR

The Master View toolbar, shown in Figure 6.17, allows you to insert, delete, rename, and preserve Slide and Title Masters. Table 6.1 describes the function of each of the buttons on the Master View toolbar.

FIGURE 6.17

Use the Master View toolbar to work with Slide and Title Masters

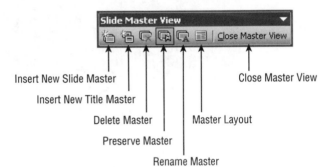

TABLE 6.1: THE SLIDE MASTER VIEW TOOLBAR

BUTTON NAME	FUNCTION
Insert New Slide Master	Adds a blank Slide Master to the presentation. You can insert and arrange placeholders, graphics, fonts, bullets, color schemes, and other slide elements to create your own master from scratch.
Insert New Title Master	Adds a blank Title Master to the presentation. Only enabled if you add a regular Slide Master first. Modify design elements on the new Title Master to create your own Title Master from scratch.
Delete Master	Removes the selected master from the presentation. Reformats slides based on that master to match one of the remaining masters.

Continued on next page

TABLE 6.1: THE SLIDE MASTER VIEW TOOLBAR *(continued)*

BUTTON NAME	FUNCTION
Preserve Master	Prevents PowerPoint from automatically deleting a master when no slides are based on that master or when you apply a new design to slides that were originally based on that master.
Rename Master	Opens the Rename Master dialog box, where you can type a new name for the selected master. Renaming one master in a Slide–Title Master pair also renames the other.
Master Layout	Opens the Master Layout dialog box, where you can enable or disable certain elements (date, footer, slide number) on the selected master.
Close Master View	Returns you to Normal view after you finish changes to the master.

TIP   If you want to save slight modifications to a master while retaining the original, PowerPoint now lets you copy any slide, including a master. Choose Insert ➤ Duplicate Slide Master, modify the copy, and then rename the copy if you wish. In Normal view you can choose Insert ➤ Duplicate Slide to copy the selected slide.

Adding Slide Footers

Slide footers are the text elements that appear at the bottom of every slide. This may include a company name, slide number, date, or other similar data. When you use the AutoContent wizard to create a presentation, one of the steps in the wizard prompts you to include the system date, slide number, and other text in a slide footer. These elements are placed in the Slide Master. You can edit the footers inserted by the AutoContent wizard and you can insert footers on slides you created yourself.

To edit footers adding in the AutoContent Wizard, start by opening the Slide Master (View ➤ Master ➤ Slide Master). Whether or not you chose to display Date/Time and Slide Number, only placeholders appear in the Slide Master. Select any of the placeholders and press Delete to delete the placeholder. To add text in the Footer area, select the Footer placeholder and type the text you want to appear. To add a date or slide number, keep reading—you will want to use the Header And Footer dialog box to do that.

To insert date/time, slide number, or text footers into slides that do not display them, choose View ➤ Header And Footer from the menu in Normal view or Slide Master view. The Header And Footer dialog box (shown in Figure 6.18) allows you to edit, add, or delete footer text on slides. Turn on the items you want to display, activate Don't Show On Title Slide, if desired, and click either Apply to place a footer on the current slide only or Apply To All to change the Slide Master. (If you opened the dialog box from the Slide Master, you can only choose Apply To All.)

FIGURE 6.18

Edit headers and footers on the Slide Master or in the Header And Footer dialog box.

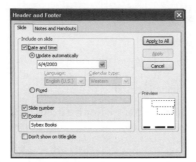

Customizing and Refining a Presentation's Design

With PowerPoint 2003, you have lots of flexibility in customizing design templates. You can change the color scheme, design your own color scheme, and even add your own custom background. To make sure your presentation meets all your expectations, you can also use PowerPoint built-in tools to check formatting and other style choices.

Changing a Presentation's Color Scheme

When you're ready to make changes, open the task pane and choose Slide Design ≻ Color Schemes from the drop-down arrow in the task pane to display color scheme options, as shown in Figure 6.19. If the task pane is already displaying the Slide Design task pane, just click Color Schemes to wind up in the same place. For most templates, PowerPoint displays several standard schemes with the ability to edit them, creating your own custom color schemes. With only a few exceptions, like the Whirlpool template, the standard color schemes include the current color scheme, at least one alternate scheme, and one black-and-white choice. The number of standard schemes you see depends on the design template. The color schemes with the white background are designed for overheads, but they can be used for kiosk or web presentations.

FIGURE 6.19

Change design template colors using the color scheme options in the task pane.

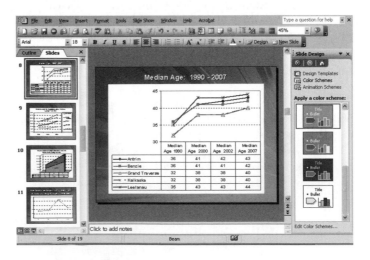

A scheme can be applied to selected slides or to all of the slides in the presentation. To apply a new color scheme to all slides in a presentation, just click the thumbnail of the color scheme you like. With PowerPoint 2003, color scheme changes are made in real time so you can see modifications immediately and undo any you don't like.

To change only selected slides in the presentation, do the following:

1. Display the presentation in Normal view with slide miniatures showing in the left pane.

2. Select the slides to be modified.

3. Click the drop-down arrow on the color scheme you want to use. Choose Apply To Selected Slides.

If none of the standard schemes trips your trigger, create your own scheme. Select the scheme that's closest to the scheme you want and click Edit Color Schemes at the bottom of the task pane. This opens the Edit Color Scheme dialog box to the Custom tab, as shown in Figure 6.20. Select the element color you want to change and click the Change Color button to open the Colors dialog box. Choose a color from the array of colors presented, or if you want to mix your own, select the Custom tab to open the Color Picker.

FIGURE 6.20

Change colors used in the selected scheme to create custom color schemes

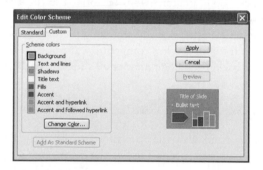

If you wish, you can save the color scheme of the current design for future use by clicking the Add As Standard Scheme button on the Custom tab (see Figure 6.20). Added schemes are displayed on the Standard tab of the Edit Color Scheme dialog box. (If you need to switch between color schemes depending on what room you are in or some other factor, check out Chapter 19, "Using Macros to Do More with Office." We show you how to record a macro to automate a scheme switch.)

Customizing the Background of a Presentation

When you choose to apply a design template, the template includes, among other things, the color scheme and background color. Often, the background is more than just a solid color. It might have a shaded effect, a pattern, or a texture. A picture or graphic object may be part of the background. All these characteristics—shading, patterns, textures, and objects—form the background of the slide. Text and objects that you place on the slide are positioned on top of the background.

To change the background, choose Format ➤ Background, or in Normal view right-click the background and choose Background from the shortcut menu to open the Background dialog box.

As with the color scheme, you can apply changes to selected slides or to the Slide Master. If the background graphic elements interfere with an object you've placed on a slide, remove the background graphics by enabling the Omit Background Graphics From Master check box and clicking Apply. The master background graphics won't be applied to the selected slide, but all other slides will retain background graphics. You may see slight differences in other slide elements, but the slide retains the general presentation design. By removing the background objects, the chart, table, or image you've placed on the slide has less competition. If your presentation is chock-full of charts and graphics, omit the background graphics for all slides by enabling the check box and clicking Apply To All.

NOTE *When you select Omit Background Graphics, you also omit the footer.*

To change the background, click the drop-down arrow in the Background Fill area of the Background dialog box to open a drop-down list of the color scheme options.

Choosing Automatic fills the background with the default fill color. Select one of the color-scheme colors or choose More Colors (which opens the Color Picker) to select a solid background color. For a walk on the wilder side, choose Fill Effects to open the Fill Effects dialog box.

In this dialog box, you can select a background from four different types of fills, as demonstrated by the four tabs: Gradient, Texture, Pattern, or Picture. Figure 6.21 shows the Texture tab of the Fill Effects dialog box. You are probably familiar with gradients, textures, and patterns from Excel, WordArt, or Word.

FIGURE 6.21

Using the Texture tab of the Fill Effects dialog box, you can create a background from a variety of available textures.

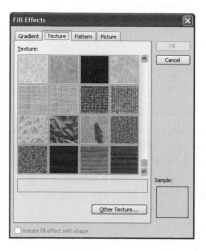

TIP   *You can apply the same Fill Effects options to chart elements in Excel and any object you draw using the Drawing toolbar throughout Office 2003.*

Creating Custom Backgrounds from Your Photos

If your job includes sitting through a lot of PowerPoint presentations, you probably know all the design templates by heart. Nothing can make a presentation more boring than seeing the same old templates over and over again.

Rather than relying on backgrounds supplied by Microsoft, you can create PowerPoint backgrounds using your own digital photos. A background should be subtle enough to sit behind text and not overpower it and yet distinct enough to set your presentation apart. Look around you and try to find something that could fill the bill. You may want to look for an unusual pattern or design, like the one that may be on the floor in the entrance to your corporate headquarters or on the side of the building. Or you could set up a photo with the special items, scenery, or people you want to include. The possibilities are endless.

NOTE   *If a photo has a lot of background colors, you may want to change the font color to a lighter color on the Slide Master so it is visible through the background.*

To use a picture as a slide background, do the following:

1. Choose Format ➢ Background from Normal or Slide Sorter view or right-click a slide (outside of any text boxes or objects). Choose Background from the shortcut menu.

2. Open the fill drop-down list and choose Fill Effects.

3. Select the Picture tab of the Fill Effects dialog box.

4. Click the Select Picture button to open the Select Picture dialog box.

5. Locate the picture you wish to use. Click OK.

6. Preview the new pattern and click Apply or Apply To All.

Formatting and Checking Text

When you format text on individual slides, the formatting takes precedence over formatting from the Slide Master. Even if you apply a new design to the master, formatting applied to individual slides won't change, so you should make sure you are pleased with the overall design before formatting individual slides. You can apply standard Office text enhancements to text in your PowerPoint slides. Select the text you want formatted and then change font typeface, size, and attributes using the Formatting toolbar or the Format menu.

TIP PowerPoint designers spend a considerable amount of time putting together templates with colors, fonts, and other attributes that provide a coordinated look. If you sometimes arrive at work wearing a striped shirt and plaid pants and still want to experiment with your own designs in PowerPoint, ask a colleague to review the presentation after you make formatting changes.

The text formatting is displayed by default in both Normal and Slide Sorter views. However, you can decide whether or not to display formatting. The Show Formatting button on the Outlining toolbar toggles between displaying and hiding text formatting. In Slide Sorter view, the Show Formatting button toggles between displaying the slide thumbnail and slide titles.

Two buttons that do not appear in Word or Excel are the Increase Font and Decrease Font buttons. Each click changes the font size in standard increments that increase as font size increases. Fonts 10 points and smaller change in 1-point increments; larger fonts change in greater increments.

Add a shadow to selected text by clicking the Shadow button.

Change the color of selected text by clicking the down-arrow on the Font Color button on either the Formatting or Drawing toolbar to display the current color Scheme. Select the color you want to apply or click More Colors to apply a color that is not part of the current color scheme.

Select View ➤ Toolbars ➤ Drawing to turn the Drawing toolbar on or off. You can also right-click any toolbar and turn the Drawing toolbar off and on from the shortcut menu.

A WORD ABOUT FONTS

Fonts fall into five categories: serif, sans serif, script, decorative, or symbol.

Serif fonts, like Times New Roman, are easily recognizable from the serifs attached to the ends and tips of letters. For example, the uppercase *N* shown below has feet, and the lowercase *t* has a curvy bottom. Serif fonts are best for body text in paragraphs because the serifs provide cues for the reader.

Continued on next page

This is Times New Roman, a Serif font
This is Arial, a San Serif font
This is Brush Script MT, a script font
This is Magneto, a decorative font
Wingdings is a symbol font. Here are some Wingdings: ♨☜■◗☒

Sans serif fonts, like Arial, do not have fancy ends and tips on letters. These plain-vanilla fonts work well for headings.

Script fonts, such as Lucida Handwriting or Brush Script, are designed to look like cursive handwriting. Avoid script fonts at the office, since they project a more personal, rather than corporate, style.

Decorative fonts, like Old English or Broadway, add impact to documents like flyers and banners. You will see decorative fonts used on formal documents like wedding invitations. If you are the person in charge of creating and posting flyers for the annual company picnic, consider using a decorative font to draw people's attention to the posted document.

Symbol fonts are for inserting special characters like the copyright symbol (©) or for choosing bullet characters. You have probably seen the trademark symbol (™) used in business publications, and the Greek capital letter Sigma (Σ). Other symbols work well for bullet characters.

Aligning Text

Text can be left-aligned, centered, right-aligned, or justified. Align Left, Center, and Align Right are options on the Formatting toolbar. To justify text, position the insertion point in the paragraph you want to format and choose Format ➢ Alignment ➢ Justify from the menu bar. The paragraph containing the insertion point is now justified. If you wish to justify multiple paragraphs, select them before choosing the menu commands.

Replacing Fonts

Use the Replace Font dialog box to substitute one font for another globally in a presentation. You might choose to replace fonts to change the look of a presentation, but there is sometimes a more pressing reason. If you open a presentation on a computer that doesn't have the presentation's fonts installed, another font is automatically substituted—unless the fonts were embedded in the presentation. This substitute font may not be good looking and occasionally it is not even readable. Rather than changing various levels of the master, you can have PowerPoint change each occurrence of the missing font by following these steps:

1. In Normal view, select the text box that includes the font you want to replace.

2. Choose Format ➤ Replace Fonts to open the Replace Font dialog box.

3. Select a replacement font.

4. Click Replace.

5. Click Close to close the dialog box.

To replace fonts for *all* text boxes on *all* slides, switch to Slide Sorter view, select all slides (Ctrl+A is the fastest way), and follow steps 2 through 4.

Adjusting Line Spacing

In PowerPoint, you can add or subtract space between lines and before or after paragraphs, much as you add leading in desktop publishing. Rather than entering extra blank lines between points or subpoints, you can use the Line Spacing dialog box to adjust the spacing between lines.

In Normal view, select the text you want to space. (This process works whether the text you select is on the outline or on the slide.) Choose Format ➤ Line Spacing to open the Line Spacing dialog box. Then set the lines or points (1 point = 1/72 inch) you want as Line Spacing (between each line, even within a point or subpoint), Before Paragraph, or After Paragraph, and click OK.

Adjusting Tabs and Indents

The distance your insertion point moves when you press the Tab key is preset at one-half-inch. You can see the default tab stops on the ruler in Normal view. Choose View ➤ Ruler to turn your ruler on, if necessary. To change the default tab settings for your presentation, do the following:

1. Switch to Normal view and display the ruler (View ➤ Ruler).

2. Select the text you want to change the tabs for.

3. On the ruler, drag the first default tab stop to its new position. All other tab stops will adjust so that the distance between each tab stop is the same.

If you click in a text box with multiple levels of main points and subpoints, you will see indent markers appear on the ruler, as shown in Figure 6.22. Each level of points has its own set of three indent markers. If you have only first-level bullets, you will see only three markers. If you have first- and second-level bullets, you will see six, and so on. You can use these indent markers to move text and bullets to the left or right, or you can indent just the text, moving it farther from the bullet that precedes it.

FIGURE 6.22

You can use indent markers on the ruler to move bulleted points or indent text.

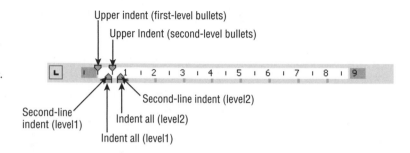

The upper marker sets the indent for the first line of the paragraph. Adjust the marker instead of pressing Tab if you want to give the appearance of a tabbed first line. Just drag the upper indent marker to the right; the other lines in that paragraph (and all paragraphs at that bullet level) will wrap to the left margin of the text box.

When you drag the triangular part of the lower indent marker, it adjusts all lines in the paragraph below the first line. If the first and subsequent lines of the paragraph are at the same setting (alignment), dragging this marker moves the entire paragraph in relation to the bullet. (The rectangular portion of the marker also moves when you drag the triangular portion.)

Drag the rectangular part of the lower marker to move the entire paragraph while maintaining the relationship between the first-line indent and the rest of the lines.

Take these steps to change indent settings for the current slide:

1. In Normal view, select the text for which you want to set indents.

2. If the ruler isn't displayed, turn it on (View ➢ Ruler).

3. Drag the upper indent marker to change the indent for the first line of a paragraph.

4. Drag the lower indent marker to set the indent for other lines in a paragraph.

5. To change the indent for an entire paragraph, drag the rectangular box beneath the lower indent marker to move both upper and lower markers while maintaining the relationship between the upper and lower indent.

6. To change the distance from a hanging paragraph to the bullet that precedes it, drag the triangular portion of the bottom indent marker.

PowerPoint 2003 has buttons for increasing and decreasing the indent setting on selected text. Click the Increase Indent button to move text to the right one level at a time. Click Decrease Indent to move text left one level at a time. If you think this sounds just like promoting and demoting, you're correct! The buttons do essentially the same thing.

Using the Style Checker

PowerPoint 2003 can automatically check your presentation for consistency and style. When there are problems with punctuation or visual clarity, they are marked with a light bulb. You can fix or ignore these inconsistencies, and there are options for changing the style elements PowerPoint checks. Automatic style checking is off by default. Turn it on by clicking Tools ➤ Options ➤ Spelling And Style and then enabling the Check Style control.

NOTE *The Office Assistant must be displayed to check styles.*

1. Open the presentation you want to check for style and consistency.

2. Activate the Office Assistant, if it isn't already showing, by choosing Help ➤ Show The Office Assistant.

3. Locate slides that are flagged for errors.

4. Click the light bulb to see a list of options.

5. Click the option you want to apply.

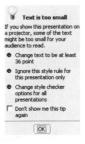

To change the elements that PowerPoint checks for, choose Change Style Checker Options For All Presentations in the list of options. If your presentation doesn't have any inconsistencies, choose Tools ➤ Options to open the Options dialog box. On the Spelling And Style tab of the dialog box, click Style Options to open the Style Options dialog box, as shown in Figure 6.23.

FIGURE 6.23

Open the Style Options dialog box to change the style elements that are checked

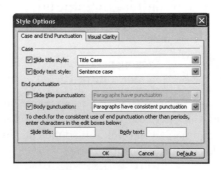

In the Case And End Punctuation tab of the dialog box, enable or disable case and end punctuation options so that your presentation is consistent. The default settings shown in Figure 6.23 would implement a very common style, applying Title Case (like newspaper headlines or the section titles in this book) with no ending punctuation to slide titles and sentence case with consistent ending punctuation to the body text. But that's by no means the only appropriate style. For example, in a presentation where every slide title was an "action item" for a team, you might use sentence case with ending punctuation: "Identify and eliminate time-wasting duplication of effort." In other presentations, the body text might be a bullet list of phrases that shouldn't be punctuated. In any case, it is usually a good idea to check for consistent end punctuation on paragraphs. When you choose to use end punctuation, PowerPoint checks for periods by default. If you're using question marks or other end punctuation, type the punctuation symbols in the edit boxes so the style checker can look for them.

Click the Visual Clarity tab of the dialog box to enable or disable font and legibility checking. Use the spin boxes to set options for the number of fonts per presentation, font sizes, number of bullets, and number of lines of text.

If you wish to return to the original style options without readjusting manually, simply click the Defaults button in the Style Options dialog box.

Chapter 7

Pushing PowerPoint to the Limit

AFTER YOUR PRESENTATION'S CONTENT is under control, it's time to think about ways to add visual impact that supports and extends your message. Objects add interest that text cannot; well-chosen graphics provide another way for the audience to understand your message. Why not include your company logo on the introductory slide? Consider displaying those month-end sales figures in a Word table. Emphasize a particularly important point with a graphical bullet. This is your opportunity to add the design elements that turn a good presentation into a great presentation.

◆ Inserting clip art, media, and other objects

◆ Adding transitions between slides

◆ Animating text and objects

◆ Adding and animating charts

◆ Preparing handouts and notes

◆ Adding timings and setting up the show

Adding Objects

PowerPoint treats each item placed on a slide as an object. Most slides have at least two text boxes—one for the title and one for the bulleted text—and each text box is an object. We covered the title box and text box objects in Chapter 6, "Adding Electronic Punch to Your Presentations." In this chapter, we will focus on other, catchier, objects that support content. The PowerPoint Online Help uses the term *text boxes* to refer to title boxes and text boxes (or simply text boxes) and uses the term *objects* to refer to objects other than the title box and text box. We will use the same convention in this chapter. To add objects to slides, switch to Normal view.

TIP   If an object (like a company logo or custom background) must appear on every slide, add it to the Slide Master (see Chapter 6).

Using Slide Layouts with Object Placeholders

The easy way to insert an object is to begin with a slide layout that includes the object, whether the object is text, clip art, a table, a chart, a sound or video clip, or any other object. To insert a new slide and display layout options, choose Insert ➤ New Slide from the menu. If you just want to see layouts without inserting a new slide, choose Slide Layout from the drop-down list at the top of the task pane. Figure 7.1 shows several examples of slide layouts that include text and objects.

FIGURE 7.1

Choose a layout that includes an object in the Slide Layout task pane

Select a slide layout that includes the object you want to use. There are layouts with placeholders for charts, tables, organizational charts, media clips, and clip art, as well as generic objects. After selecting a layout, double-click the object's placeholder in the slide, and PowerPoint launches the appropriate application to either insert or create the indicated object (see Chapter 6 for more information on slide layouts).

TIP   An easy way to build immediate rapport with your audience is to include pictures that are meaningful to them. When you use an image of a customer's building as the background to a presentation, it's a powerful way to say, "We visited your manufacturing facility." When you're collecting information for a proposal, use a digital camera to take photos of client sites for use in project and sales presentations (however, don't include images of people unless you have obtained their permission). If you don't have a digital camera with good resolution, you can take 35mm photos and scan them on a high-resolution scanner.

Inserting Objects

You can insert objects on any slide without changing the layout. In the absence of the placeholder that the layout provides, you must manually resize and position inserted objects. The PowerPoint grid takes the guesswork out of sizing and aligning. You can turn it on with a click of a button. Show/Hide Grid is available on the Standard toolbar.

As you drag an object near a guide, the object "sticks" to the guide so you can easily align objects on the guide. This Snap To Grid feature is *on* by default. To adjust specifics of how the grid works, choose View ➤ Grid And Guides (or press Ctrl+G) to open the Grid And Guides dialog box.

Clear the Snap Objects To Grid check box if you don't want objects to stick to the grid as you drag. Enable Snap Objects To Other Objects if you want to automatically line up objects that are positioned on the same gridline. Use the Grid Settings area of the dialog box to adjust spacing between gridlines. Enable the check box to Display Drawing Guides On Screen if you want to display two nonprinting lines that divide each slide into four equal quadrants. Design and graphics professionals often use layout guides for placing objects in ways that create a balanced look.

USING THE TASK PANE TO INSERT CLIP ART

You can insert clip art into a slide by using the search feature on the Clip Art task pane.

To insert a clip on any slide, click the Insert Clip Art button on the Drawing toolbar, or choose Insert ➤ Picture ➤ Clip Art to open the Clip Art task pane. Use the drop-down lists to refine your search and click Go. Clip art meeting your criteria appears in the search Results box, as shown in Figure 7.2. Use the scroll bar to view the search results. Click the clip you want to use and the clip appears on the slide. Move and resize the clip as necessary.

FIGURE 7.2

Use the Clip Art task pane to find and enter a clip.

NOTE *If this is your first contact with clip art, you should become familiar with the Clip Organizer, the Office 2003 tool for grouping and cataloging clip art and media clips. Chapter 5, "Beyond Text: Making an Impression with Multimedia," presents detailed information about using this tool. To begin working with it, click the Organize Clips link at the bottom of the task pane to open the Clip Organizer. When you have completed organizing your clip art, existing picture files on your computer are available when you search for clip art in the Clip Art task pane.*

USING THE SELECT PICTURE DIALOG BOX TO INSERT CLIP ART

If you need the clip art in a specific position relative to text or other objects, choose Slide Layout from the drop-down menu in the task pane and click the layout that best suits your needs. Click the Insert Clip Art icon on the slide to open the Select Picture dialog box, as shown in Figure 7.3.

Search or scroll to find the clip you want to use. Click to select and then click OK. The dialog box closes and the picture you selected appears on the slide, sized to the frame of the placeholder.

FIGURE 7.3

The Select Picture dialog box offers hundreds of clip art images you can add to presentations.

If you insert an object without a placeholder on a slide that's already "full," PowerPoint automatically adjusts the slide layout to accommodate the new object. Often, you get results you don't want when this AutoLayout feature kicks in. Click the Automatic Layout Options icon to see a list of choices related to the slide layout.

Choose Undo Automatic Layout to return the object to its original position. The inserted object stays on the slide, but you'll have to move and resize it to not obscure other slide objects (unless, of course, you want them partially obscured). Choose Stop Automatic Layout Of Inserted Objects if you never want PowerPoint to adjust the slide layout when you insert additional objects. Or you can choose Control AutoCorrect Options to open a dialog box and disable automatic features you don't need.

POWERPOINT SUPPORTS DIFFERENT GRAPHIC FILE FORMATS

When you are deciding what art you want to use in your presentation, you may need to explore what graphic format a particular picture comes in. PowerPoint supports the following common graphic formats directly (in other words, you don't need a special filter for them):

- Enhanced Metafile (.emf) and Windows Metafile (.wmf)
- Graphics Interchange Format (.gif)
- Joint Photographic Experts Group (.jpg)
- Portable Network Graphics (.png)
- Microsoft Windows Bitmap (.bmp, .rle, .dib)
- Tagged Image File Format (.tif)

The following graphic formats require special filters to access them:

- Computer Graphics Metafile (.cgm)
- CorelDRAW (.cdr)
- Hanako (.jsh, .jah, and .jbh)
- Macintosh PICT (.pct)
- Word Perfect Graphics (.wpg)

These filters are available on the Office 2003 installation disks and can be installed using the Custom Installation option. Many other filters for commonly-used file types are available from Microsoft Office Online (http://office.microsoft.com).

Aligning and Rotating Art

To quickly align or space objects, including clips, hold Shift and select the objects. On the Drawing toolbar, choose Draw ➢ Align Or Distribute and then choose an alignment or distribution option from the menu. If you want to distribute the objects horizontally or vertically relative to the slide, you must select the Relative To Slide option on the Align Or Distribute menu before the Distribute Horizontally and Distribute Vertically options are available.

You can also drag objects into position but, before you do, you may want to turn on the grid. The grid helps to align objects by forcing them into a horizontal and vertical position on a 1 × 1-inch grid. Click the Show/Hide Grid button on the Standard toolbar to activate the grid on the slide. If you find a need to rotate a picture, select the graphic and then position the mouse pointer over the green handle and drag left or right.

Recoloring a Clip Art Object

The Picture toolbar opens automatically when you select a clip art object in PowerPoint. If you or another user previously turned it off, click View ➤ Toolbars ➤ Picture to display it again.

If you find some clip art that illustrates your point perfectly, but clashes with your presentation's color scheme, you do not have to choose between leaving out the clip art and changing the presentation's color scheme. If the clip is a Microsoft Windows Metafile, the Recolor Picture button on the Picture toolbar solves the problem. Click the Recolor Picture to open the Recolor Picture dialog box, shown in Figure 7.4.

NOTE   *You must use an image-editing program to recolor bitmapped files (usually with extensions* `.bmp`*,* `.tif`*,* `.gif`*, or* `.jpg`*).*

FIGURE 7.4

Swap clip art colors in the Recolor Picture dialog box.

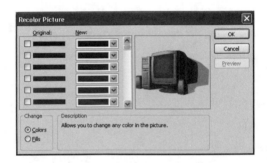

In the Change area, click either Colors to change any color in the picture, or Fills to change only background or fill colors in the picture. Select the check box for each color you want to change. Select a new color from the corresponding New drop-down list. The sample changes as you assign new colors for the clip.

TIP   *The Recolor Picture feature is available only in the Picture toolbar in PowerPoint. If you need to recolor a clip art image in any other Office application, copy the image and paste it in a PowerPoint slide. Recolor the image in PowerPoint and then use the Clipboard to return it to the other Office application.*

Inserting Media Clips from Clip Organizer

PowerPoint includes sounds and animation you can play during your slide shows. Some sounds, like the typewriter or laser sound, are accessed from animation effects (more on this later in the chapter). Other sounds and motion clips are in Microsoft Clip Organizer. Just as with clip art, you may find it easiest to insert clips by choosing a slide layout that includes a media clip placeholder. Simply click the Insert Media Clip icon on a slide with a media clip placeholder to open a dialog box with available clips.

To insert a sound or video file on any slide, follow these steps:

1. In Normal view, display the slide you want to add a media clip to.

2. Choose Insert ➤ Movies And Sounds ➤ Movie From Clip Organizer or Sound From Media Gallery.

3. In the Clip Art task pane, select the sound or motion clip (animated GIF) you want to add. Click the drop-down arrow and choose Preview/Properties to preview the selected sound or motion clip.

4. Click Insert from the drop-down menu or simply click the thumbnail icon to insert the object and place a sound icon or video object on the slide. When you insert a media clip, PowerPoint prompts you to choose to play the clip Automatically or When Clicked. If you choose When Clicked, single-click the clip to activate in Slide Show view.

5. Preview a sound or video clip by double-clicking it in Normal view.

NOTE *You need speakers (or headphones) and a sound card to play music and sounds. To view the current settings for sound on your computer, open the Control Panel and check the Sounds And Multimedia settings (Windows 2000) or Sounds and Audio Devices (Windows XP).*

Inserting Other Sound and Video Files

Microsoft provides a fine selection of sound clips, and you can download more sound and video clips from Clip Organizer online. But you're not limited to the Microsoft clips. You can download royalty-free sounds and video from a number of websites. Grab a camera or microphone and hit the field to interview customers, or use the Windows Sound Recorder or Media Player to capture sound and video with your PC. To insert a sound or video file stored on your computer or network, follow these steps:

1. Choose Insert ➢ Movies And Sounds ➢ Sound From File or Movie From File.

2. Locate and select the file you wish to insert.

3. Click OK to insert the file.

If you need video for a presentation and don't have a video capture card or a digital video camera, don't despair. Most computer graphics companies and many full-service camera shops can create video files from your videotape or 8mm tape.

TIP *The optimal screen display size for a video depends on your screen resolution. To have PowerPoint estimate the best video size, select the video object and choose Format ➢ Picture to open the Format Picture dialog box. On the Size tab, enable the Best Scale For Slide Show check box. Choose the resolution for the monitor or projector you'll use for playback from the drop-down list. When you click OK, PowerPoint resizes the object.*

PowerPoint supports a number of sound and video formats, but the Windows Media Player supports even more. If PowerPoint doesn't support the type of multimedia file you want to play in your presentation, insert the object as a Windows Media Player object instead of a PowerPoint movie or sound file. To do so, follow these steps:

1. Choose Insert ➤ Object from the menu to open the Insert Object dialog box.

2. Choose Media Clip from the list of objects.

3. Verify that Create New is selected (you are creating a new Media Clip object even if you will be playing an existing media file).

4. Click Insert.

5. Click OK. The media clip appears on the slide and the Windows Media Player toolbar replaces the PowerPoint toolbars.

5. Choose Insert Clip from the menu. Select the type of clip you want to insert.

6. In the Open dialog box, select the clip and click Open.

7. Edit the media clip as desired (volume control, frame by frame editing, etc.).

8. Click in the background of the slide to end the editing session.

To reopen the Windows Media Clip object for editing, right-click the object, and choose Media Clip Object ➤ Edit. For more information about the Windows Media Player, choose Help while editing a media clip to open Windows Media Player Help.

TIP *To hide the media clip icon from your audience, drag it off the slide in Normal view. In this case, you'll probably want to use custom animation (covered later in this chapter) to have the media clip play automatically when the slide is displayed.*

Customizing Bullets

You're probably used to choosing bullet characters in PowerPoint and Word from the myriad font sets installed with Windows and Office. If you thought Wingdings and Monotype Sorts were cool, fasten your seatbelt. In PowerPoint 2003, you can create a custom bullet from any picture file, giving you endless possibilities for emphasizing points on slides.

Before you change bullet characters, decide whether you want to make the change on all slides or on just the selected slide. If you wish to make the change for all slides, be sure you are working from the Slide Master (View ➤ Master ➤ Slide Master). Then do the following:

1. Select the text that will use the new bullet. If you are working on the Slide Master, click in the appropriate level.

2. Choose Format ➤ Bullets And Numbering. The Bullets And Numbering dialog box opens, as shown in Figure 7.5.

FIGURE 7.5

Use the Bullets And Numbering dialog box to customize bullet characters.

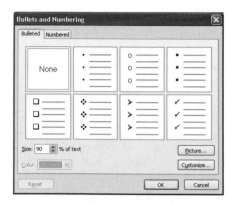

3. Select one of the seven bullet types displayed here and click OK.

    A. Alternatively, you can click Customize to open the Symbol dialog box. Click the Font drop-down list to switch character sets. Select the character you wish to use and click OK.

    B. A third alternative is to click Picture to open the Picture Bullet dialog box. Choose one of the displayed bullets or, to choose a picture from a file, click the Import button, select the file you wish to use, and click Import.

When you wish to use the picture bullet, look for it among others in Clip Organizer. To adjust the size of a custom bullet, use the Size spin box in the Bullets And Numbering dialog box.

Modifying and Adding Transitions

An electronic presentation, or slide show, is a presentation displayed on a computer screen or projected on a screen. Since slides are "changed" by the computer rather than by hand, you can add computerized special effects to a slide show that aren't possible when you use regular overheads for a presentation (unless you're an incredibly talented presenter who moonlights as a magician).

A *transition* is a special effect added to the slide's initial appearance on-screen. If a presentation has no transitions, each slide simply appears in place of the previous slide—very plain vanilla. Apply transitions to have the slide appear from the right, dissolve in gradually, or fade through the background of the previous slide.

Individual slides can also include *animation*—different steps used to construct the slide, one object at a time. For example, the slide can appear with just the title and with bulleted points following one by one.

When you give a slide show, you want the audience to remember your presentation's *content*—not just the flashy effects. Just as your choices in slide design are basic to an effective presentation (see Chapter 6), your choices in transitions and animation effects can go a long way in setting and maintaining the right mood. In general, you should develop an overall animation theme, apply it consistently, and vary from the theme to highlight key points. If you don't incorporate any movement, your presentation might appear boring and incomplete, which may, in turn, reflect badly on you. If, on the other hand, you choose a different transition for every slide and have text and other objects jumping in and flying out from all directions, you present a chaotic and out-of-control image. Using subtle transitions and carefully planned animation effects can add just the momentum needed to keep people interested.

Use one or two similar transitions throughout the presentation. For example, alternating left and right or top and down transitions of the same type provides variety without irritating your audience. (Avoid alternating rapid left/right transitions if you're keynoting after a big meal unless you have a supply of those small bags that the airlines use.) When a presentation has transitions, slides without transitions stand out, so No Transition effectively becomes another type of transition. Sound can be attention grabbing, but new sound on every slide is too much.

The same tips apply to animation. Choose a small group of animation effects. Text that flies in from the right feels normal because the words we read first enter first; so the majority of body text should enter the screen from the right rather than the left, particularly if your audience might include low-level readers. To add emphasis, then, have text enter from the left, top, or bottom, but make sure to leave the text on the screen for a longer period of time; it takes longer to begin reading text that enters from the left.

NOTE *Many of the PowerPoint 2003 design templates already include transitions and/or animation. Think of these as default settings. Modify or add transitions in Normal or Slide Sorter view, and animations in Master view.*

In PowerPoint 2003, you can apply and preview transitions in either Normal or Slide Sorter view. In Slide Sorter view, simply click the Transition button on the Slide Sorter tool bar to open the Slide Transition task pane. Choose the effect you wish to use from the list box in the task pane.

In Normal view, display the task pane (View ➤ Task Pane) and choose Slide Transition from the task pane drop-down list. The Slide Transition task pane displays current transition settings, as shown in Figure 7.6.

FIGURE 7.6

The Slide Transition task pane is available in both Normal and Slide Sorter views.

To apply a transition in either Normal or Slide Sorter View, select the slide(s) and then choose an effect from the Apply To Selected Slides list box.

TIP   *To select a slide, click it. To select multiple noncontiguous slides, click the first slide, hold down Ctrl, and click the other slide(s) you want to select. To select all slides, select a slide and press Ctrl+A.*

Many of the transitions listed differ only in direction—for example, Cover Up, Cover Down, and Cover Up-Left. PowerPoint 2003 has several more exciting transition effects as well. Check out Newsflash, Comb, Shape, and Wedge & Wheel. Any time you select a transition from the list, PowerPoint provides a preview of the transition using the selected slide. (Look carefully—it doesn't take long.) To see the transition again, click Play at the bottom of the task pane. If you don't like seeing the automatic preview each time you make a transition selection, disable the AutoPreview check box at the bottom of the task pane. You can still click Play to see a preview when *you* decide to.

In Slide Sorter view, an *animation icon* below the lower-left corner of a slide indicates that the slide has an assigned transition or animation. You can't tell from looking at the icon whether it has transitions, animations, or both. Click the icon to see a preview in the slide miniature.

TIP   *To quickly return to Normal view from Slide Sorter view, double-click a slide.*

Setting Transition Speed and Sound

Each transition has a default speed. You can change the speed for transitions, choose a different transition, or add sound effects to accompany a transition in the Slide Transition task pane, shown previously in Figure 7.6.

Select the slide(s) you want to adjust. Choose a new transition effect (if you wish) and then choose one of the Speed options from the drop-down list in the Modify Transition area of the Slide Transition task pane. If you assign a transition sound from the Sound drop-down list, you can choose to have the sound loop until another sound begins playing. The last choice on the drop-down list, Other Sounds, opens a dialog box so that you can select a sound file. PowerPoint uses WAVE sounds (.wav extension). You will find some WAVE files in the Media folder in the Windows folder, but you can purchase CDs of wave files at many computer stores and download free sound bytes from the Internet (see Chapter 5 for more about music).

Use the Advance Slide settings to enter timings for automatic slide advances. Any settings you choose are applied immediately to selected slides. If you wish, you can choose Apply To All Slides to apply the transition settings to every slide in the presentation. Effects, including sound, can be previewed by clicking the Play button in the task pane.

Adding Animation

Transition effects occur *between* slides; animation effects occur *within* a slide. You can add each title, bulleted point, or object on a slide separately. Animating a point focuses the viewer's attention on the individual point under discussion in the presentation. PowerPoint 2003 has new preset *animation schemes* that include separate effects for the slide title and bulleted paragraphs. You can apply preset animation schemes from either Slide Sorter or Normal view.

In Slide Sorter View, simply click the Slide Design button on the Slide Sorter tool bar to open the Slide Design task pane.

In Normal view, display the task pane (View ➤ Task Pane) and choose Slide Design-Animation Schemes from the task pane drop-down list. The Slide Design task pane opens, as shown in Figure 7.7, with animation schemes categorized as Recently Used, No Animation, Subtle, Moderate, and Exciting.

FIGURE 7.7

The Slide Design–Animation Schemes task pane is accessible in both Normal and Slide Sorter views.

NOTE   *If the task pane is already in Slide Design mode, but does not display animation schemes, click the Animation Schemes icon near the top of the task pane.*

To apply an animation effect, select the slide(s) you want to animate and choose a scheme from the scroll list in the task pane.

Schemes are applied to selected slides in real time. You'll see a preview as soon as you choose a scheme from the list. (If you don't see the preview, enable the AutoPreview check box at the bottom of the task pane.) Click Apply To All Slides if you wish to use the selected animation scheme on all slides.

WARNING   *Preset animation schemes override existing transitions. If you don't want to lose the transitions you've applied, you must use custom animation (discussed in the next section).*

When you animate some but not all elements on a slide, Slide Show view opens the slide displaying those objects and graphics that are *not* animated. Click, or press Enter on the keyboard, to animate the first slide element. Repeat for each additional object on the slide.

Adding Custom Animation

Sound and motion can be combined in unique ways to generate a memorable electronic presentation. PowerPoint's custom animation tools help you to display objects in a specific order, highlight important points and add exciting action to what might be not so exciting text. With Custom Animation, you can really begin to have some fun.

Options for applying entrance, emphasis, path, and exit effects allow you to animate an object to bounce in and then bounce out. You can even apply simultaneous animation so that multiple slide elements appear at once.

Switch to Normal view to apply custom animation. (This feature is disabled in Slide Sorter view). Custom animation involves two basic steps: select a slide object and then apply the custom effects you want for that object. Repeat these steps for each object on the slide that you wish to animate. It is helpful to animate items in the order you want them added to the slide during the slide show. However, as described below, you can change the animation order with just a few clicks. Let's take a closer look at the steps you'll follow to apply custom animation:

1. In Normal view, navigate to the slide you want to animate.

2. Display the task pane and choose Custom Animation from the task pane drop-down menu to open the Custom Animation task pane, as shown in Figure 7.8.

FIGURE 7.8

PowerPoint displays helper text to assist with custom animation on unanimated slides.

3. Select an object on the slide (the slide title, for example) and click the Add Effect button in the task pane. The Custom Animation drop-down menu opens, as shown in Figure 7.9.

FIGURE 7.9

Click the Add Effect button to access custom animation options.

4. Then you must decide *how* and *when* you want to animate the selected object. Choose from these options:

    Entrance   Applies an effect when the object enters the slide in Slide Show view. Objects animated with entrance effects do *not* appear on the slide when it transitions from the previous slide.

Emphasis   Uses an effect to draw attention to a particular slide element. Objects with emphasis animations appear on the slide when it transitions from the previous slide.

Exit   Applies an effect as the object leaves the slide. As with emphasis effects, objects appear with the slide transition.

Motion Path   Creates a set of specific directions for the object to follow when it animates. Objects might or might not appear on the slide when it transitions—it depends on where you place the object in Normal view. If you position the object *off* the slide, it follows the motion path *onto* the slide (unless you goof and choose a path that doesn't move the object toward the slide!).

5. Select the animation effect you want applied. The choices available depend on which of the four animation types you chose in step 4. For example, when you click Add Effect and choose Entrance for the selected slide title, you're presented with a list of most-frequently/recently used entrance effects, as shown in Figure 7.9. Choose one of these or click More Effects, shown in Figure 7.10, to see additional choices in a dialog box. The dialog box choices are categorized as Basic, Subtle, Moderate, and Exciting. If the Preview Effect check box is enabled, you can click an effect to get an idea of what it does (you may have to drag the dialog box out of the way to see the preview on the slide). When you find the effect you want to use, click it and then click OK.

FIGURE 7.10

Choose More Effects to open the Entrance Animation dialog box.

TIP   Many effects—Wipe Fly, Checkerboard, and Cover, to name a few—have an adjustable direction component. Choose the effect as you normally would and then, if you wish, select something other than the default from the Direction drop-down list in the task pane.

6. Repeat the procedure for each element you wish to animate. PowerPoint displays the *animation sequence*—the order in which animations occur—in the task pane (shown here) and places a

nonprinting, numbered animation tag next to animated slide elements in the Slide pane. Tag numbers correspond to the numbered item in the task pane.

Any time you wish to preview the effects applied to a slide, just click Play at the bottom of the task pane. In preview mode, effects display automatically even if objects are set up to animate on mouse-click. To get a feel for how the slide will behave during the actual presentation, click the Slide Show (From Current Slide) button.

To adjust the animation sequence, click the animated object in the task pane list, and then use the Re-order buttons (below the list) to adjust its placement in the list. PowerPoint automatically adjusts the tags on the slide to reflect the new animation order.

But wait, there's more! What if you decide to use more than one animation on an object? For example, bulleted points with entrance effects can include an exit effect as well. To apply a second animation to an already-animated object, select it and follow steps 3 through 5. PowerPoint might display more than one tag on slide objects with multiple animations, or you might see the tag number followed by an ellipsis (...). The slide displayed in Figure 7.11 contains objects with multiple animations.

APPLYING PATH ANIMATION

We've frequently heard questions like these from longtime PowerPoint users:

◆ Can I make the racecar drive up the side of the slide and then across the top?

◆ Can I make a butterfly clip art flit across the screen?

◆ Can my drawn arrow make a figure eight and then come to rest in the upper-right corner of the slide?

The answer is "Yes, and it's simple to do!" PowerPoint 2003's path animation makes it easy for objects to follow virtually any path. Several dozen path selections are built in, and you can choose to draw a custom path. Path animation might seem a bit tricky at first, but here's what you need to know to be successful with it.

◆ Objects using path animation have a starting and ending point.

◆ The object's placement on the slide determines its starting point.

◆ The path animation you select determines the object's ending point. You can reverse the animation path, which also swaps starting and ending points.

◆ Paths can be locked or unlocked. *Locked* means the animation path is tied to that location on the slide, even if you move the object. When you choose *unlocked*, the path moves automatically any time you move the object.

To apply a path animation, follow these steps:

1. Select the object you wish to animate.

2. In the Custom Animation task pane, click Add Effect ➤ Motion Paths to open a menu of choices. Choose one of the menu options, or choose More Motion Paths to open the Add Motion Path dialog box. The dialog box displays motion paths in Basic, Lines & Curves, and Special categories. Click a path to see its effect (make sure Preview Effect is enabled and move the dialog box out of the way if necessary). When you find the one you want to use, click it and click OK.

3. If you don't see an effect that suits your needs, you can choose Add Effect ➤ Motion Paths ➤ Draw Custom Path to create your own. (See Sidebar "Perfecting Path Animation," below.)

4. After you've applied a path animation, the path is displayed on the slide as a nonprinting dotted line (see Figure 7.11). A green arrow indicates the starting point, and a red arrow indicates the ending point.

FIGURE 7.11

Slide objects show nonprinting numbered tags to indicate the order in which they are animated.

Adjusting Path Animation

At times you will want to make minor modifications to the animation path: Make the curve a little wider or make the bounce a little lower. PowerPoint lets you edit the path at certain points. Just select the object with the path animation you want to tweak and then click the Path drop-down list in the Custom Animation task pane. Choose Edit Points to display handles on the animation path. Drag the handles—one at a time—to adjust the path.

To tie an animation path to a location on the slide and not the object you're animating, choose Locked from the Path drop-down list. If you later move the object, the path stays put. To have the path move with the object, choose Unlocked.

You can also reverse the direction the object travels along the animation path. Select the object and choose Reverse Path Direction from the Path drop-down list in the Custom Animation task pane. Essentially, you are swapping the object's starting and ending points when you reverse the path.

MASTERING THE OPPORTUNITIES: PERFECTING PATH ANIMATION

So you've grown tired of using the canned path animations (even though there are over 60 of them!). No problem; PowerPoint 2003 lets you draw your own custom path. The secret to having success with this feature is selecting the correct drawing tool and knowing the click sequence that produces the desired results with that tool. Select the slide object you wish to animate. Click Add Effect ➢ Motion Path ➢ Draw Custom Path from the Custom Animation task pane and then use one of these tools:

◆ Choose the *Line* tool if you want to draw a straight path. Once the tool is selected, drag from the object to the ending point. Release the mouse, and the animation path immediately appears on the slide.

◆ Click the *Curve* tool to make a wavy path. Click once at the starting point, move the mouse to where you want the first curve, and click. Repeat until you have all the curves you need. Double-click to end the curve and display the path on the slide.

◆ Select the *Freeform* tool if you want to create a path that includes both straight and curvy line segments. Use clicks to create straight-line segments; drag when you want to draw wavy lines or other shapes. Double-click to finish.

◆ Use the *Scribble* tool to create virtually any path. One caution here: You'll have difficulty drawing straight lines. If you're going for that erratic look, Scribble will do it. Select the tool and drag from the object to the ending point. Release the mouse button to end the path.

Changing Speed, Timing, and other Custom Animation Settings

So far we've discussed how to apply animation effects and how to adjust the animation sequence. But there's much more to it than that. For example, you can adjust the speed at which an object animates, apply sounds to accompany animation effects, change text color after animation, and create simultaneous animations. You can also determine whether each animation occurs with a click of the mouse or automatically based on timing. With all these choices, you can spend hours on animation alone!

To adjust the speed of an animation effect, first select the object (by clicking it on the slide or in the animation sequence, or by clicking its animation tag on the slide). Then choose a different animation rate from the Speed drop-down list in the Custom Animation task pane.

TIP   To get an idea of the exact timing of an animation, display the Advanced Timeline. Just click the drop-down arrow next to the object in the Custom Animation task pane animation list and choose Show Advanced Timeline.

Animations that are adjacent in sequence can be set up to occur simultaneously. When you want animations to happen at the same time, make sure they are next to each other in the animation list. Use the Re-order arrows to position them if necessary. Then follow these steps:

1. Select the one that appears *farthest down* the list.

2. Click the Start drop-down list at the top of the Custom Animation task pane.

3. Choose With Previous.

Items that animate simultaneously have the same numbered tag on the slide. You can still apply more than one animation to items that animate at the same time.

NOTE *It's fairly easy to understand an animation sequence from the tags on the slide. However, to see the specific effect applied to an object, you must click its tag. The effect appears at the top of the task pane below the Change icon. And remember, you can always click Play to get the full visual effect.*

WORKING WITH TEXT FRAMES

Although graphics can add pizzazz to an otherwise dull presentation, slide text usually conveys your message in the most straightforward way. Therefore, it pays to spend a few minutes introducing and emphasizing your slide text in ways that make it easy to understand and remember. One way to do this is with an emphasis effect (discussed previously). However, if an audience member glances away during the critical moment, they may miss the emphasis and lose track of which bulleted point you are addressing. Using an after-animation dim color can help the audience keep up. (Just make sure you don't dim to a color that makes the text unreadable or your note-takers may become annoyed.) Alternately, you might choose to repeat the emphasis until you click for the next bulleted point. Fortunately, there are several ways to fine-tune animation.

With PowerPoint 2003 you can choose a different effect for each bulleted point. This feature gives you much more control and increases the likelihood of overkill at the same time! Seriously, though, there are ways to use varying effects without stupefying your audience. Here are some quick ideas:

◆ Wipe in the first several points and bounce in the last. (Or combine any two effects in this way.)

◆ Alternate two effects: one paragraph dissolves in, the next flies in.

◆ Use the same effect on each point, but vary the direction: stretch across, from bottom, from left, from right.

◆ Choose a different effect and direction for each point, but use the same effect sequence for every slide: wipe right, then ascend, curve up, and checkerboard across on every slide. We wouldn't recommend this for slides with more than four bulleted points, and that might be pushing it, depending on any other effects included in the presentation.

Consistency is the key. Choose one or two settings to alter between slides; don't change everything under the sun! Once the audience sees a consistent pattern (the earlier the better), they'll quickly know what to expect and focus more on content.

The task pane displays animated text frames collapsed by default.

When you select the collapsed item and apply animation, the effect settings are the same for each paragraph in the text box—a quick and easy way to animate if you want to use the same effect within a frame. To access individual paragraphs within the text frame, click the double down-arrows to display them. Click the double up-arrows to collapse the detail at any time.

TIP   *You can also select a specific paragraph by clicking its numbered slide tag. The list in the task pane expands automatically.*

ADJUSTING EFFECT OPTIONS

Each animated object listed in the task pane contains a menu of choices related to the animation. Now that you know the difference between selecting a text box and selecting a specific item within a text box, we can proceed with modifying default animation settings. Select any text object you've previously animated, or animate one now if you are starting from scratch. Click the drop-down arrow next to the animated item in the Custom Animation task pane to display a menu of choices for that item.

Choose Effect Options to open a dialog box with options for that animation. Figure 7.12 shows effect options available for a text box with a Strips animation. Proceed as follows:

1. Select a different direction from the Direction drop-down list if you don't like the current choice. The Direction list varies according to the type of effect you've chosen. These same choices are available in the Custom Animation task pane, but you can change them here too.

2. Choose a sound to accompany the animation if you wish. Click the sound icon to adjust the volume of the sound. Keep in mind that, depending on which object you selected in the task pane, you might be applying a sound to every bulleted point in the frame—overkill in most situations.

3. Select an After Animation color to change the color of animated text as the next animation occurs. You can use this in multiple-point slides with rather dramatic effect; for example, you can have each point animate as white text and then change to gray when the next point enters, drawing the viewer's attention immediately to the new point and away from the previous point. If you're creating a presentation for an audience that includes members with lower reading levels—and that includes most audiences—make sure you dim points after animation so that they stay visible but are no longer emphasized. It's a simple way to make sure you don't leave slow readers in the dust.

WARNING   *Over 30 percent of the adult population learns best when taking notes. It's not that they don't trust your handouts; the physical act of writing triggers learning. If you don't want to really irritate a third of your audience, select an After Animation color that doesn't get lost in the background. Gray works well with many backgrounds (unless, of course, the background color of your template is gray).*

4. The Animate Text list determines how you introduce text: all at once, by word, or by letter. If you introduce by word or letter, you must select a delay percentage.

WARNING   *Be careful here. It's exciting to see an occasional slide title fly in by letter, but you'll lose your audience at the second bulleted point if you animate text-heavy slides by word or letter.*

5. When you have finished adjusting effect options, click OK to apply them. PowerPoint provides an immediate preview.

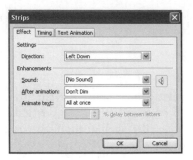

FIGURE 7.12

Modify animation effects to achieve the exact look and feel that you need to keep the attention of your audience.

Effect options are available for any slide object. You can't introduce graphics by letter, of course, but you can choose a sound and a dim color for most. In addition, path animations offer the following options:

Smooth Start Causes the animation to build speed gradually rather than starting abruptly.

Smooth End Slows the animation as it reaches its ending point.

Auto-Reverse Plays the animation twice: once forward, once in reverse, and so requires double the time.

MODIFYING ANIMATION TIMING

You can introduce a slide object automatically or as a *triggered effect*, which means it animates on mouse-click. You needn't make the same choice for all slides, but if you're varying triggers on or between slides, you should practice the presentation until you've memorized where to click and where automatic advances occur.

To adjust timing, select an animation from the task pane list and click the drop-down arrow to display its menu. Then follow these steps:

1. Choose Timing to open the Timing page of the effect dialog box shown in Figure 7.13.

FIGURE 7.13

Use the timing page of the Effect dialog box to fine-tune animation timing.

2. Choose a Start option. If you wish to automate the animation so that it proceeds without mouse-clicks, choose After Previous. (The With Previous choice creates simultaneous animation, as previously discussed.)

3. If you wish to apply a time delay between the Start action and the animation, set the number of seconds in the Delay spin box.

NOTE   *The times here are somewhat relative based on your processor speed and available memory. Five seconds may actually take 8 or 10 seconds on a slower computer, while on a faster computer with tons of available memory, five seconds may zoom by.*

4. Use the Speed control to adjust how fast the animation occurs. For entrance, exit, and path animations, the speed setting determines how fast it takes the object to go from start to end position. With emphasis effects, the timing control establishes how long the animation lasts. These same timing choices are available from the Speed drop-down list in the Custom Animation task pane.

5. If you want to see an animation more than once, you can repeat it. Choose an option from the Repeat list to see an animation multiple times, until the next click, or until the next slide is displayed.

TIP   *You can use the repeat feature in conjunction with some of the emphasis effects. This is helpful in keeping the audience focused on the bulleted point you're currently addressing. As always, consider the annoyance factor and make sure the effect you're using doesn't obscure the message.*

6. If you want an object to return to its original position after animation, enable the Rewind When Done Playing check box. This is particularly helpful with path animations. It causes the object to move from starting to ending point, pause for a moment, and then return to its original placement (which could even be off the slide).

7. Adjust triggers if needed. Choose Animate As Part Of Click Sequence to play the animation in the order in which it appears in the task pane sequence, regardless of *where* you click during the slide show. Choose Start Effect On Click Of and select an object if you want to specify an exact click location to trigger the animation.

8. When you're finished, click OK. PowerPoint provides a preview that plays even triggered events automatically. To preview the show using actual triggers, click the Slide Show button in the Custom Animation task pane.

Using Charts in Presentations

In Office 2003, there are two programs that create charts: Excel and Microsoft Graph. If you already have a chart in Excel you can easily copy it and embed it in or link it to your slide. In early versions of Office, PowerPoint created the largest (possibly the only) user group for Microsoft Graph, because PowerPoint didn't support animation for objects created in Excel. Excel charts can be animated in PowerPoint 2000, 2002, and, of course, PowerPoint 2003.

NOTE   *While Graph is a decent charting tool, it's only useful for simple charts. Excel is the best tool for creating and formatting charts.*

To place an existing Excel chart in a PowerPoint slide:

1. Open Excel.

2. Select the chart you want to use.

3. Copy the chart to the Clipboard.

4. In PowerPoint's Normal view, select the slide you want to contain the chart.

    You can choose to embed or link the chart.

5. To *embed* the chart, click Paste or choose Edit ➤ Paste from the menu.

6. Alternatively, to *link* the chart, choose Edit ➤ Paste Special to open the Paste Special dialog box.

    A. Select the Paste Link option on the left. (To display an icon that you can click to display the chart, enable the Display As Icon check box.)

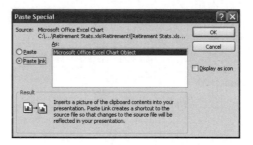

    B. Click OK to paste the linked chart.

If the workbook that the chart was copied from contains macros, you'll be notified and prompted to proceed or cancel.

NOTE *When you link rather than embed a chart (or any other object), there are obvious trade-offs. Your chart contains current data, but if someone moves or renames the file containing the chart, or if you e-mail the presentation to someone who does not have access to the file, the slide cannot display charted data.*

To insert a Microsoft Graph chart, click the Insert Chart button on the Standard toolbar or double-click a slide that has a chart placeholder. Microsoft Chart is a fine tool for creating a basic chart. However, we recommend creating your charts in Excel and importing them into PowerPoint. Your data is probably there anyway and if it's not, Excel is a better place to keep it. If you want to play around with Microsoft Chart, go ahead. You'll find help for it from the Help menu as soon as you double-click a chart placeholder.

Animating Charts

Charts illustrate numeric data; animation breathes life into the illustration. During your slide show, you can introduce an entire chart all at once or have chart elements appear by category, by data series, or as individual data points. Adding the data separately lets you apply emphasis where needed, and it allows your audience to digest one piece of information before you deliver another. You must animate the entire chart first, even if you are planning to animate individual elements. Navigate to the slide with the chart you wish to animate, select the chart, and choose Slide Show ➢ Custom Animation to open the Custom Animation task pane.

1. Click Add Effect and choose an entrance, exit, emphasis, or path animation. If you're planning to animate individual chart elements, be careful here. All the animation effects are available when chart elements are introduced all at once (see step 3). Only certain effects allow you to animate by element. For example, you can't have chart elements spiral in by category, but you can have them strip down.

NOTE *Many, but not all, of the directional effects work with individual chart elements: Blinds, Strips, Wipe, Stretch, Checkerboard, and Expand all work. Surprisingly, Fly does not. Experiment until you find one you like. Chances are, you'll use it again and again in your presentations.*

2. Display effect options for the chart you just animated. (Click the drop-down arrow next to the object in the task pane and choose Effect Options.) Choose the Chart Animation tab of the dialog box. Chart Animation is available only if the selected object is a chart.

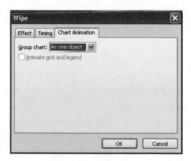

3. In the Group Chart drop-down list, select how you want the chart elements to appear.

As One Object   Brings the chart in like a picture; the entire object appears.

By Series   Causes all bars from a data series (all the bars, columns, or line segments that are the same color) to appear at once. For example, you might have all four quarters of the West Coast data appear, then the East Coast, etc.

By Category   Brings in each x-axis cluster separately (all first-quarter, then all second-quarter, and so on).

By Element In A Series and By Element In A Category   Works essentially the same as By Series and By Category, respectively. The difference is that only one bar appears at a time rather than several bars at once. Choose By Series or By Category to set the order in which to animate the individual data points.

4. Turn on Animate Grid And Legend if you want to apply effects to those chart elements as well.

5. Use the Effect tab of the dialog box to assign a sound and an After Animation option if you wish. Adjust timings on the Timing tab just as you would with any object.

6. Click OK when you're finished. PowerPoint provides an immediate preview as long as the AutoPreview check box is enabled in the task pane.

NOTE   *As you add effects to a live presentation, you should increase your practice time. For a perfectly polished presentation, practice until you have memorized which slides animate automatically and which advance on mouse-click. If you find it difficult to memorize during practice, your presentation is probably overanimated.*

Animating Video and Sound

Multimedia settings work just like text animation settings. Select a sound or video object and open the Timing tab of the effect options (shown earlier in the "Modifying Animation Timing" section of this chapter). If you choose to start After Previous, you don't have to click the object to play it. You can hide the object until it plays by assigning an entrance effect. To have the video loop, choose a Repeat setting other than None. Rewind a video clip automatically by enabling the Rewind When Done Playing check box. If you wish, assign a sound to play as the video plays. (Use the Effect tab for this.)

If you'd like to know more about using music and narration in your presentations, refer to Chapter 5.

Hiding Slides

Many presentations contain "emergency slides" that are displayed only if certain questions or topics arise during the presentation.

 In Slide Sorter view, select the slide you want to hide, and then click the Hide Slide button on the Slide Sorter toolbar. In Normal view, right-click the slide in the left pane and choose Hide Slide from the shortcut menu. A null symbol appears over the slide's number. To display the hidden slide during the presentation, you have three choices:

If you have access to the computer's keyboard, type *H* while displaying the slide preceding the hidden slide.

If you are using a mouse or a remote pointing device, you can right-click the slide before the hidden slide, choose Go ➤ Go To Slide, and select the title of the hidden slide from the shortcut menu. However, the shortcut menu intrudes on your presentation. Further, anyone in the audience who uses PowerPoint will know that the slide titles displayed in parentheses on the shortcut are hidden slides. That defeats the purpose of hiding them. If you won't have access to a keyboard during a slide show, keep reading to see how to insert a hyperlink on a slide—a much slicker way to show hidden slides.

Adding Links to Other Slides

PowerPoint 2003 supports hyperlinks to other slides, other presentations, and URLs. Clicking a hyperlink moves the user from the current slide to another slide, another presentation, or a site on the Internet.

To create a hyperlink, switch to Normal view and select the text or object you want used as a hyperlink. Normally, text tells the user where they will end up: "Click Here To Exit The Presentation," for example, or "Click To View More Options." However, you can also tie a hyperlink to a piece of clip art, a photograph, or any other object. In a presentation, you probably don't want to display "Click Here To Go To Another Slide," so select some existing text or an object that forms a logical jump-off point. With the text/object selected, right-click and choose Action Settings from the shortcut menu, or choose Slide Show ➤ Action Settings from the menu bar, to open the dialog box shown in Figure 7.14.

FIGURE 7.14

Create hyperlinks in the Action Settings dialog box.

You can activate a hyperlink in two ways: by clicking it or by moving the mouse over it. Both pages of this dialog box are identical—choose a page based on which mouse action you want to trigger the hyperlink. Click the Hyperlink To option and select the slide you want to link to.

Choosing Next Slide shows the next slide, even if it's hidden. To choose a specific slide, choose Slide from the Hyperlink To drop-down list to open the Hyperlink To Slide dialog box.

Choose a slide from the Slide Title list box, and then click OK. Click OK in the Action Settings dialog box to create the hyperlink.

When text is turned into a hypertext link, its formatting is changed. The text is underlined, and a contrasting font color applied. You won't be able to change the color or remove the underlining on the slide. If you want to camouflage hyperlinks, change their color to match surrounding text by using the Custom tab of the Edit Color Scheme dialog box (click the Edit Color Scheme link at the bottom of the Color Schemes pane of the Slide Design task pane). If you use another type of object for the hyperlink, you will not notice any changes in the object.

WARNING   *Don't change the hyperlink color scheme to match surrounding text if you are creating a kiosk presentation for users to click through themselves. They won't know it's a hyperlink if it doesn't stand out. (And if you're presenting a slide show created a few months ago, it's possible to forget the hyperlink without a visual cue.)*

If you prefer, you can apply hyperlinks directly by selecting text or another object and clicking Insert ➤ Hyperlink or clicking the Insert Hyperlink button on the Standard toolbar. Specific steps for creating hyperlinks this way are discussed in Chapter 10, "Taming Complex Publications."

Preparing Handouts and Notes

Handouts are pictures of the slides or the outline from a presentation that you give to participants. You can arrange handouts so they have two, three, four, six, or nine slides to a page, or you can choose to create a handout from your outline.

The Handout Master

You use the Handout Master to view and select the handout layouts. Choose View ➤ Master ➤ Handout Master to open the master, shown in Figure 7.15. The Handout Master toolbar opens automatically.

Figure 7.15

The Handout Master is a tool for preparing handouts from your slides.

TIP   *Settings for the masters, including the Slide Master and the Handout Master, are saved as separate workspaces within PowerPoint. If you close, for example, the Handout Master toolbar before switching out of the Handout Master, the next time you open the Handout Master the toolbar will not be displayed. Right-click any command bar or choose View ➤ Toolbars to display toolbars that were turned off in an earlier session.*

The unlabeled placeholders (rectangles with dotted-line borders) show where slides are positioned in the layout selected in the Handout Master View toolbar. Click the appropriate button on the Handout Master View toolbar to select the number of slides you'd like to display on each page of the handout.

The Handout Master contains placeholders for the footer, header, date, and page number. By default, the footer area displays the title of your presentation (not to be confused with the presentation's filename). If you have chosen to number slides or display the date and time in the presentation, the Handout Master also includes these fields.

To display or delete placeholders for date/time and page number, or to format or automatically update the date/time field, open the Header And Footer dialog box (View ➢ Header And Footer). Switch to the Notes And Handouts tab, shown in Figure 7.16. The header, footer, page, and date information you enter in the dialog box replaces the appropriate placeholders in the Handout Master when you print handouts.

FIGURE 7.16

Change settings to display date and/or time, page numbers, and fixed text in the Header And Footer dialog box.

If you delete a placeholder and later change your mind about the deletion, PowerPoint offers a quick and easy way to bring it back. Just click the Handout Master Layout button on the Handout Master View toolbar to display the Handout Master Layout dialog box.

Enable the check box next to any placeholder you wish to restore. If the placeholder already exists on the master, it is "grayed out" in the dialog box.

NOTE *Click in any of the labeled placeholders to add text to the placeholder. It's easiest to edit the master if you change the Zoom setting to* **75%** *or* **100%** *so you can see the text.*

Insert art or other graphics (a company logo, for example) just as you would on a slide. (Choose Insert ➢ Picture ➢ Clip Art or Insert ➢ Picture ➢ From File.) Format the background of your handouts by choosing Format ➢ Handout Background from the menu. To modify the slide color scheme for handouts, do the following:

1. Display the color scheme options in the task pane. (Choose View ➢ Task Pane, and then choose Slide Design—Color Scheme from the task pane selection menu.)

2. Click the arrow next to the color scheme you want to use.

3. Choose Apply To Handout Master.

Printing in PowerPoint

When you click the Print button on the Standard toolbar, PowerPoint prints the entire presentation in the default setting—usually the Slide pane from Normal view. If the slides have a background, this can take some time, even on a laser printer. More important, it's rarely what you intended to print. In Power-Point, it's always best to choose File ➢ Print to open the Print dialog box (shown in Figure 7.17) so you can select whether to print slides, handouts, notes, or an outline.

TIP   You can replace the standard Print button with a button that opens the Print dialog box. Right-click any toolbar and choose Customize. With the Customize dialog box open, drag the Print button off the toolbar and drop it in the application window. On the Commands tab of the dialog box, choose the File category. In the Commands pane, select the Print... button and drag it onto the Standard toolbar. Close the Customize dialog box.

FIGURE 7.17

Change print settings for your presentation in the Print dialog box.

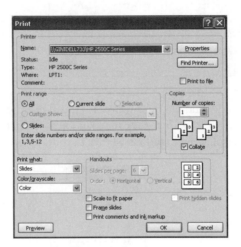

The default print setting is All Slides. To print some, but not all, slides, select the Slides option button and enter their numbers in the Slides text box. Choose what you want to print (slides, handouts, notes, or an outline) from the Print What drop-down list. If you are printing a color presentation on a noncolor printer, choose Pure Black And White from the Color/Grayscale list. This helps speed up the printing process. Choose Grayscale from this list to print black-and-white on a color printer.

NOTE   Choose Tools ➢ Options and select the Print tab of the Options dialog box to change the default print settings for the current presentation and the default settings for printing graphics for all presentations.

If you're printing handouts with multiple slides per page, you must choose either a vertical or a horizontal printing order. Click the Frame Slides check box to print a simple box around each slide; this is a good idea if the slides themselves don't include a border. If there are hidden slides in your presentation, the default is to print them. You can disable that option by clearing its check box.

You can also choose how many slides per handout page to print in the Print dialog box. If you previously used the Handout Master to choose the number of slides per page, you can override that choice here.

To preview what you're about to print, click the Preview button on the Print dialog box to display the presentation with current print settings.

NOTE *If you are in the presentation, you can click the Print Preview button on the Standard toolbar (or choose File ➢ Print Preview) to preview the presentation at any time.*

The Print Preview toolbar, shown here, provides several options for changing print settings without reopening the Print dialog box.

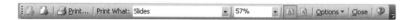

You can use the scroll bar to browse the document preview, but there are also buttons on the toolbar for viewing previous and next pages. Change what you're printing by choosing from the Print What drop-down list. The Options button has settings for framing slides, printing comments, setting color options, adjusting print order, and more. About the only thing you can't do there is choose a different printer. You can even change from portrait to landscape orientation by clicking the appropriate button on the toolbar. This is particularly helpful if you're experimenting with different handout layouts.

When you're finished adjusting settings, click Close to leave the preview and return to work on your presentation, or click the Print button to open the Print dialog box (shown previously in Figure 7.17) and proceed with printing.

NOTE *You can't change the page orientation if Print What is set to Slides.*

Creating Handouts in Word

You can use the power of Office automation to create handouts and reports for a PowerPoint presentation in Word. The Send To Word feature transfers the text or slides from the current presentation to a Word document, which you can then edit (adding titles and additional text), format, and print to use as handouts. Choose File ➢ Send To ➢ Microsoft Word to open the Send To Microsoft Word dialog box, shown in Figure 7.18.

Select how you want the presentation to appear: in one of the four handout-style layouts or as an outline. Choose whether you want to paste a copy from your presentation or link the Word document to the presentation. If you choose Paste Link, changes to the presentation will be updated in the Word document; however, you'll lose some of the editing flexibility in Word.

After selecting layout and paste options, click OK. PowerPoint launches Word and exports your outline or slides. Edit and print the document as you would a Word document. If you send slides (instead of an outline), this may take a few minutes because each slide is exported as a graphic object.

FIGURE 7.18

PowerPoint provides options for creating handouts in Word.

TIP   If you're only transferring an outline, click the Color/Grayscale button on the Standard toolbar and choose Grayscale or Pure Black And White before opening the Send To Microsoft Word dialog box for easier formatting in Word. When you want to refocus on the presentation, click Close Grayscale View or Close Back And White View on the Grayscale View toolbar that opens.

Setting Slide Timings

After you have finalized your slides, including transitions and animation, you are ready to rehearse your slides in preparation for the actual presentation. Rehearsal is vital—it's better to discover problems in private than have them projected to a large audience.

Automated vs. Manual Advance

Advancing an electronic presentation can happen in one of two ways. If the presentation is designed to run on its own—for example, in a booth at a trade show—you'll want to advance slides automatically. If your finished presentation will be used to illustrate a verbal presentation or will be posted on an intranet, you'll probably prefer to advance slides manually. If slides should advance automatically, only a bit more work is required to set the timings for each animation and transition.

If you are using manual advance, then your presentation is essentially completed. Rehearse the presentation a few times, making sure that you know how many times to click on each slide to display all the objects.

TIP   You can always manually advance slides in a presentation, even if it includes slide timings. Choose Slide Show ➢ Set Up Show from the menu and choose an Advance option: Manually or Using Timings, If Present.

Setting Automatic Timings

There are also two ways to set slide timings: through rehearsal or manually in the Slide Transition task pane. (You can only enter animation timings by rehearsal.) It's easiest to create timings through rehearsal and then alter individual advances manually. Before setting timings, run through the entire slide show two or three times. Try not to advance slides and animations too quickly for your audience, because they will be seeing the slides for the first time. Make sure that your audience will have time to read the title, read each point, and see how a graphic illustrates the points. It helps to read the contents of each slide out loud, slowly, while rehearsing and setting the timings. When you're ready to record timings, switch to Slide Sorter view and follow these steps:

1. Click the Rehearse Timings button on the Slide Sorter toolbar or, in Normal view, choose Slide Show ➤ Rehearse Timings. The first slide appears, and the Rehearsal toolbar opens.

2. The Rehearsal toolbar has two timers. The timer on the right shows the total time for the presentation. The left timer is the elapsed time for the current slide. Click anywhere on the slide for your next animation or your next slide. The timers automatically record the number of seconds that pass between transitions and animations.

3. The Rehearsal toolbar has three buttons: Next, Pause, and Repeat. Click the Next button (or anywhere on the slide) to move to the next slide or animation.

4. If you are interrupted in the middle of rehearsal, click the Pause button, and then click Pause again to resume.

5. If you make a mistake while rehearsing a slide, click Repeat to set new timings for the *current* slide. If you don't catch a mistake before a slide has been advanced, you can either finish rehearsing and then edit the slide time manually or close the toolbar and begin again.

6. When you complete the entire rehearsal for a presentation, or if you press Esc to end the rehearsal, you are prompted to save the timings:

7. Choose Yes to save the timings as rehearsed. Choose No to discard the timings. In Slide Sorter view, the total time for each slide appears below the slide.

EDITING SLIDE TIMINGS

To edit an individual transition time, select the slide in Slide Sorter view and click the Slide Transition button on the Slide Sorter toolbar. The rehearsed time, which you can edit, is displayed in the Advance Slide area of the task pane.

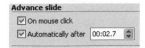

To re-rehearse timings for one or more slides:

1. Choose Slide Show ➤ Set Up Show from the menu to open the Set Up Show dialog box, shown in Figure 7.19.

2. In the Show Slides section, set the From and To controls to the range of slides you wish to change animation timings for.

3. Click OK to close the dialog box.

4. Choose Slide Show ➤ Rehearse Timings, or click the Rehearse Timings button on the Slide Sorter toolbar, to rehearse new timings for the selected slides. Save timings when prompted.

5. Choose Slide Show ➤ Set Up Show and set the Show Slides option to All.

FIGURE 7.19

The Set Up Show dialog box lets you choose the slides for which you wish to re-rehearse timings.

Customizing Shows for Different Audiences

Sometimes you need to create multiple versions of the same slide show to present to different audiences. For instance, you might have an East Coast and a West Coast version of the same sales presentation. Both versions use identical slides 1–12, but slides 13–25 are different, depending on where the client is located. You don't have to save each version as a separate file. In PowerPoint 2003, you can create a presentation within a presentation using the Custom Shows feature. To begin customizing, choose Slide Show ➤ Custom Shows from the menu to open the Custom Shows dialog box. Click New to open the Define Custom Show dialog box.

Name your show, overwriting the default name Custom Show 1. Select the slides you wish to include in this version of the show and click Add to move them to the Slides In Custom Show list. Use the Remove button to remove selected slides from the list.

Use the Move Up and Move Down arrows to change the slide order. Click OK to save the custom show and return to the Custom Shows dialog box. Define another custom show using the New button, or click the Edit button to edit a selected show. To remove the selected custom show, click the Remove button.

During a presentation, you can right-click, choose Go ➢ Custom Show on the shortcut menu, and select the custom show you want to display. The shortcut menu, however, is rather intrusive. You may prefer to set up the presentation so it displays the custom version when you start the slide show (see the upcoming section, "Setting Up the Slide Show").

TIP   You can switch to a custom show during a presentation by creating a hyperlink to that show. Select the text or object you want to link from and choose Slide Show ➢ Action Settings or Insert ➢ Hyperlink from the menu. For more information, see the section "Adding Links to Other Slides" earlier in the chapter.

Setting Up the Slide Show

You've designed a good presentation, had it reviewed by a colleague, and practiced moving through the slides. Now you're ready to specify the settings that you'll use to deliver the show. Before you present the slide show, choose Slide Show ➢ Set Up Show to open the Set Up Show dialog box, shown previously in Figure 7.19.

In the Show Type area, select a presentation method and then choose whether or not to use narration, animation, and looping in the Show Options area. In the Advance Slides area, choose Manually or Using Timings, If Present. To show the presentation continuously, choose Using Timings, If Present and click the Loop Continuously Until 'Esc' check box in the Show Options area. In the Show Slides area, you can choose to show the entire presentation, certain slide numbers, or a custom presentation.

During the presentation, you can use the mouse pointer to draw on the slides to emphasize a point (see "Drawing on Slides" later in this chapter); select a pen color that contrasts with both the background and the text colors used in the slides.

Viewing on Two Screens

One of the challenges of being a presenter is how you manage to see your printed notes, handle a mouse or remote control to control the presentation, and still attend to your audience. Well, now you can get the benefits of online broadcasting even if you're doing a live presentation to a group. Power-Point's View On Two Screens option allows you to set up a show with one computer as the presenter and the other (a computer with a large monitor) as the audience. You get to see slides and notes while the audience sees only the slides.

First, your computer must have the capability to display on more than one monitor. In other words, you must be able to plug more than one monitor into the video card, have more than one video card (with an appropriate adaptor), or have a TV-Out or S-Video port. If so, connect the second monitor to the computer. You may need to change the settings of each monitor in the Windows Display Properties (right-click the Windows Desktop and choose Properties, then click the Settings tab) to set the monitor you want to be primary (the one you'll be viewing should be primary).

Then, choose Slide Show ➤ Set Up Show to open the Set Up Show dialog box (refer to Figure 7.19, shown earlier). Open the Display Slide Show On drop-down list and select the monitor you wish to use to show the presentation. The other monitor displays your presentation in Normal view. Enable the Show Presenter Tools check box to see a navigation panel on one screen, shown in Figure 7.20, making the presentation easier to navigate during the show.

FIGURE 7.20

Presenter Tools provide an easy means to navigate the slide show when you're using multiple monitors.

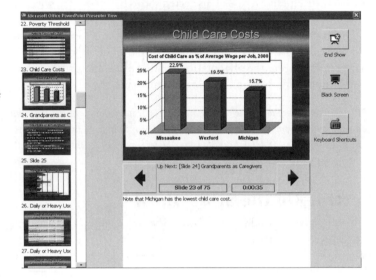

Adjusting Performance

PowerPoint 2003 offers performance settings to help achieve smooth-running presentations when your processor speed may not be up to it. Choose Slide Show ➤ Set Up Show to display the Set Up Show dialog box, shown previously in Figure 7.19. If your video card supports it, enable the check box Use Hardware Graphics Acceleration to improve animation speed. If your presentation is running too slowly, you may want to reduce the resolution. Select a resolution from the Slide Show Resolution list.

NOTE   If reducing the resolution causes the slide image to shift, return the resolution to Use Current Resolution or choose another resolution from the Slide Show Resolution list.

When you've finished adjusting show settings, click OK to close the Set Up Show dialog box and save the slide show settings with the presentation.

IMPROVING SLIDE SHOW PERFORMANCE

Technical problems are the last thing you need during a big presentation. Plan to spend at least an hour setting up and testing your equipment before the audience enters the room. In a perfect world, you should test everything a day before the presentation and again just before show time. Ah … would that it were a perfect world!

Continued on next page

IMPROVING SLIDE SHOW PERFORMANCE *(continued)*

PROJECTOR RESOLUTION IS FUZZY

Ideally, the resolution on the computer should match the resolution of the projector. Adjust computer resolution in the Settings tab of the Display Properties dialog box (right-click the Windows Desktop and choose Properties) or use the Set Up Show dialog box to choose a different resolution for the show (Slide Show ➢ Set Up Show). With some laptops, you may have to disable the display to get ideal resolution from the projector.

NOTHING APPEARS ON THE PROJECTION SCREEN

If there's no light or sound from the projector, check the simple things: Is it plugged in? Is the power strip turned on? Is the projector turned on? Is the bulb good? Is the lens cap off?

If you have power and light but still no image from the computer, check the following: Is the laptop toggled so that the video port is active? Are cables plugged in correctly and securely? Have you tried turning both machines off and back on? (Turn the projector on first, then the computer.)

PRESENTATION RUNS TOO SLOWLY; ANIMATIONS ARE CHOPPY

Enable graphics acceleration and/or choose a lower resolution in the Set Up Show dialog box. You can also set color depth to 16-bit to get the best performance. (Use the Settings tab of the Display Properties dialog box; use the Control Panel to get there.) You might also consider compressing pictures in the presentation.

PRESENTATION STILL RUNS TOO SLOWLY

Resize animated pictures so that they are smaller. Use less "exciting" transitions and animations. Fading, spinning, spiraling, and scaling are resource hogs. Use Fly, Wipe, Dissolve, and other basic effects instead. Use fewer simultaneous animations, and reduce the number of by-word and by-letter animations.

Displaying the Slide Show

Choose Slide Show ➢ View Show or press F5 to start the presentation. To advance to the next slide or animation, click anywhere on the slide background, or if you're using a keyboard, press Enter, Page Down, down-arrow, or N.

Right-click anywhere on the slide to open the shortcut menu.

The shortcut menu provides additional options for navigating through your presentation. From the menu, you can move to the previous or next slide. To move to a specific slide, choose Go To Slide and choose the slide you want to display, as shown in Figure 7.21.

FIGURE 7.21

Use the shortcut menu to move to a specific slide in Slide Show view.

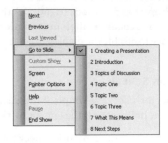

Online Presentations

With Microsoft Windows Media Services and Online Presentation Broadcasting, you can show a presentation over a TCP/IP network or the Internet. Members of the audience view the presentation on their computers. You can schedule the meeting in advance either by phoning participants or by using Microsoft Outlook to schedule the meeting. During the presentation, you can take complete control while audience members watch (or you can use online collaboration, allowing participants to make changes to the presentation). For more about Online Presentation Broadcasting, see Chapter 11, "Creating and Modifying Documents for the Web." For more about collaborating on PowerPoint presentations see Chapter 8, "Collaborating on Documents."

Drawing on Slides

During the slide show, you can underline or circle an object or text to make a point, check off points that have been discussed, or use lines to connect related points on-screen. Press Ctrl+P, or choose Pointer Options from the shortcut menu, to turn the mouse pointer into a Ballpoint Pen, Felt Tip Pen, or Highlighter. Select the desired pen type from the list and drag the pointer to draw on the current slide.

NOTE   If you have a Tablet PC, you can use the tablet pen to add ink to the slides during a presentation.

You can change the color of the pen tool (but not the pen type) before you begin a presentation by choosing Slide Show ➢ Set Up Show from the menu. Select a color from the drop-down list. You can also change pen colors during your presentation. In Slide Show view, right-click and choose Pointer Options ➢ Ink Color from the shortcut menu or move the pointer to the lower left of the screen and click the pointer arrow to select a type of pen, the ink color, the highlighter, arrow, and erasing options.

TIP   The Slide Show toolbar contains the Previous and Next buttons as well as two buttons that display menu commands for common tasks: the pointer arrow to access pen options and the slide navigator to navigate between the slides in your presentation.

If you discover that you've made a mistake after you have drawn on the screen, you can erase what you've drawn. Right-click the slide and choose Pointer Options again but this time choose Eraser. The eraser works just like a pen—just drag over what you want to erase.

To turn the pen off, choose Arrow from the shortcut menu, or press Ctrl+A. When you end the presentation, PowerPoint gives you the option to discard or save the ink annotations you made. When you choose to not save the drawing, no changes are made to the slide.

TIP   If members of the audience (or you) want a hard copy of a slide that's been illustrated with the pen, hold Alt and press Print Screen to copy the slide and drawing to the Clipboard. After the presentation, paste the image from the Clipboard into a Word document. To capture up to a dozen illustrated slides during a presentation, open the Office Clipboard before starting the presentation. Screen shots captured with Alt+Print Screen are copied to the Office Clipboard if it is already open.

Packing a Presentation for CD

New!   If you've ever tried to transfer a PowerPoint presentation from one computer to another, you've experienced the pain of finding out your file is too large to go on a floppy disk. Although the increase in the number of CD writers has made life easier, you have to assume the recipient has PowerPoint and knows how to run a presentation. Well, PowerPoint 2003 has made life a whole lot easier with the introduction of its Package for CD feature. This new tool copies a presentation to a CD, but it doesn't stop there. You can copy multiple presentations and set them up to play automatically and in a specified order, using the PowerPoint viewer. That means you can run them on a machine that doesn't even have PowerPoint. You can also set it up so the recipient can choose in which order to play the presentations. If you are not ready to put the package on a CD, you can write the files to a folder location and even add support documents that are not PowerPoint presentations. Here are the steps for creating your own CD package:

1. Choose File ➤ Package For CD.

2. In the Package For CD dialog box, shown in Figure 7.22, enter a name for the CD. You are limited to 16 characters, so be clear but brief.

FIGURE 7.22

In the Package For CD dialog box, you can add files, access options, and choose to copy the package to CD or a folder location.

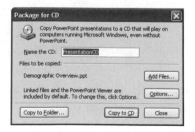

3. Click Add Files to add presentations and other files to the package. The open presentation is added automatically. If you are including only one presentation, you can skip to step 4.

4. Select a file and click the up-arrows and down-arrows in the Package For CD dialog box, shown in Figure 7.23, to change the order of the file, or click Remove to remove a file from the package.

FIGURE 7.23

After adding files, you can change the order of the presentations in the Package For CD dialog box.

5. Click the Options button to determine how you want the presentation(s) to play. In the Options dialog box, shown in Figure 7.24, you can choose to include the PowerPoint viewer by leaving the PowerPoint Viewer check box checked.

FIGURE 7.24

In the Options dialog box, you can set how you want the presentations to play, whether to include linked files and embedded fonts, and set passwords.

6. If you choose to include the PowerPoint Viewer, click the Select How Presentations Will Play In The Viewer drop-down list to choose between the following:

◆ Play All Presentations Automatically In The Specified Order. With this option, as soon as the CD loads in the drive, the PowerPoint viewer launches and plays the presentations one after another.

◆ Play Only The First Presentation Automatically. After the first presentation completes, the Microsoft Office PowerPoint Viewer dialog box opens and lets the user select another presentation.

◆ Let The User Select Which Presentation To View. As soon as the CD loads in the drive, Microsoft Office PowerPoint Viewer dialog box opens and lets the user select a presentation to run.

◆ Don't Play The CD Automatically. The CD does nothing until the user opens it in My Computer and opens a file.

7. Choose to include Linked Files by leaving the Linked Files check box selected. With this option, any documents, such as an Excel worksheet that is linked to a slide, are also included in the CD package.

8. To assure that the recipient has the fonts you carefully selected to make your presentation beautiful, select the Embed TrueType Fonts check box. If you leave this unchecked, Windows might replace a font it doesn't have with something pretty unattractive. If you are using anything out of the ordinary, it's generally best to include them.

9. If this is confidential material, you can include a password to open and a password to modify the files. If you do this, be sure the recipient knows the password to open or they won't be able to get much further. A password to modify will prevent a user from making changes to your work and repackaging it to send it out under their moniker.

10. Click OK to close the Options dialog box.

11. When you are ready with a brand new CD in your CD writer drive, click the Copy To CD button. If any of your presentations contain comments, revisions, or ink annotations, you'll be prompted about whether you want to continue. You may not want an important client to see you've raised the price by 20 percent in the last few days. If you choose *No*, you can make corrections to the presentation and start over with packaging it for CD. If you say *Yes*, the copying process begins.

12. When the CD package is complete, the CD ejects from the drive and you are prompted about whether you want to create another. Saying *Yes* gives you a chance to insert another CD before writing the second one. If you say *No*, you are returned to the Package For CD dialog box.

13. To make a backup copy for yourself of the CD you prepared, or if you are not ready to cut the CD yet, click the Copy To Folder button.

14. This prompts you for a folder name and location. Enter those and click OK to copy the presentations and other files to a folder at the specified location.

15. Click Close to close the Package For CD dialog box.

After you package a CD, it's a good idea to play it yourself to make sure everything works as expected. If you instructed it to play automatically, it should start up by itself, load the PowerPoint Viewer, and start the presentation. The first time you run the PowerPoint Viewer, you are asked to accept the license agreement before continuing. Your recipients will get this same prompt, so you might want to prepare them for it.

If you set the options for users to decide in which order they want to play the presentations, be sure to let them know what to expect and how to select the presentation they want to view.

And that's all there is to it. The only other thing you might want to do is design a cool label to go on the CD. You'll find some great, easy-to-use templates on Microsoft Office Online. Just open Word and, from the New Documents task pane, choose Templates on Office Online. Search for "CD Cover" to find jewel case covers and face labels. Of course, you'll probably have to buy the CD covers and labels but it's worth it to make your presentation package one your clients will remember.

Chapter 8

Collaborating on Documents

COLLABORATION IS THE BUZZWORD of the new millennium. If you aren't working together to accomplish your objectives, you are probably not making the best use of your organization's resources and talents. In Office 2003, collaboration is a central theme. Everywhere you look in Office 2003, you can find tools that make collaboration easier. From fundamental tools such as revision tracking in Word to elaborate tools such as Windows SharePoint Services, you can work with others on documents, workbooks, and presentations. You can schedule and hold online meetings, share contacts and calendars, and create complex document libraries for any member of your team to access.

In this chapter, we'll examine sharing and tracking changes in Word, Excel, and PowerPoint documents. Then we'll see how to take revision tracking and all kinds of other collaborative activities to the next level with Windows SharePoint Services.

- ◆ Sharing Word documents and Excel workbooks
- ◆ Revising shared documents
- ◆ Reviewing and commenting on PowerPoint presentations
- ◆ Discussing documents with others over a network or the Web
- ◆ Creating ad hoc team websites with Windows SharePoint Services
- ◆ Creating Documents Workspaces
- ◆ Creating Meeting Workspaces
- ◆ Sharing contacts, tasks, and events
- ◆ Creating SharePoint Services lists from Excel data

Saving Versions of Word Documents

Word, Excel, and PowerPoint each include features that are designed for multiple reviewers. These features, including Versions, Tracking Changes, and Comments, make it possible to incorporate new ideas with an understanding of where they came from and, if necessary, to restore earlier work without having to re-create it. In this section, we'll discuss Versions and then move on to Tracking Changes and Comments.

When working with others, you will find that one of Word's most useful features is its capability to save multiple versions of a document. For example, if you are sending an online document to be reviewed by team members or supervisors, you can save the original version, and then save the version that includes the changes suggested by reviewers.

NOTE   *In case you are wondering, versioning is only available in Word.*

Prior to versioning, if you wanted to change and save a document and keep the original intact, you had to remember to open it as a read-only copy or, more often than not, remember to save the revised document using a different filename. If you're like most people, there were those inevitable times when you saved without thinking and, with one click of the mouse, wiped out any vestige of the original document. Word's versioning feature allows you to save multiple versions of a document within the document itself and open a different version to edit.

NOTE   *Word saves only the changes that were made to the document, not the entire document, when you save a version.*

To save a version of the active document, follow these steps:

1. Choose File ➢ Versions to open the Versions In [*Document*] dialog box, shown in Figure 8.1. Previous versions (if any) appear in the list box with information about each saved version. (More on this below.)

FIGURE 8.1

If you've saved previous versions of a document, they appear in the Versions In [*Document*] dialog box.

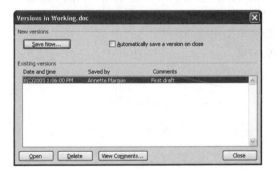

2. Click Save Now to open the Save Version dialog box. The date, time, and name of the person creating this version are displayed at the top of the dialog box.

3. Type any comments you want to make about this version of the document in the Comments On Version text box.

4. Click OK. The Versions icon appears on the right side of the status bar to let users know that this document contains a version.

Word can automatically save a version of the document each time it is closed. This feature is useful if you need to keep track of who made changes to the document and when they were made. The most recently saved version of the document displays by default the next time you open the file.

Word also allows you to manage the versions in other ways. For example, you can see how many versions of the document have been saved, the date and time each was saved, and the name of the person who created each version. The most recent version appears highlighted at the top of the list in the Versions dialog box.

Any existing version can be saved to a separate file. When the version is in a separate file, you can make sure that the reviewers are evaluating the most recent version (by circulating only that version), or you can compare it to another file to find changes that were made with Track Changes (discussed later in this chapter) turned off. You can also delete a saved version, which is useful when your file becomes large and seems to open and navigate more slowly.

WARNING *When you save a document as a web page (see Chapter 11, "Creating and Modifying Documents for the Web"), any versions it contains are lost. Save the file as a regular document before you save it as a web page, and use the document file to create any subsequent versions.*

Use the following options to manage your versions and the size of the file:

1. Choose File ➤ Versions to display the Versions In [*Document*] dialog box, shown previously in Figure 8.1.

2. Check the Automatically Save A Version On Close check box to have Word save the document each time the file is closed.

3. Click Save Now to display the Save Version dialog box (shown in Figure 8.2) if you want to save the current version of the file. Alternatively, highlight the version you want to manage, and then use any of the following options:

   Open Opens the selected version in another window on your screen. (The document is also open and appears in its own window.)

   Delete Deletes the selected version when you no longer need it. After selecting this option, click Yes in the message box that appears to confirm the deletion.

   View Comments Displays a message box containing all of the comments that were entered by the reviewer when the selected version was saved (see "Adding Your Two Cents through a Comment" later in this chapter).

4. If necessary, click Close to return to your document.

FIGURE 8.2

In the Save Version dialog box, you can enter comments to identify the details of the version you are saving.

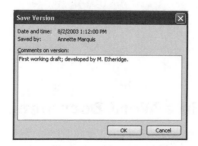

NOTE   *When you delete a version of a document, you're only marking it for deletion. The version isn't deleted until you save the document.*

Tracking Changes in Documents, Worksheets, and Presentations

The most powerful document-based collaboration tool is the Track Changes feature, available in various forms in Word, Excel, and PowerPoint. With this feature, you can make revisions to your heart's content and then in a single motion accept them or reject them all. You can also review each one and choose whether to accept or reject the change. When you distribute a document in which you've activated Track Changes, you are able to maintain a record of every insertion, deletion, and move, including who made the change and when it was made.

Figure 8.3 shows a Word document that has been revised with revision tracking turned on. Word gives you several options for how you'd like revised text to appear. In this example, inserted text is underlined, and deleted text is crossed out. Revision tracking also assigns each author a different color so it's evident at first glance that revisions were made by different people. Pointing to any revision shows a screen tip with the reviser's identity, the date and time of the revision, and what was done.

FIGURE 8.3

With revision tracking active, you can immediately see what text was revised and, by pointing to the text, find out the identity of the reviser.

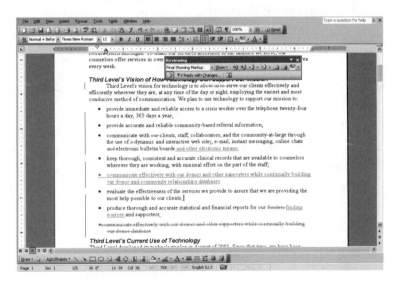

Because of the difference in revision tracking in Word, Excel, and PowerPoint, we'll focus here on one application at a time.

Tracking Changes in a Word Document

Although saving each version of a Word document is helpful, it can still be difficult to identify where all the changes were made. To make that easier, Word can track each change to a document and indicate those changes on the screen. You can even choose to print them when you print the document.

To preserve document layout, Word now shows some of the changes inline and others in balloons in the margin of the document. Depending on the options you choose, inline changes, such as newly inserted text, can appear both underlined and in a different color; deleted text may appear with a strikethrough character through it and in a different color. In all cases, a vertical line in the outside margin indicates each line in the document where text has been changed.

NOTE *You must be in Print Layout or Web Layout view to see tracked changes in balloons.*

You can easily access all of the Reviewing tools from Word's Reviewing toolbar, shown in Figure 8.4. To display the toolbar, right-click any toolbar and then choose Reviewing.

FIGURE 8.4

The Reviewing toolbar has tools to assist in reviewing and tracking changes.

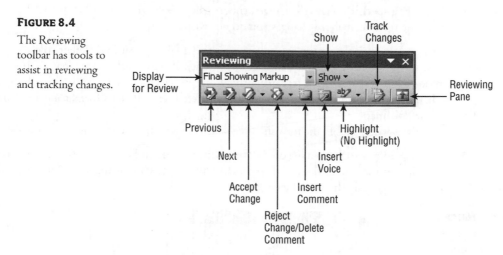

To begin tracking changes, use one of the following methods to enable the feature:

- ◆ Click the Track Changes button on the Reviewing toolbar. The button is a toggle switch, so you can click it again to turn off the Track Changes feature.

- ◆ Double-click the dimmed TRK option on the status bar or right-click it and select Track Changes. This option is also a toggle switch, so you use the same method to turn off Track Changes when you are finished editing the document.

- ◆ Choose Tools ➤ Track Changes from the menu.

By default, each user's changes are visible. If a number of changes are made to the same section of a document, it gets pretty difficult to tell what text the document really includes. You can modify the tracking feature so that only formatting changes are visible, only insertions and deletions are visible, comments are not visible, or changes for a specific reviewer are visible and others are hidden. To do so, follow these steps:

1. Click the Show drop-down list on the Reviewing toolbar.

2. Hide comments, insertions and deletions, and/or formatting by clicking the appropriate choice to remove the check mark.

3. To select a specific reviewer's changes, choose Show ➢ Reviewers and clear the check marks from the reviewers whose changes you do not wish to see.

As other people open the document, any changes they make appear in different colors (up to eight authors can work on one document before colors repeat). If you would prefer that all inserted text appear in one color and all deleted text in another, you can select a specific color for each. In addition, you can change the way Word indicates inserted and deleted text, changed formatting, or changed lines of text in the document.

Follow these steps to specify the formats and characters you want Word to use when tracking changes:

1. Click the Show drop-down list on the Reviewing toolbar and choose Options, or right-click the TRK icon on the status bar and then choose Options, or choose Tools ➢ Options to display the Track Changes tab, shown in Figure 8.5.

FIGURE 8.5

Display the Track Changes dialog box when you want to modify the way changes to the document appear on screen and in printed copies.

2. Make these choices in the Markup area:

  ◆ Choose an option from the Insertions drop-down list. Select (None), Color Only, Bold, Italic, Underline, Double Underline, or Strikethrough as the format to apply to inserted text.

◆ Select one of these same options as the format to apply to Deletions and one to apply to changes in Formatting.

3. In the Color drop-down lists adjacent to Insertions, Deletions, and Formatting, choose the By Author option to have Word assign a different color to the first eight reviewers who insert text, delete text, or change the formatting applied to the document text. Alternatively, you can assign a particular color to all insertions, all deletions, and all formatting changes.

◆ To indicate lines that are changed, choose Left Border, Right Border, or Outside Border from the Changed Lines drop-down list. Assign a color from the adjacent Color drop-down list.

◆ Choose a color for comments inserted into the document from the Comments drop-down list. You can choose By Author to assign a different color by author or choose a particular color for all comments.

4. In the Balloons area:

◆ From the Use Balloons In Print And Web Layout drop-down list, choose Always to show balloons, Never to disable balloons, or Only for Comments/Formatting if you'd prefer to display comments and formatting changes in balloons and text changes inline in the document.

◆ If you leave balloons enabled, use the spin control to select a Preferred Width and change the Measure In setting to reflect your preferred unit of measurement. Select whether to display the balloons in the right or left margin, and enable or disable the Show Lines Connecting To Text option depending, again, on your preference.

5. To set options for how Word prints with balloons, select a paper orientation from the drop-down list:

Preserve Prints using the orientation specified in the Page Setup dialog box.

Auto Lets Word print using the layout it deems best for the document.

Force Landscape Prints the document in landscape orientation, leaving the most room for balloons

NOTE *These orientation options apply only if you choose Document Showing Markup in the Print dialog box. If you choose to print just the document, the regular page setup settings remain in effect.*

6. Click OK when you have finished adjusting Track Changes options.

To display information about a change, just point to the marked text to see a screen tip that indicates the type of change, who made it, and the time and date it was made.

Choosing a Display for Review

When a document "makes the rounds," it is often examined by people with different purposes in mind. For example, an author is usually interested in seeing changes in relation to how the original text was written. A proofreader needn't see changes at all. In fact, displaying multiple changes might interfere with accurate proofreading. Word allows you to display tracked changes from different points of view. Now it is even easier to review changes prior to accepting or rejecting them.

By default, Word displays Final Showing Markup. Select from the Display For Review drop-down list on the Reviewing toolbar if you wish to see the document from another point of view. Choose from the following options:

Final   Shows how the document will look if you accept all changes.

Original   Shows how the document will look if you reject all changes.

Final Showing Markup   Displays deleted text in balloons and inserted text inline. Changes to formatting are visible. With this display, you can easily review suggested insertions because they are displayed inline.

Original Showing Markup   Leaves deletions inline and displays insertions and changes to formatting in balloons. Authors generally prefer this display for easy review of proposed changes.

Working with Changes in the Reviewing Pane

There may be times when you prefer to view a list of changes outside of the document text. Word's Reviewing pane allows you to do just that! Simply click the Reviewing Pane button on the Reviewing toolbar or click Show ➢ Reviewing Pane to display the pane below the horizontal scroll bar, as shown in Figure 8.6.

FIGURE 8.6

The Reviewing pane allows you to view and modify changes outside of the document text.

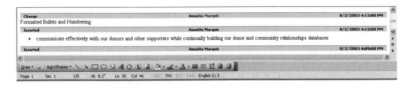

Six different sections in the Reviewing pane separate changes made to different parts of the document. Scroll the pane to see Main Document Changes And Comments, Header and Footer Changes, Text Box Changes, Header and Footer Text Box Changes, Footnote Changes, and Endnote Changes. If no changes have been made to a particular part, Word displays *None*.

You can adjust changes directly in the Reviewing pane if you wish. To do so, follow these steps:

1. Scroll to the change you wish to modify.

2. Click once in the pane to activate it, and then click again to place the insertion point.

3. Select, delete, insert, and format text as desired.

The Reviewing Pane button is a toggle. To hide the Reviewing pane, simply click the button again.

Accepting or Rejecting Changes

After everyone else has had a crack at the document, you, as the document's originator, still have the final word—you can decide which changes to accept and which ones to reject. Here are your options on the Reviewing toolbar:

- ◆ (*a*) and (*b*): To navigate through the document, click the Previous button to select the change preceding the position of the insertion point, or the Next button to select the change following the position of the insertion point.

NOTE *If the Reviewing pane is turned on, the Previous and Next buttons automatically scroll the pane as needed.*

- ◆ (*c*) and (*d*): Click the Accept Change button to agree to the selected change, or the Reject Change button to remove the proposed change and return the document to its original text in this instance.

- ◆ To accept all changes to a document, click the drop-down arrow next to the Accept Changes button and choose Accept All Changes In Document.

- ◆ To reject all changes in a document, click the drop-down arrow next to the Reject Changes button and choose Reject All Changes In Document.

- ◆ If you've chosen not to display certain tracked changes—turned off formatting changes under the Show menu, for example—you can choose Accept All Changes Shown or Reject All Changes Shown from the drop-down lists on the Accept and Reject buttons. Only changes you have chosen to display are affected.

TIP *Click the Undo button on the Standard toolbar immediately after accepting or rejecting a change to return to the original edit.*

Printing Tracked Changes

You can choose to print a document showing tracked changes and comments (for more about Comments, see the section, "Adding Your Two Cents through a Comment," later in this chapter). Or you can print the list of changes without the document text. In either case, choose File ➤ Print to display the Print dialog box.

If you want to print the document showing comments and tracked changes, choose Document Showing Markup in the Print What drop-down list. Word adjusts the zoom level and page orientation as needed to display changes on the printed page.

To see a list of changes and comments, choose List Of Markup from the Print What drop-down list in the Print dialog box. The document changes and comments are printed consecutively along with the number of the page on which the comment is located.

Collaborating on Excel Workbooks

Collaborating on Excel workbooks allows multiple users to make changes to a workbook simultaneously and then merge the changes to produce the final product. Before you can track changes in Excel, you must share the workbook.

Sharing allows more than one user to access a workbook at the same time. Tracking stores information about workbook changes by user. In this way, sharing and tracking are intertwined. You can track changes only in a shared workbook; tracked changes are kept for a duration that you set in the Share Workbook dialog box.

Sharing Workbooks

If you want others to be able to use a workbook while you have it open, you need to share the workbook and ensure that it is stored on a shared drive that other users can access. Choose Tools ➢ Share Workbook from the menu to open the Share Workbook dialog box.

By default, the current user has exclusive rights to a workbook. On the Editing tab, enable the Allow Changes check box to make the file accessible to other users. Then move to the Advanced tab to set options for tracking changes and resolving conflicts explained in the next sections.

If you choose to track changes in a *change history*, select the number of days the change history should be kept.

TIP   You can track changes only in shared workbooks. To use the tracking feature on workbooks that only you use, password-protect the shared workbook and don't give anyone the password.

Whether you track changes or not, you need to set when changes are updated. The default is to update changes only when the file is saved. This means that each time you (or another user) save, Excel will save your changes and update your workbook with changes made by other users. You can choose to have your workbook updated Automatically every set number of minutes; if you then choose the Save My Changes option, your changes will be saved when the update occurs. If you update changes Automatically, other users still won't see your changes until you save—unless they also choose to see saved changes Automatically rather than waiting until they save.

When two or more users make different changes in the same cell, it causes a conflict. Set the Conflicting Changes option to indicate how conflicts should be resolved. Excel can prompt you to resolve conflicts or automatically accept the saved changes.

The Personal view contains your print and filter settings for the workbook. These settings do not affect other users' view of the workbook. Use the check boxes to include or exclude these settings when the workbook is saved.

When you close the dialog box, Excel will prompt you to save the workbook. If you return to the Shared Workbook dialog box, you'll notice that you no longer have the workbook open exclusively, because other Excel users can now open it.

TRACKING AND UPDATING CHANGES

When you track changes in a workbook, Excel notes each change in each workbook cell. Display the changes by choosing Tools ➤ Track Changes ➤ Highlight Changes and enabling Track Changes While Editing.

When tracking is enabled, a changed cell has a cell indicator in the upper-left corner, color-coded by user. Hover over the cell, and Excel displays a screen tip to show you the changes that have been made.

6/2/2001	6/4/2001	**Annette Marquis, 8/3/2003 12:51 PM:**	
6/2/2001	6/7/2003	Changed cell R27 from '6/6/2001' to '6/7/2003'.	
6/2/2001	6/5/2001		
6/2/2001	6/5/2001		
6/13/2001	6/11/2001		
6/13/2001	6/11/2001		

Working in a Shared Workbook

When Highlight Changes is enabled, each change made is noted in a comment, and changed cells are flagged with a cell indicator in the upper-left corner. Excel assigns a different triangle color to each user who modifies the workbook, so you can visually inspect the workbook to find all the changes made by one user. When you save the workbook, you accept the changes, so the triangle and comment disappear.

Some Excel features aren't available in shared workbooks. For example, while a workbook is shared, you can't do any of the following:

- Delete worksheets

- Add or apply conditional formatting and data validation

- Insert or delete ranges of cells (you can still insert and delete individual cells, rows, and columns), charts, hyperlinks, or other objects (including those created with Draw)

- Group or outline data

However, you can use the features before you share a workbook, or you can temporarily unshare the workbook, make changes, and then turn sharing on again. See Excel's Online Help for the complete list of limitations of shared workbooks.

WARNING   If you unshare a workbook, it cannot be merged with other copies of the shared workbook. For more information, see the section, "Merging Workbook Changes," later in this chapter.

RESOLVING CONFLICTS

If changes you are saving conflict with changes saved by another user, you'll be prompted to resolve the conflict (unless you changed the Conflicting Changes setting in the Advanced tab of the Share Workbook dialog box). In the Resolve Conflict dialog box, you can review each change individually and accept your change or others' changes, or accept/reject changes in bulk.

VIEWING THE CHANGE HISTORY

You can examine all the changes that have been saved in a workbook since you turned on the change history. Choose Tools ➢ Track Changes ➢ Highlight Changes to open the Highlight Changes dialog box.

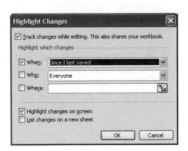

In the dialog box, select the time period for the changes you want to review, and specify the users whose changes you want to see. If you only want to see changes for a particular range or sheet, select the range you want to view. You can view the changes on screen or on a separate worksheet in the workbook.

When you view the change history on a separate worksheet, you can filter the changes to find changes made by different users or on specific dates. When you remove a workbook from shared use, the change history is turned off and reset. If you want to keep the changes, select the information on the History worksheet and copy it to another worksheet before unsharing the workbook.

Accepting or Rejecting Changes

You can review a workbook and accept or reject changes in bulk or individually as you do in Microsoft Word. To begin reviewing, choose Tools ➤ Track Changes ➤ Accept Or Reject Changes to open the Select Changes To Accept Or Reject dialog box.

Specify the time period, users, and cell range you wish to review. If you don't specify a range, you'll review the entire workbook. Click OK to open the Accept Or Reject Changes dialog box.

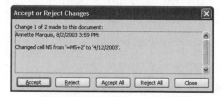

To accept or reject all changes, click the Accept All or Reject All button. To accept or reject a specific change, select the change and then click the Accept or Reject button. Click Close when you are finished reviewing changes.

Merging Workbook Changes

If you anticipate many conflicting changes in a shared workbook, or if you want users to be able to make changes independently and then review all changes at once, make and distribute copies of the shared workbook. To create the copies, use Save As and give each copy of the workbook a different name. Then you can merge the copies when users are done with their changes. You can merge only those workbooks that have the same change history, so it's important that none of the users turns off sharing while using the workbook (see the sidebar "Protecting Workbooks for Merging"). The history must be complete when you merge the workbooks.

If, for example, you set the number of days for the history at 30 days and users keep the workbooks for 32 days, you won't be able to merge the workbooks. Before you make copies of the shared workbook, make sure you set the history to allow enough time for changes and merging. If you're uncertain, set the history to 1000 days or an equally ridiculous length of time.

Follow these steps to merge shared workbooks:

1. Open your copy of the shared workbook that you want to merge changes into.

2. Choose Tools ➤ Compare And Merge Workbooks. If you haven't saved your copy of the workbook, you'll be prompted to do so.

3. In the Select Files To Merge Into Current Workbook dialog box, choose the copy (or copies) of the shared workbook containing the changes you wish to merge. Click OK.

PROTECTING WORKBOOKS FOR MERGING

To prevent users from turning off sharing or changing the change history, password-protect the workbook before sharing and distributing it. Here are the steps to follow:

1. Choose Tools ➢ Share Workbook to open the Share Workbook dialog box.

2. Select the Editing tab and make sure the Allow Changes By More Than One User At The Same Time check box is enabled.

3. On the Advanced tab, select Keep Change History For, and enter a number of days that vastly exceeds the number of days the workbooks will be shared. If you're not sure, enter 1000. Set any other options you wish on the Advanced tab.

4. On the Editing tab, turn the Allow Changes check box back off so the workbook is not shared. Click OK.

5. Choose Tools ➢ Protection ➢ Protect And Share Workbook.

6. Enable the Sharing With Track Changes check box.

7. Type a password in the Password text box.

8. Reenter the password when prompted.

9. Close all open dialog boxes. You might be prompted to save the workbook again.

Getting Feedback on Your Presentation from Your Workgroup

Most of us wouldn't deliver new sales materials to a client without first having a colleague proofread them. Nor should you give a presentation that hasn't been scrutinized by someone else whose opinion you trust. There's nothing quite like the feeling you get when you and a few hundred of your closest friends notice a spelling or grammatical error projected in five-foot-high letters in an auditorium.

The people who proof your presentation don't have to be in the next office. They could be anywhere in the world! Attach your PowerPoint presentation to an e-mail message so others' comments can be added, or use online collaboration, where you actually build your presentation with the help of a person or team at another location. Either way, you're getting suggestions from a second or third person as you're polishing your presentation.

Incorporating Feedback into a PowerPoint Presentation

PowerPoint 2003 now offers the same robust reviewing features as Word, although there is a slightly different process for working with them. When you send a presentation for review (see the "Sending Documents, Workbooks, and Presentations for Review" section later in this chapter), PowerPoint tracks changes in content, color schemes, animation settings, transitions, layout, formatting of text and objects, and much more.

When you receive a file with a reviewer's changes, do one of the following to display those changes in your original presentation:

◆ If you used Outlook to send the presentation for review, open the message and double-click the attachment. Click Yes when Outlook displays a message box prompting you to merge changes.

♦ If you used any other means for distributing the presentation to reviewers, open the original presentation and then click Tools ➤ Compare And Merge Presentations to display a dialog box where you must locate and select the reviewer's file. Click Merge.

PowerPoint 2003 displays markers next to the slide objects that have been changed. Point to a marker to see the reviewer's name and a description of the change. Use the Previous Item and Next Item buttons on the Reviewing toolbar to browse markers in a presentation.

For each marker you see, decide whether to keep or discard the reviewer's changes. Click the Apply button on the Reviewing toolbar to keep the selected change, or click Unapply to reject it. The drop-down lists on these buttons offer options for applying/unapplying all changes to a particular slide or all changes in the active presentation. After you have chosen Apply or Unapply, you may wish to delete a change marker. To do so, click it and press Delete on the keyboard.

WARNING *Be sure to address the change marker by clicking Apply or Unapply before deleting it.*

Click the Reviewers button if you wish to review changes by one or more particular reviewers. Disable the check boxes next to the reviewers whose changes you don't want to see.

The Revisions Pane button toggles the Revisions task pane on and off. If you prefer to see changes and comments in a list, as shown in Figure 8.7, turn it on. You can select reviewers, browse changes, and apply and reject changes in the Revisions pane.

FIGURE 8.7

The Revisions pane shows tracked changes in list format color-coded by reviewer.

Click a list item to see details about its changes.

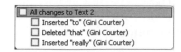

Enable a check box to apply a change. Clear a check box to unapply it. Apply all changes to an object by enabling All Changes To [*object name*]. If you prefer to see miniatures of slides with changes, select the Gallery tab in the Revisions pane. Click the slide miniature to toggle between the original slide and the revised slide.

TIP   *When you're finished looking at changes for a particular reviewer, switch to the Gallery tab of the Revisions pane, locate a miniature slide with changes from that reviewer, and then click the Down arrow on that slide and choose Done With This Reviewer.*

ENDING A REVIEW CYCLE

As soon as you combine a reviewed presentation with your original, an End Review button appears on the Reviewing toolbar. Click it when you are finished reviewing file modifications.

Confirm the end-review command in the message box, keeping in mind the following:

◆   You can no longer combine reviewed presentations with the original.

◆   Any unapplied changes remain unapplied, and you can't view them again.

If you have applied (or unapplied) all reviewer modifications, deleted all change markers, and saved your presentation, PowerPoint ends the review automatically.

Adding Your Two Cents through a Comment

Comments provide another way for reviewers to add input to a document, workbook, or presentation without directly impacting the content. Comments can be used separate from or in combination with revision tracking. You can enter comments in Word documents, in Excel worksheets, and in PowerPoint presentations. Comments are an effective way of communicating with team members about something in a document, reminding you of work left to be finished, and documenting the purpose of a document.

When thinking about how you might use comments, it's important to note that comments aren't part of the printed document but can be viewed on screen. You can insert comments, view comments from one or all reviewers, and print the comments. In Word, you can even insert and play back voice comments.

Making Comments in Word

When you insert a comment in Word, a comment indicator appears at the insertion point and displays the text of the comment in a balloon. If you are in Normal view, balloons are not visible, so the Reviewing pane opens instead.

To insert a comment, follow these steps:

1. Position the insertion point where you want to place the comment, and then either click the New Comment button on the Reviewing toolbar or choose Insert ➤ Comment.

2. Type the text of your comment in the Reviewing pane (for Normal view) or directly in the balloon (for Web Layout and Print Layout views).

3. To insert another comment in Normal view, press F6 (which toggles between the document and Reviewing panes) or click in the document pane, and then repeat steps 1 and 2. To insert another comment in any other view, place the insertion point at the appropriate place in the document and repeat steps 1 and 2.

4. Toggle the Reviewing Pane button to hide the comments and other tracked changes in Normal view.

The steps for inserting a voice comment are slightly different, but no more difficult:

1. Place the insertion point at the appropriate location in the document.

2. Click the Insert Voice button to open the Sound Object In [*Document*] dialog box.

NOTE   *If the Insert Voice button is not visible, click the Toolbar Options button (Down arrow) on the Reviewing toolbar and then click Add Or Remove Buttons ➤ Reviewing ➤ Insert Voice*

3. Click the Record button—it's the only one enabled—and then say (or sing, if you are so inclined) your comment.

4. Click the Stop button when you're done commenting.

5. If you wish to rerecord your comment, click the Seek To Start button and repeat steps 4 and 5.

6. When you're finished, click the Close button to close the dialog box.

WARNING   *If you're having trouble rerecording a comment, make note of its position and length as displayed in the dialog box. If you wish to rerecord a comment (rather than just add to it), make sure you speak over the entire position and length of the original sound.*

Text comments are visible in balloons by default in Outline, Web, and Print Layout views. To make them visible in Normal view, or if you've disabled balloons in the Track Changes options, you must display the Reviewing pane. You can hide comments in Print Layout view by choosing Show ➤ Comments on the Reviewing toolbar to remove the check mark.

Voice comments are indicated by the sound icon at the point the voice comment was inserted (or in the appropriate position in the Reviewing pane). Double-click the sound icon to hear a voice comment.

NOTE   *If you can't hear comments on playback, you may need to adjust the volume of your speakers. If sound quality is still poor (or if you can't hear a thing) on a recording you made, check your microphone setup.*

To see information about the comment's author, and the date and time commented, just position the mouse pointer over the comment balloon or sound icon for a moment—the information appears in a box above the text. If you're using the Reviewing pane, this information is automatically displayed with each comment.

NOTE   *Word pulls the author's name from the User Information tab of the Options dialog box. If a generic or unrecognized name is being used for comment information, edit it there.*

You have several choices for editing comments:

◆ Click directly in the balloon and edit the comment there.

◆ Click in the Reviewing pane and edit the comment's text as usual.

◆ To edit a voice comment, right-click the sound icon and choose Sound Recorder Document Object ➢ Edit to display the Sound Object In Status Report dialog box. Click the Record button and say your new comment.

You can browse comments right along with other tracked changes using the Next and Previous buttons on the Reviewing toolbar. After all comments are addressed, you can delete them from the document. You can delete them one at a time, by reviewer, or all at once.

To delete a single comment, do any one of the following:

◆ Click the balloon you wish to delete and click the Reject Change/Delete Comment button on the Reviewing toolbar.

◆ Right-click the balloon you wish to delete and choose Delete Comment from the short-cut menu.

◆ Click the comment you wish to delete in the Reviewing pane and proceed with any of the above three actions.

◆ Select the sound icon of a voice comment and press Delete on the keyboard.

To delete comments by a particular reviewer:

1. Choose Show ➢ Reviewers on the Reviewing toolbar and clear the check boxes for the reviewers with comments you *don't* want to delete.

2. Click the drop-down arrow next to the Reject Change/Delete Comment button and choose Delete All Comments Shown.

To delete *all* comments in a document, click the drop-down arrow next to the Reject Change/Delete Comment button and choose Delete All Comments In Document.

Commenting in Excel

Excel's Comment feature is similar to Word's in many ways. The primary difference is that you are commenting on cells of a worksheet, rather than text. You can insert a comment using the Reviewing toolbar or just right-click and cell and choose Insert Comment. After you type the comment, click outside of the comment to insert it. Excel places a red cell indicator in the top-right corner to mark the cell. Point to cell to make the comment appear.

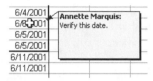

If you'd like the contents of a comment to appear in the onscreen and printed versions of the worksheet, right-click the comment and choose Show/Hide Comments. To hide a comment again, right-click it and choose Hide Comment.

When a comment is visible, it might hide a valuable portion of the worksheet. You can point to the border of the Comment text box and drag it to a better location. The comment's connector line retains its connection to the cell regardless of where you move it.

Comments are a great way to include worksheet instructions for new users or to document the reasoning behind a particular entry. Be creative and you'll probably come up with lots of ways to incorporate comments into your worksheets.

Adding Comments to Presentations

In PowerPoint, reviewers can annotate individual slides with comments. The comments can be hidden, so you can keep the comments with the presentation as you're working on it. Figure 8.8 shows a slide with a comment added in the default comment location.

To add a comment, switch to Normal view and choose Insert ➢ Comment from the menu bar. The Reviewing toolbar and a comment text box open. Your name appears at the top of the comment. Begin typing, and the comment appears in the text box. Comments are not visible in Slide Show view.

FIGURE 8.8

A slide with a reviewer's comment

Slide comments in PowerPoint 2003 are indicated by *markers*, small boxes with the reviewer's initials and a comment number, similar to the reviewing comments discussed earlier. Point to a marker to see the text of a comment. Click a marker to display the comment until your next click.

You can place more than one comment on a slide. To insert another comment, click the Insert Comment button on the Reviewing toolbar. Click the Show/Hide Markup button on the Reviewing toolbar to display or hide all comments in the presentation. Hidden comments are hidden in all views. Use the comment's handles to move or resize the comment as you would any other text box. Modify the text of a comment by clicking the Edit Comment button on the Reviewing toolbar or right-clicking the comment and choosing Edit Comment.

You can delete each comment as you address it. Simply click at the edge of the comment to activate the frame and press Delete, or click the Delete Comment button on the Reviewing toolbar. If you want to keep the comments (perhaps for future enhancements to the presentation), you can either hide them or move them out of the display area if they are interfering with your work (i.e., drag comment markers into the gray background area of Normal view).

Sending Documents, Workbooks, and Presentations for Review

Being connected to your colleagues—by a local or wide-area network, or through electronic mail—makes sharing and exchanging documents a snap. With Office, you dispatch a document by sending it for review or you can route it from one reviewer to another.

Sending Files for Review

When you're satisfied with the first draft of the document, workbook, or presentation, you are ready to send it to your reviewer(s). If you want to send the document to multiple reviewers all at once, or if you just want to send it to one person, you can use the Send For Review feature. Office produces an e-mail message with the file attached. Because the Reviewing toolbar and revision tracking are already turned on, even reviewers unfamiliar with those features should be able to make their changes and return the document to you. If you have concerns, it's not a bad idea to include explicit instructions in the body of the message about how to return the document after they have finished reviewing it.

NOTE   *When you wish to send a document to a list of reviewers one at a time and in order, use the Routing features discussed in the next section.*

To send a document for review, choose File ➤ Send To ➤ Mail Recipient (For Review). Then follow these steps:

1. Address the message as you normally would.

2. Change the subject and message text if you wish.

3. Click Send.

WARNING   *When you send a document for review, be sure to consider what protection you want on the document. Using Protection (Tools ➤ Protect Document in Word, Tools ➤ Protection in Excel, or Tools ➤ Options ➤ Security in PowerPoint) to control what kind of changes reviewers can make and/or the new Information Rights Manager to restrict access to specific people. For more about protection and rights, refer to Chapter 12, "Securing and Organizing Documents."*

When the recipient opens the attachment, the Reviewing toolbar is already in place. After the reviewers make their changes, they can follow the same procedure to return the document to you. When you've decided to end the review cycle, click the End Review button (it's visible only when a document is sent using the above procedure) on the Reviewing toolbar. Confirm your decision in the message box and click OK.

TURNING OFF REVISION TRACKING

When you are ready, turn off revision tracking on the document. In Word, double-click the TRK icon on the status bar. In Excel, choose Tools ➢ Track Changes ➢ Highlight Changes and clear the Highlight Changes In Document check box. In PowerPoint, you're all set unless you use Compare and Merge to merge in another presentation.

Using a Routing Slip

Word includes a routing slip feature, which specifies how to send an outbound document to reviewers. The routing slip can dispatch a document in either of the following ways:

◆ Use a routing slip to send a copy of the document simultaneously to all reviewers.

◆ Use a routing slip to send the same document to each reviewer, one at a time, in the order you specify so that subsequent reviewers can see the changes proposed by earlier reviewers. You can keep track of the location of the document when it is routed this way.

The routing slip can be saved with your document. A routed document is sent as an attachment to an e-mail message.

Routing requires a MAPI-compliant e-mail program, such as Outlook or Outlook Express, or a VIM-compatible program such as Lotus cc:Mail.

To attach a routing slip to a document, follow these steps:

1. Choose File ➢ Send To ➢ Routing Recipient to display the Routing Slip dialog box shown in Figure 8.9.

FIGURE 8.9

Use the options in the Routing Slip dialog box to send a document as an e-mail attachment to reviewers.

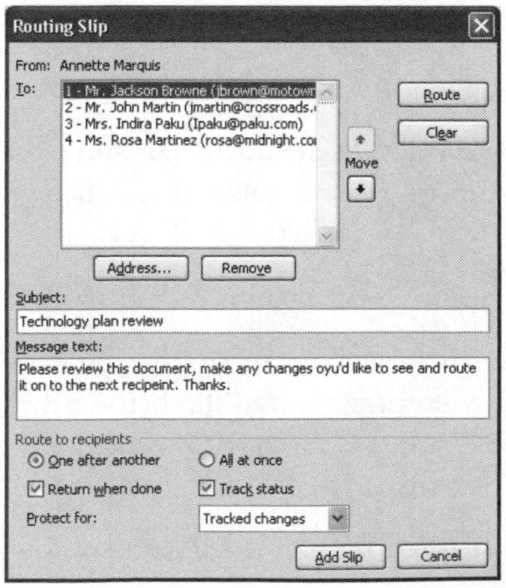

NOTE   *If you use Outlook, you may be prompted to authorize access to your Outlook address book for a specific length of time. This is a security measure to protect against unauthorized access by malicious code, such as viruses, worms, and Trojan horses.*

2. Click the Address button to display your e-mail system's address book. Highlight the name of a reviewer, and then choose To to place the name in the Message Recipients list box. Choose the name of each reviewer in this way, and then click OK to return to the Routing Slip dialog box. Each name you selected appears in the To list box.

3. Type a subject for the e-mail message in the Subject text box. By default Word uses the word *Routing* followed by a colon and the title as entered in the document's properties (File ➤ Properties).

4. Type the e-mail message to send with the attached document in the Message Text box.

5. Choose one of the following options to specify how the document is to be routed to the reviewers:

    One After Another   Sends the document to each reviewer in the order in which they are listed in the To list box at the top of the Routing Slip dialog box. Click the ↑ or ↑ Move button to change the order of the highlighted name.

    All At Once   Simultaneously sends a copy of the document to each person listed in the To list box.

6. Check either of the following check boxes as necessary:

    Return When Done   Automatically sends the routed document back to you when the last reviewer closes it.

    Track Status   Automatically sends you an e-mail message as the document is sent to the next reviewer in the list when the document is routed using the One After Another option.

7. Select (None), Tracked Changes, Comments, or Forms as the method of protection for the document in the Protect For drop-down list.

8. Click one of the following buttons to send the routing slip with the attached document:

    Add Slip   Adds the routing slip to the document and closes the Routing Slip dialog box without sending the document. Choose this option when you want to edit the document before sending it.

    Route   Adds the routing slip to the document and sends it.

If you are routing the document to One After Another, you can choose to use the route settings previously established, or you can alter the routing slip before sending the document. To use existing settings, choose File ➤ Send To ➤ Next Routing Recipient to open the Send dialog box, and then choose either of the following options:

Route Document To *Reviewer Name*   Sends the document to the next person on the list when you click OK.

Send A Copy Of Document Without Using The Routing Slip   Opens a new message in Outlook with the document already attached. Select the name of the reviewer in the address book, type any accompanying e-mail message in the text area, and then click Send to place the message in your Outbox. Click Send And Receive to actually send the message.

Alternatively, choose File ➤ Send To ➤ Other Routing Recipient to open the Routing Slip dialog box again so that you can change any of the route settings, or even add someone new. When you're done making changes, click Route to send the document right away or click Add Slip to close the dialog box and return to the document. If you've chosen Add Slip, you can route the document later by choosing File ➤ Send To ➤ Next Routing Recipient.

As each reviewer finishes reviewing a document that is sent One After Another, he or she must select File ➤ Send To ➤ Next Routing Recipient to send the document to the next reviewer in the list.

You can't remove a routing slip once it's added to a document. But you can make changes to it as we've described above, and you can choose not to use it. When you close a document with a routing slip, Word reminds you that the document is set up for routing.

Click Yes to close the document and send it using existing route settings. Click No to close the document and ignore the routing slip. Click Cancel to return to the document.

Using Compare and Merge

So what happens if a novice user, thinking they are being extra careful, opens a routed file and uses the Save As command to give the document a new name? Their changes are now on a different copy than those of the other reviewers. Fortunately, Office's Compare and Merge feature can get you through the inconvenience in a snap—before you even have time to enroll the novice user in a training class.

When you use Compare And Merge, the document shows differences between the documents as tracked changes. In Word, that means you see balloon indicators in the margins. You can merge changes from multiple reviewers into a single document before you decide whether to accept or reject changes. To identify changes between two different documents and choose how to reconcile those changes, do the following:

1. Open one of the documents for comparison.

2. Choose Tools ➤ Compare And Merge Documents (Workbooks, Presentations). The Compare And Merge Documents dialog box appears (it looks very much like the Open dialog box).

3. Locate and select the other file for comparison. In Word only, enable or disable the Find Formatting and Legal Blackline check boxes as desired. The Legal Blackline option creates a new document that shows only the differences between the two documents without changing the original documents. Word creates the new document by assuming that all previously tracked changes in those documents are accepted.

4. Click the Merge button in PowerPoint or OK in Excel. In Word, choose one of the following from the Merge drop-down list in the bottom-right corner of the dialog box:

Merge   Displays all changes in the target document (the one you just located in the Merge And Compare dialog box).

Merge Into Current Document   Displays all changes in the current document (the one you opened first).

Merge Into New Document   Displays results in a new, third document that you can choose to save.

Compare   The only choice available if you enabled Legal Blackline. When the documents you are comparing contain tracked changes, you must confirm that Word can accept those changes and proceed. Remember, the original documents remain unaltered. Word creates a third document that shows where the two differ once changes are accepted.

NOTE   *If you've used the Versions command to maintain a history of changes and want to compare an earlier version, you must first save the earlier version under a different name.*

With the documents merged, you can now proceed with accepting or rejecting changes as you see fit.

CONCURRENT EDITING

With concurrent editing, multiple users can edit the same Word document at the same time. You don't get real-time simultaneous editing—no user can see what another is changing. But two or more people can now open the file for modification, where previously only one could modify while the other users could open only a read-only copy. When the first user saves and closes his file, other users are given options to see that document and use Compare and Merge to update their own file with the first user's changes. All changes are noted with revision tracking so you always know who made what changes when.

Collaborating Online

If you and your associates aren't satisfied with the passive methods of collaboration discussed in this chapter so far, hold on to your seats. Office 2003 includes a number of options for working together virtually. You can hold virtual meetings, collaborate on documents, conduct document-centered web discussions, share contacts and calendars, create document libraries, and prepare for meetings with a Meeting Workspace. Each of these methods provides options for collaboration and input impossible to obtain before the Web existed. Although in-depth coverage of these tools is beyond the scope of this book, we want to introduce to you the possibilities and give you a taste for the future of collaboration.

Holding a Virtual Meeting

Virtual meetings allow a group of geographically separated people to work together on documents over the Web. Microsoft NetMeeting adds full meeting functionality to the online experience. With

NetMeeting, participants have the power to simultaneously examine a document and make changes to it through each person's workstation, share a whiteboard, take control of another computer, use audio and video, and transfer files to each other.

NOTE *Microsoft NetMeeting is not included with Office 2003. However, it comes preinstalled with Windows 2000 or XP. Talk with your network administrator to find out if NetMeeting is available through your network.*

You can access NetMeeting from Outlook's Calendar to schedule a NetMeeting—just click the This Is An Online Meeting check box in an open Meeting form. If you'd like to hold a meeting regarding a specific document at a later time, choose Tools ➢ Online Collaboration ➢ Schedule Meeting from the menu of the active application. This also opens an Outlook Meeting form where you can enter information about the NetMeeting. You'll need to include the following:

◆ the address of the Directory Server you want to use

◆ the organizer's e-mail address

◆ the path to an Office document you want to share during the meeting

When the meeting time comes, Outlook automatically starts NetMeeting and signs you in to the meeting. Figure 8.10 shows the NetMeeting window when a meeting is in progress.

FIGURE 8.10

From the NetMeeting window, you can click one of the buttons at the bottom to share an application, chat, use the whiteboard, or transfer files.

If you would like to hold a NetMeeting with just a couple of people, you can use your standard Internet connection. However, if you plan to have a large group meeting, you should have access to a conferencing server, such as Microsoft Exchange Conferencing Server, to manage the conference for you. For more about Microsoft Exchange Conferencing, visit www.microsoft.com.

NOTE *Microsoft used to maintain a group of conferencing servers for public use. Because of the amount of unseemly traffic they were receiving, they have discontinued access to these servers. If you would like access to a public NetMeeting server, you can still find out where to find one at* http://communities.msn.com/TheNetMeetingZone *(word of caution: this is now considered an adult content site).*

Using a Windows SharePoint Site for Team Collaboration

If you need to collaborate with anyone about anything, Windows SharePoint Services is an exciting new way to collaborate. Whether you are managing a workgroup in a large corporation, supervising home-based employees, or planning a conference, Windows SharePoint Services (WSS) provides you with a valuable organizational and communication tool. WSS is a web-based toolset that combines web publishing, file sharing, and workgroup tools into a flexible and manageable website. Using the SharePoint services site structure, you can do all of the following and more:

◆ Post announcements

◆ Advertise events

◆ Publish useful links

◆ Hold discussions

◆ Post document libraries

◆ Collaborate on documents in a Document Workspace

◆ Prepare for meetings with a Meeting Workspace

◆ Share contact data

◆ Assign tasks

Figure 8.11 shows the home page of a WSS site developed for TRIAD Consulting. Since TRIAD is a consulting firm consisting of staff who work primarily from their homes, this site provides a great way for the staff to stay on top of what is happening, share ideas, pose problems, collaborate on documents, share mutual contacts, and manage small projects. Assigning user roles enables TRIAD's management to control who can post announcements to the site, who can participate in discussions, and who can customize the site's design.

FIGURE 8.11

A WSS site is a great way to help people stay in touch with each other.

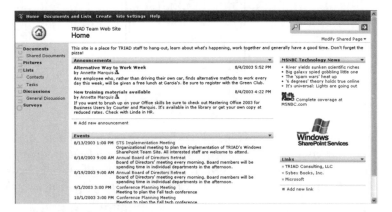

Working with a WSS site is pretty intuitive once you have a sense of what you can do with it. In this section, we'll provide you with an overview of the way a WSS site is organized and introduce you to the possibilities this type of site holds for Office collaboration.

NOTE   *Windows SharePoint Services comes with Windows Server 2003. You can run a Windows SharePoint Services site on a server in your organization or you can purchase a hosting plan from an outside vendor. For more information about WSS hosting plans, visit* `www.triadconsulting.com/resources`*.*

Exploring a Windows SharePoint Services Site

When you access a newly created site for the first time, it looks like an already developed website. It has graphics, links, a navigation bar, and a welcome message. But if you take a closer look, you can see that the site is really an empty container waiting for you to add content. In Figure 8.11, you can see several of the major sections of a default site: Announcements, Events, and Links. These sections, built on Windows .NET technology, are referred to as Web Parts. In addition to the default Web Parts, this site was customized to include a publicly available Web Part from MSNBC to display up-to-date technology news. Web Parts form the technological basis of every WSS site.

For everyday users of a WSS site, these Web Parts are displayed as the libraries, discussion boards, forms, and lists that provide the information they need to participate in a team. Users are assigned permissions that control how much they can participate. Four levels of permissions guide a site's access:

1. *Readers* have read-only access to the site. They can visit but not touch.

2. *Contributors* can add items to existing lists. For example, a Contributor could add an announcement or upload a document to an existing library.

3. *Web Designers* can create new lists, add new document libraries, and insert new Web Parts.

4. *Administrators* can add users, set permissions, and manage the overall site.

Web Designers and Administrators can add the appropriate lists, libraries, and Web Parts to the site based on the specific needs of the team. Table 8.1 shows the available elements of a WSS site.

TABLE 8.1: THE LISTS, LIBRARIES, AND WEB PARTS OF A SHAREPOINT SERVICES SITE

ELEMENT TYPE	LIST/LIBRARY/WEB PART	DESCRIPTION
Document Libraries	Document Library	A collection of documents or other files that you want to share
	Form Library	A collection of XML-based business forms, created with Microsoft Office InfoPath or other compatible XML editor
	Picture Library	An album of photos with options for thumbnails, a slide show, and download
Lists	Links	List of web links
	Announcements	Announcements, news items
	Contacts	Shared contacts list; compatible with Outlook Contacts

Continued on next page

TABLE 8.1: THE LISTS, LIBRARIES, AND WEB PARTS OF A SHAREPOINT SERVICES SITE *(continued)*

ELEMENT TYPE	LIST/LIBRARY/WEB PART	DESCRIPTION
	Events	Shared meetings, appointments, and events; compatible with Outlook Calendar
	Tasks	Team tasks and task assignments
	Issues	Issues lists that you can assign, prioritize, and track progress
Custom Lists	Custom List	A list with your own items such as inventory or price lists
	Custom List in Datasheet View	A spreadsheet-like custom list; requires a Windows SharePoint Services–compatible list datasheet control and ActiveX control support
	Import Spreadsheet	An imported spreadsheet from Excel or other compatible application
Discussion Boards	Discussion Board	Hold a newsgroup-style discussion with managed threads
Surveys	Survey	Customized survey tool to gather input and opinions
Web Pages	Basic Page	A basic web page with your own custom content
	Web Part Page	A page containing predesigned Web Parts, including everything from STS lists to news, weather, and sports.
	Sites and Workspaces	Sub-webs for special projects; also includes special sites including a Meeting Workspace to plan and prepare for a meeting scheduled through Outlook and a Document Workspace to collaborate on documents

As the team develops, designers can add new elements to respond to the growing needs of the team. Because these elements are all predesigned, it literally just takes a minute to add a new document library, an issues list, or even a discussion board.

In the remainder of this section, we'll show you how you can use a WSS site to collaborate throughout Office.

COLLABORATING IN A SHARED DOCUMENT WORKSPACE

When you are working on a large document creation project, such as developing a personnel manual, in which you have multiple contributors, you may find a WSS Document Workspace, such as the one shown in Figure 8.12, to be just the answer. In a Document Workspace, you can post one or more documents, assign and track team tasks, and share useful links. A Document Workspace is a fully functioning web with all the same options as the main WSS site.

FIGURE 8.12

A Document Workspace is an excellent way to work on complex documents that are being written collaboratively.

If you have Web Designer or Administrator privileges to a WSS site, you can create a Document Workspace. You have the option of creating the Document Workspace from the WSS site or directly within an Office application. To create a Document Workspace from within Word, Excel, or Power-Point, follow these steps:

1. Open any one of the documents you want to share and click Tools ➤ Shared Workspace. This opens the Shared Workspace pane, as shown in Figure 8.13.

2. In the Shared Workspace pane, enter the name you want to give to the Shared Workspace and, in the Location text box, enter the site address of the WSS site or select a prelisted site where you want the Document Workspace.

3. Save the open document when prompted.

4. Enter your username and password to the site if prompted.

FIGURE 8.13

In the Shared Workspace pane, you can identify the name and location of the new workspace.

When the Document Workspace is complete, you can continue to work with the document in the open application or you can switch to the browser to open the site. These options and others related to the workspace are available on the Shared Workspace pane. You can use the task pane to do the following:

◆ Check the status of a document and get document updates.

◆ See which members of the team are online and add members to the team. The Document Workspace relies on Windows Messenger (or MSN Messenger) to identify which members of the team are online.

◆ View, add, and update tasks.

◆ View a list of documents in the workspace, add new documents, and set alerts about documents. Figure 8.14 shows the types of alerts you can set.

◆ Add and access links.

◆ View document information such as who created the document and who last modified it. You can also restrict permissions to the document using Information Rights Management and view a versions history.

FIGURE 8.14

Document alerts keep you up to date on changes team members make to shared documents.

To set options related to the Shared Workspace pane and workspace updates, click the Options link at the bottom of the pane. As shown in Figure 8.15, you can choose to automatically update the document and the workspace when you open the document, at regular intervals while it is open, and when you close the document.

If you'd like to open the workspace in a browser, click the Open Site In Browser link at the top of the workspace pane. This opens the Document Workspace site shown earlier in Figure 8.12. Through the website, you get access to the entire Document Workspace where you can access other shared documents and view workspace announcements. A site designer or administrator can custom-design the site and also add other lists, libraries, and Web Parts to the workspace as needed.

FIGURE 8.15

You can set options regarding the Shared Workspace pane and the frequency with which documents are updated.

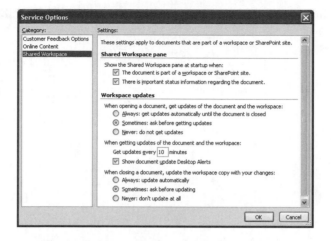

When you close a shared document in Office, you are reminded that this document is stored in a Document Workspace and you are prompted to update the workspace copy before closing.

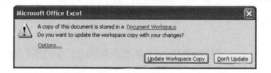

Using Document Workspaces is a great way to keep a team on task and track changes in and status of a shared project. Meeting Workspaces provide a similar tool for you to use when preparing for a big meeting.

PLANNING MEETINGS IN A MEETING WORKSPACE

Meeting Workspaces are to meetings what Document Workspaces are to documents. In a Meeting Workspace, you can post an agenda, develop meeting objectives, track attendees, and share documents. You can create a Meeting Workspace anytime you schedule a meeting in Outlook. Follow these steps to create and prepare a Meeting Workspace.

1. Plan a meeting in Outlook (see Chapter 3, "Taking Control of Your Time and Tasks").

2. Click the Meeting Workspace button on the open Outlook Meeting form.

3. Click the Create button on the Meeting Workspace pane.

4. Enter your username and password, if required, to access the WSS site.

5. After the workspace is created, click the Go to Workspace link on the Meeting Workspace pane to open the Meeting Workspace, shown in Figure 8.16, in your Web browser.

FIGURE 8.16

The Meeting
Workspace

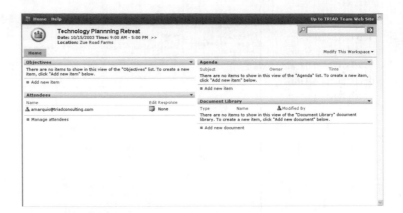

6. Click the Add New Item button to enter a meeting objective or an agenda item.

   A. Enter the information on the New Item page, as shown in Figure 8.17.

   B. Click the Attach File button if you want to attach a document to the item.

   C. Click Save and Close to return to the Meeting Workspace Home page.

FIGURE 8.17

Enter information
about the agenda
item or objective in
the New Item page.

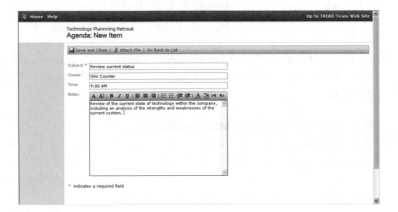

7. Click Manage Attendees in the Attendees section to review the status of attendees, add attendees, and edit attendee information.

   A. If you would like to add comments or change an attendee's attendance or response, click the Edit icon next to the attendee's name.

   B. Click Save and Close to return to the Attendee list page.

   C. Click Home on the top navigation bar to return to the Meeting Workspace Home page.

8. Click Add New Document to open the Document Library to share any document pertinent to the meeting.

- ◆ To upload a single document, click Browse to locate the document you want to share, locate the document in the Choose File dialog box, and click Open.

OR

- ◆ To share several documents, click the Upload Multiple Files link. Check the documents you want to upload and click Save and Close. Click OK to Confirm the documents you want to upload. When finished, you are returned to the Meeting Workspace Home page.

9. When you are finished working with the Meeting Workspace, you can click the Up To [*website name*] Website link in the top-right of the Home page to go to the main WSS site or close the browser to return to the Outlook meeting form.

NOTE   *You may have to click the Outlook Meeting form on the Windows Taskbar to reopen it.*

When you send a meeting invitation to a meeting that has a workspace, a link is added to the Notes pane of the Meeting form so attendees can easily access the workspace.

> Meeting Workspace: <u>Technology Plannning Retreat</u>
> Visit the workspace to learn more about this meeting or edit its contents.

You can identify meetings in Outlook that have a workspace by the Meeting Workspace icon that is added to the meeting.

When a meeting is over, you can choose to retain the workspace as part of the WSS site and, if you want, even update it with any finished documents that came out of the meeting. If you want to delete the workspace, click Documents And Lists on the WSS main navigation bar and then click Meeting Workspaces on the Quick Launch pane on the Documents And Lists page.

Click the Delete icon next to the Meeting Workspace you want to delete.

ACCESSING SHARED CALENDARS, CONTACTS, AND TASKS IN OUTLOOK

Most teams have a list of contacts, calendars, and task lists that they maintain in some form. It is rare, however, unless you are using Microsoft Exchange Public Folders, that these lists are ever shared with all the members of the team. Team members end up maintaining their own lists, all with various degrees of accuracy. With a WSS site, you can maintain central lists that everyone on the team shares. You can import data from Outlook and have access to the shared contacts and event lists from within your Outlook mailbox.

The process for accessing shared lists, entering data, importing data, and linking the lists to Outlook are pretty much the same for Contacts, Tasks, and Events on a WSS site. We'll show you the steps for managing a list and point out any differences in the three types of lists you should be aware of.

1. Click the Contacts link on the Quick Launch pane on the WSS site Home page to open the Contacts list. For Tasks, click the Tasks link on the Quick Launch pane. For Calendar appointments, meetings, or events, click Events in the Center pane of the site's Home page.

2. Click New Item to enter data related to a new contact, task, or event.

3. When finished, click Save and Close to return to list.

4. If you are entering a number of new items at once, you may find it easier to click Edit in Datasheet on the navigation bar to open a datasheet view of the list.

   A. Tab between fields as you enter data.

   B. Click New Row to add a new, blank row to the datasheet.

   C. Click Task Pane if you would like to work with the data in Excel or Access.

   D. If you have numeric data in the datasheet, click Totals on the navigation bar to add a totals row to the datasheet.

   E. Click Show in Standard view to return to the list.

5. To import contacts from any Outlook/Exchange address book, click Import Contacts on the Contacts list navigation bar (you cannot import tasks or events).

   A. Select the contacts you want to import from the Select Users To Import dialog.

   B. Click the Add button to add the selected contacts to the list.

   C. Click OK to import the contacts (you may have to authorize access to Outlook for a minute or two if prompted).

NOTE Contacts might appear in the address book more than once if they have multiple e-mail and fax addresses. If you select the contact only once, all of the data is imported.

6. If you want to view of subset of the list—for example, all contacts from Michigan—click Filter on the list's navigation bar to activate filter buttons similar to Excel's AutoFilter function (see Chapter 14, "Designing and Building Data Sources"). Click Hide Filter Choices to return to the standard list.

7. In Tasks and Contacts, click My Tasks or My Contacts in the Select A View list on the left of the page to see only tasks assigned to you or contacts you entered or imported. These views help to keep you from becoming overwhelmed with everyone else's data and lets you focus on your own.

8. To make shared contacts and events accessible in Outlook, click Link To Outlook on the list's navigation bar. If the site is not a trusted site, you might receive this warning:

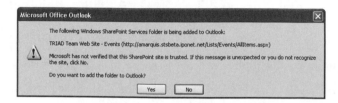

A. Click Yes to add the folder to your Outlook mailbox (see more about shared lists in Outlook later in this chapter).

9. To see the details of an individual item in a list, double-click the item or open the drop-down list and choose View or Edit.

10. To delete an item, point to the item, open the drop-down list, and choose Delete.

11. To be notified whenever a specific item changes, choose Alert Me from the item's drop-down list. You can choose to be e-mailed immediately or receive a summary of any changed items daily or weekly.

12. Click Home on the WSS site navigation bar to close the list you are viewing.

If you've chosen to link a Contacts list or an Event list to Outlook, it appears under Other Calendars or Other Contacts on the Outlook bar in your Outlook mailbox, as shown here.

Keeping your shared contacts, tasks, and calendars up-to-date and making sure everyone who needs the data has access to it goes a long way toward improving collaboration in your organization. In this last section, we'll look at another way to collaborate in a WSS site using Excel data.

CREATING CUSTOM WSS LISTS FROM EXCEL

If you already have data in Excel that you want to make available in a WSS site, you have several options. You can upload the document or create a Document Workspace. The problem with either of these options is that you are still working with an Excel workbook. Now, that may be appropriate in some cases but what if you would like to create a WSS list from data you have in Excel? With a WSS list, users can access it in datasheet view or in standard view and don't need to have any knowledge of Excel to use it. To create a WSS list from data that exists in Excel, follow these steps:

1. Open the Excel workbook that contains the data you want to use to create the list.

2. Select the list of data, leaving out any summary rows or columns.

3. Choose Data ➤ List ➤ Create List.

4. Verify that you've selected the correct range and if the list has headers and click OK.

5. From the List toolbar that opens, click List ➤ Publish List.

6. In Step 1 of the Publish List To SharePoint site dialog box, shown in Figure 8.18:

   A. Enter the address of the WSS site.

   B. Click the Link to the New SharePoint List check box if you want to keep a link to the list to update changes when you synchronize.

   C. Enter a name and description for the list.

   D. Click Next.

7. In Step 2 of the Publish List to SharePoint site dialog box, shown in Figure 8.19, verify the data types of each column in the list. A published list can only contain one data type per column. If Excel determined the data type from the first row, it shows only the data type. If it determined it from another row, the key cell address appears. If the data type is incorrect, you must cancel the process, fix the data type and publish the list again (return to step 5).

8. Click Finish to publish the list.

FIGURE 8.18

In Step 1 of the Publish to List dialog box, you can enter the site and list information.

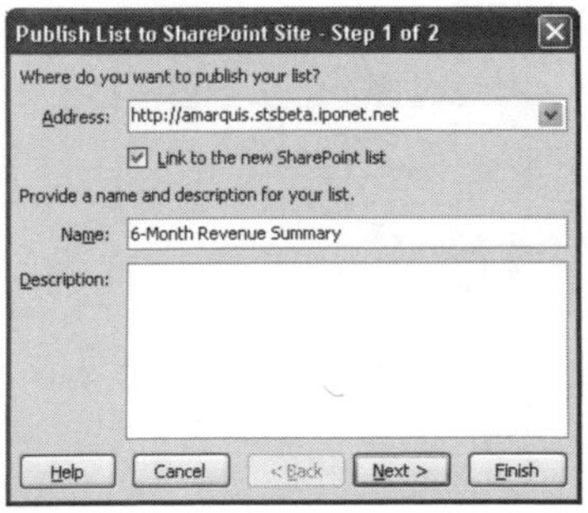

FIGURE 8.19

In Step 2 of the Publish to List dialog box, you can verify that the data types are correct.

Excel verifies that the list was published successfully and provides a link to the list on the WSS site.

Click the link to see the list. The list appears in WSS like the one shown in Figure 8.20.

FIGURE 8.20

The published list appears in the WSS site.

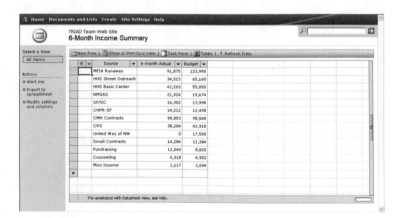

If you make changes to the list in Excel that you want to synchronize with the WSS list, right-click the list and choose Synchronize List.

NOTE *To be able to synchronize, you must have clicked the Link to the New SharePoint List check box in Step 1 of the Publish To List dialog box (see step 6.b. earlier).*

Creating a custom list from Excel is just one of the many ways you can make a WSS site valuable to your team. In this discussion of Windows SharePoint Services, we just barely scratched the surface of all the things you can do with a WSS site. We hope you experiment on your own with this exciting new collaboration tool—we're confident your team will find it useful to their work.

Chapter 9

Streamlining Mailings and Messaging

ANY TIME YOU WANT to send the same information to more than a few people, Office 2003's mail merge features can make your life a whole lot simpler. Mail merge allows you to combine data with form letters, labels, and reports to produce customized documents with a fraction of the effort you would spend replicating the document for each individual recipient. With mail merge you can input data directly into a Word table or import data stored in an Excel spreadsheet, an Outlook address book, or an Access database. Choose the data receptacle that is best for you, and Word will work with you to put your data to work in a variety of useful ways. In this chapter, we'll explore all the commonly used mail merge options and a few that might just surprise you.

- ◆ Understanding mail merge
- ◆ Creating a main document
- ◆ Choosing recipients
- ◆ Using existing data
- ◆ Creating a new data source
- ◆ Sorting and filtering the data source
- ◆ Creating envelopes and labels
- ◆ Merging documents
- ◆ E-mailing to a group

Making Sense of Mail Merge

Whether you want to send a form letter to 5 people or 500, you can use Word to personalize each one and to address mailing labels or envelopes. You've heard about mail merge and you might even have used it, but you might not have realized that Word's mail merge feature is much more than a tool to create form letters and mailing labels. Don't let the term *mail merge* limit your thinking: you can use mail merge to create telephone directories, birthday lists, nametags, or any type of list or customized document you can imagine.

A mail merge requires two documents: a *data source* (also called a *recipient list*) in which the individual records are stored and a *main document* that refers to the fields in the data source. These two documents then come together to create the final *merge document*, a document that uses the text and layout in the main document and the data in each record of the data source.

There are five types of main documents:

Letters   Letters, memos, or reports you want to personalize

E-mail messages   Electronic mail items sent through Outlook

Envelopes   Envelopes fed directly into your printer

Labels   Address labels or any other kind of label, such as nametags, videotape or disk labels, and file folder labels

Directories   Lists of data, such as phone lists, course catalogs, or membership directories

A data source consists of a number of individual *records*. A record contains all the information gathered about the item. For example, a record about a person might contain a name, address, telephone number, and date of birth. Each record is made up of a series of *fields*; a field is the smallest unit of data collected. A record about a person probably contains quite a few fields. The person's name, such as Ms. Mary A. Smith, might consist of four fields in the record—SocialTitle, FirstName, MiddleInitial, and LastName. The address, Magic Manufacturing, 555 Marl Lane, Buckley, MI 49620, might contain a separate field for the OrganizationName, StreetAddress, City, State, and PostalCode. Any item you might need to work with individually should have its own field. The ability to store data such as your personal or business contacts, product catalog information, or purchasing records puts extra power in your hands. Using Word, you can access the data stored in any of the following:

◆   A data source file created using Word

◆   A file created with other Microsoft Office products such as an Excel database (list), Outlook contacts, or an Access database

◆   A database file created using any type of software and saved in a supported file format or as a delimited text file

NOTE   *Word merge supports dBASE, FoxPro 2003, and HTML data files, as well as any database you can query with Microsoft Query, including Oracle and SQL Server.*

Creating or Specifying the Main Document

The Mail Merge task pane helps you create a main document, create or select a data source, and then produce merged documents. You must create a main document, or at least specify which document is the main document, before you create or select a data source. Your main document can be any Word document, including a new, blank document.

Follow these steps to create a main document:

1. Open an existing document or create a new document to serve as the main document. You can also create a new main document after you've started the Mail Merge task pane.

2. Choose Tools ➢ Letters And Mailings ➢ Mail Merge to display Step 1 of the Mail Merge task pane, shown in Figure 9.1. (If the task pane is already visible, you can choose Mail Merge from its selection menu.)

3. Choose a document type from the list that appears in Step 1 (in this example, choose Letters. We'll go into more depth about other types of main documents later in this chapter). Then click Next: Starting Document at the bottom of the task pane to move to Step 2.

FIGURE 9.1

Display the Mail Merge task pane when you want to create either a main document or a new Word data source file.

4. Choose a start option:

Use The Current Document   Allows you to work with the active document, whether it is a file you have already opened or a blank page you will edit later.

Start From A Template   Lets you select from the Template's dialog box, introduced in Chapter 15, "Creating Templates to Handle Your Repetitive Tasks." For more about using mail merge templates, see the section "Using a Mail Merge Template for a Main Document," later in this chapter.

Start From Existing Document   Allows you to open a previously created Word file.

5. After choosing a start option you can, at any time, modify the document by adding text or changing formatting.

6. Although Word doesn't prompt you to do so, if you've spent a fair amount of time working on the content of the main document, now is a good time to save it.

NOTE   When you save a merge document, you might find it helpful to indicate the type of document somewhere in the file-name. We suggest that you begin main documents with the word Main *and, when appropriate, the name of the data source it is linked to (*Main_Acknowledgment Letter to Customers*) so that you can identify your main documents easily.*

Although this is by no means the end of the mail merge process, this is the biggest part of what you must do to create a main document. The rest involves adding merge codes for the data fields you want to use. Since you must select recipients before you add merge codes, we will discuss recipients next. To learn about merge codes, see "Adding Merge Fields to a Main Document," later in this chapter.

Selecting Recipients

The next step (Step 3 of 6) in the Mail Merge task pane is to create or select a data source to use with your main document. Your data source can be used over and over again, with more than one main document. For example, if you want to send a form letter to your company's customers, you can use the same data source file for both the main form letter document and the main mailing labels document.

TIP   Although selecting recipients is Step 3 of the Mail Merge task pane, you probably want to think about this list before starting the mail merge process. You know you are going to need the recipient list and the sooner you put effort into getting it into shape the easier mail merge will be.

You are given three options for selecting recipients:

◆ Use an existing list if you've already created a data source in Word, Excel, Access, dBASE, or another ODBC-compliant program.

◆ Select From Outlook Contacts if you're planning to send the document to people in your Outlook contacts list.

◆ Type a new list if you don't have an existing data file and you're not using Outlook contacts.

Using an Existing Data Source

If you already have data in an Excel worksheet, an Access database, an Outlook address book, or a dBASE, FoxPro, or delimited text datafile, there is no need to re-create that data in Word. (In fact, there is never a need to house data in Word and we strongly recommend against it—the other applications listed are all much better for organizing and maintaining data.) A data source file usually consists of a table with a *header row* (the first row in the table, which contains the names of the fields for which you will enter data). Each field name is in a separate column in the row. The records, which contain the data, are entered in subsequent rows in the table. For example, each cell in the column that contains the LastName field will contain the last name of an individual.

Follow these steps to use an existing data source:

1. In Step 3 of the Mail Merge task pane, choose Use An Existing List.

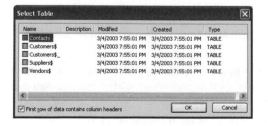

2. Click the Browse icon to open the Select Data Source dialog box. By default, the Look In field is set to the My Data Sources folder. Select another folder if appropriate; then select and open the file you'd like to use for this merge.

3. If you're using an Excel workbook or Access database, Word displays the Select Table dialog box (shown in Figure 9.2) so that you can select the sheet, named range, or table that contains the data you need for the merge. If you're using spreadsheet data, be sure to enable or disable First Row Of Data Contains Column Headers as appropriate. Then click OK to display the Mail Merge Recipients dialog box shown in Figure 9.3.

4. In the Mail Merge Recipients dialog box, choose the records you want for the merge. Deselect the records you don't want by clearing the check boxes in front of them. You can also sort and filter records by using the column headers in this dialog box. (Sorting and filtering are discussed in greater depth later in this chapter.) Click OK when you're finished selecting recipients.

TIP   If you plan to use most of the records, click Select All and clear the check marks from the ones you don't want. If you plan to use only a few of the recipients listed, click Deselect All, and then check the ones you want.

5. Once you've selected recipients, Word closes the dialog box and displays information about the selected recipients in the task pane. If you wish, you can select a different list or edit the existing recipient list. Select either option and repeat the steps above to modify the data source as needed.

This completes the recipient selection part of the mail merge process. Click Next: Write Your Letter to proceed to Step 6 where you insert merge codes and finalize the main document.

FIGURE 9.2

The Select Table dialog box allows users to choose a worksheet, named range, or table as a data source.

FIGURE 9.3

The Mail Merge Recipients dialog box is used for selecting records from a data source.

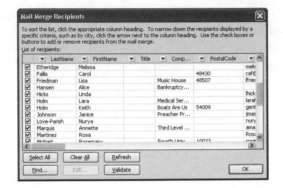

USING AN EXCEL WORKSHEET AS A DATA SOURCE

Excel worksheets are also tables, which, as you've seen, can be used to create a data source. An Excel data source is called a *list*. In Excel, each column is described with a label (the field name), and each row contains an individual record.

There are several things to keep in mind when you are using an Excel worksheet as your data source:

◆ It's easiest if the data source does not contain any blank rows or columns. If you have used Mail Merge in earlier versions of Word, you might expect Word to recognize the end of a list when it comes to a blank row or column. This is no longer the case. In Word 2003, Mail Merge enters zeros in the place of blank rows and columns in an Excel worksheet and keeps right on going. To get around this in worksheets that contain additional data, use the Name tool described later in this sidebar.

◆ The column labels (field names) must be in the first row of the list. You can add special formatting, such as bold, to the column labels to differentiate them from the data entered in each record.

◆ Items in the list can be sorted by multiple fields in Word when you're selecting recipients, or in Excel when you're setting up the data.

If you typically use only *some* of the data in the worksheet as the data source, you might find it easier to name a range in Excel, rather than spend extra time selecting recipients in Word. In Excel, select the range of cells that contains the list items, including the column labels in the first row of the list, and then assign it a range name. Make sure you include the column labels as the first row in the named range, because Excel uses the data in the first row as the merge field names. Use one of the following methods to create a range name:

◆ Select the range of cells and then type the name you want for that range in the Name box at the left of the formula bar.

◆ Select the range of cells and then choose Insert ➢ Name ➢ Define to display the Define Name dialog box. Type the name in the Names In Workbook text box and then choose Add. Choose OK when you are finished entering range names.

Make sure you re-save the file after you name the range. When you're ready to use the named range as a data source, simply follow the same steps you would in any merge. When Word displays the Select Table dialog box, the named range(s) appear in the list along with the sheet tab names. Select the one you want and click OK.

Creating a New Data Source in Word

If you haven't created a data source before you start the mail merge, Word provides the means to do so as part of the process. We never used to recommend using Word to create a data source because it just wasn't the best tool for the job. However, in this version (and Word 2002), when you create a data source as part of the mail merge process, Word creates an `.mdb` file (Access database) for the data, not a Word `.doc` file as in previous versions. The data is infinitely more usable this way, so we no longer object if you want to give it a try.

Here's everything you need to know about creating a data source in Word.

NOTE *Even if you are using another data source besides Word, the information presented in this section is helpful in creating field names that cross applications seamlessly.*

You can use the default address fields Word provides, or create your own fields. In fact, with Word 2003 it is possible to use just about any field name you can imagine. However, this freedom in naming fields could have adverse effects if you share a data source with another user who isn't running Office 2003. To be safe, it is a good idea to follow these rules when creating a data source in any application. These rules are absolutes in earlier versions of Word and in other data applications:

- ◆ Field names should be less than 40 characters long. Some programs won't recognize larger names, and shorter is better for easy reference.

- ◆ Each field name must be unique—no two fields in a data source can have the same name.

- ◆ Field names should not contain spaces and should begin with a letter rather than a number. You can use the underbar (_) character to separate words, but it is easier to omit spaces and underlines and simply capitalize the first letter of each word in a name, such as StreetAddress or DateOfBirth.

- ◆ Stay away from using periods, commas, colons, semicolons, slashes, or backslashes in field names.

This is a good time to think about how you will use your data. If you use only one field, Name, for both first and last names, you can't open a letter with "Dear Joe." By separating names into FirstName and LastName fields, you have more options for how you can use the name in your main document. If you're feeling formal and might want to use "Dear Mr. Smith" as the salutation, you will want to include a Title or Honorific field for Mr., Mrs., Ms., and other social titles.

Addresses should be separated into StreetAddress or Address, City, State or Province, and ZipCode or PostalCode. Later, you can choose to print labels that are sorted by ZipCode, or print envelopes and letters only for clients in Arkansas.

If you are creating several different data source files, it's helpful to use the same field names in each data source. For example, if you use "FirstName" in one data source, use this field name consistently—don't use "FNAME" or "First" in other source files. When you use the Mail Merge task pane to create your data source, you can select many commonly used field names from a built-in list to help you keep your field names consistent. If you use the same field names, you'll often be able to use the same main documents with different data source files, rather than creating new main documents.

Creating a recipient list from scratch starts at Step 3 of the task pane. Choose Type A New List.

Click the Create icon to open the New Address List dialog box shown in Figure 9.4. You'll see the list of commonly used address fields Word provides for you. If these fields are all you need, simply type the data you want in the appropriate field, and press Tab or Enter to move to another field. You don't have to enter data in every field, but if you're not going to use a field, consider deleting it as described below.

FIGURE 9.4

The New Address List dialog box provides fields to enter data for a new recipient list.

To add, delete, reorder, or rename fields, click the Customize button and Word displays the Customize Address List dialog box shown in Figure 9.5. You can do any of the following:

◆ Select a field you don't need and click the Delete button to remove it from the data source. Confirm the delete by clicking Yes in the message box, but be aware that if you've previously entered data in that field, you are deleting the data as well as the field.

◆ Change the name of a field by selecting it and clicking the Rename button. Type a new name for the field in the Rename Field dialog box, overwriting its original name—remember to use the field name naming rules outlined earlier so your field names can be used in other applications.

◆ Adjust the order of the fields by clicking the Move Up and Move Down buttons. This is particularly helpful if you are typing data from a written page and the fields are in a different order on the page than they are in the New Address List dialog box.

◆ Add another field by clicking the Add button and typing the name of the field you wish to add in the Add Field dialog box.

FIGURE 9.5

The Customize Address List dialog box allows you to add, delete, rename, and reorder fields in a recipient list.

When you've adjusted the fields to your satisfaction, click OK to close the Customize Address List dialog box and proceed with entering data in those fields.

It's easy to enter records in your new recipient list using the data form in the New Address List dialog box shown previously in Figure 9.4. Although it's possible to open the data source file (once it's saved) and enter the records directly in the data source's table, that is typically more difficult. The advantage to using the data form is that it displays only one record at a time. If you open the data source file, all the records are displayed, which can make it difficult to keep track of the field you're entering data for. And you need to know a bit about Access to work with the data directly.

Follow these steps to enter data in the new data source:

1. Type the information for the first field in the text box beside its name and then press Tab or Enter to move the insertion point to the next field's text box.

2. Repeat Step 1 until you've entered data for each field in the first record. Then choose New Entry or press Enter to place the current data in the data source and to display the next empty record. Continue entering data.

3. Use the navigation buttons at the bottom of the New Address List dialog box to view the Next, Previous, First, and Last records. You can also type the number of a record and press Enter to display it. If you wish to remove a record, navigate to it and click the Delete Entry button.

NOTE *You can sort and filter data as you create the data source. These features are discussed in the next few sections.*

4. Click Close to finish entering records. Before the Mail Merge Recipients dialog box opens, Word prompts you to save the data source.

TIP *When you save a data source file, it's a good idea to name the document so that it is easily identifiable as a data source file. You might want to begin all of your data source file names with Data—for example, Data-Customers.*

If you are finished with the recipients list for now, click OK to close it and return to the mail document. You can always reopen it later if you want to work with the list. The task pane displays the filename and path of the data source you just created. If you want to make changes to the data in the list, click Edit Recipient List to open the Mail Merge Recipients dialog box. You also have the option from the task pane to open another data source if you don't want to use the one you just created.

EDITING RECORDS

Your data source records can be edited within the Mail Merge Recipients dialog box shown previously in Figure 9.3. You can enter new records, edit, delete, search, sort, filter, and validate records. If it is not still open, click Edit Recipient List in the task pane to open the Mail Merge Recipients dialog box.

To add a new record, select any record and click the Edit button. Word displays the data form that you saw previously in the New Address dialog box. Click the New Entry button to navigate to a blank form. Enter the data as you normally would. When you're finished, click Close to return to the Mail Merge Recipients dialog box. The new records appear with the others.

To delete a record, select it and click Edit. Make sure the record you want to delete is displayed in the data form, and then click the Delete Entry button. Click Yes to confirm the deletion. Click Close to return to Mail Merge Recipients.

To add, remove, reorder, or rename fields in the data source, click Edit to bring up the data form, and then click Customize to open the Customize Address List dialog box, shown previously in Figure 9.5.

SORTING RECORDS

By default, the data form and Mail Merge Recipients dialog box display records in the order you entered them. Therefore, Word merges them in the order you entered them unless you modify that order by sorting. You can organize your data source by sorting any field that you find useful. For example, you may want to see a list of the names of your customers in alphabetical order by their last names. Records can be sorted in *ascending order* (A to Z or 0 to 9) or in *descending order* (Z to A or 9 to 0).

To sort, open the Mail Merge Recipients dialog box at Step 3 of the Mail Merge task pane. (Just click Edit Recipient List in the task pane.)

As you already know, Word displays recipients in table format with field names at the top of each column of data. Click any field name for an ascending sort on that field. Click the field name again for a descending sort.

There may be times when your data requires a *multilevel sort*—by last name and then first name, for example, or by company and then by last name. In any multilevel sort, there is, at the very least, a primary sort field and a secondary sort field. Word allows you a *tertiary* (third-level) sort field as well. For example, an elementary school's student list would typically be sorted by grade level (the primary field), last name (the secondary field), and then first name (the tertiary field.) This ensures that Sam Smith the second-grader appears in the list before Judy Smith the fourth-grader. And Judy appears in the list before Zack Smith, who is also in the fourth grade.

You can't perform multilevel sorts in the Mail Merge Recipients dialog box. Each sort works independently of the next. Instead, click the down arrow on any field name to open a menu of choices. Select Advanced to open the Filter And Sort dialog box, and click the Sort Records tab to display the sorting options shown in Figure 9.6.

FIGURE 9.6

Word allows up to three levels of sorting in a data source.

Select the primary, secondary, and tertiary sort fields from the down arrows, choose whether you want an ascending or descending sort on each field, and click OK. Figure 9.7 shows the Mail Merge Recipients dialog box after sorting by the fields shown in Figure 9.6. Notice that the Mail Merge Recipients dialog box does not indicate the sort order in any way. If you are unclear about the sort order, reopen the Filter And Sort dialog box and review it there.

FIGURE 9.7

The Mail Merge Recipients dialog box displays this data sorted by company and then by last and first names.

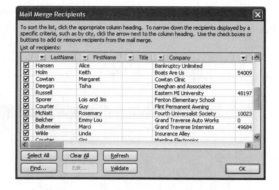

FILTERING RECORDS

Often, a data source contains more records than you want to use in a merge. As you know, you can deselect individual records by clearing the check box in front of the record in the Mail Merge Recipients dialog box. You can also *filter*, or separate, records based on criteria that you establish. Click the down arrow on any field in the Mail Merge Recipients dialog box. You'll see a list of unique values for that field and two other typical filtering choices. Choose from the following options:

Unique Values   Selects only those records that contain that value. Using the data in Figure 9.7, you might choose to send a sales promotion only to those customers at Insurance Alley.

Blanks   Selects only those records with no data in the field. For example, you might want to send a memo to individuals who are not associated with a company.

Non Blanks   Selects records that have data in a field. If you're mail-merging to an e-mail, you certainly want to filter the data for those records with e-mail addresses.

Advanced   Establishes filter criteria through a query.

In the database world, a *query* is a tool used to select a group of records that meet specific criteria. To use a query to filter the records before you merge the main document and the data source, follow these steps:

1. In the Mail Merge Recipients dialog box, click the down arrow on any field and choose Advanced. The Filter And Sort dialog box opens as shown in Figure 9.8. Make sure the Filter Records tab is selected.

2. In the Field drop-down list, select the field you want to use to select records.

3. Select one of the comparison operators in the Comparison drop-down list.

4. In the Compare To text box (at the far right of the dialog box), enter the text string you are looking for in the selected field.

5. Choose OK to filter the records with one criterion.

For example, if you wanted to include everyone from Michigan, you would choose the State field from the Field drop-down list and Equal To from the Comparison drop-down list. Then you would type **MI** in the Compare To text box (assuming the State field in the data uses two-letter abbreviations). Table 9.1 indicates the results from using other Comparison operators when you choose State as the field and enter a Compare To value of MI.

FIGURE 9.8

The Filter Records tab of the Filter And Sort dialog box allows you to specify the criteria necessary to merge only the records you want.

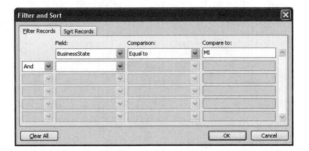

TABLE 9.1: EFFECT OF COMPARISON OPERATORS

COMPARISON	SELECTS RECORDS
Equal To (the default)	With the State value of MI
Not Equal To	With any State value that is not MI
Less Than	With State values in the alphabetical range of AA to MH
Greater Than	With State values in the alphabetical range MJ to ZZ
Less Than Or Equal	With State values AA to MI
Greater Than Or Equal	With State values MI to ZZ
Is Blank	Where there is no value in the State field
Is Not Blank	Where any State value is included
Contains	The string "MI" is somewhere in the field
Does Not Contain	The string "MI" is not in the field

Using And and Or

After you enter a Compare To text string, the word *And* appears in the drop-down list to the left of the second row of the Filter Records tab in the Filter And Sort dialog box. You can enter multiple query criteria and select, for example, the records for people in California where the data source doesn't list a zip code. The single most confusing thing about writing queries is knowing when to use *And* and when to use *Or*. Hopefully, we can shed some light on that for you here.

Choosing *And* means both comparisons must be true for a match. If you enter this information: Field: ZipCode, Comparison: Is Blank in the second row after the *And* in Figure 9.8, shown earlier, the results include all records where the State is Michigan *And* the ZipCode field in the data source is blank. Both conditions must be true. Records for people from Arkansas, Oregon, or Massachusetts are not selected. Records for people living in Michigan with a zip code will not be selected.

Choosing *Or* means a match is found if either comparison is true. In this case, all records from Michigan are selected, as well as anyone from any other state who doesn't have a zip code listed in the data source. Use *Or* when you want to select two different possible values for the same field. For example, when you want to send a mailing to all your customers in California and Nevada, you should select records where State is equal to California *Or* State is equal to Nevada. You wouldn't select *And* because no single record includes both states.

Of course, there is an exception to every rule (well, most of the time anyway). In this case, there is one time you use *And* when making two comparisons in the same field and that is when you want to select records within a numeric range. For example, you might want to send an advertisement to all families with annual incomes between $25,000 and $40,000. In this example, you would select Income greater than $25,000 *And* Income less than $40,000. If you used *Or*, all records would be selected, as every level of income is either less than $40,000 or more than $25,000. Make sense?

TIP   Here's a general rule for troubleshooting queries: If you expected some records to be selected but none were, you probably used And *when you should have used* Or. *If you got a lot more records than you expected, you probably used* Or *when you should have used* And.

FINDING AND EDITING RECORDS

So what happens if, after you have entered records into a Word data source, you find out that someone has moved or you spelled someone's name wrong? You can edit records by first finding the record you want to change and then editing it in the Address List dialog box. Follow these steps to search for a record and open it for editing:

1. Click the Find button in the Mail Merge Recipients dialog box (click Edit Recipient List on Step 3 of the Mail Merge task pane) to open the Find Entry dialog box.

2. Type the text you want to find in the Find text box.

3. Select a Look In option. Search all fields or choose the field where the text is stored in the This Field drop-down list.

4. Click Find Next to have Word highlight the first record in the data source that contains that text in the field. If it does not find the record you want to edit, Click Find Next until it selects the desired record. When it selects the record you want to edit, click Cancel to close the Find Entry dialog box and then Edit to open the Enter Address Information dialog box. Make any edits as necessary.

5. To locate another record, click Find Entry and repeat Steps 2–4 except you don't have to click Edit because the Enter Address Information dialog box is already open.

6. Repeat Step 5 as necessary. If Word finds no records that match your search criteria, it displays a message box saying so.

7. When you are finished editing, click Close to close the Enter Address Information dialog box and click OK to return to the active document and Mail Merge task pane.

If you want to add new records, rather than edit existing ones, you can open the Enter Address Information dialog box the same way. Click Edit Recipient List on Step 3 of the Mail Merge task pane. Click Edit on the Mail Merge Recipients dialog box and click New Entry to clear the Enter Address Information dialog box.

VALIDATING RECIPIENT DATA

Data validation has always been a powerful feature in spreadsheet programs. Excel's data validation tools are some of the best available. And now you've got that power in Word. When you're merging with a very large data source, it's impossible to hand-check every printed document for accuracy. Address validation can help eliminate certain errors ahead of time by verifying the validity of addresses and zip codes before you drop your letters in a mailbox. For example, all U.S. zip codes should have at least 5 digits. If you were using zip+4, the entries in that field would have 10 digits (5 + 4 + 1 for the hyphen.) Data-validation tools can check to make sure that all entries in the zip code field are either 5 digits or 10 and notify you if that's not the case.

Address validation is available in the Mail Merge Recipients dialog box, but you must install third-party address validation software such as FirstLogic's Postalsoft (`www.firstlogic.com`) to use this feature. If you click the Validate button with no validation software installed, Word invites you to visit the Web for information about such programs.

Using Outlook As a Data Source

If you store names, addresses, and other recipient data in Outlook, mail merge is easier than ever! At Step 3 of the Mail Merge task pane, choose Select From Outlook Contacts, and then click Choose Contacts Folder. If Outlook is closed and you use multiple profiles, Outlook prompts you to select a profile.

If prompted, choose the Outlook profile that contains the contact folder you wish to use. Once you've chosen a profile, the Select Contact List Folder dialog box appears as shown in Figure 9.9.

Select the appropriate folder and click OK. The Mail Merge Recipients dialog box opens with Outlook contact data displayed. Proceed with selecting, sorting, and filtering as you normally would.

FIGURE 9.9

The Select Contact List Folder dialog box lets you choose an Outlook contacts folder as a mail merge data source.

Using a Word Table As a Data Source

With the vast improvements to mail merge, you may find that you never have occasion to create a Word table for use as a data source. However, if you are a mail merge user from way back, chances are some of your existing data sources may be in Word table format. You can use the tools in the Mail Merge Recipients dialog box to manipulate the data in a Word table, just as you would with any data source. However, if you prefer to work with the table directly, you'll want to be familiar with the Database toolbar shown in Figure 9.10. Choose View ➢ Toolbars ➢ Database to display it.

FIGURE 9.10

Word's Database toolbar lets users work directly with records in a Word table.

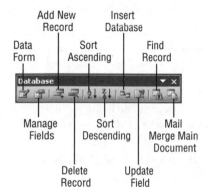

In order for a Word table to be recognized as a data source, it has to follow certain rules. It has to be the only text in the document, it cannot contain any blank rows, and it must have column headers that follow field-naming conventions (reviewed earlier in this chapter).

You can add records to the data source by inserting another row and typing the data for the record. If you prefer to enter or view records using the data form, click the Data Form button.

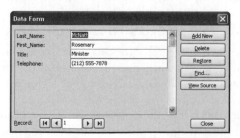

This data form is similar to the New Address List dialog box shown previously in Figure 9.4, with options for adding, deleting, and finding records. Edit as desired and click Close to return to the table. You should see your changes immediately.

To add, remove, or rename fields in your data source, open the document that contains the table and click the Manage Fields button on the Database toolbar to open the Manage Fields dialog box.

In the Manage Fields dialog box, you can perform any of the following, and then click OK when you're finished.

◆   To create a new field in the data source, type a name in the Field Name text box and click Add. The new field name appears at the end of the list in the Field Names In Header Row list box, and a new column is created beside the last column in the data source.

◆   To remove a field from the data source, highlight its name in the Field Names In Header Row list box and click Remove. Click Yes to confirm that you want to remove the field, along with the data stored in it.

WARNING   *When you remove a field from the data source, the data in that field is also removed. Be sure you don't need the data for any other purpose before removing a field because once it is gone, it's gone. If you are uncertain about your decision, it's a good idea to save a backup version of the file before removing a field.*

◆   To rename a field, highlight its name in the Field Names In Header Row list box, click Rename to display the Rename Field dialog box, type a new name for the field in the New Field Name text box, and then click OK.

The Database toolbar has a number of other tools to help you manage the data in a Word table, including buttons for adding and deleting records and sorting the records in the table. But even with all these tools available, we still recommend copying and pasting the table into an Excel worksheet and working with it from there. In Excel, you don't have to worry about whether the fields fit within a specific page width and you can easily sort and filter the data. Excel is just a better all-around data management tool.

Adding Merge Fields to a Main Document

After you have created or identified the data source, you are ready to add *merge fields* and any additional information you need to the main document. There are two kinds of text in a main document. *Regular text* is text that will be the same in each version of the merged document, such as the body text in a form letter. *Variable text* is text that will be different in each merged document and is represented by a merge field. Merge fields have the same names as the field names in the data source. For example, the recipient's name and address is variable text in the main document.

You can edit the regular text in your main document as necessary, using the same methods as those you use to edit any other document. Insert a merge field where you want variable text from the data source to appear in your final, merged document.

Move to Step 4 of the Mail Merge task pane: Write Your Letter. The task pane displays several choices for adding regular and variable text.

Follow these steps to add merge fields and other information to your main document:

1. Position the insertion point where you want the address block to appear.

2. Click Address Block to display the options for addressing your letter, shown in Figure 9.11. Choose whether or not you want to include the recipient's name, and then select a name format from the list if applicable. Enable or disable the Insert Company Name check box. If you want to include the postal address, enable that choice and choose an option for including or excluding country and region data.

FIGURE 9.11

The Insert Address Block dialog box lets you choose the fields to use in addressing letters to be merged.

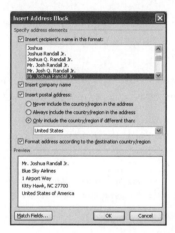

If the preview in the Insert Address Block dialog box doesn't show the address information you want, follow these steps:

A. Click the Match Fields button to bring up the Match Fields dialog box.

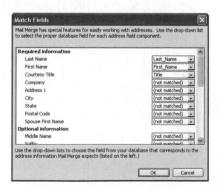

B. Use the drop-down lists on the right to select the name of the field in your data that corresponds with the address field Word displays on the left. For example, Word uses the term Postal Code, and many databases call this same field Zip Code.

C. When you're finished, click OK twice to close both dialog boxes. The address block field appears in the document with double angle brackets (<< >>) around the field name.

WARNING   Merge field codes must be entered using the options in the Mail Merge task pane. You cannot simply type << before the field name and >> after it to make it a merge field.

NOTE   Sometimes it's helpful to distinguish the field codes from the static text in the document. To have the merge fields appear with gray shading in your main document, choose Tools ➤ Options ➤ View. In the Show area, choose Always in the Field Shading drop-down list and click OK.

3. To have Word insert a greeting line for you, position the insertion point where you want the greeting line to appear and click Greeting Line in the task pane to open the Greeting Line dialog box shown in Figure 9.12.

4. Select the components you want from the drop-down lists until the preview shows the data as you want it displayed in the main document.

5. Select a backup greeting from the Greeting Line For Invalid Recipient Names drop-down list for instances where the data fields that you need to create the greeting line are empty. If appropriate, use the Match Fields feature to adjust greeting fields.

NOTE   If you don't like the greeting choices, you can type whatever you want in the first and third text boxes in Greeting Line Format and in the Greeting Line For Invalid Recipient Names text box.

6. Click OK when you're finished.

NOTE   Word offers options for inserting postal bar codes and electronic postage. These features are discussed in the section "Creating Envelopes and Labels," later in this chapter.

FIGURE 9.12

Let Word insert a greeting line for you using fields available in the Greeting Line dialog box.

7. To insert other fields from your data, position the insertion point where the field should appear in the document and click More Items in the task pane. The Insert Merge Field dialog box opens as shown in Figure 9.13.

8. Choose whether to display Word's Address Fields or the fields from your database. Select the field you want and click Insert.

9. Click Close to return to the main document.

10. Position the insertion point and repeat Steps 5–7 for each field you wish to place in your main document. It's a bit cumbersome, but you must close the Insert Merge Field dialog box each time you want to reposition the insertion point.

TIP   You may find it easier to insert all the fields you want to use with the dialog box open and then reposition them as needed after you return to the document. If you do this, be sure to select the field name and the two sets of angle brackets around it before moving it or you will disable the field.

FIGURE 9.13

The Insert Merge Field dialog box allows users to insert Word address fields or any field from the data source.

11. Continue typing and inserting fields until you are finished with the main document. If you haven't already saved, now is a good time to do so. Figure 9.14 shows a main document ready to be merged.

12. After you have saved the main document, you can attach a different data source to it. Just click Previous: Select Recipients in the task pane and follow the steps you normally would for selecting a data source. Only one data source can be attached at a time. Now you can see the advantage of using consistent field names in your data source files!

NOTE   A main document can be attached to only one data source at a time, but a data source can be attached simultaneously to multiple main documents.

13. When you have finished setting up and saving the main document, Word provides you with an opportunity to preview the merge results before completing the actual merge. Click Next: Preview Your Letters to proceed.

FIGURE 9.14

Field shading in a main merge document makes it easy to distinguish regular from variable text.

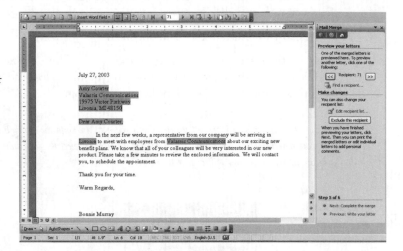

MASTERING THE OPPORTUNITIES: USING AN IF...THEN...ELSE FIELD TO VARY TEXT

From time to time when you're creating form letters, you might want to vary the text of the letter based on a field in the data source. For example, a teacher sending progress reports wants to add a sentence that reads, "Please contact me for a conference," but only for those students who have grades below C. The operations manager sending notice of a plant-wide meeting wants most employees to show up at 9:00 AM but requires employees in the Facilities department to come an hour early to set up.

An If...Then...Else field lets you vary the text of your main document based on the value in a data field. Here's what you do:

1. Proceed through Step 4 of the Mail Merge task pane as you normally would.

2. At Step 4, as you are preparing the main document, position the insertion point where you want the If...Then...Else field to appear.

3. Click the Insert Word Field button on the Mail Merge toolbar. (Choose Tools ➤ Letters And Mailings ➤ Show Mail Merge Toolbar to display the Mail Merge toolbar if it isn't already visible.)

4. Click Insert Word Field and choose If...Then...Else to open the Insert Word Field: IF dialog box.

Continued on next page

MASTERING THE OPPORTUNITIES: USING AN IF...THEN...ELSE FIELD TO VARY TEXT *(continued)*

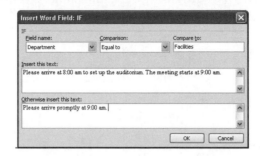

5. Use the Field drop-down list to choose the field on which you are basing the varied text.

6. Choose a comparison from the Comparison list. (See Table 9.1 earlier in the chapter for a description of comparisons.)

7. Type a value, if required, in the Compare To field.

8. Click in the Insert This Text box and enter the text you want to appear in merged documents that meet the condition you specified.

9. Click in the Otherwise Insert This Text box and enter the text you want to appear in documents that do *not* meet the condition you specified.

10. Click OK to close the dialog box and insert the field.

11. Use the Preview step to review records, making sure the text varies according to the condition you specified.

12. If you have made an error (specified the wrong condition, for example), you must delete the Word field with the error and insert a new field with the correction.

In our plant-wide meeting notice example, the operations manager would choose Department in the Field Name list, choose Equal To in the Comparison list, and enter **Facilities** in the Compare To field. In the Insert This Text field, she might say, "Please arrive at 8:00 AM to set up the auditorium. The meeting starts at 9:00 AM." In the Otherwise Insert This Text box, she could add, "Please arrive promptly at 9:00 AM."

The field you use to specify a condition need not be part of the main document. In other words, you can use any field in the data source for the If...Then...Else field. It doesn't have to appear anywhere in the main document.

Previewing the Merged Document

When the main document and data source are merged, Word generates a separate document or listing (if you are setting up a directory) for each record in the data source, based on the layout of the main document. Before you perform the merge, it is a good idea to see a sample of how the merged document will appear. Step 5 of the Mail Merge task pane provides preview and editing options, as shown in Figure 9.15.

FIGURE 9.15

At Step 5 of the Mail Merge task pane, users can preview their finished documents before actually performing the merge.

Step 5 automatically shows what the first record in the merge document will look like. To see the next record, click the double right arrow. The task pane shows which recipient number you're currently viewing. Click the double left arrow to see the previous record.

If necessary, you can make any additional edits to the main document while you're previewing the merged data. For example, if you did not place a colon or other punctuation after the greeting, you can insert it now. If you make any changes to the main document, be sure to save it again.

You can also make changes to the data source at this step. Exclude any recipient by displaying their merged record in the document window and then clicking the Exclude This Recipient button in the task pane. If you prefer, you can click Edit Recipient List to open the Mail Merge Recipients dialog box and sort, filter, or add recipients. Changes to the data source are automatically saved.

NOTE *You can sort and filter any data source in the Mail Merge Recipients dialog box. However, you can edit only fields and field names for data sources in Word table format or those created with the Mail Merge task pane. The Edit feature is disabled for other types of data.*

If you are content with the setup of both the main document and data source, you're ready to complete the merge. Skip to the "Merging Documents" section to proceed, or read the following sections to learn about alternative types of main documents.

Creating Directories

A *directory* (also referred to as a *catalog*) is a main document used to create lists. Each record is listed directly under the previous record on the same page. Word 2003's Mail Merge tool is a great improvement over earlier versions, showing little of its former awkwardness. Just as with a letter merge, you can sort and filter records before performing the merge. In some cases this makes it easier to read the directory. (See the sidebar "Inserting an External Database into a Word Document" if you need to create something more ambitious.)

A directory merge follows the same basic process as any other merge with just a couple of differences:

◆ At Step 1, select Directory from the list of Document Types.

◆ At Step 4 when you set up a directory main document, you can either create a table to hold the merge field codes or use tabs to separate the codes. Using a table produces consistent results with the least amount of hassle. Enter any text you want to appear with each record of the data source, but don't include other surrounding text. If, for example, you want a heading to appear above the records in the list, don't enter it now or your merged document will include a heading, a record, another heading, another record, and so forth.

◆ The Preview step only allows you to see records one at a time. Although you don't get a complete view of the completed directory, you can still spot problems. This is a good time to make any adjustments to the table width or to the width of any column in the main document.

After you have merged the data source and main document (see "Merging Documents" later in this chapter), you can add titles, column headings, and any other information to the merged document before you print it, as shown in Figure 9.16. You probably won't want to save the results of merged directories, particularly if the underlying data changes frequently. However, if you had to add a lot of heading and title information after the merge, go ahead and save it for future reference.

FIGURE 9.16

Insert titles, column headings, and any other general information in a directory after you have merged the main document and the data source.

Volunteer Development Committee

Last Name	First Name	Title	Telephone
McNatt	Rosemary	Minister	(212) 555-7878
Presley	Lisa	Minister	(231) 555-4876
Works	Larry and Lauren	Webmaster	(231) 555-4565
Courter	Amy	Vice President, MIS	(734) 555-3456
Fallis	Carol	Attorney	(810) 555-1111
Friedman	Lisa	Minister	(810) 555-8767
Dennett	Richard	Farmer	(231) 555-6789
Pahl	Dave		(231) 555-9234
Bultemeier	Marci	Internist	(231) 555-0850
Holm	Keith	Engineer	(715) 555-8989
Belcher	Emmy Lou	Minister	(231) 555-3116
Etheridge	Melissa	Singer/Songwriter	(231) 555-1111
Near	Holly	Activist/Singer	(231) 555-4343
Martinez	Rosa		(810) 555-4567
Paku	Indira		
Cash	Swin		
Courter	Gini	UUA Trustee	
Courter	Guy		(810) 555-3456
Cowtan	Charlotte		
Cowtan	Margaret		(416) 555-9898
Deegan	Tisha	RE Chair	(810) 555-7896
Hansen	Alice	Worship/Program Chair	
Hicks	Linda	SLUUD Extension	(905) 555-9878

MASTERING THE OPPORTUNITIES: INSERTING AN EXTERNAL DATABASE INTO A WORD DOCUMENT

As an alternative to using mail merge to create directories, Word lets you easily insert data from an external data source, such as an Excel or Access table, into a Word document. Using this feature, you can create a directory where the data is linked directly to the data source; this way, you can update data without merging again. And unlike the Directory Mail Merge feature, Insert Database allows you to insert data into a document that already contains text.

Follow these steps to insert an external database into a Word document:

1. Open a new, blank document, or open a document that contains the data source you want to replace.

2. Display the Database toolbar (View ➤ Toolbars ➤ Database).

3. Click the Insert Database button on the Database toolbar to display the Database dialog box.

4. Choose Get Data to display the Open Data Source dialog box and then select the name of the folder that contains the database in the Look In list box.

5. Select the file extension of the database file in the Files Of Type drop-down list, highlight the name of the database file that contains the records you want to insert into Word, and then choose Open. (If you would like to connect to another type of ODBC-compliant database, click the New Source button to open the Database Connection Wizard.)

6. If the Select Table dialog box appears, specify the table, query, or worksheet that contains the data. You will only see this option if the data source you're using contains multiple tables.

7. To filter or sort the data or to select specific fields, click the Query Options button and enter the criteria. Click OK to return to the Insert Data dialog box.

8. You can choose an AutoFormat for the table by clicking the Table AutoFormat button and selecting the options you want in the dialog box. Click OK when you're finished here.

9. Choose Insert Data in the Database dialog box to display the Insert Data dialog box. Then choose any of the following options, and click OK:

   Insert Records Choose All to insert all of the specified records, or choose From to insert a range of records, and then type the number of the first record in the adjoining text box and the number of the last record in the range in the To text box.

Continued on next page

Insert Data As Field   Choose this option to automatically update the data in the Word document each time the data in the original database changes.

10. If you are inserting a database into an existing data source, choose Yes to confirm that you want to replace the current data source with the records in the database.

If you chose Insert Data As Field in Step 9, click the Update Field button on the Database toolbar to have Word update the data source with any edits made in the database that you used to create it.

Creating Envelopes and Labels

Labels and envelopes are two other types of main documents. Specialty labels are available at office supply stores, allowing you to create labels for any use. Word can merge to various sizes of envelopes, including standard, business, note card, and other sizes. If your printer can print on envelopes and labels, you can create them in Word. (You must also know how to load the envelopes and labels. If you're not sure, consult your printer manual.)

Preparing Labels

Follow these steps to create labels:

1. Display the Mail Merge task pane and then choose Labels in the Select Document Type options.

2. Click Next: Starting Document.

3. Choose a Starting Document option. If you began with a blank document, you can choose Change Document Layout to create a label from scratch or choose Start From Existing Document to use an existing label setup.

4. Click Label Options to set up the label you want to use. Select the manufacturer of your labels in the Label Products drop-down list. Select the product number (or Avery equivalent) that appears on your label package in the Product Number list box. If you're using a printer that has multiple feed trays, select the one you wish to use from the Tray drop-down list at the top of the Label Options dialog box. The default for these types of printers is Manual Feed, so you may want to choose an automatic feed option if you are printing many pages. Click OK when you have finished selecting label options.

5. Click Next: Select Recipients.

6. Attach a data source by browsing to open an existing list, choosing an Outlook folder, or creating a new address list.

7. Modify the recipient list, if desired, by clicking Edit Recipient List and then sorting or filtering, or selecting individual records. Click Next: Arrange Your Labels to proceed.

8. Set up the labels with the fields you want to use. Insert and format the fields on the first label. Then click Update All Labels to place those fields on every label.

WARNING *Don't delete the Next Record field Word automatically inserts on every label but the first. If you do, the first record is repeated on every label!*

9. Click Next: Preview Your Labels to get an idea of how the final merged document will appear. Figure 10.17 shows name badges at the Preview stage.

10. Use the navigation buttons to browse through the labels in Preview mode. Just as with other main document types, you can edit the recipient list at this point if you wish.

11. Click Next: Complete The Merge when you are ready to proceed.

TIP *If you want to save the Label main document, type* **Labels** *(instead of Main) at the beginning of the filename.*

FIGURE 9.17

Create name tags using labels as the main document type.

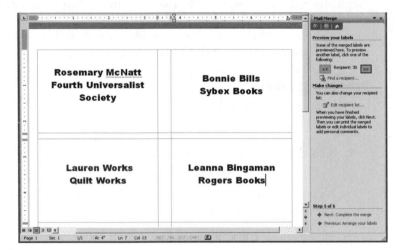

Preparing an Envelope

Creating an envelope main document is similar to creating a label main document. Follow these steps:

1. Display the Mail Merge task pane and then choose Envelopes in the Select Document Type options.

2. Click Next: Starting Document.

3. Choose a Starting Document option. If you began with a blank document, you can choose Change Document Layout to create an envelope from scratch or choose Start From Existing Document to use an existing envelope setup.

4. Click Envelope Options and set up the envelope you want to use. Select an envelope size and font options as appropriate. When you're finished, click OK and Word places the envelope in the document window.

5. Click Next: Select Recipients.

6. Attach a data source by browsing to open an existing list, choosing an Outlook folder, or creating a new address list.

7. Modify the recipient list, if desired, by clicking Edit Recipient List and then sorting or filtering, or selecting individual records. Click Next: Arrange Your Envelope to proceed.

8. Position the insertion point on the envelope and insert the fields you want to use. Word automatically includes the fields on every envelope in the merge.

9. Insert a postal bar code, if desired, to speed up the delivery process. Position the insertion point above the name fields and click Postal Bar Code to open the corresponding dialog box.

Use the drop-down lists to choose the database field that corresponds with the zip code and street address fields in Word. Click OK when you're finished; the bar code field appears on the envelope at the insertion point.

NOTE *There is a text box on the label to help place recipient address fields. To see it, just click once in the area where you would expect to insert address fields. (If you don't see the text box right away, click again in another spot.) Once the text box is visible, the insertion point appears in the appropriate position and you can insert an Address Block field.*

10. If you have electronic postage software installed, you can select that option in the task pane.

11. Click Next: Preview Your Envelopes to get an idea of how the final merged product will appear. Figure 9.18 shows an envelope in Preview mode, ready to be merged.

12. Use the navigation buttons to browse through the labels in preview mode. Just as with other main document types, you can edit the recipient list at this point if you wish.

13. If the envelope appears as you wish, save it to a file that begins with *Envelopes*.

14. Click Next: Complete The Merge when you are ready to proceed.

FIGURE 9.18

Preview envelopes
to make sure the
address fields are
placed appropriately.

Envelopes appear with the return address specified as the mailing address on the User Information tab in the Options dialog box. An envelope main document is easy to edit once you have set it up. To remove the return address from preprinted envelopes, just select it and press the Delete key.

TIP   To change the return address on your envelope main document, choose Tools ➤ Options to open the Options dialog box. On the User Information tab, type a different name and address in the Mailing Address text box and click OK.

Using a Mail Merge Template for a Main Document

Word 2003 includes templates designed specifically for mail merge. You can choose from an assortment of letters, fax cover sheets, and directories. The templates come with commonly used merge fields already inserted, which save you steps, allowing more time for the really important things—like lunch!

Using a template is even easier than using a blank main document. Start the merge process as you normally would. At Step 1, choose Letters, E-Mail Messages, or Directory as your document type. Click Next: Starting Document and then proceed as follows:

1. In the Select Starting Document area of the task pane, choose Start From A Template.

2. Click Select Template to open the Mail Merge tab of the Select Template dialog box.

3. Choose from the available templates to produce the type of mail merge document you want to create: letter, fax, or address list (directory).

4. Click OK to close the dialog box and open the template.

5. Proceed through the rest of the steps as you normally would. Depending on your data source, you might have to delete some of the fields included in the template, or replace them with correct fields from the data source before you complete the merge.

Using E-mail As Main Documents

If you are comfortable creating letters as a main document, you'll have no trouble with e-mail. The steps to create an e-mail main document are exactly the same except you choose E-Mail Messages as the document type in Step 1 of the Mail Merge task pane. You'll experience slight differences when you actually perform the merge, and those differences are discussed in the next section.

Merging Documents

After you've created a main document and attached a data source, you are ready for the actual merge. This happens at Step 6 of the task pane. If you are still at Step 5, click Next: Complete The Merge to proceed.

The choices you see at Step 6 depend on which type of main document you are using. For each main document type you will be able to perform at least one of the following options.

Print   Opens the Merge To Printer dialog box. Once again you're given the choice to merge all records, the current record, or a range of records.

When you click OK, Word sends the results of the merge directly to the printer. Therefore it is prudent to send the current record or a small range just to make sure everything goes as expected. If you send the entire merge results and something is wrong, the error is multiplied by the total number of records you have in your data source. Choose All only if you have previewed your merge and everything is in perfect order (check that nobody has left purple and green paper in the printer!).

Edit Individual Letters (or Labels or Envelopes)   Opens the Merge To New Document dialog box. (It looks just like the Merge To Printer dialog box.) Choose which records you wish to merge and click OK to have Word conduct the merge and create a new document with the results. Labels appear in columns, form letters and envelopes are separated by page breaks, and directories display each record. You can review the results of the merge (and even modify individual letters) before sending the merge document to the printer. After the merge is printed, there is no reason to save the merge results. If you need to print it again at a later date, you'll want to do the merge again in case you've updated any of the records in the data source.

NOTE   *After you've edited individual letters, labels, or envelopes, just click the Print button on the Standard toolbar to send them to the printer. At that point, they are just like any other document.*

E-mail   Opens a similar dialog box. With this option, however, you must select the database field that contains the recipients' e-mail address. If you're merging to e-mail, you may type a subject line and choose a mail format.

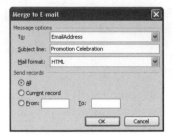

Then you can select the records you wish to merge and click OK. Word sends the e-mail messages to Outlook (or your default e-mail client). If Outlook is open, the messages are sent on their way or stored in the Outbox until Outlook's next Send/Receive.

TROUBLESHOOTING MERGE PROBLEMS

There are three basic reasons for merge problems:

◆ Document incompatibility

◆ Problems with the data source

◆ Problems with the main document

Document incompatibility means that either the data source or the main document isn't a valid Word mail merge file. A dialog box will appear, telling you that the main document has no merge codes or that the data source is invalid. Examine the file in question. If it is a data file, make sure it has field names, that there is no extra text at the beginning of the file, and that the data is in a table. If the problem is the main document, open it and check to make sure you have selected the correct data source file and that it has merge field codes. Even if both files seem to be okay, structural problems with individual records (like missing fields) can cause Word to stop in the middle of a merge.

You can have Word check the data source for omission errors before merging. With the main document active, click the Check For Errors button on the Mail Merge toolbar to open the Checking And Reporting Errors dialog box, shown below. Using this tool is much like checking spelling before printing.

Choose one of the following options, and then choose OK:

◆ Have Word simulate a merge and report errors in a new document.

◆ Merge the two documents and report errors while the merge is taking place.

◆ Merge the two documents and report errors in a new document.

Continued on next page

TROUBLESHOOTING MERGE PROBLEMS *(continued)*

If you expect errors, simulation is best. If you don't think there will be errors (always our hope), go ahead and have Word merge, stopping along the way to report any errors it finds. When Word finds an error, a dialog box opens. Depending on the kind of error, you may be allowed to fix the error and then continue merging. If you can't fix it, note the information provided and click OK to continue finding errors. When Error Checking is complete, close the merged document and fix the data source and/or main document files before merging the documents again.

Even if Word finds no errors and your documents merge, you might still find mistakes in your merged document. There is an easy way to decide if a mistake is in the main document or in the data source. If the mistake appears in every merged document, look for the problem in the main document. For example, if there is no space between the first and last names in your merged form letters, you need to put a space between the merge codes for FirstName and LastName in the main document. Spelling errors in every merged document should lead you to suspect that you forgot to check the spelling in the main document before merging.

If a mistake appears in some but not all merged documents, the problem is in the data source. If a merged first name is spelled incorrectly in one of the merged letters, it's misspelled in the data source. Close the merged file, open the data source file, correct the error, and then merge the documents again.

Although mail merge is the more traditional way to send the same letter to a group of people, the development of e-mail has resulted in another commonly used method, e-mail distribution lists. With a distribution list you can save a group of e-mail addresses as a single address book entry that you can reuse whenever you want to send a group message. In the final section of this chapter, we'll show you how to create and use your own distribution lists.

E-mailing to a Group

When you work with a team or are a member of a committee or task force, you'll often address e-mail to the same group of people—the other members of your team. *Distribution lists* streamline this process. With a distribution list, you create a named list in your Outlook Contacts folder and then add all the members of your team or committee to the group. When you address your next e-mail message, you can send it to the distribution list (and all its members) rather than adding each of the members as individual recipients.

To create a new distribution list in your Contacts folder, follow these steps:

1. Click the down arrow on the right of the New Contact button in Outlook and choose New Distribution List. You can store distribution lists in any Contacts folder as long as it is enabled as an e-mail address book (see Chapter 3, "Taking Control of Your Time and Tasks," for more about enabling Contacts folders)—if you create a subfolder in your main Contacts folder to store distribution lists, you'll discover that they are easier to find when you need them.

2. Choose where you would like to store this list and click OK to open the Untitled Distribution List dialog box.

3. Enter a name for the list in the Name text box.

4. Click the Select Members button to open the Select Members dialog box.

5. Choose the address book that contains the first member you wish to add. Double-click an address to add the address to the distribution list. Continue selecting additional members. If you are creating a large group, you might find it easier to hold Ctrl and click each member to select them and click the Members button to add them to the list.

6. When you've selected all the members of the distribution list, you may want to add some notes to describe the list in more detail. Click the Notes tab to enter any detail about the group.

7. When you've finished, click OK to close the Select Members dialog box. Figure 9.19 shows an example of a distribution list.

8. Click Save And Close to close the Distribution List dialog box.

FIGURE 9.19

In the Distribution List dialog box, enter a name for the list and select the members you want to include in the list.

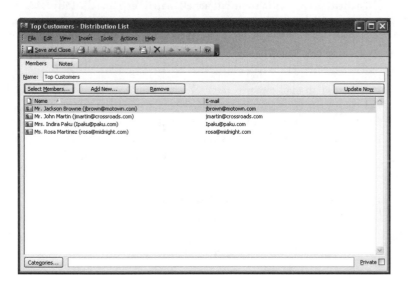

NOTE *If you click the Add New button on the Distribution List dialog box, you can enter a display name and e-mail address and check whether you want to add this person to Contacts. If you do not add the information to Contacts, this person's address is accessible only in the distribution list.*

Distribution lists are intermingled with contacts—look for the special group icon to tell them apart.

NOTE   If you're one of a group of users who need the same distribution list, you can send the distribution list via e-mail as an attached item. See Chapter 2, "Digging Out of the E-Mail Avalanche." You might also talk with your Microsoft Exchange administrator about creating global distribution lists, which are stored in the Global Address List.

Addressing Mail to a Group or Distribution List

To send mail to all members of a group or distribution list, type the group name in the To, Cc, or Bcc text box on the message form, or click one of the three buttons to open the Select Names dialog box. Group names are bold in the Select Names dialog box and address books, and they are preceded by the group icon. Select the group name and click the To, Cc, or Bcc button to add the group's members as message recipients. To check the membership of a group, right-click the group name in the message's address boxes or in the Select Names dialog box and choose Properties to open the group's Properties dialog box.

TIP   If the Bcc field is not visible in the message header, click the down arrow on the Options button on the message's toolbar and choose Bcc. To protect everyone's privacy, you might want to consider putting a distribution list in the Bcc field. Everyone gets the message but doesn't get access to everyone else's e-mail address.

ADDING OR REMOVING A NAME FROM A GROUP OR DISTRIBUTION LIST

The membership of a team or committee can change as members leave the team and new members are added. Follow these steps to add and remove names from a group or distribution list:

1. Choose Tools ➤ Address Book from the menu and select the address book that contains the distribution list.

2. Double-click the name of the list you want to change or right-click a distribution list name and choose Properties to open the Distribution List Properties dialog box.

3. Click the Select Members button to add new group members.

4. To remove a member from a group, select the name you want to delete and click the Remove button in the Distribution List Properties dialog box.

5. When you've finished adding and removing members, click OK to close the Distribution List Properties dialog box.

TIP   If you are sending a mailing that you don't want a particular individual to receive (say you are planning their promotion party) but you don't want to remove them from the distribution list for future mailings, click the Expand button (plus symbol) in front of the name of the distribution list. You are warned that after you do this you can't collapse it again but go ahead and be daring—Outlook expands the list before it sends it anyway. With the list expanded, you can select and delete an individual address and still keep everyone else apprised of the plans.

DELETING A DISTRIBUTION LIST

When a team's work is complete or a committee is disbanded, you probably won't need the distribution list anymore. To remove a distribution list, open the address book (Tools ➤ Address Book) and select the group you want to remove.

Right-click the name of the distribution list and choose Delete from the shortcut menu. When you delete the distribution list, any addresses that existed *only* in the list are also deleted.

NOTE *You can also delete the distribution list from the Contacts folder in which it resides.*

UPDATING DISTRIBUTION LISTS

Each time you use a distribution list, be sure to check the contents to make sure the addresses and membership list are still current. Distribution lists save considerable time but can be the cause of embarrassment if you include someone on a list who has been recently terminated. Use the add and remove features described earlier to clean up your lists before using them.

Chapter 10

Taming Complex Publications

To CREATE USEFUL MULTIPAGE documents, you need more tools in your toolbox than Word's editing and formatting tools. Using Word's Reference tools, you can tackle lengthy documents by including footnotes, endnotes, tables of contents, indexes, hyperlinks, and cross-references. Master documents take you a step further and help you organize multiple documents in a single volume while retaining their individual components. With a little forethought and some extra effort, you can make documents easy to follow and help your readers find what they are looking for. Word 2003 takes the headache out of these additional touches, providing you with one more way to make your work stand out. In this chapter, we'll show you all you need to know to produce functional, readable complex documents.

◆ Adding and revising footnotes and endnotes

◆ Deleting and converting notes

◆ Using bookmarks

◆ Creating cross-references

◆ Indexing for easy reference

◆ Generating and modifying a table of contents

◆ Managing large documents

◆ Creating and printing master and subdocuments

◆ Converting existing documents

Documenting with Footnotes and Endnotes

When you want to give readers more information about your topic or a reference to the source of your information, Word gives you options for inserting both *footnotes,* which appear at the bottom of the page, and *endnotes*, which appear at the end of the document. Word automatically numbers the notes for you and calculates how much space footnotes will need at the bottom on the page. In Word 2003, you can choose a number format for footnotes and endnotes and apply different formats to individual sections, all from within one dialog box. Where was this feature when *we* were typing term papers?

NOTE *You can insert both footnotes and endnotes in the same document. For example, you may want to insert footnotes to add comments to the text of a page and endnotes to add source information, such as a bibliography, at the end of a report.*

Each time you insert a footnote or endnote, Word automatically inserts a *note reference mark* (a character in the text of the document that tells the reader to look for additional information) in your document at the location where you inserted the note. The reference mark can be automatically numbered using Arabic numerals (1, 2, 3, and so on) or using the consecutive numbers or symbols you specify in a different format. You can also choose to insert a custom mark or symbol to use as the note reference mark in your document. Automatic numbering is, of course, the easiest because Word knows what the next reference mark number should be. If you choose a custom mark, you must select the symbol each time you insert a new note, even if you are using the same symbol for every note. This is much easier in Word 2003 since the Insert Symbol dialog box displays recently used symbols.

To insert a footnote or an endnote, switch to Normal, Print Layout, or Web Layout view and follow these steps:

1. Position the insertion point where you'd like the note reference mark to appear, and then choose Insert ➢ Reference ➢ Footnote to display the Footnote And Endnote dialog box shown in Figure 10.1.

FIGURE 10.1

Display the Footnote And Endnote dialog box each time you insert a note reference mark in your document.

2. Select Footnote or Endnote in the Location area to specify what type of note you want to insert. Choose a placement option from the drop-down list to the right of the note type you specified.

- ◆ Choose Bottom Of Page to place footnotes just above the bottom margin on the page that includes the note reference mark or Below Text to place the footnotes just below the last line of text on a short page of text.

- ◆ You can choose to display endnotes at the end of the document or at the end of each section.

3. Choose a Number Format from the drop-down list or, if you prefer, type the character you wish to use in the Custom Mark field or click Symbol to select a character from Word's symbol fonts.

4. If you're numbering footnotes/endnotes, enter a Start At number and then specify one of the following numbering options:

Continuous   Inserts consecutive numbers or symbols in the numbering format selected.

Restart Each Section   Restarts footnote numbering, using the Start At number you specified, at each section break.

Restart Each Page   Restarts numbering, using the Start At number you specified, at each page break.

5. Choose an Apply Changes To option.

6. Click Insert to close the Footnote And Endnote dialog box.

When you insert a note in a document, Word inserts the note reference mark you specified and then:

- ◆ In Normal and Web Layout views, the Note Pane opens. Type the text of your note beside the note reference mark. You can then press F6 to move the insertion point into the document window in the position where you inserted the note. In this way, both the Note Pane and the document window appear on your screen at the same time, as you can see in Figure 10.2. You can work in either pane by repositioning the insertion point either with the mouse or by pressing the F6 key. You can also click Close to hide the Note Pane and return to your document. Insert another note or choose View ➤ Footnotes to redisplay the Note Pane.

- ◆ In Print Layout view, the insertion point moves to the actual location where the note will appear in your document. Type the text of the note, and then press Shift+F5 or double-click the note's reference number to return to the location where you inserted the note reference mark in your document.

TIP   You can use Shift+F5 any time to return the insertion point to the last three locations in the document where you edited text.

FIGURE 10.2

In Normal and Web Layout views, you can see the document and the Note Pane at the same time.

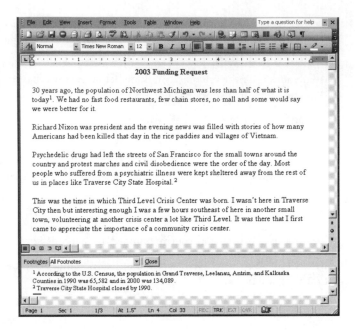

You can decide which view is easier to use when working with notes. In either view, when you want to review your note, all you have to do is point to the reference mark. The mouse pointer changes to an I-beam with a note attached to it, and a second later the note text appears. Just move the mouse pointer away, and the note disappears.

If you are not satisfied with the location of the notes, the note reference marks, and the way the notes are numbered, you can make some changes.. For example, you can change the format of automatically numbered notes (Arabic numerals such as 1, 2, 3) to uppercase or lowercase letters, Roman numerals, or a list of symbols, which Word uses in a set pattern. You can also specify a position for the location of the notes in your document. Any changes you make to the way the notes appear are applied to all the footnotes or endnotes in the document.

To change the way footnotes and endnotes appear, use the following steps:

1. Select the note reference number, the entire document, or the specific section you wish to change. Choose Insert ➤ Reference ➤ Footnote to display the Footnote And Endnote dialog box shown previously in Figure 10.1.

2. Choose a different Number Format, Custom Mark, Start At number, or Numbering type.

3. If you wish to convert a footnote to an endnote, or the reverse, choose a different option in the Location area of the dialog box. You can convert this one instance, or you can change them all. If you wish to change them all, click Convert to open the Convert Notes dialog box. Select from the following options:

Convert All Footnotes To Endnotes   Changes all footnotes into endnotes.

Convert All Endnotes To Footnotes   Changes all endnotes to footnotes.

Swap Footnotes And Endnotes Simultaneously changes all footnotes to endnotes and all endnotes to footnotes.

4. Click OK in Convert Notes dialog box, and then click Insert in the Footnote And Endnote dialog box to both insert a note in the new format and change all existing notes to the new format.

Revising Footnotes and Endnotes

Now that you have footnotes and endnotes scattered throughout your text, you may need to edit one of the notes. There are several ways to activate a note so you can edit it:

◆ Double-click any reference mark in Normal view to open the Note Pane at the bottom of the screen. All notes of the same type appear in the pane—just scroll to the one you want to edit, make your changes, and click Close.

◆ If you are looking for a specific note in Normal view, click the Select Browse Object button on the vertical scroll bar, choose Go To, select Footnote or Endnote, enter the reference mark number you are looking for, and choose Go To. The insertion point automatically moves to the note in the Note Pane.

◆ Move the insertion point into the notes area in Print Layout view and select the text you want to edit. Type the new text to replace the selected text.

To change the numbering or custom mark symbol, double-click any reference mark in Normal view to open the Note Pane at the bottom of the screen. Then choose Insert ➤ Reference ➤ Footnote so you can change the numbering or custom mark symbol. Click Apply to apply the change and close the dialog box.

TIP   If you are changing a note reference mark and know you have to retype the note text, why not select the text and copy it to the Clipboard first? Once you've modified the reference mark, you can just paste the text back into the Note Pane.

Deleting Notes

When you want to delete a note entirely, click before or after the reference mark and press the Backspace or Delete key twice—the first time selects the reference mark, and the second time deletes both the mark and the note. Deleting the text inside the Note Pane or at the bottom or end of the document does not delete the reference mark in the document.

Using Bookmarks

Bookmarks are named locations in a document. It's useful to be able to mark an item or a location that you want to return to later, especially when you are working with long documents. The bookmark could be a place where you need to insert some additional information before finishing the final draft, or a location in the document that contains information pertinent to the current topic. You can also create a bookmark to serve as the destination of a hyperlink in a document (see "Inserting Hyperlinks to Make Navigation Easy" later in this chapter). Whatever the reason, by inserting bookmarks you can easily move to specific text or objects in a document without having to scroll.

Bookmark names can include both numbers and letters, but they must begin with a letter. You can't include spaces in a bookmark name, but you can include the underline character to use instead of a space in names that consist of multiple words.

To insert a bookmark, use the following steps:

1. Select the text, graphic, table, or other object you want to mark. Alternatively, position the insertion point in the location you want to mark.

2. Choose Insert ➢ Bookmark to display the Bookmark dialog box, shown in Figure 10.3.

3. Type a name in the Bookmark Name text box.

4. Choose Add to create the bookmark and return to your document.

FIGURE 10.3

Display the Bookmark dialog box when you want to insert a bookmark in a document.

By default, you cannot see bookmarks in your document. To display bookmarks, you can do the following:

1. Choose Tools ➢ Options and display the View tab in the Options dialog box.

2. Check the Bookmarks check box in the Show area.

3. Click OK in the Options dialog box.

Large, gray brackets ([ ]) surround text or graphics to which bookmarks were added. A gray I-beam appears in the location in which a bookmark was inserted where no item was selected. The brackets are nonprinting characters, so if you're working with a lot with bookmarks, it's handy just to leave them turned on.

Use the options available in the Bookmark dialog box to delete existing bookmarks, to display hidden bookmarks, such as cross-references, or to move to a different document location that was marked. To manage your bookmarks, use the following steps:

1. Choose Insert ➢ Bookmark to display the Bookmark dialog box.

2. To edit or move to bookmarks in a document, use one of the following options:

   ◆ To delete a bookmark, highlight its name in the Bookmark Name list box and choose Delete.

- ◆ To change the order in which the bookmark names are displayed in the Bookmark Name list box, choose an option in the Sort By area. Choose Name to display the bookmark names alphabetically. Alternatively, choose Location to display the bookmark names in the order in which they are located in the document.

- ◆ To select the document location or item that is marked, highlight the name of the bookmark in the Bookmark Name list box and choose Go To.

3. When you are finished making changes or have found the location you want, click Close to return to your document.

Another way to move to and select a bookmark in your document is to use Word's Go To feature:

1. Click the Select Browse Object button at the bottom of the vertical scroll bar.

2. Select Go To in the menu that appears; this will display the Go To tab of the Find And Replace dialog box, shown in Figure 10.4.

3. Choose Bookmarks in the Go To What list box and select the name of the bookmark in the Enter Bookmark Name drop-down list.

4. Click Go To to move to the bookmark.

5. Click Close to close the dialog box and return to your document.

FIGURE 10.4

Use Go To to quickly navigate to a bookmark.

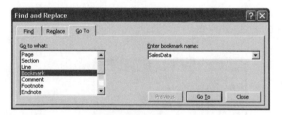

When you close the Go To dialog box, you can use the Previous Find/Go To and Next Find/Go To browse buttons, located above and below the Select Browse Object button on the vertical scroll bar, to move to and select each of your bookmarks.

Creating Cross-References

Use *cross-references* to refer to text or objects elsewhere in a document. Cross-references are used to automatically keep references within a document up-to-date throughout editing. For example, you might direct a reader to see a paragraph in a different section: "See 'Employee Benefits' in Section 5 for more information." If Employee Benefits is later moved to Section 4, you can rest assured that the reader will still look in the right place, because the cross-reference will be updated when Employee Benefits is moved.

NOTE   *If you want to insert cross-references from one document to another—for example, in chapters of a book—convert the documents into subdocuments of a master document. See "Managing Large Documents" later in this chapter for additional information.*

Cross-references can be linked to bookmarks, headings, numbered items, footnotes, endnotes, equations, figures, and tables—and you can choose how the reference will appear in the document. For example, if you want to refer to a heading, you can have the cross-reference indicate the actual text of the heading, the page number where the text is found, or just the word "above" or "below."

To insert a cross-reference in a document, use the following steps:

1. For a text cross-reference, type appropriate text before the position in which you want to insert the cross-reference. For example, type **See page** and then press the spacebar to insert a space.

2. Choose Insert ➤ Reference ➤ Cross-Reference to display the Cross-Reference dialog box.

3. Select the type of item to which the reference will refer in the Reference Type drop-down list. In Figure 10.5, Bookmark is the selected reference type. A list of the items of that type in the document appears in the list box.

4. Select the item in the For Which list box to which the cross-reference will refer.

5. Choose what you want to include in the reference in the Insert Reference To drop-down list. This item will be inserted in the position of the insertion point in the document. For example, select Page Number to have the page number of the item selected in Step 4 appear beside your optional text.

6. Choose Insert to insert the cross-reference.

7. Repeat the steps above to insert as many cross-references as necessary, and then click Close to return to your document.

FIGURE 10.5

The Cross-Reference dialog box allows you to insert a reference to information in another location in the same document.

Cross-references are inserted as fields in the document. By default, the results of the field codes appear. If you want to see the actual field code, right-click the field and choose Toggle Field Codes. To display the results of the field code, right-click the field again and choose Toggle Field Codes.

NOTE *The Field Code commands do not appear on the shortcut menu if the field codes contain a grammatical error, such as no space between the field code and the period of the previous sentence. You must correct the grammatical error before Word will display the shortcut menu with the Field Code commands.*

MASTERING FIELD CODES

Field codes are used in documents as placeholders for data that might change. Fields help you automatically enter some types of information. Some fields that are commonly used in documents include the Page field, which automatically updates the page numbers, and the Date field, which automatically inserts today's date (retrieved from Windows). In document-heavy businesses, the file name and path to a saved document are often displayed in a footer, making it easy to locate a file from a printed document. Speaking of printing, in businesses where a document undergoes several edits, it helps to use a field code to display the date each draft is printed. That way an attorney knows at a glance which version of the contract is more recent before he meets with the client to review it!

By default, the results of field codes appear in your documents rather than the field codes themselves. When field codes are displayed, they appear in braces, or curly brackets ({ }). To change the view so that the field codes, rather than the results, are displayed, follow these steps:

1. Choose Tools ➢ Options, and display the View tab in the Options dialog box.

2. In the Show section, click the Field Codes check box to place a check mark in it.

3. Click OK.

Fields are inserted when you use specific commands, some of which are located on the Insert menu. For example, to insert page numbering (the Page field code), choose Insert ➢ Page Numbers, choose the position and alignment, and then click OK. If you want to manually insert field codes, do not type the braces. Instead, press Ctrl+F9 to have Word insert the field-code braces and then type the appropriate data between them.

Word's field codes can be found in the Field dialog box, which is displayed when you choose Insert ➢ Field.

If you make any changes to the document, you should manually update the results of the field codes. You can update individual fields by right-clicking the field and choosing Update Field. To update all the fields in the document, follow these steps:

1. Choose Edit ➢ Select All to select the entire document.

2. Press F9, or right-click the selection, and then choose Update Field in the shortcut menu.

TIP   To have Word automatically update all the field codes in a document before you print it, choose Tools ➢ Options, display the Print tab, check the Update Fields check box in the Printing Options area, and then click OK.

Hyperlinking Cross-References for On-Screen Viewing

If your document is intended for use online or on screen, leave the Insert As Hyperlink check box in the Cross-Reference dialog box checked to create a more active kind of cross-reference. A *hyperlink*, which is a connection between two areas of a document or two different documents, is commonly used in Internet and intranet sites and other documents that are to be viewed online. By clicking a hyperlink, you can move to a different location in the same document, a different file, or even an address on the World Wide Web. When a user points to a hyperlinked cross-reference, a screen tip appears telling the user they will go to a location in the current document if they hold Ctrl and click the hyperlink (except in Reading Layout view where you only need to click the hyperlink). Hold Ctrl (the mouse pointer changes to a hand) and click once to move to the location in the document to which the hyperlink cross-reference refers.

NOTE *Hyperlinking cross-references is limited to reference types within the same document (or master document). If you want to create a hyperlink to another document, to a document created with another application, or to an address on the World Wide Web, read the section "Inserting Hyperlinks to make Navigation Easy" later in this chapter.*

TIP *If you prefer to follow hyperlinks with a single click as you do on the Web, disable the Ctrl+click feature by choosing Tools ➤ Options ➤ Edit and clearing the check box in front of Use Ctrl+click To Follow Hyperlink.*

To create a hyperlinked cross-reference, follow the same steps outlined earlier to create a traditional cross-reference, but substitute this first step:

1. Position the insertion point where you want the hyperlinked text to appear. For example, if you want a hyperlink to take readers to a document section called "Sales Data," create a bookmark at the sales data location, move the insertion point to the position where you want the link to be placed, and type text such as `For more information refer to the section on` .

Also, be sure the Insert As Hyperlink check box is checked in the Cross-Reference dialog box. Word automatically inserts the bookmark name, Sales Data. The user just clicks the link to jump to the "Sales Data" section.

TIP *If you find yourself moving back and forth in your document, you might find it helpful to turn on the Web toolbar. Right-click any toolbar and choose Web. Click the Back button on the Web toolbar to return to the point of origin, the hyperlink cross-reference. Click the Forward button to jump once again to the position to which the hyperlinked cross-reference refers.*

Be careful not to delete an item that is referenced or the link will be broken. If the cross-reference is a hyperlink, Word will take your readers to another location that contains similar text. Users clicking the "See Employee Benefits" hyperlink could find themselves, for example, on the "Termination of Employment" page—probably not the message you want to convey.

Inserting Hyperlinks to Make Navigation Easy

As you saw in the previous section, you can use cross-references to create hyperlinks to locations within the same document (or master document). But what if you want to create a link between a report created in Word and the Excel spreadsheet that supports the information in the report, or you want to direct readers to a website with more information? In these cases, you would create a hyperlink rather than using a hyperlinked cross-reference.

NOTE *In case you are wondering, inserting a hyperlink to a location within the same document (or master document) is another way to create a cross-reference. In this situation, you could use either one. Use Cross-reference if you want to refer readers to specific page numbers in a printed document and Hyperlink if the document will be read electronically. It's only when you want to link outside of a document that you can't use a cross-reference and instead need to insert a hyperlink.*

Hyperlinks appear underlined and in a different font color. (If they don't stand out, no one knows to click them!) By default, hyperlinks appear in a blue font on your screen. Once you click the hyperlink, it changes to magenta.

NOTE *Type the e-mail or web page address directly in a Word document to have Word automatically insert the address as a hyperlink. If the address does not appear as a hyperlink, check the Internet And Network Paths With Hyperlinks check box on the AutoFormat As You Type tab and AutoFormat tab in the AutoCorrect dialog box (Tools ➢ AutoCorrect Options). You might want to clear this check box if you are typing URLs/addresses in a print document and you do not want to show the hyperlink format (or you can reformat the hyperlink manually by changing the underline style to None).*

There are several ways to create hyperlinks in your documents. The easiest way is to right-drag (use the right mouse button to drag) into your Word document selected text or graphics from a Word document or PowerPoint slide, an Excel spreadsheet range, or an Access database object. The document that contains the selection must have previously been saved.

When you drag the selection, Word automatically knows the location of the object you dragged. It is not necessary to create bookmarks in the destination document or to name ranges in the destination worksheet before you drag a selection.

To create a hyperlink by dragging selected text or a selected object, use the following steps:

1. Open the file that contains the text or other object and also open the Word document in which a hyperlink is to be inserted.

2. Display both files on your screen. If the two files are both Word files, use the Window ➢ Arrange All command to have the two open documents arranged horizontally on your screen. If the destination file is an Access, Excel, or PowerPoint file, open the file and display the location the hyperlink will jump to and then resize both applications' windows so you can see them on your screen.

3. Select the object the hyperlink will jump to in the destination file.

4. Hold down the right mouse button and drag the selection into the position you want for the hyperlink in your Word file.

5. Release the button and choose Create Hyperlink Here from the shortcut menu.

TIP *You can also use the Clipboard to create a hyperlink. Copy the data or object to the Clipboard and position the insertion point where you want to create the hyperlink. Choose Edit ➢ Paste As Hyperlink to create the hyperlink in your Word document.*

When you point to the hyperlink, the path to its destination file appears in a screen tip. If you position the insertion point within the hyperlink text, you can then edit it.

You can also insert a hyperlink to an e-mail or web page address, specify descriptive text for the hyperlink in a screen tip, or browse for the exact path of a hyperlink's destination file using the options available in the Insert Hyperlink dialog box.

To use the Insert Hyperlink dialog box to insert a hyperlink, follow these steps:

1. Position the insertion point where you want to insert the hyperlink and choose Insert ➤ Hyperlink to display the Insert Hyperlink dialog box.

2. Specify the following options for the destination:

   ◆ Click Existing File Or Web Page in the Link To area. Then type the path to the file or the address of the web page in the Address text box. If you've entered the address previously, you can click the down-arrow on Address and select the address from the list. Alternatively, click the Look In down-arrow and select one of the files or web pages that appears in the list box. The addresses in the list box change depending on which option (Recent Files, Browsed Pages, or Current Folder) is selected in the Look In Pane.

TIP *You can click the Target Frame button to select an exact location on the page or to open the page in a separate window.*

   ◆ Choose Place In This Document in the Link To area. Then select Top Of Document, the name of a heading or a bookmark, or one of the locations listed in the Select An Existing Place In The Document list box and click OK to insert the hyperlink and close the dialog box. Figure 10.6 shows an example of linking to a bookmark.

   ◆ Choose Create New Document in the Link To area. Then type a filename for the document in the Name Of New Document field. Choose whether you wish to edit the new document now (Word will display the blank document immediately) or later (Word saves the blank document and inserts the hyperlink—you can open the blank document and edit it at any time).

   ◆ Choose E-mail Address in the Link To area. Type the address in the E-mail Address field (or select one from the list of recently used e-mail addresses). Type a subject line for the e-mail, if you wish.

3. To have descriptive text appear as the hyperlink in your document, type it in the Text To Display text box.

4. By default, the address in the Address box appears as the screen tip for the hyperlink. Choose ScreenTip to display the Set Hyperlink ScreenTip dialog box, type the descriptive text that will appear in the screen tip when you point to the hyperlink in the ScreenTip Text box, and then click OK.

5. Click OK to insert the hyperlink in your document.

FIGURE 10.6

Use the options in
the Insert Hyperlink
dialog box to insert a
hyperlink to a file, a
web page, an e-mail
address, a location
in the current
document, or to
create a new
document as
the hyperlink's
destination.

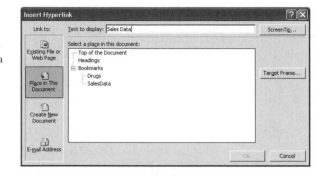

Indexing for Easy Reference

You can make lengthy documents more user-friendly by creating an index of key words and phrases. Index entries can consist of individual words, phrases, or symbols that you select in your document; a topic that extends through several pages that you have named as a bookmark; or a topic that references another index entry.

Although marking index entries is a manual process, Word automates the creation of the index along with insertion of current page numbers, and will update it on request. Word automatically inserts the XE (Index Entry) field code for each marked entry. You can either mark the entries individually or have Word mark every instance of the same entry.

To mark the first index entry, follow these steps:

1. Select the text you want to include in the index and press Alt+Shift+X to display the Mark Index Entry dialog box shown in Figure 10.7.

2. The selected text appears in the Main Entry text box. If necessary, edit the text so it appears as you want it in the index.

3. To place subentries below the main index entry when the index is generated, type up to six additional entries, separated by a colon, in the Subentry text box. For example, when the main entry is Sales, type **Sales data: Western Region** to include both of those topics below the Sales topic in the index.

4. Choose one of the following options in the Options area to specify what type of index entry you want the marked text to be:

   Cross-Reference Adds the cross-reference text you type to the index entry instead of the page number. When you select this option, type the name of another index entry after See in the corresponding text box. For example, if the main entry is Text Box, type **graphics** after See.

Current Page   Automatically adds the page number after the marked entry.

Page Range   Allows you to select a previously named bookmark, which defines text that spans multiple pages, in the adjacent drop-down list.

5. To add bold or italic formatting to the entry's page number, check the Bold or Italic check box in the Page Number Format area.

6. Choose one of the following to mark the index entry:

Mark   Labels only the selected text in your document as an index entry.

Mark All   Labels every occurrence of the selected text in your document.

NOTE   *You can also display the Mark Index Entry dialog box by choosing Insert* ➤ *Reference* ➤ *Index And Tables and then clicking Mark Entry.*

The Mark Index Entry dialog box, shown in Figure 10.7, stays open while you return to your document and select the next text you want to appear in the index. When you click back in the dialog box, the selected text appears in the Main Entry text box.

FIGURE 10.7

Use the Mark Index Entry dialog box to create several different types of entries for an index in the current document.

NOTE   *A cross-reference index entry occurs only once in the index. As a result, you can choose Mark, but not Mark All, when marking cross-references.*

MASTERING THE OPPORTUNITIES: MARKING INDEX ENTRIES USING A CONCORDANCE FILE

A *concordance file* is a regular Word file that Word uses to automatically mark index entries in your document. A concordance file contains a two-column table. The exact text to be marked in the document is typed or pasted into the first column, and the text that is to appear in the index for that entry is typed in the second column. When you are ready, Word searches through the document for the text in the first column and marks it with an index entry field that includes the text in the second column.

Continued on next page

MASTERING THE OPPORTUNITIES: MARKING INDEX ENTRIES USING A CONCORDANCE FILE
(continued)

Businesses with common terminology or technical jargon often use a concordance file to mark index entries. It saves the user from having to mark each entry individually when the same terms are marked again and again over different documents. You can always use the concordance file as a starting point and add the terms that are specific to each document.

You must first set up the concordance file. To do so, follow these steps:

1. Open a new, blank document.

2. Create a two-column table.

3. Type (or paste) the text you want Word to mark for the index entry in the first column. The text must be entered exactly as it appears in the document.

4. Press Tab to move the insertion point to the next cell and type the index entry for the text that appears in the first column.

5. Repeat Steps 3 and 4 for every index entry. To make sure Word marks all occurrences of the text you want, be sure to include all forms of the word in the concordance table. For instance, you should include *hibernate*, *hibernating*, and *hibernation* on the left column and type the word **bears** for all three in the right column.

6. Save the file.

Once you've created the concordance file, follow these steps to have Word mark the index entries in the document:

1. Choose Insert ➤ Reference ➤ Index And Tables to display the Index tab in the Index And Tables dialog box.

2. Choose AutoMark and select the name of the concordance file, and then choose Open. Word searches the document for the text in the left column of the concordance file and uses the text in the right column for the index entry.

When you are finished marking entries, get up from your chair and stretch for a minute. It's a tedious process but well worth it, because Word will use the marked index entries to automatically generate the index.

When you're ready to generate the index, follow these steps:

1. Press Ctrl+End to move the insertion point to the last page of your document, and then enter a heading for the index. Press Enter a couple of times to leave some space after the heading.

2. Choose Insert ➤ Reference ➤ Index And Tables to display the Index And Tables dialog box shown in Figure 10.8.

3. Choose any of the following options to specify how you'd like to format the index. Watch Print Preview in the dialog box to see how the options you select affect the index.

Type Select an option to specify how all subentries will appear below main entries. The Indented option places subentries below main entries; the Run-In option places subentries on the same line as main entries.

Columns Adjust the value to specify the number of columns that will appear in the index. Choose Auto to have the index appear with the same number of columns as the document.

Language Select the language for the index.

Right-Align Page Numbers Check the check box to have Word place the entries' page numbers along the right margin of the page or column. Then, in the Tab Leader drop-down list, select dots, dashes, underline, or None as the character that appears before the right-aligned page numbers.

Formats Select the styles to apply to the index. If you choose From Template, choose Modify to display the Style dialog box and then make any necessary changes to the selected index style.

4. When the sample index in the Print Preview area appears with the formatting you want for your index, click OK to generate the index in the position of the insertion point (see Figure 10.8).

FIGURE 10.8

Display the Index tab in the Index And Tables dialog box when you are ready to generate the index.

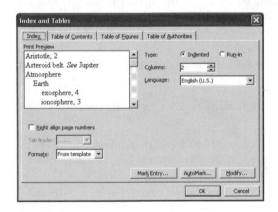

Word gathers the marked index entries and then uses them to create the index. A continuous section break mark is automatically inserted before and after the index. Go through each entry in the index to make sure it says what you want it to say and that the references are accurate. If you find any errors, you can fix them in the index, but any changes made to the index itself will be lost if you regenerate the index. Instead, make any necessary changes in the Index Entry (XE) fields inserted in the document and then regenerate the index.

NOTE *Just as with cross-references, you can't see Index entries unless the Show/Hide button on the Standard toolbar is turned on.*

To regenerate the index after making changes, follow these steps:

1. Choose Insert ➢ Reference ➢ Index And Tables and then click OK to regenerate the index.

2. Word selects the existing index and displays a dialog box asking whether you want to replace it. Choose Yes.

If you edit the document after you generate the index, some of the page numbers in the index might no longer be correct. You can update the index without regenerating it because the entire index is a field. (The index that appears is the result of entering the Index field code at the insertion point.) To update the index, click anywhere in it and press F9. Any edits or formatting you've applied directly to the index are replaced when you update it.

Generating a Table of Contents

Creating a table of contents (TOC) is similar to creating an index. However, instead of marking entries to generate the table of contents, you apply Word's built-in heading styles to the text that is to appear in the TOC. Word automatically selects the document's headings and lists them in the table of contents. If you did not apply heading styles when you created the document, you can go through the document and apply them before you create the table of contents.

NOTE *If you are unfamiliar with Styles, stick to the basics. Apply Heading 1, Heading 2, or Heading 3 by moving the insertion point into the heading text in a section of the document and selecting the appropriate heading level from the Style drop-down list on the Formatting toolbar. Use Heading 1 for the main sections, Heading 2 for subsections, and Heading 3 if your document's structure requires a lower level. By using Heading styles, you save yourself the trouble of remembering how you formatted the previous header—Word formats it for you.*

In Word 2003 the document headings are entered as hyperlinks in the table of contents. You can point to one of the headings to move immediately to that position in the document. If the document is to be printed, display it in Print Layout view so the page numbers appear along with the headings. If the document is to be viewed online, display it in Web Layout view so that the headings are displayed as hyperlinks.

To create the table of contents, follow these steps:

1. Position the insertion point at the beginning of the document and choose Insert ➢ Reference ➢ Index And Tables to display the Index And Tables dialog box, previously shown in Figure 10.8.

2. Select the Table Of Contents tab in the Index And Tables dialog box, shown in Figure 10.9.

3. Choose any of the following options for your TOC:

   Show Page Numbers Check this box to have page numbers appear when the document is viewed in Print Layout view or when the document is printed.

Right Align Page Numbers   Check this box to have displayed or printed page numbers aligned along the right margin of the page. Adjust the Tab Leader control to select None, dots, dashes, or underline as the character to appear before the page number.

Formats   Select the formatting you want for the table of contents. If you choose From Template, choose Modify to display the Style dialog box and then make any necessary changes to the TOC headings.

Show Levels   Adjust the value in the text box to display the number of heading levels you want to appear in the table of contents.

4. Click OK to generate the table of contents.

When you generate the table of contents, a page break is inserted above the insertion point, and Word enters the TOC field code on the new page.

FIGURE 10.9

The Table Of Contents tab in the Index And Tables dialog box shows you samples of the table of contents in both Print Preview and Web Preview views.

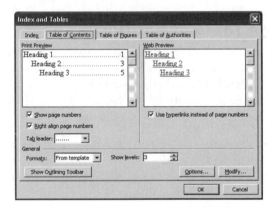

USING OTHER OPTIONS TO CREATE A TABLE OF CONTENTS

You can also create a table of contents using a combination of outline levels, existing styles (other than heading styles), and TC (table of contents entry) fields. If you want to use other styles or outlining, simply assign each style a TOC level and/or outline level. To mark table of contents entries exactly as you want them to appear in the table of contents, insert TC field codes immediately before the text entry you want to include in the table of contents. Click Insert ➢ Field and choose TC to insert a TC field code (and enter the text in the Text Entry field of Field Properties). Follow these steps to use either option to create a table of contents:

1. Position the insertion point where you want the table of contents to appear in your document.

2. Choose Insert ➢ Reference ➢ Index And Tables ➢ Table Of Contents and then click Options to display the Table Of Contents Options dialog box.

Continued on next page

3. Check the Styles check box to have Word build the table from available styles in your document and then assign each style the appropriate TOC level by typing the level in the adjacent TOC Level text box.

4. Check the Table Entry Fields check box if you inserted TC field codes in the document.

5. Enable the Outline Levels feature if you'd like to include text marked with outline levels in place of or in addition to styles in your TOC.

6. Click OK to return to the Index And Tables dialog box.

7. Choose the formatting for the table of contents from any of the available options.

8. Click OK to generate the table of contents.

Modifying a TOC

Although you can directly edit the text in the table of contents, any changes you make will be lost if you regenerate the table or update the TOC field code. Each table of contents entry is a hyperlink, so if you changed the default option requiring you to use Ctrl+click to follow a hyperlink (Edit tab on Tools ➢ Options), use the arrow keys to move to the text you want to edit.

Generally, it's a good idea to update the entire table of contents instead of editing it. For example, if you edit the text of the document, the page numbers in the table of contents might then be incorrect.

When you want to update the table, move the insertion point into the table and press F9. Or, if the Outlining toolbar is turned on, click the Update TOC button on the toolbar.

TIP   You can turn on the Outlining toolbar by right-clicking any toolbar and choosing Outlining.

If, after updating, the page numbers still don't seem to be correct, check the following:

- ◆ Index entry fields are formatted as hidden text. To hide them and other hidden text so they do not appear in the document (and increase its on-screen length), click the Show/Hide ¶ button on the Standard toolbar. Then update the table of contents.

- ◆ Remove any hidden section or page breaks from the document, and then update the table of contents.

If you decide that you want fewer (or additional) heading levels to appear in your TOC, choose Insert ➢ Reference ➢ Index And Tables ➢ Table Of Contents and adjust the number of heading levels. You can also change the tab leader by selecting a different one from the Tab Leader list. When you click OK, the TOC regenerates with the requested number of levels. In some documents, you might even want two TOCs—one with all heading levels and one with only the first-level headings.

Managing Large Documents

As a policy manual, personnel handbook, report, contract, or similar document gets longer, it uses more resources to open, save, or print. It takes forever to scroll down a couple of pages, and editing becomes a nightmare. With a little foresight, you can avoid this dilemma by starting with an outline and then dividing the entire document, called the *master document*, into various related documents, called *subdocuments*. You—and others in your work group—can then work with subdocuments as separate entities. However, at any point you can work with the entire master document so that you can have continuous page numbering, add headers and footers, create a table of contents, attach an index, and insert cross-references—all those things you cannot do with individual, unrelated documents.

What if you're already 10 chapters into a large document? Don't despair—those kind people at Microsoft were thinking of you when they created master documents. Word 2003 can combine separate documents into one master document and divide one long document into several subdocuments. So there's no excuse for working with a document that's out of control—the remedy is right at your fingertips.

Creating Master Documents and Subdocuments

To create a new master document from scratch, open a new document and display it in Outline view. To change to Outline view, choose View ➢ Outline or click the Outline View button next to the horizontal scroll bar.

The Master Document tools appear on the Outlining toolbar. Create an outline by entering headings and subheadings into the document. Use the same heading level (generally Heading 1) for each section that you want subdivided into its own document.

When you have finished creating the outline, select the headings and text you want to split into subdocuments. Click the Create Subdocument button on the Outlining toolbar, and Word creates individual subdocuments using the highest-level heading text you selected as the subdocument name.

The master document displays each subdocument in a box with a small subdocument icon in the upper-left corner when displayed in Master Document view (the default). Click the Master Document View button on the Outlining toolbar to display the master document in Outline view. When you do, the subdocument icon and box no longer appear, and the display shows the section break marks that Word inserted before each selected heading when you created subdocuments.

When you save the master document, each subdocument is automatically saved in a separate file in the same folder as the master document, using the first part of the heading text as the filename. In addition, each subdocument automatically becomes a hyperlink in the master document. When the master document is open, you can simply click the hyperlink of a subdocument to open it for editing. In addition, you can open a subdocument when the master document is not open, using the same methods you would use to open any other file.

NOTE *To open a subdocument before you save the master document, double-click its subdocument icon.*

The primary purpose of creating a master document is to be able to work with discrete sections of the document. It makes sense, then, to collapse the master document so that just the document names are visible. Word automatically displays the master document with collapsed subdocuments when you open the master document file. If you want to see all the text in the entire document, click the Expand Subdocuments button on the Outlining toolbar. The button is a toggle switch—clicking the Collapse Subdocuments button on the Outlining toolbar will collapse the subdocuments again.

The subdocuments of a master document can be *locked*, which makes them read-only files. Read-only files can be viewed, but no changes can be saved to them. To lock a subdocument, click the Expand button to expand the subdocument and then click the Lock Document button on the Outlining toolbar. Click the Lock Document button again to unlock a locked subdocument.

NOTE *In Master Document view, subdocuments are collapsed by default and always appear to be locked—the subdocument icons have padlocks—even if they are not. To see whether the subdocuments in a master document actually are locked, click the Expand Subdocuments button on the Outlining toolbar.*

Word automatically locks an open subdocument. If the document is saved to a shared directory on a network and someone else opens a subdocument that is already open, it opens as a read-only document. In addition, subdocuments that are shared as read-only are locked, as are subdocuments stored on a read-only file share.

When the master document is expanded, you can work with it as if it were one document by switching to Normal, Print Layout, or Web Layout view. You can insert page numbers, headers and footers, a table of contents, an index, and cross-references, and adjust styles just as you would in a normal document. The styles in the master document's template are used for all the subdocuments when the document is printed. If you want to use different formatting for a subdocument, change the formatting in the master document section that contains the subdocument. The page numbers, borders, headers, margins, and columns can be changed in individual sections of a master document.

NOTE *You can use a different template in a subdocument. To do so and then print the subdocument with different styles from those in the master document, open the subdocument in its own window and print it from there. You can also change the section's formatting by opening the subdocument in its own window and then making the changes.*

CONVERTING EXISTING DOCUMENTS

For a document to be converted to a master document, you must apply Word's built-in heading styles to some of the text so you can work with it in Outline view. After you have applied heading styles, you can switch to Master Document view and follow the same steps you would to create a new master document.

If you have several documents that you want to combine into one master document, follow these steps:

1. Open a new, blank document or a document based on the template you want to use for the master document. Make sure you are in Outline view or you won't see the tools you need on the Outlining toolbar.

2. Position the insertion point where you want to insert an existing document and click the Insert Subdocument button on the Master Document toolbar to display the Open dialog box.

3. Locate and select the name of the file to insert and click Open. The subdocument appears expanded by default.

4. Click the Collapse Subdocument button if you wish to collapse the subdocument. Word prompts you to save if you have created a new master document.

5. Click a subdocument's icon to select it. Press the Shift key while you click to simultaneously select another subdocument.

Once you've selected files, you can do the following:

◆ To merge two subdocuments, select both files and click the Merge Subdocuments button on the toolbar.

◆ To split one subdocument into two, place the insertion point where you want to split and click the Split Subdocument button. Usually, you will choose to split the subdocument at a natural breakpoint, such as a major heading. Word assumes you are doing this; by default, it takes the first line as the document name. If you split a subdocument at a point where there is no heading, it's a good idea to add one for Word to use as the document title.

◆ To delete a subdocument, select it and press the Delete key.

◆ To convert a subdocument to master document text, select it and click the Remove Subdocument button.

Printing Master Documents

When all the text is entered in the subdocuments and all the formatting is applied to the master document along with a table of contents, index, and any other document items, you are ready to print the master document. Word allows you to print the entire master document or only specified details, depending on the heading levels and text displayed on your screen.

To print the entire master document, do the following:

1. Click the Expand Subdocuments button on the Outlining toolbar to expand the subdocuments.

2. Change the display to Normal or Print Layout view.

3. Print as you would any other document.

To print only some of the details of the master document, follow these steps:

1. Click the Expand Subdocuments button on the Outlining toolbar to expand the subdocuments.

2. Use the Show Heading buttons and the Expand and Collapse buttons on the Outlining toolbar to specify the amount of detail you want to print.

3. Print the document as you would any other document.

The printed master document is now ready to be bound, copied, and distributed as you sit back and wait for the accolades that will surely be showered upon you for your Herculean effort!

Chapter 11

Creating and Modifying Documents for the Web

MICROSOFT OFFICE 2003 WAS designed with the Web in mind. In fact, many of the enhancements to Office overall are related to the Web. Creating a web page is the easy part; making it attractive, responsive, and interactive takes some knowledge and an array of special tools. Microsoft has worked to simplify the tools included in the Office suite. Although it has some limitations, Office 2003 has sufficient power to make quality web development a realistic possibility for Office users.

NOTE   *A website is a collection of web pages and other files such as graphic files. The only major difference between a website and a folder you've organized on your hard drive is that, in a website, documents are linked together with hyperlinks and are available for others to view through a web browser.*

Let's say your supervisor has just asked you to create a series of web pages for your corporate intranet. If you haven't created web pages but have heard the lunchroom rumors about HTML, this new assignment can be pretty intimidating. Fear no more—Office 2003 can do the job for you. All you need to do is add a few new skills to your Word, Excel, and PowerPoint repertoire and you'll be producing dazzling pages in no time.

In this chapter, we'll help you differentiate the web-related tools in Office 2003 so you can pick the tools that work best for your situation. We'll also review the general web publishing options and how to save, publish, and manage a published web page. Finally, we'll show you how to create web content by focusing on the most commonly used tools—Word, Excel, and PowerPoint.

- ◆ Choosing from among the Office web design tools
- ◆ Setting web publishing options
- ◆ Saving documents as web pages
- ◆ Publishing and managing web pages
- ◆ Creating web pages
- ◆ Creating web-based forms
- ◆ Working with frames

◆ Publishing an Excel spreadsheet to the Web

◆ Posting presentations to the Web

Filling Your Web Design Toolbox

Every one of the Office 2003 applications offers something for the Web. With some applications, such as Word, Publisher, and FrontPage, you can create fully functioning websites. Other applications, such as Excel and Access, offer tools to create individual web pages and special objects that you can include in existing pages. Access, through the use of Data Access Pages, makes database data available to your web visitors. In PowerPoint, you can create presentations for the Web and even broadcast presentations to a select audience. Although Outlook doesn't include any web design tools, you can use Outlook as a browser, display home pages for folders, access contacts' web pages, and store URLs on the Outlook bar. And, if you use Word as your e-mail editor to create HTML mail, you can use all of Word's web design tools to create e-mail messages.

Let's examine each Office 2003 application and identify the strengths and limitations of its web tools.

Access   Makes live database data available to the Web with Data Access Pages.

Strengths   Data Access Pages can be used for interactive reporting, data entry, and data analysis. Pages are reasonably easy to design once you decide what you want users to do. You can open any HTML page in Access as a Data Access Page.

Limitations   Users must have Internet Explorer 5 or higher and a Microsoft Office 2003 license, so Data Access Pages are not for general distribution on the Web. They have limited flexibility from a web design perspective.

Excel   Publishes static or interactive spreadsheets and pivot tables.

Strengths   Users can save and publish workbooks or individual pages. Excel tools are included with the worksheet object for direct data manipulation.

Limitations   You need to open the page in a web editing program such as FrontPage or be able to edit the HTML code directly in Notepad to add additional content.

FrontPage   Creates and manages small- and large-scale websites and Windows SharePoint Services sites. It has most of the tools you need for web page creation and website management and provides web page templates and wizards.

Strengths   Web page editing and formatting tools are as consistent with Word as HTML allows. Reports and views help manage websites. Explorer-type interface offers easy file management.

Limitations   It creates extraneous HTML code. The shared borders and navigation bars are great when they work but can be difficult to master. FrontPage server extensions must be installed on a server to take full advantage of the tools.

InfoPath   Creates forms using user-defined XML schema that integrates with XML web services. (Only available in the Enterprise Edition of Microsoft Office.)

> **Strengths**   Uses the familiar Office interface to make usable XML forms requiring little or no custom programming.

> **Limitations**   A brand-new tool in Office 2003 that requires a change in the way organizations think about data.

Outlook   Adds web links to contacts. Opens web pages directly in Outlook. Assigns home pages to folders and adds URLs to the Outlook bar.

> **Strengths**   Integrates the Web with other contact and folder management activities.

> **Limitations**   Cannot create web content. You must edit folder home pages in FrontPage.

PowerPoint   Publishes presentations and creates online broadcasts. Creates hyperlinks to web pages in typical presentations.

> **Strengths**   Easy way to present summary information to users. Few new skills are needed to learn to design and publish presentation. The full-screen slides look great.

> **Limitations**   Presentations run as web pages. You cannot add additional content to the pages.

Publisher   Creates web pages and entire websites.

> **Strengths**   Built-in wizards and templates make web design easy and fun.

> **Limitations**   A limited set of automated components and no website management tools.

Word   Creates web pages in HTML, including themes, frames, and form-creation tools.

> **Strengths**   Little new to learn. Great for intranet content providers who have to update and maintain a limited number of pages.

> **Limitations**   No website management tools.

Introducing the Best Web Tools

Given all the web tools at your fingertips, here is a summary of what we think works best for the common web-related tasks:

♦ If you are planning to create and maintain a full-service website with multiple pages, hyperlinks, user forms, graphics, and maybe even a little sound and video, we recommend that you start in FrontPage and use that as your primary web design tool

♦ If you have other users who are creating and updating simple web pages that you want to incorporate into a larger website, you may want to encourage them to use Word or Publisher rather than taking the time to teach them FrontPage. They will be eternally grateful!

♦ Use Excel, Access, and PowerPoint to add interactive content where appropriate.

♦ Take advantage of Outlook's web tools, particularly adding hyperlinks to contacts' websites.

♦ Use InfoPath to create dynamic, interactive forms to capture user input.

In the rest of this section, we'll take you through some of the common web publishing options you will find throughout Office 2003. Although these are a bit technical, it helps to know what's available before you start creating and publishing web pages.

Setting Web Publishing Options

In each Office 2003 application where you can create HTML web pages—Word, Excel, PowerPoint, Publisher, and to a lesser degree Access and Outlook—you can change the default settings for HTML publishing in the Web Options dialog box. The available options differ slightly, depending on the application you are using. However, several of the options are available in most applications; we'll review those for you here.

NOTE   *Because FrontPage is dedicated to web publishing, all of its options are related to web publishing. To learn more about FrontPage, see* FrontPage 2003 Savvy, *by Christian Crumlish and Kate Chase (Sybex, 2004).*

To access the web options in Word, Excel and PowerPoint, choose Tools ➤ Options. Click the Web Options button on the General tab to open the Web Options dialog box, like the one shown in Figure 11.1 for Excel. Use the pages of this dialog box to set specific options for creating web pages in Office 2003.

FIGURE 11.1

Set options for your web page in the Web Options dialog box.

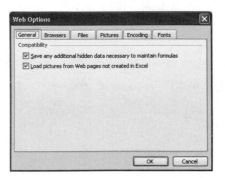

NOTE   *Check the Web Options dialog box in each Office application to see the options that are specific to that application.*

General Options

The General options vary the most depending on the application. Word has no General options. In Excel, you can set options for the inclusion of hidden data and to indicate whether pictures from web pages not created in Excel should be loaded. While in Access, you can only adjust the color of hyperlinks.

Browser Options

If you are creating web pages for use on your company's intranet, you probably have a pretty good idea which browser most people have access to. If you select that browser as the target browser from the drop-down list on the Browsers tab shown in Figure 11.2, you can make sure everyone will have access to the cool stuff you add to your website. The options listed at the bottom of the page turn on and off based on which target browser you choose. Supported features are selected, and unsupported features are unselected.

FIGURE 11.2

Use the Browsers tab to set options related to browsers, such as how graphics are handled.

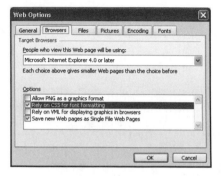

Use these options to set how you want to display graphics. Advanced browsers like Internet Explorer (IE) 5 support Vector Markup Language (VML) and Portable Network Graphics (PNG). Displaying graphics in VML and allowing PNG as an output format result in smaller web graphics files, which download and save much more quickly. If you've ever waited while your low-speed modem slowly downloaded a dozen graphics, you know that VML and PNG are very good news. The bad news is that when you use VML, users with older browsers like IE 4 won't see any graphics at all—and IE 4 isn't all that old.

NOTE   *Internet Explorer 5.0 or later supports saving new web pages as Single File Web Pages, also called* web archives. *Use this option to save snapshots of web pages in single MIME-encoded files using the* .mht *or* .mhtml *file format. See "Saving a Single File Web Page" later in this chapter.*

File Options

The settings on the Files tab, shown in Figure 11.3, determine how the application saves files when you publish your document. These file options are available in many of the Office 2003 applications.

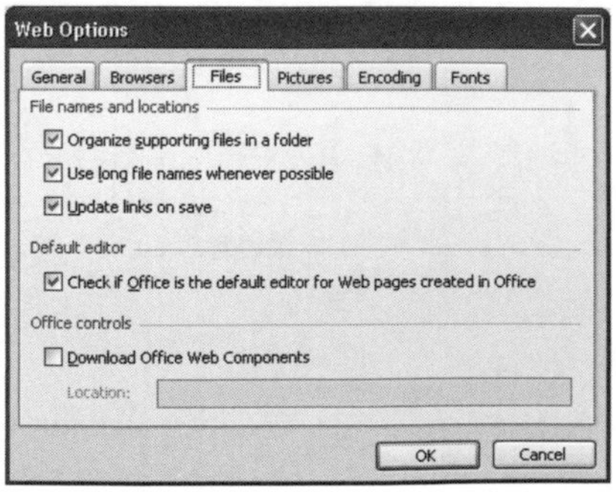

FIGURE 11.3

Use the Files tab to set how you want web documents saved when you publish the files to the Web.

Organize Supporting Files In A Folder   Enabled by default; this option creates a separate folder for supporting files such as graphics when the document is saved. The folder's name is the document's name with _files appended. For example, the folder of supporting files for My Presentation is named My Presentation_files. This option helps keeps your files organized and looking more like a website. If you clear the check box, be sure you can keep track of all of the files associated with the pages you create.

Use Long File Names Whenever Possible   Disable this option if you're saving your presentation on a network file server (rather than a web server) and Windows 3.1 and/or non–Windows users on your network need to open your presentations.

Update Links On Save   This option automatically checks to make sure the links to supporting files such as graphics, background textures, and bullets are updated when the web page is saved.

Check If Office Is The Default Editor For Web Pages Created in Office   Clear this option only if you want to use a non-Office application as your default web page editor. Otherwise, Office will ask you every time you try to save a web page in Office if you want to make an Office application the default editor for the page. If you are setting Word options, you can specifically set Word as the default editor for the page.

In Excel, use the Files tab options to set a location from which you want to download Office Web Components from your corporate intranet. When you designate a file location, Office Web Components are loaded and installed automatically when you open an Excel workbook that uses them. This download location must be set up by your system administrator.

Picture Options

On the Pictures tab, shown in Figure 11.4, you can set the size of a target display monitor, and the number of pixels per inch, to improve layout and resolution. An 800 × 600 display is still the most common resolution used today, but the proliferation of laptops and high-resolution monitors makes this difficult to predict. Choosing 800 × 600 is probably still a safe bet for most web development.

FIGURE 11.4

Use the Pictures tab options to set the size of the target monitor.

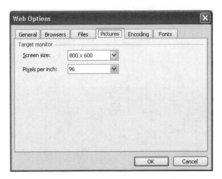

Encoding and Font Options

On the Encoding tab, you can choose the language code you want to save with the web page. If you are using another language from the Microsoft Office Multilingual User Interface Pack to create the web page, be sure to save the corresponding encoding with the web page.

The Fonts tab, shown in Figure 11.5, sets the appropriate character set—Arabic, Cyrillic, English/Western European, and so forth—to use with your web page. This is also where you set the default font and font size on the web page. If a user opens the web page and they have the default font on their system, that's the font the page will use. If they don't have the default font, their browser substitutes another font. It's a good idea to choose a common font that you can be confident most users will have available to them if you want your pages to display correctly.

FIGURE 11.5

On the Fonts tab, you can choose the character set and the default Proportional Font and Fixed-Width Font to use on your pages.

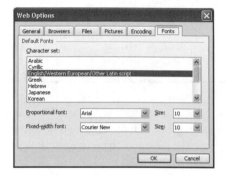

ASSIGNING A HYPERLINK BASE FOR A DOCUMENT

If you are creating web pages for a corporate intranet (or a website where all linked pages reside on the same domain), you can establish a hyperlink base for a document that provides a consistent path to where linked documents are located. This makes it easy to link to documents because you don't have to enter the entire path. It also means that if you change the location of the linked documents, all you have to do is change the hyperlink base and all the links in the document will still be viable. To set a hyperlink base for a document:

1. Open the document's Properties sheet (File ➤ Properties) and click the Summary tab.

2. In the Hyperlink Base box, type the path you want to use for all the hyperlinks you create in this document.

If you want to override the hyperlink base and identify a fixed location for a particular link, just enter the full path to the link in the Insert Hyperlink dialog box.

Saving Documents as Web Pages

In some of the Office 2003 applications, you can save documents as web pages using the Save As Web Page option on the File menu. The Save As Web Page dialog box from Word is shown in Figure 11.6.

Click Change Title to open a dialog box where you can enter a title to appear in the browser's title bar when the page is displayed. (The filename is the default title.) In Word, you simply click Save to save an HTML version of the document. With PowerPoint and Excel, you can set other options, and with Publisher, you can create more than just web pages—you can create an entire website. In Outlook, you can use the File ➤ Save as Web Page option to save the Calendar and e-mail messages.

FIGURE 11.6

When you save as a web page, you have the option of saving a page title that is different from the filename.

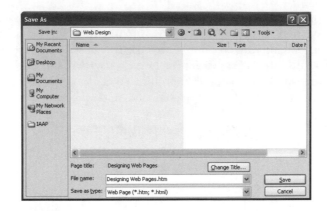

When Office saves the web page, it creates a separate folder called [*filename*]_files to house supporting documents such as graphics. Before you save a document as a web page, we recommend creating a folder in which to save the page and any related web pages. This organizes the web files and makes the supporting subfolders easy to find.

NOTE *If you move or copy a web page to another location, you must also move or copy the supporting folder in order to maintain all links to the web page.*

Saving a Single File Web Page

If you want to send a snapshot of a web page you created in Office 2003 to someone and don't want to send all the accompanying supporting files, you can save the page as a Single Page Web File or Web archive. This file format applies MIME encoding, used to encode e-mail attachments, to the page so it can be saved as a single document. It is only supported by Internet Explorer 4.0 or higher, so make sure your recipient has at least this version of IE.

To save a web page as a Single Page Web File, choose File ➤ Save As Web Page and then select Single Page Web File (*.mht, *.mhtml) from the Files Of Type drop-down list.

You can open Single Page Web Files directly in Internet Explorer or in the Office application you used to create it.

TIP *If you use Word to create a Web page and are sending it to someone who will open it in a browser or publishing it to a web site, you can reduce the file size by saving the file as a filtered web page. Filtering a web page removes any HTML tags that are specific to Microsoft Office programs. The downside? If you reopen a filtered web page in Word, some of the Office functionality, such as automatic bullets, will not be available. To save a filtered web page, choose File ➤ Save As and select Web Page, Filtered (*.htm, *.html)*

Saving vs. Publishing

Excel and PowerPoint each have two ways to save web documents:

◆ Saving as a web page

◆ Publishing a web page

NOTE *Office 2003 Help uses the terms save and publish interchangeably, but there are differences between them that are worth knowing about.*

Saving a document as a web page saves the document in HTML format and makes the page viewable in a browser. You may want to save a document first as an Office document and then save it again as a web page. When you want to make changes to the web page, open the Office document, make the changes there, and resave it as a web page. This reduces the formatting losses you may experience if you open an HTML document in an Office application.

The option to publish a web page is available in Excel, PowerPoint, and Publisher. *Publishing* a web page automatically makes a copy of the page, requiring you to enter a different name or path for the file. It also provides you with options that are not available by simply saving. For example, publishing a PowerPoint presentation allows you to set such additional options as which slides are displayed and whether Speaker's Notes are available. Figure 11.7 shows the Publish As Web Page dialog box that opens when you click the Publish button on the Save As dialog box in PowerPoint.

Excel allows you to publish individual worksheets, but you have to save a workbook as a web page before you can access the entire book in a browser. So why would you want to publish? Publishing allows you to select a range of cells or append a worksheet or a range of cells to an existing web page. If you'd like to find out more about publishing Excel pages, refer to the section "Creating Web Pages with Excel" later in this chapter.

FIGURE 11.7

Publishing a PowerPoint presentation as a web page allows you to select additional options that aren't available by saving.

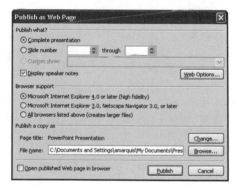

Managing Published Web Pages

Managing web pages you create in Office applications can be a bit tricky unless you also have Microsoft FrontPage 2003. FrontPage includes a number of website management tools that give you control over your published website. A major part of managing a web page is verifying that the hyperlinks work; FrontPage includes a tool to verify hyperlinks. When you don't have FrontPage, one way to do this is to access the page just as any other user would and check the hyperlinks in your browser. If the links work there, they are probably fine. If they don't, correct the hyperlinks in your copy and republish the page to the web server.

NOTE *It's best if you check hyperlinks from a computer other than the one on which you created the site. On your primary computer, a link might work because the file is on your local machine, however, other users couldn't access it.*

Creating Web Pages with Word

Creating and editing web pages in Word is not much different than creating and editing other Word documents. You have access to all of Word's formatting and editing tools, including fonts, paragraph formatting, bullets, tables, and borders and shading. Web pages also include features that are not typically used in print documents: themes, hyperlinks, active graphics such as scrolling text boxes, forms and form controls, and frames, These tools are described in this section. If you learn to use these tools effectively, you'll be able to design web pages that are dynamic, attractive, and effective. The Web Page wizard, used to create full websites in previous Word versions, is no longer available in Word 2003. You can still use Word to create websites but you'll want to use FrontPage or Publisher to create websites that contain more than a few pages.

To create a web page, choose File ➤ New and choose Web Page from the New Document task pane. You can also create a normal new Word document and then save it as a web page. In either case, choose File ➤ Save As Web Page to save the new page, as described earlier in the chapter.

NOTE   *Remember to create a new folder before saving the web page so you can keep the entire website's content together.*

You can add content and design elements to the web page in any order you prefer. We'll start with applying themes and then move through hyperlinks, graphics, forms, and then frames.

Applying Themes

Themes were first introduced in FrontPage 98 and are now included in several Office 2003 applications. A theme, similar to a PowerPoint design template, is a collection of colors, fonts, graphics, backgrounds, bullet characters, and heading styles that fit together. Office includes over 65 themes that can be applied to print publications, online documents, and web pages. To select a theme, choose Format ➤ Theme.

The Theme dialog box, shown in Figure 11.8, displays a preview of each theme listed on the left. Options for Active Graphics (typically appearing as animated bullets and horizontal lines) and Background Image are on by default. If you would also like to use Vivid Colors, click the check box. You can see the results of turning these options on or off in the preview window on the right, although you won't see active graphics actually move.

After you decide on a theme (you can also choose No Theme from the top of the list), click OK to apply the theme to the page.

FIGURE 11.8

You can apply web themes to web and print documents to create a consistent look and feel for all your publications.

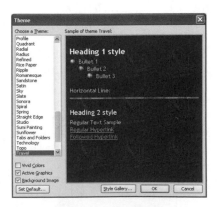

To use the formats of the theme you applied, select a style from the Style drop-down list on the Formatting toolbar and enter some text. Figure 11.9 shows a web page using the Heading 1, Heading 2, and Outline Number styles with the Travel and Compass themes.

FIGURE 11.9

Using styles with predefined themes gives your web page a distinctive, professional look.

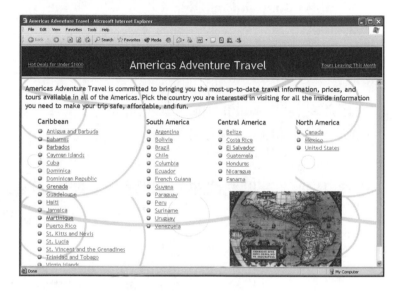

Adding Content to a Web Page

Editing web pages in Word is not much different than editing other Word documents. You have access to all of Word's formatting and editing tools, including fonts, paragraph formatting, bullets, tables, and borders and shading. Web pages also include features that are not typically used in print documents: hyperlinks, frames, form controls, active graphics such as scrolling text boxes, and other special multimedia features. These tools are described in this section. If you learn to use these tools effectively, you'll be able to design web pages that are dynamic, attractive, and effective.

Creating Hyperlinks

Hyperlinks are what make the World Wide Web what it is. When Tim Berners-Lee, CERN researcher, developed HTML, his primary interest was in being able to access related documents easily—without regard to computer platform or operating system— by connecting the documents through a series of links. Hyperlinks allow readers to pursue their areas of interest without having to wade through tons of material searching for specific topics, and hyperlinks take readers down paths they might never have traveled without the ease of clicking a mouse. Adding hyperlinks to your documents moves information down off the shelf, dusts it off, and makes it a living, breathing instrument that people can really use.

Creating a hyperlink in an existing web page is easy. Just follow these steps:

1. Enter some descriptive text or select existing text or an image in the page to define the link; this is the text or image you want users to click.

2. Right-click the selected text or image and choose Hyperlink to open the Insert Hyperlink dialog box, as shown in Figure 11.10.

3. Type a file or web page name in the Address text box, or click the Existing File Or Web Page buttons to browse for the file. Click the Place In This Document button to create a link to another location in the same document, or click the E-mail Address button to create a link to an e-mail message form.

4. If you want to change the hyperlink text, enter new text in the Text To Display box (not available when linking to images).

5. Add a screen tip to the hyperlink by clicking the ScreenTip button and entering the text you want to appear in a screen tip.

6. Click OK to create the link.

For more about creating hyperlinks and bookmarks in Word documents, refer to Chapter 10, "Taming Complex Publications."

FIGURE 11.10

Create hyperlinks to other documents, web pages, e-mail addresses, and other places in the same document by using the Insert Hyperlink dialog box.

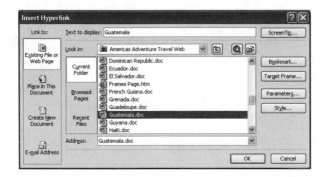

NOTE *Word automatically creates a hyperlink when you type an address it recognizes as an Internet or file path address. If, for example, you type* www.train2k.com, *Word creates a hyperlink to that address. To turn hyperlink automatic formatting on or off, choose Tools ➤ AutoCorrect. Click AutoFormat As You Type and check or clear the Internet And Network Paths With Hyperlinks check box.*

ADDING HYPERLINKS TO NEW PAGES

If you want to create a multi-page website and you haven't created the additional pages yet, you can use the Insert Hyperlink dialog box to do it for you. Follow the same steps as you would to create a link to an existing document, except click the Create New Document button to open options related to a new document.

By default, Word creates Word DOC files. If you want to create an HTML document instead, click the Change button and select Internet Files from the Save As Type dialog box. You can also identify the location of the new document in the Create New Document Dialog box. When you return to the Insert Hyperlink dialog box, you can choose to edit the new document now or later.

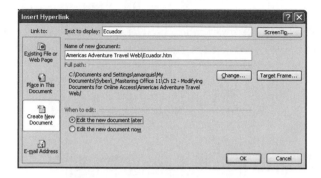

Inserting Graphics

Visitors to a website expect to see more than just text. Fast-loading graphics add impact to your web pages. The trick is to use small, attention-grabbing graphics on main pages and give visitors the option to view larger, more elaborate graphics by clicking to another page.

Inserting a graphic into a web page is no different than placing one in a Word document. The Insert Clip Art task pane opens when you select Picture ➢ Clip Art from the Insert menu; from the task pane you can choose art or any other clip art or photos you want to use (for more about inserting graphics in Word, see Chapter 5, "Beyond Text: Making an Impression with Multimedia"). You can also use Insert ➢ Picture ➢ From File to access images that are not available in the Clip Organizer.

Web browsers don't support all the graphics features available in Word. To ensure that your web pages look as good when viewed in a browser as they do in Word, features that are unsupported have been disabled. Only some of the wrapping styles available in Word documents, for example, are available for use in web pages. As a result, you may find that once you've inserted a graphic, you have difficulty positioning it where you want it. To change how text wraps around the picture so you can more easily place the graphic where you want it, right-click the graphic and choose Format Picture or choose Format ➢ Picture from the menu. Select the Layout tab and change the Wrapping Style, as shown in Figure 11.11.

FIGURE 11.11

By changing the Wrapping Style, you can more easily position graphics.

You can also access the wrapping styles from the Picture toolbar that opens when you select a picture. Click the Text Wrapping button and choose a wrapping style from the menu that opens.

INSERTING ALTERNATIVE TEXT

A number of other options are available in the Format Picture dialog box. Because not all browsers can display graphics and some people just don't have the patience to wait for your beautiful graphics to appear on a web page, it's possible to insert alternative text that describes the graphic. When the web page opens, the alternative text appears while the page is loading, allowing visitors to click when they find the text they want without waiting for the graphic. To specify alternative text, select the Web tab of the Format Picture dialog box.

NOTE   Alternative text not only makes your site friendlier, it makes it more accessible to people with vision impairments who use text readers. For that reason alternative text is required for any site that needs to be Section 508-compliant. (Section 508 is the law that requires Federal agencies to make their electronic and information technology accessible to people with disabilities.) For more information about the requirements for becoming 508-compliant, refer to www.section508.gov. *Also check out* www.bobby.cast.org *for a free service that reviews your web pages to test for accessibility.*

MAKING GRAPHICS STAY WHERE YOU WANT THEM

If you are having trouble positioning graphics on a web page, you might want to try a web designer's trick. Insert a table into the page. Three columns are usually sufficient, but add more columns if you want to line up a series of graphics. Then, position the graphic inside a cell of the table and change the table properties so the table expands to fill the size of the screen. To do so, follow these steps:

1. Click inside the table and choose Table ➤ Table Properties.

2. Select the Table tab and change Preferred Width to 100% Measure In Percent. (Although this step is not necessary, it makes it easier if you aren't sure about precise placement and sizing.) Click OK.

3. Now place the graphic inside the cell of the table that corresponds to the position you would like for the graphic. Click the Center button on the Formatting toolbar to center the graphic in the cell.

Before publishing the web page, you can change the table's borders to No Borders. To do this, select the table, choose Format ➤ Borders And Shading, click the Borders tab, and click None. Your table won't be visible on the page, but the graphics will stay where you put them.

Using the Web Tools Toolbar

Word comes equipped with a Web Tools toolbar, shown in Figure 11.11, to help you add sounds and video, create forms, access and edit source code, and add scrolling text. To turn on the Web Tools toolbar, choose View ➤ Toolbars and click Web Tools (be careful not to choose Web or you'll get the browser toolbar).

FIGURE 11.12

The Web Tools toolbar can help you add sounds, video, forms, and scrolling text.

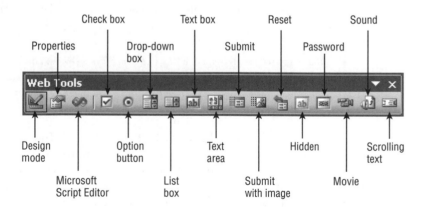

ADDING BACKGROUND SOUNDS AND MOVIES

Even though we don't seem to mind being constantly barraged by sounds from radio and television, most of us have not yet developed a fondness for sounds emanating from the Web uninvited. Only occasionally will you happen upon a website that opens with background music drawing you in—or turning you away, as the case may be. However, if you'd like to add background sounds to your site despite all the evidence to the contrary, Word makes it easy for you to do.

To add a sound file to a page, follow these steps:

1. Check to see that you are in Web Layout view (View ➤ Web Layout).

2. Turn on the Web Tools toolbar by choosing View ➤ Toolbars ➤ Web Tools.

3. If you'd like to see the sound icon on the page, click the Design Mode button on the Web Tools toolbar, otherwise you can skip this step.

4. Move the insertion point to any obvious place on the page—it doesn't matter where you insert it.

TIP   You can move into Design mode from any view, not just Web Layout view, but if you're working on a web page, it's best to begin in Web Layout view so you know what your finished product will look like.

5. Click the Sound button on the Web Tools toolbar.

6. Enter the name of a WAV file or click Browse and locate the file.

7. Click the Loop down-arrow to choose the number of times you want the sound to play, either 1–5 or Infinite.

8. Click OK.

9. Click the Design Mode button to return to your previous view. The sound file should begin playing immediately and will play whenever you open the page, as many times as you instructed it to.

NOTE   Your browser (along with add-ins like RealPlayer—www.realplayer.com—and the Microsoft Windows Media Player) determines the types of sound files you can play. MIDI and WAV files are common, but MP3 (MPEG audio) files are becoming the most common. After you insert the file, test it in your browser and in browsers that your site's visitors would commonly use.

To add a movie file, click the Movie button on the Web Tools toolbar (remember to click the Design Mode button and position the insertion point first if you want to see the Movie icon on the page). Enter the settings in the Movie Clip dialog box, as shown in Figure 11.13. It's a good idea to include an alternative image to display in browsers that do not support movie clips, or you can put the clip on a page so that users can choose whether or not to download it. However, even if a browser does support movie clips, the image will be small and difficult to see on most systems. If possible, test the display on several machines with different browsers to see how the movie file looks before making it a permanent part of your web page. Click the Design Mode button to play the movie clip.

FIGURE 11.13

To display a movie clip on a web page, enter the settings for the clip you want to play and an alternative graphic for those browsers that do not support clips.

To remove a sound or movie clip, switch to Design mode. Locate the Sound or Movie icon, like the ones shown here. Select the icon you want to delete and press Delete or choose Edit ➤ Clear Contents.

NOTE   Movie clips consume a lot of bandwidth, so be cautious about using movie clips if most of your visitors use a dial-up connection to reach your site.

ADDING SCROLLING TEXT

Scrolling text is a way to grab your visitors' attention with a special announcement or notice. If you've used the Windows Scrolling Marquee screensaver, you're already familiar with the concept. To add scrolling text, follow these steps:

1. Click the Design Mode button on the Web Tools toolbar.

2. Position the insertion point where you want the scrolling text to appear.

3. Click the Scrolling Text button on the Web Tools toolbar.

4. Enter the text in the text box.

5. Set the options for Behavior, Direction, Background Color, Loop, and Speed.

6. Click OK to insert the scrolling text box.

7. Click the Design Mode button to exit Design mode; the text box doesn't scroll in Design mode.

You can resize or move the scrolling text box in Design mode as you would any text box in Word. To delete a scrolling text box, switch to Design mode, click the box to select it, and press Delete or choose Edit ➤ Clear Contents.

Viewing a Word Web Page in a Browser

If you are working on a website in Word, the easiest way to take a look at your work in a browser is to click File ➤ Web Page Preview. You'll want to do this on a regular basis to make sure the page looks the same in the browser as it does in Word. You don't want any surprises after you've finished your work on the website. Use the navigation links on the page you preview to see other pages in the website.

If you have your browser open and the website you want to view is not open in Word, follow these steps to view the website in the browser:

1. Start the browser.

2. Click File ➤ Open and locate the home page for the website you want to view. Click OK.

3. Use hyperlinks to move from the home page of the website to the page you are working on.

Creating Web-Based Forms

To make the website truly interactive, information has to go in both directions. Web users need the ability to send information to the site owners, and website owners need to know who their visitors are and what they are looking for. Web forms provide a way for visitors to respond to surveys, register with a site, voice their opinions about issues, search your site, or submit feedback.

You can add a form to any web page. When you add a form control from the Web Tools toolbar, Word automatically adds Top Of Form and Bottom Of Form boundaries to the form, as shown in Figure 11.14:

FIGURE 11.14

Word's Web form controls automatically designate the top and bottom of a form on a web page.

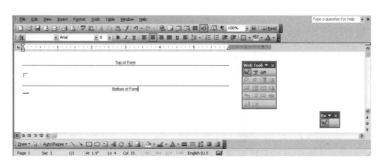

Word comes equipped with 11 built-in controls on the Web Tools toolbar for you to use on forms. Here's a quick look at each one.

 Checkbox   lets users select more than one option within a group. For example, you could have your check box say something like, "Send me more information about:" and then list various choices for the user to select from.

 Option Button   indicates that users can select only one item from a group of options, such as indicating that they would like to receive information Daily, Weekly, or Monthly.

 Drop-Down Box   gives users a list of specific options from which they can choose one. For example, from a drop-down list of cities, you can pick yours to see its weather report.

List Box is similar to a drop-down box in that they give users a list of options to choose from. However, instead of clicking an arrow to open a list, users use scroll buttons to scroll through the list. List boxes allow users to select multiple choices by using Shift or Ctrl while clicking.

 Text Box is a field where users can enter text, such as a name, address, or other specific information.

 Text Area is an open text box with scroll bars where users can write a paragraph or more to give feedback, describe a problem, or provide other information.

 Submit Button adds a Submit button, an essential element on a form for a user to send the data they entered to the web server for processing.

 Submit With Image lets you substitute an image for the standard Submit button. Make sure users know they have to click this button to submit their data—and that clicking the button submits the data. For example, don't use the same image for a Next Page button and a Submit button.

 Reset Button is a command button form control that clears the data in the current form so the user can start over.

 Hidden is a form field, invisible to the user, that passes data to the web server. For example, a hidden control could pass information about the user's operating system or web browser.

 Password creates a control where typed text is replaced with asterisks so users can type passwords confidentially.

LAYING OUT A FORM

Tables are a big help in laying out a form so that it looks organized. Create the table so it has twice the number of columns you would want to display in a single row. For example, in Figure 11.15, the third row contains three fields, so the table contains six columns. After you have inserted all the field names and form controls, save the page and open it in Internet Explorer or another browser to see how it looks.

FIGURE 11.15

Using a table to lay out form fields helps to align them in organized columns.

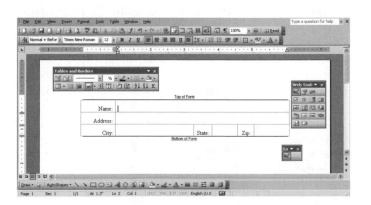

To make the table look more attractive, remove the cell borders. The easiest way to do this is the click the Tables and Borders button to turn on the Table and Borders toolbar. Select the table, and click the No Border button on the Borders menu. You can also merge cells where there is only one field in a row. Select the cells you want to merge and click the Merge Cells button on the Borders and Tables toolbar.

NOTE   *Because of the way different browsers display form fields, it is impossible to make every field line up perfectly with the fields above it unless you use tables.*

Insert the appropriate form controls in the corresponding cells of the table. For example, in the table we began in Figure 11.15, we inserted text boxes in each cell except for State, where we inserted a drop-down box. We then resized the text boxes by selecting each one and dragging the horizontal field handle to the appropriate size. We also dragged the cell borders for the City and Zip Code fields to make them larger. Here is our final result:

SETTING FORM FIELD PROPERTIES

All form controls have properties that determine how they behave. Some form controls require that you set the properties before the control can be used. For example, you must enter the values that you want to appear in a drop-down list so the user has options to choose from. To set or edit a control's properties, double-click the control to open the Properties dialog box, like the one in Figure 11.16.

If you haven't worked with control properties before, these dialog boxes can be a bit intimidating. Once you understand what you are looking at, you can choose which of the property settings to change and which to just leave alone. Each of the Properties dialog boxes has two tabs: Alphabetic and Categorized. They both contain the same properties in different order. The Alphabetic tab displays the properties in, you guessed it, alphabetical order. The Categorized tab groups the properties into various types: Appearance, Data, Miscellaneous, and so on.

FIGURE 11.16

Set or edit form field properties in the Alphabetic tab of the Properties dialog box or view the same properties in collapsible and expandable groups on the Categorized tab.

To make changes, double-click any of the properties to enter Edit mode. One change you should always make is to rename the control from the default HTMLName to a name that describes the field—for example, change *HTMLText1* to *FirstName*. Control names cannot contain spaces, but they can contain numbers and both uppercase and lowercase letters. It's also useful to rename the HTML Name, which is more like a label. This name is used when the information is sent to a web server and it can contain spaces.

Entering Values for Drop-down Lists and List Boxes

To enter options for a drop-down list or a list box, type the first value in the DisplayValues property. Enter a semicolon and no space before entering the next value. Figure 11.17 shows you the values in the control properties and the end result in a drop-down list. As you can see, each value you type appears on a separate line in the list. To test the drop-down list box, exit Design mode and click the Down arrow on the form control.

FIGURE 11.17

Enter values for a drop-down list in the DisplayValues property. When you view the page, the values you entered appear on separate lines in the drop-down list.

For more information about form control properties, refer to the Word Help topic "Form Controls You Can Use on a Web Page."

ADDING SUBMIT AND RESET BUTTONS

After a user fills out your fabulous form, it would be nice if the data actually went somewhere. Every web form needs Submit and Reset buttons to complete the form's functionality. The Submit button must be tied to some action so that the data knows where to go. The Reset buttons clears the form when the user makes mistakes and wants to start over. To insert Submit and Reset buttons, move to the end of the form—stay above the Bottom Of Form marker—and click the Submit or Reset buttons on the Web Tools toolbar.

To make the Submit button really work, you might need the help of your web server administrator. Data can be stored in a comma-delimited text file, an Access table, or other database format. But before it can do that, it has to have a script, referred to as a *CGI script* or *form handler*, to tell it what to do with the data it collects. If you don't know how to write this script and you don't have a web server administrator to help you, consider taking your form into FrontPage. FrontPage makes it easy to create these scripts by just answering a few questions in a dialog box.

Working with Frames

A *frame* is a structure that displays a web page within another web page. The page that displays the frames is called a *frames page*. A web page can contain one frame or multiple frames but two or three is usually the desired limit.

TIP   There's a Frames toolbar that you can use to add, delete, and set the properties of frames. Right-click on any toolbar and choose Frames to display the toolbar.

To add a frame, choose Format ➤ Frames to open the Frames menu. If you want to add only a table of contents to the existing document, choose Table Of Contents In Frame. This option creates a table of contents for the displayed document based on heading styles used in the document. Figure 11.18 shows an example of a table of contents frame for this chapter. A link is created for each heading formatted using a heading style.

FIGURE 11.18

The Table Of Contents In Frame option creates a table of contents for the displayed document based on the heading styles.

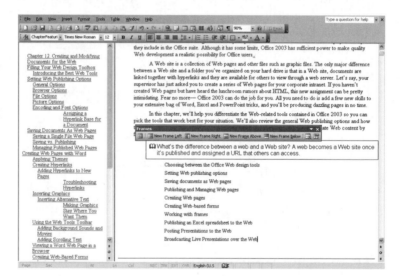

To create a page that you can use with frames, choose Format ➤ Frames ➤ New Frames Page to create the frames page. Choose Format ➤ Frames again to choose the position of the frame you would like to add. You can choose from several options about where to place the frame on the page. New Frame Above creates a header frame, and New Frame Below creates a footer frame. If you plan to add horizontal and vertical frames, add header and footer frames first so they extend the width of the page. Resize frames by dragging the frame border in the direction you want. After adding a horizontal frame, click in the main body of the page before clicking New Frames Left to add a vertical frame. Otherwise, you divide the header into two sections. Click in each frame to add content.

SAVING A FRAMES PAGE

If you save the frames page before adding any content, Word saves all three frames as a single document. Unlike other web pages, however, Word doesn't give this document a title in the Save As dialog box. As soon as you add content to a frame, Word also saves the frame as an individual document the next time you save. Because you are going to end up with several documents for each frames page you create, it's a good idea to create a folder to save in before saving a frames page. This keeps the main frames page and all the individual frames together in one easy to find place. Give the main frames page a name that reminds you it's a frames page. If it is the home page of the website you are creating, however, save it as default.htm.

If you add graphics or other objects to a frame, Word creates subfolders to house them in. The subfolder has the name of the page followed by an underscore and the word files. For example, let's say you insert a graphic on a frame that you saved as Registration Form. Word creates a folder called Registration Form_files to store the graphic. It also creates an XML document in the folder called filelist.xml that keeps a list of all the images in the document. Each frame gets its own subfolder to hold image files. The example in Figure 11.19 shows the results of creating a frames page with three frames and inserting text and graphics on each page. In saving the main page as TRAIN2K.htm, Word also saved each frame as an individual document and created folders in which to store the images from each frame.

FIGURE 11.19

Word saves each frame individually and creates folders in which it saves image files.

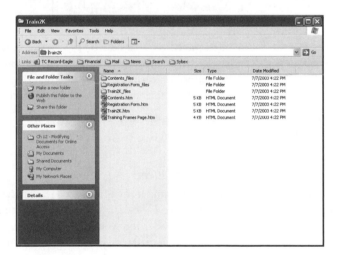

RENAMING FRAMES PAGES

After Word creates folders in which to store images related to a frames page, the process of renaming a frame document is a little more complicated than renaming a normal document. To maintain the association between the document and the folder, you must first open the document you want to rename and resave it using File ➢ Save As to give it the new name. Word creates a new folder to store the image files. You must then choose File ➢ Open and delete the original document and associated *_files folder. It's an awkward process but it works. The key thing is to remember to discard the old document and folder so it doesn't confuse you down the road.

SETTING FRAME PROPERTIES

Right-click any frame, or select the frame and click the Frame Properties button on the Frames toolbar, to open the Frame Properties dialog box, shown in Figure 11.20. The initial page should be set to the frame that is open. However, you can change the page that opens in a frames page by selecting a different initial page from the drop-down list or clicking Browse to search for one. Give the frame a name by selecting or entering one in the Name box. Adjust the size of the frame by adjusting the size controls. By default, frames are set to a relative size. You can change the relative size to a specific pixel size or a percentage of the screen display by changing the Measure In option.

FIGURE 11.20

Use the Frame Properties dialog box to adjust the size of frames, borders, and other frame settings.

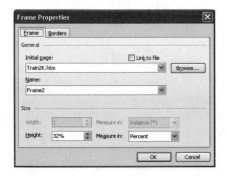

On the Borders tab of the Frame Properties dialog box, set whether you want to display frame borders and, if you do, what size and color you want them to be. You can determine if users will be able to adjust the frame size or not by clearing or checking the Frame Is Resizable In Browser check box. Turn scroll bars on or off using the Show Scrollbars In Browsers setting.

WARNING   *If you move a frames page to a different folder or drive location, you must copy all of the related frames documents to the same location.*

REMOVING A FRAME FROM A FRAMES PAGE

If you decide you want to remove a frame from a frames page, click in the frame and choose Format ➢ Frames ➢ Delete Frame or click the Delete Frame button on the Frames toolbar. You may want to save the frame under a different name before you delete it in case you decide you want to use it at a later time. To save the frame under a different name, right-click in the frame and choose Save Current Frame As.

TIP   *Although Word 2003 provides some exciting web page design options, creating a complex website requires some knowledge of HTML and other web programming tools. While you are creating web pages in Word, Word is writing the HTML and XML code behind the scenes. You can view this code and even edit it directly by choosing View ➢ HTML Source. This opens the Microsoft Development Environment design window where you can edit HTML and active server page (ASP) files. If you are not a programmer, this is a good place to take a look at what it takes to produce the content you are creating and see HTML in actual application. If you are a programmer, you can edit the HTML file and add Microsoft Visual Basic, JScript, and VBScript to your files.*

Making a Website Available for Others to View

When you have your website looking just the way you want, it's time to put it out there for others to use. In today's environment, you may be publishing a website to your company's intranet, an extranet, or the World Wide Web. If you are developing for your company's intranet, contact the web administrator to see how to proceed from here. It may be as simple as saving the files to a shared network folder.

If you want your web pages to be available for the whole world to see, you need to publish the site to a web server that others can access. The web server may be within your company or run by a web-hosting company. The cost of having a website hosted by an external company has come down dramatically, so unless you have a burning desire to run your own server, the smartest choice is to let a specialist do it. A good web-hosting company is sure to have fast equipment, T1 lines for fast connections, and multiple phone lines to handle the heavy traffic that will be generated by your site. The company you choose can give you instructions on how to publish the website to their server.

TIP   If you need to find a company to host your website, HostSearch.com (`www.hostsearch.com`) can help. HostSearch.com maintains an unbiased directory of web-hosting companies and lets you search for a host using a number of criteria including cost, space, and features. You can read reviews by actual users and compare up to five plans that meet your criteria.

Creating Web Pages with Excel

Excel 2003 is well equipped to work with the Web. Not only can you save Excel worksheets as web pages, you can open HTML files directly from Excel and drag-and-drop HTML tables from your browser directly into Excel worksheets. When you save or publish Excel 2003 worksheets as web pages, the pages you create are either interactive or non-interactive. Non-interactive pages are simply static pages that users can look at to examine data, like those you could publish in prior versions of Excel. With the interactive opportunities made available by using the Office Web Components, users can work with the data via the browser using some of the same tools they would in Excel 2003.

Excel 2003 includes three Office Web Components, and each one supports specific kinds of interactivity. The components are:

◆   The Spreadsheet component inserts a spreadsheet where users can add formulas, sort and filter data, and format the worksheet.

◆   The Charting component is linked to data in the Spreadsheet component so that the chart can display changes when the data in the spreadsheet changes.

◆   The PivotTable component lets users analyze database information using most of the sorting, filtering, grouping, and subtotaling features of PivotTable Reports.

UNDERSTANDING OFFICE WEB COMPONENTS

The Office Web Components are based on *COM*, the *Component Object Model*. With these components, you don't need to learn Java to create the slick interactive interface your users are asking for. The COM standard defines groups of functions called *interfaces*. Interfaces like the Office Web Components are grouped into component categories, which are in turn supported by applications like Excel, Access, and Internet Explorer 4 higher. COM objects used in Office 2003 are only interactive if the user's browser supports COM. Users with an older browser will still see the spreadsheet, chart, or pivot table, but they will not be able to manipulate it in their browser.

To create either an interactive or non-interactive web page, open the spreadsheet you want to save to the Web. Then choose File ➢ Save As Web Page from the menu to open the Save As dialog box.

You'll notice a couple of differences between this and the typical Save As dialog box. You can choose to save the entire worksheet or just the selected sheet. To create interactive pages that website visitors will be able to work with, enable the Add Interactivity check box to add Office Web Components to your page. When you save the entire workbook, the sheet tabs are available by clicking the visible sheet tab and selecting another form the list that opens, as shown in Figure 11.21.

FIGURE 11.21

Saving an interactive workbook lets users access all of the sheets in the book.

Referrals

	A	B	C	D	E	F	G	H
1								
2	**Sept-Feb**	**Referred**	**Followed-through**					
3	Shelter	6	4					
4	Motels	5	5					
5	FIA Housing Locator	0	0					
6	Group home/Foster Care	0	0					
7	Permanent Housing	0	0					
8	Family/Friends	8	8					
9	**Total**	**19**	**17**					
10								
11	**Mar-Aug**							
12	Shelter	15	6					
13	Motels	4	4					
14	FIA Housing Locator	2	2					
15	Group home/Foster Care	2	1					
16	Permanent Housing	1	1					
17	Family/Friends	0	0					
18	**Total**	**24**	**14**					
19								
20	**FY 03**							

03 Shelter Referrals ▼

To have Chart functionality, you must first create a chart in the worksheet and select it before opening the Save As dialog box.

Publishing the Active Sheet

If you want to publish the active sheet in the open workbook to a web server, click File ➢ Save As Web Page and then click Publish to open the Publish As Web Page dialog box, as shown in Figure 11.22.

FIGURE 11.22

In the Publish As Web Page dialog box, you can select the parts of the sheet you want to publish, the viewing options, and where you want to publish it.

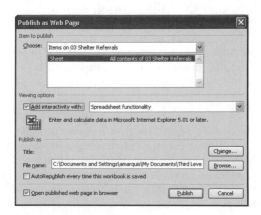

Choose what part of the workbook you want to publish. You can choose to publish the entire workbook without interactivity, you can choose a range of cells, or you can choose any of the sheets in the workbook.

If you have enabled interactivity, choose the component you wish to use from the drop-down list by selecting the kind of functionality you want users to have: Spreadsheet Functionality or PivotTable Functionality.

In the Publish As section of the Publish As Web Page dialog box, click the Change button if you want to designate a page title. Click Browse to find the web folder you want to publish to. In Excel 2003, you can select the AutoRepublish Every Time This Workbook Is Saved check box to take the hassle out of remembering to republish the worksheet every time you make a change.

If you want to immediately view your work in the web browser, select the View In Web Browser button before you click Publish. When you are ready to publish, click the Publish button. Excel creates the web page, including any interactivity you have specified. Figure 11.23 shows a web page that includes the PivotTable component.

FIGURE 11.23

An interactive Excel web page that includes the PivotTable component

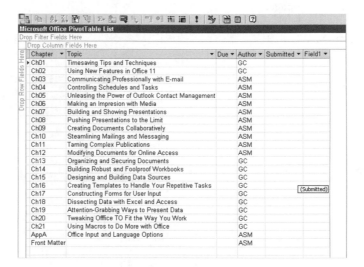

Most of the toolbar buttons on a published Excel worksheet are familiar Excel buttons. There are two additions: the Export To Excel button and the Commands And Options button. The Export To Microsoft Office Excel button re-creates the Excel worksheet at a user-specified location. The Commands And Options button opens additional user tools. Figure 11.24 shows the Commands and Options dialog box for PivotTable functionality. Use this dialog box to change the format of a worksheet, work with formulas in the sheet, find worksheet data, and change worksheet and workbook options.

FIGURE 11.24

Users can change the properties of selected cells.

The Chart component displays both the chart and the underlying data (see Figure 11.25). Users manipulate the data to change the chart, just as they would in Excel. They can't change the chart type or other chart features, so make sure you create a chart that's useful before saving it as an interactive page.

FIGURE 11.25

The Chart component reflects changes in the underlying data.

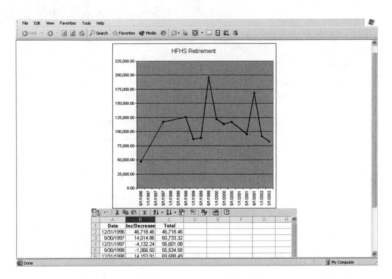

Appending to an Existing Web Page

If you already have a published spreadsheet and you'd like to add another web component such as a chart or a pivot table to it, you can append the data to the existing page. To place a second component on a single web page, choose File ➤ Save As Web Page and then click Publish to open the Publish As Web Page dialog box. Enter the existing HTML file in the File Name text box. When you click Publish, Excel prompts you to replace or add to the page. Choose Add To File to display more than one component on the page.

Preparing Presentations for the Web

If you have a presentation to give and your audience is spread out across the continent or across the globe, save the expense of bringing them all together. With PowerPoint 2003, you can save or publish presentations for individuals to use online at their convenience.

PowerPoint 2003 gives you two methods for making presentations available for browsing on the Internet or your company's intranet: saving and publishing. When you save a presentation, other PowerPoint 2003 users connected to your network can access the HTML document, which allows them to edit the presentation. A published presentation, however, is like a published website: other users can view it and follow its links, but they cannot edit it. You'll probably want to save a presentation to a network file server while you and any colleagues are working on it; then, once it's ready to "go live," you can publish it to a web server.

Before saving or publishing your presentation, it's a good idea to preview (File ➤ Web Page Preview) the way the presentation will look in your default browser. Then choose File ➤ Save As Web Page from the menu bar to open the Save As dialog box.

Saving a Presentation as a Web Page

The page title for the presentation is displayed near the bottom of the Save As dialog box. The title appears in the title bar of the user's browser; the default title is the presentation's title (from the title slide). To change the page title, click the Change Title button and enter a new title in the Set Page Title dialog box.

Click OK to return to the Save As dialog box. Click the Save button to save the presentation and close the dialog box.

Publishing a Web Presentation

With PowerPoint 2003, you can publish an entire presentation, selected slides, or even a single PowerPoint slide. The first page of a PowerPoint publication, displayed in Internet Explorer 6, is shown in Figure 11.26.

FIGURE 11.26

The published presentation includes navigation controls browser users expect to see.

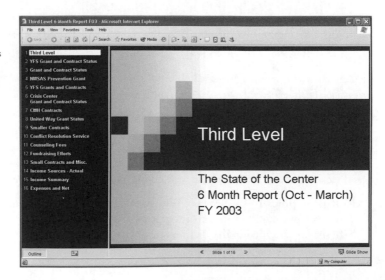

To publish your presentation, first choose File ➢ Save As Web Page; then click the Publish button in the Save As dialog box to open the Publish As Web Page dialog box, shown in Figure 11.27.

FIGURE 11.27

Set options for your Web presentation in the Publish As Web Page dialog box.

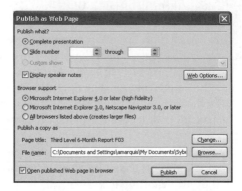

In the Publish What section, choose to publish the entire presentation, a range of slides, or a custom show you created using the Slide Show ➢ Custom Shows command. Enable the Display Speaker Notes check box if your presentation includes speaker's notes that you want users to see in a separate Notes pane.

SETTING WEB PUBLISHING OPTIONS

Click the Web Options button on the Publish As Web Page dialog box to open the Web Options dialog box. Use the six tabs of this dialog box to set options for publishing the current presentation. The General options available only in PowerPoint are detailed here.

TIP   You can also access Web Options from the General tab of the Options dialog box. From the main PowerPoint window, choose Tools ➢ Options, select the General tab, and click the Web Options button.

Add Slide Navigation Controls   Your presentation will include an Outline pane with a collapsible outline (see Figure 11.26) in the color scheme you select, a Notes pane, and navigation buttons below the presentation. Turn this option off if you're publishing a single slide.

NOTE   In order to display Outline and Notes panes in your published presentation, these panes must be turned on in the presentation before you publish. Also, you must have entered Notes on at least one slide prior to publishing.

Show Slide Animation While Browsing   Your slide show will display animations within slides. If animations are manually advanced, the user will click the navigation buttons to switch slides and click the slides to move through the animations. There are no instructions to tell the user to do this, so we suggest you set automatic timings for all animations if you enable this check box.

Resize Graphics To Fit Browser Window   This option is enabled by default. When you publish your presentation, this option automatically resizes graphics so they'll display best in the Screen Size setting specified in the Picture options.

When you've finished setting web options, click OK to close the Web Options dialog box and return to the Publish As Web Page dialog box.

TROUBLESHOOTING WEB PRESENTATIONS

After you publish a presentation, you might notice that the slide show (in PowerPoint) and the same presentation viewed as pages in your browser behave differently. Functionality that comes from PowerPoint isn't available in your browser. For example, when you right-click during a web presentation, the presentation shortcut menu does not appear. This makes sense—your browser probably doesn't have a Power-Point shortcut menu the rest of the time, either!

There are a number of PowerPoint features that don't work on a web page, regardless of the browser support you select when you publish your presentation. Features that do not have web support include the following:

- Embossed and shadow effects for fonts
- OLE multimedia objects
- Multislide sound effects (moving to another slide stops sound)
- Dimming effect on previous points on a slide
- Text animated by letter or by word rather than by paragraph
- Chart effects
- Spiral, stretch, swivel, and zoom effects

The browser you're using (or the browser you chose to support when you published) also affects the published product. Internet Explorer 3, for example, doesn't support sound and video playback.

Chapter 12

Securing and Organizing Documents

Documents AREN'T JUST WORD documents, but all your work products. There is a common set of issues to consider when storing documents, whether your documents are Excel workbooks, Power-Point presentations, Outlook items, Access databases, or Word DOC files. In this chapter we'll discuss strategies and reveal best practices for storing and protecting documents in Office 2003.

◆ Password-protecting documents

◆ Protecting workbooks, worksheets, and ranges

◆ Hiding formulas in Excel worksheets

◆ Securing Access databases

◆ Saving messages as messages on your network or hard drive

◆ Using Outlook rules to tame your wild inbox

◆ Setting up the Out Of Office Assistant

◆ Setting permissions and delegate status in Outlook

◆ Understanding protection with Information Rights Management (IRM)

Strategies for Document Protection

Office 2003 supports several levels of document protection:

◆ File-level password protection in Word, Access, and PowerPoint

◆ Windows read-only protection for all documents saved as files (and Windows file permissions when using an NTFS-formatted drive)

◆ A new level of protection via Information Rights Management (IRM)

◆ Workbook, worksheet, and range-level protection in Excel

◆ Message encryption in Outlook

◆ Object and record-level protection in Access

Before protecting a document, you need to decide what you're trying to accomplish, and then choose the appropriate type of protection. *Read-only* protection allows users to open and edit a file, but they can't save changes to the original file. There are two types of *password* protection: a password to open a document, and/or a password to make changes to a document.

You can also use the new Protect Document task pane, which allows you to set specific types of restrictions such as formatting and editing restrictions with Word documents.

This chapter focuses on document protection strategies in Windows and Office 2003, but if your organization has a network, there are other ways to limit access to documents. If you need to allow a specific group of users access to a set of documents (for example, all the files pertaining to a project), you can tap into Microsoft's new method of protecting intellectual property with Information Rights Management.

Saving a Document as Read-Only

A read-only document can be opened and read, but can't be edited. A user who changes the document text must save the changed document with a new name or in a new location.

CHANGING A FILE'S READ-ONLY PROPERTY IN WINDOWS

You can change any file to a read-only file in Windows. The file will be read-only until it is changed again in Windows. To change a document to read-only in Windows:

1. Open My Computer or the Windows Explorer and locate the file.

2. Right-click the file and choose Properties from the shortcut menu to open the file's Properties dialog box:

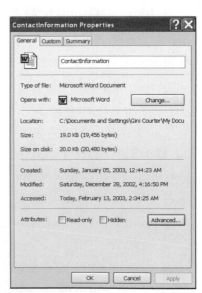

3. Enable the Read-Only check box. Click OK to close the dialog box.

When you open the file, a glance at the title bar lets you know the file is read-only:

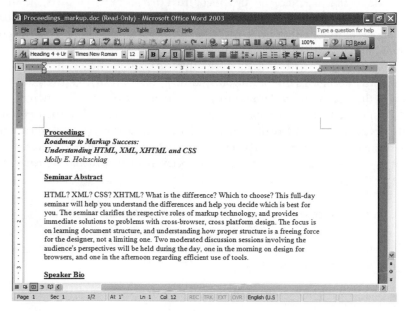

If you change the file and attempt to save it without changing the file name or location, Windows opens a message box to notify you that the file is read-only. You must enter a new file name and/or location if you want to save your changes; the original read-only file is always preserved.

SETTING A WORD DOCUMENT TO PROMPT FOR READ-ONLY OPEN

In Word you can change a file's properties so that a user is prompted to open a read-only copy when they open the file. Follow these steps.

1. Choose File ➤ Save As (or Save if this is the first time you're saving the document) to open the Save As dialog box.

2. Click the down-arrow on the Tools button in the Save As dialog box and choose Security Options to open the Security dialog box.

3. Enable the Read-Only Recommended check box. Click OK or Protect Document to close the Security dialog box and return to the Save As dialog box. Enter a file name and location and click Save to save the document.

When you open a document with the read-only recommended setting, a dialog box asks you to open the file as read-only:

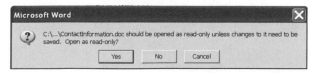

You can choose Yes to open the document as read-only, but you can as easily choose No to open the document as a read/write document.

If you want to protect your document from changes by rookie users, recommending read-only is not enough. Users who don't understand what read-only means almost always choose No in this dialog box. If you want to force the user to open the document as read-only, change the property in Windows or apply a Password To Modify as explained in the next section.

While Word's read-only feature doesn't provide much protection from other users, it may be enough to protect documents that *you* might accidentally overwrite. If you have a document that you frequently use as the basis for other documents, you might open it with the intention of executing a File ➤ Save As command later to retain the original. On those occasions, when you forget to do this and just click the Save button, you overwrite the original with your changes. (In our experience this only happens with very important documents!) Turning on the read-only-recommended check box gives you the opportunity to be intentional when you open the document rather than have to remember to choose Save As rather than Save later in your work session.

PROTECTING WORD DOCUMENTS USING THE TASK PANE

A new feature in Microsoft Office 2003 is the task pane, with which you've become familiar throughout this book. If you'd like to protect a Word Document using the task pane, you can do so by following these steps:

1. Open the document you'd like to protect. Make sure the task pane is at the ready by selecting View ➤ Task Pane.

2. From the Task Pane drop-down, select Protect Document. Examine the pane. You'll see two types of restrictions: Formatting and Editing (see Figure 12.1).

FIGURE 12.1

The Protect Document task pane in Word

3. To restrict formatting, click in the Limit Formatting To A Selection Of Styles check box.

4. Click the Settings link in the Formatting restrictions section. The Formatting Restrictions dialog appears.

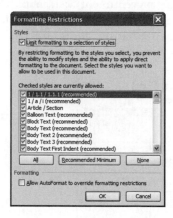

5. By default, all styles are checked. You can limit this by making sure the Limit Formatting To A Selection Of Styles check box is checked, and by unchecking those styles you don't wish to have included. You can also decide to let AutoFormat override these restrictions; to do so, check the box next to Allow AutoFormat To Override Formatting Restrictions. Click OK.

6. To manage editing restrictions, check the Allow Only This Type Of Editing In The Document check box in the Editing Restrictions section of the Protect Document pane. Then, from the drop-down menu, select the changes you'd like to apply.

7. If you'd like to, you can now make exceptions based on groups by simply checking those boxes next to existing users who you'd like to allow to freely edit the document. Click the More Users link if you'd like to find more users to add as exceptions.

8. If you're set with the restrictions and exceptions, click the Yes, Start Enforcing Protection button. The Start Enforcing Protection dialog appears. Here, you can select a variety of options including prevention of accidental changes, password protection, and prevention of intentional or malicious changes. Make your selections, then click OK.

Once your permissions are set up, The Protect Document pane appears with the options available for you (Figure 12.2).

FIGURE 12.2

The Protect Document pane displays set permissions.

Password Protection in Word, PowerPoint, and Excel

When you password-protect a document, users (including you) must enter a password before they can open and/or modify the document. Password-protecting a Word document, Excel spreadsheet, or PowerPoint presentation is a process that is almost the same in all three, with minor differences in the dialog boxes and menu options available.

To password-protect a document in one of these programs, choose File ➤ Save As from the menu to open the Save As dialog box. Click the down-arrow on the Tools button and choose Security Options (General Options in Excel) to open the Security Options dialog box shown in Figure 12.3.

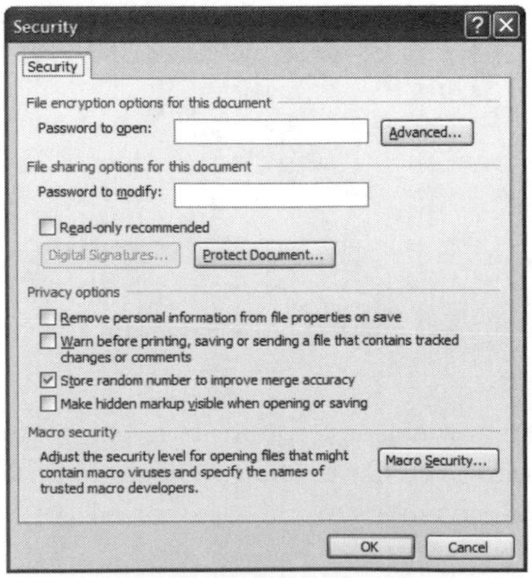

FIGURE 12.3

Use the Security dialog box to set password protection and read-only settings in Word.

You use the Password To Open and Password To Modify settings together to protect your document. Table 12.1 describes three different protection scenarios.

TABLE 12.1: PASSWORD PROTECTION SETTINGS	
SCENARIO	**SETTINGS**
Any user who knows the password can open and modify the document.	Password To Open only
Any user can open the document in read-only mode. Only users with a password can open and modify the document.	Password To Modify only
Any user who knows the password can open the document. Only selected users can modify the document.	Password To Open and different Password To Modify

To require password protection, type a password in the appropriate text box. When you click the OK button in PowerPoint or the Protect Document button in Word, you'll be prompted to re-enter each password you entered.

When you attempt to open a file that requires a Password To Open, you are prompted to supply the password. If you don't enter the correct password, the document won't open. When you open a file that needs a Password To Modify, you're prompted to supply the password. If you don't know the password, you can still open a read-only version of the document:

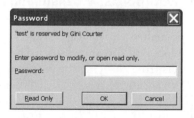

PowerPoint's Security Options dialog box doesn't include a Read-Only Recommended check box. Use the Password To Modify setting if you want to force users to open the file as read-only.

TROUBLESHOOTING PASSWORDS

Password protection is one means of document protection that is better than nothing, but less than perfect. There are password-recovery utilities available via the Internet for all the Office products. You can use them to recover a password for your files, but others can use them to "crack" the password for your files. Password recovery programs quickly run through thousands of character combinations per second until one of the combinations matches your password. The best passwords are a long combination of uppercase letters, lowercase letters, and numbers, because they are more difficult to crack). The easy availability of tools to break passwords means basic password protection protects your documents from only those people who don't know these programs exist or who are too honest—or afraid of being caught— to use them on other people's files.

The biggest problem with passwords isn't their vulnerability to recovery utilities: it's users failing to carefully choose and protect their passwords. Many users choose passwords that can easily be guessed by their coworkers: names of their spouse or partner, children, or pets. Users store their passwords on notes near their desks, in their Rolodexes and planners, and in files stored on their computers. They use their "regular" password to password-protect shared files and provide it to other users.

To keep your documents secure:

◆ Choose passwords that you can remember but others can't easily guess.

◆ Use at least two sets of passwords: one set that is never shared for documents that only you should be able to open and another set for workgroup or team documents that you create and share with coworkers.

◆ Use long passwords with strong encryption (128 bit).

If you can't remember your passwords, consider purchasing a program that stores passwords in a password-protected database. You need to remember only one password—the password that opens the database. This puts all your eggs in one basket, but is more secure than keeping your passwords on a note in your desk drawer.

Protecting Excel Workbooks, Worksheets, and Ranges

Excel has three specific levels of protection that secure workbooks, worksheets, and ranges. With range protection, you can allow different groups of users to edit different ranges in a worksheet. Worksheet protection locks cells in a worksheet that you haven't explicitly unlocked. Workbook protection prevents users from changing the properties of the workbook's sheets so that, for example, a user can't display a worksheet that you've hidden. A protection strategy may include all three levels of protection.

PROTECTING WORKBOOKS

To protect a workbook, choose Tools ➤ Protection ➤ Protect Workbook from the menu to open the Protect Workbook dialog box:

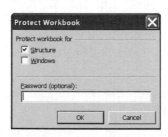

To protect the structure of a workbook so that worksheets can't be hidden, unhidden, renamed, moved, inserted, or deleted, enable the Structure check box. To lock in the size and position of the workbook's windows when the workbook is opened, enable the Windows check box. To prevent other users from turning off the protection, type a password and then click OK. You'll be prompted to confirm the password by typing it again. If you lose your password, you won't be able to turn off workbook protection without resorting to password-recovery software.

Protection without a password is no protection. Many users spend their first few minutes with any new program simply opening menus and choosing commands. This is scary, but true. Without a password, Tools ➤ Protection ➤ Unprotect Workbook turns the protection off.

While a workbook is structurally protected, commands that affect a workbook's structure are not enabled:

PROTECTING WORKSHEETS AND RANGES

Worksheet and range protection are used to protect parts of a workbook. Typically you'll protect formulas and labels, but allow users to enter values. Each cell has a Locked property, which is enabled by default. Although the cell is locked, the Locked property is enforced only when you protect the cell's worksheet. When protecting a worksheet, you first unlock all cells where you'll want users to enter data or all the cells in the sheet will be locked. There are two ways to do this:

◆ Unlock the range by turning off the Locked property feature for the cells within that range. This unlocks the range for all users, so anyone who can edit any sheet in the workbook can enter, edit, or delete data in these cells.

◆ Use the new Allow Users To Edit Ranges feature to provide specific users with permission to edit the cells.

With either option, after you've "opened up" specific cells, you must protect the worksheet to lock the remaining cells.

Unlocking Ranges

To unlock cells, select the cells and then choose Format ➤ Format Cells or right-click and choose Format Cells from the shortcut menu to open the Format Cells dialog box. On the Protection tab shown in Figure 12.4, turn off the Locked check box.

FIGURE 12.4

Turn off the Locked property on cells that you want users to be able to edit before protecting the worksheet.

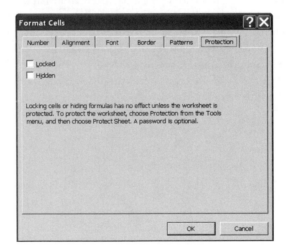

After unlocking where users will enter or edit data, turn on worksheet protection for the sheets you want to protect (see the section "Protecting Worksheets," later in this section).

MASTERING THE OPPORTUNITIES: HIDING FORMULAS TO PROTECT YOUR BUSINESS ADVANTAGE

We're amazed at how much company information Excel users routinely send to vendors and customers. We see workbooks with formulas that include proprietary information like markups, hourly rates, and details of project proposals and other information that shouldn't be shared with outsiders. But face it—if you send your organization's information to a customer or vendor, you can't guarantee that it won't end up in the hands of your competitors.

Continued on next page

MASTERING THE OPPORTUNITIES: HIDING FORMULAS TO PROTECT YOUR BUSINESS ADVANTAGE *(continued)*

When a user selects a locked cell in a worksheet, that user can view contents of the cell in the formula bar even if the cell is locked. If your worksheet includes business-rule formulas that you don't want your users to see, follow these steps to hide all the cells with formulas before sending the workbook outside your organization:

1. Select the worksheet that contains the formulas you want to protect.

2. Click the Select All button at the left end of the column headers.

3. Press F5 or Ctrl + G or choose Edit ➢ Go To from the menu to open the Go To dialog box.

4. Click the Special button to open the Go To Special dialog box:

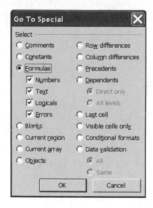

5. Choose the Formulas option. To hide all formulas, leave all four check boxes enabled.

6. Click OK to close the dialog box and select only the worksheet cells that contain formulas.

7. Choose Format ➢ Cells or right-click in the worksheet and choose Format Cells from the shortcut menu. (Don't click in the worksheet or you'll deselect the cells with formulas and you will need to return to step 2.)

8. On the Protection tab enable the Hidden check box and the Locked check box. Click OK.

When you protect the worksheet, all the formulas will be hidden and locked.

Excel will let you hide cells without locking them. This is not a good idea. The cells look empty (because the formulas are hidden), but when a user enters data in the cell, it overwrites the formula.

Allowing Users to Edit Ranges

Excel's range editing feature provides two types of security: user-based and range-based. Permission can be granted based on either passwords or network authentication, and different permissions can be granted for specific ranges of cells. For example, in a customer table, you might allow one user to edit customer address information and another user to edit only customer discount data.

NOTE   *This feature is operating-system-dependent and works only with Windows 2000 or XP.*

You grant permission to edit ranges before protecting a worksheet using the Allow Users To Edit Ranges dialog box shown in Figure 12.5.

FIGURE 12.5

Use the Allow Users To Edit Ranges dialog box to give users permissions for specific ranges.

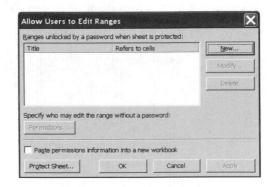

Follow these steps to set permissions in the worksheet:

1. Choose Tools ➤ Protection ➤ Allow Users To Edit Ranges to open the Allow Users To Edit Ranges dialog box.

2. Click the New button to open the New Range dialog box:

3. Enter a Title for the range. You can title it Range1, but a functional title (like CustomerDiscounts) is better. You can also use a range's name as its title in this dialog box.

4. Specify the range in the Refers to Cells text box. Hold Ctrl to select noncontiguous ranges.

5. If the workbook will be used by users who aren't on your network, enter a password for this range. Users will be required to enter the password to edit cells.

   If possible, use your users' network logins to establish their identity. Users like it because they don't have to remember an additional password. We like it because users almost never lend their network password to other users.

6. If all the users you will allow to edit the range will be logged onto your network, click the Permissions button to open the Permissions dialog box, shown in Figure 12.6.

FIGURE 12.6

Set permissions for network users in the Permissions dialog box.

7. Click the Add button to open the Select Users, Computers, Or Groups dialog box. Select users or groups from your network by using the Object Types button within the Select Users Or Groups dialog, then selecting which types you'd like to have added. When you have finished selecting users and groups, click OK to return to the Permissions dialog box.

8. For each user or group, confirm or deny editing rights without a password. Click OK to return to the Allow Users To Edit Ranges dialog box.

9. Repeat steps 2–8 for each unique group of users that you want to grant permissions to.

TIP   To document the protection information, enable the Paste Permissions Information Into A New Workbook check box in the Allow Users To Edit Ranges dialog box before you protect the worksheet. Excel opens a new workbook and pastes the range and user permission information.

When you are finished setting password or network-authenticated permissions for users, click OK or click the Protect Sheet button to open the Protect Sheet dialog box.

PROTECTING WORKSHEETS

When you're finished unlocking cells, hiding formulas, and allowing users to edit ranges, you are ready to protect your worksheet. Choose Tools ➢ Protection ➢ Protect Sheet to open the Protect Sheet dialog box shown in Figure 12.7.

FIGURE 12.7

Use the Protect Sheet dialog box to specify the sheet features you wish to protect.

Enter a password (which you'll need to know if you ever want to change permissions for the worksheet) and verify the worksheet actions that users are allowed to take in this worksheet after it is protected:

Select Locked Cells (on by default)

Select Unlocked Cells (on by default)

Format Cells

Format Columns

Format Rows

Insert Columns

Insert Rows

Insert Hyperlinks

Delete Columns

Delete Rows

Sort

Use AutoFilter

Use PivotTable Reports

Edit Objects

Edit Scenarios

Unless you change the default settings, users will only be allowed to select cells and enter or edit data using an input device or copy and paste. But you might want to change a couple of these settings:

Select locked cells   If you turn this off, users can't move to a cell that is locked. This is nice because users can tab or use the arrow keys to move quickly between unlocked cells.

Sort   If users need to be able to sort rows in the worksheet, remember to turn this on.

When you're finished setting allowable actions, click OK to protect the worksheet. Test your password out, confirming that all is working properly.

TIP   Turning off the Select Locked Cells option isn't a substitute for hiding formulas. You can see all the non-hidden formulas in a worksheet (even if you can't select them) by exposing the formula layer: just hold Ctrl and press ` (the key to the left of the 1 key). Press Ctrl+` again to hide the formula layer.

When users try to edit a locked cell after the worksheet has been protected, they see this message:

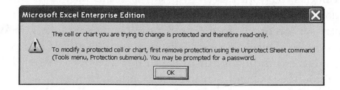

Check this message out! Excel tells the user how to unprotect the sheet. Protection without a password is no protection at all.

Unprotecting a Worksheet

To unprotect a worksheet so that you can make changes to locked cells, choose Tools ➢ Protection ➢ Unprotect Sheet. You'll be prompted for the password you entered in the Protect Sheet dialog box. Remember to protect the worksheet again before saving the workbook.

Securing Access Databases

Access has two types of protection: password protection to open the database and protection for individual objects. Database protection is easy; protecting individual objects is much more complex and beyond the scope of this book. Object-level security is normally done by an Access database developer, not by end users. If you need information on securing tables, queries, forms, and other objects, you'll find information in the Access help files as well as in the Knowledge Base on the Microsoft website.

To password-protect an entire database, have the database open for exclusive use. To do this, browse to locate the database and select it. Then, in the Open dialog, click the arrow to the right of the Open button and choose Open Exclusive. Then, choose Tools ➢ Security ➢ Set Database Password to open the Set Database Password dialog box. Enter the password in both the Password text box and the Verify text box and then click OK to set the password.

The next time the database is opened, the user is prompted to enter the password:

If the user can't supply the correct password, Access won't open the database.

Organizing and Securing Outlook Items

Ten years ago, a well-thought-out set of Windows directories (now called folders) was all you needed to organize your work. But if you're like the majority of today's business users, many if not most of the documents you work with arrive by e-mail as a message or its attachments. You'll open a message, edit a document, forward the message to other users, and save changes to the message, thereby saving the edited version of the document. But the document isn't in your Windows folders, it's in your Outlook folders. Organizing your e-mail may be as important as designing a good folder structure for other documents. In this half of the chapter we'll discuss strategies that can help you gain and keep control of e-mail messages and other Outlook items.

TIP   Outlook 2003 premieres a new organizational feature—search folders—that crosses folders. Search folders and the Ways To Organize Inbox pane are discussed in Chapter 2, "Digging Out of the E-Mail Avalanche."

Saving Outlook Items as Items

One strategy is to save Outlook items, particularly e-mail messages, in the same places you would save other Office documents. This is a good strategy if you meet the following requirements:

◆ Have a well-developed set of folders on your local and network drives that you know how to use effectively

◆ Struggle to keep your mailbox within the size limits set by your network administrator

There are four main ways that you can save messages from Outlook 2003. If the mail message is in HTML format, you can save it as HTML. You can also save your file as text (.txt), Outlook Template (.oft), and Outlook Message Format (.msg). Each of these has specific uses.

When you save your e-mail messages as text files, you only need one set of folders (in Windows) and you can keep all the documents related to a project or client in one folder (in Windows). But the disadvantages loom large; perhaps the biggest disadvantage is losing the ability to work with the saved messages as *messages*. Open the saved text documents and they're just text: no Reply, Reply To All, or Forward buttons, no way to save attachments along with the text. So, while saving as text can offer document management advantages, you lose the functionality of working with them as actual e-mail messages.

But here's the good news: you *can* save an Outlook message as an Outlook message, complete with attachments, Reply buttons, and recipient information. And when you open the Windows folder that contains the message, you know immediately that the document came from Outlook and will open in Outlook just as surely as an Excel workbook opens in Excel:

Maps for CANA Project
Outlook Item
13 KB

NOTE *The Outlook Template format allows you to save any e-mail message as a template. This is mostly used for saving the HTML and styles associated with a given message for further use as stationery.*

To save an Outlook e-mail message as a message, follow these steps:

1. Select the message in the **Inbox** (or other folder).

2. Choose File ➤ Save As from the Outlook menu.

3. In the Save As Type drop-down list choose Outlook Message Format.

4. Edit the file name, select a location, and then click Save.

After you've saved the message you can delete the original from the Outlook folders. When you double-click the message icon in Windows or open it from the My Recent Documents list, it opens in Outlook.

Creating Outlook Folders

Outlook uses folders to organize content, and depending upon your configuration, you might have multiple sets of folders. The folders in your mailbox or personal folders list (for example, **Calendar**, **Inbox**, and **Deleted Items**) are under your control. In your mailbox, you can perform the following actions:

◆ Create new folders

◆ Create, edit, and delete items in the folders

◆ Delete folders you've created

◆ Grant other users permission to view or work with folders and the items in the folders if you're using Exchange

Public folders are controlled by your organization's Exchange Administrator. If you can see a public folder, you were given permission to see it. The administrator has the same control over public folders that you have over the folders in your mailbox.

UNDERSTANDING PUBLIC FOLDERS

Public folders play an important organizational role. Public folders are used for workgroup collaboration and can be customized to create applications. Out of the box, public folders allow users to perform these actions:

◆ Share contacts (such as a list of vendors)

◆ Create custom calendars (such as organizational events)

◆ Receive and store messages in a common location (such as messages that can be handled by anyone in a department or workgroup)

Talk to your Exchange Administrator if you have ideas about how public folders can benefit your workgroup or organization.

The default Outlook mailbox includes a minimal number of folders. You can create additional folders and use them to organize Outlook items. Follow these steps to create a new folder:

1. Select the existing folder that will contain the new folder.

2. Right-click the folder icon and choose New Folder from the shortcut menu to open the Create New Folder dialog box shown in Figure 12.8.

FIGURE 12.8

Create new folders to organize e-mail, contacts, appointments, and tasks.

3. Enter a name for the folder. Folder names can contain letters, numbers, and most punctuation marks including periods, underscores, spaces, and hyphens. Some of these characters (particularly periods) make it more difficult to write programs that use the folder, so it's best to not use periods in folder names.

TIP   *When the folder list is sorted alphabetically, names beginning with underscores appear at the top of the list.*

4. When you opened the Create New Folder dialog box, Outlook set the Folder Contains drop-down list to the type of item displayed in the folder you chose in step 1. For example, when you create a new folder in the Inbox, Mail And Post Items is selected. Verify that the type of item is correct. The folder you selected in step 1 should be selected in the folder list. Click OK to create the new folder.

Don't start dragging and dropping items in your new folder before you read the next section. There's an easier way to move messages between folders.

Using Rules to Tame Your Wild Inbox

As you are struggling to keep up with the daily avalanche of e-mail, wouldn't it be nice to have a personal assistant who sorts and processes e-mail for you? *Rules* take the headache out of managing your Inbox by letting Outlook handle much of your mail automatically. In the Ways To Organize Inbox pane (discussed in Chapter 3, "Taking Control of Your Time and Tasks"), you can create simple rules to automatically move messages based on the sender or recipient to a specific folder. In this section we'll look at more complex rules that use other criteria. You can build rules using one of eight templates. The templates are described in Table 12.2.

TABLE 12.2: OUTLOOK RULE TEMPLATES

TEMPLATE	DESCRIPTION/USE
Move messages from someone to a folder	Move messages based on the sender: move messages from your project leader to that project's folder.
Move messages with specific words in the subject to a folder	Move messages based on text in the subject: move messages with "idea" in the subject to the Ideas folder.
Move messages sent to a distribution list to a folder	Move messages based on the recipient: move messages sent to *HelpDesk@yourcompany.com* to the Help Desk folder.
Delete a conversation	Move messages to Deleted Items based on text in the subject: delete all messages with "free camera" in the subject.
Flag, with a colored flag, messages from someone	Flag messages based on the sender: apply a green flag to all messages from your project leader.
Display mail from someone in the New Item Alert window	Immediately display mail based on the sender: display mail from your boss as soon as it arrives.
Play a sound when I get messages from someone	Associate a specific sound file with a specific sender: play "We're in the Money" when a message arrives from the Payroll Department.
Send an alert to my mobile device when I get a message from someone.	A message will be sent to your cell phone, PDA, or other wireless mobile device when a message is received.

If these templates don't handle the rule you want to create, you can easily build it from scratch using a wizard. Outlook rules can handle all the day-to-day management of your e-mail by sorting mail into folders, forwarding and copying mail, deleting junk, and responding to mail automatically.

TIP   In Exchange, you can't create rules when Outlook knows you're working offline. Create rules when you're connected to Exchange.

To create an e-mail rule using a template, follow these steps:

1. Open the Inbox and choose Tools ➤ Rules And Alerts to open the Rules And Alerts dialog box.

2. On the E-mail Rules tab, click the New Rule button to open the Rules Wizard, shown in Figure 12.9.

FIGURE 12.9

Use the Rules Wizard to create rules for handling e-mail messages.

3. Select one of the eight templates in the Step 1 pane.

4. Click a link in the Step 2 pane to edit the rule. For example, if you are using the Move Messages From Someone To A Folder template, then click the People Or Distribution List link to open the Rules Address dialog box. Then, from the Rules Address dialog, you can type in a name, or select the address of the sender from your address book by highlighting it, then clicking OK. Then, you'd click the Specified link and select the folder you want the mail to move to in the Rules And Alerts dialog box. (Click the New button if you want to create a new folder for these messages.)

5. Click Next to move to the next page of the Rules Wizard, shown in Figure 12.10. Select any conditions you want checked before the rule is applied. For example, if you want the mail from this sender moved to the folder you specified only if you are the only recipient, enable the Sent Only To Me condition check box. After you set the conditions, click Next.

FIGURE 12.10

Set additional
conditions to iden-
tify mail this rule
should handle.

FIGURE 12.10

Set additional
conditions to iden-
tify mail this rule
should handle.

6. On the next page, shown in Figure 12.11, choose any additional actions you want to take with
messages that meet the conditions. In this example, Move It To The Specified Folder is already
selected. We might also choose to forward the messages to someone else. Click Next when you
are finished specifying actions.

FIGURE 12.11

Specify actions for
messages handled by
the rule.

7. Identify any exceptions to the rule. For example, perhaps you don't want the message moved if
its Importance setting is High or if the word "urgent" appears in the subject. After you set
any exceptions, click Next.

8. In the final step of the Rules Wizard, shown in Figure 12.12, enter a name for the rule and indicate whether you would like to run the rule immediately on messages in the current folder. This

is a great way to test the rule to see that it does what you want it to, and saves the time you'd spend taking the action(s) yourself. Click Finish to return to the Rules And Alerts dialog box.

FIGURE 12.12

Use the final step of the Rules Wizard to name your rule and review its settings.

9. If you want to create additional rules, repeat steps 2–8.

10. You can change the order in which rules are processed so that a message that might be affected by more than one rule is handled appropriately (see the sidebar, "Mastering the Opportunities: Organizing Folders and Rules in the Workplace," for an example). Click the Move Up and Move Down buttons to rearrange rules.

If you'd like to turn a rule off without deleting it, clear the rule's check box. You can then enable it when you want the rule to run again. Click OK to close the Rules And Alerts dialog box. If you set the rule to run now, it will do so.

MASTERING THE OPPORTUNITIES: ORGANIZING FOLDERS AND RULES IN THE WORKPLACE

College teachers receive a lot of e-mail from students; organizing and managing the mail is a time-consuming task—time they'd rather spend reading and responding to the messages. Here's how we suggested faculty members at one of our clients use folders and rules to help them with e-mail management; you can use these concepts to organize incoming mail in any situation where you can tell senders what to include in their e-mail subject.

At the beginning of the term, the instructor creates a folder for the term, and a folder for each class they're teaching. For example, in the fall of 2003 Deborah is teaching a biology lecture (BIO140), three biology labs (BIO140A, BIO140B, and BIO140C), and one microbiology lecture course (MCR240). Deborah creates one folder named Fall 2003. Inside the Fall 2003 folder she creates five folders using the course numbers as the names.

Continued on next page

MASTERING THE OPPORTUNITIES: ORGANIZING FOLDERS AND RULES IN THE WORKPLACE (continued)

In her course outlines, Deborah informs students that they must include the course number somewhere in the subject of any e-mail they send about the course: "If you have a question about the microbiology lecture, include MCR240 in the subject of your e-mail message. For example: "Need test dates for MCR240.""

Deborah then creates five rules using the Move Messages With Specific Words In The Subject To A Folder template. The order of the rules is important. The rule for BIO140 must be listed below the three rules for BIO140A, BIO140B, and BIO140C. If BIO140 is listed first, all the messages for the labs will be moved to the BIO140 folder.

For Deborah (and the other instructors), the students' messages are organized automatically, making it easy to check student e-mail before class without sorting through all the messages in their Inbox folders.

SHARING RULES WITH OTHER USERS OR COMPUTERS

You don't need to re-create rules on every machine you use. You can export rules to other computers, for your own use or for your coworkers to import and use. To import or export rules, choose Tools ➤ Rules And Alerts to open the Rules And Alerts dialog box. On the E-Mail Rules tab, click the Options button to open the Options dialog box:

Click Export Rules to save your rules in a RWZ file. Click Import Rules to import rules from an RWZ file.

TIP *Use this technique as a means to create a backup of your rules.*

AUTOMATICALLY RESPONDING TO MESSAGES

Business users spend a lot of time communicating stock answers to questions. For example, you might:

- Reply to a message simply to let the user know you received it
- Send meeting agendas when team members request them
- E-mail product information in response to customer requests

If you can set criteria that define the messages that should receive a specific response, you can set up Outlook to handle a fair amount of your low-level communication.

Here's an example: In a recent workshop, attendees were interested in a list of the steps required to use the Work menu in Word. Rather than repeat the steps in slow motion, we told the audience that we would create a handout, put it on our website, and send a link to the handout to anyone who requested it ("Please put 'Work menu' in the subject of your e-mail"). We then created an auto-reply system to handle the requests:

◆ A message template (WordWorkMenu) that includes text and the hyperlink

◆ A folder (Handout Requests) for messages that have been answered

◆ A rule (WordWorkMenuRequests) that sends the reply and moves the original message to the Handout Requests folder

Creating the Template

You must create the template and folder before you create rules that use them. We created an Outlook message template that includes the text we want to send in response to the requests. Outlook templates have file names with the OFT extension. Here's what our template looks like:

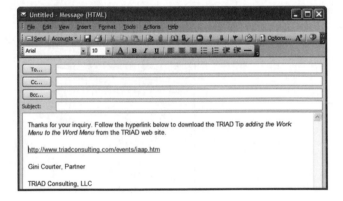

When you save a new message as a template while Word is your e-mail editor, the template is a Word template with a DOT extension, not an Outlook template. When you create a message template, you need to temporarily switch to an e-mail editor other than Word. Here are the steps to create a message template:

1. Choose Tools ➤ Options to open the Options dialog box.

2. On the Mail Format tab, turn off the Use Microsoft Word To Edit E-mail Messages check box. Click OK to close the Options dialog box.

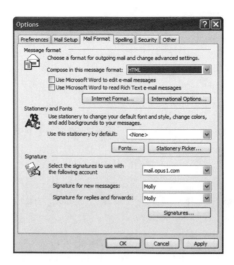

3. Click New to create a new e-mail message. A new, untitled message will appear.

4. Enter any text that you want to include in the message body. The text can include hyperlinks; you can attach files to the message.

5. Choose File ➤ Save As from the message menu to open the Save As dialog box.

6. In the Save As Type drop-down, select Outlook Template.

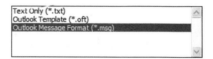

The Save In location is automatically switched to your templates folder.

7. Enter a file name for the template and click Save.

8. Close the template. When you're prompted to save the changes, click No.

9. If Word was your e-mail editor, return to the Mail Format tab in the Options dialog box and enable the Use Microsoft Word To Edit E-mail Messages check box.

Creating the Folder

We followed the steps in the "Creating Outlook Folders" section earlier in this chapter to create a Handout Requests folder in the Inbox. We could have created the folder as a peer to the Inbox to display the folder in the Folder List without expanding the Inbox, but in Outlook 2003 it's just as easy to click the Mail group header and drag the folder into the Favorite Folders list.

Outlook normally displays the number of unread messages in a folder, but we want to monitor the total number of requests we get for this handout to help us decide if this was a good way to provide information to this audience. In the Favorite Folders list, we right-clicked the `Handout Requests` folder and chose Properties from the shortcut menu. On the General tab we chose the Show Total Number Of Items option:

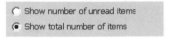

Creating the Rule

There isn't a template for an auto-reply message, so we used the Rules Wizard to create our rule. Here are the initial steps we followed:

1. Choose Tools ➤ Rules And Alerts and click New Rule to fire up the Rules Wizard. If you're using Exchange, be sure you are connected prior to doing this step.

2. Choose Start from a blank rule. Then, highlight the Check Messages When They Arrive option. Click Next.

3. In the second step, enable the With Specific Words In The Subject check box. In the Rule Description pane, click the Specific Words link to open the Search Text dialog box. Type **Work menu** in to the list of search terms and click Add. Click OK to close the dialog box, then click Next.

    We also added **Work Word menu** as a likely phrase someone would put in the subject. We did not, however, add **Word menu**—we don't want to automatically reply to messages that aren't about this specific feature. And we didn't add **Word Work menu**. It contains text that we're already searching for—Work menu—so it would be redundant.

4. Select the actions you want the rule to take, as shown in Figure 12.13: Reply Using A Specific Template and Move It To The Specified Folder.

FIGURE 12.13

Choose one or more actions that the rule should take.

5. Click the A Specific Template link in the Rule Description to open the Select A Reply Template dialog box.

6. In the Look In drop-down list, select User Templates In File System to switch to your templates folder:

7. Choose the template you created earlier (if you don't see it, choose Browse to locate the template). Click Open to return to the Rules Wizard.

8. Click the Specified folder link and set up the folder you want messages moved to after the auto-reply has been sent: Handout Requests in our example. In the Rules Wizard, click Next.

9. Set exceptions, if any, and then click Next.

10. Name the rule. Click Finish and then click OK to close the Rules And Alerts dialog box.

When the next message arrives with your specific text in the subject, Outlook will reply to the message and move it to the folder you specified.

MASTERING THE OPPORTUNITIES: SENDING AUTO-REPLIES FROM THE SERVER

If you need to have a reply sent whether or not Outlook is running and if you are using an Exchange account, you'll need to do a few things differently when you create the rule. Exchange uses the default Outlook template, so you'll enter message text rather than creating a template. Here are the differences:

◆ Follow the first three steps in the "Creating the Rule" section.

◆ In step 4, choose the Have Server Reply Using A Specific Message check box instead of the Reply Using A Specific Template check box.

◆ Click the A Specific Message link in the Rule Description pane.

◆ Enter text in the message body and subject.

◆ Click Save and Close, and then click Next.

◆ Set exceptions and name the rule. Click Finish and OK to save the server-side rule.

NOTE   *During a session, Outlook will remember the list of users to whom it has sent an auto-reply. This way, if you reply using a specific template, the reply will be sent to only one sender during a session as opposed to multiple replies being sent. Once you close and restart Outlook, the list will be deleted, so remember that this feature is session-specific.*

Using the Out of Office Assistant

The Out of Office Assistant, and Exchange-specific feature, is auto-reply with one significant improvement: from the time you turn it on until you return to the office, the Assistant replies once and only once to each e-mail address. If Beth sends you 15 e-mails, she'll receive only one Out of Office reply while you're out of the office this time.

Out of Office also supports rules: if you want to reply to, forward, or take other action with specific messages while you are out of the office, create rules and then turn them on in the Assistant.

To use the Out of Office Assistant, choose Tools ➤ Out Of Office Assistant from the menu to open the Out Of Office Assistant dialog box. The dialog box with a sample Out of Office message is shown in Figure 12.14.

FIGURE 12.14

Use the Out of Office Assistant to reply to messages received when you are on vacation or working from a remote site.

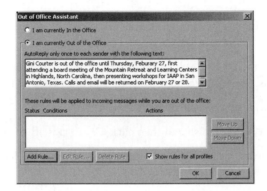

Enter your message in the upper pane. Minimally you should let people know the following:

◆ When you will return

◆ Whether you will respond to messages and/or voice mail while you are gone

◆ Who they should contact with urgent business in your absence

If you don't want to apply any rules, choose the I Am Currently Out Of The Office option and then click OK to turn on the Assistant. When you return to the office, choose I Am Currently In The Office to turn off the Assistant.

NOTE   The text you enter in the Out of Office Assistant will be there the next time you open the Assistant.

PLAYING BY THE RULES

If you have rules that should be enforced only when you're out of the office, create them in the Out of Office Assistant. Here are some situations where rules would be used while you're out of the office:

◆ You have coworkers who handle some of your clients when you're on vacation. Create rules to forward messages from specific senders to specific coworkers.

◆ You forward specific messages to your home e-mail account or cell phone while you're working from home or on the road.

◆ Some customers need more detail than others about why you're out of the office. Create a template with the detail and a rule that replies using the template.

NOTE   *You should check with your IT department before forwarding e-mail outside your organization.*

To add a rule, click the Add button in the Out Of Office Assistant dialog box to open the Edit Rule dialog box, shown in Figure 12.15.

FIGURE 12.15

Use the Edit Rule dialog box to create rules that work when you're out of the office.

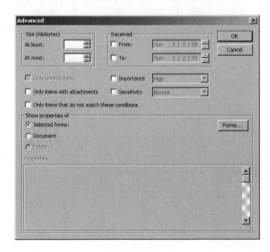

This isn't like the Rules Wizard: There are only two dialog boxes with criteria and actions combined. Use the Edit Rule dialog box to set the criteria in the top section and actions in the bottom. (Note that one of the actions is to reply with a specific template.)

Click the Advanced button to access a few more specific criteria: size, date received, and attachments. You could, for example, create two rules to forward messages with attachments to a separate personal e-mail account while forwarding other messages to your cell phone.

As with the Rules and Alerts, rules are processed in order in the Out of Office Assistant.

Granting Other Users Permissions to Your Outlook Folders

At the beginning of the Outlook section of this chapter, we noted that the folders in your mailbox are your personal folders. By default, you are the only person who can examine the contents of your Inbox, Calendar, and other folders. If you're working with Exchange, there are valid reasons you might want to grant other users permission to work in your folders. For example, one or more specific users might need these permissions:

◆ View and/or edit your contacts

◆ Schedule appointments on your calendar

◆ Send messages on your behalf

Outlook has two ways to allow other users to work with your Outlook items: permissions and delegates. When you give another user permission to use your folders, it is as if you are using the folder. For example, if you give someone permission to create items in your Inbox, the messages they create will look like they come from you. If you give another user permission to create appointments in your calendar, meetings they create look like you set them up.

When someone is your delegate, it is clear that they are not you. The sender for a message sent by a delegate reads "on behalf of": Abby Adams (the delegate) on behalf of Barbara Johnson (who gave her delegate permission).

We'll show you how to set up delegate roles first and then discuss folder permissions.

TROUBLESHOOTING TIP: STEERING CLEAR OF IDENTITY "THEFT"

We've worked with organizations where assistants were given permission to send messages from their executive's Inbox because the executive correctly noted that "on behalf of" makes it clear that the message was sent by someone else. We're going to risk great candor here: This is a very bad idea for both the executive and the assistant. Executives are responsible for all messages sent in their name; they can't prove that someone else actually created the message. And the assistant can too easily be accused of authoring a message sent by the executive if that's how business is normally conducted.

In a time of increased focus on corporate responsibility, identity theft, and litigation where e-mail is entered into evidence, it's important to use best practices:

◆ Never let anyone else use your electronic identity

◆ Never agree to "be" someone else

There are resources that will help you consider (and perhaps take a leadership role in formulating) electronic policy for your organization. Visit the ePolicy Institute at www.epolicyinstitute.com/ for white papers, case studies, and other information.

DELEGATING PERMISSION TO OTHERS

You can delegate permission to your `Calendar`, `Inbox`, `Tasks`, `Contacts`, `Notes`, and `Journal`. There are four delegate roles:

Role	Permissions
None (the default)	No permissions
Reviewer	Delegate can view items in the folder
Author	Delegate can view items and create new items in the folder
Editor	Delegate can view, create, and modify (including delete) folder items

This is mix and match. A delegate may, for example, be a reviewer in your `Calendar`, an Editor in your `Contacts` folder, and have no permissions in your other folders. Follow these steps to delegate permission to your folders.

1. Choose Tools ➢ Options from the menu to open the Options dialog box.

2. On the Delegates tab, click the Add button to open the Add Users dialog box shown in Figure 12.16.

3. Select the user(s) you want to give the same delegate permissions to and then click the Add button to add them to the list. (You can hold Shift or Ctrl to choose multiple user names).

FIGURE 12.16

Select users to whom you will give the same delegate permissions and Add them to the list.

4. Click OK to open the Delegate Permissions dialog box, shown in Figure 12.17.

FIGURE 12.17

Choose delegate roles for the selected user(s) in the Delegate Permissions dialog box.

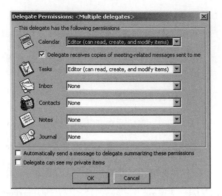

5. To automatically have a user delegated as an Editor on your calendar receive all meeting-related messages, enable the check box below the Calendar drop-down list.

6. At the bottom of the dialog box, enable the Automatically Send A Message To Delegate Summarizing These Permissions check box. When you close the Options dialog box, Outlook will send all delegates a message informing them that they are delegates and summarizing the permissions you have granted.

The last check box lets your delegates see the details of items marked as private in any folder where they are a Reviewer, Author, or Editor. After setting a role for each folder, click OK to return to the Options dialog box. Click OK to close the Options dialog box and set the delegate permissions.

TIP   Some executives have assistants who handle all their appointments. If someone else is responsible for setting up the meetings on your calendar, you can remove yourself as a recipient so you don't have unnecessary messages in your Inbox while your delegate is managing your calendar. When you return to the Options dialog box, click the corresponding check box on the Delegates tab and Outlook will send meeting and appointment items to your delegates only.

GRANTING PERMISSIONS TO FOLDERS IN EXCHANGE

To set permissions for a folder, right-click the folder and choose Properties from the shortcut menu. Click the Permissions tab to view the current permissions for the folder, as shown in Figure 12.18.

NOTE   Only the folder owner can set permissions. If there's no Permissions tab in the Properties dialog box, you're not a folder owner.

FIGURE 12.18

Grant very specific permissions to individual users in a folder's Properties dialog box

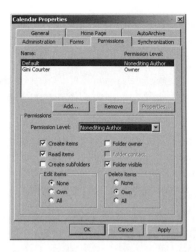

There are a number of separate permission items that are summarized into nine levels. At any permission level other than None, the folder is visible to the user. In addition to the specific permissions listed, the owner has permission to grant permission to other users. The permission levels are described in Table 12.3.

TABLE 12.3: OUTLOOK PERMISSION LEVELS

PERMISSION LEVEL	CREATE ITEMS	READ ITEMS	CREATE SUBFOLDERS	EDIT ITEMS	DELETE ITEMS
Owner	Yes	Yes	Yes	All	All
Publishing Editor	Yes	Yes	Yes	All	All
Editor	Yes	Yes	No	All	All
Publishing Author	Yes	Yes	Yes	Own	Own
Author	Yes	Yes	No	Own	Own
Non-editing Author	Yes	Yes	No	None	Own
Reviewer	No	Yes	No	None	None
Contributor	Yes	No	No	None	None
None (default)	No	No	No	None	None

To set permissions, first click the Add button and add the user to the list in the upper pane. Select a user in the upper pane (or hold Ctrl or Shift and select multiple users) and then choose a permission level or use the check boxes and option buttons to set the user's permissions.

WARNING   Make sure you select the user before setting permissions. It's easy to accidentally set permissions for the default user, which is all users. If, for example, you make the default user a Reviewer on your Inbox, any user on your network will be able to read your e-mail.

When you're finished setting permissions, close the Options dialog box.

If you're accountable to a large group of people, consider changing the permission level for the default user to Reviewer. This allows anyone on your network to see your calendar. Users will be able to see the details of appointments and meetings, but only the time and date of items marked private.

Understanding Protection with Information Rights Management (IRM)

With today's networking and collaborative environment, the protection of company ideas, documents, and people is becoming more of a concern. Even where security and protection options are available, their use is still inconsistent, so as a result, there's a great need to protect digital information more explicitly.

Microsoft Office 2003 has added a number of features to help support Information Rights Management (IRM) concerns. Using Windows Rights Management Service (RMS) technology in Microsoft Windows Server 2003, it becomes easy to add protection to documents created with Outlook, Word, Excel, and PowerPoint.

NOTE   IRM is based on the concept of Digital Rights Management (DRM). DRM attempts to address both the legal and ethical concerns rising out of today's information security needs. DRM is in and of itself a controversial subject, with its critics claiming that companies use DRM in unfair ways. Learn more about Microsoft's approach to DRM and IRM at `www.microsoft.com/windows/windowsmedia/drm.aspx` *and* `http://www.microsoft.com/office/editions/prodinfo/technologies/irm.mspx`. *For alternative viewpoints and DRM activity, please see the Electronic Privacy Information Center (EPIC) web page on DRM,* `www.epic.org/privacy/drm/`.

IRM Technology in Outlook

You can protect e-mail documents in Outlook from being copied, forwarded, and printed by recipients.

NOTE   To activate Information Rights Management technology in Office, you'll need to download the Windows Rights Management client software. This step-by-step list includes the download. Once the client is downloaded, it can then be accessed by other Office 2003 products without having to be downloaded again.

To use IRM technology to protect an e-mail message in Outlook, follow these steps:

1. Create a new e-mail message.

2. From within the message window, click the Permission button on the standard toolbar.

3. If you haven't installed IRM technology during your Office 2003 install, or haven't used IRM in Outlook yet, you'll get a pop-up message asking you if you wish to download and install the Rights Management client software now. Click Yes.

4. The Rights Management client Setup Wizard appears (Figure 12.19).

FIGURE 12.19

The Windows Rights Management client setup wizard

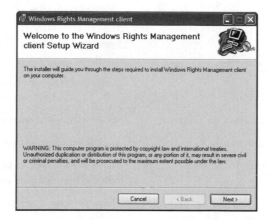

5. Click Next, read and accept the privacy statement provided and click the I Agree radio button if you agree with the statement.

6. Click Next again. You'll reach a Confirm Installation window. Click Next to start the installation.

7. The client will download. Once complete, click OK and return to your message in Outlook.

You can now click the Permissions button to toggle from Unrestricted Access to Do Not Forward access, which will prevent messages from being forwarded, copied, and printed.

NOTE   *If you don't have access to the proper server features, Microsoft will allow you to access their IRM service. You won't be able to send the message if you don't have some sort of access, so check with your systems administrator before using these features.*

Using IRM in Word, Excel, and PowerPoint

You can use IRM in Word, Excel, and PowerPoint to restrict access by setting a range of permissions for a given document. Table 12.4 shows the type of IRM restrictions you can place on a document created in any of these Office 2003 programs.

Table 12.4: IRM Permissions in Word, Excel, and PowerPoint	
Permission Option	**What it Does**
Read	Users can read but not change, print, or copy the document.
Change	Users can read, edit, and save changes, but cannot print the document.
Expires on	Expires a document on a given date, making it unusable after that date.
Print content sions but no print available.	Enables print options for those with Read or Change permis-
Allow users with read access to copy content	Allows users with read access to copy document.
Access content programmatically	Allows users to access the content via programmatic means.
Request additional permissions from	Allows users to request additional permissions from the individual(s) who can grant permissions via e-mail.
Allow users with earlier versions of Office to read with browsers supporting Information Rights Management. (Increases file size)	Allows content to be viewed in browsers that are considered trusted via the security level within a given browser.
Require a connection to verify a user's permission	Requires users to be connected to the network in order to verify permissions.

Adding IRM Permission Features to a Document

Whether you're in Excel, Word, or PowerPoint, you can modify the options shown in Table 12.3 by following these steps:

1. With the document, workbook, or presentation open, click the Permissions button on the toolbar. The Permission dialog opens.

2. Check the Restrict Permission To This Workbook check box to activate the permissions (see Figure 12.20).

FIGURE 12.20

Read and Change permissions are set in the Permission dialog.

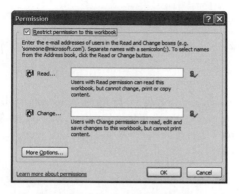

3. To set Read permissions, enter the e-mail addresses of those users to whom you'd like to offer Read permissions into the available text box. Separate the e-mail addresses using a semicolon (;) as stated by the Permission dialog.

4. To set Change permissions, enter the e-mail addresses in the same way, this time into the Change text box.

5. Click the More Options button to bring up the full Permission dialog with additional IRM options (Figure 12.21).

FIGURE 12.21

The Permission dialog with additional permission options

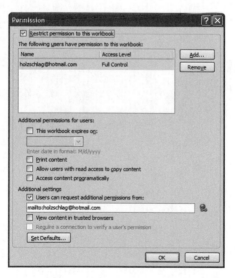

6. Add additional options as required according to Table 12.3. When you're finished, click OK.

Your permissions are now applied.

TIP   *If at any time you'd like to restore the permissions to default, simply click the Set Defaults button in the Permission dialog.*

NOTE   *To get more information and updates to the Rights Management Add-On for Internet Explorer, see* www.microsoft.com/windows/ie/downloads/addon/. *More about the RMS technologies can be explored at* http://www.microsoft.com/windowsserver2003/evaluation/overview/technologies/rmenterprise .mspx.

Chapter 13

Building Robust and Foolproof Workbooks

FIVE YEARS AGO, MOST knowledge workers who used Office spent the majority of their time in one application: Microsoft Word. That same year, e-mail applications including Outlook were the "second home" to the vast majority of Office users. Over the past five years, we've seen the numbers change as an increasing number of knowledge workers spend equal amounts of time in Excel and Outlook, and much less time in Word. This movement away from creating Word documents to creating reports and analysis tools in Excel reflects a sea change in the job duties of business users.

This chapter isn't the place to learn Excel from scratch: There are many courses and other books that cover the basics of Excel. This chapter focuses on the skills that self-taught users often miss, or find just beyond their reach:

◆ Inserting, copying, and moving worksheets

◆ Using the logical and lookup functions to make decisions and retrieve information

◆ Using functions that clean up and split text

◆ Using functions that manipulate dates

◆ Simplifying your workbooks with names

Changing Workbook Layout

By default, an Excel workbook includes three worksheets: Sheet1, Sheet2, and Sheet3. There's nothing magic about the number. Earlier versions had a five-worksheet default.

Changing the Number of Sheets in a New Book

If you commonly use a number of worksheets other than three, it makes sense to change the default. To do so, choose Tools ➤ Options to open the Options dialog box. On the General tab, shown in Figure 13.1, change the Sheets In New Workbook setting to your preferred number of worksheets.

FIGURE 13.1

Set the default
number of sheets
for a new workbook
in the Options
dialog box.

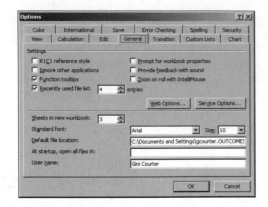

Each new workbook you create will include the new default number of sheets.

Inserting and Deleting Sheets

Regardless of the default number of worksheets, you will occasionally need to insert or delete worksheets in a workbook. You insert sheets when the scope of your work changes. If your workbooks contain sheets that aren't used, you should delete them so they don't confuse novice users.

The quick way to insert a new worksheet is to use the menu. Choose Insert ➢ Worksheet to insert a new worksheet to the left of the currently selected sheet. The worksheet will use the first worksheet number not in use in the workbook (or previously used in this session). For example, if you have renamed all your worksheets, the new sheet will be named Sheet1.

TIP   To rename a worksheet, double-click the sheet tab. Type a new name and press Enter.

There's one exception to this "quickest" rule: if you want to insert a new worksheet that's a template rather than the blank default worksheet, use the shortcut menu attached to the sheet tabs:

1. Right-click any sheet tab and choose Insert from the shortcut menu to open the Insert dialog box.

2. Select the template you want to use then click OK to insert the template as a worksheet in the current workbook.

NOTE   For information on creating and using templates, see Chapter 15, "Creating Templates to Handle Your Repetitive Tasks."

Moving and Copying Within a Workbook

Use the sheet tabs to move or copy sheets within a workbook to rearrange the workbook. To move a worksheet, use the mouse to drag the sheet's tab to its new location and then drop it. To copy a sheet, hold down Ctrl while you release the mouse button.

Moving and Copying between Workbooks

There are a number of scenarios where you might want to move or copy sheets between books:

◆ You want to consolidate sheets from different workbooks into one workbook. Move—don't copy—the sheets to one workbook and then delete the empty workbooks. If you copy the sheets, it's too easy to update the wrong workbook.

◆ You're sending a workbook to another user who needs only two worksheets from the book. Copy the worksheets they need to a new workbook rather than sending the original workbook and its extra (and unnecessary) worksheets.

TIP   If you're sending only one worksheet by e-mail, select the sheet you want to send and then choose File ➤ Send To ➤ Mail Recipient and choose Send the Current Sheet as the Message Body in the E-mail dialog box.

◆ You want to use some, but not all, of the sheets in the current workbook as part of another workbook. Group the sheets you want to copy and then copy them all to the other workbook. Remember to ungroup the sheets when you're finished copying.

◆ Your workbook contains so many sheets that navigating the sheets is difficult. Group and move a logical subset of the worksheets to a new book, then comment the name and location of the new book in cell A1 of the first sheet in the original book.

NOTE   To group sheets, select the first sheet's tab, then hold Ctrl and click on other sheet tabs. If the sheets are next to each other, you can select the first sheet and then hold Shift while selecting the last sheet you want to select. Groups are temporary; when you select any sheet that's not in the group, the grouping is removed. For tips and uses for grouping, see in Chapter 1, "What's New in Office 2003." For information on inserting comments, see Chapter 15.

To move or copy selected sheets between workbooks, follow these steps:

1. Open the workbook that contains the sheets you want to move/copy, as well as any workbooks that you want to move/copy to. If you're moving or copying to a new workbook, you do not need to create it first.

2. Select the sheet or group the sheets you want to move or copy.

3. Right-click any selected sheet's tab and choose Move or Copy from the shortcut menu to open the Move or Copy dialog box, shown in Figure 13.2.

FIGURE 13.2

Use the Move or Copy dialog box to move sheets between Excel workbooks.

4. From the To Book drop-down list, select the book you want to move or copy the sheet(s) into.

5. To copy, enable the Create a Copy checkbox at the bottom of the dialog box. To move, leave it turned off. Note that you can move the sheets before a specific sheet in the target workbook, or place them at the end. Don't spend too much time on the placement of the moved or copied sheets. You can always rearrange them later.

6. Click OK to move/copy the sheets.

7. If you grouped sheets in Step 2, right-click any sheet and choose Ungroup from the short-cut menu.

Working with Excel's Functions

Functions like SUM are used to calculate results used in statistics, finance, engineering, math, and other fields. *Functions* are structured programs that calculate a specific result: a total, an average, the amount of a monthly loan payment, or the geometric mean of a group of numbers. Excel includes hundreds of functions. Most are included in the typical installation, but others, like the Engineering functions, must be installed separately. Each function has a specific order, or *syntax*, that must be used for the function to work properly.

Functions are formulas, so all functions begin with the equal sign (=). The equal symbol is followed by the *function name*, followed by one or more *arguments* separated by commas and enclosed in parentheses. Excel's functions are grouped into the 10 categories listed in Table 13.1.

TABLE 13.1: EXCEL FUNCTIONS

CATEGORY	EXAMPLES
Financial	Calculates interest rates, loan payments, depreciation amounts, and so on; additional financial functions are included in the Excel Analysis Toolpak Add-in.
Date & Time	Returns the current hour, day of week or year, time, or date.
Math & Trig	Calculates absolute values, cosines, logarithms, and so on.
Statistical	Includes common functions used for totals, averages, and high and low numbers in a range; advanced functions for t-tests, Chi tests, deviation.
Lookup & Reference	Searches for and returns values from a range; creates hyperlinks to network or Internet documents.
Database	Calculates values in an Excel database table.
Text	Converts text to uppercase or lowercase, trims characters from the right or left end of a text string, concatenates text strings.
Logical	Evaluates an expression and returns a value of TRUE or FALSE; used to trigger other actions or formatting.

Continued on next page

TABLE 13.1: EXCEL FUNCTIONS *(continued)*

Information	Returns information from Excel or Windows about the current status of a cell, object, or the environment.
Engineering	Included with Office, but must be installed separately from the Analysis Toolpak.

You don't have to learn all the functions—but you should know the common functions thoroughly and know enough about other functions so that you can find them as you need them. The AutoSum functions (SUM, COUNT, AVERAGE, MIN, and MAX) are the only functions included on the Standard toolbar. You access all the functions (including SUM) using the Insert Function button on the formula bar, or by selecting More Functions on the AutoSum button menu.

Relative and Absolute Cell References

Before we launch into functions, we'd like to spend a minute on the difference between absolute and relative cell references. If you're already comfortable with absolute cell references, you can skip this section.

When you copy a formula from one cell to another, Excel automatically adjusts each cell reference in the formula. If, for example, the formula in cell J15 includes a reference to cell H15 and you copy the formula down a row to J16, the new formula's reference is automatically changed to refer to cell H16. In this example, H15 is a *relative cell reference*—the kind of reference Excel creates when you simply click in a cell or type a cell address when creating a formula. It doesn't matter how you copy the formula from J15 to J16. Excel treats formulas the same way, regardless of the copy method you employ.

Most of the time, this is exactly what you want Excel to do. When you copy a formula from one column to another, you want Excel to adjust the column references. A copy from one row to another should result in a change in the row numbers in the cell references. However, there are exceptions. Sometimes you want Excel *not* to adjust a cell reference when you copy a formula. One such exception is shown in Figure 13.3. On the left, you see the worksheet formulas. The formula =B2/B9 was created in cell C2, then filled to the other cells in the column. The results are shown on the right of Figure 13.3: the correct formula from C2 results in a DIV/0 error when copied to C3, C4, and so on.

FIGURE 13.3

The formula in cell C2 was correct, but yielded wrong results when copied down the column.

	A	B	C
1		July Sales	State %
2	Alabama	103451	=B2/B9
3	Georgia	254980	=B3/B10
4	Mississippi	99435	=B4/B11
5	Florida	212997	=B5/B12
6	South Carolina	109368	=B6/B13
7	Louisiana	121093	=B7/B14
8			
9	Total	=SUM(B2:B8)	=SUM(C2:C8)

	A	B	C
1		July Sales	State %
2	Alabama	103,451	11%
3	Georgia	254,980	#DIV/0!
4	Mississippi	99,435	#DIV/0!
5	Florida	212,997	#DIV/0!
6	South Carolina	109,368	#DIV/0!
7	Louisiana	121,093	#DIV/0!
8			
9	Total	901,324	#DIV/0!

So what happened? When the formula was filled from C2 to C3, Excel changed both cell references. B2 was changed to B3 (which works) and B9 was changed to B10—an empty cell. When you fill this type of formula, you want Excel not to change the cell reference of the total (or average, or other number that appears only once in the worksheet). To instruct Excel not to change the cell address in a formula, you make the reference to the cell *absolute*—not changeable.

CREATING ABSOLUTE CELL REFERENCES

The row and column in an absolute cell reference are preceded with dollar signs: $B$9. The dollar signs "lock in" the reference so Excel doesn't change the row or column when you fill or copy the formula. The dollar sign in front of the B instructs Excel not to change the column; the dollar sign in front of the 9 locks in the row.

You create the absolute cell reference in the original formula—the one you want to fill. If you never intend to copy a formula, you don't need to use absolute references, and they won't fix a formula that doesn't work correctly to begin with. If you are typing the formula and know you want to create an absolute reference, just precede the column and row addresses with a $. Using point and click, click on the cell and then press the F4 key on your keyboard. To change an existing formula, select the cell with the formula and then select the reference you want to change in the formula bar and press F4.

TIP   *Another way to handle this situation is by naming cell B9. See the "Using Names" section later in this chapter.*

USING A MIXED CELL REFERENCE

You can also create a *mixed reference*, making part of a cell address absolute and part relative, by locking in either the column or the row. Use mixed references when you want to copy a formula down *and* across to have a reference change relatively in one direction but not in the other. For example, E$5 will remain E$5 when copied down because the row reference is absolute, but it can change to F$5, G$5, and so on when copied across because the column reference is relative.

TIP   *The Absolute key (F4) is a four-way toggle. The first time you press it, it locks both the column and row: $B$9. Press it again, and only the row is locked: B$9. The third time you press the Absolute key, the column is locked: $B9. Press it a fourth time, and both row and column are relative: B9.*

Using Logical, Lookup, and Information Functions

Logical operators, such as greater than, less than, and not equal to, allow you to compare two or more values or text strings to filter or sort values or text strings. Excel's Logical functions place that decision-making power inside a formula to determine what action should be completed based on a condition. Uses for logical functions abound in business—every time you choose one action or another based on a value, you're probably doing work that Excel could do for you.

The related lookup functions are used to retrieve information from a list (database) based on a value in a specific cell. Lookups are widely used to return, for example, a customer name and address when a user enters the customer number. Lookups are relatively easy to create and can make you incredibly popular with the people who use your workbooks because users can enter minimal data and return accurate results.

The third group in this section, the Information functions, returns information about a cell: Is it blank? Does it contain text? A number? An error? Information functions are almost always used with the logical functions.

Decision Making with IF

Use logical functions (also referred to as conditional or IF functions) any time you need to take different actions based on a condition: to apply one formula or another (or no formula), based on the contents of a cell, such as:

- Calculating shift premiums: two or three different gross pay formulas based on an employee's shift

- Concatenating text strings: formulas that create full names from columns of first names, middle initials, last names, and titles (Dr., Ms., etc.) without adding inappropriate spaces when some fields are blank

- Calculating gross pay with overtime: different formulas for employees who work more than 40 hours and those who work 40 hours or less

- Commission calculations using rates that vary based on the total sales volume, region, products sold, or other specific values

WHEN AND HOW TO USE IF

The sales worksheet in Figure 13.4 shows committed sales closed by our sales staff this quarter. At the end of each quarter, salespeople get a bonus. Here's how it's calculated:

- For sales under $500,000, there is no bonus.

- There is a 7% bonus for all sales in excess of $500,000.

FIGURE 13.4

In the sales worksheet, a bonus is earned on sales over $500,000—a great place to use a formula containing IF.

C4		f_x =IF(B4>500000,(B4-500000)*7%,0)		
A	B	C	D	E
1 Fourth Quarter Bonus Calculation				
2				
3 Name	Sales	Bonus		
4 Alex	515,940	$ 1,116		
5 Bonnie	612,098	$ 7,847		
6 Calvin	650,209	$ 10,515		
7 Katie	455,877	$ -		
8 Tamara	695,766	$ 13,704		
9 Linda	510,978	$ 768		

Without using a function, we would need two different formulas: one for salespeople who were getting a bonus, and another for those who were not. IF allows us to combine the two formulas and the condition into a single formula. This is a "textbook" use of the IF function: two possibilities with a clear condition (sales greater than $500,000) that separates the two.

The formula in C4 is relatively straightforward, especially if you create it using the Function Arguments dialog box. Choose one of these approaches to create the formula:

Locating and selecting a function   Click the down-arrow on the AutoSum button and choose More Functions to open the Insert Function dialog box, shown in Figure 13.5. Locate the function, either by selecting a category and then the function or by entering a description (or the function name) in the text box at the top of the dialog box. Select the function to open the Function Arguments dialog box, shown in Figure 13.6.

FIGURE 13.5

Select IF—or any other function— from the Insert Function dialog box.

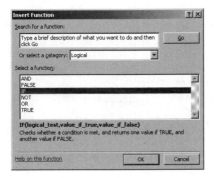

Typing the start of the formula   If you know the name of the function, type the equal symbol, the function name, then the opening parenthesis: **=IF(**. Then click the Insert Function button at the left end of the formula bar to open the Function Arguments dialog box for the IF function, shown in Figure 13.6.

The Functions Arguments dialog box has a text box for each argument. Required arguments are labeled in bold (like Logical_Test in Figure 13.6). Click in a text box to see a description of the argument. Click in the worksheet or type to enter the arguments. Excel provides the commas that separate arguments, as well as the opening and closing parentheses that surround the arguments. Excel does not enter parentheses within formulas, so in our example, we have to enter the parentheses around B4-500000.)

FIGURE 13.6

In the Function Arguments dialog box, enter each argument in its text box. Excel will provide the punctuation for your formula.

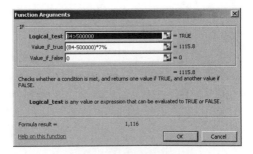

Typing the entire formula   Some users prefer to create formulas without the dialog box, and Excel provides some support for this method. After you type the opening parenthesis for the function arguments, the syntax for the function is displayed as a screen tip near the cell. If you create the formula without using the Insert Function dialog box, you're responsible for entering the appropriate commas and parentheses.

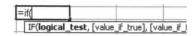

Table 13.2 explains the three arguments for the formula in our example.

TABLE 13.2: ARGUMENTS FOR FIGURE 13.5

ARGUMENT	VALUE	DESCRIPTION
Logical_test	B4>500000	The test that Excel should use to determine which formula to execute. The test must have only two possible outcomes: True or False.
Value_if_true	(B4-500000)*7%	The formula that Excel uses if the result of the logical_test is True. The parentheses are required to force Excel to subtract the 500000 before performing the multiplication. For more information on why this is required, open the Office Assistant and search for **order of operations**.
Value_if_false	0	The formula that Excel uses if the result of the logical_test is False.

There is no commission if the result of the logical test is false. However, if you leave the value_if_false text box empty, the text FALSE will appear in the cell whenever the result of the logical test is false. In this case, the value_if_true is a number, so we used zero (0) for the value_if_false. The corresponding text argument is two quotes with nothing between them—""—literally no text.

TIP   You can quickly fill a formula down a column by selecting the first cell with a formula, pointing to the fill handle, and double-clicking. Excel stops when it hits a blank cell in the column to the left.

USING IF TO CONCATENATE NAMES
Here's another common situation: you have a list of names and addresses in Excel, properly separated into columns, that you need to convert into full names for an address label or Word merge. There are some empty cells because some names don't include middle initials. A sample list of names is shown in Figure 13.7.

FIGURE 13.7

The list of names includes these fields: Title, First Name, MI, and Last Name

	A	B	C	D
1	Salutation	First Name	MI	Last Name
2		Karla	J.	Browning
3	Mr.	Michael		Young
4	Ms.	Annette	S.	Marquis
5	Ms.	Kay		Montgomery
6	Dr.	Norma		Poinsett
7		Pat	M.	Andrews

First we'll create a full name that uses only the first and last names. Every entry has a first name, so we don't need to use IF in this formula. The ampersand (&) is used to concatenate two text strings. The formula =B2&D2 is almost a good formula—almost because it concatenates the contents of the two cells, but doesn't leave a space between the two names:

	A	B	C	D	E
1	Salutation	First Name	MI	Last Name	Full Name
2		Karla	J.	Browning	KarlaBrowning

We want a space between the first and last names, so we need to include a space in the formula by concatenating a space (enclosed in quotes) between the contents of the two cells: =B2&" "&D2.

	A	B	C	D	E
1	Salutation	First Name	MI	Last Name	Full Name
2		Karla	J.	Browning	Karla Browning

Now, we'll create a full name that includes the middle initial. A formula that would do this is =B2&" "&C2&" "&D2. However, two of our four entries don't have a middle initial and this formula will put spaces around the middle initial, even if cell C2 is empty. The result: two spaces between the first and last name when there's no middle initial. The formula works for Karla, but not for Michael—a sure clue that it's time to use the IF function:

	A	B	C	D	E
1	Salutation	First Name	MI	Last Name	Full Name
2		Karla	J.	Browning	Karla J. Browning
3	Mr.	Michael		Young	Michael Young

The condition in the IF formula needs to determine if the cell in column C is empty. If it is, it should use the full name formula that skips the middle initial: the formula that works for all records. If, however, there is a middle initial, Excel should use the formula that includes the middle initial: the formula that worked for Karla. The Function Arguments dialog box for the completed formula is shown in Figure 13.8. The arguments are for the formula in cell E2 detailed in Table 13.3.

FIGURE 13.8

The function arguments for the IF function that concatenates strings to create a full name

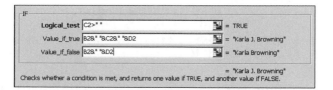

TABLE 13.3: ARGUMENTS FOR THE IF FUNCTION IN FIGURE 13.8

ARGUMENT	VALUE	DESCRIPTION
Logical_test	C2>" "	The logical_test checks to see if there's "more than" a space in cell C2.
Value_if_true	B2&" "&C2&" "&D2	If the logical_test is True (there's an entry in C2), use the formula that includes B2, C2, and D2.
Value_if_false	B2&" "&D2	If the logical_test is False (C2 is blank, or contains only a space), use the formula that only concatenates B2 and D2.

The formula in Figure 13.8 tests one condition: is there a middle initial entry? We have a similar problem with the Title field, which we could solve with a similar formula. To create a formula that includes both a Title and a middle initial whether either or both could be blank, we need more than one IF statement as you'll see in the next section, "Nesting IF Functions."

MASTERING THE OPPORTUNITIES: MOVING LISTS FROM WORD TO EXCEL

The power of functions makes Excel the perfect application for managing text lists. If many of your lists are in Word, don't worry—they're no more than two steps away from Excel. If the list is in a table, simply copy the list in Word and paste it in Excel. Excel will convert each table cell to a worksheet cell.

If the text is in Word tabbed columns, select the text then choose Table ➤ Convert Text to Table from the Word menu to turn the text into a table, which you can then copy and paste into Excel.

NESTING IF FUNCTIONS

If you need to test for more than one condition or apply more than two different calculations in a formula, nest one IF function inside another. In our sample workbook, there are four fields that can be combined to create a Full Name field: Title, First Name, MI (middle initial), and Last Name. Either Title or MI may be empty. In the previous section we created a formula that tests to see if there's a middle initial, then executes one of two operations to create a Full Name: =IF(C2>" ",B2&" "&C2&" "&D2,B2&" "&D2). To check whether the Title field is empty, we need another IF function: IF(A2>" ",…). The resulting formula using two levels of IF looks pretty complex, but the parts detailed in Table 13.4 should look familiar:

```
=IF(A2>" ",IF(C2>" ",A2&" "&B2&" "&C2&" "&D2,A2&" "&B2&" "&D2),IF(C2>" ",B2&"
"&C2&" "&D2,B2&" "&D2))
```

TABLE 13.4: ARGUMENTS FOR THE IF FUNCTION FOR SALUTATIONS AND MIDDLE INITIALS

ARGUMENT	VALUE	DESCRIPTION
Logical_test	A2>" "	The logical_test checks to see if there's "more than" a space in the Title (cell A2)
Value_if_true—another IF function	Logical_test: IF(C2>" ",	There's a Title in A2, so test to see if there's a middle initial in C2
	Value_if_true: A2&" "&B2&" "&C2&" "&D2	If there's a middle initial in C2, then use the formula that concatenates A2, B2, C2, and D2
	Value_if_false: A2&" "&B2&" "&D2	If there's no middle initial in C2, use the formula that concatenates A2, B2, and D2
Value_if_false—another IF function	Logical_test: IF(C2>" ",	There is no salutation in A2, so test to see if there's a middle initial in C2
	Value_if_true: B2&" "&C2&" "&D2	If there's a middle initial in C2, use the formula that concatenates B2, C2, and D2
	Value_if_false: B2&" "&D2	If there's no middle initial in C2, use the formula that concatenates B2 and D2

The key to creating nested logical functions is knowing how they work. As soon as any IF condition is met, Excel processes the *result if true* argument for the function and ignores any other functions nested within the IF statement. If the logical_test is true, Excel ignores the value_if_false. If the logical_test is false, Excel ignores the value_if_true. That's why we need three IF functions: we need to test for a middle name twice, once when there's a Title, and again if there is no Title.

But There's Another Way to Do This

We'd be remiss if we didn't point out that there's an Office application that runs this function automatically: Microsoft Outlook. Outlook converts name fields into full names and never includes extra spaces. When you receive an Excel workbook like the workbook in our example with names separated into fields, you might prefer to work with the data in Outlook, particularly if your end result will be created in an application other than Excel (like a Word merge). See Chapter 3, "Taking Control of Your Time and Tasks," to learn how to import Excel name and address data into Outlook.

USING NESTED IFS WITH VALUES AND DATES

When you create an IF based on ranges of values or dates, start at one end of the range or the other, and work through the range sequentially. For example, imagine you need to age your accounts receivable, separating them into accounts that are more than 90 days overdue, 61–90 days overdue, and 30–60 days overdue. Working from one end of the range to the other, you should handle the 90-day-plus accounts first, then the 61–90 day accounts, then the 30–60 day accounts. A sample accounts receivable worksheet is shown in Figure 13.9.

FIGURE 13.9

The Accounts Receivable worksheet lists customer invoices and due dates. We'll use a nested IF formula to complete the aging information.

	A	B	C	D	E
1	Customer	Invoice	Invoice Date	Due Date	Age
2	ABC Excavating	97854	5/15/2003	6/14/2003	
3	Burleigh Printing	97855	5/15/2003	6/14/2003	
4	Curl Up and Dye	97862	6/18/2003	7/18/2003	
5	Draftmasters	97869	7/13/2003	8/12/2003	
6	Enterprise Tire	97876	8/5/2003	9/4/2003	

TIP   *You can nest up to seven IF functions in one formula.*

In this example, we'll walk through each of the steps required so you can see how to efficiently create the nested IF formula in cell E2. We'll also use another function, the TODAY function, which retrieves the current date from Windows. TODAY is followed by a set of empty parentheses because it has no arguments: TODAY(). TODAY is classified as a *volatile* function because its value changes. Excel recalculates any formulas that use volatile functions each time the workbook is opened and whenever any other calculations are performed.

Here are the steps to create the nested IF aging formula:

1. After selecting cell E2, type **=IF(** and then click the Insert Function button at the left end of the Formula Bar to open the Function Arguments dialog box.

2. Our first test is for invoices more than 90 days overdue. In the Logical_test text box, enter **TODAY()-D2>90**.

3. In the Value_if_true text box, type the text string to display in E2 if the logical test is true: **"90+ days"**.

4. Select the Value_if_false text box.

5. Click the function button (it should be labeled IF) displayed where the Name box normally appears. Excel opens a new Formula Arguments dialog box for this IF function. Next we test for invoices between 61 and 90 days overdue:

6. In the Logical_test text box, enter **TODAY()-D2>=61**. We don't need to test to see if the date is also 90 days or less—all results over 90 days were handled by the first logical test.

7. In the Value_if_true text box, type **61-90 days**.

8. Select the Value_if_false text box and click the IF function button to open another Function Arguments dialog box.

9. Finally we test for invoices between 30 and 60 days overdue. In the Logical_test dialog box, enter **TODAY()-D2>=30**. We don't need to test to see if the date is also less than 61 days—all results over 60 days were handled by the two previous logical tests.

10. In the Value_if_true text box, type **30-60 days**.

11. This is our last test, so we need to specify how Excel should handle any value in D2 that fails all three tests: accounts that aren't yet overdue. We could put some text here (like "Not Overdue"), or a null string: quotes with no text in them (""), sort of a non-entry, but a value from Excel's point of view. If we don't specify a Value_if_false, Excel displays FALSE in the cell where the final logical test fails. In the Value_if_false text box, enter a null string: **""**.

12. Click OK to enter the formula.

TIP   The Function Arguments dialog box is a very versatile tool when used in concert with the formula bar. When you select a cell with a formula and click the Insert Function button, Excel opens the dialog box. Click any function name in the formula bar (IF, TODAY) to see the arguments for that function.

Incorporating the TODAY function makes this formula relentlessly useful. Every time you open this workbook, Excel updates the values in column E.

Using AND and OR

Two related functions, often used with IF in conditions, are AND and OR. AND and OR both return one of two values: TRUE or FALSE. These functions have an easy syntax: the function name, followed by a list of conditions separated by commas.

The AND function returns a value of TRUE if every condition in the list is true: =AND(1<2,1>0,2>0) returns TRUE. If one or more conditions are not true, AND returns a value of FALSE: =AND(1<2, 1>0, 2<0) returns FALSE.

OR returns TRUE if any condition in the list is true, and only returns FALSE if all conditions are false.

Use AND and OR in combination with IF when you are looking for two conditions at the same time. For example, in the Accounts Receivable worksheet in the previous section, if you were focused only on accounts that were between 30 and 60 days old, you could find them with a single IF logical test using the AND function: =IF(AND(TODAY()-D2>=30,TODAY()-D2<=60,…).

Using Lookups

The lookup functions use a value to find a record in an Excel list. When the record is found, the lookup returns the data from one other column in the list. For example, if you enter a part number, a lookup function can return the name of the part, or the description or the quantity on hand. If you enter an employee number, a lookup function can return the employee's name, or department, or e-mail address.

To use lookups, you need a good database of parts, or employees, or other items you want to look up. It's easiest to create lookups in the workbook that contains the database. But don't worry if the data is in another workbook, or another program like Access. You can still use lookups, but you must first create a query to bring the data into Excel. For more information on queries and lookups, see Chapter 14, "Designing and Building Data Sources."

There are three lookup functions: LOOKUP, VLOOKUP, and HLOOKUP. Two other functions, MATCH and INDEX, are often used in combination to look up information in a table. VLOOKUP and HLOOKUP search vertically through a column and horizontally through a row to find a specified value. VLOOKUP is the more frequently used function because Excel lists are normally arranged with each row representing a record; searching vertically in a column searches in all records.

We'll start with an example that illustrates how lookups are used. The worksheet shown in Figure 13.10 has a number of VLOOKUP formulas. When the user enters an employee's last name in cell C3, four lookup formulas return the employee's full name (cell C5), e-mail address (D6), department (D7), and extension (D8). We'll take this worksheet apart in a moment. But first, let's consider why lookups are useful.

FIGURE 13.10

The Employee Directory uses lookup functions to return employee information based on last name.

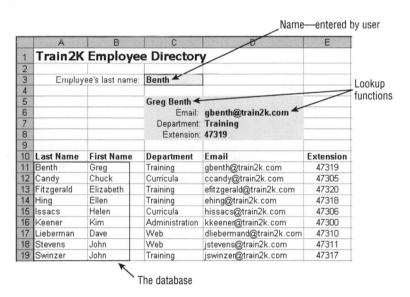

Lookups provide three useful pieces of functionality: user convenience, a minimal level of error prevention, and flexibility. Lookups are convenient because a user doesn't need to enter all of the information about an employee, or a customer, or an inventory item. Enter unique information about the record, and use lookups to have Excel return corresponding fields from the same record. Lookups provide a minimal level of error control because they return an error when a user enters incorrect information. In Figure 13.10, this also means that if you can't spell an employee's last name, you won't be able to find them in the directory. Lookups are flexible because you can change the database and the lookups will still return accurate information: if telephone extensions, e-mail addresses, or names change, the values returned by the lookup formulas will also change.

Each of the lookup functions has unique advantages and limitations, the most important being the use of wildcards like A* to search for names starting with the letter A. Table 13.5 describes reasons to use each function.

TABLE 13.5: SUMMARY OF THE LOOKUP FUNCTIONS

FUNCTION NAME	ADVANTAGES
VLOOKUP	Use when you want to look up values in the first column of a table and don't need to use wildcards.
HLOOKUP	Use when you want to look up values from the first row of a table and don't need to use wildcards.
LOOKUP	Use when you need to look up values from any column or row of a table, are able to sort the table, and don't need to use wildcards.
INDEX/MATCH	Use when you need to search using wildcards, whether or not the table is sorted.

Using VLOOKUP

The syntax for VLOOKUP is =VLOOKUP(*lookup value, table, column index number, range lookup*). The arguments are detailed in Table 13.6.

TABLE 13.6: VLOOKUP ARGUMENTS

ARGUMENT	DESCRIPTION
Lookup_value	A value or a reference to the cell that contains the value you want to find in the first column of the table.
Table	The table/database range. Make the range absolute if you intend to copy the formula.
Column_index_Number	The number of the column that contains the value you want to return. The first column of the table is column 1.
Range_lookup	Either False or True (you can leave this blank for True), indicating whether the table is sorted or not.

The range_lookup argument is somewhat subtle. If you want the lookup to return only when it finds an exact match for the lookup_value, you must set the range_lookup to FALSE, whether or not the database is sorted. If you don't need an exact match, the table must be sorted and range_lookup set to TRUE or left blank, which defaults to TRUE. Excel will return the largest value from the list that is not larger than the lookup_value.

MASTERING TROUBLESHOOTING: AVOIDING DUPLICATE VALUES

Whether or not you use an exact match, duplicate values present a problem when using the lookup functions. Excel grabs the first occurrence that matches the lookup_value, which may not be what you're looking for. For example, we can't guarantee unique last names in our employee directory: the company might hire another Benth, Hing, or Keener. If possible, a lookup should use unique lookup_values such as employee numbers, social security numbers, or unique SKUs or UPC codes.

When you're creating formulas that use lookup functions, don't overlook the usefulness of the Function Arguments dialog box. When you use the dialog box, you don't have to remember the order of the arguments, and help with the function is just a click away. Here are the formulas used in the worksheet in Figure 13.10:

The Employee's full name formula in C5 is the most complex; it concatenates two lookups and a blank space to return the first name from column 2, followed by a space, followed by the last name in column 1: =VLOOKUP(C3,A11:E19,2,FALSE)&" "&VLOOKUP(C3,A11:E19,1,FALSE)

Email address (D6): =VLOOKUP(C3,A11:E19,4,FALSE)

Department name (D7): =VLOOKUP(C3,A11:E19,3,FALSE)

Extension (D8): =VLOOKUP(C3,A11:E19,5,FALSE)

In the employee directory worksheet, we only want to return information if Excel finds an exact match in the first column of the table, so we set the range lookup argument to FALSE even though the list is sorted.

NOTE *Lookup functions return an error #NA if the lookup value is blank. For now, enter a value in the lookup_value cell before saving your workbook so that users don't see the error when they initially open the book. We'll show you a more elegant solution in "Trapping Errors with Logical Functions" later in this chapter.*

When you have a database that lists the first value in a range (for example, a sales commission database), the Range Lookup argument should be TRUE (or left blank). In a commission table like the table shown in Figure 13.11, Excel doesn't need to find an exact match. An exact match isn't even desirable; your sales staff won't be pleased to find that you're only paying commissions on sales of exactly $200,000, $250,000, and $300,000. Excel needs to return the closest match.

FIGURE 13.11

The commission formulas in column E use the VLOOKUP function to look up a value in the table at the bottom of the worksheet.

	A	B	C	D	E
1	Commission Worksheet				
2					
3	**Number**	**Name**	**Region**	**Sales**	**Commission**
4	AJ45	Allison	North	151,985	7,599.25
5	AL13	Barb	West	180,637	9,031.85
6	AJ47	Don	North	212,637	11,695.04
7	AJ91	Barry	East	129,874	6,493.70
8	AJ57	Myha	South	172,658	8,632.90
9	AL21	Jamal	East	176,692	8,834.60
10	AL22	Betty	South	247,958	13,637.69
11	AL23	Scott	West	309,987	20,149.16
12					
13					
14	**Sales Over**	**Percent**			
15	-	5.0%			
16	**200,000**	5.5%			
17	**250,000**	6.0%			
18	**300,000**	6.5%			

The formula in E4 is =VLOOKUP(D4,$A$15:$B$18,2,TRUE)*D4. The absolute reference to the commission table allows us to copy the formula to the other cells in column E.

NOTE   *Use HLOOKUP when your table is presented horizontally, with unique values in the top row. HLOOKUP is exactly the same as VLOOKUP, except it looks horizontally across the top row of the lookup table rather than down the first column. If your lookup table is arranged horizontally, you have two choices: transpose the table with Paste Special (copy the selection, click in the destination, and then choose Edit ➤ Paste Special ➤ Transpose) or use HLOOKUP. The syntax for HLOOKUP is almost the same as VLOOKUP: specify the row index number rather than a column index number.*

Using LOOKUP

LOOKUP searches either horizontally or vertically, and has one other huge advantage: the column (or row) you're searching doesn't need to be the first column in the database. For example, in the Employee Directory shown in Figure 13.10, the only column we can use for a lookup range with VLOOKUP is column A, so with the current arrangement of columns, we must look up employees by last name. With LOOKUP, we can do a reverse search and enter an e-mail address or extension and return the employee's name. Two caveats: with LOOKUP, the values in the lookup range *must* be sorted in ascending order, so you have to sort the database on the column you're searching. And LOOKUP searches either by column or row depending on the array dimension. If your table has more columns than rows, LOOKUP will search the first row rather than the first column. Excel returns an error message if the lookup value is less than the value in the first cell of the lookup range.

However, sorting a table is much less of a problem than rearranging the columns, especially if you're not the only person using the table. There are two forms of the LOOKUP function: vector and array. The array form of the function is included in Excel for compatibility with other spreadsheet programs. The syntax for the vector form is LOOKUP(*lookup_value,lookup_vector,result_vector*). The arguments are explained in Table 13.7.

Table 13.7: LOOKUP Function Arguments	
Argument	**Description**
Lookup_value	The cell that contains the value you want to look for in the lookup_range
Lookup_range	The range of cells that should be searched for the lookup_value
Result_range	The range of cells that the result will be returned from

In Figure 13.12, we modified the Employee Directory worksheet to look up employee information based on Extension. Extension isn't the first column, so we can't do this with VLOOKUP. However, we must sort the table by column E to use the LOOKUP function.

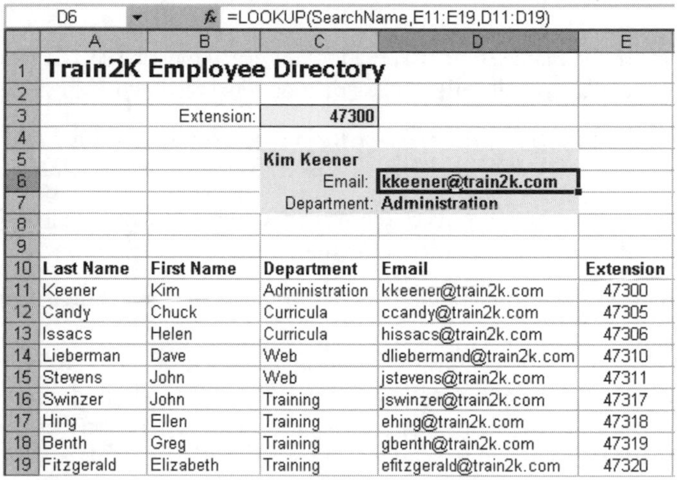

D6 =LOOKUP(SearchName,E11:E19,D11:D19)

	A	B	C	D	E
1	Train2K Employee Directory				
2					
3		Extension:	47300		
4					
5			Kim Keener		
6			Email:	kkeener@train2k.com	
7			Department:	Administration	
8					
9					
10	Last Name	First Name	Department	Email	Extension
11	Keener	Kim	Administration	kkeener@train2k.com	47300
12	Candy	Chuck	Curricula	ccandy@train2k.com	47305
13	Issacs	Helen	Curricula	hissacs@train2k.com	47306
14	Lieberman	Dave	Web	dliebermand@train2k.com	47310
15	Stevens	John	Web	jstevens@train2k.com	47311
16	Swinzer	John	Training	jswinzer@train2k.com	47317
17	Hing	Ellen	Training	ehing@train2k.com	47318
18	Benth	Greg	Training	gbenth@train2k.com	47319
19	Fitzgerald	Elizabeth	Training	efitzgerald@train2k.com	47320

Figure 13.12
Use vector LOOKUP when the column or row you need to search follows the column or row that contains the results you want to return.

The worksheet uses the following formulas, which all use the vector form of the LOOKUP function:

Employee name (C5): `=LOOKUP(C3,E11:E19,B11:B19)&" "&LOOKUP(C3,E11:E19,A11:A19)`

Email address (D6): `=LOOKUP(C3,E11:E19,D11:D19)`

Department name (D7): `=LOOKUP(C3,E11:E19,C11:C19)`

Using MATCH and INDEX

The MATCH and INDEX functions, used in combination, are an alterative to the VLOOKUP and LOOKUP functions. The resulting formulas are more complex, but there's a huge bonus: unlike the lookup functions, the MATCH function supports wildcards.

MATCH returns the position of a cell in an array: a table with rows and columns. The syntax for the MATCH function is MATCH(*lookup_value,lookup_array,match_type*). Table 13.8 describes the arguments.

TABLE 13.8: MATCH FUNCTION ARGUMENTS

ARGUMENT	DESCRIPTION
Lookup_value	A value or the cell that contains the value you want to look for in the lookup_array
Lookup_array	The range of cells that should be searched for the lookup_value—usually a single column or row
Match_type	Either 1 (sorted in ascending order), -1 (sorted in descending order), or 0 (unsorted)

- If the match_type is 1, the lookup_array must be sorted in ascending order. MATCH returns the largest value that is less than or equal to the lookup value.

- If the match_type is -1, the lookup_array must be sorted in descending order. MATCH returns the smallest value greater than or equal to the lookup value.

- If the match type is 0, the array does not need to be sorted. MATCH will only return a value that exactly matches the lookup value.

The MATCH function returns the position of a matching entry: "I found it in the fourth cell I looked at."

There are two versions of the INDEX function. The reference version returns a reference to another cell. The array version of the INDEX function returns a cell from a range. Here's the syntax: INDEX(*array,row_num,column_num*). Table 13.9 describes the arguments for the array version of the INDEX function.

TABLE 13.9: INDEX FUNCTION ARGUMENTS

ARGUMENT	DESCRIPTION
Array	Range of cells you want to search—usually in a single column or row
Row_number	The row to return a value from
Column_number	The column to return a value from

When you combine the two functions in a formula, you use the MATCH function as either the row number or column number argument for the INDEX function. In Figure 13.13 we've recreated the original Employee Directory worksheet from Figure 13.10 using INDEX and MATCH. In the revised worksheet, users can search with wildcards, so the user doesn't need to know exactly how to spell an employee's last name to search for them by last name in the directory.

FIGURE 13.13

Create a lookup formula with the INDEX and the MATCH functions and your lookups will allow wildcard searches.

	A	B	C	D	E
1	**Train2K Employee Directory**				
2					
3	Employee's last name:		F*		
4					
5			**Elizabeth Fitzgerald**		
6			Email:	**efitzgerald@train2k.com**	
7			Department:	**Training**	
8			Extension:	**47320**	
9					
10	**Last Name**	**First Name**	**Department**	**Email**	**Extension**
11	Benth	Greg	Training	gbenth@train2k.com	47319
12	Candy	Chuck	Curricula	ccandy@train2k.com	47305
13	Fitzgerald	Elizabeth	Training	efitzgerald@train2k.com	47320
14	Hing	Ellen	Training	ehing@train2k.com	47318
15	Issacs	Helen	Curricula	hissacs@train2k.com	47306
16	Keener	Kim	Administration	kkeener@train2k.com	47300
17	Lieberman	Dave	Web	dliebermand@train2k.com	47310
18	Stevens	John	Web	jstevens@train2k.com	47311
19	Swinzer	John	Training	jswinzer@train2k.com	47317

The INDEX/MATCH lookups in Figure 13.13 use the following formulas:

Employee name (C5): `=INDEX(B11:B19,MATCH(C3,A11:A19,0))&" "&INDEX(A11:A19,MATCH(C3,A11:A19,0))`

Email address (D6): `=INDEX(D11:D19,MATCH(C3,A11:A19,0))`

Department name (D7): `=INDEX(C11:C19,MATCH(C3,A11:A19,0))`

Let's unpack this last formula used to return the employee's department name. The MATCH function uses the value in C3 to search the range A11:A19 (the first column). In Figure 13.13, the match is the third cell of the array. We then used the results of the MATCH function as the row_number argument for the INDEX function, instructing the INDEX function to return the value in the third cell in the array C11:C19: Training. We only had to specify one column number/row number argument in our formulas because INDEX is returning a value from an array that is within one column or row.

The INDEX/MATCH combination is powerful, but the formulas can be complex to figure out, particularly at first. As you're working with INDEX and MATCH, remember that Excel includes two tools to assist you: the Function Arguments dialog box and the function help files. Choose either INDEX or MATCH in the Function Arguments dialog box and then click the Help With This Function link to see syntax and examples.

Creating Complex Lookups Quickly

The Lookup Wizard Add-in creates INDEX/MATCH lookup formulas with a few easy steps. The Lookup Wizard is designed to search a two-dimensional table in *both* directions. The Lookup Wizard returns the intersection of a row and column. If the row and column labels are not unique, the formula will use the first instance of the row or column label that it happens to stumble across—but this is also true of the LOOKUP and VLOOKUP functions. We'll show you two examples, one using the familiar Employee Directory and a second using a budget summary.

If the Lookup Wizard is installed, the command Lookup appears on Excel's Tools menu. If it is not installed, choose Tools ➤ Add-ins. Check Lookup Wizard in the Add-ins dialog box and install the wizard. To use the wizard, select any cell in the array and choose Tools ➤ Lookup.

In the first step of the Lookup Wizard, shown in Figure 13.14, select the table in which you're looking up values, including the row and column labels. If you click in any cell of the database before starting the wizard, Excel will select the database.

FIGURE 13.14

In the first step of the Lookup Wizard, select the table.

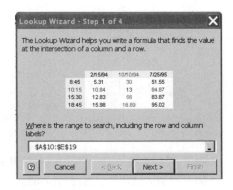

In the second step of the wizard, shown in Figure 13.15, from the drop-down lists choose the column and row of the data you wish to return. In our example, we're selecting the Department column and the first record, Benth.

FIGURE 13.15

In the second step, select the row and column that contain the data you want to return.

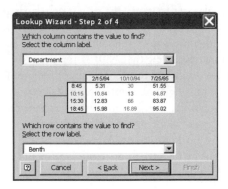

You can't scroll at this stage. If you're selecting a column or row that doesn't appear on the screen (like the 110th row in the table), choose No Row/Column Label Matches Exactly to open the Lookup Wizard dialog box. Type the row or column label and click OK.

In the third step, shown in Figure 13.16, choose how you want the data displayed. This is where it gets interesting. If you choose the default Copy Just the Formula To a Single Cell, you get one formula that returns Benth's department. If you need to find another intersection of a row and column, you'll need to modify the formula or run the Lookup Wizard again. If you choose the default, you've taken a lot of steps to return a single value.

FIGURE 13.16

In the third step of the wizard, choose a data display method.

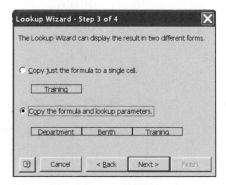

If, however, you choose the second option, Copy the Formula and Lookup Parameters, you create a lookup formula *and* a criteria range where you can enter a different row label and column label and see the results.

If you chose the default data display option, Step 4 prompts you for a location for your formula. If you chose to copy the formula and parameters, Steps 4–6 will prompt you for a location for each parameter and the formula. In our worksheet, we placed the column heading Department in C7, Benth in C3, and the formula in D7, as shown in Figure 13.17. To test the lookup, enter another last name in C3 and another column heading (Email or Extension) in C7. The formula returns the value you requested in D7.

FIGURE 13.17

Enter new parameters to return different values.

	A	B	C	D
1	**Train2K Employee Directory**			
2				
3	Employee's last name:		Benth	
4				
5				
6				
7			Department **Training**	
8				

We could, of course, use the Lookup Wizard to create a series of formulas to return the e-mail, extension, and first name, or create and combine two formulas to display the full name.

Now we'll turn to another example based on a budget summary. With their unique account names and account numbers, budgets are almost custom designed for use with the Lookup Wizard. Figure 13.18 shows a summary of a four-year budget overview. Note that each row and column has a unique label.

FIGURE 13.18

This budget summary can be searched with the Lookup Wizard; each column and row has a unique label.

	A	B	C	D	E
1	FY 2002-2005 Budget Summary and Forecast				
2					
3	Enter a fiscal year (ex: FY2005):			FY2004	
4	Enter a Category:			Telephone	
5	Expense:			9,270	
6					
7	Category	FY2002	FY2003	FY2004	FY2005
8	Telephone	7,640	8,500	9,270	17,920
9	Postage	5,850	5,850	6,300	7,700
10	Internet	7,200	7,200	9,600	10,200
11	Travel	58,460	167,810	144,000	122,000
12	Software	28,124	32,233	26,665	28,000
13	Printing	1,124	1,690	3,950	3,995
14	Supplies	2,280	3,100	3,100	3,100
15	Marketing	11,894	43,022	41,454	60,099
16	Materials	389,056	393,100	567,405	567,000
17	Payroll Expense	711,664	694,048	962,011	800,329
18	Capital Expense	54,115	61,671	57,994	63,397

NOTE   The shading in every other row in the budget summary is a conditional format to improve readability.

In the last steps of the Lookup Wizard, we pasted the parameters in D3 and D4 (and added some labels to help the user enter information). The INDEX/MATCH formula created with the Lookup Wizard uses the parameters to locate a specific cell:

`=INDEX($A$7:$E$18, MATCH(D4,$A$7:$A$18,),MATCH(D3,$A$7:$E$7,))`

CHOOSING PARAMETERS FROM DROP-DOWN LISTS

Two additions would make this worksheet much easier to use: drop-down lists for the two parameters. Drop-down lists make it easy for users to enter information quickly and correctly. To create the drop-down list for fiscal years, select cell D3 and then choose Data ➤ Validation from the menu. On the Settings page, choose List, then select the four fiscal years in row 7:

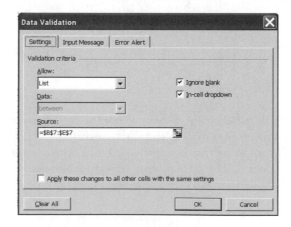

Click in D4 and repeat the steps for the categories, selecting the cells that contain the category names in column A.

NOTE   *Drop-down lists and other types of validation are discussed in depth in Chapter 14.*

Trapping Errors with Logical Functions

One of the most common errors in Excel, the Division By Zero error, occurs when you divide a number by 0. This often happens when you create a worksheet, complete with formulas, but the non-formula data isn't entered yet. If, for example, cell B27 is empty and cell B30 contains the formula =B10/B27, the error message #DIV/0 appears in cell B30. A user opening the workbook to enter data is greeted with an error message: not the way to increase user confidence in your worksheet. You can use Excel's functions to anticipate DIV/0 errors and other common errors so they don't appear in your worksheet.

In this case, the DIV/0 error is easily handled with IF. Wrap the formula =B10/B27 in an IF formula that tests if B27 has a value greater than zero to omit the error message: =IF(B27>0, B10/B27,0). (If B27 could contain either positive or negative values, but not zero, use B27<>0 as the condition.)

Let's return to the Employee Directory worksheet with lookups. When there is no value in cell C3 (the lookup value), the worksheet is filled with the error code #N/A as shown in Figure 13.19. An N/A error occurs when a value that a function needs (in this case, the lookup value) is not available.

FIGURE 13.19

When the lookup value cell is empty, the lookups return NA errors.

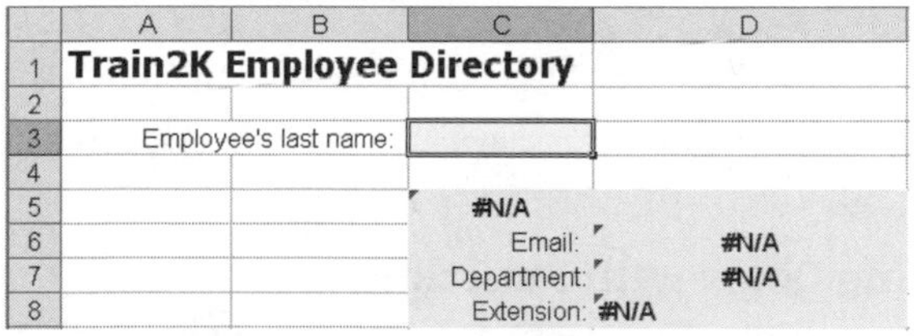

	A	B	C	D
1	**Train2K Employee Directory**			
2				
3		Employee's last name:		
4				
5			#N/A	
6			Email:	#N/A
7			Department:	#N/A
8			Extension:	#N/A

There are a number of reasons why a lookup returns an N/A error: the lookup value cell is empty; the range array option is set to FALSE and the value in the lookup value cell can't be found in the database; or you entered a range rather than a single cell for the lookup value. Before you modify your formula to handle the possibility of an empty lookup value, make sure the VLOOKUP formula works when a valid value is entered in the lookup value cell. Then, modify the formula using IF and ISBLANK.

The ISBLANK function returns one of two values, TRUE or FALSE. Its only argument is a cell address: =ISBLANK(C3) returns TRUE if C3 is absolutely empty. The current formula in D6 (the email address) is =VLOOKUP(C3,A11:E19,4,FALSE). This modified version checks to see if C3 is blank before attempting to use it in the lookup function. If C3 is blank, an empty string (" ") appears in D6 instead of an error: =IF(ISBLANK(C4)," ",VLOOKUP(C3,A11:A19,4,FALSE).

ISBLANK is one of a family of information functions that return Boolean (true or false) values. Every information function has a single argument: a cell reference. The information functions are described in Table 13.10.

TABLE 13.10: INFORMATION FUNCTIONS

FUNCTION	RETURNS TRUE WHEN
ISBLANK	the cell is blank
ISERR	the cell returns an error other than N/A
ISERROR	the cell returns an error, including N/A
ISLOGICAL	the cell contains or refers to a Boolean value
ISNA	the cell returns an N/A error
ISNONTEXT	the cell is blank or contains a number
ISNUMBER	the cell contains a number
ISTEXT	the cell is nonblank and contains text

Use the information functions with IF to determine whether a cell meets the following specifications:

◆ Contains text before concatenating it with another cell: in our formulas earlier in the chapter that concatenated first names, middle initials, and last names, we used IF(C3>" ") as our test. We could have used IF(ISBLANK(C3) instead.

◆ Contains a number before performing a mathematical operation (using ISNUMBER).

◆ Contains an entry before doing lookups (using ISBLANK).

◆ Contains an error so you can display an error message in a nearby cell (using ISERROR).

Manipulating Dates with Functions

Excel includes a number of formats for dates and times, but ideally, the date or time is stored as a value rather than text. In Figure 13.20, the date December 20, 2003 is displayed in a number of formats, but the values entered in column B are all the same: 12/20/2003. Date and Time formats are applied on the Number tab of the Format Cells dialog box.

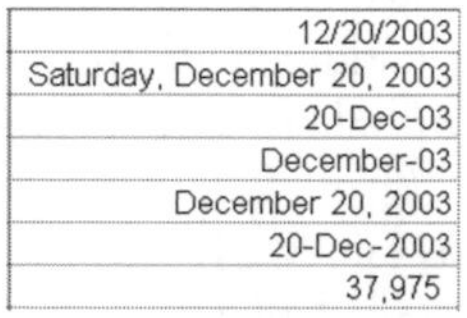

FIGURE 13.20

The format doesn't change the underlying value of the dates in this worksheet.

12/20/2003
Saturday, December 20, 2003
20-Dec-03
December-03
December 20, 2003
20-Dec-2003
37,975

Microsoft Excel stores dates as sequential numbers called serial values. January 1, 1900 is assigned the number 1. December 20, 2003 is serial number 37975 because it is 37,975th day after January 1, 1900. Times are stored as decimal numbers because each hour, minute, and second is a fraction of a day. Noon on 12/20/2003 is 37975.5. Six hours later at 6 PM, the time/date value is 37975.75.

The fact that dates and times are numbers means you can complete mathematical operations on cells that contain dates or times. The following are examples of the calculations you can complete in Excel:

◆ Subtract today's date from a book's due date to see if it is overdue.

◆ Add days to a project's beginning date to calculate the date when the project should be completed.

◆ Determine how many days fall between two dates.

◆ Sort dates in chronological order.

◆ Subtract the start time for a task from the ending time to determine how long it took to complete the task.

Excel includes time/date conversion and mathematical functions. The conversion functions convert or extract date and time data and include tools to handle dates and times stored as text. The mathematical functions are used for addition and subtraction.

MASTERING TROUBLESHOOTING: AVOIDING TROUBLE WITH DATES

When you enter dates, Excel generally recognizes them as dates. If, for example, you enter 1/1/2004, 1-1-2004, or January 1, 2004, Excel will recognize it as a date. Dates with two-digit years, or those imported from another application, may not fare as well. Imported dates are often stored as text entries, and two-digit years are converted to four-digit years. How the date is converted depends on the computer's operating system settings or an internal rule in Excel that converts the years 00–29 to 2000–2029 and numbers greater than 29 to dates in the 20th century: 1930–1999. If you're entering dates, enter a four-digit year to minimize errors. Use the date and time conversion functions to convert text dates to number dates (see the "Converting Text Strings to Dates" sidebar later in this section).

Table 13.11 lists commonly used date and time conversion functions. Following the table, we'll provide some examples of how the functions are used in business settings.

TABLE 13.11: COMMON DATE AND TIME CONVERSION FUNCTIONS

FUNCTION	DESCRIPTION	SYNTAX
DATE	Creates a serial value (which you can format using any of the date formats) from three numbers: the year, month, and day	=DATE(*year, month, day*)
TIME	Creates a decimal number time from three numbers: hour, minute, and second	=TIME(*hour, minute, second*)
NOW	Returns the serial value for the current date and decimal fraction for the current time from your computer's system clock	=NOW()

Continued on next page

TABLE 13.11: COMMON DATE AND TIME CONVERSION FUNCTIONS *(continued)*

FUNCTION	DESCRIPTION	SYNTAX
TODAY	Returns the serial value for the current date from the computer's system clock	=TODAY()
DAY	Returns the day number (1 to 31) from a text string, date, or serial value	=DAY(*date*)
MONTH	Returns the month value (1 to 12) from a text string, date, or serial value	=MONTH(*date*)
YEAR	Returns the year value (1 to 9999) from a text string, date, or serial value	=YEAR(*date*)
HOUR	Converts a text string or decimal fraction to an hour	=HOUR(*string* or *fraction*)
MINUTE	Converts a text string or decimal fraction to a minute	=MINUTE(*string* or *fraction*)
WORKDAY	Returns the first workday (nonweekend day) based on a starting date, a number of days, and optionally, a list of holiday dates (in Analysis ToolPak)	=WORKDAY(*start date, days, list of holidays*)
NETWORKDAYS	Returns the number of days, excluding weekends and optionally holidays, between a start date and an end date (in Analysis ToolPak)	=NETWORKDAYS(*start date, end date, list of holidays*)

Use the DATE and TIME functions to construct dates and times when the arguments (year, month, day, hour, minute, or second) are supplied by a cell entry or another formula. For example, you can use the TODAY function or a user-entered date and then use the MONTH, YEAR, and DATE functions to determine the first day of the month or year. Here's the formula to determine the first day of the current month: =DATE(YEAR(TODAY()),MONTH(TODAY()),1)

TIP   The NOW and TODAY functions have no arguments. Both consult the computer's system clock. TODAY returns the current date; NOW returns the current date and time. The NOW function can be nested in the TIME function to calculate the current time.

When you sort a list of birth dates or hire dates, the dates are sorted in chronological order. If you have every employee's birth date or hire date in an Excel workbook, you can use the MONTH and DAY functions to create a birthday list or anniversary list that you can sort by month and day, rather than by date. Figure 13.21 shows a list of birth dates, months, and days sorted by month, then date. In cell D2, the formula is simply =MONTH(C2). The day formula in cell E2 is =DAY(C2). In column F, the days and months are used in a DATE formula to create a series of dates in the same year: =DATE(1900,D2,E2). We could have used any year for this formula. Column F was then sorted, and the dates formatted with a format that hides the year: for example, the custom format d-mmm.

FIGURE 13.21

Use the MONTH and DAY functions to extract birth months and days from a list of birth dates.

	A	B	C	D	E	F
1	**Last Name**	**First Name**	**Birthdate**	**Birthmonth**	**Birthday**	**List**
2	Garrison	Kent	1/5/1962	1	5	5-Jan
3	Poinsett	Norma	1/22/1946	1	22	22-Jan
4	Nygen	Myha	2/3/1965	2	3	3-Feb
5	King	James	2/3/1988	2	3	3-Feb
6	Smith	Mary	2/14/1978	2	14	14-Feb
7	Jones	David	2/20/1952	2	20	20-Feb
8	Cowtan	Charlotte	2/28/1946	2	28	28-Feb
9	Courter	Gini	3/8/1957	3	8	8-Mar

We did this in three columns so you could see the separate days and months. It could be done in one formula in cell D2: =DATE(1900,MONTH(C2),DAY(C2))

MASTERING THE OPPORTUNITIES: CONVERTING TEXT STRINGS TO DATES

When you import dates from another application, they may be imported as text strings, just as if you'd typed an apostrophe in front of a date entered in Excel, or applied the text format before typing the date in the cell. You can easily tell that a date is text rather than a value by widening the column that the date appears in. Dates are numbers, so they should be right-aligned in the cell. Text entries are left-aligned.

The DATEVALUE function converts a text string date to a serial value; the syntax of the function is DATE-VALUE(*text string date*). There's only one catch: DATEVALUE only works for dates in the 20th century. Use DATEVALUE when dates prior to 12/31/1999 from another application are imported as strings to convert them to serial values. There is no corresponding function for dates beginning in 2000, or prior to 1900. Instead, you need to use a nested formula to create a serial value.

If cell B30 contains the text string 1/12/1899, the following formula, using the DAY, MONTH, YEAR, and DATE functions, will convert the string to serial value: =DATE(YEAR(B30),MONTH(B30),DAY(B30)).

FUNCTIONS THAT EXCLUDE WEEKENDS

A life without weekends sounds incredibly unattractive, so Excel has two functions that take weekends into consideration. WORKDAY and NETWORKDAYS automatically exclude weekends when calculating results, and both can be beefed up to also exclude holidays.

NOTE *The WORKDAY and NETWORKDAYS functions are part of the Analysis ToolPak add-in. To install the add-in, choose Tools ➤ Add-ins. Enable the Analysis ToolPak check box and click OK to install the ToolPak. If the ToolPak does not appear on the list of add-ins, run Office Setup to install the Analysis Toolpak. After installation, choose Tools ➤ Add-Ins in Excel and click the Analysis Toolpak check box.*

The WORKDAY function takes a start date, then adds a number of workdays, and then returns the result as a serial value, which you can then format as a date. If you add, for example, one day to a Friday, the WORKDAY function will return the serial value date for the following Monday. The formula =WORKDAY(A4,3) takes the date in cell A4 and adds three workdays. If you have a list of holiday dates, enter the range as the third argument for the function to have Excel treat dates on the list as nonworking days: =WORKDAY (A4,3,*range of holidays*).

The NETWORKDAYS function returns the number of workdays between a starting date and an ending date, excluding Saturdays and Sundays (and optionally holidays).

Using Names

Names are one of Excel's often-overlooked gems. A *name* is an alias for a range of cells (or a constant or calculation, which we'll discuss later in this chapter). A range can be as small as one cell or as large as a worksheet. Names provide multiple benefits, which become more important as you create increasingly complex workbooks:

◆ Names can be used in formulas and are easier to remember than cell addresses.

◆ When a range moves within the sheet, the name moves with it.

◆ You can use a name in place of a cell or range address in a formula or function argument.

◆ Names identify the range's contents: *PayRate*, *TotalSales*, and *Quantity* are more descriptive formula references than cell addresses or range references.

◆ When you copy a formula that uses a name, the effect is the same as using an absolute cell reference.

The rules for using range names include the following:

◆ Names can be up to 255 characters long and can include letters, numbers, underscores, or periods.

◆ The name must begin with either a letter or the underscore character.

◆ You cannot use spaces, commas, exclamation points, or other special characters.

◆ Names cannot be valid cell addresses: FY2001 cannot be used as a name, but FYr2001 can be.

◆ Names are not case-sensitive: GrossPay, grosspay, and GROSSPAY are all the same name.

◆ A name must be unique within a workbook; you can't use the same name on two different sheets.

The tradition is to mix uppercase and lowercase letters, beginning each word within the name with an uppercase letter: *GrossPay*.

Excel lets you assign names that might be disallowed in many programs—and should be disallowed here, too. For example, you can assign the names of program features like cell, column, and row to cells or cell ranges. You're also allowed to assign names that are the names of functions: SUM, COUNT, and so on. To avoid confusion, you probably shouldn't do this, even though Excel allows it.

There are three ways to name a range:

◆ Use the Name box in the formula bar.

◆ Use the Define Name dialog box.

◆ Create names from a row or column of labels.

Naming a Range Using the Name Box

The easiest way to name ranges is using the Name box at the left end of the formula bar:

1. Select the range to be named; hold Ctrl if you need to select noncontiguous cells.

2. Click in the Name box.

3. Type a valid name for the range and press Enter.

You must press Enter to create the name; you can't simply click in another cell. Click the drop-down arrow in the Name box to open a list of the named ranges in your workbook.

Using the Define Name Dialog Box

The Define Name dialog box, shown in Figure 13.22, is another place to name ranges, and is the only place you can change or delete existing range names. The dialog box displays a list of names already defined in the active workbook. Here are the steps for defining a range name using the dialog box:

1. Select the range of cells you want to name.

2. Choose Insert ➢ Name ➢ Define from the menu bar.

3. Type a name for the range in the Names In Workbook text box and click Add.

4. Click OK to close the dialog box.

FIGURE 13.22

In the Define Name dialog box, you can define, delete, or edit a range name.

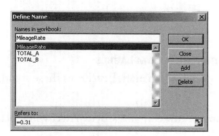

Changing a name or the range referred to by a name is equally easy. First, choose Insert ➢ Name ➢ Define to open the Define Name dialog box.

◆ To change the name used to refer to a range of cells, select the name from the list of named ranges. Select the name in the Names In Workbook text box, overtype the old name with the new name, and click Add.

◆ To change the cells referred to by a name, select the name from the list of names. Select the range in the Refers To text box. Select the correct range of cells in the worksheet (you can click the Collapse button in the Refers To text box to hide the dialog box) then click Add.

To delete a name, select the name from the Names In Workbook list and click the Delete button.

TIP   Names are very persistent. When you delete a sheet that contains named ranges, either global or local, Excel does not delete the names. Open the Define Names dialog box and delete the names.

Creating Names from a Row or Column

You can define a group of names using row or column labels using the Create Names dialog box, shown in Figure 13.23.

FIGURE 13.23

Create names from labels in the Create Names dialog box.

1. Select the range to be named, including the column and/or row labels you want to use as names.

2. Choose Insert ➢ Name ➢ Create from the menu bar to open the Create Names dialog box.

3. In the Create Names In area, select the row (Top or Bottom) or column (Left or Right) that contains the labels you want to use to name the selected range.

4. Click OK to apply the names and close the dialog box.

HOW EXCEL CREATES RANGE NAMES FROM LABELS

Excel edits text as needed to make valid names. Excel uses these standards to generate names from labels or other text:

◆ If the label for a column or row contains spaces, Excel will replace the space with an underscore: `Interest_Rate`.

◆ If the cell contents begin with a number, like `8-Mar` or `4 bags`, Excel will add an underscore to the beginning of the name: `_8-Mar` or `_4_bags`.

◆ Excel will not create a name for a cell that contains *only* a number (like 1998, 78, or 1254.50). Excel will let you go through the motions, but it won't create the name.

Using Names

After you've defined a range, you can enter the range name anywhere a regular cell reference is valid. For example, you can enter the name of a range as an argument for a function: `=SUM(Totals)` to add the cells in the range named `Totals`. To insert a name in a formula, type the name or choose Insert ➢ Name ➢ Paste from the menu to open the Paste Names dialog box, shown in Figure 13.24.

FIGURE 13.24

Fire up the Paste Names dialog box to paste a name into a formula.

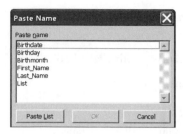

Select the name from the list and click OK to paste the name into the formula. (If you simply select the named range when creating the formula, Excel will substitute the name for the cell references.) When you fill or copy the formula that contains a name, the name is not changed in the pasted or filled cells. In Excel, range names are always absolute.

TIP   If you don't want Excel to convert the cell or range address to a name, type the cell address rather than selecting the cells when you create the formula.

Names also serve a valuable navigation function in large workbooks and complex worksheets. To move to and select a named range anywhere in a workbook, click the drop-down arrow in the Name box and select the name from the list.

Names created from column and row labels can be used to refer to specific cells at the intersection of the named row and column. For this example, we'll use a single-year budget worksheet showing the details of the FY2005 figures in the summary sheet shown previously in this chapter. We used the Create Names dialog box to create names from the category names in column A and the month abbreviations in row 3. Now, we can use these names in formulas. Figure 13.25 shows the creation of one such formula. When we enter =Jan Materials, Excel selects the Jan range (B4:B14) and the Materials range (B12:M12) and returns the value at B12, the intersection of the two ranges.

FIGURE 13.25

The formula in this worksheet uses names to return the value at the intersection of Jan and Materials

Range: Jan

	A	B	C	D	E	F	G	H	I	J	K	L	M	N
1	FY 2005 Budget Forecast													
2														
3	Category	Jan	Feb	Mar	Apr	May	Jun	Jul	Aug	Sep	Oct	Nov	Dec	Totals
4	Telephone	1,493	1,493	1,493	1,493	1,493	1,493	1,493	1,493	1,493	1,493	1,493	1,493	17,920
5	Postage	1,283	-	1,283	-	1,283	-	1,283	-	1,283	-	1,283	-	7,700
6	Internet	2,550	-	-	2,550	-	-	2,550	-	-	2,550	-	-	10,200
7	Travel	20,333	5,083	20,333	5,083	40,667	5,083	5,083	5,083	5,083	5,083	5,083	-	122,000
8	Software	-	-	-	15,000		3,000			10,000				28,000
9	Printing	400	-	400	-	400	-	400	-	400	-	400	1,595	3,995
10	Supplies	100	-	1,000	-	-	1,000	-	-	1,000	-	-	-	3,100
11	Marketing	5,000	5,000	5,000	5,000	5,000	5,000	5,000	5,000	5,000	5,000	5,000	5,000	60,099
12	Materials	47,250	47,250	47,250	47,250	47,250	47,250	47,250	47,250	47,250	47,250	47,250	47,250	567,000
13	Payroll Expense	66,694	66,694	66,694	66,694	66,694	66,694	66,694	66,694	66,694	66,694	66,694	66,694	800,329
14	Capital Expense	34,000	-	-	-		29,397	-	-	-	-	-	-	63,397
15														
16														
17		=Jan Materials												

Range: Materials

TIP   To list all the names in the active workbook and the cells they refer to, go to an empty area of a worksheet, open the Paste Name dialog box, then click the Paste List button.

Stretching Names to the Max

Names are incredibly versatile. In this section, we'll create less traditional names:

External names that refer to ranges in other workbooks

3-D range names that cross multiple sheets

Local names that repeat within a book

Constant names that refer to values rather than ranges

USING NAMES TO LINK TO RANGES IN OTHER WORKBOOKS

You can use the Define Name dialog box to create names that refer to cells in any open workbook. Rather than copying or linking to values in other workbooks, you can create names for these ranges, then use the names in formulas in the current workbook whether or not the other workbook is open. When you refer to a cell in another workbook, the reference is an *external reference*. You name external ranges as you would name ranges in the current workbook, then use the names as external references in formulas. Follow these steps to name a range in another workbook for use in the current workbook:

1. Open both workbooks.

2. Switch to the workbook where you want to create the name.

3. Open the Define Names dialog box (Insert ➢ Name ➢ Define).

4. Type a name for the reference in the Names In Workbook text box.

5. Click in the Refers To text box. Click the Collapse button.

6. Switch to the workbook that contains the range you want to name.

7. Select the range.

8. Click the Expand button to expand the Define Names dialog box.

9. Click Add to create the range name and click OK to close the dialog box.

External ranges don't appear on the Names drop-down list in the active workbook, but they are listed in the Define Names dialog box. You use them in formulas as you would internal named ranges. Type the range name, or choose Insert ➢ Name ➢ Paste to paste the named range into a formula.

External named ranges are an excellent way to create links to other workbooks. When you link to another workbook by just selecting the cell or using copy and paste, the resulting formula includes the workbook name, the worksheet name, and the cell reference, which makes your formulas really difficult to read and edit. With the named range, only the name appears in the formula. External named ranges have the same downside as links created using the "regular" methods—if the other workbook is deleted, moved, or renamed, Excel won't be able to easily find the named range. External named ranges and other links can be checked or fixed using the Edit Links dialog box (Edit ➢ Links).

CREATING NAMES THAT SPAN WORKSHEETS

A *3-D name* refers to the same cell in more than one worksheet in a book. For example, you have a budget workbook where the total sales figure is in cell D87 of each monthly worksheet. You can create a 3-D name that refers to D87 across multiple worksheets. Follow these steps to define a 3-D range name:

1. Choose Insert ➢ Name ➢ Define from the menu bar.

2. In the Names In Workbook text box, type the range name.

3. Delete any reference in the Refers To text box, and type =.

4. Click the tab for the first worksheet you want to reference, hold Shift, and select the tab for the last worksheet to be referenced.

5. Select the cell or range to be named.

6. Click Add to add the name, and click OK to close the dialog box.

While 3-D range names have almost no navigation use, they're very useful in summary formulas for workbooks that contain a series of periodic worksheets. With 3-D range names, formulas are easy to create and edit.

CREATING THE SAME NAME IN MULTIPLE WORKSHEETS

By default, names have workbook *scope*: they're available anywhere in the workbook. If, for example, you create the name TotalExpenses on Sheet1, you can use that name in a formula on Sheet2, so you can't also name a range of cells on Sheet2 TotalExpenses. There are times, however, when that's exactly what you want: a name with worksheet scope that refers to a specific range in the current worksheet rather than just one range in the workbook. It takes only a bit more effort to create names with worksheet scope, allowing you to use the name TotalExpenses to describe a similar range of cells that appears on multiple sheets in a workbook. Names with worksheet scope are called *local names* or *worksheet names*.

Follow these steps to define a name with local scope:

1. Select the worksheet that you want to create the name in.

2. Select the cells you want to name.

3. Choose Insert ➢ Name ➢ Define to open the Define Name dialog box.

4. In the Names in Workbook text box, enter the sheet name, an exclamation point, and the range name. For example, to name a range TotalExpenses on Sheet1, enter **Sheet1!TotalExpenses**. If the sheet name includes a space, put single quotation marks around the sheet name: **='Jan Sales'!TotalExpenses**.

5. Click Add to add the name and OK to close the Define Name dialog box.

You can have global and local names that are the same. For example, a five sheet workbook could include the following:

◆ A range on Sheet1 named TotalExpenses

◆ A range on Sheet2 named `Sheet2!TotalExpenses`

◆ A range on Sheet3 named `Sheet3!TotalExpenses`

In the workbook, the name TotalExpenses appears only once on the list in the Name box. That single reference always refers to the appropriate named range: the local name on Sheet2 and Sheet3, and the global name where there is no local name on Sheet1, Sheet4, and Sheet5. The local name always overrides the global name.

TIP   *If you copy a sheet with a named range, Excel creates a local version of the same name, resulting in extra local-scope names you don't need. Do this on purpose, and you've quickly created local names—a smart move. If, however, you don't mean to create local names, open the Define Names dialog box and delete the extra names.*

Local names are useful because they allow you to create short names that still work in formulas. If you type a range name into a formula or use the Paste Name dialog box, the same rules apply. However, you can use a local name in a formula in another worksheet if you enter the entire name, including the sheet name.

NOTE   *When you list range names by clicking Paste List in the Paste Name dialog box, the list shows only local names on the active worksheet.*

USING NAMES TO STORE CONSTANTS

Most users know about naming cells, but don't realize that you can use the Define Name box to name constants as well as cell ranges. Why is this useful?

◆ Rather than entering values for fixed items like markup percentages, interest rates, or hourly rates in worksheet cells where they're visible and accessible, you can enter them as named items where they're accessible but invisible.

◆ All formulas that use the named constant can be updated at once just by changing the value in the Define Names dialog box.

To create a named constant, choose Insert ➤ Name ➤ Define to open the Define Names dialog box. Enter a name in the Named in Workbook text box. In the Refers To text box, type = and then the constant. In Figure 13.26, we're creating a constant named VolumeDiscount that's =3.25%. To calculate the discount on a cost in cell C2, we'll enter the formula `=C2*VolumeDiscount`.

Named constants can include calculations. For example, `=10% * 45` is a valid Refers To entry, which makes names a great way to embed business logic and rules in a worksheet.

FIGURE 13.26

Use the Define Name dialog box to create constants that can be used throughout a workbook.

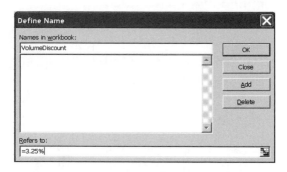

NAMING RANGES FOR FREQUENTLY USED FORMULAS

Now, let's take names one step further: you can include functions in names. For example, if you have a list of prices in B12:B28 and you use the average of those prices frequently in your workbook, you can define a name AveragePrice that refers to =AVERAGE(B12:B28). The name is valid anywhere in the workbook, and will always reflect the current average of the range.

TIP   There's an easy trick you can use to view the named ranges in a worksheet: change the zoom to 25%, or any zoom less than 40%, and Excel places the range names in the worksheet display like watermarks.

Names are one of the most powerful, and most overlooked, features in Excel because they stretch the boundaries of traditional worksheets. Almost any feature that has worksheet scope can be extended past the worksheet to the entire workbook by using names.

Chapter 14

Designing and Building Data Sources

A WELL BUILT OFFICE data source is a treasure trove, an information store that supports your work, which you can use with other applications. You can enter and save data in Word, Excel, Access, InfoPath, Outlook, and on Windows SharePoint sites. So where *should* you store data? This chapter will help you answer that question in terms of your own needs. We begin with an overview of the data capabilities of the three "core" applications (Word, Excel, and Access), then dive into the specifics of data sources created in Word, Excel, and Access.

- ◆ Choosing an Office application for your data
- ◆ Sorting Word tables
- ◆ Converting text to tables
- ◆ Converting Word databases to Excel
- ◆ Creating, sorting, and filtering an Excel list
- ◆ Using Excel's List toolbar
- ◆ Creating tables in Access
- ◆ Validating data entry in Excel and Access
- ◆ Creating drop-down lists in Excel and Access tables

NOTE *Two Office data sources are discussed in other chapters: SharePoint lists are discussed in Chapter 8, "Collaborating on Documents." See Chapter 16, "Constructing Forms for User Input," for help customizing Outlook data sources.*

Storing Data in Office

In its simplest form, a *database* or *data source* is a list with a specific structure, defined by its *fields:* the categories of information it contains. In the database shown in Figure 14.1, for example, the database fields include Last Name, First Name, Department, Email, and Hourly Rate.

FIGURE 14.1

A database is data organized into fields and records.

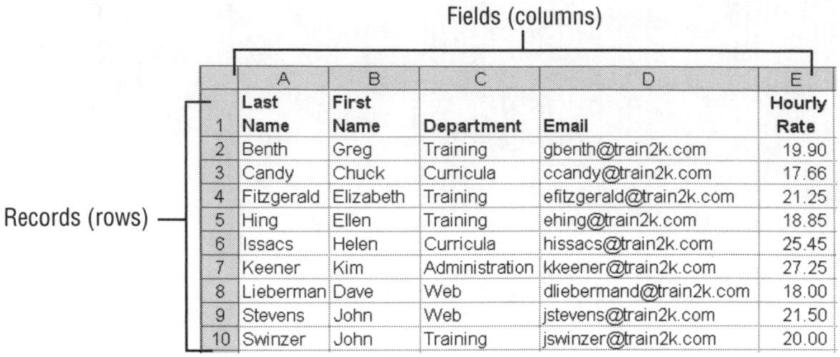

Fields (columns)

Records (rows)

	A	B	C	D	E
1	Last Name	First Name	Department	Email	Hourly Rate
2	Benth	Greg	Training	gbenth@train2k.com	19.90
3	Candy	Chuck	Curricula	ccandy@train2k.com	17.66
4	Fitzgerald	Elizabeth	Training	efitzgerald@train2k.com	21.25
5	Hing	Ellen	Training	ehing@train2k.com	18.85
6	Issacs	Helen	Curricula	hissacs@train2k.com	25.45
7	Keener	Kim	Administration	kkeener@train2k.com	27.25
8	Lieberman	Dave	Web	dliebermand@train2k.com	18.00
9	Stevens	John	Web	jstevens@train2k.com	21.50
10	Swinzer	John	Training	jswinzer@train2k.com	20.00

An individual listing in the database is a *record* containing a single set of the fields: one person's last name, first name, and so on. In most data sources, each field must have a unique *field name:* LastName, last name, LASTNAME, and LastNameforListing are all possible field names for a field containing last names.

NOTE   Access and some Excel features use the terms field and record to refer to organizing categories and individual items in a data source. Elsewhere in Office, these features are normally called columns and rows.

Features to Look For in a Data Source Application

To be useful, the application that holds your data should make it easy for you to do the following:

Sort   organize the data in a specific order (for example, alphabetized by last name)

Filter   query the data to find specific information (for example, all the entries for a specific city)

If an application doesn't allow you to sort and filter, it's not database software. Based on this definition, Word isn't database software: it sorts, but it doesn't filter. Find is the closest thing to filtering in Word. Other features that are useful when working with data include these:

Validation   limits the values that can be entered by a user

Input support   automatically formats phone numbers as phone numbers, separates addresses into separate fields, etc.

Summarization methods   perform functions like sum, average, and count

Word can sum, but validation is more difficult. Outlook has data type validation (you can't enter text in number fields) and excellent input support, but few summarization methods.

NOTE   In this section, we're evaluating the features that are built into the applications. With Visual Basic code you can make any Office application do nearly anything that another application can do.

Security is another issue you must consider. For more information about Office document security, see Chapter 12, "Securing and Organizing Documents."

Storing Relational Data

The type of database you can create in Word, Outlook, or Excel is known as a flat file: a single table, folder, or worksheet. More elaborate databases consist of many tables related by common fields; for example:

◆ Customers and orders

◆ Parts and suppliers

◆ Teachers, classes, and students

When you need to create more than one data source and relate the sources, you need a *relational database*. In a relational database, each type of information has its own table, and queries are used to pull together information from different tables to answer complex questions. Microsoft Access and Microsoft SQL Server are both relational databases.

There's another factor that some users need to consider: database size. Excel databases, called *lists*, are limited to the number of rows in a worksheet: you can store only 65,535 records in a worksheet. If you're creating a database with lots of fields—for example, to store and analyze the results of a multi-page survey—you'll notice another limitation: Excel can handle only 256 fields. While a single Access table has the same limitation, Access's relational ability means you can separate fields into two or more tables without compromising your ability to analyze data across the tables.

Importing, Exporting, and Linking

There's one final factor to consider before you put data into an application: how easy is it to get the data back out? For Office power users, this may be the most important factor because you want to use Excel data in Word and Access data in Excel; you also might want to drop data and charts into PowerPoint presentations. Access, Excel, and Outlook support easy importing and exporting to other formats. Excel supports the widest range of export and import formats, but Outlook and Access export to Excel, so they're just one step away from any format that Excel can create. Outlook and Excel are also OLE-DB servers: that means you can link directly to data stored in these applications. Data stored in Word tables can be exported to Excel only; you can't link to Word tables from other applications.

NOTE   *See Chapter 17, "Dissecting, Importing, and Exporting Data," for details on importing and exporting in Office.*

If you want to work with data in a variety of applications, store it in Outlook, Excel, or Access, not in Word. You may be wondering: if Word isn't a great container for data, why do so many users put data in Word tables? Here are three of the numerous answers to this question:

Installed user base   More people use Word than any software except Windows. Word is pretty close to a universal application. If you send someone a Word document that contains a data source, there's a good chance they'll know how to open it.

Presentation   Word's formatting tools are fabulous.

User skills   Some people work in Word only, so all their data is entered and edited there.

Previous versions of Word mail merge were partially responsible; data sources created in Word were put in Word tables. In Word 2003, Word mail merge data sources are stored in Access databases.

The number and percentage of users who spend the majority of their computer time in Excel or Outlook rather than Word is growing rapidly. This means more users know exactly what to do with an Excel data source or Outlook folder, and prefer to receive data in a more robust format than Word. Table 14.1 summarizes the data features of the Office applications.

TABLE 14.1: STORING DATA IN OFFICE APPLICATIONS

APPLICATION	ACCESS	EXCEL	OUTLOOK	SHAREPOINT	WORD
Sort	Yes	Yes	Yes	Yes	Yes
Filter	Yes	Yes	Yes	Yes	No
Validate	Yes	Yes	Some	Some	Minimal
Input Support	Some	Minimal	Excellent	Some	No
Summarize	Yes	Yes	Some	Some	Minimal
Security	Excellent	Great	Great	Great	Good
Relational	Yes	No	No	No	No
Link/Export	Yes	Yes!	Yes	Yes	Excel Export only

We have an opinion (in case you hadn't noticed) on where you should store data sources that you create:

◆ Contacts and appointments should be stored in Outlook. Create additional folders if you need to segregate the data.

◆ Store shared contacts on your Windows SharePoint Services site. Link the contact list to Outlook, where it will appear as an address book.

◆ Mission-critical data that needs different permissions for different users can be stored and secured in Excel. For more robust permissions, nothing beats a well-designed Access database. Relational data must be stored in Access or linked to an Access database from Excel or Outlook.

◆ Other data should be stored in Excel.

◆ Use Word tables very sparingly: for data that will be used only once or discarded when you're finished with it.

WHY THIS CHAPTER DOESN'T INCLUDE CREATING AN ACCESS DATABASE

Most businesses have data that must be stored in a relational database, so this chapter and others show you how to create Access tables, create queries, and build reports. However, we did not include Access *database* creation in this book. Here's why we left it out:

Relational databases (databases with more than one table) need to be carefully designed, and design includes a lot of theory. Database designers understand normalization and relationships, and how to apply them to the specific data they want to store. They know about data types and referential integrity. If you create a good database but don't understand the theory, your success is due to luck, not skill.

There are hundreds of thousands, if not millions, of poorly designed Access databases that prove the truth of this statement. Behind these databases are smart, hardworking people, many of whom stayed late or worked weekends to create the database that never really worked right. If the database almost works, they spend too much time supporting the database and its users. If you're one of these folks, you know what we mean.

What if you need to create an Access database and don't know about database design? Get some help from your Information Technology department. If you work for a small organization with no IT department or don't get sufficient help from your IT staff, start with a course on database design, or a great reference, or both.

◆ There are Microsoft certified courses on database design for Access; classes and locations are listed on the Microsoft website. Your local college or university might also have classes.

◆ There are also many good books available on database design; check your local bookstore or an online retailer.

Our recommendation: Don't agree to create an Access database without negotiating the resources you'll need: references, perhaps a course, time to create the database, and time to support users after the database is completed.

Now that you know what we're *not* covering in this chapter, let's get back to the topic at hand: working with your data in Office 2003.

Working with Word Data

Most Word users have data stored in Word documents. Some Word data is tabbed data: data entered in columns created with tab stops like the tabbed columns shown in Figure 14.2. This is a legacy from early versions of Word and WordPerfect that couldn't create tables but could create parallel columns for tabular data. WordPerfect had two features that Word 2003 does not have: a way to select a column of tabular data without selecting the surrounding data; and the ability to sort based on the values in columns 2, 3, and so on. Word text can be sorted by paragraphs or fields, but not by tabular columns. Tabular columns are old school, and they're not pretty. It's time to move up to tables.

FIGURE 14.2

This data was entered
as tabbed columns.
Notice the tab stops
on the ruler that
mark each column.

Start Time	End Time	Event	Location
8:15 am	4:00 pm	Book Nook	Ballroom
8:15 am	9:00 am	Complimentary Continental Breakfast	Regency Foyer East
9:00 am	11:45 am	Technology Tools for Admins	Live Oak
9:00 am	11:45 am	Applying Management Tactics	Pecan
10:15 am	10:30 am	Complimentary Refreshment Break	Regency Foyer East
12:00 noon	1:00 pm	Complimentary Networking Lunch	Garden Terrace
1:00 pm	3:45 pm	Desktop Management	Live Oak
1:00 pm	3:45 pm	Creativity	Pecan
2:15 pm	2:30 pm	Complimentary Refreshment Break	Regency Foyer East

With tables, you *can* select and format columns. You can sort by the values in any column. You enter data the same way: by tabbing from column to column. When you press Enter, you get another line in the same cell, which keeps your data intact. If table lines are all that's preventing you from moving tabular text to tables, you can format the table so it looks like tabbed data by removing all the borders.

NOTE *If you need to know how (and why) to create and format Word tables, See Chapter 11, "Creating and Modifying Documents for the Web."*

Converting Text to Tables

Tabbed data can be converted to tables. Select the data and choose Table ➤ Convert ➤ Text to Table to open the Convert Text to Table dialog box shown in Figure 14.3.

FIGURE 14.3

Use the Convert Text
to Table feature to
turn tabbed data
into a data table.

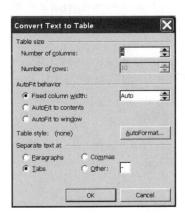

Make sure the number of columns is correct and that you've chosen the Tabs option in the Separate Text At section. If the columns aren't correct, you probably have additional tab stops in the ruler that don't mark data. You can choose Cancel and remove the extra tab stops, or continue and delete the extra columns in the table after conversion.

Choose an AutoFit option. The default setting, Fixed Column Width (Auto) breaks the columns at the current tab stops. Click OK to convert the text to table. The tabbed data from Figure 14.2 would look like this:

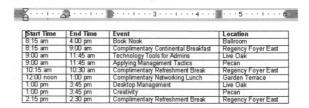

If you don't like the results, click Undo to return to the tabbed data. Make whatever adjustments are required and convert the text again.

Sorting Word Tables

To sort a table, click anywhere in the table and choose Table ➤ Sort from the menu to open the Sort dialog box shown in Figure 14.4. This dialog box is almost the same as Excel's Sort dialog box, and you'll use it the same way.

FIGURE 14.4

Use the Sort dialog box to order table rows or paragraphs.

First, visually check the My List Has option. If the table's first row is headings, Header Row should be selected. If the first row is a record, choose No Header Row.

In the Sort By drop-down list choose the heading of the column you want to sort by. If your table has no header row, choose the column number you want to sort the table by.

Verify that the field type matches the kind of data stored in the column. Choose Number for numbers and monetary values; choose Date for dates and times. If it's neither a number nor a date, choose Text. Choose the Descending option to sort numbers from highest to lowest or dates with the latest date on top.

If you want to sort on the values in one column, click OK to sort the table. To sort on more than one column (for example, to sort by last name and then by first name), make choices in the first Then By section. Use the third section to sort by three columns (for example, to sort by state, city, and company name).

TIP   You can only sort by three columns in Word. In Excel, Outlook, and Access, you can sort by as many columns as your data contains.

DATA TYPES AND SORTING

When you sort numbers, make sure you choose Numbers in the Type drop-down. If you sort numbers with the Type set to Text, Word sorts numbers as it would names: all the entries that begin with *1*, followed by all the entries that begin with *2*, and so on. Figure 14.5 shows a column of numbers sorted as text, then sorted as numbers.

FIGURE 14.5

When you understand how Office applications sort, it's easy to spot numbers incorrectly sorted as text.

Original List	Sorted as Text	Sorted as Numbers
1	1	1
10	10	2
2	14	10
20	2	15
15	20	20
30	21	21
21	30	30

You'll see the same sorting problem in Excel, but Excel's Sort dialog box doesn't allow you to choose a data type. Like Word, Excel automatically detects the data type of each entry, but when Excel sorts numbers as text, you need to fix the data.

Converting Word Tables to Excel

Word tables pasted into Excel worksheets are automatically converted to Excel's native format. To convert a Word table to Excel, follow these steps:

1. In Word, select and copy the entire table.

   The quickest way to select an entire table is to click anywhere in the table then click the table selection icon at the upper left corner of the table.

2. Switch to Excel. Select the first (upper-left) cell where you want to begin pasting the data.

3. Click the Paste button, right-click, and choose Paste, or choose Edit ➤ Paste from the menu to paste the table.

4. Click the Paste Options button to open the paste options menu:

Choose Keep Source Formatting to keep table borders, fonts, and other formatting from the Word table. Choose Match Destination Formatting to discard the Word formatting and use the formatting that was previously applied in Excel.

Building and Using Excel Lists

For reasonable amounts of data (other than contact and calendar data) you can't beat an Excel list. You can create the list quickly, and the tools are both powerful and easy to use. There isn't much that's new and amazing in this version of Excel, but the new Create List feature and List toolbar, discussed at the end of this section, certainly qualify.

Creating an Excel list is as simple as creating any other Excel worksheet, but there are additional rules for worksheets that you intend to use as lists:

Blank rows and blank columns signal the end of a list. *Don't* leave a blank row between column headings and data records. *Don't* leave blank columns within a list, and make sure there are no blank columns hiding between the columns of a list that you inherit. *Do* leave a blank row after all records and before totals, averages, or other summary rows.

Field names at the tops of columns must be unique within a list. Be consistent: label every column. If a label is too wide for the column and you're tempted to enter it in two cells, enter it in one cell and handle it with formatting: wrap or rotate the entry (Format ➤ Cells ➤ Alignment).

NOTE *See Chapter 13, "Building Robust and Foolproof Workbooks," if you're new to Excel and want help creating a worksheet.*

Any existing worksheet can be used as a list, but you might have to delete or insert rows, delete columns, or edit column labels so that your worksheet meets Excel's requirements. The list we'll use to illustrate Excel list concepts is the User Support Call Log shown here. Note the blank row (6) that separates the Start Date and End Date from the Excel list.

	A	B	C	D	E	F	G	H	I
1	User Support Call Log		Total Calls	12					
2			Total Time	2:57					
3									
4									
5	Start Date	6/1/2003	End Date	6/30/2003					
6									
7	User	Department	Date	Start Time	End Time	Length	Application	Type	Platform
8	Benth	Training	6/1/03	8:15 AM	8:18 AM	0:03	Outlook	App Error	Desk/Laptop
9	Keener	Administration	6/1/03	9:20 AM	9:30 AM	0:10	Excel	Code	Desk/Laptop
10	Lieberman	Web - IT	6/1/03	11:40 AM	12:00 PM	0:20	Word	Beginning	Desk/Laptop
11	Hing	Training	6/1/03	1:35 PM	1:55 PM	0:20	Data Analyzer	Intermediate	Desk/Laptop
12	Benson	Accounting	6/1/03	1:55 PM	2:10 PM	0:15	Excel	Advanced	Desk/Laptop
13	Turik	Info Tech	6/1/03	2:14 PM	2:30 PM	0:16	Connectivity	Beginning	PDA
14	Laramie	Manufacturing	6/1/03	3:00 PM	3:40 PM	0:40	Data Analyzer	Advanced	Desk/Laptop
15	Smith	Communications	6/1/03	3:45 PM	3:50 PM	0:05	Excel	Intermediate	Desk/Laptop
16	Keener	Administration	6/1/03	4:10 PM	4:13 PM	0:03	Excel	Code	Desk/Laptop
17	Fitzgerald	Training	6/2/03	8:32 AM	8:50 AM	0:18	FrontPage	Intermediate	Desk/Laptop
18	Song	Manufacturing	6/2/03	9:02 AM	9:18 AM	0:16	Excel	Intermediate	Desk/Laptop
19	Wilson	Maintenance	6/2/03	9:22 AM	9:33 AM	0:11	Outlook	Intermediate	PDA

NOTE   *This worksheet is the sample used in this chapter. An enhanced version is used in Chapters 17 and 19. If you'd like to play along with the examples in these chapters, download the User Support Call Log worksheet from the Sybex website.*

With the extended formats and formulas option enabled, you don't need to copy formatting or formulas when you add records. When you enter a new record at the bottom of the list (row 20 in our Call Log), Excel 2003 automatically does the following:

◆ Copies the formatting from the previous row to the new row

◆ Copies formulas from the previous row to the new row

Just type or paste in the row directly below the last list row, and Excel handles formatting and formulas. The Extended Formats and Formulas option is enabled by default. If it has been turned off, follow these steps to turn it on:

1. Choose Tools ➤ Options to open the Options dialog box.

2. On the Edit tab, enable the Extend List Formats and Formulas check box.

Quick Data Entry in Excel Lists

Most Excel users are familiar with the AutoComplete feature. AutoComplete is particularly useful in lists because it kicks in when you begin entering text that matches existing text in the same column. AutoComplete isn't useful when the column contains *nearly* identical text entries like those shown here:

University of Michigan
University of Michigan - Flint
University of Michigan - Dearborn
Michigan State University
Michigan State University Management Center

In this example, AutoComplete won't kick in until you enter at least 22 characters—at that point, you might as well just keep typing. Instead of typing the next entry, right-click in the cell and choose Pick From Drop-down List to open the list of AutoComplete entries:

Michigan State University
Michigan State University Management Center
University of Michigan
University of Michigan - Dearborn
University of Michigan - Flint

Pick the entry you want from the list. Pick From Drop-down List doesn't work with numbers—only with text entries. Both AutoComplete and Pick From Drop-down List use the text entries from cells in the same list range. If a blank row separates the current cell from some entries, those entries will not appear on list:

An empty cell doesn't cut off AutoComplete and Pick From Drop-Down List, but an empty row does.

NOTE   *You can create your own drop-down lists in Excel. See the "Validation: Making Sure Data is Correct" section later in this chapter. Drop-down lists in Word are discussed in Chapter 16.*

AN ALTERNATIVE TO SCROLLING: DATA FORMS

Excel data forms provide an easy way to enter or search for data. Because data forms have a portrait orientation, they're particularly helpful when your list has too many columns to display on the width of the screen. Using the form allows you to see all the list fields at once without scrolling horizontally.

To create a data form, select any cell in the list and choose Data ➢ Form. The first record in the list will be displayed in the data form. Use the vertical scroll bar or the up-arrow and down-arrow keys to browse the records. Use the Tab key to move between fields in the form; pressing Enter moves to the next record.

If you're an experienced Excel user, data forms aren't terribly exciting until you consider the other users who enter data in your workbooks. Data forms offer a nearly bulletproof way to let a less-accomplished user enter data. The contents of *calculated fields* are displayed without a text box, so users can't accidentally overwrite formulas.

Sorting in Excel

When you work with an Excel list, the rule is *select one cell.* Then, when you choose one of the list commands, Excel will select all cells above, below, to the right, and to the left of the cell you selected until it encounters a blank column and row.

To sort the data in a list, select any cell in the list and then choose Data ➢ Sort from the menu to have Excel select the records in the list and open the Sort dialog box, shown in Figure 14.6.

FIGURE 14.6

Order the rows in an Excel list with the Sort dialog box.

Specify whether or not you have a header row in the My List Has options, then open the Sort By drop-down list and make sure all your column headings are listed. Choose a column to Sort By. If some of the records have the same value in the Sort By column, use the two Then By drop-down lists to set up secondary and tertiary sorts. Choose Ascending (alphabetical) or Descending (reverse—highest values first) order for each sorting level. When you have made all the sort selections, click OK to sort the list according to your specifications.

NOTE   *If you don't select a cell within the list before choosing Data ➢ Sort, Excel will notify you that there was no list to select. Close the message box, select a cell in the list, and choose Data ➢ Sort again.*

SELECTING BEFORE YOU SORT

Normally you select only one cell in a list and allow Excel to select the list when you sort. But occasionally you need to sort a list that has adjoining data. For example, the data we want to sort here, the Issue column, is in the middle of other columns of data. This is not one list, but several unrelated single-column lists:

Departments	Issue	Types
Accounting	Access	Beginning
Administration	Excel	Intermediate
Communications	Word	Advanced
Curricula	PowerPoint	Code
Engineering	SharePoint	Error
Info Tech	FrontPage	User Fault
Logistics	MapPoint	
Maintenance	Data Analyzer	
Manufacturing	Windows	
Personnel	Outlook	
Training	Connectivity	
Warehouse		
Web - IT		

To sort data like this and *not* sort the surrounding columns, start by selecting the data you want to sort. Then choose Data ➤ Sort from the menu bar. A message warns that there is other surrounding data:

The default in this message box is Expand The Selection. If you want to sort the selected data only, choose the Continue With The Current Selection option and then click Sort to open the Sort dialog box.

TIP   When you're working with a database that includes blank columns or rows, you can select the entire database before sorting. Of course, you'll need to make sure you always select the entire database before you use any of the Data commands: sort, filter, subtotal, and so on. It makes a lot more sense to simply delete the extra columns or rows so the database has the structure that Excel is designed to recognize.

USING THE SORT BUTTONS

You can also sort a list using the sort buttons on the Standard toolbar. Select a single cell within the column you want to sort by. Click the Ascending Sort or Descending Sort button to sort the list.

This is an easy way to sort, but it has one major drawback: Excel doesn't allow you to verify the list or header row settings. We recommend that you sort a list once using the Data ➤ Sort dialog box to ensure that you and Excel agree on what should be included in the list. After the first sort, use the toolbar buttons.

WARNING   If some columns of data are not selected, the selected columns will be sorted but the unselected columns will not be, ruining the integrity of the data by mixing up the records. (This is why you never include empty columns in a list.) Click Undo immediately if some columns were omitted in a sort.

When you know how Excel sorts, you can use the sort buttons to do secondary and tertiary sorts. When Excel sorts the records in a list, it only rearranges records when necessary. If a list is already sorted by city, sorting it by state will create a list sorted first by state, and then by city within each state, because the existing city sort will only be rearranged to put the states in order.

SORTING BY MORE THAN THREE COLUMNS

To sort by more than three fields, use the toolbar buttons. Sort the least important field first and work backward through the sort fields to the primary sort field.

Filtering an Excel List

There are many times you'll want to view or print a group of records in the list. For example, you might want to print all sales records for one salesperson, all the orders from one client, or all the customers who haven't made a purchase this year. A *filter* is used to select records that meet specific criteria and temporarily hide all the other records.

APPLYING AN AUTOFILTER

New!

To set up an AutoFilter, select any cell in the list and choose Data ➤ Filter ➤ AutoFilter. Excel reads every record in the list and creates a filter criteria list for each column. Click the drop-down arrow that appears next to each column header (see Figure 14.7) to access the column's criteria list. In Excel 2003, the sort commands appear at the top of the list for each column.

FIGURE 14.7

Click the drop-down arrow next to the column heading to choose AutoFilter criteria.

User	Department	Date	Start Time	End Time	Length	Application	Type	Platform
Benth	Sort Ascending	6/1/03	8:15 AM	8:18 AM	0:03	Outlook	App Error	Desk/Laptop
Keener	Sort Descending	6/1/03	9:20 AM	9:30 AM	0:10	Excel	Code	Desk/Laptop
Lieberman	(All)	6/1/03	11:40 AM	12:00 PM	0:20	Word	Beginning	Desk/Laptop
Hing	(Top 10...)	6/1/03	1:35 PM	1:55 PM	0:20	Data Analyzer	Intermediate	Desk/Laptop
Benson	(Custom...) Accounting	6/1/03	1:55 PM	2:10 PM	0:15	Excel	Advanced	Desk/Laptop
Turik	Administration	6/1/03	2:14 PM	2:30 PM	0:16	Connectivity	Beginning	PDA
Laramie	Communications Info Tech	6/1/03	3:00 PM	3:40 PM	0:40	Data Analyzer	Advanced	Desk/Laptop
Smith	Maintenance Manufacturing	6/1/03	3:45 PM	3:50 PM	0:05	Excel	Intermediate	Desk/Laptop
Keener	Training	6/1/03	4:10 PM	4:13 PM	0:03	Excel	Code	Desk/Laptop
Fitzgerald	Web - IT	6/2/03	8:32 AM	8:50 AM	0:18	FrontPage	Intermediate	Desk/Laptop
Song	Manufacturing	6/2/03	9:02 AM	9:18 AM	0:16	Excel	Intermediate	Desk/Laptop
Wilson	Maintenance	6/2/03	9:22 AM	9:33 AM	0:11	Outlook	Intermediate	PDA

All   is the default criterion setting in each field, which means that the contents of the field are not being used to filter the records so you're seeing All of the records.

Top 10   is used in numeric fields to display the top or bottom 10, 5, or any other number or percentage of values.

Custom   prompts you to create a custom filter (see the section "Creating a Custom Filter," below) for choices that don't appear on the list.

When you apply a filter, all the records not included in the subset are hidden, as shown in Figure 14.8, where the records are being filtered so we see only support calls from the Training department.

FIGURE 14.8

Only support calls from the Training department are shown. Records displayed as filter results keep their original row numbers.

	User	Department	Date	Start Time	End Time	Length	Application	Type	Platform
8	Benth	Training	6/1/03	8:15 AM	8:18 AM	0:03	Outlook	App Error	Desk/Laptop
11	Hing	Training	6/1/03	1:35 PM	1:55 PM	0:20	Data Analyzer	Intermediate	Desk/Laptop
17	Fitzgerald	Training	6/2/03	8:32 AM	8:50 AM	0:18	FrontPage	Intermediate	Desk/Laptop

Each record retains its original row number; the row numbers of filtered records appear in blue. The number of records found and the total number of records in the list are displayed at the left end of the status bar. The drop-down arrow for the filtered field turns blue to show that it is being used to filter the list. To open the AutoFilter list in a column, either click the filter arrow or select the column heading with the AutoFilter arrow and press Alt+↓ . Table 14.2 lists keyboard shortcuts you can use with AutoFilter.

TABLE 14.2: AUTOFILTER KEYBOARD SHORTCUTS

KEY	ACTION
Alt+↓	Open the list
Alt+↑	Close the list
↓	Move down one list item
↑	Move up one list item
Enter	Apply the selected item

Filtering on More Than One Column

When you apply more than one filter, only records that meet all the criteria you select are displayed. In our list, there were three calls from the Training department and two calls related to Outlook. But if we filter for Training in the Department column and Outlook in the Application column, only one record is returned: the individual in the Training department who called with an Outlook question.

To display the entire list, change the filter criteria for all filtered fields back to All, or simply choose Data ➢ Filter ➢ Show All.

Using the Top 10 Filter

Top 10 filters display records based on their value. When you choose Top 10 as your filter criterion, the Top 10 AutoFilter dialog box opens:

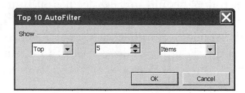

In the first drop-down list, choose Top or Bottom, depending on whether you want to see the highest or lowest values in the list. In the spin-box control, enter a number larger than 0. In the last control, choose Items or Percents. For example, to see the 5 calls that took the greatest time to handle, choose Top, enter **4** and then choose Items. To see which half of the calls were handled most quickly, choose Bottom, enter **50**, and select Percent. The Top 10 filter only works with values: numbers, dates, and times.

NOTE   *If you use a handful of filters frequently, consider saving filtered versions of the list as views. See Chapter 1 7.*

CREATING A CUSTOM FILTER

When you filter using the drop-down criteria, you are looking for records that exactly equal specific criteria. Custom filters give you access to other ways to set criteria:

◆ All records with fields that are *not* equal to a criterion

◆ Records that are greater than or less than a criterion

◆ Records that meet one condition *Or* another

To create a custom filter, choose Custom from the drop-down criteria list to open the Custom AutoFilter dialog box, shown in Figure 14.9.

FIGURE 14.9

Set multiple criteria in a field, or filter for a range of values, in the Custom AutoFilter dialog box.

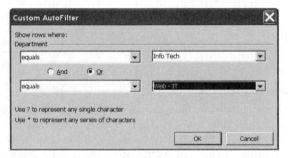

Click the filter operation drop-down list to choose an operator. The list includes common logical operators like Equals and Is Greater Than Or Equal To, as well as complex operators to filter for records that do or do not begin with, end with, or contain a *string* (one or more characters) you specify. The values drop-down list on the right is populated with the record entries in the field from the field criteria list. To find all calls that were not in the Training department, for example, choose Does Not Equal as the operator, and select Training from the Department drop-down list. You can also enter text in the criteria controls. Notice in the dialog box that you can use the wildcard characters * and ? to broaden the search string.

The And and Or options are used when you want to filter by more than one criterion in a column. *And* is used to establish the upper and lower ends of a range and is almost always used with numerical entries, as with this custom filter where we're finding the calls that took between 10 and 20 minutes to handle:

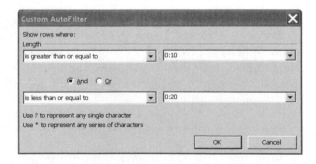

Or is used to filter by two different criteria: Training *Or* Web - IT. If you use And when you mean Or, you'll often get a *null set:* no records. There were no calls from employees in Training *And* Web - IT—employees work in one department or the other. If you use Or when you mean And, you'll get all the records. Every call took either more than 10 minutes or less than 20 minutes to resolve.

Filtering on screen is a great way to answer ad hoc questions. To communicate your answers, print the list. The filter criteria drop-down arrows don't print, so there's no need to turn the AutoFilter off until you are done working with a list.

At first glance, filtering looks like it would be useful when you need to chart the list's data. You could filter the records you want to chart, then select and chart the information as you would normally. This is true. Bear in mind, however, that when the filter criteria change, the chart will change.

To turn the AutoFilter off, choose Data ➤ Filter ➤ AutoFilter.

NOTE *If you need to create charts for specific filtered data sets or subtotals, see the section "Creating a Subset" in this chapter and Chapter 17.*

CREATING A SUBSET

There are times when you will want to work with or distribute a subset of a list. For example, you have a list with 5000 records—but only 700 of them pertain to your current project. It would be easier to work with a smaller list that includes only the 700 records you need. You can quickly create a subset of the 700 records using copy and paste:

1. Filter the active list to display the records you wish to copy.

2. Select the filtered list, including the column labels and any other titles you wish to copy.

3. Click the Copy button, choose Edit ➤ Copy, or right-click and select Copy or hold Ctrl and press C.

4. Select the first cell where you want the new list to appear.

5. Press Enter to paste the list.

Remember that this filtered data is not linked to the original list, so changes in the original aren't reflected in the subset. Don't invest time updating and maintaining this as a separate list. If you need to work with a subset that remains up to date, use Microsoft Query (discussed in Chapter 17) to link directly to the Excel list.

Filtering on Complex Criteria

Complex filters quickly outgrow the Custom dialog box. You need the Advanced Filter if you need to create subsets like these, filtered by more than two criteria in a field, or with a combination of And and Or statements:

♦ Support calls from end users during "prime time": that is, calls from departments other than Info Tech and Web - IT that we receive at the start or end of the workday (i.e., between 8 AM and 9:30 AM or after 3:30 PM).

♦ Support calls that our business rules define as complex: calls over 20 minutes and any call related to Code

If you want quick information, you can filter the list in place just as you do with AutoFilter. You create subsets based on complex criteria by *extracting* the subset's records from the list using Excel's Advanced Filter. The term *extract* is a bit misleading. Nothing is removed from the original list; Excel creates a copy of the records that meet your criteria.

The Advanced Filter is more complex than AutoFilter, but incredibly powerful. To use the Advanced Filter you establish:

◆ A *criteria range* that includes the column labels from your list and one or more criteria that you enter directly below the labels

◆ An optional *extract range* where Excel places a copy of the data

Excel filters the list through the criteria range to create the subset. The criteria range is the heart of advanced filtering. If the criteria range is incorrect, the extracted data will be wrong—so take your time with this. The column headings must be precisely the same as they are in the list, so begin by copying the column headings to another location in your workbook (a separate worksheet that you name *Criteria* is good).

Then, type the criteria you want to establish. Let's take our second example, support calls that our business rules define as complex: calls over 20 minutes and any call related to Code. Here's what the criteria range looks like:

	A	B	C	D	E	F	G	H	I
1	User	Department	Date	Start Time	End Time	Length	Application	Type	Platform
2						>=0:20			
3								Code	

There are two ways to filter for two criteria in separate columns, based on whether you want to use And or Or. Enter criteria on the same row for an And condition. Here's the criteria range for Code calls over 15 minutes with both criteria in the same row:

	A	B	C	D	E	F	G	H	I
1	User	Department	Date	Start Time	End Time	Length	Application	Type	Platform
2						>=0:15		Code	

Compare this with the previous criteria, where the criteria were in two different rows—an Or condition. You can create the And criteria with AutoFilter. You can't create the Or criteria with an AutoFilter: AutoFilter always uses And for criteria in two different columns. Here's another filter that requires an advanced filter: calls over 5 minutes from the Training department and calls over 10 minutes from the Info Tech department:

	A	B	C	D	E	F	G	H	I
1	User	Department	Date	Start Time	End Time	Length	Application	Type	Platform
2		Info Tech				>=0:10			
3		Training				>=0:05			

TIP   You'll need to refer to the criteria range in the Advanced Filter dialog box, so you might want to name it (Insert ➤ Name ➤ Define). Name the range including the column headers Criteria, and Excel will automatically enter the range in the Advanced Filter dialog box.

After the criteria range is set, click anywhere in the list and open the Advanced Filter dialog box (Data ➤ Filter ➤ Advanced Filter) shown in Figure 14.10.

FIGURE 14.10

Select the list, criteria range, and location for the extracted data in the Advanced Filter dialog box

Excel will automatically select your list for the List Range text box (but it never hurts to double-check!) Use the Criteria Range text box to identify your criteria range, including the column labels. If you named your range Criteria, it's automatically entered, too.

Choose whether you want to filter the records in their current location (as AutoFilter does) or extract the records by copying them to another location. If you choose the Copy To Another Location option, the Copy To text box will be enabled so that you can select the first cell of the range where the filtered records should be copied. As with any copy operation, just select one cell—if you select a range, it must match exactly the size and shape of the range required by the extracted data.

Be sure that there is room below the Copy To cells for all the extracted rows. You can enter a cell in any open workbook in the Copy To text box, so you can put the extracted data in a different workbook or a different worksheet than the original list. If you want to eliminate duplicate records from the filtered list, turn on the Unique Records Only check box. Finally, click OK and Excel will filter in place or extract data as you have indicated.

TIP   Suppose you've received a list with 10,000 records, many of them duplicate records. Don't eliminate the duplicates manually. Set up a criteria range without criteria (column headings only) and use the Unique Records Only option to extract a list without duplicates. Before you start creating the queries to eliminate duplicates in Access, consider exporting the table to Excel, where it's far easier to eliminate duplicates.

When you use advanced filtering to filter in place, the filtered subset will have blue row numbers, just as it does with AutoFilter. To turn the filter off, choose Data ➤ Filter ➤ Show All.

Using the New Create List Feature

New!   There's a nifty new feature in Excel 2003: a Create List command on the shortcut menu. Create List quickly turns on the AutoFilter and opens a new List toolbar with additional list commands.

To create a list, select any cells in the range and choose Data ➤ List ➤ Create List from the menu or right-click any list cell and choose Create List from the shortcut menu to open the Create List dialog box shown here:

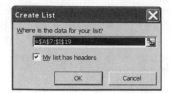

Verify the range for your list and click OK to create the list and open the List and XML toolbar as shown in Figure 14.11.

FIGURE 14.11

When a list cell is selected, the List and XML toolbar is displayed.

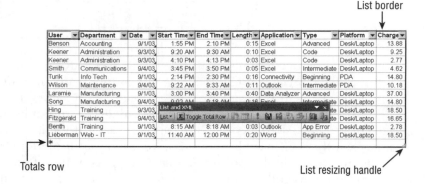

List border

Totals row

List resizing handle

CHANGING THE LIST

Excel's list includes one extra row. The asterisk in the first cell is an indicator. When you hover over it, the screen tip reminds you that data entered or pasted into the extra row is added to the list. There's a resizing handle on the lower-right corner of the list border. Drag the handle to include columns and rows or remove them from the list.

NOTE *You can also change the area defined as a list by opening the List menu on the List toolbar and choosing the Resize List command.*

One of the benefits of the list isn't immediately obvious: Excel segregates the list from the rest of the worksheet, so you can select a column within the list as easily as you'd select a worksheet column. Point to the top edge of the list header and the pointer will change to the column selection tool you've seen in Word tables. Click to select the column within the list. This is really convenient when you want to format list columns or rows without affecting nearby cells.

USING THE LIST AND XML TOOLBAR

The List And XML toolbar, shown in Figure 14.12, offers a wonderful compilation of list commands from the List drop-down menu, and includes easy total commands for filtered lists that were a bit complex in previous versions of Excel.

FIGURE 14.12

Use the List And XML toolbar to handle common list tasks that aren't built into the list itself.

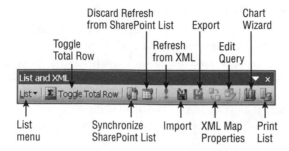

The List Menu

If you'd like to insert or delete rows and columns, you simply use the List drop-down menu. The first two commands on the List menu, Insert and Delete, will allow you to insert or delete rows and columns. Sort sorts the list on the current column in ascending order. Form opens a data form for the list.

NOTE *The Synchronize SharePoint List and Discard Refresh from SharePoint List commands are used with Windows SharePoint Services. For information on publishing to and using WSS sites, see Chapter 8.*

When you enter new data in the empty row, Excel extends the list to include a new empty row. If you copy and paste a group of new rows, use the Resize List command to open the Resize List dialog box, shown below, and resize the list. If you change your mind and delete the data, you can't resize the list with the resizing handle; you must use the Resize List dialog box.

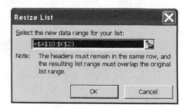

Publish List, X List, and View List On Server publish and synchronize your list with your Windows SharePoint site. Unlink List detaches the list in your workbook from the SharePoint site, creating a "local copy" that will neither receive nor send updates to the SharePoint site list.

NOTE *For information on working with SharePoint, see Chapter 8.*

Choose Convert To Range to remove the list but leave the contents of the list cells in the worksheet.

The Data Range Properties command is enabled when your list is linked to another list, usually a SharePoint site or data returned by a query. For more information on Data Range Properties, see Chapters 8 (for SharePoint) and 17 (for Microsoft Query).

Creating Dynamic Totals in the Total Row

The Total Row is, in our opinion, the best aspect of the Create List feature. The Total Row is a row that's set to create summary functions for the list. The Total Row uses Excel's Subtotal function, so the totals area is recalculated each time the list is filtered. If, for example, you filter the list to show calls from the Training department only, the results in the Total Row are for the Training department's calls. Show all records and the totals show the results for all records.

When Excel creates the list it creates one total for the right-most column in the list. Click the Toggle Total Row button to show or hide the total. To total other columns:

1. If the Total Row is not displayed, click the Toggle Total Row button.

2. Click the Total Row cell in the column you want to total.

3. Click the arrow to open the list of total functions:

4. Choose a total function to create the total formula.

After you create a total, you'll see this message box when you hide the Total Row using the Toggle Total Row button:

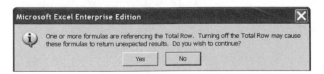

Click Yes to hide the Total Row. When you show the total row again, your totals will still be there. To remove a total, choose None from the list.

Creating and Modifying Access Tables

If you have a data set that has or will soon have more than 65,535 records, you'll run out of rows in Excel, so you must put the data in an Access table. Just as Excel lists live in Excel workbooks, Access tables live in Access databases. Before you can create a table, you must create a database to store it in. Follow these steps to create a blank Access database:

1. Start Access.

2. In the New File section of the task pane click the Blank Database link to open the File New Database dialog box.

3. In the dialog box enter a location and database name and then click Create. Access saves the database and opens the database window, shown in Figure 14.13.

FIGURE 14.13

The Access database window. Use the icons in the Objects bar to choose the type of object you want to work with.

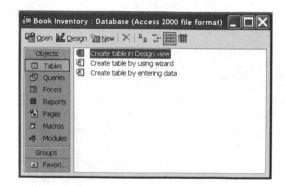

In a new database, tables are displayed in the database window. If you're looking at forms, reports, queries, or some other type of object, click the Tables icon in the Objects bar. Three table-creation methods are shown:

◆ Create Table In Design View

◆ Create Table By Using Wizard

◆ Create Table By Entering Data

To create a table with fields commonly used in business, begin with the Table Wizard, which includes a variety of tables and fields. Fields chosen from the wizard include useful extras. For example, if you choose a phone number field from the Table Wizard, the field is already formatted with the parentheses and hyphens used to format a telephone number. After finishing the wizard you can further modify the table in Design view. At that point you also have the options of entering data either directly or via a form the wizard creates.

For tables that include fields specific to your organization only, start in Design view. In Design view, you enter field names and specify all the properties of each field.

We'd encourage you to simply ignore the third choice, Create Table By Entering Data. It's very limiting: you can change the names of fields, add lookup columns, enter data, and that's about it. Access assigns attributes to the fields, sometimes incorrectly. You get the idea: use Design View or the Table Wizard. We'll tackle the Table Wizard first. Before we do, we need to discuss one table design element: primary keys.

Choosing (or Not) a Primary Key for a Table

A primary key is the field (or set of fields) that is unique and can, therefore, be used to identify one record in a table. For example, when you need to find a specific book on amazon.com, a search by the primary key for books, the ISBN, will find the single correct result. Examples of data that serve as primary keys include the following:

- ◆ Social Security numbers, student numbers, and employee numbers for people
- ◆ Product numbers (SKUs or UPCs) for products
- ◆ ISBNs for books
- ◆ FEINs for U.S. companies
- ◆ Vehicle numbers (VINs) for cars and trucks
- ◆ Credit card and bank account numbers

When a field is set as the primary key, Access won't allow you to enter a duplicate value. In the Amazon.com database, if an employee tries to enter an ISBN that has already been entered, the database will kick it back and ask for a new ISBN. In this way, primary keys help prevent accidental duplicate data entry.

If you're creating a database that will have only one table, a primary key isn't absolutely necessary (but it's still a good idea to include one). In a relational database with *more* than one table, however, every table *must* have a primary key for multi-table queries, reports, and forms to work properly. When a single field can't serve as a primary key, it's OK to create a key by using two or three fields. If no combination of fields is unique, include a field with the AutoNumber data type to use as a primary key.

Creating a Table Using the Table Wizard

The Table Wizard is a fast way to create a table. As with most Office wizards, the Table Wizard offers limited choices that are prepackaged. When you choose a field in the wizard, you're also choosing other settings related to the field. The wizard includes sample tables and fields; browsing the lists may prompt you to include other useful fields in your table.

To create a table using the Table Wizard, double-click Create Table By Using Wizard on the Tables tab of the Database window.

1. In the first step of the wizard, shown in Figure 14.14, choose a category option, Business or Personal, and select a table from the Sample Tables list that's similar to the table you want to create.

FIGURE 14.14

Select a sample table and fields in the Table Wizard.

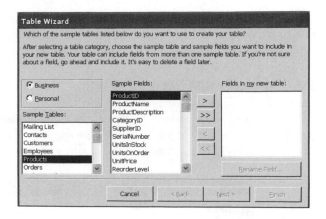

2. To include a field from the Sample Fields list, double-click the field name or use the pick buttons (with the arrows) to move the field to the list of Fields In My New Table.

3. To rename a field, select the field in the Fields In My New Table list. Click the Rename Field button to open the Rename Field dialog box. Enter a name for the field, and click OK.

4. Continue selecting tables and fields for your table. When you've selected all the fields you want to include in this table, click Next.

5. In the second step of the wizard, type a name for your table and select a primary key option.

    a. If you let Access set the primary key, it adds an AutoNumber field to the table. Do this if none of the fields you selected can serve as a primary key. Click Next.

    b. Choose No, I'll Set The Primary Key if the fields you selected include a field you want to use as the primary key. Click Next to advance to the next step of the wizard. Select the key field from the list of fields in your table and choose the data type for that field using the option buttons. Click Next.

6. In the last step of the wizard, you have three choices. You can select Modify The Table Design to open the finished table in Design view (so you can further tweak the design); you can select Enter Data Directly Into The Table (so you can start entering data in Datasheet view); or you can let Access automatically create and display a form that will allow you to enter data into the table. Select the option you want, and click Finish.

If there are other tables in your database, the last step of the wizard prompts you to create relationships to the existing tables. If this is the first table in your database, you won't be asked about relationships.

Access saves the table design and opens the table so you can begin entering data. Use tab to move from one field to the next, and to move from the last field in a record to the next record. When you're finished entering data, close the table. Access automatically saves your data.

Creating a Table in Design View

When you can't find the fields you need in the Table Wizard, you can create a table from scratch (or modify a table you created in the wizard) in Design View. Double-click the Create Table In Design View to open a new table in Design view. Design view for the table we'll create as our example is shown in Figure 14.15. Feel free to create the table as you work through this section.

FIGURE 14.15

Enter field names, types, and descriptions, and set properties in the table Design view.

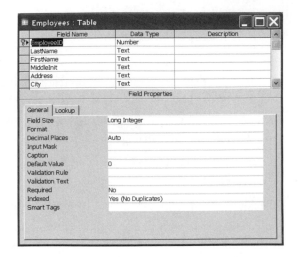

Follow these steps to create a table:

1. Type the field name for the first field. If your table will include a primary key, enter that field first, then right-click the field name and choose Primary Key from the shortcut menu. Field names should be descriptive and as unambiguous as possible. The convention is initial caps, no spaces (like *LastName*), but spaces are allowed.

2. Press Tab to move to the Data Type column. Select a data type from the drop-down list. You can select a data type from the list by typing its first letter; for example, if you know you want a Number data type, type **n**.

The *data type* describes and limits the kind of data that can be entered in the field. If, for example, you select the Number or Currency data type for a field, users won't be able to enter any character other than a digit, minus symbol, plus symbol, decimal point, or dollar sign. Choose the data type that reflects the type of data you want users to be able to enter in the field. There are 10 items on the Data Type drop-down list:

Text Used for both words and numbers that won't be used in calculations, such as phone numbers and Social Security numbers. The maximum length for a Text field is 255 characters. Text is the default data type because it is used most frequently.

Memo An open field that is used for comments. Although you can enter more characters than you can with a Text field (65,536), you can't easily sort or filter on a Memo field, so use this field type sparingly.

Number Numbers that are negative or positive values; unlike Excel, Access does not treat dates as numbers.

Date/Time Dates, times, and combinations of the two.

Currency Numbers in dollars or in dollars and cents.

AutoNumber A numeric field automatically entered by Access; it is used for a primary key field when none of the fields in a table is unique.

Yes/No A logical field that forces a user to choose one of two values. Data in this field can be displayed in different ways: Yes or No, On or Off, True or False, or with a check box.

OLE Object An object, such as a photograph, a bar code image, or a document, that was created in another application.

Hyperlink URLs and e-mail addresses.

Lookup Wizard Not really a data type, this is used to create a lookup field, which lets the database user select a value from a list, enhancing data accuracy by preventing typos (see the section "Creating Lookup Field Lists in Access" later in this chapter).
Starting again with the numbered steps from above:

3. Tab to move to the Description area. Enter a description for the field if you wish.

There are two uses for the description. While you're creating a database, this is a fine place to keep your notes. When the database is completed and you're ready to let others use it, the field descriptions provide a passive help system. When a user moves to a field in a table or form, the text in the description appears in the status bar. If you've used the descriptions for your own notes, you can either turn off the status bar display or return to Design view to clean up the descriptions.

4. Press Enter or Tab to drop to the next blank row and enter the information for the next field. Continue until you have entered all fields.

5. Click the Save button on the toolbar or choose File ➢ Save to save the table. Enter a table name when prompted.

Close the table or click the View button to switch to Datasheet view and begin entering data.

Validation: Making Sure Data is Correct

The best source for data is the person who knows whether or not the data is correct. For example, if you type your own business address or hourly rate incorrectly, you're likely to notice it. This observation is the reason behind an entire field of endeavor called *source data entry:* trying to capture data at the source. However, there are many times it doesn't work this way. Often the person entering data is far removed from the reality the data represents. In this kind of environment, it's easy for data to be entered incorrectly.

Even when knowledgeable people enter data, mistakes occur. When you're in a hurry, you don't have time to check every entry. Numerical data is easily transposed, so you're suddenly credited with working 21 hours in a day instead of 12, or selling an order for $950 instead of $590.

Data validation builds business rules into your data source so that grossly incorrect entries produce error messages. Business rules are the policies and procedures, formal and informal, which govern how a business operates. Examples of business rules include: no refunds after 30 days; no one ever works more than 80 hours in a week; and all employees must be at least 16 years of age. Both Excel and Access include tools to assist with data entry and validation.

Validating Data in Excel

Validation rules limit the range or type of entry that's valid for a cell. When you set up validation, you tell Excel what to do when a user enters data that breaks the rules. There are two choices:

◆ Show an error message that tells the user to try again

◆ Skip the message; accept and track incorrect entries so you can review them later

NOTE *You can't add validation to a list that is linked to a Windows SharePoint site.*

If a person using the worksheet is familiar with the data, an error message like the message in Figure 14.16 is useful. The user can immediately correct invalid data. The rule and message took about a minute to set up—less time than it would take to make one phone call to check on an incorrect worksheet entry.

FIGURE 14.16

The error message tells the user the entry is invalid, and explains values that are acceptable for this cell.

Users hate message boxes, particularly when the message tells them that they made a mistake. If a worksheet is used infrequently, has unusual rules, or is often used by new employees, it's smart to include an input message that appears when the user selects a cell with a validation rule. The input message looks like a comment, and provides help before the user makes a mistake:

> **Entering Call Dates**
> The Call Date must be between the start date for this log (in cell B5) and today's date.
> TIP: To enter today's date, hold Ctrl and press ;

You don't have to include an error message as part of data validation. You might prefer to let users enter data and then have Excel identify invalid data upon demand. Figure 14.17 shows a worksheet with invalid data marked as invalid by Excel.

FIGURE 14.17

The validation rule allows users to enter invalid data. The Formula Auditing tools are used to identify invalid data.

Start Date		9/1/2003	End Date	9/30/2003
User	**Department**	**Date**	**Start Time**	
Benson	Accounting	8/28/03	1:55 PM	
Keener	Administration	9/3/03	9:20 AM	
Keener	Administration	9/3/03	4:10 PM	
Smith	Communications	9/4/03	3:45 PM	
Turik	Info Tech	9/1/03	2:14 PM	
Wilson	Maintenance	9/4/03	9:22 AM	
Laramie	Manufacturing	9/1/03	3:00 PM	
Song	Manufacturing	9/4/02	9:02 AM	
Hing	Training	9/3/03	1:35 PM	
Fitzgerald	Training	9/4/03	8:32 AM	
Benth	Training	9/1/03	8:15 AM	
Lieberman	Web - IT	9/1/03	11:40 AM	

NOTE   *See the "Identifying Invalid Data" section later in this chapter to learn how to use the Formula Auditing toolbar.*

CREATING A VALIDATION RULE

You create validation rules one rule at a time. In our sample worksheet we have five different validation rules, so we had to go through the steps below five times. Here are the steps:

1. Select the cells you want to validate with the same rule (Ctrl-click to select noncontiguous cells).

2. Choose Data ➤ Validation to open the Data Validation dialog box.

The Data Validation dialog box shown in Figure 14.18 has three tabs:

FIGURE 14.18

Use the Data Validation dialog box to set up rules for valid data in your worksheet.

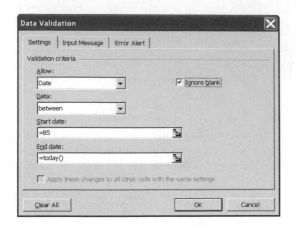

Settings   used to create the rule

Input Message   message that appears when a user selects the cell

Error Alert   message that appears when a user enters invalid data

3. Set the range of acceptable values on the Settings page. Choose an option from the Allow list, described in Table 14.3.

TABLE 14.3: DATA ALLOWED IN VALIDATION RULES

ALLOW	TO LIMIT VALID ENTRIES TO	USE THIS WHEN YOU WANT TO
Any Value	Any entry	Provide an input message, but not validate user entries.
Whole Number	Integers in a range you specify	Validate data about non-divisible units like people and jobs.
Decimal	Numbers in a range you specify	Validate data when decimal values are appropriate.
List	Items on a list you create	Force the user to choose from a limited list of choices like gender or credit cards' names
Date	Dates in a range you specify	Validate that a date is within a range: for example, not before today
Time	Times in a range you specify	Validate that a time is during working hours or within a specific range.
Text Length	A string with specific length	Make sure the user enters the correct number of characters like 9-digit Social Security numbers
Custom	Based on criteria you specify in a formula	Use other data in the worksheet to validate the entry in this cell.

After you choose a rule type from the Allow drop-down list, Excel opens other text boxes so you can fill in the rest of the rule. You can enter values or formulas in the open text boxes. For example, the rule in Figure 14.18 requires dates between the date in cell B5 and today's date. You can compare the data to another value in the same row, a constant, or a formula. If you use a formula or cell address, double-check the cell reference to make sure it is appropriately absolute, relative, or mixed.

NOTE *Validation lists offer some other choices. Don't let that put you off. They are easy to create and incredibly useful, so we walk through the steps in detail later in this chapter. If you choose List, see "Creating a Drop-Down List In Excel."*

By default, validation rules apply only to cells with entries. If a user clears the data in a cell, the validation rules aren't applied. Turn off the Ignore Blank check box to require an entry in cells validated with this rule.

4. To provide information when a user clicks on the cell, enter a message and optional title on the Input Message page, shown in Figure 14.19. Enable the Show Input Message When Cell Is Selected check box.

FIGURE 14.19

An input message is displayed when a user selects the cell: an ideal time to offer helpful hints for data entry.

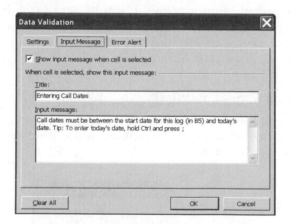

5. If you want to notify users when they enter invalid data, check the Show Error Alert After Invalid Data Is Entered check box on the Error Alert tab, shown in Figure 14.20.

FIGURE 14.20

To reject invalid data, enter an error message on the Error Alert page.

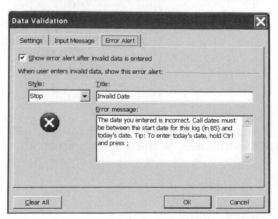

6. Enter text for a customized error message explaining why the user-entered data is invalid. If you don't provide error message text, Excel uses a default error message that's not helpful or friendly.

7. Choose the Warning style for the error message. The alert styles—Stop, Warning, and Information—are the standard styles for Windows error messages; Warning is the appropriate style for validation messages.

8. Click OK to turn on Validation.

9. Test the input message, validation, and error message by entering invalid data in one of the cells for each validation range.

To remove Validation, select the cells, open the dialog box, and click the Clear All button to clear all three pages of the dialog box.

People who use the same worksheet regularly are annoyed by input messages. To provide less intrusive help, create two different validation rules. In the first data row, include the input message. Omit the message on the remaining rows. The easy way to do this is to create the validation rule, including the input message, for all the cells, then select the cells that shouldn't have an input message and turn the input message off. After you turn off the input message for some cells in the range, Excel treats the two ranges as separate validation ranges.

SELECTING CELLS WITH VALIDATION RULES

Use the Go To Special dialog box to select all cells with validation rules, or all cells that have the same validation rule as the active cell. Choose Edit ➤ Go To to open the Go To dialog box. Click the Special button to open the Go To Special dialog box.

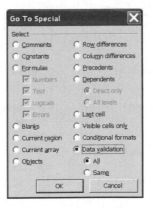

Select the Data Validation option, then choose either the All option (for all cells with validation) or Same (which selects all cells with the same validation rule as the active cell).

Using Validation to Create a Drop-Down List

In Excel, validation can also be used to create a drop-down list of values for a cell:

There are other tools that do this, such as Visual Basic list boxes, but validation is vastly easier to use. There's only one disadvantage to validation drop-down lists: the list of values must be included in the same worksheet (but you can hide the rows or columns that contain the list) or in a named range elsewhere in the workbook. Follow these steps to create a drop-down list in Excel:

1. Somewhere in the worksheet, create, in order, the list of values that should appear in the drop-down list. The list for the Type column in our User Support Call Log worksheet is shown here:

2. Select the cells where you want the drop-down list to appear and choose Data ➤ Validation to open the Data Validation dialog box.

3. On the Settings page, shown in Figure 14.21, choose List from the Allow drop-down list.

FIGURE 14.21

Use Validation to create drop-down lists of acceptable values in Excel.

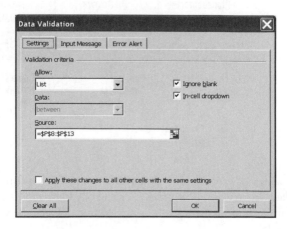

4. In the Source control, select the list of values you created in Step 1 above.

5. Make sure the In-Cell Drop-Down dialog box is enabled.

6. Enter an input message on the Input Message tab if you wish. Click OK to create the validation rule.

7. Click in any cell you selected in Step 2 above. A drop-down arrow appears at the right edge of the cell. Click the arrow to open the list and select a value.

Identifying Invalid Data

Even with validation rules in place, users can enter invalid data. Data validation only validates data that's typed by a user. Validation doesn't check data that's pasted or filled, entered by a macro, or the result of a calculation.

You can, of course, ask users not to copy or fill in your workbook, but that's not a real fix for the problem. It's better to disable drag and drop copying. Choose Tools ➤ Options to open the Options dialog box. On the Edit tab, turn off the Allow Cell Drag and Drop check box.

Use the tools on the Formula Auditing toolbar to find and circle cells that contain invalid data, whether it was copied/pasted by users, or created by a macro or formula. The Formula Auditing toolbar includes the tracing tools from the Circular Reference toolbar, a Trace Error button to check the precedents for error codes, and buttons to circle or clear circles from entries that violate validation rules. The Formula Auditing toolbar is one-stop shopping for error checking in your worksheet. Turn on the toolbar by choosing Tools ➤ Formula Auditing ➤ Show Formula Auditing Toolbar from the menu. The toolbar is shown in Figure 14.22.

FIGURE 14.22

The commands used to circle invalid data are on the Formula Auditing toolbar.

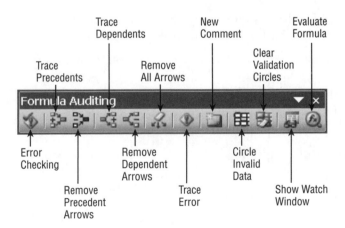

If you don't assign an error alert to your validation rules, there's no visible indication when a user enters invalid data. To view invalid entries, click the Circle Invalid Data button on the Formula Auditing toolbar. Each invalid entry will be circled in red. Click the Clear Validation Circles button to remove the circles.

Validating Data in Access

In Access, there are three ways to validate data, based on what you're trying to check:

◆ Field validation checks the value a user enters in a field and is used, for example, to make sure a hire date is less than or equal to today's date.

◆ Table validation compares values entered in two fields in the same record and is used, for example, to make sure a termination date is later than the employee's hire date.

◆ Lookups are used to create lists (like the validation list in Excel). You can then limit data entry to items on the list.

Validation is more tedious to set up in Access because of this fragmentation. On the positive side, Access validation is much more reliable. Excel allows a user to enter invalid data; Access chews it up and spits it out.

SETTING FIELD VALIDATION

Field and table validation are both set in a table's Design view. Field validation is a field property; table validation is a table property. To open a table in Design view, select the table in the database window and then click the Design button on the window's toolbar.

Follow these steps to validate a field:

1. Select the field in the grid. The properties of the selected field appear in the list beneath the field grid:

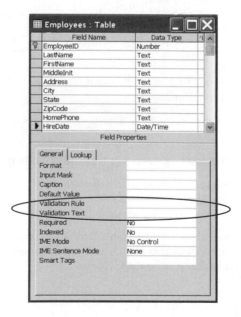

2. In the Validation Rule property, enter the criteria Access should use to determine if the entry is valid. You can compare the entry to a fixed value or the result of a formula. For example, if a field can't include future dates, enter **<=NOW()** in the Validation Rule property. (Click the Build button at the right end of the Validation Rule property text box to open the Expression Builder and list of Built-in Functions.)

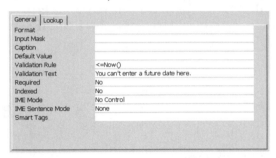

3. In the Validation Text property, enter the error message you want a user to see when they enter invalid data.

4. Save the table. This message box is displayed:

5. Click Yes to test the existing records for validity, or No to accept invalid existing records but check all future records.

6. Enter invalid data in the table to test your changes.

MASTERING THE OPPORTUNITIES: SETTING ACCESS DATA TYPE PROPERTIES

Excel's validation rules are also used to limit the data type of a cell entry to dates, times, integers, or text of a particular length. In Access, data type is set for each field. Specific subtypes (like integers) and sizes (like the maximum length of a text string) are properties of the field.

If you've already entered records in the table, Access will check the data to make sure it conforms to your changes. If it does not, you will not be able to save the changes, so it's a good idea to check the data first, before you invest time changing the field properties.

Continued on next page

MASTERING THE OPPORTUNITIES: SETTING ACCESS DATA TYPE PROPERTIES *(continued)*

To set field properties in a table, open the table in Design view. Select a field to display the field properties below the field grid. The properties depend on the field's data type. Here are the properties for a field with the Number data type, followed by the properties that control data subtypes for each data type:

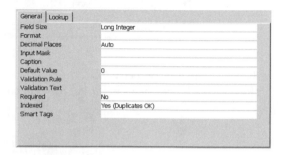

◆ Text: Set text string length with the Field Size property.

◆ Number and Currency: Set field formatting with the Format property (for example, Long Integer for whole numbers). Set the number of digits after the decimal in the Decimal Places property.

◆ Date/Time: Choose a Format appropriate to the field's data.

◆ Yes/No: Choose one of three formats: Yes/No, True/False, On/Off. Switch to the Lookup tab and choose a Display Control (Check box, Text box, Combo box) that users will work with. Save the table when you're finished setting properties.

VALIDATING ONE FIELD COMPARED TO ANOTHER

Use Table Validation when you want to check the value in one field against another field in the same record. This is often used with date/time fields that must be in sequence; for example:

◆ Equipment rental date before the check-in date

◆ Date hired before termination date

◆ Shift start date/time before shift end date/time

◆ Numbers in two or more fields total 100% or another specific number

Table validation happens just before Access saves the record. Follow these steps to set up table validation:

1. Open the table in Design view.

2. Right-click an empty area of the grid and choose Properties from the shortcut menu or choose View ➢ Properties from the menu to open the Table Properties.

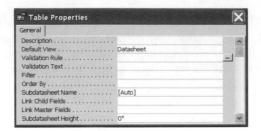

3. Click in the Validation Rule property. Click the Build button to open the Expression Builder, shown in Figure 14.23. The folders in the left pane contain the table, functions, constants, and operators.

FIGURE 14.23

Use the Expression Builder to create field or table validation rules.

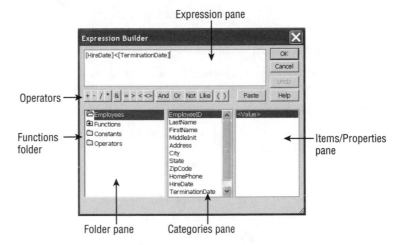

4. Open the folder to display the folder's contents in the center and right panes. Double-click an item to add it to the expression. Type **operators**, or click the Operator buttons just below the expression pane.

In Figure 14.23 we opened the Employee folder, double-clicked Hire Date in the center pane, clicked the Less Than operator button, then double-clicked Termination Date. Click the Help button for assistance with using the Expression Builder.

5. Click OK to close the Expression Builder.

6. In the Validation Text property, enter text to display when the record is invalid. Table validation occurs when the record is saved, so the feedback might not happen immediately after the user has entered the invalid data, but after they've entered data in other fields. Therefore, your validation text should include the name of the field so the user knows what to correct. For example, "The termination date must not be earlier than the hire date."

7. Save the table. Test the rule and text by entering invalid data.

MASTERING TROUBLESHOOTING: WORKING WITH DATABASES CREATED BY THE MAIL MERGE WIZARD

When you create a new mail merge data source in Word 2003, Word stores the data in an Access database table (and opens a form in Word for data entry and editing). You can open and modify the database in Access, adding validation, input masks, even adding and deleting table fields. Access won't stop you—but it should. Changes to the table aren't reflected in the Word form, which creates a mismatch between the form and the table. If a user then enters invalid data in the form, Access rejects the data but the message that appears doesn't let you know that this is a permanent problem. Instead, you're encouraged to check back later to see if Access is in a better mood.

It's best to think of the table created by the Mail Merge Wizard as unchangeable. If you want to add validation to a mail merge data source, create the data source in Excel or directly in Access.

CREATING LOOKUP FIELD LISTS IN ACCESS TABLES

The Access equivalent of an Excel validation list is a *lookup field*. A lookup field gets its entries from one of two sources: a table or a list of values. Lookups are more powerful than the Excel lists in one respect: users can type the first letter or two of an entry to choose from the list. In Excel you must click on, or "arrow down," to the item you want to select from the list.

Lookup fields speed data entry and ensure data accuracy because the user can't inadvertently misspell an entry chosen from a list. But lookup fields aren't just convenient for users. The enforced accuracy of lookups really pays off when you create reports that sort or group on the values in a field. It's easy, for example, to present all the orders from North Dakota as a group when every user enters North Dakota the same way—**ND** or **North Dakota** or even **N. Dakota**. If the table includes several different renditions of North Dakota, your reports will include a total for each version and, therefore, no true total for orders from North Dakota.

Lookup fields are created with a Lookup Wizard. To create a lookup field, decide whether you want to present a list of values from another table or from a fixed list. A fixed list is good if the possible values are few and seldom change, because you don't need to create another table to hold the entries. For example, if you need to enter a credit card type (such as Visa, MasterCard, or American Express) in an Orders table, your database works faster if you create a fixed list of these names for the lookup field. If, however, your organization decides to start accepting Discover, you'll have to correct the list in the table.

Base your lookup on a table if the list of items will change. It's easier to change values in a table, and the user always sees the current list of items. The table must exist before you can create a lookup field that uses it, and can be a simple table with just one field. The table does not need to have records; however, it is easier to size the text boxes used to display table information if the table has a few sample records.

Creating a Lookup Based on a List

To create a lookup based on a typed list of values, open the table in Design view and follow these steps:

1. If you're creating a new field, enter the field name.

2. Choose Lookup Wizard as the data type.

3. In the first step of the Lookup Wizard, choose whether the data in the lookup will come from a typed-in list or an existing table. Click Next.

4. In the next step of the wizard choose a number of columns for the list and type in each item, as shown here:

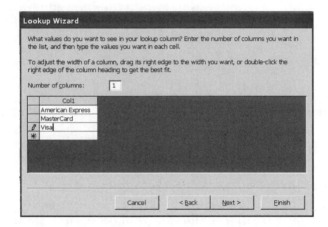

Press Tab after each item; if you press Enter you'll end up in the next step of the wizard.

5. Adjust the width of each column so that it is slightly wider than the longest entry and click Next.

6. If you have more than one column of data, you'll be prompted to choose a column that uniquely identifies the row: usually the primary key field.

7. Click Finish. Edit the field name if you wish.

Creating a Lookup Based on a Table

To create a lookup based on a table, open the table in Design view and follow these steps:

1. If you're creating a new field, enter the field name.

2. Choose Lookup Wizard as the data type.

3. In the first step of the Lookup Wizard, choose whether the data in the lookup will come from a typed-in list or an existing table. Click Next.

4. Select the table that includes the values for your lookup field. Click Next.

5. Double-click a field to add it to your lookup.

If you choose more than one field, all the fields will be visible when the user opens the lookup list. Make sure the users are familiar with the fields first. The primary key field will be included automatically and is the value that is stored in the table where you're creating the lookup.

6. When you have selected all the fields you wish to display in the lookup, click Next.

7. Choose a sort order for the list. Click Next.

8. Set the width of each column by dragging the right border of the column label. Unless the primary key field has meaning for your users, leave the Hide Key Column check box enabled. Click Next.

9. In the last step of the Lookup Wizard, edit the label (if you wish) and then click Finish. You'll be prompted to save the table so that Access can create the relationship between the table you're working on and the table that provides the values for the new lookup field.

To test the lookup, open the table and click in the lookup field. Click the arrow to open the list of choices from the table.

Chapter 15

Creating Templates to Handle Your Repetitive Tasks

ALMOST ANY WORD, EXCEL, or PowerPoint document can be saved as a template. Templates prove their worth when you need to create documents with identical or similar features: much faster than copying an existing document, presentation, or workbook and then deleting the information you don't want to keep. Templates help enforce consistency, not just of formatting, but of data. If, for example, you have a number of clients that send you data, you can send them an Excel template with data validation to ensure that the data is accurately entered, appropriately formatted, and entered in the proper columns. In this chapter you'll learn to create and use templates in PowerPoint, Word, and Excel. (For information on Outlook templates, see Chapter 12, "Securing and Organizing Documents." Topics in this chapter include:

- ◆ Understanding templates

- ◆ Creating presentation templates in PowerPoint

- ◆ Using and creating workbook templates in Excel

- ◆ Adding comments in Office documents

- ◆ Creating document templates in Word

- ◆ Downloading templates from Microsoft

Understanding Templates in Your Organization

Templates might be an important element in your organization's communication strategy. Just as they have stock designs for business cards, most mid-size and large organizations require employees to use specific approved templates when creating presentations, documents, and workbooks. These templates include corporate branding elements like the company's logotype, colors, and fonts.

If your organization doesn't have official templates, you have some room to create templates for your workgroup and projects. You might want to create templates for the same reasons companies have official corporate templates: so your communications have a consistent look and therefore "speak with one voice." If all the presentations (and other documents) that communicate information about a project use the same templates, the project looks more organized.

Even if you work in an organization that has templates for external documents, you can create templates to support internal processes for your workgroup—or your desktop. Any frequently used document that requires numerous formulas or extensive, precise, or consistent formatting is a good candidate for a template.

Templates don't just include formatting; your templates can include anything that a document can include. For example:

◆ Formulas, validation, and conditional formatting in Excel templates

◆ Custom styles and AutoCorrect entries in Word

◆ Color schemes in PowerPoint

◆ Macros in any application

In PowerPoint, creating templates focuses largely on design elements with minimal content, so PowerPoint is a good place to begin. With the PowerPoint templates in place, we will create templates with the same "voice" for Word and Excel. Word templates often include content, and Excel templates almost always focus on content more than design.

STORING TEMPLATES: LOCATION, LOCATION, LOCATION

There are several ways to distribute a template. In Word and Excel, for example, you can choose a default template that's used for every new document or workbook. To store a template for your own use, save it in your Templates folder or one of its subfolders. There are a number of ways to share a template, including:

◆ Save a Word template in the folder for workgroup templates (set this folder on the File Locations page of the Options dialog box)

◆ Save the template in a shared folder and then create a link to the template on your intranet so others can open and save it as a template

◆ Save the template in your shared workspace

◆ E-mail the template to co-workers

This last option can cause problems if your template includes macros, even if your macros are digitally signed (see Chapter 19, "Using Macros to Do More with Office"). If you need to send templates with macros, use the Windows Zip utility or a third-party compression utility like WinZip to package your templates for e-mail.

Creating Presentation Templates in PowerPoint

PowerPoint templates include all the attributes of a presentation, including a slide design and color scheme, transitions and animation. Most templates include at most one slide. Elements for all slides are established on the slide masters.

Saving the Template with a Custom Name

We'll begin by selecting a slide design: for our organization the built-in Curtain Call template is a good fit. After opening the template and before making any changes, we'll save our template so we don't affect the original Curtain Call template. Follow these steps to open and save the template:

1. Open PowerPoint and choose File ➤ Open.

2. In the Files Of Type drop-down list, choose Design Templates (`*.pot`).

3. Navigate to the Office templates folder usually installed in this path: `\Program Files\Microsoft Office\Templates\Presentation Designs`.

If you have difficulty finding the folder, choose Start Ø Search on the Windows menu and search for `*.pot`.

4. Select and open the `Curtain Call.pot` template.

5. Choose File ➤ Save As.

6. In the Save As dialog box change the Save As Type to Design Template. PowerPoint will automatically switch to the folder where your templates are stored. Depending on your operating system, however, this might not be the folder you wish to use. Two local template folders are available when Office 2003 is installed on a Windows XP computer:

   A personal template folder usually installed in this path: `\Documents and Settings\`*username*`\Application Data\Microsoft\Templates`

   The Office templates folder usually installed in this path: `\Program Files\Microsoft Office\Templates\Presentation Designs`

The slide designs in *both* of these folders are loaded each time you start PowerPoint. If you save the template in your personal template folder, it is listed in the Slide Design Pane only when you're logged onto the computer. If you save the template in the Presentation Designs folder, anyone who uses your computer can use the template.

7. Choose the folder you want to store your template in.

8. Specify a filename (we named ours `ABC Theater`).

9. Click Save to save the template. PowerPoint templates are saved with the POT extension.

Modifying the Template

Now you can modify the template using the techniques you would use to modify a presentation—with one exception: all of your changes should be made on the Slide Master and Title Master, including animation and transitions.

TIP   Animating the master does not cause a problem when you create presentations. Many presentation designs include transitions and animation. Transitions and animation applied to a slide override those assigned to the slide master.

DELETING EXTRA COLOR SCHEMES

We want to restrict the color schemes that users can apply in our template to two color schemes: the scheme with the blue background (for electronic presentations) and the scheme with the white background (for overheads and handouts). To delete the other schemes, switch to the Slide Design Pane and click the Color Schemes link or choose Slide Design - Color Schemes from the Other Task Panes drop-down list to open the Color Schemes Pane. Click the Edit Color Schemes link at the bottom of the pane to open the Edit Color Scheme dialog box. Click the Standard tab, shown in Figure 15.1.

FIGURE 15.1

Edit, save, and delete color schemes in the Edit Color Scheme dialog box.

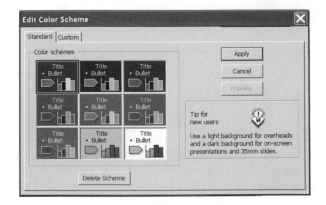

Select and delete each unneeded color scheme; then choose the blue background color scheme and click Apply to apply the scheme and close the Edit Color Scheme dialog box.

RESAVING THE TEMPLATE

When you've finished creating the template, save it again and then close the template. Your template will appear in the designs Available For Use in the Slide Design Pane the next time you launch PowerPoint.

APPLYING THE POWERPOINT TEMPLATE

Apply your PowerPoint templates as you apply the existing design templates: Format ➤ Slide Design (or choose Slide Design from the task pane drop-down list if the task pane is already open), and then choose the design from the list.

PROTECTING TEMPLATES FROM ACCIDENTAL MODIFICATION

After you create a template in an Office application, the list at the bottom of the File menu will include the template you just created. If you or another user opens the template from the File menu, the template—not a new document based on the template—will open. Any changes will be saved as modifications to the template. The easiest way to prevent this from happening is to hide the recently used file list. To clear this list from the File menu, first save and close the template; then choose Tools ➤ Options to open the Options dialog box. On the General page, turn off the Recently Used Files check box and then click OK to close the Options dialog box and clear the list. Reopen the Options dialog box and enable the check box, and the application will resume displaying recently used files with the next files you save.

Creating Templates in Excel

Excel includes some templates and additional templates are available for download from the Microsoft site. You can create templates from scratch, but it's good practice to check the existing templates first to see if there's a template that has some or all of the functionality you desire. Microsoft encourages you to modify the templates before using them.

Any workbook can be turned into a template. Examine the Excel files on your drives and see how many of them are different variations on the same workbooks to discover where you can save time and effort by building templates.

For example, you might track hours worked by your department's employees, with each week's hours on a separate worksheet and a consolidating worksheet to track monthly totals for analysis: five or six sheets in all, depending on the number of weeks in that month. Rather than constructing a new workbook each month, you can create a monthly payroll template. Each month you can create a new workbook from the template instead of copying and gutting an existing payroll workbook or, worse yet, starting from scratch.

An Excel template differs from a regular workbook in five specific ways:

◆ The file is saved as a template (XLT file extension) rather than a regular workbook (XLS). Excel creates new workbooks based on the template but the template isn't changed when you use it. The template is saved in the Office Templates folder or a workgroup templates folder for others to use.

◆ The workbook template contains only the worksheets, text, formulas, and formatting that remain the same each time the workbook is used. Blank sheets are deleted.

◆ The template includes visual formatting clues and comments (see "Creating Templates for Other Users" later in this section).

◆ Cells where users should enter data are unlocked and the worksheets and workbook are protected (see Chapter 12).

You can create a template from scratch or base it on an existing workbook. If you're using an existing workbook, first make sure that all the formulas work and that numbers and text are formatted appropriately. Remove the text and numbers that will be entered each time the template is used. Don't remove formulas—although the results of the formula change, the formulas themselves remain the same. If you're creating a template from scratch, you'll need to enter (and then remove) values in the data entry cells to test the template's formulas before saving the template.

Saving a Template in Excel

Follow these steps to save an Excel template:

1. Choose File ➢ Save As.

2. In the Save As Type control, choose Template from the drop-down list. The Save In control will change to the default `Templates` folder.

3. Enter a name for the template in the File Name text box.

4. Click the Save button.

Editing a Template

To modify a template, open the template from the Templates folder using File ➢ Open rather than File ➢ New. When you are finished editing, save and close the template.

As you gain experience with Excel, you can add other features to templates, like command buttons and custom toolbars. Use Excel's Help feature to find more information on template design and modification. Refer to Chapter 19 for information on recording simple macros that you can attach to buttons or menus.

CREATING EDIT-FREE FORMULAS

We often find users editing formulas because the formula they're using (and modifying with each use) is too wimpy to do the job. And because the formulas require user intervention, the workbooks aren't worth saving as templates.

For example, one of our users routinely edited formulas that calculated the average daily sales for each salesperson. The formulas divided the sales for the month by the number of weekdays in the month, which the user faithfully calculated by counting the Mondays, Tuesdays, Wednesdays, Thursdays, and Fridays for the month on his wall calendar. Modifying the formula to use Excel's NETWORKDAYS function got him out of the calendar counting business, and made the workbook functions powerful enough to handle the task when saved as a template.

Another user added formulas to workbooks after the data was entered by other people in her department. The formulas were added later because some of the formulas resulted in Division By Zero errors until data was entered. Adding the IF and ISBLANK functions to the formulas to complete calculations only if the precedent cells contained data took care of the problem.

If a workbook contains predictable data, formulas shouldn't change unless your business rules change. The next time you open a workbook or a copy of a workbook and edit formulas, determine why you're changing the formulas—then replace them with formulas that won't require editing in the future.

Creating Templates for Other Users

When you create a template for other users, you can't assume that they know how to use the template. Even if your colleagues who use the template initially are experienced users, those who succeed them may know little or nothing about your organization, Excel, or your template. If you don't invest the time required to create a solid template, you'll get to be the trainer and help desk for your template when other employees use it. Build in the following features to make your template easier to use:

Borders and fill color   to let users know where they should—and shouldn't—enter text or other information. In the templates included with Excel, cells with a back color like pale yellow or green contain formulas; users enter data in cells with no fill.

Comments   to provide assistance where users might have questions about data entry. The Excel 2003 templates include almost no comments, but we suggest that you err on the side of too many, rather than too few, comments. See the next section, "Inserting Comments in Excel."

Data Validation to provide input messages and error messages to guide data entry.

Focus the user on the template by removing extra worksheets. Hide rows and columns that will never be used. Hide worksheets that provide background information like data used by the Lookup functions (see "Hiding Worksheets," below).

Protection for cells that shouldn't be altered (see Chapter 12).

When you're finished creating the template, choose File ➤ Save As and save the workbook as type Template. You can create folders within the `Templates` folder to hold your personal templates. Other than the General tab, tabs in the New Workbook dialog box represent folders in the `Templates` folder. The template will be included on the General page (or a page representing a folder you created) of the New dialog box. Save the template in a shared folder to make it accessible to other users.

Inserting Comments in Excel

 A comment is a text box connected to a cell. You format a comment as you would any other text box to change the font attributes, fill color, shadow and 3-D effects, and other settings. Use comments to do the following:

- Explain worksheet features
- Unpack the logic behind formulas
- Tell a user what information should be entered in a cell

Select the cell you want to comment, then choose Insert ➤ Comment or right-click and choose Insert Comment from the shortcut menu to insert a comment in the active cell. The comment includes your username in bold (you can delete it if you wish). Enter your text and then drag the comment handles to size the comment text box appropriately.

	A	B	C	D
1	Meeting Na	**Gini Courter:** For information on this template contact info@triadconsulting.com		
2	Meeting Lo			
3	Meeting Da			
4				

When you click outside the comment, the text box is hidden. A red comment indicator in the top-right corner of the cell shows that the cell contains a comment. Hover over the indicator to display the comment. This is the default display for comments.

A comment is a text box attached to a specific cell. You can format the comment as you would any other text box: for example, you can change the font or apply font colors and background color.

Showing and Hiding Comments

You can set options to show all comments or hide the indicators. To change comment options, choose Tools ➤ Options to open the Options dialog box. On the View tab, shown in Figure 15.2, choose an option to show None, Comment Indicator Only, or Comment & Indicator.

FIGURE 15.2

Set comment display options on the View tab of the Options dialog box.

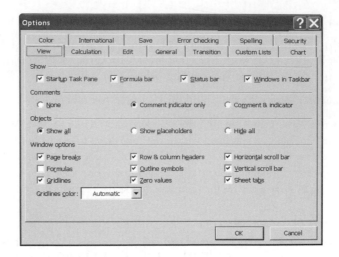

While we're on the View tab, there are a few other view options often used in templates:

◆ Turn off the sheet tabs if there's only one visible sheet in the workbook

◆ Hide rows and column headers

◆ Turn off the gridline display

Display or hide individual comments on the cell's shortcut menu. Right-click and choose Show/Hide Comments to display a cell's comment. Choose Hide Comment to hide a comment that is currently displayed.

TIP   Right-click on a cell that contains a comment to edit the comment—even if it is hidden.

Printing Comments

There are times when you want to print a worksheet's documentation, and comments might form part of that documentation. On the Sheet tab of the Page Setup dialog box, choose from three print settings for comments:

None (the default)   comments do not print, even if they're displayed

At end of sheet   all comments are printed as a separate listing at the end of the print job

As displayed on sheet   the worksheet, including displayed comments, prints as it appears on the screen. Hidden comments (and their comment indicators) are not printed.

As with other Page Setup options, these settings apply to the selected worksheet(s).

HIDING WORKSHEETS

Your template might contain supporting data that you don't want your users to edit or view. For example, you might have criteria ranges to support advanced filters, or data tables used for lookup formulas. Place supporting data on a separate worksheet and hide the worksheet to make your worksheets less cluttered. Select the sheet(s) you wish to hide, and choose Format ➤ Sheet ➤ Hide to hide the worksheet.

To unhide hidden sheets in a workbook, choose Format ➤ Sheet ➤ Unhide to open the Unhide dialog box. Select the sheet you wish to display and click OK to display the worksheet. Seems too easy to unhide worksheets, doesn't it? To keep template formulas safe, remember to protect your template's worksheets and workbook. See Chapter 12 for more information on protecting your work.

Creating Document Templates in Word

Word 2003 ships with a number of templates, and there are dozens of additional free templates on Microsoft's Office website. You can modify any of the templates to include your personal and organization data then resave the changed template. To open a template, choose File ➤ New (don't click the New toolbar button) to open the New Document task pane. Use the task pane links to open the template.

◆ From the New Document pane in word, click the On My Computer to open the Templates dialog box, shown in Figure 15.3, and view your templates.

FIGURE 15.3

Open your personal and workgroup templates from the Templates dialog box

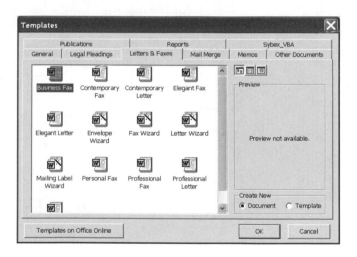

◆ Your organization's templates might be stored on the intranet. Click the On My Web Sites hyperlink to open the New From Templates on My Web Sites dialog box, which is filtered to show locations from My Network Places.

◆ Enter a search term and click Go or click the Templates Home Page link to find templates on the Microsoft Office website.

To create a template from an existing document, remove any variable text before choosing File ➤ Save As. Choose Document Template from the Save As File Type drop-down list to switch to the templates folder (or the folder you selected when you saved or opened a template previously in the session).

Storing Templates in Word

As with Excel and PowerPoint, Word templates are stored in a default templates folder, which is the folder that opens when you choose Document Templates from the file type drop-down list. If you want to categorize your templates, create subfolders within the templates folder, then save your templates in the subfolders.

Word includes another template location for workgroup templates, typically a shared folder where members of your team save templates that all team members can use. There are obvious reasons to share templates; storing them in a workgroup template folder (rather than e-mailing them to each user or having each user download the template) ensures consistency and makes it easier to update the template. If every user has a copy of a template, you must make sure each user has the new, revised version each time the template changes. If the template is stored in and used from the workgroup templates folder, you only need to change one template.

Templates can be stored anywhere, but when you click the On My Computer link, Word shows you only the templates stored in your user templates folder (and its subfolder) and the workgroup templates folder (and its subfolder). There is no default workgroup templates folder: you need to set it in Word. To set a workgroup templates folder, choose Tools ➢ Options and click the File Locations tab (see Figure 15.4).

FIGURE 15.4

Set an alternate location for Workgroup Templates.

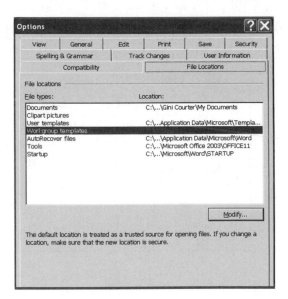

Choose Workgroup Templates in the list of file locations. Click the Modify button to open the Modify Location dialog box. Find and select the folder where your workgroup templates are saved.

NOTE   If templates with the same name appear in both template locations, the template stored in your user templates folder has precedence. If you want to maximize the usefulness of the workgroup templates folder, make sure people in your workgroup don't copy workgroup templates to their user templates folder.

Applying a New Template to an Existing Document

Word templates can include macros, custom toolbars, styles, and other settings. If, for example, you need to use a macro and it's not available in the current template, you can attach the template that includes the macro to access the macro. You can choose whether or not to update the styles in the active document to use the styles in the attached template.

Follow these steps to attach a different template to the current document:

1. Choose Tools ➤ Templates and Add-ins to open the Templates and Add-Ins dialog box, shown in Figure 15.5.

FIGURE 15.5

Use the Templates and Add-ins dialog box to attach a different template to the active document.

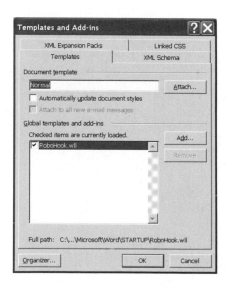

2. Click the Attach button to open the Attach Template dialog box. Select the template you want to attach and then click the Open button.

3. In the Templates And Add-Ins dialog box enable or disable Automatically Update Document Styles to copy or discard the styles from the template.

4. Click OK to attach the template.

If you update the document styles, styles in the template are added to the document's styles. If the same style name occurs in both the document and the template, the style in the template over-writes the document's style.

Finding Templates Online

Office 2003 includes a number of templates for each application, but more templates are available on the Microsoft website. New templates are regularly added to the online collection, so it's worth checking online before creating new templates—someone might have already created a template that you can use as a starting point.

To locate a template for use in a specific Office 2003 application, launch the application then choose File ➢ New. In the New task pane, enter a search term:

Then click Go to search the Microsoft Office site for templates that match your search term:

Business Plan Presentation
Templates > Management and Planning

To view the template, click the link in the Search Results task pane to open the Template Preview window, shown in Figure 15.6.

FIGURE 15.6

Preview and download templates in the Template Preview window.

If your search resulted in more than one template, use the Next and Previous buttons to move through the templates. Click the Download button to download the template.

TIP *Choose File ➤ Save As and change the Save As Type drop-down list to save the template as a template. If you don't change the type, the template is saved as a document.*

To view the entire collection of templates on the Microsoft site, click the Templates Home Page link in the New task pane. On the Templates Home Page the templates are arranged by category with featured templates posted for holidays, seasons, and important events in the business cycle. If you'd like to be informed when new templates are posted, click the Sign Up To Hear About New Templates link in the link list. Click the Suggest A Template link to post your idea about the perfect template.

Microsoft isn't the only source for Office templates. If you're looking for a specific template for Word or Excel (and might even be willing to pay for it), open your browser and search for Microsoft Office templates.

There are thousands of PowerPoint templates. Some are expensive, but a number of sites feature free templates. A few of our favorites were designed by Microsoft MVP (Most Valuable Professional) Sonia Coleman. Here's the URL for Sonia's site: `www.soniacoleman.com/templates.htm`.

Chapter 16

Constructing Forms for User Input

Forms ARE A CRITICAL means of getting and saving input from others as well as improving your own work flow. You can create forms in six different Office applications: Access, Excel, FrontPage, InfoPath, Outlook, and Word.

◆ Creating Word forms

◆ Building Excel forms

◆ Creating, saving, publishing, and distributing Outlook forms

◆ Assigning an Outlook form as the default for a folder

◆ Converting existing Outlook items to a new form

◆ Creating forms to capture user input from a web page

◆ Assigning a data source to a web page form

◆ Using the Access Form Wizard

In many cases, you'll create your forms using the form tools in the application that houses your data.

Which Application to Use?

You'll want to choose your data application carefully; part of the decision should be based on the types of forms you want to create.

NOTE *See Chapter 14, "Designing and Building Data Sources," for more information on this topic.*

There are some guidelines that will help you decide which application to use when creating forms. These guidelines are summarized in Table 16.1.

TABLE 16.1: CHOOSING A FORM CREATION APPLICATION

APPLICATION	USES
Access	Large quantities of data, any amount of relational data including data from multiple linked data sources
Excel	Forms with complex calculations that rely, for example, on Excel's financial or statistical functions
FrontPage	Web form to be filled out by visitors to your website. Data can be forwarded by e-mail or stored in a text file or database
InfoPath	Flexible, easy to use forms that export pure XML
Outlook	Customized versions of existing Outlook forms, including e-mail messages, appointments, and contacts
Word	Manual (printed) forms, forms for distribution to a wide variety of users, forms that include complex formatting, simple web forms

There are two types of forms: input forms and display forms. Input forms, the topic of this chapter, are used to gather information from a user. Display forms are used to show information on screen, much as a report is used to provide printed output.

NOTE   *The Office 2003 applications can also use forms created in Visual Basic.*

Creating Word Forms

Every organization uses forms. Here are some of the forms that have appeared on our desks in the past week:

◆ Business line of credit application

◆ Expense reimbursement form

◆ Medical insurance renewal

◆ Request for speaker information and bio

◆ Chamber of commerce directory information

The last two forms were Word documents attached to e-mail messages. Electronic forms can be a real bonus. We don't have a typewriter in our office, so paper forms need to either be scanned and converted to electronic forms (not really worth doing for most forms) or filled out by hand. However, some of the electronic forms we receive are so difficult to fill out on computer that we convert them into manual forms. We print them, put pen to the paper, then stuff the forms in envelopes. Surely this isn't what the sender intended. Here are clues that a form isn't all it could be:

◆ You must use the arrow keys or mouse to move from one blank to the next. If you press Tab, text and lines on the form move around.

♦ Unless you switch to overtype mode when you type, the blank lines move across the page to the right of the text.

♦ Switch to overtype and the line disappears where you enter text, leaving a stubby line where you haven't typed:

> Name: _Gini Courter_____
> Email: _____

♦ You can accidentally select and delete text and objects on the form.

♦ If the form includes a calculation, you have to press F9 to make Word calculate. (Or, worse yet, you have to calculate yourself and type in the answer!)

It doesn't have to be this way. In this section, we'll show you how to create a structured Word form that works—where fields stay put, lines don't disappear, and calculation happens automatically. In the second section, we'll use the FILLIN mail merge field to create a form for unstructured data.

Building the Basic Form for Structured Data

You can create electronic forms in many of the Office applications, but forms created in Word have a winning advantage over forms created in the other applications: a vastly larger number of potential users. Word is the most used office application, and might be the only application other than Solitaire that home users are comfortable with. If you're creating forms to e-mail to a diverse group of users, Word is your best bet.

Fortunately, it's easy to create forms in Word. Here are the steps:

1. Use tables to lay out the form

2. Use borders and shading to create lines and boxes for users to enter information

3. Add form controls from the Forms toolbar

4. Lock the form

5. Distribute the form

Some users assume you need Excel if your form includes formulas, but this isn't true. Word forms support basic calculation:

♦ Addition (including a SUM function)

♦ Subtraction

♦ Multiplication

♦ Division

If your form must include complex formulas (for example, a form that estimates mortgage payments), use Excel. But for simple arithmetic, Word is sufficient.

Understanding the Word Form Controls

Choose View ➤ Toolbars or right-click any toolbar to display the shortcut menu. Choose Forms to display the Forms toolbar, shown in Figure 16.1.

FIGURE 16.1

The Forms Toolbar

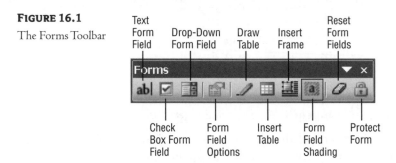

Word forms support three controls, described in Table 16.2

TABLE 16.2: THE WORD FORM CONTROLS

NAME	DESCRIPTION
Text Form Field	Text data: letters, numbers, dates
Check Box Form Field	Logical (Yes/No) data
Drop-Down Form Field	A list of text choices

A *control* is any element of an interface that a user can interact with or a developer can place, delete, move, or size: a text box, a button, a label, and so on. Labels describe other controls. Text boxes, check boxes, and drop-down form fields are data controls. Data controls are *bound* (connected) to fields in a data source or in the case of Word, *unbound*. In Word, data is stored directly in the control.

NOTE   *You'll see the term control often in this chapter and Chapter 19, "Using Macros to Do More with Office," because controls are the building blocks for both forms and reports.*

There are two sets of form controls in Word. The controls on the Forms toolbar are used to create Word forms. The ActiveX controls in the Control Toolbox are used with Visual Basic code.

Using Tables as Your Form's Foundation

Tables have two roles in forms: layout and data entry areas. Use tables as you would when creating a web page: to align form elements like text and images. Display and hide cell borders to create data entry areas in your form.

The sample form for this section began as an Excel spreadsheet used by staff and volunteers to document expenses for reimbursement. The Excel spreadsheet is shown in Figure 16.2.

FIGURE 16.2

The original form is an Excel spreadsheet.

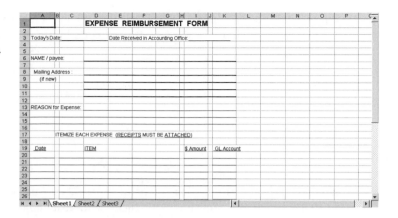

The draft expense form isn't a great form, but even if it was, this input form should be created in Word, not Excel. This organization's staff members all have Excel on their desktops, but volunteers may not be Excel users. By creating a Word form, the organization is providing an easy-to- use form that won't require staff support time.

If you're beginning with an existing form, start by analyzing the form to determine how many rows and columns are required to display the labels (text) and blanks needed in the form. As with any Word table, it's easier to add rows than columns without messing up the layout, so focus on the columns.

Include a column for each column of data or labels, as well as extra columns to provide horizontal spacing. For example, this section of the form will need seven columns: Date, a spacer, Item, a spacer, $ Amount, a spacer, and the GL Account column:

Date	ITEM	$ Amount	GL Account

Providing User Clues with Borders and Shading

After creating the tables and adjusting columns (don't forget to use the Merge Cells and Split Cells features on the Table menu!) insert extra rows for vertical spacing, then enter labels in the appropriate cells. As an example, here's the table that provides the top section of our form. We've added shading so you can see the blank rows and extra cells, inserted to provide space in the form:

Today's Date			Date Rec'd in Acct.	
Name/Payee				
check if new address	Street Address			
		City	State	Zip Code
Reason for Expense				

You need to decide how much the form should look like a table when it's printed/viewed on screen. We chose to use boxes on the top for user input, but to use an Excel-like format for the bottom section:

	ITEMIZED EXPENSES		
Check one: Receipts attached Receipts already mailed Receipts will be mailed on			
Date Incurred	**Item**	**$ Amount**	**GL Account**

You'll find all the formatting tools you need on the Tables And Borders toolbar. Click the Draw Table button on the Forms toolbar or right-click any toolbar and choose Tables And Borders to turn on the toolbar, shown in Figure 16.3.

FIGURE 16.3

The Tables And Borders toolbar is the best collection of design tools anywhere in Word.

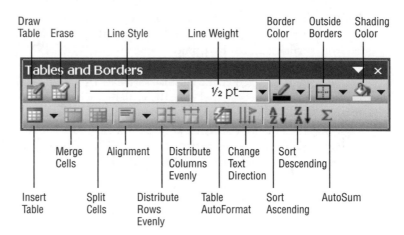

TIP   If you'd like to have the Borders and Shading buttons become floating toolbars, click the arrow to open the option from the Tables And Borders toolbar. Then, drag the sub-toolbar off the main Tables And Borders toolbar and drop it into the document window.

Apply a bottom border to provide a horizontal line for users to "type on," or border all four sides of the table cell to create a box for user input. When you have numerous cells to which you want to apply only one border (like the bottom border), remember that the shortcut to repeat the last command is Ctrl+Y. A preview of our form layout is shown in Figure 16.4.

FIGURE 16.4

This form includes four distinct areas: logo, contact info, expense lines, and a calculation area.

Adding Form Controls

You can complete all the form design before placing controls, or place them as you design each section. If the Forms toolbar isn't on, turn it on now (View ➤ Toolbars ➤ Forms).

Make sure the Form Field Shading button is enabled; when the form fields aren't shaded, they're invisible in the form.

To add a form control, position the insertion point where you want to place the control. Then click one of the three form field buttons on the Forms toolbar to place the control at the insertion point.

After placing the field, double-click the form field to open the field's Options dialog box. The Text Form Field Options dialog box is shown in Figure 16.5.

FIGURE 16.5

Use the field's Options dialog box to set the field's data type, bookmark name, and other options.

SETTING A BOOKMARK NAME AND ENABLED OPTION

You don't need to set all the options for any field. It's a good practice to enter a Bookmark name so you'll know what to call each field if you refer to it later in a formula or a macro. For example, our form contains 15 rows for expenses. Each row has four text form fields, one for the expense's date, one for item description, one for dollar amount, and one for general ledger account:

In the first row, the text form fields are named Date1, Item1, Amt1, and Acct1. Similar bookmark names are used for rows 2–15. When we need to add all the expenses in the calculation area of our form, we won't have to guess the names of the fields: they're Amt1 through Amt15.

Every form field has an Enabled option: Fill-in Enabled is the option for Text fields. The option is turned on by default. When this option is turned off, users can't enter data in the field.

Other form field options are discussed in the sections that follow.

SETTING DATA TYPE FOR TEXT FORM FIELDS

For text form fields, you'll also want to set the data type. There are six types to choose from, described in Table 16.3.

TABLE 16.3: TEXT FORM FIELD DATA TYPES

DATA TYPE	OTHER OPTIONS
Regular Text	Format as uppercase, lowercase, first capital, or title case
	Specific length or unlimited
	Default text
Number	Format number of decimals and currency or percent
	Specific number of digits or unlimited
	Default number
Date	Various date, time, and date/time formats
	Default date
Current Date	Various date formats
Current Time	Various time formats
Calculation	Formula

SETTING DROP-DOWN LIST OPTIONS

Once you create a drop-down list, you must set options or your list won't have any items to choose from! Click the Form Field Options button on the Forms toolbar or double-click the form field to open the Drop-Down Form Field Options dialog box, shown in Figure 16.6.

FIGURE 16.6

Enter the values for a drop-down list in the Drop-Down Form Field Options dialog box.

You create the list one item at a time. Type the first entry and click the Add button to add the entry to the list. Type the next entry and Add it. Use the Remove button to delete a list item; use the two Move buttons to rearrange the list.

TIP   The first item on the list is the default item. If you don't want to specify a default, enter a placeholder (see Figure 16.6) or a blank space as the first entry on the list.

After creating the list, don't forget to supply a descriptive value for the bookmark name before clicking OK to close the dialog box.

SETTING CHECK BOX OPTIONS

Check box form fields are nice and simple; you'll set three options: bookmark name, size, and default value (checked or not) in the Check Box Form Field Options dialog box, shown in Figure 16.7.

FIGURE 16.7

Set check box options in the Check Box Form Field Options dialog box.

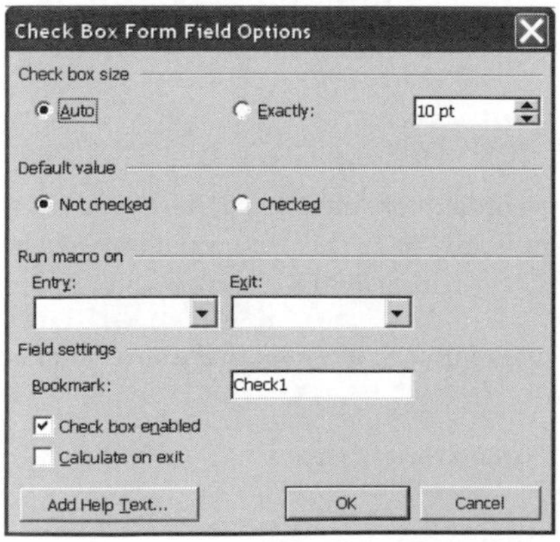

ADDING CALCULATED FIELDS

You can only "do math" with Text form fields and constants (typed-in values). You can't include drop-down list form fields in formulas.

For calculated fields, choose the Calculation data type. In the Expression text box, enter a formula using the bookmark names. For example, to add Amt1 and Amt2, enter the formula =Amt1+Amt2. The order of operations works here, so if a formula includes multiplication/division and addition/subtraction, use parentheses to indicate when addition/subtraction should occur before multiplication/division.

Enabling Calculation

After adding the calculated fields, you'll need to set the options for fields that should trigger a calculation. Open the Options dialog box and enable the Calculate On Exit check box for any field that should trigger calculation.

When the user tabs out of any field where Calculate On Exit is enabled, all calculated fields on the form are calculated. You can calculate manually at any time by pressing the F9 key.

TIPS FOR CALCULATED FIELDS

Make sure you set default values for fields used in calculations.

If you mistype any of the bookmark names, Word will display an error when you click OK to close the Options dialog box. Therefore, if you're creating a formula with a lot of calculations (in our form, adding fields Amt1 through Amt15 to calculate the Subtotal), begin by entering just a few of the bookmarks in the calculation (for example, =Amt1+Amt2+Amt3+Amt4) and closing the dialog box. If there's an error, you have a limited area to search in. Then reopen the dialog box and edit the formula, adding a few more bookmarks and operators. If there's an error this time, it's in the edited portion of the formula.

Like Excel, Word returns an error when you divide by zero. Don't enable Calculate On Exit for the number you're dividing (the dividend); enable it on the divisor (the number you're dividing by). That way, the calculation won't happen until the user has entered the divisor.

PROTECTING YOUR FORM

You must protect the form before anyone can use it. To protect the form, click the Protect Form button on the Forms toolbar. When the form is protected, users can then tab from field to field.

USING MACROS FOR FORM NAVIGATION

Let's say you want to control tab order more effectively, having your users input required fields first, and then move on to less significant fields. To do this, you must record a macro that goes to field J, and then assign that macro as an action when exiting field X. Here are the steps to record the macro:

1. If your form is locked, be sure to unlock it. Then, make sure you know the name of the field you want to go to.

2. Choose Tools ➤ Macro ➤ Record New Macro.

Continued on next page

3. Name the macro—for example, GoToFieldJ.

4. Change the Store Macro In entry to the current document.

5. Choose Edit ➢ GoTo from the menu.

6. Choose Bookmarks. Select field **J** from the list of Bookmarks.

7. Click Go To to go to the field.

8. Click the Stop button to save the macro.

Now, open the options for field X. In the Exit drop-down, choose your macro. Click OK. When you're finished, click the Protect Form button on the Forms menu again to protect your form.

Protecting Your Form from User Changes

The Protect Form button does little more than allow data entry. If you want to really protect your form, you should apply document protection, then save the form as a template. Here are the steps:

1. Choose Tools ➢ Protect Document to display the Protect Document task pane:

2. In Editing Restrictions enable the Allow Only This Type Of Editing In The Document check box.

3. Choose Filling In Forms from the drop-down list.

4. Click the Yes, Start Enforcing Protection button.

5. Type a password in the Enter New Password box, then confirm the password by typing it again. The password allows you to unprotect and modify the document.

6. Save the form as a template.

There are a number of ways to distribute your document: as an e-mail attachment, by saving it in a workgroup or personal templates folder, or by uploading or saving it on a Windows SharePoint Services site.

Creating Forms for Unstructured Data

You've probably used Word's Mail Merge feature to create personalized letters or labels by merging a data source into a main document. Mail merge includes a Fill-in field that prompts the user to enter information in a form. When you open a template, Word checks to see if it includes Fill-in fields. A dialog box opens for each field, prompting the user to enter the information to fill the field:

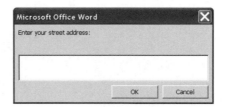

Templates using Fill-in fields are easy to create and ideal when you want to convert an existing unstructured document like a letter to include user input. You can begin with an existing document, or create a new form from scratch.

Follow these steps to insert a Fill-in field in a document:

1. Place the insertion point where you want to insert the field.

2. Choose Insert ➤ Field to open the Field dialog box, shown in Figure 16.8.

FIGURE 16.8

Use the Field dialog box to insert a Fill-in field.

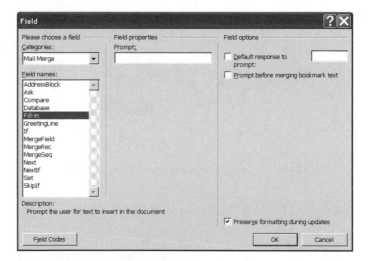

3. Choose Mail Merge from the Categories drop-down list.

4. In the Field Names list, choose Fill-in.

5. In the Prompt text box, enter the text to display to the user. For example, if you want the user to enter their address, you might type *Enter your street address:* as the prompt.

6. Optionally, you can supply a default value (for example, *United States* for a Fill-in field for Country Name). Enable the Default Response To Prompt check box, then enter the default value in the text box.

7. Click OK to close the Field dialog box and display the message window.

Follow the steps above to create all the Fill-in fields in your document. When you're finished, save the document as a template.

TIP   To view all the fields in a document, hold Alt and press F9. If you press Alt-F9 again, your fields will once again be hidden.

To test your saved template, choose File ➤ New to open the New Document task pane. In the Templates section, click the On My Computer link. Select and open the template. Word will immediately begin prompting you to enter contents for the Fill-in fields.

Fill-in isn't the only useful Word field. Table 16.4 describes other fields frequently used in document automation.

TABLE 16.4: FREQUENTLY USED FIELDS

FIELD	CATEGORY	DESCRIPTION
FileName	Document Information	Inserts the filename of the current document. Enable the Add Path To Filename option to include the path.
DocProperty	Document Information	Inserts the value of the document property (from the Properties dialog box) you specify.
Date	Date and Time	Inserts the current date in the specified format.
PrintDate	Date and Time	Inserts the date document was last printed.
SaveDate	Date and Time	Inserts the date document was last saved.
=Formula	Calculations and Formulas	Inserts the results of the formula you specify.
UserName	User Information	Inserts the user's name as specified in the Options dialog box.

There are over 100 field codes. If Word has access to information you want to enter from the Options dialog box, the Properties dialog box, or from the document (such as the current page number), there's usually a field code to insert the information in your document.

TIP   If you know the code for a field, you can type it directly in your document instead of opening the Field dialog box. Press Ctrl+F9 to insert field brackets in the document and then type the code within the brackets. If you type field codes, text (such as prompts) must be typed within a pair of quotes: for example, {FILLIN "Enter your street address:"}.

Building Forms in Excel

Excel works with built-in forms to enter data in lists and provides the tools needed to design online and paper-based forms. You'll choose a form type based on what you want to accomplish with the form, and how (or whether) the form will be distributed:

Built-in forms Valid only for a list or range, these are the forms that open when you select any cell in a list or range and choose Data ➣ Form. Data forms display one record at a time. You can't publish or distribute data forms outside Excel, and users have the habit of closing them and then not being able to open them again.

NOTE *For information on built-in forms, see Chapter 14.*

Built-in and user-designed templates Some of the Excel templates are forms—for example, the invoice and expense statement templates. Other freeform templates are available from Office Update on the Microsoft website.

User-designed forms Forms that you create using Excel form controls. User-designed forms can be used online or printed to create manual forms.

You can add web scripts to Excel forms and use your forms as part of a website. But if you're creating web forms, you should use FrontPage, which automatically creates most of the scripts that you must create manually in Excel.

Creating an Excel Form

Excel has two toolbars with form controls. The controls in the Control Toolbox are used with Visual Basic (VB). The Forms toolbar includes many of the same controls used in Word forms, and doesn't require VB. To display the Forms toolbar, right-click any toolbar and choose Forms from the list of toolbars.

Three of the controls aren't enabled: Edit Box, Combination List-Edit, and Combination Drop-Down Edit. You'll use cells as Edit boxes in Excel forms.

The sample form we'll use for this section is the order entry form shown in Figure 16.9, which uses many of the Excel form controls.

After designing your form, here are the steps you'll take to create an Excel form using the Form controls:

1. Create supporting data for list boxes and combo boxes.

2. Add labels and create formulas.

3. Unlock cells where user data will be stored.

4. Add controls and set control properties.

5. Save the form as a document or template.

Start by entering descriptive labels as you would when creating any template. Then add formulas.

FIGURE 16.9

The LogoWear
Order Entry form

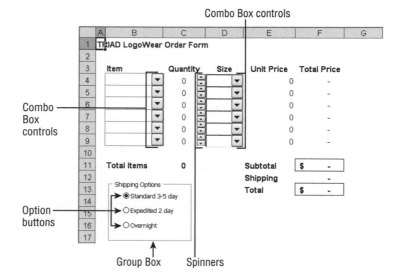

UNDERSTANDING EXCEL FORM CONTROLS

In Word forms, data that a user enters in a text box is stored in the text box. In Excel, data is always stored in one of the worksheet cells, called the control's *cell link*. In many forms, the form control is placed directly on top of the cell link. Depending on the type of control you use, Excel will store either the value selected by the user or a reference to the selection's ordinal value.

The differences in form controls have several implications for form design in Excel:

Formulas In Word, you create calculation form controls that refer to the bookmarked form controls. In Excel, you'll use regular formulas that refer to the worksheet cells. Create the formulas first, before adding the form controls (particularly if you're going to place the form controls on top of their linked cells).

Protection If you're going to lock your worksheet, you must unlock all the cells used as cell links or users won't be able to enter data in the form controls.

Data storage Some controls store the displayed data; others do not. For example, when a user chooses a Quantity using the spinner control in our form, Excel stores the number the user selected in the cell link.

In contrast, when users choose from a combo box list of items, Excel stores the item's ordinal value from the combo box list. For example, when a user chooses Navy Polo (the second item in the list) in our form, the value 2 is stored in the cell link.

If you want to take an action based on the user's choices, you need to know what value is stored. Table 16.5 lists the data stored by each control.

TABLE 16.5: EXCEL FORM CONTROLS

CONTROL TYPE	DESCRIPTION	DATA STORED IN CELL LINK
Check Box	Used for logical data (Yes/No)	TRUE if checked, FALSE if unchecked
Combo Box	Allows user to select one item from a drop-down list	Ordinal value of selection in list
Group Box	Groups option buttons for mutually exclusive choices	Ordinal value of option button selected by user
List Box	Allows user to select one or multiple items from a list	Ordinal value of single selection from the list
Option Button	Used for logical data (Yes/No)	0 if unchecked, 1 if checked (see Group Box for value if used in Group Box)
Scroll Bar	Scroll box for numeric data; typically used for a large range of numbers (for example 1–5000)	User-selected number
Spinner	List box for numeric data; typically used for a small range of integers incremented by 1 (for example 1–10)	User-selected number

Control type is dictated by the type of data you want to collect. If you're not sure which control to use, open the Print dialog box in any application and see how the controls are implemented: check boxes for yes/no choices, grouped option buttons or combo boxes for mutually exclusive choices, and so on. If you use controls in familiar ways, users will find your form easy to use.

NOTE *Button controls are used to run macros. For more information on macros and button controls, see Chapter 19.*

CREATING SUPPORTING DATA FOR TEXT CONTROLS

Every list box control, combo box control, and lookup function in your form needs a list of supporting data. We entered the supporting data for our form on a separate worksheet (named Data), which we'll hide before saving the form. The three sets of supporting data are shown in Figure 16.10.

FIGURE 16.10

Create lists of supporting data for combo box controls, list box controls, and lookup functions.

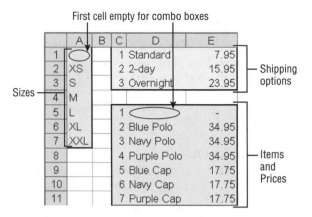

Creating Lists for Combo and List Boxes

Lookup functions are often used in forms to return a specific value based on the choice a user makes. In our sample form (see Figure 16.9) the user chooses an item from the first combo box and Excel stores the ordinal value of the user choice in the linked cell, B4. Assume that the user chooses a purple polo shirt. The value 4 will be stored in the cell linked to the combo box. If we create a table of the ordinal values, items, and prices (see Figure 16.10), we can look up the price for item 4 with a VLOOKUP function:

```
=VLOOKUP(B4,Data!$C$5:$E$11,3,FALSE)
```

For more information on lookup functions including VLOOKUP, see Chapter 13, "Building Robust and Foolproof Workbooks."

Notice that the first item (ordinal value 1) in each list is blank. The first item is the default item for a combo or list box. By including a blank item, the combo box will be "empty" until the user chooses an item (see Figure 16.9).

Creating Lists for Grouped Option Buttons

A user chooses a shipping method using the grouped option buttons. The buttons are enclosed in a group box. This changes the option buttons' behavior in two ways:

◆ Clicking one option button turns the other option buttons off.

◆ All buttons in the group use the same linked cell. The ordinal value of the button selected is stored in the cell: 1 for Standard, 2 for Expedited, and 3 for Overnight.

There is no extra "empty" item in the list of shipping options. In an option group, one of the buttons (by default, the first button) is turned on when the form opens.

The table of shipping options in Figure 16.10 is used with a VLOOKUP function to return the shipping cost based on the option selected by the user. This VLOOKUP formula uses an IF function so the formula doesn't calculate shipping until the user has selected at least one item. The total items are calculated using a simple SUM function in cell C11: =SUM(C4:C9). Here's the VLOOKUP for shipping cost from cell F12: =IF(F11>0,VLOOKUP(C12,Data!C1:E3,3,TRUE),0).

TIP   *If you're using a lot of controls and lookup functions, name each of the supporting data tables.*

ENTERING LABELS AND FORMULAS

After you've created supporting data, enter the labels, sample data, and formulas in your form. Figure 16.11 shows the form's sample data and formulas before the controls are placed.

FIGURE 16.11

Enter the labels, sample data, and formulas required by the form.

	A B	C	D	E	F
1	TRIAL				
2					
3	Item	Quantity	Size	Unit Price	Total Price
4	1	1	1	=VLOOKUP(B4,Data!$B$1:$D$7,3,FALSE)	=C4*E4
5	1	1	1	=VLOOKUP(B5,Data!$B$1:$D$7,3,FALSE)	=C5*E5
6	1	0	1	=VLOOKUP(B6,Data!$B$1:$D$7,3,FALSE)	=C6*E6
7	1	0	1	=VLOOKUP(B7,Data!$B$1:$D$7,3,FALSE)	=C7*E7
8	1	0	1	=VLOOKUP(B8,Data!$B$1:$D$7,3,FALSE)	=C8*E8
9	1	0	1	=VLOOKUP(B9,Data!$B$1:$D$7,3,FALSE)	=C9*E9
10					
11	Total	=SUM(C4:C9)		Subtotal	=SUM(F4:F9)
12		1		Shipping	=IF(F11>0,VLOOKUP(C12,Data!A11:C13,3,TRUE),0)
13				Total	=F11+F12

The sample data has one purpose: to let you check your formulas and supporting data before placing the form controls. Change the sample data and test the formulas before adding controls.

ADDING AND POSITIONING CONTROLS

To add a control to the form, click the control on the Form toolbar, then click in the spreadsheet where you'd like the control to go. You can place the control on top of the cell that contains your sample data, or move the control after setting its properties by selecting it. Once you see the four-way arrow, you can drag it anywhere you like. Combo and list boxes are usually placed on top of the linked cell. Spinners are placed at the right side of the linked cell, and the cell alignment is changed to center. (If you leave the default right alignment, the cell contents are hidden by the spinner.)

TIP   *Worksheet rows and cells are measured in points. Form controls are measured in inches or centimeters (based on the Windows system settings). When you place a new form control in the worksheet, it won't match the height/width of the cells. You can drag the control's handles to manually resize the control, but most of the controls have a minimum height that's slightly taller than the default row height. Resetting the row height (to 15 for combo boxes and 18 for list boxes) makes it easier to place these controls within a row.*

If you need several controls that are the same, create the first control then hold Ctrl and drag and drop the control to create copies.

For information on the properties of specific controls, see "Setting Control Properties" later in this section.

Creating Groups of Option Buttons

Use an option button group when the user must choose one and only one item from a list. First, place and size the group box control. To change the default text (GroupBox N), select and delete or overtype the default text.

With the group box in place, click the Option Button button on the Form toolbar and then click in the group box to place the first option button. With the option button still selected, type the label for the button. You can copy and paste the remaining buttons, or add new buttons using the Form toolbar.

SELECTING CONTROLS

When you click off a control, the control is enabled. The next time you click the control, you're using rather than editing it. To select a control to reposition it, delete it, or change its properties, either right-click the control or hold Ctrl, click the control, then release the Ctrl button.

SETTING CONTROL PROPERTIES

You must set the control properties for every control. With the first control selected, click the Control Properties button on the Form toolbar, right-click the control, and choose Format Control from the shortcut menu, or choose Format ➤ Control from the menu to open the Format Control dialog box.

Controls, like cells, are locked by default, so you don't need to change the Protection tab. Controls automatically move and size with cells; if you want to change this behavior, choose another option on the Properties tab.

Control Properties for Scroll Bars and Spinners

Scroll bar and spinner controls are used to enter numbers. The Control tab of the spinner control is shown in Figure 16.12.

FIGURE 16.12

Set the range, increment, and cell link for spinner and scroll bar controls.

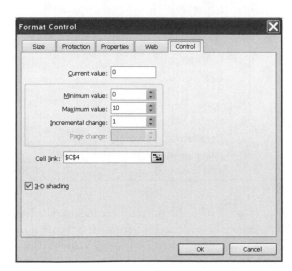

Use the spinners to set the Minimum Value, Maximum Value, and Incremental Change—how much the value should change when the user clicks the spinner once. In Figure 16.12, the spinner accepts whole numbers between 0 and 10.

Set the Cell Link to the cell where Excel should store the data from the spinner or scroll bar control. Typically, this will be the cell directly under the spinner or scroll bar control.

There are two ways to change the value in a scroll bar control: by clicking the arrows at the top and bottom to change by increments, or clicking the background of the scroll bar (behind the scroll box) to change by larger increments called pages. With a scroll box control, set the Incremental Change to the smallest interval and the Page Change to a larger number. For example, if a scroll bar is used to capture values between 1 and 100, set the Incremental Change to 1 and the Page Change to 10. Clicking either arrow moves the value by 1; clicking the scroll bar background changes the value by 10.

TIP *Form controls print by default. If you don't want a scroll box or spinner control to print, turn off the Print Object check box on the Properties tab. With the control set as non-printing, the contents of the cell under the controls are printed.*

Control Properties for Combo Boxes

Use a combo box when you want a user to choose one non-numeric item from a list. The Control properties for a combo box are shown in Figure 16.13.

FIGURE 16.13

Set the input range, cell link, and number of drop-down lines for combo boxes.

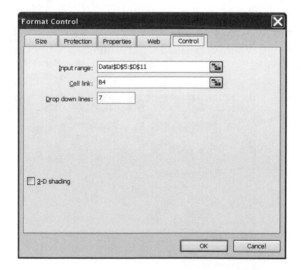

In the Input Range text box, select the cells that include the list of items for the list. In the Cell Link box, enter the single cell where Excel will store the ordinal value of the user's choice. Drop-Down Lines is the number of items that are displayed when the user clicks the drop-down arrow. If the number of cells in the Input Range is larger than the Drop-Down Lines value, the list will have a scroll bar on the right edge so users can scroll the item list:

If there are fewer items than drop-down lines, the list will open to display all the items. It will not include extra blank lines.

Control Properties for List Boxes

List boxes are used less often than combo boxes. There are a couple of reasons for this. The list doesn't open, so you must choose between creating a larger list box to show all the items and requiring the user to click the arrows to move between items. If the list's contents aren't self-evident (like Female/Male or Yes/No), the user might make a less accurate choice rather than scroll enough to see the best choice.

A list box has a scroll bar even if all items are displayed. If the list box is too large, there will be empty space below the list.

On the plus side, list boxes let the user choose more than one item, but if you allow multiple or extended selection, you must add VB code to read and deal with the choices. Excel only knows how to store the results of a single selection. If you're not using VB in your form, use list box controls when there are a limited number of choices and you want the user to be able to see all the choices and select without opening a drop-down list. The Control tab of the Format Control dialog box for a list box control is shown in Figure 16.14.

FIGURE 16.14

Choose the Single selection type to store the results in a worksheet cell.

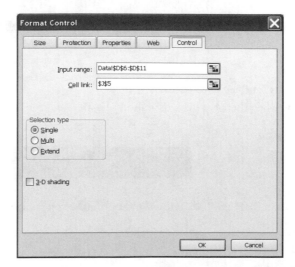

Control Properties for Option Button Groups

Option button groups are used to present a small group of mutually exclusive choices. When one button is checked on, the others are turned off:

In a group of option buttons, either one or none of the buttons can be turned on. Turn on a button to make it the default option, or set all buttons to Unchecked if there is no default option. You only need to set the options for the default button (which should also be the first button in the list). The remaining buttons will use the same Cell Link and will remain unchecked. The Control tab for one option button from a group is shown in Figure 16.15.

FIGURE 16.15

Set the options for the default button in an option button group.

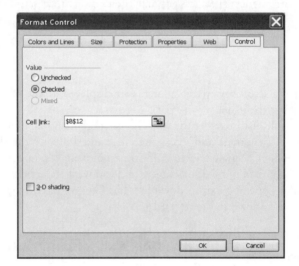

Control Properties for Check Box Controls

Use a check box when there are two possibilities: Yes or No, True or False, On or Off, Checked or Unchecked:

The Control tab for check box controls and option button controls (see Figure 16.15) is the same.

NOTE *The check box control supports a third "maybe" choice: Mixed. The user can't select Mixed; it can only be chosen as a default or set programmatically with Visual Basic. When the check box value is mixed, the N/A error code is stored in the link cell (in other words, Excel can't store the "mixed" value).*

FINISHING YOUR FORM

After setting all control properties and testing your form, you may choose to further modify your form:

◆ hide extra rows, columns, and worksheets

◆ turn off sheet tabs and column/row headings in the Options dialog box

◆ protect the form (Tools ➤ Protection ➤ Protect Worksheet) so that users can only select unlocked cells

When you're finished, save the form as a workbook or template (File ➤ Save As).

Creating Outlook Forms

Every Outlook folder is a database of items. You can look at all the items using a view, or individual items using a form.

Outlook forms and views provide an easy way to create personal applications. You can customize forms to include fields that are part of an item, but not reflected in the form. Most forms have extra tabs that are hidden; you can display the hidden tabs and add controls for existing data or new fields that you add to the folder. If your organization also uses Microsoft Exchange Server, you can create entire groupware applications using Outlook forms, views, and Exchange public folders.

Whether you're creating an application for yourself or your entire workgroup, here are the steps you'll follow to create your application:

1. Choose the form you want to customize.

2. Customize the form.

3. Publish the form in the appropriate folder.

4. Set the form as the folder's default form.

Choosing a Form to Customize

There are two broad types of applications created using Outlook forms: folder-based applications, and routing applications. With a folder-based application, users complete a form and save it (post it) to a specific folder. Routing applications send and receive e-mail messages.

Custom forms are created by modifying one of the existing Outlook forms. Choose the form to customize based on the kind of application you want to create. Table 16.6 lists the default Outlook forms and their uses.

TABLE 16.6: OUTLOOK FORMS AND USES

DEFAULT FORM	APPLICATION TYPE	USES
Message	Routing	Container to send or receive user information
Contact	Folder	Track contact information
Post	Folder	Store requests or conversations in a public folder
Task	Folder	Assign and track task information
Appointment	Folder	Set meetings and events
Distribution List	Support for other applications	Alias for a list of contacts and their e-mail addresses
Journal Entry	Support, Folder applications	Log activities about other items
Meeting Request	Routing	Hidden form used to create a meeting
Task Request	Routing	Hidden form used for task assignment
Note	N/A	Cannot be customized

Use what you already know about the default Outlook forms to choose the form that will serve as the basis of your custom form. If your application will send and receive e-mail, use a message form. If you're tracking information about people, start with a contract form; for activities, use a task form. If the primary goal is to have users post information about parts or services in a public folder, use a post form.

We're going to create a customized Contact form that is used to track membership information. For our example, we'll post and test forms locally.

TIP   After customizing, publishing, and testing a form locally, talk with your Exchange administrator to publish the form so that your coworkers can use the form.

Here are the steps we'll follow to create our form:

1. Create a new folder for items created using the form.

2. Open the default form in design mode.

3. Modify the form by hiding/showing pages and adding/removing controls.

4. Publish the form.

5. Set the new form as the default for the folder.

Creating the Customized Membership Application

To create the membership form, we'll add some existing fields and new fields to an extra page in the default contacts form. The customized Member Info page is shown in Figure 16.16.

FIGURE 16.16

The Member Info page is customized by adding fields and setting field properties.

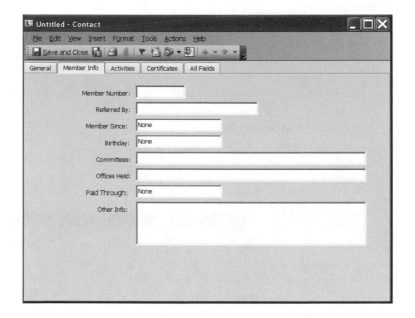

CREATING A MEMBERS FOLDER

The membership form won't be used for all our contacts—just for the contacts who are members of our organization. We'll still use the default form for contacts in other folders. While you can choose Tools ➢ Forms ➢ Choose Form from the Outlook menu and select any appropriate form to create an item, it's easier to separate items that use a specific form by placing them in a separate folder. We'll begin, then, by clicking the Contacts folder and creating a new Members folder as a subfolder of the Contacts folder:

1. Right-click the Contacts folder and choose New Folder from the shortcut menu to open the Create New Folder dialog box:

2. In the Name text box, type **Members** as the name for the folder.

3 In the Folder Contains box, choose Contact Items.

4. Click OK.

Outlook creates a new folder and assigns IPM.Contact as the folder's default form.

CREATING THE MEMBERS FORM

Switch to the Members folder. To open the default form, choose File ➤ New ➤ Contact from the main Outlook menu to open a new form. Choose Tools ➤ Forms ➤ Design This Form to open the Design Form dialog box shown in Figure 16.17.

FIGURE 16.17

The Advanced information includes the form's message class

Select the Contact form and click Open to open the form and display the form and the Field Chooser, as shown in Figure 16.18.

Some forms have pages that can't be modified. You can hide the page, but it can't be changed. To quickly see if a page can be edited, click the page tab then check the Control Toolbox button on the form's Standard toolbar. If the button is enabled, the page can be edited. (Most editable pages also have a grid.) Table 16.7 indicates whether the default pages of forms can be customized.

FIGURE 16.18

The Contact form in design view with the Field Chooser.

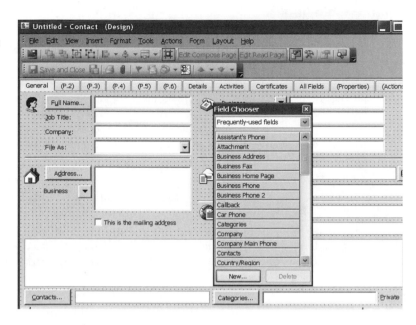

TABLE 16.7: FORMS AND CUSTOMIZABLE PAGES

FORM	DEFAULT PAGES CUSTOMIZABLE?
Appointment	No
Contact	General page only
Distribution List	No
Meeting Request	No
Message	Yes
Post	Yes
Task	No
Task Request	No

Displaying a Hidden Page

As you can see in Figure 16.18, the Contact form includes extra pages labeled (P.2), (P.3), and so on. When a page tab's label is enclosed in parentheses, the page is hidden. We want to add controls to a new page. Select page 2 (P.2) and choose Form ➢ Display This Page from the form menu to unhide page 2.

Hiding a Default Page

If a default page can't be customized (such as the Details page) and you don't want to include it in your custom form, hide the page. To hide the Details page, select the page then choose Form ➤ Display This Page to turn off the checkmark.

Renaming a Page

Select P.2. Choose Form ➤ Rename Page to open the Rename Page dialog box. Enter a name to display on the page tab (*Member Info*) and click OK to rename the page.

Adding Field Controls to the Form

The Field Chooser opens with the list of frequently used fields for this form type. To view other field lists, click the drop-down arrow at the top of the Field Chooser and select the field list you wish to use. We want to add several fields that are used in Contacts, so choose the All Contacts fields category. Drag the following fields from the Field Chooser onto the Member Info page of the form as shown below: Organizational ID Number, Anniversary, Birthday, Referred By.

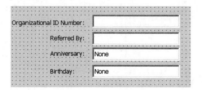

When you drop a field from the Field Chooser into the form, Outlook adds two controls: a label and a text box. The text box is bound to the data field you dragged from the Field Chooser. Later in this section we'll change the labels for Organizational ID Number to Member Number and Anniversary to Member Since, but the text box controls will still be bound to the original fields.

We need four more fields that don't already exist in the list of All Contact Fields. To create a new field, click the New button at the bottom of the Field Chooser to open the Field Properties dialog box. Enter the field's name, data type, and data format, and then click OK to create the field and add it to the list of User-Defined Fields In This Folder. Create these four fields:

Field Name	Type	Format
Committees	Text	Text
Offices Held	Text	Text
Paid Through	Date/Time	Short Date (ex: 11/30/2003)
Other Info	Text	Text

Drag each of the fields from the Field Chooser and place them on the Member Info page. Place fields in the order you want them to appear in the form.

TIP   *Outlook includes four placeholder fields named UserField1, UserField2, UserField3, and UserField4 in the* Contacts *folder. You can use these fields for any purpose, but you might want to save them for something special. Some handheld devices will automatically synchronize the contents of these four fields, but will not synchronize user-defined fields.*

Positioning and Sizing Controls

Click a control once to select it. To select multiple controls, either hold Ctrl and click each control you wish to select, or hold Shift and select the first and last control. Or, hold the mouse button and drag a rectangle around the controls you want to select. Drag selected controls to move them.

 To align controls, select two or more controls and then choose the appropriate alignment from the drop-down menus on the Align buttons on the toolbar. To resize controls, select two or more controls, then click the down-arrow on the Make Same button and choose Height, Width, or Both.

To adjust the space between controls, select the controls, then choose Layout ➤ Horizontal Spacing or Layout ➤ Vertical Spacing and select a command from the menu.

Previewing the Form

Choose Form ➤ Run This Form to preview the form. (Tab through the controls if you wish.) Close the form without saving to return to design view.

Setting Field Properties

If you tabbed through the fields, you might have noticed that the Anniversary and Birthday fields are plain text boxes, not the calendar control that appears in the default contact form IPM.Contact. The calendar control used in the default form isn't available when you customize a form, so Outlook simply uses a text box.

 The date format used in the calendar control is the verbose date format. If a user enters 11/11/2003, the control will display November 11, 2003. To change the format (or the format for any other control), you modify the field properties.

The Other Info text box will be used for comments, so it should be a larger text box that support multiple lines of text. Select the Other Info text box control, then click the Properties button to open the Properties dialog box, shown in Figure 16.19.

FIGURE 16.19

Change field settings in the control's Properties dialog box.

On the Display page, enable the Multi-line check box and click OK to change the property for the Other Info field. Now drag the text box sizing handles to make the box wider and taller:

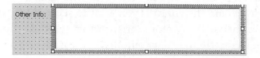

To edit a label control, select the label, open the Properties dialog box, and edit the Caption property (see Figure 16.19).

We made the following change to the properties and sizes of the form controls:

Control	Property	Change
Organizational ID Label	Caption	Member Number:
Anniversary Label	Caption	Member Since:
Referred By		Widen text box
Committees		Widen text box
Offices Held		Widen text box

Validating Data Entry

Validation properties restrict the data that must be entered in a control. Our organization has a business rule that states, "Every member must be assigned a member number before they can be entered in the database." We can use validation to enforce the rule. To validate the member number field, select the Organizational ID Number field and click the Properties button to open the Properties dialog box. On the Validation page, shown in Figure 16.20, enable the A Value Is Required For This Field check box. Click OK to apply the validation and close the dialog box.

FIGURE 16.20

Use Validation to require users to provide data in specific fields.

```
Properties                                    ☒
 Display │ Value │ Validation

  ☑ A value is required for this field

  ☐ Validate this field before closing the form
    Validation Formula:
    [                              ]  [ Edit... ]
    Display this message if the validation fails:
    [                              ]  [ Edit... ]

  ☐ Include this field for Printing and Save As




              [  OK  ] [ Cancel ] [ Apply ]
```

You can also create validation formulas so that users can enter only those values that fall within a specific range. For example, the Anniversary date entered should not be later than today. The validation formula to ensure the date is less than or equal to the current date is shown in Figure 16.21.

FIGURE 16.21

Create validation formulas to check the value entered by the user.

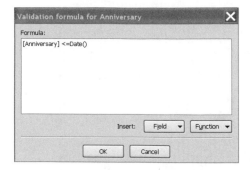

To create the formula:

1. Select the field you want to validate (Anniversary).

2. Click the Properties button on the toolbar.

3. On the Validation page, click the Edit button next to the Validation Formula text box to open the Validation Formula for Anniversary dialog box (see Figure 16.21).

4. Click the Field button.

5. Choose All Contact Fields.

6. Select Anniversary from the list of fields.

7. Type <=

8. Click the Function button. Choose Date/Time from the list of categories.

9. Choose Date() from the list.

10. Click OK to save the formula and return to the Properties dialog box.

Use the second text box on the Validation page to display a message when incorrect data is entered. The validation formula and validation message are shown in Figure 16.22. After entering the message, click OK to save the property settings and close the dialog box.

FIGURE 16.22

Enter a validation message to provide feedback when users enter invalid data.

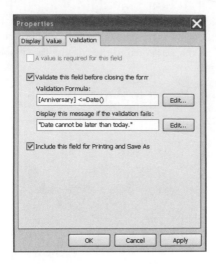

NOTE   *Outlook's Date( ) function retrieves today's date from Windows. The Now( ) function retrieves the current date and time.*

Choose Form ➤ Run This Form once more and check the form's design before publishing the form.

PUBLISHING THE FORM

When you publish a form, it is saved as part of the e-mail system, not as part of the Windows file system. Before publishing your form, it's smart to save your form as a template in the Windows file system. If there's a problem during publishing, you can open the template and publish again. And if someone else likes your form, you can send them the template and they can publish it on their computer.

Saving the Form as a Template

To save your form as a template:

1. Choose File ➤ Save As from the menu.

2. In the Save As Type drop-down, choose Outlook Template (*.OFT)

3. Enter a name for the template.

4. Click Save.

Publishing the Form in a Form Library

You can't use your form in Outlook until you publish it in a form library. To publish the form, make sure you're still in form design view and follow these steps:

1. Click the Publish Form button or choose Tools ➤ Forms > Publish Form As to open the Publish Form As dialog box shown in Figure 16.23.

FIGURE 16.23

Use the Publish Form As dialog box to save the form in a form library.

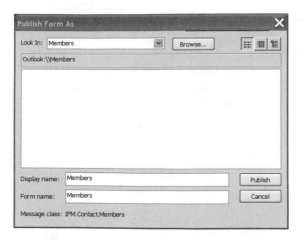

2. Choose a form library from the Look In drop-down list. This form will be used in the Members folder created earlier, so choose the Members folder as the location.

3. Enter a Display Name for the form. If the Display Name has spaces, it's a good idea to remove the spaces from the text in the Form Name text box.

4. Click Publish to publish the form.

5. Close the form. When prompted to save, do **not** save. (You're being prompted to save the item, not the form.)

Assigning an Outlook Form as the Folder Default

There's one more step to take so that new items created in the Members folder use the Members form: assigning the Members form as the folder's default form. Follow these steps:

1. In the Outlook Folders list or the My Contacts list, locate the Members folder. Right-click the folder and choose Properties from the shortcut menu to open the Members Properties dialog box.

2. On the Forms tab, you'll see the Members form is listed in the Forms Associated With This Folder list.

3. On the General tab, shown in Figure 16.24, choose Members from the When Posting To This Folder Use drop-down list.

FIGURE 16.24

Choose your new form as the default form for posts to the Members folder.

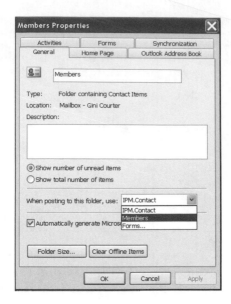

4. Click OK to close the Properties dialog box.

In the Members folder, double-click in the Information Viewer, choose File ➤ New Contact, or choose Actions ➤ New Member to open your customized form and enter a new member.

TROUBLESHOOTING FORM PUBLISHING AND PERMISSIONS

You must have Owner, Editor, or Publishing Editor permissions to add forms to a folder. You're the owner of all folders created in your mailbox, so you can create all the forms you want for your own use. If another user wants one of your forms, you can e-mail the template to that user. They would then open the template in design view, publish the template in one of the folders in their mailbox, and set the folder default to the new form.

Workgroup applications are usually created in public folders rather than user mailboxes. You'll follow the same steps to create and publish forms in public folders, but you must have adequate permissions. If you want to publish a form for use in a public folder, talk to your Exchange Administrator.

Changing Items' Message Class

Every item contains a message class field that stores the name of the form that Outlook uses to display the item. The message class for all Outlook items begins with IPM. The message class is assigned when an item is created. For example, a contact created with the default form uses the message class IPM.Contact. The custom Member form was based on the Contact form, so the internal name for the form is IPM.Contact.Member.

CONVERTING ITEMS BASED ON A CUSTOMIZED FORM

If you need to modify a custom form after it has been published and used to create items, follow these steps to change the message class of the existing items in the folder:

1. Open a blank item using the existing form.

2. Modify the form.

3. Republish the form with the same name.

All items in the folder that used the old form will now use the new form.

CONVERTING EXISTING ITEMS BASED ON A DEFAULT FORM

Sometimes you don't realize you need a custom form until you've created a lot of items using the default Outlook form. The existing items are based, for example, on IPM.Contact, not on the new form IPM.Contact.Member. Your new items, however, will be based on the IPM.Contact.Member. Don't delete and reenter the items using the new form—there's an easier solution.

For every version of Outlook, Microsoft provides a Word document with a set of macros that will change the message class of existing items to a new message class that you specify. To download the document, follow these steps:

1. In your browser, go to www.microsoft.com.

2. In the search box, enter **201089** to search for Knowledge Base Article 201089: Word Document to Change Message Class of Outlook Items.

3. Follow the instructions in the article to download and use the file.

Creating Access Forms

Access forms let users enter or view data without needing to know how the database tables are designed or related. A form doesn't need to include all of a table's fields, so the form may omit fields where users can't enter data, such as AutoNumber fields. A form can include data from multiple tables, providing one-stop data entry. You can design the form so that it looks just like a physical document that serves as the source document—a membership application, a customer data form, or another document used to collect data—to make it easier for users to enter data correctly. Access provides three form-creation methods: AutoForms, the Form Wizard, and form Design view.

We'll use the Northwind database for illustrations in this chapter so you can play along. Northwind.mdb is the sample database included with Office System 2003. To open the database, choose Help ➤ Sample Databases ➤ Northwind Sample Database from the Access menu. You'll get a security warning here, but go ahead and click Open. The database opens with a "splash screen" form with a picture of a lighthouse. Click the OK button to close the splash screen. Click the Close button the Main Switchboard form to close the switchboard and display the database window.

NOTE *If the database is not installed, you'll be prompted to install it. You will need your Office System 2003 CDs to complete the installation.*

Selecting a Form Layout

Most data entry forms are based on one of three layouts: datasheet, tabular, or columnar. Figure 16.25 shows a datasheet form for the Customers table. The datasheet form layout looks just like the table's Datasheet view, right down to the navigation buttons. Users can rearrange the columns and rows using drag and drop as they would in the table's Datasheet view. Using this form is a lot like working in an Excel worksheet: the arrow keys move the cursor between fields and records, and PgUp and PgDn scroll screen by screen.

FIGURE 16.25

A datasheet form resembles the table's Datasheet view.

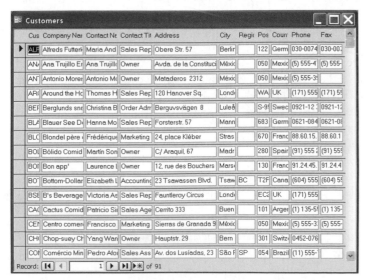

A tabular form for the Customers table is shown in Figure 16.26. Like the datasheet form, the tabular form presents multiple records. However, the form itself looks a bit more polished, and movement within the form is limited. Tab and Enter allow you to move from field to field within each record and from the last field in one record to the first field in the next record. You'll use the navigation buttons at the bottom of the form, not the arrow keys, to navigate between records.

FIGURE 16.26

A tabular form is a more polished version of the datasheet form.

A columnar form, like the form shown in Figure 16.27, displays one record at a time. If the primary purpose of a form is data entry or editing, a columnar form is best. Click the navigation buttons to move between records or enter a new record.

FIGURE 16.27

Columnar forms display one record at a time.

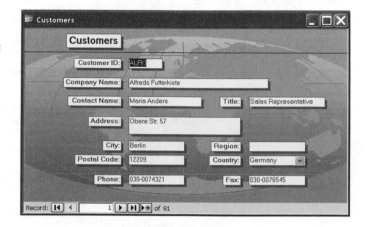

Both the tabular and datasheet forms display multiple records. A common use for a datasheet or tabular form is as a subform: a form within another form. For example, the Northwind Customer Orders form is a columnar form that includes two datasheet subforms, as shown in Figure 16.28. A form and subforms are used to display data from a primary table (Customers) and related tables (Orders and Order Details).

FIGURE 16.28

This form displays data from three tables. The columnar form displays customer data; the datasheet subforms display orders and order details from related tables.

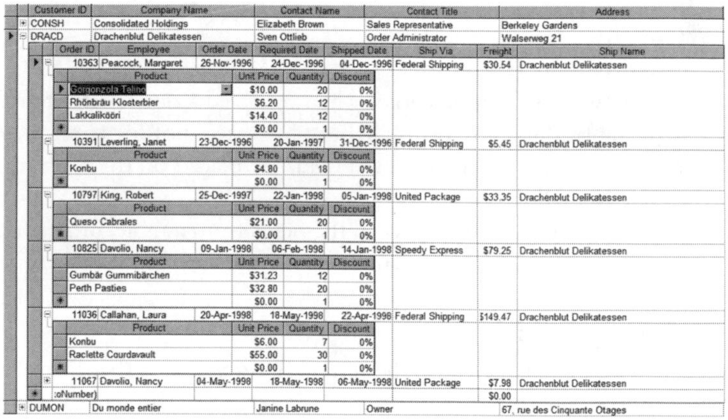

Tabular and columnar forms display each data field in a *text box control*: an editable area on a form that is bound to a field in a table. To move to the next record in a form, tab out of the last text box control for the current record, or simply press Ctrl+Page Down. In all forms, you can use the navigation buttons to move between existing records and use the Delete Record button on the toolbar to delete the current record or selected records.

Creating AutoForms

AutoForms are quick, no-frills forms created with a few clicks on the Access toolbars. AutoForms are based on a single table or query. You select the table or query and choose a layout, and Access creates the form. To create an AutoForm:

1. Select a table in the Database Window.

2. Choose Insert ➢ Form from the menu.

3. To create a columnar form, choose AutoForm: Columnar (you can create any type of form you require that's listed, of course).

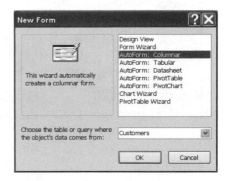

4. Choose the source table or query.

5. Click OK to create and display the form.

NOTE   *When you close the form, you are prompted to save it.*

AutoForms are a good choice when you need a quick form that includes all the information from a single table. But AutoForms are built for speed, not for comfort: AutoForms are labeled with field names rather than captions; all the fields are placed on the form in the order in which they appear in the table.

If you don't want to display all the fields from a table, or if you need data from multiple tables, use the Form Wizard or Design view to create your form.

Printing Forms

Forms print as displayed on the screen. But don't click that Print button yet! When you click the Print toolbar button, Access prints every record in the active record set—in this case, that's your entire database. If the form is a columnar form, each record prints on a separate page; this can amount to a lot of dead trees.

NOTE   *Access reports are designed for printed output, so they provide many more options for printing single or multiple records.*

To print the current record or selected records, displayed in a table's Datasheet view or in a tabular form, use the mouse to select the records you want to print. Choose File ➢ Print from the menu bar to open the Print dialog box, choose Selected Record(s) under Print Range, and click OK.

PRINTING FORMS TO FILL IN OFFLINE

One reason to print a form is to create a blank form that you can distribute to others so they can fill it out by hand. To print a blank form, open the form and display a new record (choose Records ➤ Data Entry from the menu or click the New Record button on the navigation bar). If you print a totally blank record, the text boxes do not appear. Type a space or period in one field so that the record is not blank, and choose File ➤ Print Preview to preview and print the form. (If the underlying table has other data entry requirements, you'll have to meet those before you can print the record.)

Creating Forms for Multiple Tables

Users rarely get to work with one table at a time. Customers don't call to set up a new account and then call later in the day to place their first order. Forms based on multiple tables are necessary to support the kinds of data entry users require. The person who takes an order needs to be able to set up the account and take an order, all at one time. When you base a form on multiple tables, the result is two forms: one form (a *subform*) nested within another form (the *main form*), or a main form with a button that opens the related form. Use the Form Wizard to create forms that display data from related tables—the *related* part is important, because if there isn't a relationship between two tables, you can't relate them in a form.

TROUBLESHOOTING DATABASE RELATIONSHIPS

If you're not familiar with table relationships, open the Northwind database and choose Tools ➤ Relationships to open the Relationships window. Then choose Relationships ➤ Show All from the menu to display all the relationships in the database. Relationships are the lines that link a field in one table to the corresponding field in another table. The Northwind database has all the appropriate relationships so you can easily create forms and reports that return data from two separate tables: for example, Suppliers and Products, or Customers and Orders.

Before creating multi-table forms and reports in any database, it's a good practice to verify the relationships. If there are no relationships (or very few relationships), there are two possible reasons. It could be that the tables don't really reside in Access, but are stored in SQL Server—an increasingly common scenario, particularly for large databases—or another data source like Excel. In the Tables list in the Database Window, tables that are linked from other data sources have an arrow in front of the icon from the external data source.

The second possibility is that the tables are in Access, but the person who designed the database didn't create the relationships.

In either case, talk with the database designer to get some guidance before creating forms. You can create queries to link related tables. This works well for reports, but can be tricky for forms. If you plan on creating a lot of forms or reports, it's best to have the designer relate the tables using the Relationships window in Access.

UNDERSTANDING MULTIPLE TABLES, FORMS, AND SUBFORMS

When you create a form with fields from more than one table, the Form Wizard prompts you to select either a single form or a form and a subform. The choice depends on the use for the form. If you select the Customers and Orders tables in the Northwind database, switching between By Customers and By Orders changes the sample in the Form Wizard. Figure 16.29 shows the sample form when By Customers is selected; it's a main form that shows one customer at a time with a subform that shows all the orders a specific customer has placed.

NOTE   The Customers and Orders tables have a one-to-many relationship: one customer can place many orders, but each order has only one customer.

If the main form contains many fields, if there are a lot of records in the subform, or if the data in the related table is used infrequently, choose the Linked Forms option to display the subform as a linked form, as shown in Figure 16.30. The main form contains a button that opens the linked subform.

FIGURE 16.29

Multiple-table form arranged by Customers (the primary table)

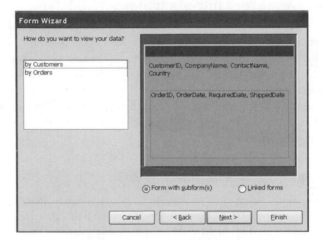

FIGURE 16.30

To ease crowding in the main form, create a linked subform.

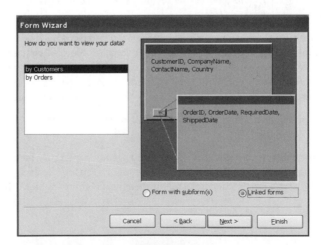

The sample form arranged By Orders is shown in Figure 16.31. When the primary focus of the form is the table that contains many records (Orders) rather than Customers, there is no subform. Each order was placed by one customer, so there is no need for a subform to display multiple customers for a single order.

FIGURE 16.31
Determine how you'd like to view your data in this screen.

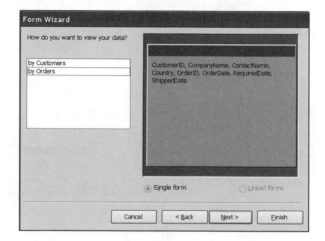

Create forms for a single table with the Form Wizard if you want to omit fields or ensure that the form is labeled with captions rather than field names. When you're creating forms for multiple tables, the Form Wizard is the best tool. While creating the forms, the wizard sets the form properties so that users cannot make changes—such as deleting a linked record—that would violate relationships between the tables.

You can create forms with data from multiple tables in Design view, but it's tedious and time-consuming. If you're interested in efficiency, start every form by using either the Form Wizard or an AutoForm, and then modify the form in Design view. Very few forms (most of them very complex) can be created more quickly when you work solely in Design view.

Creating Forms with the Form Wizard

To create a form with the Form Wizard, follow these steps:

1. Select the Forms tab in the Database window and click the New button, or choose Form from the drop-down menu on the New Object toolbar button to open the New Form dialog box.

2. Choose Form Wizard and click OK to open the Form Wizard. Click Next.

3. Select one of the tables you want to use in the Tables/Queries drop-down list (tables are listed first, followed by queries).

4. In the Available Fields list, double-click the fields to include, or use the pick buttons to move fields, in order, to the Selected Fields list:

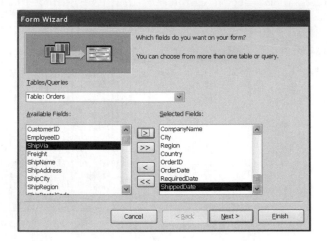

5. If your form will have data from more than one table, select a related table from the Tables/Queries drop-down list.

6. Select the fields to include from the related table.

7. Repeat steps 5 and 6 until all fields are selected. Click the Next button.

8. In the next step of the wizard, select how you want to view your data. If the tables have a one-to-many relationship, you are asked how you want to view your data—which table should be the primary focus. If you select By [*primary table*], set the Form With Subform(s) or Linked Forms option. Click Next.

NOTE   *If you choose fields from unrelated tables, the Form Wizard displays an error message. Close the wizard, set the relationships (Tools ➤ Relationships), and start the Form Wizard again.*

9. If the form includes a subform, choose the Tabular or Datasheet format. Click Next.

10. Select a style for the main form; Standard is recommended. Click Next.

11. Enter names for the form (and the subform if you created one). Click Finish to create the form(s).

Modifying Access Form Design

The forms created with the Form Wizard have limited visual appeal. Fortunately Access includes many tools for modifying a form's design. To switch to Design view in an open form, click the Design View button on the Database toolbar. To display a form in Design view, select the form in the Database window and click the Design button on the toolbar. The form in Figure 16.32 is shown in Design view.

TIP   You spend a lot of time switching between Design view and Form view as you're working in Access. Use Ctrl+>
and Ctrl+< to toggle between Form view and Design view.

FIGURE 16.32

A form and subform
in Design view with
the Field List and
Toolbox toolbar
displayed.

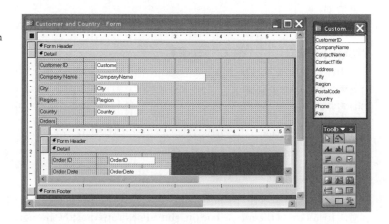

The Design View window includes horizontal and vertical rulers, Form Design, Formatting, and
Toolbox toolbars, and the Field List. The Toolbox button includes tools to add controls to the form.
If the Toolbox doesn't appear when you open a form in Design view, click the Toolbox button on the
Form Design toolbar.

In Design view, a form includes several sections and a number of different controls. The sections are:

Form Header   Appears at the beginning of the first page of the form and is usually used for titles.

Form Footer   Appears at the end of the last page of the form and is used for user tips or other
miscellaneous information.

Page Header   Is used for printing information at the top of every page in a form.

Page Footer   Is used for printing information at the bottom of every page in a form.

Detail Section   Displays a record's data.

The form shown previously in Figure 16.32 doesn't have Page Headers and Footers, so those sections
don't display by default. If the Form or Page Header and Form Footer bars aren't visible and you
want to use these sections, choose View ➤ Form Header/Footer or View ➤ Page Header/Footer
from the menu bar to display them. The Detail section includes the form background and controls,
including text boxes that display table data and labels, and the caption or field name from the table.
In tabular and datasheet forms, labels appear in the Form Header section, and text boxes appear
below the labels in the Detail section.

If you want to rearrange a form, it's easiest to begin by enlarging the form's area. Move the mouse
pointer to the bottom of the Detail section, just above the Form Footer. When the pointer changes
to an adjustment tool, drag the Footer bar down to increase the height of the Detail area. To increase
the Header section, drag the Detail bar down to make the Header area larger. Adjust the form width
by dragging the right edge of the form.

TIP   The Design View window includes an extra toolbar and rulers that aren't displayed in Form view, so you can't precisely resize the Form View window with the mouse. To resize the Form View window after you finish working in Design view, switch to Form view, make sure the form window is not maximized, and then choose Window ➤ Size To Fit Form from the menu.

Working with Form Controls

To select a control, click it. Handles indicate the control is selected. If you click a control that's already selected, the insertion point appears inside the control so that you can edit text in the control. To reselect the control, click anywhere outside the control and then click the control again.

NOTE   In Access, controls that display data, such as text boxes and check boxes, are bound (directly tied) to fields in the underlying table; labels are just text on the form and are unbound.

To select multiple controls:

◆ Move the pointer to either ruler bar. The pointer changes to a bold arrow pointing toward the form. Press the mouse button, and a line drops directly through the form. Drag along the ruler to select controls within a vertical or horizontal area. When you release the button, all the controls that the line passed through are selected.

◆ If the controls you want to select aren't grouped together, you can select one control and hold the Shift key while selecting additional control(s).

◆ Starting outside any control, drag a rectangle over the controls you wish to select. Hold Shift and click to unselect controls that you don't want to include in the selection.

TIP   To specify whether you need to touch or enclose controls to select them, choose Tools ➤ Options to open the Options dialog box. On the Forms/Reports page, choose Partially Enclosed (the default setting) for the touch method, or Fully Enclosed to select only those controls completely included in the rectangle.

Delete selected controls by pressing the Delete key on the keyboard.

MOVING AND SIZING CONTROLS

To move a control, first select it; then move the pointer to an edge of the selected object, being sure not to point directly at any of the resizing handles. The pointer changes shape to a small hand. Hold the mouse button and drag the object to its new location. If you move an object beyond the bottom or right edge of the form, the form area increases.

When you select certain Access controls—text boxes, check boxes, and option buttons—the corresponding label control is also selected. Point to the edge of the text box (not on a handle) to see the Hand pointer. Move the text box *and* the label by dragging the Hand. To move one control but not the other, point to the move handle on the upper-left corner of the text box or label control. The pointer changes to a finger pointing at the move handle. Drag the control to move it.

TIP   When you click to select a text box, the corresponding label is only partially selected. It moves with the text box, but if you change the format of the text box, the label format does not change. To format the label, you must select it.

Adjust the size of controls by dragging the resizing handles at the corners and sides of the object. Changing the size of a text box control does not change the size of its underlying field. To change field size, you must go to the table's Design view and change the field size properties.

TIP   For extra precision, select a control and use Shift+arrow keys to resize and Ctrl+arrow keys to move the control.

Adding and Formatting Labels and Controls

You can place and format labels in any section of a form. All labels can be edited and formatted with impunity. Click on a selected label to edit the text in the label.

WARNING   Don't change the field name that appears in a text box control. You'll break the binding between the control and its underlying field, and data from the table won't appear in that control. If you're not sure whether a control is a text box or a label, right-click the control and choose Properties. The control type appears in the property sheet title bar.

ADDING A TITLE

The Form Header section is generally used for a form title. Use the Toolbox Label tool to create a title. In the Toolbox, click the Label tool; when you move the pointer back into the design area, it changes to a large letter *A* with crosshairs. Move the pointer into the header area, click where you want to place the label, and type the label text. When you are done entering text, click elsewhere in the form to close the label control. Then you can select the control and use the Formatting toolbar to format the title.

TIP   If you make a mistake, you can click the Undo button to reverse your last action. You can click the button more than once to reverse several actions.

FORMATTING TEXT

Select one or more controls and then choose Properties from the Formatting toolbar, or right-click on the control(s) and select Properties from the shortcut menu.

Font/Fore Color is the color used for text. Some colors, such as dark blue, make an attractive form that is easy to read. Other colors, such as yellow, are very hard to read and should be used sparingly, unless you make the background dark and contrasting (which is itself a bad idea).

The Fill/Back Color is the color for the fill behind the text. The default for labels is transparent, which means the color from the form background appears as the label's background color. The default background color for text boxes is white.

To change the appearance of text, select the controls that contain the text you want to change (to save time, you can select and format several controls at once). Use the Font, Font Size, Weight And Style, Alignment, and Color buttons on the Formatting toolbar to format the selected controls.

TIP   A form that's cluttered can be hard to use. Separate your forms into individual pages or use graphic lines and rectangles to segment the form visually to make your forms easy to use. Use the Page Break, Line, and Rectangle controls in the Toolbox to insert page breaks, lines, or rectangles.

CHANGING BORDERS

Every Access control has a border. Borders have three properties: color, line width, and special effect. Although you can't delete the border, you can effectively disable all three properties by choosing Transparent from the Line/Border Color button menu. (This is effective for labels, but text boxes should have borders so that users know where to enter data.)

TIP The brief history of PCs is littered with obsolete applications that were functional but made their users feel stupid. Keeping your form design close to the Windows standards makes it easier to use, which helps your users feel reasonably smart. If you're not sure how a control should be formatted, look at any Office dialog box (Print, Save As, Open) for guidance.

Change the border width using the Line/Border Width button on the Formatting toolbar, selecting widths from a hairline thickness to a 6-point width. Typically, a 1- or 2-point border is appropriate for a text box control, but thicker borders can be used for titles and graphic design.

Border effects differentiate types of controls and draw the user's attention to important controls. The six special effects you can access from the Special Effects button's drop-down list are:

Flat   Appropriate for controls, such as labels, that are not used for data entry.

Sunken   The best choice for text boxes, for editing or entering data.

Shadowed   A good choice for titles.

Raised   Another useful choice for data entry or titles, or to draw attention to a part of the screen.

Etched   The standard choice for text boxes that cannot be changed.

Chiseled   Good for titles. It applies a single inverted line underneath the control.

When you apply the Sunken, Raised, Etched, or Chiseled effects, you turn off any other choices for border color and line width. Only Flat and Shadowed are affected by the border-color and line-width formatting options.

Changing several controls one by one can be a time-consuming task. Use the Format Painter to paint all the formatting—color, borders, special effects, and alignment—from one control onto another. Just follow these steps to do so:

1. Format one control so that it appears as you want it.

2. Select the formatted control.

3. Click the Format Painter.

4. Click an unformatted control. The formatting from the selected control is immediately copied to the second control.

If you're going to apply the selected format to more than one other control, double-click the Format Painter button to lock it on. Click it again to turn it off.

NOTE For information on formatting controls based on the value displayed in the control, see Chapter 19.

Relative Sizing and Alignment

A form's background has a grid of horizontal and vertical guidelines and points. (If the grid points aren't visible, choose View ➤ Grid.) When you move a control, it automatically lines up with the grid, both horizontally and vertically. If you try to place the edge of the control between two grid points, Access moves it to align with one grid point or the other. This is a feature called *Snap To Grid*.

TIP   *For easier formatting in forms and reports, move the gridlines farther apart. Choose Format on the menu to ensure Snap To Grid is on. Right-click on the form to open the property sheet for the entire form (or report). The Section: Detail dialog opens. Click the Format tab, change the Grid X and Grid Y property values to a larger number: 5 or 10.*

Sometimes you might want to place controls so they aren't on a grid point, for example. To do this, you must first turn off Snap To Grid by choosing Format ➤ Snap To Grid. The Snap To Grid feature is not one you need to turn off very often, but working without Snap To Grid is essential for small refinements in your Access forms.

TIP   *When you create a form with the Form Wizard or AutoForms, controls are not aligned with the grid. See the next section for hints on lining up controls irrespective of the grid.*

Aligning, Sizing, and Spacing Controls

You can manually adjust the size and position of every control on a form. However, Access automates size and positioning features so you can manipulate multiple controls simultaneously for perfect layout results.

ALIGNING CONTROLS

Begin by selecting two or more controls, and then choose Format ➤ Align or right-click and choose Align from the shortcut menu to open the list of alignment options.

Align ➤ Left aligns the left edges of all selected controls with the leftmost of them. Align ➤ Right works the same way but to the right. Use Align ➤ Top or Align ➤ Bottom to adjust controls on the same horizontal line.

TIP   *Access can't align controls that are overlapped, but that doesn't stop it from trying. The results aren't pretty. Separate overlapping controls before attempting to align them.*

SIZING CONTROLS

Choosing Format ➤ Size ➤ To Fit or double-clicking any sizing handle instantly resizes labels to fit their text. You can select two or more controls and use the other sizing options to resize all the selected controls to the same size. Tallest and Shortest refer to vertical height, and Widest and Narrowest refer to horizontal width.

SPACING CONTROLS

Spacing allows you to increase or decrease the relative position of selected controls by one grid point either horizontally or vertically. This is valuable if you need to spread out controls or move them closer together for a neater visual layout. You can also use spacing to make sure controls are evenly spaced. Select the controls, and choose Format ➢ Vertical Spacing (or Horizontal Spacing) ➢ Make Equal (or Increase or Decrease).

Rearranging the Tab Order

A form's *tab order*—the sequence of controls you move through when pressing Tab—is assigned when the form is created. After you rearrange controls on a form, the tab order may be out of sequence. Users expect to be able to move through the form sequentially, so an inconsistent tab order almost guarantees data entry errors. To change a form's tab order, choose View ➢ Tab Order, or right-click and choose Tab Order, to open the Tab Order dialog box.

You can set the tab order for each of the three sections on the form, but you'll usually only care about the Detail section. Clicking Auto Order generally rearranges the fields in the correct order, so it always makes sense to try this option first. If the auto order is not correct, you can set the order manually. Click the row selector for a control; then drag the control up or down into position in the tab order.

TIP   You should test how well your forms work each time you make any substantive change. Enter sample data and make sure everything operates as you expect it to.

Formatting Subforms

Making formatting changes to a form that has a subform is in most ways no different than formatting a single form. You can format it just as you would any form, using the Toolbox and the Formatting toolbar. To size a subform, stretch the borders of the subform control in the main form, not in the subform itself. If the subform has a datasheet format, open the main/subform combination in Form view and resize the columns by dragging or double-clicking the column headers.

TIP   When you open a main form that includes a subform, often the subform controls are not accessible. Right-click the subform and choose Subform In New Window from the shortcut menu to work with the two forms separately.

Adding Controls to Existing Forms

If you add a field to a table, existing forms won't include the field. And sometimes you change your mind about fields you omitted when you originally created a form. In both cases, you must add the field to the form in order for users to enter data in the field. To add a field's text box control to the form, click the Field List button on the toolbar or press F8 to open the Field List (see Figure 16.32).

You can resize the Field list by dragging its borders as necessary. Select the field you wish to add and press Enter, or drag the desired field from the Field list into the design surface and drop it in place. Controls created from the Field list are automatically bound to their table fields.

TIP   To add a control that enables users to look up a record in the form, don't choose from the Field list. Instead, insert a combo box control from the Toolbox. Make sure the Control Wizards button on the Toolbox is turned on; then click the combo box control and click in your form to launch the Combo Box Wizard.

Changing Properties of Forms and Controls

Every Access object—including controls—has properties. As with field properties and data types, the specific properties for a control depend on the control type. For example, the properties of a text box include its color, font, size, and control source: the table or query and the field that supplies data to the text box. Field properties include size, input masks, and the field type. Form properties include the size of the form, how the form can be viewed, and its record source: the table or query the records come from.

It's not essential to know every available property to work successfully in Access. However, whenever an object doesn't behave as you expect it to, it's a good idea to look for a property that might be affecting its behavior. To view the properties for a control, double-click the control in Design view to open the property sheet, or right-click the control and choose Properties from the shortcut menu.

To open a form's property sheet, double-click the form selector (at the intersection of the vertical and horizontal rulers). A form has four categories of properties (the All tab lists all the properties found on the other four tabs):

Format   Properties related to formatting—what the form or control looks like, what buttons and bars are activated, what views are allowed

Data   Properties that indicate the record or control source and whether the data can be edited

Event   Properties that control events to which you can attach macros and programming code

Other   Miscellaneous properties that relate to the object, including, for example, a field's tab order

The property sheet title bar includes the name of the selected object. If you want to look at properties for another control, don't close the property sheet—just click the control to display its property sheet or select from the drop-down list at the top of the property sheet.

TIP   Access 2003 includes voluminous help on each of the control and object properties. With a property sheet open, choose Help ➤ What's This [?] from the menu, and then click the property you'd like information about.

Changing Property Settings on Multiple Fields

Often, you'll want to change the property settings on multiple controls at the same time. If you select more than one control and open the property sheet, only those properties that affect all the selected controls are displayed. For example, if you select a label and a text box, no Data or Event properties are displayed; the text box has Data and Event properties, but the label does not.

TIP   *Unless you're feeling very adventurous, you should leave the default settings for properties that you are unfamiliar with.*

Hiding Form Features

A number of elements are enabled by default on every form, including scroll bars, record selectors, and navigation buttons. All these elements can be turned off in the form's property sheet. For example, the scroll bars are only needed if parts of the form don't fit on the screen. Record selectors may or may not be necessary. Navigation buttons are generally not needed on a subform. All these features take up valuable screen space and can cause confusion during data entry. You can turn off features you don't need by opening the form's property sheet and changing the item's setting to No on the Format property sheet. These changes, relatively easy to make, can make the form much easier to use.

If you've come this far, you'll eventually want to know more about form and control properties and events. Information is close at hand. We recommend the Microsoft Access 2003 Help files. For more information, we suggest *Mastering Access 2002 Premium Edition,* by Alan Simpson and Celeste Robinson (Sybex, 2003).

Chapter 17

Dissecting, Importing, and Exporting Data

THE WORDS *data* AND *information* are often used interchangeably, but they don't mean the same thing. Data is to information what flour, water, and yeast are to bread, or what petroleum is to gasoline: raw materials that can be turned into a finished product. Information supports decision making; data often confuses the decision-making process. The language we use to describe data, information, and the processes used to convert the former to the latter clearly reflect the difference: data is "raw" and needs to be "refined." Reports that use *data* where *information* is needed have conclusions that are "half baked."

Just as it's damaging to put crude oil in your car's gas tank, it's a bad idea to give users data when they need information. Office 2003 has two powerful data analysis programs: Excel and Access. This chapter focuses on using Excel and Access queries to dissect, analyze, and summarize: to extract information from data. In the next chapter we turn to the tools used to present the information in useful and appropriate ways.

- ◆ Using Excel's what-if tools

- ◆ Understanding data tables

- ◆ Using Goal Seek to find a specific solution to a business problem

- ◆ Using Solver to solve complex business problems

- ◆ Summarizing scenarios to compare and report on options

- ◆ Creating and saving views

- ◆ Using Excel's database functions

- ◆ Creating and using pivot tables and pivot charts

- ◆ Importing and exporting data

Answering Questions with Excel's Analysis Tools

You already know how to use many of Excel's analysis tools. You can learn a lot about data simply by using functions and formulas. For more advanced work, Excel includes specialized forecasting tools often referred to as *what-if* tools, used in what-if analysis: data tables, Goal Seek, and Solver. These tools are used to answer very simple as well as incredibly complex questions.

Understanding Data Tables

Data tables are used within the context of what-if analysis, which is a means of forecasting outcomes by changing values within the cells of the table. Data tables are used to show the results of changing either one or two variables used as arguments in a formula.

For example, the table in Figure 17.1 is the sort of list you've seen in event brochures and ticket windows: a total price table for tickets in different quantities at different prices.

FIGURE 17.1

This table of ticket prices was created using Excel's data table feature.

	A	B	C	D	E	F	G	H	I	J
1	Ticket Sales Worksheet									
2										
3			1	2	3	4	5	6	7	8
4	Balcony	42.50	42.50	85.00	127.50	170.00	212.50	255.00	297.50	340.00
5	Loge	52.50	52.50	105.00	157.50	210.00	262.50	315.00	367.50	420.00
6	Front	73.00	73.00	146.00	219.00	292.00	365.00	438.00	511.00	584.00
7	Rear	87.50	87.50	175.00	262.50	350.00	437.50	525.00	612.50	700.00

In Figure 17.1, this formula with two mixed references works in C4 and can be copied down and then over to the remaining cells in the table: =$B4*C$3. If you don't like creating formulas with mixed cell references, you might prefer creating a table like that shown in Figure 17.1 using the data table feature. But there's a more important reason to know how data tables work: other users create data tables and then pass their workbooks on to you.

We're going to unpack the table shown in Figure 17.1 so you know how to work with tables in workbooks you inherit. The data table cells contain formulas.

The table here was created by entering values in column B and row 3 and a formula in the upper-left corner of the table in cell B3. The formula, however, is not what you might expect. It refers to two empty cells in the worksheet: =C1*C2. The data table feature uses two *input cells* outside of the table to temporarily store each value from column B and row 3 as it calculates results and creates the table.

With the row and column data and formula in B3 entered, here are the steps to create the table:

1. In a single selection, select the data table range, including the formula, data series, and results cells: in our worksheet, the range A3:J7. The selection cannot include the input cells or any extra cells, and must be one contiguous selection.

2. With the cells selected, choose Data ➤ Table to open the Table dialog box shown below. Click in two empty cells outside of the selection that Excel should use as the Row Input Cell and Column Input Cell.

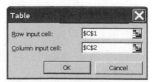

3. Click OK to create the data table.

The formulas in the results cells identify this as a table:

$$fx \quad \{=TABLE(C1,C2)\}$$

If you want to find the "edges" of the table, select any cell with a formula that uses the TABLE function and choose Edit ➤ Go To. In the Go To dialog box, click the Special button. In the Go To Special dialog box, choose Current Array, then click OK to select the results cells, row and column values, and table formula.

Using the Forecasting Tools

Forecasting is a common business activity. A forecast is a set of predictions of future values. Online services that estimate the future prices of stocks use forecasting. Department, project, and company budgets and production schedules are forecasts. Companies buy materials, hire employees, and assign prices to their products and services based on forecasts. The forecasts are based on a mix of these points:

♦ Company historical data: actual budget values, weighted averages of past performance, and experience from similar business units or similar projects

♦ Judgments or educated guesses by people in a position to help predict future performance: managers, customer focus groups, marketing specialists, sales staff

♦ Information about the external environment: for example, prices charged by competitors, the local employment level, regulatory changes, and the current interest rate

♦ Relevant models for the industry, size, geography, or other attributes of the organization

The more good sources of information you consider, the more accurate your forecast will be. There are different ways to construct forecasts. In Excel, forecasting always involves creating one or more worksheets with formulas to show how different variables interrelate.

DOCUMENTING ASSUMPTIONS WITH COMMENTS

Forecasting is always based on assumptions. Each model has specific assumptions, but there are general assumptions common to most models. One such assumption is that the future will be much like the present. You also assume that a forecast will not be perfect. There will always be some neglected piece of information that affects the forecast because your worksheet and its formulas are a simulation of reality, not reality itself.

Another assumption is that the distant future is more difficult to predict than the near future. That's why it is difficult to get 50-year mortgages or place bets on the 2009 World Series. No one could have accurately predicted the last four years of stock market prices, airplanes as terrorist weapons, or the recent success mapping the human genome. As the time involved in a forecast increases, the accuracy of the forecast decreases, even if the model was essentially accurate in the short term when it was constructed.

There are other assumptions that are specific to your workbook. For example, you might assume that the wage for painters next year will be this year's hourly wage, adjusted for the cost of living, so that's the adjusted wage you'll use when you create the formulas for the cost of painting the new offices. You should always document this type of assumption in your workbook, and document as many of the general assumptions as seem appropriate. The easiest way to document assumptions is by inserting a comment. Chapter 15, "Creating Templates to Handle Your Repetitive Tasks," shows how to do that.

Building a Good Worksheet Model

Several steps are involved in building a model and using it to forecast performance or solve business problems:

1. Determine what you need to forecast with the model: Gross sales? Best price? Optimal staffing level? Total profit for your department next year?

2. Define and collect information for the model.

3. Create the model in an Excel workbook. Use comments to document the assumptions behind your formulas.

4. Use the model to forecast the future value of variables.

5. Compare real performance to the model and adjust the model (or change actual performance) as necessary so it's ready the next time you need to use it.

Spend appropriate time and effort on the model. Don't spend hours researching a decision to save 50 dollars. But you need to spend sufficient time when you are creating a model to support decision making that involves hundreds of thousands of dollars.

Using Goal Seek to Find a Specific Value

Goal Seek is used to calculate backwards—to determine the values necessary to reach a specific goal. If you have a worksheet model, you can use Goal Seek to get a specific answer. The Conference Planner worksheet shown in Figure 17.2 is a simple model used to calculate costs for a conference. We'll use it to demonstrate the usefulness of Goal Seek.

FIGURE 17.2

Examining the Conference Planner worksheet

	A	B	C	D	E
1	**Conference Planner**				
2					
3	Attendees	125		Days	2
4				Fee	300
5	Meeting Space	25,000			
6	Meals	11,250			
7	Publicity	2,000			
8	Overhead	5,000			
9	**Total Cost**	**43,250**			
10					
11	Registrations	37,500			
12					
13	**Net Income/Loss**	**(5,750)**			

The worksheet includes three named cells: the number of attendees in B3 (**Num**), the number of days in E3 (Days), and the registration fee in E4 (Fee). The worksheet formulas are shown in Figure 17.3.

FIGURE 17.3

Formulas used in the Conference Planner worksheet

	A	B	C	D	E
1	**Conference Planner**				
2					
3	Attendees	125		Days	2
4				Fee	300
5	Meeting Space	=100*Num*Days			
6	Meals	=45*Num*Days			
7	Publicity	2000			
8	Overhead	5000			
9	**Total Cost**	**=SUM(B5:B8)**			
10					
11	Registrations	=Num*Fee			
12					
13	**Net Income/Loss**	**=B11-B9**			

There are three values we could change: the number of attendees, the number of days, and the registration fee. We'll start with the example using the number of attendees and unpack the example to see how Goal Seek found a result. Here's the problem we're trying to solve: the registration fee for our two-day conference is $300. How many attendees do we need so we don't lose money? Here are the steps to solve the problem:

1. Enter the values that can't change: **2** in E3 and **300** in E4.

2. Select the goal cell: Net Income/Loss in B13. The goal cell must contain a formula.

3. Choose Tools ➢ Goal Seek to open the Goal Seek dialog box. Excel automatically enters the active cell as the Set Cell.

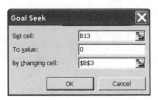

4. Enter a To Value (0 in our example) that Excel will try to achieve as the result in the Set Cell.

5. Click in the By Changing Cell text box and then click the cell that Excel should change: the number of attendees in B3. The By Changing Cell must contain a value, not a formula.

6. Click OK to have Goal Seek find a solution:

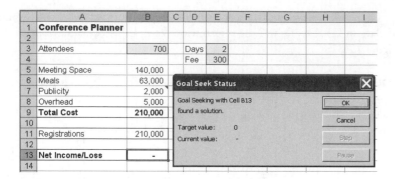

7. Click OK to accept the solution and enter the value in B3 or Cancel to keep the original value.

HOW GOAL SEEK WORKS

Goal Seek changes the number in the By Changing Cell until the result of the formula in the Set Cell is equal to the To Value. Excel begins by trying an upper and lower value for the number of attendees. If the result in the Set Cell falls between the initial values, Goal Seek then narrows the value in small increments until the Set Cell value is within 0.01 of the goal. If the goal value is outside the initial range, Goal Seek will try a wider range of values. Each attempt to meet the goal is an *iteration*. The default settings (Tools ➤ Options ➤ Calculation) instruct Excel to try 100 iterations before giving up.

NOTE   *Some problems don't have a solution. When Goal Seek can't solve the problem, the message reports that a solution can't be found. Even when Goal Seek can't find a solution, however, you know more than you knew before. Given the other values in your model, there is no solution.*

You can use Goal Seek with the Conference Planner worksheet to find the number of attendees, or the registration fee, or the number of days as long as you know the other two values. When you want to change two of the variables at the same time, you need another analysis tool: Solver.

Solving Complex Business Problems

Solver is used to find an *optimal* solution: the solution that strikes a good balance between competing or conflicting requirements, rather than a specific value goal like a Net Income/Loss of 0.

Optimization has many business applications. Solver can be used to find the least expensive solution to a problem, or a solution that maximizes income. As you'll see in our second example, you can add constraints that describe the limit of acceptable values.

Solver can also be used, like Goal Seek, to find a specific value. Use Solver rather than Goal Seek when you need to change values in multiple cells or apply constraints.

INSTALLING SOLVER

Solver is not included in a typical Excel installation. If you don't see Solver on the Tools menu, click Tools ➣ Add-Ins and choose Solver Add-in in the Add-Ins dialog box.

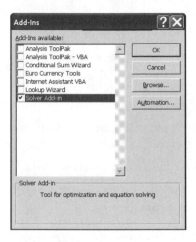

Excel may prompt you for the CD to install this feature.

In the first example, we'll use Solver to find the perfect number of conference attendees from a profit/loss point of view.

1. Choose Tools ➣ Solver to open the Solver Parameters dialog box, shown in Figure 17.4.

FIGURE 17.4

Use Solver to find the optimal solution to a problem.

2. Enter references or values in the following controls:

Set Target Cell   Solver's Target Cell is the same as Goal Seek's Set Cell: the cell that the final result should appear in. If you select the cell before you fire up Solver, it's automatically entered in the dialog box.

Equal To   Choose the Max, Min, or Value Of option to solve for the largest or smallest possible number, or a set value.

By Changing Cells   As with Goal Seek, the By Changing Cells is the cell that Solver is to change to find the solution indicated. You can select the cell(s), or click the Guess button to have Solver examine the formula in the Target Cell and find all of its predecessor cells that contain values. Delete any guessed cells that Solver should not change as part of the solution.

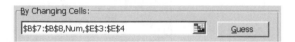

The settings to optimize income in the Conference Planner worksheet are shown in Figure 17.4: B13 is the target cell, B3 is the changing cell, and we chose the Max option.

3. Click the Solve button to put Solver to work.

Like Goal Seek, Solver will try 100 iterations before reporting that it cannot find a solution. A successful solution is shown in Figure 17.5.

FIGURE 17.5

Keep or discard the Solver solution.

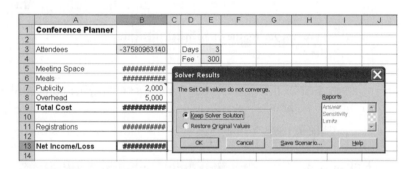

Choose to Keep Solver Solution or Restore Original Values. (The other option, saving scenarios, is discussed later in this chapter.) If you choose Keep Solver Solution, the original values will be overwritten. You cannot undo this change. You could, of course, close the workbook without saving changes if you really needed to get the original values back.

Our solution has a few problems: to maximize profit for a two-day conference with a $300 registration fee, we need to invite negative 37 billion people to our conference. In this "solution," 37.5 billion people *don't* attend, and we therefore receive income for each non-attendee—the money we would have spent for meeting space and meals if they registered and attended.

Even if there were this many people, we couldn't do it. Negative people can and do attend conferences, but you can't have a negative number in cell B3. The value in B3 can't be less than zero. The same is true of cells B5 and B6. Even in a bad economy, conference centers and caterers aren't paying customers to not show up. We know this, but Excel doesn't. We need to add some constraints to cells B3, B5, and B6 so Excel knows what we know, and then try again.

NOTE   *There's another piece of information in this "solution"—we're losing money on each registration. If we were making money on each registration, the optimal answer would be a positive number of attendees. Either the costs are too high or the registration fee is too low (or both). More on this in the next section.*

ADDING CONSTRAINTS IN SOLVER

In the Solver Parameters dialog box, click the Add button to open the Add Constraint dialog box:

Enter a cell reference, choose an operator, and enter a value or cell reference as a constraint. Click Add to add the constraint and create another. Here, we've referenced the cell, and constrained the parameters by setting them to greater than or equal to 0. Click OK when you are finished to return to the Solver Parameters dialog box:

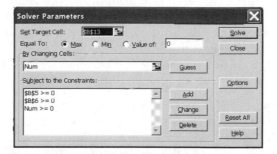

When we solve this time, the answer lets us know that with the current registration fee and costs, this three-day conference is a money-losing proposition with no attendees. We'll lose less money if we simply cancel the conference and eat the Publicity and Overhead costs. We can continue adding different constraints to see how many attendees would be necessary to meet or exceed expenses.

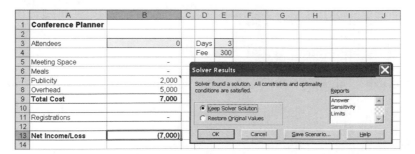

SAVING A SOLUTION AS A SCENARIO

There's been a lot of discussion about the registration fee on the conference planning committee. Some are firm that we can't charge more than $300 for conference registration; the largest number that's been seriously considered is $750. It's worth saving our solutions so we have the results for future discussion. To save a solution, click the Save Scenario button in the Solver Results dialog box to open the Save Scenario dialog box:

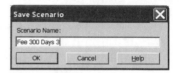

Enter a name for this scenario and then click OK to save it. We'll show you how to access and summarize your saved scenarios later in this chapter.

USING SOLVER WITH MULTIPLE VARIABLES

Our current model has only one changing variable—Attendees—and no constraints except forcing some numbers to be positive. We need to expand the options that Excel has to solve this problem. We could go in a half-dozen directions right now, which is a natural outcome of a good model: it helps you explore a wide range of possible solutions. The conference center we're using can handle up to 2000 people. We'll instruct Solver to change the attendees *or* fee and we'll use constraints to limit the values Solver can use. Here are the scenario names we'll use, the possibilities we want to explore, and the constraints:

Max Income Fee 750 Days 3   Maximize income assuming a registration fee cap of $750 (note that Solver can change two variables: attendees and fee)

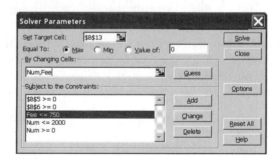

Max Income Fee 500 Days 3   Maximize income assuming a registration fee of exactly $500

Min Fee Attendees 1500 Breakeven   Minimize the registration fee assuming that 1500 people attend and we don't make or lose money. This one's a bit tricky on the surface. We can't make Fee the target cell because it's not a formula. Instead, we'll constrain the number of attendees and change the Set Cell option to Value Of 0:

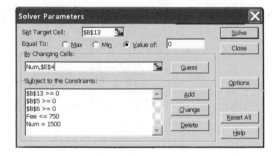

The Solver solution for Min Fee Attendees 1500 Breakeven is shown in Figure 17.6.

FIGURE 17.6

This solution answers the question, "If we don't need to make money, what's an appropriate registration fee for 1500 attendees?"

	A	B	C	D	E
1	**Conference Planner**				
2					
3	Attendees	1500		Days	3
4				Fee	440
5	Meeting Space	450,000			
6	Meals	202,500			
7	Publicity	2,000			
8	Overhead	5,000			
9	**Total Cost**	**659,500**			
10					
11	Registrations	659,500			
12					
13	**Net Income/Loss**	-			

There are other possibilities we could explore, but these four possibilities will answer the questions that have been raised so far in our conference planning committee. In the next section, we'll use the four scenarios to present the Solver solutions.

MASTERING THE OPPORTUNITIES: SAVING SOLVER MODELS

If you're working with a number of constraints and possible solutions, you might want to save the model so you can adjust it and run it again instead of creating it from scratch. In the Solver Parameters dialog box, click the Options button to open the Solver Options dialog box.

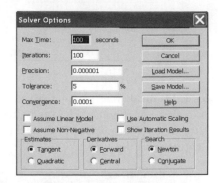

Click the Save Model button to open the Save Model dialog box, shown here:

A vertical range of cells beginning with the target cell is suggested. You don't need to save the model in the suggested range, but you need to select either a single cell or the same number of cells as the suggested range. Click OK to save the model.

To re-use a model, open the Solver Parameters dialog box, click the Options button, and click Load Model. In the Load Model dialog box, select the entire range of cells saved as the model.

Making Your Case with Scenarios

The Scenario Manager uses scenarios that you create to forecast a given result. By creating values within your worksheet, you can then switch to a scenario that you've developed to see and compare different results. The scenarios you might like to develop include models that reflect different situations for your forecast: best case, worst case, current, and most likely. In the context of our conference planning example, you would create scenarios and then compare the input you have to those scenarios, further clarifying the forecast results.

CREATING A SCENARIO

Goal Seek and Solver both support scenarios. To save the results of an analysis operation as a scenario, click the Save Scenario button in the Solver or Goal Seek Results dialog box. We saved scenarios in Solver, but you can create simple scenarios directly in the Scenario Manager. Follow these steps:

1. Choose Tools ➤ Scenarios to open the Scenario Manager shown in Figure 17.7.

FIGURE 17.7

Use the Scenario Manager to create, display, and summarize scenarios

2. Click the Add button to open the Add Scenario dialog box:

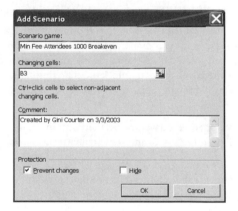

3. Type a name for the scenario (like Min Fee Attendees 1000 Breakeven) in the Scenario Name field.

4. Enter the address of the cell or cells you wish to change in the Change Cells field. Enter additional details about the scenario in the Comment field.

TIP If you're sharing the workbook with other users, you may choose to protect the scenario by preventing changes or hiding it. The scenario is not protected until you protect the worksheet (Tools ➤ Protection ➤ Protect Sheet).

5. Click OK to open the Scenario Values dialog box and enter the value for this scenario:

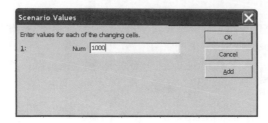

Only the cells you specified as Change Cells will be changed. In this example, we didn't include the Fee cell as a Change Cell, so Excel will use the cell's current value: $440.

6. Click OK to return to the Scenario Manager. Click Add to create another scenario. Close the Scenario Manager when you're finished.

SHOWING A SCENARIO

To display a scenario, open the Scenario Manager (Tools ➤ Scenario) and choose a scenario from the list. Click the Show button to display the scenario results in your worksheet.

MASTERING THE OPPORTUNITIES: COLLABORATING WITH OTHER USERS ON SCENARIOS

The merge feature makes it easy for members of a team to create scenarios independently and then consolidate the scenarios into one workbook. You can merge scenarios from multiple workbooks, provided that each scenario has been created from the same base model and uses the same values except for the changing cells. Create the model worksheet, unlock the changing cells, and protect the worksheet before sending it to other users. (See Chapter 12, "Securing and Organizing Documents" for help protecting workbooks and worksheets.)

To merge workbooks, open all the workbooks that contain scenarios. Activate the workbook that will receive all the scenarios. Choose Tools ➤ Scenarios to open the Scenario Manager dialog box, shown previously in Figure 17.7.

Users might forget to enter comments or they might provide descriptions that are too brief—or lengthy—to be useful. To edit a scenario description before merging the scenario, open the workbook, open the Scenario Manager, select the scenario, and click the Edit button to open the Edit Scenario dialog box. When you've finished editing the scenario, click OK to return to the Scenario Manager. Excel automatically appends your user name and the current date to the scenario's description when you modify a scenario. You can remove the added text if you wish by editing the scenario again and deleting it.

Click the Merge button to open the Merge Scenarios dialog box. For each workbook that you want to merge scenarios from, follow these steps:

1. Select the workbook from the drop-down list.

2. Choose the worksheet that contains the scenarios.

3. Click OK to merge the worksheet's scenarios into the workbook.

Continued on next page

> **MASTERING THE OPPORTUNITIES: COLLABORATING WITH OTHER USERS ON SCENARIOS** *(continued)*
>
> If two scenarios have the same name, Excel appends the worksheet creator's name to the end of the scenario name.
>
> If a worksheet contains more than one scenario, all scenarios are merged. To remove a scenario, select the scenario in the Scenario Manager and click the Delete button.

Summarizing Scenarios

Use the Scenario Manager's summarization feature to compare the results of different scenarios in a single table or pivot table—like an executive summary. The worksheet in Figure 17.8 summarizes the five scenarios saved in the Conference Planner worksheet.

FIGURE 17.8

Summarize the results of several scenarios in a single table for side-by-side comparison.

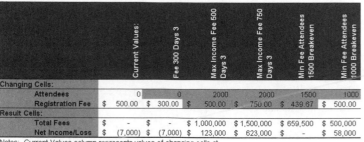

	Current Values:	Fee 300 Days 3	Max Income Fee 500 Days 3	Max Income Fee 750 Days 3	Min Fee Attendees 1500 Breakeven	Min Fee Attendees 1000 Breakeven
Changing Cells:						
Attendees	0	0	2000	2000	1500	1000
Registration Fee	$ 500.00	$ 300.00	$ 500.00	$ 750.00	$ 439.67	$ 500.00
Result Cells:						
Total Fees	$ -	$ -	$ 1,000,000	$ 1,500,000	$ 659,500	$ 500,000
Net Income/Loss	$ (7,000)	$ (7,000)	$ 123,000	$ 623,000	$ -	$ 58,000

Notes: Current Values column represents values of changing cells at time Scenario Summary Report was created. Changing cells for each scenario are highlighted in gray.

In the summary, each column of data represents one scenario. The scenario name is used as the column label, with the description immediately below. The description can be hidden easily using the outline symbols on the vertical outline bar.

The description is followed by two sections: the changing cells and results cells. The row labels are the names of the results cells. If you do not name the results cells, Excel uses the cell address to label the row, but you can edit the labels in the Scenario Summary worksheet.

Activate the worksheet that contains the scenarios, open the Scenario Manager (Tools ➤ Scenarios), and click the Summary button to open the Scenario Summary dialog box:

Choose the Scenario Summary or Scenario PivotTable report type. Changing Cells are automatically included in the summary. In the Result Cells text box, select any other cells you want to show. In the summary shown in Figure 17.9, we chose the cells with net income/loss (B13) and registration income (B11). Click OK to generate the summary on a new worksheet.

A summary pivot table for the same scenarios is shown below. The summary pivot table is less flashy than the scenario summary, but is a better data source for a chart. If you're working with merged scenarios, the pivot table has one other advantage: it automatically includes a filter so you can show scenarios developed by specific users.

	A	C	D
1	Num,Fee by		
2	Num by		
3			
4		Result Cells ▼	
5	Num,Fee ▼	$B$11	$B$13
6	Fee 300 Days 3	300000	-142000
7	Max Income Fee 500 Days 3	1000000	123000
8	Max Income Fee 750 Days 3	1500000	623000
9	Min Fee Attendees 1500 Breakeven	659500	0

TIP *If you intend to summarize scenarios in a pivot table, you'll save lots of time by naming any results cells before creating the summary.*

There's more information about pivot tables in the section, "Creating Pivot Tables and Pivot Charts to Analyze Lists," in this chapter.

Totaling and Subtotaling Excel Lists

Excel 2003's List feature includes almost all of the commands on the Data menu. One conspicuous omission is the Subtotals command. You can create subtotals based on any column in a list or range of cells. As with totals, a *subtotal* is not necessarily a sum: it can be an average, count, minimum, maximum, or other statistical calculation based on a group of records.

NOTE *If you need a subtotal for only one group in a list, use the Total Row and filter the list to hide other rows. See Chapter 13, "Building Robust and Foolproof Workbooks," for more information on the Total Row.*

Before subtotaling, sort the list or range on the column you wish to subtotal on (so the rows you want to subtotal are grouped together). For example, if you want a subtotal for each month's orders, first sort the list by month. Follow these steps to create subtotals:

1. Sort the list by the field you wish to subtotal on.

2. Click anywhere in the list. Choose Data ➢ Subtotals to open the Subtotal dialog box, shown in Figure 17.9.

3. Choose the field you sorted by from the At Each Change In text box.

In Figure 17.9, we're subtotaling the charges attributable to each application. In the first step, we sorted by Application, and in step 3 we chose Application in the first drop-down list.

4. Select a type of subtotal from the Use Function drop-down list.

5. In the Add Subtotal To control, select each field you want to subtotal. You can subtotal more than one field at a time, but you have to use the same function: average three fields, sum three fields, and so on.

FIGURE 17.9

Create summary totals and averages for lists and ranges in the Subtotal dialog box

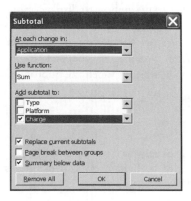

6. If necessary, change the following settings:

Enable Replace Current Subtotals   Replaces a former subtotaled set with new subtotals. If you want both sets of subtotals to appear (for example, sums and averages), deselect this check box.

Page Break Between Groups   Places each subtotaled set of records on a separate page.

Summary Below Data   Places a summary (grand total, grand average) row at the bottom of the list.

7. When you have entered the information for subtotals, click OK to generate subtotals, as shown in Figure 17.10.

FIGURE 17.10

The Call Log worksheet with subtotals

		A	B	C	D	E	F	G	H	I	J
	6										
	7	User	Department	Date	Start Time	End Time	Length	Application	Type	Platform	Charge
	8	Benson	Accounting	1/03	1:55 PM	2:10 PM	0:15	Excel	Advanced	Desk/Laptop	13.88
	9		**Accounting Total**								13.88
	10	Keener	Administration	9/3/03	9:20 AM	9:30 AM	0:10	Excel	Code	Desk/Laptop	9.25
	11	Keener	Administration	9/3/03	4:10 PM	4:13 PM	0:03	Excel	Code	Desk/Laptop	2.77
	12		**Administration Total**								12.02
	13	Smith	Communications	9/4/03	3:45 PM	3:50 PM	0:05	Excel	Intermediate	Desk/Laptop	4.62
	14		**Communications Total**								4.62
	15	Turik	Info Tech	9/1/03	2:14 PM	2:30 PM	0:16	Connectivity	Beginning	PDA	14.80
	16		**Info Tech Total**								14.80
	17	Wilson	Maintenance	9/4/03	9:22 AM	9:33 AM	0:11	Outlook	Intermediate	PDA	10.18
	18		**Maintenance Total**								10.18
	19	Laramie	Manufacturing	9/1/03	3:00 PM	3:40 PM	0:40	Data Analyzer	Advanced	Desk/Laptop	37.00
	20	Song	Manufacturing	9/4/03	9:02 AM	9:18 AM	0:16	Excel	Intermediate	Desk/Laptop	14.80
	21		**Manufacturing Total**								51.80
	22	Hing	Training	9/3/03	1:35 PM	1:55 PM	0:20	Data Analyzer	Intermediate	Desk/Laptop	18.50
	23	Fitzgerald	Training	9/4/03	8:32 AM	8:50 AM	0:18	FrontPage	Intermediate	Desk/Laptop	16.65
	24	Benth	Training	9/1/03	8:15 AM	8:18 AM	0:03	Outlook	App Error	Desk/Laptop	2.78
	25		**Training Total**								37.93
	26	Lieberman	Web - IT	9/1/03	11:40 AM	12:00 PM	0:20	Word	Beginning	Desk/Laptop	18.50

When you apply subtotals, Excel automatically applies an outline and displays the outline symbols as shown in Figure 17.10. Use the outline symbols to display the level of detail you wish to see or print.

NOTE *If the outline symbols do not appear, choose Tools ➢ Options and enable the Outline Symbols check box on the View tab of the Options dialog box.*

 To display a specific level of the outline, click the appropriate Row Level Detail symbol.

 Click the Show Detail and Hide Detail symbols to display or hide details for a subtotal. The outline symbols do not print, but if you've added a couple of layers of subtotals, you may wish to turn off the outline symbols to regain the space they occupy at the left edge of the Excel window. To remove the outline symbols but retain the subtotals, choose Data ➢ Group and Outline ➢ Clear Outline. To remove subtotals from a worksheet, open the Subtotal dialog box again and click the Remove All button.

COPYING SUBTOTALS

When you copy a *filtered* list, Excel copies only the rows that are visible. If you copy *subtotals*, even with the detail collapsed, Excel copies (and pastes) the hidden rows. There's an easy way to copy subtotals, but you could spend the better part of a workday trying to find it.

1. Begin by collapsing the subtotals so that only the data you wish to copy is visible. Select the data you wish to copy.

2. Choose Edit ➢ Go To to open the Go To dialog box.

3. Click the Special button to open the Go To Special dialog box.

4. Enable the Visible Cells Only option and click OK.

5. Click the Copy button on the Standard toolbar.

6. Move to the first cell where you want to paste the copied selection and click Paste from the Standard toolbar.

Creating Views

A *view* is a specification for the appearance of an Excel workbook. The default view is the appearance of a workbook when it was last saved. If you close a workbook with the third sheet activated, it opens with the third sheet activated. A view always includes the following:

◆ The size and position of the Excel application window and child windows, including split windows

◆ The hidden/unhidden status of worksheets and columns

◆ The active sheet and active cells when a view is created

◆ Column widths

◆ Display settings including the zoom ratio

Optionally, a view can also include:

◆ Print settings, including print area

◆ Hidden/unhidden settings for columns and rows

◆ Filter settings

Saving custom views enables you to quickly switch between different view settings: for example, a managerial view that displays cost columns and a customer view that hides detailed costs.

For example, in our workbook, we'll create a custom view for the Call Report that hangs on the wall in the Help Desk area. The report hides the start and end times and chargeback information and when printed excludes the first six rows above the data. Before setting up the wall report view, we'll save the current settings (no hidden columns, default print area) as a custom view called All Columns. Then we'll modify the workbook (hide columns and set the print area) for the Call Report and save the Call Report view.

To create a custom view, first set the print and display options and hide any rows, worksheets, or columns that you wish to hide. Activate the sheet and cells that should be activated when the view is initially enabled. Then follow these steps:

1. Choose View ➤ Custom Views to open the Custom Views dialog box.

2. Click the Add button to open the Add Custom View dialog box:

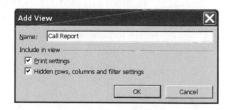

3. Enter a name for the view.

4. Disable the check boxes if you wish to omit the current print settings and hidden rows/columns and filter settings from the view.

5. Click OK to create the view and add it to the Custom Views dialog box.

To apply a view, choose View ➤ Custom Views. Select the view in the Custom Views dialog box and click Show:

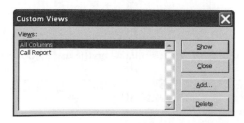

Using Functions with Lists

Excel 2003 includes two types of functions designed specifically for lists. The conditional functions SUMIF and COUNTIF combine a summary function with the IF condition so you can easily total based on a condition. The database functions, or *Dfunctions*, are similar to the Advanced Filter command: they apply a criteria range to a list.

Summarizing Based on a Condition

The specialized IF functions are statistical functions with a logical basis. Use SUMIF and COUNTIF to total or count values in a range based on the value in that range or a corresponding range. To demonstrate how these incredibly useful functions work, we'll use the two functions in our Call Log worksheet to display the number of calls and total charges for a department that the user selects.

First we inserted some blank rows directly above the list's header row and set up three "data areas": a drop-down list where a user can choose the department name and cells for Calls and Charge. We put this above the list so the user doesn't have to scroll to the bottom of what is often a long list when they need to quickly determine their department's help desk usage. Now we're ready to create the two formulas for Calls and Charge.

HOW THE SUMIF FUNCTION WORKS

The syntax for the SUMIF function is =SUMIF(*criteria range, criteria, range to sum*). The *criteria range* and *range to sum can* be the same, but rarely are in SUMIF functions. If you don't specify a range to sum, it is assumed that it is the same range as the criteria range.

In cell H6 of the Call Log worksheet shown in Figure 17.11, we've entered the formula to total the charges in column J, but only for the department (column B) that the user chose from the drop-down list in cell B6.

FIGURE 17.11

Use the SUMIF formula to total based on a condition.

	A	B	C	D	E	F	G	H	I	J
6		Manufacturing	Choose from List		Calls		Charge	=SUMIF(B10:B500,B6,J10:J500)		
7								SUMIF(range, criteria, [sum_range])		
8										
9	User	Department	Date	Start Time	End Time	Length	Application	Type	Platform	Charge
10	Benson	Accounting	9/1/03	1:55 PM	2:10 PM	0:15	Excel	Advanced	Desk/Laptop	13.88
11	Keener	Administration	9/3/03	9:20 AM	9:30 AM	0:10	Excel	Code	Desk/Laptop	9.25
12	Keener	Administration	9/3/03	4:10 PM	4:13 PM	0:03	Excel	Code	Desk/Laptop	2.77
13	Smith	Communications	9/4/03	3:45 PM	3:50 PM	0:05	Excel	Intermediate	Desk/Laptop	4.62
14	Turik	Info Tech	9/1/03	2:14 PM	2:30 PM	0:16	Connectivity	Beginning	PDA	14.80
15	Wilson	Maintenance	9/4/03	9:22 AM	9:33 AM	0:11	Outlook	Intermediate	PDA	10.18
16	Laramie	Manufacturing	9/1/03	3:00 PM	3:40 PM	0:40	Data Analyzer	Advanced	Desk/Laptop	37.00
17	Song	Manufacturing	9/4/03	9:02 AM	9:18 AM	0:16	Excel	Intermediate	Desk/Laptop	14.80
18	Hing	Training	9/3/03	1:35 PM	1:55 PM	0:20	Data Analyzer	Intermediate	Desk/Laptop	18.50
19	Fitzgerald	Training	9/4/03	8:32 AM	8:50 AM	0:18	FrontPage	Intermediate	Desk/Laptop	16.65
20	Benth	Training	9/1/03	8:15 AM	8:18 AM	0:03	Outlook	App Error	Desk/Laptop	2.78
21	Lieberman	Web - IT	9/1/03	11:40 AM	12:00 PM	0:20	Word	Beginning	Desk/Laptop	18.50
22										
23										
24										
25										
26										

Here are the results of the formula when the user chooses the Manufacturing department:

	A	B	C	D	E	F	G	H
6		Manufacturing	Choose from List		Calls		Charge	$ 51.80

You don't need to point to a cell (like B6) for the criteria. You can enter a number. For example, you could enter a department name in the formula if you were sending a worksheet to a specific department.

How the COUNTIF Function Works

The syntax for the COUNTIF function is =COUNTIF(*range, criteria*). The COUNTIF function works like COUNTA, rather than COUNT, so you can count the number of cells in a range that match a text string or a number. Here's the formula to count the number of cells in column B that match the department the user chooses in cell B6:

f_x =COUNTIF(B10:B500,B6)

The two formulas, driven by user input, create the type of summary area that's useful in a wide range of worksheets because it delivers immediate value. Novice users don't need to learn Excel to get answers to basic questions about the state of the business:

	A	B	C	D	E	F	G	H
6		Manufacturing	Choose from List		Calls	2	Charge	$ 51.80

TIP   *Divide SUMIF by COUNTIF to calculate the average as if Excel included an AVERAGEIF function.*

Using the Database Functions

The database functions, or Dfunctions, are much like the SUMIF and COUNTIF functions. The generic syntax for the Dfunctions is:

```
=FUNCTIONNAME(list range, column to search, criteria range)
```

Like SUMIF and COUNTIF, the Dfunctions are needed when the criteria that serve as the basis of a summary change. In the list we've used thus far in this section different users might want to summarize based on departments, applications, type, or platform. With Dfunction formulas, the results will change based on the criteria we use. Most of the Dfunctions mirror Excel's regular set of summary functions. Use DSUM, DCOUNT, DAVERAGE, DMIN, and DMAX as you would use the regular versions of the same functions.

TIP   *DGET works differently. It returns a unique value (if there is a single record that meets the criteria) from a list.*

The Dfunctions use a separate criteria range (like the range used in Advanced Filter.) Construct a criteria range by copying and pasting the column headings in another area of your workbook. The list and the criteria range are used in every Dfunction, so it makes sense to name both ranges. In Figure 17.12 we've cleared out the summary area we used for SUMIF and COUNTIF inserted rows and named the range of labels and the row immediately beneath the labels *Criteria*. We selected the current list area (down to row 500 to accommodate more data) and named it *Calls*. Three formulas and corresponding labels were added above the criteria range:

```
In H2: Total Charge: =DSUM(Calls,"Charge",Criteria)
In H3: Total Calls: =DCOUNT(Calls,"Charge",Criteria)
In H4: Average Charge: =DAVERAGE(Calls,"Charge",Criteria)
```

The second argument, the column to search, can be either the column header label in quotes or the index number of the column (in our example, column J is column 10).

FIGURE 17.12

The Dfunctions summarize data in a column based on values—or lack of values—in a criteria range.

	A	B	C	D	E	F	G	H	I	J
1	*User Support Call Log*									
2	Total Time	2:57					Total Charge	$ 163.73		
3							Total Calls	12		
4	Start Date	6/1/2003	End Date	6/30/2003			Average Charge	$ 13.64		
5										
6	User	Department	Date	Start Time	End Time	Length	Application	Type	Platform	Charge
7										
8										
9	User	Department	Date	Start Time	End Time	Length	Application	Type	Platform	Charge
10	Benson	Accounting	9/1/03	1:55 PM	2:10 PM	0:15	Excel	Advanced	Desk/Laptop	13.88
11	Keener	Administration	9/3/03	9:20 AM	9:30 AM	0:10	Excel	Code	Desk/Laptop	9.25
12	Keener	Administration	9/3/03	4:10 PM	4:13 PM	0:03	Excel	Code	Desk/Laptop	2.77
13	Smith	Communications	9/4/03	3:45 PM	3:50 PM	0:05	Excel	Intermediate	Desk/Laptop	4.62
14	Turik	Info Tech	9/1/03	2:14 PM	2:30 PM	0:16	Connectivity	Beginning	PDA	14.80
15	Wilson	Maintenance	9/4/03	9:22 AM	9:33 AM	0:11	Outlook	Intermediate	PDA	10.18
16	Laramie	Manufacturing	9/1/03	3:00 PM	3:40 PM	0:40	Data Analyzer	Advanced	Desk/Laptop	37.00
17	Song	Manufacturing	9/4/03	9:02 AM	9:18 AM	0:16	Excel	Intermediate	Desk/Laptop	14.80
18	Hing	Training	9/3/03	1:35 PM	1:55 PM	0:20	Data Analyzer	Intermediate	Desk/Laptop	18.50
19	Fitzgerald	Training	9/4/03	8:32 AM	8:50 AM	0:18	FrontPage	Intermediate	Desk/Laptop	16.65
20	Benth	Training	9/1/03	8:15 AM	8:18 AM	0:03	Outlook	App Error	Desk/Laptop	2.78
21	Lieberman	Web - IT	9/1/03	11:40 AM	12:00 PM	0:20	Word	Beginning	Desk/Laptop	18.50

When there are no criteria in the Criteria range, the Dfunctions sum, count, and average all the records in the list.

Adding Dfunctions to a worksheet makes the worksheets ad hoc reporting sheets. DCOUNT, DAVERAGE, and DSUM are the most commonly used Dfunctions. For information on the other Dfunctions—DVAR, DVARP, DSTDEV, DSTEVP, and DPRODUCT—search Excel Help for database functions.

Creating Pivot Tables and Pivot Charts to Analyze Lists

PivotTable Reports, Excel equivalent of an Access cross-tab query, is a powerful data summarization tool. A *pivot table* summarizes the columns of information in a database in relationship to each other. A *pivot chart* is the graphical representation of a pivot table. When you need to present thousands of rows of data in a meaningful fashion, you need a pivot table. The Call Log database is a small database, but it would still take several subtotal operations to answer the following questions:

◆ How many calls were received for each application?

◆ How many calls were received from each department?

◆ What is the charge for each department for each application?

You could sort the list and then add subtotals to answer any one of these questions. Then, to answer any other question, you would have to sort and subtotal again. A single pivot table, shown in Figure 17.13, will allow you to answer all of these questions, and more.

FIGURE 17.13

This PivotTable Report for the Call Log summarizes calls by Department and Application.

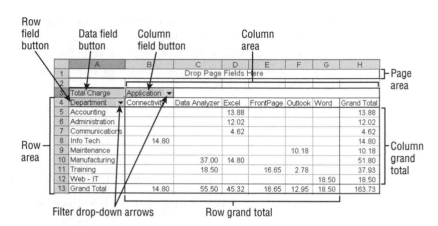

Not all lists are good candidates for pivot table analysis. Lists contain many different types of information. Pivot tables focus on two broad types of information:

◆ Columns of numerical data that can be summarized, like the Charge column in the Call Log

◆ Columns of text that describe the data, such as the Department, Application, Type, and Platform columns

Numeric data fields can be summarized using SUM, AVERAGE, MAX, MIN, and the other aggregate functions including COUNT, which can also be used to summarize text fields.

While pivot tables are often associated with reporting data in two dimensions (for example: sales by month and county, or registrations by term and academic major), you can create one-dimensional pivot tables too. The pivot table shown in Figure 17.14 summarizes charges by department.

FIGURE 17.14

A one-dimensional pivot table, reporting each department's charges.

Sum of Charge	
Department ▼	Total
Accounting	$ 13.88
Administration	$ 12.02
Communications	$ 4.62
Info Tech	$ 14.80
Maintenance	$ 10.18
Manufacturing	$ 51.80
Training	$ 37.93
Web - IT	$ 18.50
Grand Total	$163.73

You can easily extract this same information from the database using the Subtotals feature, but the pivot table has three distinct advantages over subtotals:

◆ Subtotals require a database sorted on the field you wish to subtotal by. We didn't need to change the sort order of the database to create the pivot table. If another user sorts the database, it won't affect the pivot table.

◆ The subtotals feature inserts rows in the database, which makes it temporarily useless as a data source for mail merges, queries, and analysis. The pivot table is created separate from the subtotals.

◆ The most exciting aspect of pivot tables is that they are dynamic. After you create a pivot table, you can rearrange the columns and rows, add and remove data fields, and add calculated fields and items to glean more information from the data. You can pivot the summaries around the detail data, providing different points of view of the details: hence the name *pivot table*. Subtotals are static.

Excel 2003's PivotTable Report feature is simple, and simply incredible, too. So fasten your seatbelt, open a workbook that includes a list, and let's go to work.

Creating a Table with the Wizard

To create an Excel pivot table, you'll use the PivotTable and PivotChart wizard. Follow these steps:

1. Select any cell in a database, and choose Data ➢ PivotTable and PivotChart Report to launch the wizard.

2. The next step in the wizard asks you to select the type of data you need to work with (Figure 17.15). For our purposes, we'll select the data from an Excel database, but other options include the following:

   ◆ data in an Excel database

   ◆ data from an external source like Microsoft Access

   ◆ data that you want to consolidate from several worksheets or sources

   ◆ data from an existing PivotTable

   Basing a pivot table on an existing pivot table results in a smaller file. Specify whether you want a PivotTable or a PivotChart with a PivotTable Report.

FIGURE 17.15

In step 1 of the PivotTable and PivotChart wizard, identify the type of data you want to summarize.

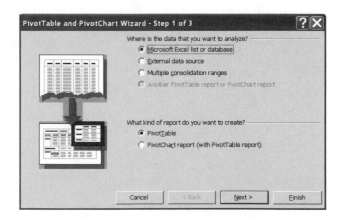

3. Now you'll verify the range of the list, as shown in Figure 17.16. If no range is selected, or if the range is incorrect, select the correct range before clicking the Next button.

FIGURE 17.16

Make sure the database is selected.

4. Specify the destination, layout, and options. The default destination is a new worksheet. To place the pivot table in an existing worksheet, click Existing Worksheet. Identify a cell address for the upper-left corner of the pivot table (Figure 17.17).

FIGURE 17.17

In step 3 of the PivotTable and PivotChart wizard, set options and select a destination.

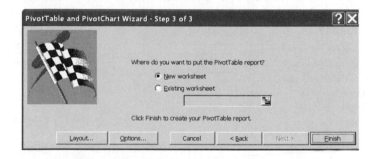

If you're an experienced PivotTable user and prefer to use the structured layout tool, click the Layout button to display the PivotTable and Pivot Chart Wizard Layout dialog box, shown in Figure 17.18.

Each of the four pivot table areas has a corresponding layout area in the Layout dialog box. At the right side of the dialog box is a group of *field buttons*, one for each field name in the database. Design the pivot table layout by dragging the field buttons into one of the four sections of the layout area.

FIGURE 17.18

Designing a table's layout in the Layout dialog box.

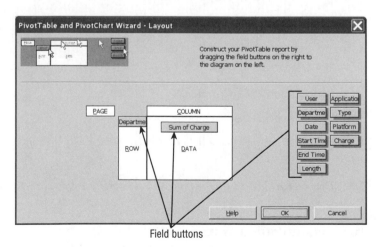

Field buttons

If you're new to pivot tables, skip the Layout dialog box and see the next section, "Changing PivotTable Layout," to learn the best way to lay out pivot tables in Excel 2003.

The other button in the third step of the PivotTable Report and PivotChart wizard is the Options button. Although you can set options in the wizard, it's easier to determine the appropriate settings for some options while you're working in the table. See the section, "Setting Pivot Table Options," later in this chapter for information on options.

Click Finish to create the Pivot Table.

Changing PivotTable Layout

When you complete the wizard, Excel displays the pivot table, the PivotTable toolbar, and the PivotTable Field List, as shown in Figure 17.19. A pivot table contains four areas, which are clearly labeled: the Page area, the Column area, the Row area, and the Data area.

FIGURE 17.19

Create the PivotTable by dragging fields from the Field List to the Data, Row, Column, and Page areas of the report.

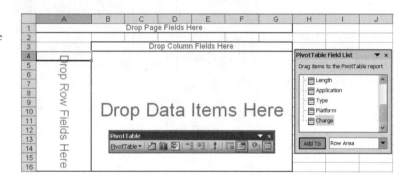

You create a table by placing fields in the data area, the column and Row areas, and optionally the Page area.

1. In the Field List, select a field in the Field List.

2. Choose an Add To location in the drop-down list.

3. Click the Add To button.

   or

1. Choose an Add To location.

2. Double click a field to move it there.

You can also simply drag a field button from the Field List and drop it into one of the PivotTable areas.

TIP   Drag the Field List to the left or right edge of the window to dock it as a task pane.

THE ROW AND COLUMN AREAS

If you want to compare text fields, you place the text fields in question into the Row and Column areas. For example, in our list we could analyze departments and dates, or departments and applications, or departments and call lengths. The Row and Column areas are somewhat interchangeable;

however, your pivot table is easier to use if it isn't too wide. When the table is created, each unique entry becomes a row or column heading—an *item*—in the pivot table. If one of the fields has fewer entries than the other, it's a better candidate for the Column area.

THE PAGE AREA

While you can filter items in the Row area and Column area, the Page area is used specifically to filter the entire pivot table. If you need to create separate reports for values in one or more columns, drag their field buttons to the Page area.

THE DATA AREA

Information in the Data area is summarized (SUM, AVERAGE, COUNT), so numeric fields are generally placed there. If you place a text field in the Data area, you can only COUNT the number of entries for each column and row.

As you drop a field button into the Data area, Excel indicates the default summary type for the data. SUM is the default for values; COUNT is the default for columns that contain text entries, dates, or times.

TIP   If a column of numbers includes text entries, you're limited to COUNT, even if most entries are numeric: a good reason not to use text values like None or NA to indicate the absence of a value. Use Replace (Edit ➤ Replace) to replace text entries like NA with blanks; simply leave the Replace With textbox blank. Blanks are also easier to filter than the text entries used to indicate blanks. To quickly locate all the blank entries in a column, turn on an AutoFilter (Data ➤ Filter ➤ AutoFilter) and choose Blanks from the list of values on the column's filter list.

REMOVING AND ADDING PIVOT TABLE FIELDS

When you're analyzing a database, you'll often want to summarize it in a number of ways. What you learn from one pivot table raises questions that only another pivot table can easily answer. Rather than create a new pivot table, you can change the layout of an existing pivot table by dragging a field button to another area. Excel automatically updates the pivot table.

To remove a field from the pivot table, follow these steps:

1. Drag the field button out of the pivot table area. A large *X* appears on the button.

2. Release the mouse button to drop and delete the field.

3. To add a field to the pivot table, drag a button from the Pivot Table in the Field List.

4. Add, delete, or rearrange the field buttons as needed.

5. Click the Finish button to return to the pivot table.

TIP   The PivotTable toolbar and Field List are displayed only when you select one or more cells in a pivot table. If the toolbar does not appear, right-click any toolbar and select PivotTable from the list. If neither the toolbar nor Field List appears, click in the pivot table and choose Data ➤ PivotTable and PivotChart Report to open the last step of the wizard. Click OK to close the wizard and display the pivot table tools.

You can place more than one field in each area to create a richer analysis. In Figure 17.20, for example, the Row area contains both the Department and Application fields. The Department field has been filtered to display three specific departments.

FIGURE 17.20

The pivot table areas can include multiple fields.

Sum of Charge		Type ▼			
Department ▼	Application ▼	App Error	Beginning	Intermediate	Grand Total
Info Tech	Connectivity		$ 14.80		$ 14.80
Info Tech Total			$ 14.80		$ 14.80
Training	Data Analyzer			$ 18.50	$ 18.50
	FrontPage			$ 16.65	$ 16.65
	Outlook	$ 2.78			$ 2.78
Training Total		$ 2.78		$ 35.15	$ 37.93
Web - IT	Word		$ 18.50		$ 18.50
Web - IT Total			$ 18.50		$ 18.50
Grand Total		$ 2.78	$ 33.30	$ 35.15	$ 71.23

The type area isn't filtered; there are only three columns because, in these three departments, there were only three different call types.

FILTERING ITEMS

To filter data displayed in the pivot table, click the filter drop-down arrow on the field button for the field you wish to filter to open a list of items in the field. Enable the checkboxes for the items you want to display and then click OK to close the list and filter the pivot table.

TIP   Do you want to include this filtered table in a report you're creating in Word? Select and copy the filtered pivot table. Open the Word document and place your insertion point where you want to place the pivot table. Click Paste to embed the pivot table in the Word document. Click anywhere in the pivot table to fire up the Excel toolbars so you can format the table.

GROUPING ITEMS

Grouping combines items, and is usually used for date fields to combine them into months or years. For example, if we dropped the Date field from the Call Log worksheet for the entire third quarter into the Column area of a pivot table, there would be almost as many columns as there are in the original database.

That's fine if the goal is a day-by-day analysis of calls. To analyze by month, quarter, or year, we need to group the data in the Date field. To group a field, right-click the field and choose Group and Show Detail ➤ Group from the shortcut menu to open the Grouping dialog box, shown in Figure 17.21.

FIGURE 17.21

Use the Group and Outline dialog box to group data by month or year.

The list box in the Grouping dialog box is a multi-pick list; choose Month if you want to group by month regardless of year (that is, if details from March 2000 and March 2001 should be combined into a single row). Choose both Month and Year (see Figure 17.23) if the same month in different years should be in separate rows. The pivot table, grouped by month and year, is shown in Figure 17.22.

FIGURE 17.22

The Third Quarter Call Log pivot table report, grouped by month.

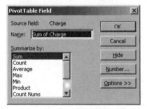

Sum of Charge	Years ▾	Date ▾		
	2003			Grand Total
Department ▾	Jul	Aug	Sep	
Accounting	24.98	24.98	24.98	74.93
Administration	76.78	76.78	76.78	230.33
Analysis	18.50	37.00		55.50
Communications	37.00	37.00	37.00	111.00
Info Tech	58.28	58.28	58.28	174.83
Maintenance	44.40	44.40	44.40	133.20
Manufacturing	13.88	13.88	13.88	41.63
Sales	19.43	19.43	19.43	58.28
Training	56.43	56.43	56.43	169.28
Web - IT	2.77	2.77	2.77	8.32
Grand Total	352.43	370.93	333.93	1,057.28

Changing the Summary and Format for Data Fields

To change the summarization method for a data field, click the Field Settings button on the PivotTable toolbar or double-click the field button in the Data area to open the PivotTable Field dialog box. Choose the type of summary you want to use from the list box:

The default number format in a pivot table is General. Click the Number button in the Pivot Table Field dialog box to change formats, or use the Formatting toolbar and Format Cells dialog box to format the completed pivot table.

Click the Option button to extend the PivotTable Field dialog box and you can perform custom calculations (see "Using Custom Calculations in Pivot Tables," later in this chapter). While you're in the PivotTable Field dialog box, you can enter a new name for the field that's less verbose than "Sum of Charge" or "Count of Charge." You cannot give the pivot table field the same name as the underlying database field (Charge in our example), but you can name it Charge_. The underscore is almost invisible on the field button.

TIP   You can rename fields in your pivot table without opening the PivotTable Field dialog box. Click the field button, overtype the name in the formula bar, and press Enter.

Setting Pivot Table Options

Pivot tables are constructed objects. Unlike a regular worksheet, the pivot table is just a description of the data used to create the table. The pivot table rows and columns are created and populated based on the description. The PivotTable Options dialog box is anything but optional; you'll save lots of time if you know what you can change in this dialog box.

Right-click anywhere in the pivot table and choose Table Options, or open the PivotTable menu on the PivotTable toolbar and choose Table Options to open the PivotTable Options dialog box, shown in Figure 17.23. If you're going to create several pivot tables in a worksheet, name them. If you don't name a pivot table, Excel will give it the default name: Pivotable1 for the first, PivotTable2 for the second, and so on.

FIGURE 17.23

Name the pivot table and set options for totals in the Options dialog box.

The default settings for Format Options and Data Options are shown in Figure 17.25. Table 17.1 describes the pivot table formatting options.

TABLE 17.1: PIVOT TABLE FORMAT OPTIONS

OPTION	DESCRIPTION
Name	Name for the pivot table. The default name is PivotTable*n*.
Grand Totals for Columns	Places a row of grand totals at the bottom of the pivot table. Enabled by default.
Grand Total for Rows	Places a column of grand totals at the right edge of the pivot table. Enabled by default.
AutoFormat Table	Applies an AutoFormat to the pivot table. Enabled by default.
Subtotal Hidden Page Items	Includes hidden items in the Page area in the subtotals.
Merge Labels	Merges the cells for row and column labels to make the table more compact and readable.
Preserve Formatting	Retains user-applied formatting when the table is updated. Enabled by default.
Repeat Item Labels on Each Printed Page	Used to set row titles that appear on each page of a printed report.

Continued on next page

TABLE 17.1: PIVOT TABLE FORMAT OPTIONS *(continued)*

OPTION	DESCRIPTION
Mark Totals With *	Displays an asterisk * after subtotals and grand totals to denote they may include hidden items. Only available for pivot tables based on an OLAP data source.
Page Layout	Order of printed pages.
Fields Per Column	Number of page fields that should be displayed before Excel starts another row of page fields.
For Error Values Show	Value to display for pivot table cells that show an error.
For Empty Cells Show	Value to display for pivot table cells that are blank.
Set Print Titles	Used to set column titles that appear on each page of a printed report.

If you don't want grand totals in your pivot table, this is the place to turn them off. Enable the Empty Cells check box to suppress the automatic display of zeros for empty pivot table cells.

The pivot table data options determine how the data in a table is accessed and refreshed. Table 17.2 describes the pivot table data options.

TABLE 17.2: PIVOT TABLE DATA OPTIONS

OPTION	DESCRIPTION
Save Data With Table Layout	Creates a pivot table cache so the table can be more quickly refreshed.
Enable Drilldown to Details	Allows drilldown into individual items in the data area. Enabled by default.
Refresh On Open	Refreshes data each time the workbook containing the database is opened.
Refresh Every X Minutes	Specifies how often data from an external database is refreshed.
Save Password	Stores the password for the external database in the workbook.
Background Query	Runs the external database query in the background so you can continue working during refresh operations.
Optimize Memory	Reduces the amount of memory used during refresh operations.

Applying a Format

There are 22 different AutoFormats designed specifically for pivot tables. The first 10 AutoFormats captioned Report 1 through Report 10 are indented formats designed to resemble traditional printed database reports, which were, in turn, based on outlines used in text documents.

These PivotTable Reports look very little like pivot tables, and a lot like reports you'd spend a fair amount of time creating and formatting in Access or a reporting application. The indented levels allow users to read section values down a column, and clearly demarcate the breaks between values.

Table 1 through Table 10 and the Classic Pivot Table formats resemble tables more than reports.

To apply an AutoFormat, click the Format Report button on the PivotTable toolbar to open the AutoFormat dialog box, shown in Figure 17.24. Select a format and click OK to apply the format. If the results aren't what you intended, click Undo.

FIGURE 17.24

Select an indented report format or traditional pivot table format for your table.

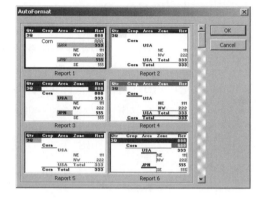

Using External Data Sources

In applications other than Excel, pivot tables are often called cross-tab reports. If you've worked with cross-tab reports in Microsoft Access or a reporting tool like Crystal Reports, you already appreciate the ease of use of Excel's PivotTable Report feature. Both Crystal Reports and Access are great software, but neither compares to Excel for ad hoc cross-tabular reporting, particularly if you want to quickly change the report layout. The good news is that you can use Excel to create pivot tables for external data from other data sources, including these:

- ◆ Access databases

- ◆ SQL Server databases

- ◆ Oracle databases

- ◆ Any ODBC- (Open DataBase Connectivity) compliant application for which you have a driver

There are two ways to retrieve external data for a pivot table: by opening an Office Data Connection (ODC file) or using Microsoft Query.

USING AN OFFICE DATA CONNECTION

To use an Office Data Connection in Excel, open the data source by choosing Data ➢ Import External Data ➢ Import Data from the menu. Excel opens your Select Data Source dialog box shown in Figure 17.25 and displays the data sources in the My Documents\My Data Sources folder. Select the data connection, import the data, then start the PivotTable Report Wizard.

FIGURE 17.25

Select an Office Data Connection to supply data for a pivot table.

USING MICROSOFT QUERY IN A PIVOTTABLE REPORT

If you want to use an existing query or any data source other than the current workbook or an Office Data Connection, use Microsoft Query. Microsoft Query is not installed during the typical Office System 2003 installation, so have your Office CD on hand when you start the PivotTable and PivotChart wizard:

1. Select Data ➢ PivotTable and PivotChart Report and choose External Data Source in the first of the three wizard steps.

2. In the second step of the wizard, click the Get Data button.

3. The Microsoft Query Choose Data Source dialog box appears. Follow the steps in the wizard to choose your data source and create a query. In the final step of the wizard, choose Return Data To Excel to return to the PivotTable Report wizard.

Keeping Your Pivot Table Updated

A pivot table is dynamically linked to the database used to create the table. If you edit values within the database, simply choose Data ➢ Refresh Data or click the Refresh Data button on the Pivot Table toolbar, and Excel will update the pivot table to reflect the database changes.

However, if you add columns to the database or add rows of data at the bottom of the database, you *cannot* simply refresh the data. You must return to the Pivot Table and PivotChart wizard and identify the new range of records that should be included in the table. If you don't, the pivot table values won't include the added data.

To update the range being used in the pivot table, choose Data ➢ PivotTable and PivotTable Chart Report from the menu or open the PivotTable menu in the Pivot Table toolbar and choose Pivot Table Wizard. Move to the second step of the wizard and reselect the database. Click the Finish button to close the wizard and return to the updated pivot table.

Using Custom Calculations in Pivot Tables

Excel 2003 supports two types of custom calculations in pivot tables: you can change the summarization function and basis for a Data field, or add a calculated field or item to a pivot table.

CALCULATED FIELDS AND ITEMS

The pivot table report includes data from the database. You can perform calculations on the data by inserting a calculated field in the data area or a calculated item in the columns or rows area. For example, we could add a field to our pivot table to calculate the actual cost (instead of the chargeback cost) for the calls summarized in the pivot table. Calculated fields perform calculations on the totals in the pivot table, not on the values in the individual records.

Inserting a Calculated Field

To insert a calculated field:

1. Select any cell in the PivotTable.

2. Open the PivotTable menu on the PivotTable toolbar.

3. Choose Formulas ➤ Calculated Field to open the Insert Calculated Field dialog box:

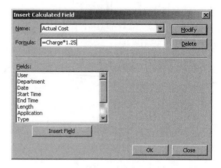

4. Type a name for the field in the Name text box.

5. Enter a formula for the calculated field in the Formula box. Use the Fields list and Insert Field button to use a field in the formula.

6. Click Add to create the field.

7. Click OK to close the dialog box and return to the pivot table.

The calculated field is added to the pivot table and the pivot table field list, as shown in Figure 17.26. To change the order of the data fields in the table, right-click the field you wish to move, then choose Order from the shortcut menu and select from the menu choices, or use drag and drop to move the field as you would any other pivot table field.

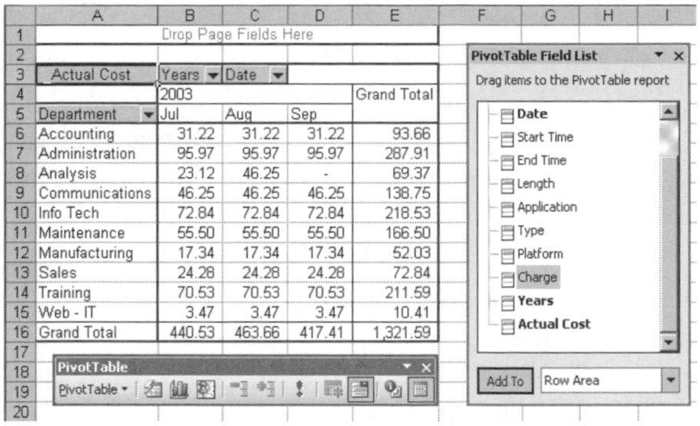

FIGURE 17.26

Calculated fields are added to the PivotTable Field List, so you can use them as you would other pivot table fields.

NOTE *Calculated item formulas are calculated for each record in the database and then summarized in the pivot table. You add a calculation to all items in a field, but you can modify the calculation for individual items. To insert a calculated item select the field or any item in the field that you want to create a calculation for. Choose PivotTable ➢ Formulas ➢ Calculated Item from the PivotTable toolbar. You can't use calculated items and grouping in the same pivot table.*

Drilling Down in a Pivot Table

If you need to see both a summary and the underlying detail, pivot tables are the tool of choice. Even though the cells in the Data area of a PivotTable contain summary information, you can *drill down* into a pivot table to view all the detail that underlies an individual summary figure. Double-click any nonzero value in the Data area, and Excel opens a new worksheet to display the records that were used to create that cell of the summary.

If you can't drill down in a worksheet, the option may be disabled in the Table Options dialog box. Right-click inside the pivot table and choose Table Options to open the dialog box.

TIP *Disable the drill down option to prevent users from seeing the underlying data in a table. Use this option when you want to present aggregate data—for example, employee attendance or student test scores—while keeping the details about individual employees or students confidential.*

Creating Separate Pivot Tables

Rather than printing different departments' or counties' pivot tables on different pages, you might want to create a series of pivot tables—one for each department or county. You can do this quite simply. First, make sure that the field you want to create individual tables for (such as Department in our example) is in the Page area of the table. Then take the following steps:

1. Arrange the layout so that the field that you want to use to separate the tables is in the Page area.

2. On the PivotTable toolbar choose PivotTable ➢ Show Pages.

3. Choose the field you want to create separate pivot tables for, and click OK.

Excel inserts new worksheets and creates a pivot table for each item in the selected field.

Creating Pivot Charts

Pivot charts help users understand data in a way that conventional database reports cannot. You can base a PivotChart on an existing pivot table or a database. If you create a PivotChart based on a database, Excel creates an *associated pivot table* before creating the chart, so if you need to create a table and a chart, save a step by simply creating the chart. The default PivotChart type is a two-dimensional column chart, but you can switch to any of the chart types that are suitable for summary data.

You can rearrange the way the data fields appear in the chart, but the pivot chart will start out with the pivot table's row fields assigned to the category axis (the horizontal, or x-axis) in the chart. Similarly, the column fields in the table become the series (the vertical, or y-axis) fields in the chart. Pivot charts also have optional page fields.

Here are the steps for creating a pivot chart:

1. Click anywhere in the database, then select Data ≻ PivotTable and PivotChart Report.

2. In the first step of the wizard, select PivotChart Report (with PivotTable report) and click Next.

3. In the second wizard step, verify that the correct data range is selected and click Next.

If you have already created a pivot table with the selected data range, Excel prompts you to create a chart based on the existing pivot table. If you don't intend to delete the existing pivot table, this is a good idea. If more than one pivot table exists for the data, Excel will prompt you to pick the one you want to use.

4. In the third step in the wizard, choose a location for the associated pivot table. Click Finish.

TIP   *Both PivotChart and PivotTable objects can be copied and pasted into documents in other applications. If you want to use your PivotChart in a PowerPoint presentation, create it in Excel as an object rather than on a new worksheet. Then select and copy the object, switch to PowerPoint, click the slide, and paste or paste link (Edit ≻ Paste Special).*

If you based your chart on an existing pivot table, or visited the Layout dialog box in the wizard, your chart will have columns, labels, and a legend, as shown in Figure 17.27. If not, you'll have a blank pivot chart and the PivotTable toolbar and field list. Drag fields onto the labeled chart areas to create the chart.

FIGURE 17.27

The Pivot Chart has many of the same options as the pivot table, including filter drop-down lists.

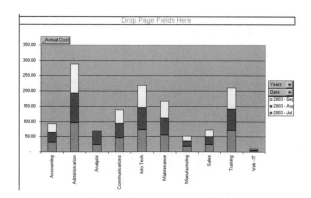

The chart fields have many of the same properties as pivot table fields. Use the filter drop-down lists to filter chart items, select a button to rename the field, or double-click a data button to change the summarization method. Use the Chart toolbar and menu to modify the chart elements as you would any Excel chart.

TIP To use calculated fields to a pivot chart, add the fields to the associated pivot table. The fields will be available for the associated pivot chart.

Importing and Exporting Data in Office

In the first section in this chapter, we compared the import and export features in the Office applications. Excel is an "Excel-lent" data application because it imports and exports data from and to a large number of file formats, but Access and Outlook are no slouches when it comes to data transferability. Table 17.3 summarizes frequently encountered file formats you can open directly in each of the Office 2003 applications.

TABLE 17.3: COMMON FILE FORMATS AND OFFICE 2003 COMPATIBILITY

FILE FORMAT	DESCRIPTION	OPEN WITH
csv	Comma delimited text	Excel
dbf	dBASE	Excel
doc	WordPerfect	Word
htm, html, mhtm, mhtml	Web pages	Word, Excel
iqy, oqy, rqy, dqy	Queries	Excel
prn	Text	Excel
pwi, pdt	InkWriter, NoteTaker	Word
txt	Text files	Word, Excel
wk?	Lotus 1-2-3	Excel, PowerPoint, Word
wk1	Quattro Pro	Excel, PowerPoint, Word
wks	Works spreadsheet	Excel
wps	Works	Word
xml	eXtensible Markup Language	Word, Excel

Importing and Exporting in Word

In Word, most importing and exporting is done in the Open and Save As dialog boxes. To convert a file from another format, simply open the file. Word automatically converts the document.

TIP   *To have Word alert you when it converts a document from another format, Choose Tools* ➤ *Options to open the Options dialog box. On the General tab, enable the Confirm Conversion At Open check box.*

To convert a Word document to another format, choose File ➤ Save As. Select the file format you want from the Save As Type drop-down list.

If you want to convert a group of files from another format to Word or convert a bunch of Word documents to a different format, use Word's Batch Conversion wizard. Follow these steps:

1. Move all the documents to one folder.

2. Choose File ➤ New from the menu.

3. In the Templates section of the New Document task pane, click On My Computer to open the Templates dialog box shown in Figure 17.28.

FIGURE 17.28

To use the Batch Conversion wizard, begin by opening the Templates dialog box.

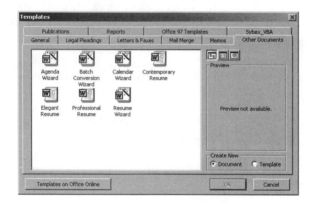

4. On the Other Documents tab, double-click the Batch Conversion Wizard icon.

5. Follow the steps in the wizard to select the format you want to convert from or to (see Figure 17.29) and the folder that contains the documents.

FIGURE 17.29

Select the file format you want to convert from or to in the Batch wizard.

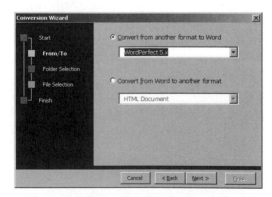

6. Choose the files you want to convert and then complete the wizard.

Importing and Exporting in Access

Access can work with information in almost any PC spreadsheet or database format. You can add copies of tables from other applications to your database or connect directly to tables that exist in a separate database, including spreadsheet files. Access can import (copy) or link (connect to) data from prior versions of Access, non-Microsoft databases like dBASE and Paradox, XML data sources, spreadsheets like Excel and Lotus 1-2-3, and HTML tables from the Internet or an intranet. You can even link to an Outlook Address Book, an Exchange folder, or a folder on a SharePoint site. Programmers will appreciate that the Import command now lets you choose XML (eXtensible Markup Language) documents.

The capability to work with data from a variety of sources makes Access a powerful tool in today's workplace, where data can originate in a variety of applications. Before you retype data that already exists, it's worth your time to see whether you can import it directly into Access or transfer it to a program that Access can use.

Access 2003 can turn almost any data file into an Access database table. Choose File ➢ Open to open an existing data file, then set the Files Of Type drop-down to "All Files (*.*)". The Open dialog box will now show multiple data file types (Excel spreadsheets, other database types, text files) in the folder. Opening a file created in an application like Excel starts the Link Spreadsheet wizard, which guides you through setting up a new database based on the data file. The new database contains a single table, linked to the original file, so you can use the data in Access without duplicating data. Creating an entire database for a single linked table isn't always the most efficient way to work with data, however, so read through the following sections on importing and linking tables into existing databases to determine which method is appropriate.

IMPORTING VS. LINKING

Importing data creates a copy of the data in a table in your database. Because a copy is created, the original data isn't affected, and further changes in the original data are not reflected in Access. With *linked* data, you are working with original data; when the source file changes, the changes are reflected in Access, and changes you make in Access are reflected in the source file.

Before you can bring external data into your Access database via importing or linking, you need to decide which method you want to use. For example, let's say that you're creating a new database, and a colleague in another department offers you an Excel spreadsheet that lists all the cities, states, and zip codes for your region. Should you import or link? If you know that the spreadsheet isn't routinely updated, you should import it. Cities, states, and zip codes rarely change, so updating isn't an issue with this data. When you import data, you can change field properties and rearrange or delete fields if you need to, so importing is more flexible from your point of view.

Contrast this with an Excel spreadsheet maintained by the Purchasing Department that lists current products in the inventory. New products are constantly added, and products are removed. You don't want salespeople who use your database to sell products you no longer carry, or fail to sell products that are in stock. You should *link* to this spreadsheet so your users always have access to current data.

IMPORTING DATA

To import external data, have an existing database or new database file at the ready. Then, choose File ➢ Get External Data ➢ Import to open the Import dialog box. Select the type of file you want to import from the Files Of Type drop-down list. Locate and select the file, and click Import. See the following sections for details on importing from different types of applications.

Importing Data from Spreadsheets and Other Databases

You can easily import data from Excel or Lotus 1-2-3. (Other spreadsheet filters are available with a custom Office installation.) To do so, follow these steps:

1. Choose File ➢ Get External Data ➢ Import to open the Import dialog box.

2. Select the file you wish to import. Click the Import button. (If you can't see Excel or Lotus files, change the Files Of Type drop-down list at the bottom of the Import dialog box.)

3. If you're importing from an Excel workbook with more than one named range or worksheet, you are prompted to select a worksheet or range, as shown in Figure 17.30. Select the range or worksheet you want to import, and click Next.

FIGURE 17.30

Select a worksheet or range in the Import Spreadsheet wizard.

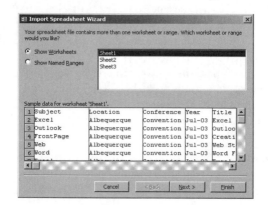

4. In the next step of the wizard (the first step you see if there is only one data source in the file you selected), indicate whether the spreadsheet's first row is data or column labels. Click Next.

TIP   If some of the column headings aren't valid Access field names, Access notifies you that it will convert the names (using names like Field1, Field2, etc.). If you're importing this data into a new table, you can change these names in Design view after importing the data. If you intend to import the data directly into an existing table, however, this is a problem. Cancel the wizard, make sure the column headings in the spreadsheet match the field names in the existing table, and start again.

5. In the next step, choose whether you want Access to create a new table with this data or place it in an existing table. If you choose an existing table, the column labels in the spreadsheet and the field names in the table must be identical. Click Next.

6. If you've chosen to import the data into a new table, the next step of the wizard allows you to indicate whether the data in each column is indexed; you can omit any columns of data you don't want by enabling the Do Not Import Field (Skip) check box. Click Next.

7. In the next step, choose whether to have Access add an AutoNumber primary key (not always the best idea), select an existing column as the primary key, or indicate that there is no primary key field.

TIP *If the primary key includes more than one field, choose No Primary Key Field, and set the primary key in table Design view after you've imported the data. If you're not sure, choose No Primary Key.*

8. In the last step of the wizard, name the table and click Finish. Access will import the data.

After the table is imported, you may want to make some changes in Design view. For example, if a Social Security Number column was imported as numbers, you'd want to change the data type to Text and add an input mask to speed up data entry. Numbers that won't be calculated, such as zip codes and part numbers, should be changed if necessary to the Text data type to retain leading or trailing zeros. Data types and field properties (like input masks) are discussed at length later in this chapter.

When you import from a database other than Access, the Import Database wizard opens, and the steps are similar to the steps in the Import Spreadsheet wizard.

TROUBLESHOOTING DATA IMPORT GLITCHES

Access can successfully import or link only to valid databases. Most database applications can only be used to create valid databases; spreadsheet, text, HTML, and XML files may not be valid databases unless they are set up properly.

When you try to import invalid data, Access reports zero records imported at the end of the Import wizard. Open the file in its native application and make whatever corrections are necessary to make it a valid database; then resave the file and try again.

If, for example, you try to import 50 rows of data from Excel, and Access reports that zero rows were imported, the Excel spreadsheet is probably not a valid Excel database. Open the Excel workbook, select any cell in the database range, and choose Data ➤ Sort. Excel will select the database range or display a message box indicating that no list is found—that the active cell is not part of a database.

If some, but not all, rows and columns are selected, check for blank rows or columns within the database. If there is no list, look for advanced formatting in the range. An Excel database can't have merged cells; and multiline cells (created by pressing Alt+Enter when entering data) aren't accurately imported. When you've corrected the Excel database, save the workbook and try importing again.

You can also use Excel's tools to check text and mark up databases. Launch Excel and open the HTML, XML, or text document to see how it performs with Excel's data tools.

If you import from another Access database, you aren't limited to importing just data. You can import forms, reports, macros, and even relationships. When you choose an Access database in the Import dialog box, the Import Objects dialog box opens. Click the Options button to extend the dialog box to show other available options.

Importing from Outlook or Exchange

You can import items from any of the MAPI folders or address books in Outlook, and import or link to an Exchange address book. Follow these steps to import your Contacts folder from Outlook or Exchange:

1. Choose File ➢ Get External Data ➢ Import.

2. In the Files Of Type drop-down list, choose Outlook or Exchange to open the Import Exchange/Outlook wizard.

3. Locate and select your Contacts folder. Click Next.

4. Select whether you wish to import the contacts into a new table or an existing table. If you select an existing table, the field names must match the field names in Outlook. Click Next.

5. If you're importing the data into an existing table, you're done. Simply click Finish and wait while Access imports the data.

6. If you chose to import the data into a new table, verify the data type for each field. Enable the Do Not Import check box to skip the selected field. Click Next.

7. Next, choose whether to have Access add an AutoNumber primary key (still not the best idea), select an existing column as the primary key, or indicate that there is no primary key field. You can assign a primary key later in Design view if you want. Click Next.

8. In the final step enter a name for the new table. Click Finish to import the data.

Relax and grab a beverage—this operation can take a few minutes. Access notifies you when the import is complete.

NOTE *You can't use this method to import user-created or custom fields. The import includes only the standard fields from the folder. If you need to import Outlook custom fields, you'll need a bit of Visual Basic code. On the Microsoft site, search for Knowledge Base article Q208232 for information on importing user-defined fields from Outlook into Access.*

LINKING TO A SPREADSHEET OR DATABASE

If the data you want to include from another source gets updated periodically, you should link to the data rather than importing it. Examples of *dynamic data* include lists of customers or products, price schedules, current course offerings, etc. Linking to a table or worksheet is even less complex than importing. You can't change the structure of the linked table or worksheet, so you don't get an opportunity to skip columns.

Follow these steps to link to an external data source:

1. Choose File ➢ Get External Data ➢ Link Tables.

2. Select the type of data source you want to link to in the Files Of Type drop-down list, select the file you want to link to, and click Link to open the Link wizard.

3. If you're linking to a spreadsheet or other non-Access file, select the worksheet, named range, or table you want to link to, and click Link. If you're linking to a table or set of tables in another Access database, select the table name(s) and click OK.

If you're linking to another Access table, the table is linked and you're finished. If you're linking to a non-Access file, continue with step 4.

4. In the wizard, indicate whether the first row contains data or column labels, and click Next.

5. Enter the name you will use to refer to the external table or worksheet, and click Finish.

You can tell which tables in a database are links to other tables. Linked Access tables have a link arrow in front of the Access table icon; other linked file types have their own icons with the link arrow.

If you decide later that you don't want to maintain the link, select and delete the link in the Table tab of the Database window. The link is deleted, but the original data source is not affected.

Importing and Exporting in Excel

It's easy to import data files from other Microsoft Office applications, but getting the stuff from non-Office programs can be more challenging. Fortunately, Excel readily opens files saved as plain text, and most programs can save files in this format. Formatting doesn't import well. Be prepared to reformat columns, reapply fonts, and apply other formatting changes that are lost during an import operation.

Here are the steps to open a non-native file (a file created in another application) in Excel:

1. Select File ➤ Open. In the Files Of Type list box, find the relevant file type (for example, XML, Text, or an earlier version of Excel) from the Files Of Type drop-down menu.

2. Locate and select the file you want.

3. Click Open. The file opens (Figure 17.31).

FIGURE 17.31

Opening an HTML song list in Excel.

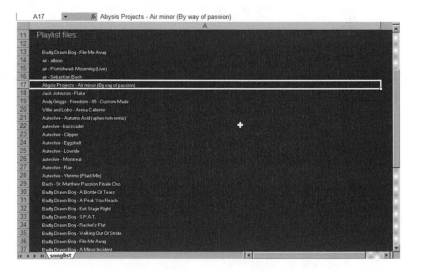

WARNING *If your file does not open, or looks very garbled in Excel, open it in the original application and save the file as an Excel file, or save it as a text file and use the steps in the next section to get it into Excel.*

In some instances, an attempt to open a file results in a "file not valid" error message. There are two possible reasons for this message: Excel doesn't support the file type, or the type is supported but the converter is not installed. Excel supports a number of file formats, including Lotus 1-2-3 and Quattro Pro. The Lotus 1-2-3 converter is installed by default; the Quattro Pro converter is installed in a custom installation only.

If the file type you wish to open isn't supported by Excel, return to the original application, save the file as a delimited text file, and reopen it in Excel with the Text Import Wizard, described in the next section.

TIP Most files can be imported if you have access to the file's native application or an application that can convert the document. If you're familiar with the file formats that each of your applications supports, you'll often be able to find an application to use as a translation tool to move from one format to another. For example, Excel imports WordPerfect tables poorly. However, with the appropriate converters installed, Word opens WordPerfect documents and appropriately displays WordPerfect tables. And you can copy/paste data directly from Word to Excel. To move data from WordPerfect to Excel, then, either save the WordPerfect document as a Word document, or open the WordPerfect document directly in Word and save it as a Word document. Copy the table, and paste it in the Excel worksheet.

Parsing Imported Data with the Text Import Wizard

When Excel can't open an imported file directly, you can use the Text Import wizard to open the file and parse it into an Excel spreadsheet. When you *parse* a file, Excel examines it, converts text items to appropriate data types, and places the data in rows and columns. In order to be parsed successfully, a text file must already resemble a spreadsheet or table, with each paragraph corresponding to a record or row, and with a consistent character, usually a comma or tab, used to mark the column breaks.

Here's how to open a text file, parse its contents, and import it using the Text Import wizard:

1. Select File ➢ Open and select Text Files in the Files Of Type list box.

2. Locate and select the file. Click Open. The first step of the Text Import Wizard appears.

3. The wizard attempts to determine what type of text file it is opening. Set or verify the data type option:

   Delimited Text files where data fields are separated by commas, tabs, or another consistent symbol or character

   Fixed Width Nondelimited files in which each field is a specific length; space between fields is padded with zeros or spaces

4. Use the Start Import At Row spin-box control to skip titles or blank rows at the beginning of the file. The row you select should contain column headings if the file contains them or the first row of data.

5. If you are importing a Mac or DOS file rather than a file created in a Windows application, select the appropriate operating system from the File Origin drop-down list. Click Next to move to the second step of the wizard.

6. Excel adds the column boundaries. If the columns aren't correct, change the symbol used as the delimiter. When you have selected the correct delimiter, each column will contain data from one field. Click Next.

TIP   This is your only chance to correctly separate the data into fields. If you've tried each of the delimiters and the columns are still incorrect, your file may have fixed-width fields, or consecutive delimiters. Click Back to return to the first step to set the Fixed Width option. Enable the Treat Consecutive Delimiters As One check box in the second step to have Excel disregard consecutive delimiters.

7. In the final step in the Text Import wizard, choose the format for each of the newly defined columns. Select a column and choose the format. (Double-check the formats for date columns, which Excel often assumes are Text.) Select the Do Not Import option to skip the selected field. The default format setting is General. The format used in the column appears in the header. If you want all of the columns to have the same format, but something other than General, hold Shift and click each column until all are selected. Choose a format from the options in the Column Data Format area.

TIP   Eurodata alert: click the Advanced button to choose separators if you're importing data that uses decimal and thousands separators other than the period and comma.

8. Click Finish when the formats have been set.

TIP   You can use Excel's internal parsing tool to separate a column of data into two columns (for example, a column of full names into first and last names). First insert a blank column to the right of the existing column. Then select the column of data and choose Data ➤ Text To Columns.

Using Refreshable Text Importing

If you will be updating the original text file containing the data you plan to import, you can establish a link to this source file so that every time it is changed, those modifications will appear in the Excel file, too. This process, known as *refreshable text importing,* uses the Text Import Wizard, too, but accesses it through a different menu command.

To implement refreshable text, use these steps:

1. Select the first cell where you will place the imported data.

2. Choose Data ➤ Import External Data ➤ Import Data from the menu.

3. Select your data source. You can use the Files Of Type drop-down to limit or expand your file type options.

4. Select the file and click Open to launch the Text Import wizard.

Your text data is now imported, and you can make changes as needed.

Importing and Exporting in Outlook

Outlook can import and export a number of different file formats used by Outlook itself as well as competing products.

IMPORTING FILES INTO OUTLOOK

The following file types can be imported into Outlook from external programs:

- ACT! 3.x, 4.x, 2000 Contact Manager for Windows
- Comma Separated Values (DOS and Windows)
- Lotus Organizer (4.x and 5.x)
- Microsoft Access
- Microsoft Excel
- Personal Address Book
- Personal Folder File
- Schedule Plus Interchange
- Schedule+ 7.0
- Tab Separated Values (DOS and Windows)

Follow these steps to import a file into Outlook:

1. Choose File ➢ Import and Export to open the Import and Export Wizard dialog box, shown in Figure 17.32

FIGURE 17.32

The Outlook Import and Export Wizard

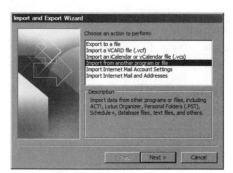

2. Choose From Another Program Or File. Click Next.
3. Select the file type you'd like to import by highlighting it. Click Next.

4. Browse until you find the file you'd like to import. Determine replacement values by selecting the radio button next to one of these options:

   ◆ Replace duplicates with items imported

   ◆ Allow duplicates to be created

   ◆ Do not import duplicate items

5. Click Next. Choose a destination folder within Outlook for the imported items. Click Next.

Your items will be imported into Outlook.

EXPORTING ITEMS FROM OUTLOOK

You can export Outlook data to a file. To do so, follow these steps:

1. From within Outlook, choose File ➢ Import and Export. The Import and Export wizard opens.

2. Select Export To A File from the list of options. Click Next.

3. Choose which file type you'd like to export your Outlook data to. You can export to a range of types suitable for later import into other programs.

4. Click Next. Choose the folder you'd like to export. Click Next.

5. Name the file and select a location for saving. Click Next.

6. Outlook will take you to the Export To A File dialog, which shows you which folder you're exporting from. If the export is correct, click Finish.

This process may take some time, depending upon how much data you're exporting.

WARNING   *Once you've chosen to export a folder and click Finish in the final wizard dialog, you cannot undo this action.*

Chapter 18

Tweaking Office to Fit the Way You Work

MICROSOFT OFFICE 2003 WAS designed with a whole host of different users in mind. Some users prefer to use keyboard shortcuts, while others depend heavily on point-and-click; some users like menus, while others prefer icons. Most users are content to learn one or two ways to complete a task while others use various methods depending on the task at hand. To make one application suite respond to the needs of so many different work styles, Microsoft incorporated a variety of ways to customize Office to make it easier for any dedicated user to become an efficient Office user. To get the most out of Office, you must invest a bit of time to tweak the options so the Office apps will respond to your personal preferences.

In this chapter, we'll show you how to customize toolbars and menus in applications and set options that increase your efficiency and maximize your productivity.

◆ Modifying toolbars and menus

◆ Creating new toolbars

◆ Customizing shortcut menus

◆ Setting application options

◆ Changing the default templates in Word and Excel

Adding Shortcuts to Office 2003 Applications

Office 2003 doesn't include an Office Shortcut bar. You can create your own shortcuts to the Office applications on the Windows XP Start menu or the Quick Launch bar in Windows 2000 or Windows XP.

Adding a Shortcut to the Quick Launch Bar

The Quick Launch bar is docked within the Windows Taskbar. Drag the vertical bar on the left end of the Quick Launch bar to resize the bar, position it within the Taskbar, or drag it onto the desktop.

NOTE *In Windows XP, the Taskbar needs to be unlocked to add shortcuts to it. To unlock the taskbar, right click on the task bar, and make sure there is no check next to Lock the Taskbar on the menu.*

CUSTOMIZING THE QUICK LAUNCH BAR IN WINDOWS XP

Follow the commands below to display the Quick Launch bar and add commands to it.

1. Right-click the Taskbar and choose Properties from the shortcut menu.

2. On the Taskbar tab, enable the Show Quick Launch check box. Click OK.

3. Open My Computer. Locate and open the `Microsoft Office` application folder (in the `Program Files` folder). Open the `Office` folder.

4. Drag the application icon and drop it on the Quick Launch bar.

TIP *A quick way to display Quick Launch: Simply right-click on the Taskbar, highlight Toolbars, and then select Quick Launch.*

CUSTOMIZING THE QUICK LAUNCH BAR IN WINDOWS 2000

Follow the commands below to display the Quick Launch bar and add commands to it.

1. Right-click any empty area of the Taskbar. (If you have a number of applications running, you may need to close a couple to create an empty area.)

2. Select Toolbars from the shortcut menu. A submenu will appear, be sure that Quick Launch is checked.

3. Open My Computer. Locate and open the `Microsoft Office` application folder (in the `Program Files` folder). Open the `Office` folder.

4. Drag the application icon and drop it on the Quick Launch bar.

Adding a Shortcut to the Start Menu

Follow these steps to add an application to the Windows 2000 Start menu:

1. Open My Computer. Locate and open the `Office` folder (`Program Files\Microsoft Office\Office`).

2. Drag the application icon and drop it on the Start button to add the application to the Start menu.

To remove a Windows 2000 Start menu item, right-click the item and choose Delete.
Follow these steps to pin an application to the Windows XP Start menu:

1. Choose Start ➢ Programs ➢ Microsoft Office.

2. Right-click the Office application you want to add to the Start menu.

3. Choose Pin to Start Menu from the shortcut menu.

To unpin a Windows XP Start menu item, right-click the item and choose Unpin From Start Menu from the shortcut menu.

Customizing Application Menus and Toolbars

When you initially launch an Office application, the app displays one row of buttons containing the most frequently used buttons from the Standard and Formatting toolbars. The menus show similarly limited options. In order to see all choices under a menu, you must pause a moment or click the Expand button at the bottom of the collapsed menu.

As you use an application, Office personalizes the toolbars and menus by displaying the commands you have already used: When an entire toolbar or menu is not displayed, the buttons you have used most recently are displayed and others are hidden. For many users, this is enough customization. The default Office user interface settings are fine for those users who long for less-powerful software with fewer features and who are confident that they won't demand more from their software tomorrow than they do today.

For most knowledge workers, personalized toolbars and menus are exactly wrong. If, for example, you use more buttons than can be displayed in the space allowed for a toolbar, some of your frequently used buttons will be hidden. If you're familiar with your toolbars and find buttons as much by location as by their icon, spontaneously regenerating toolbars makes your work harder, not easier. But in our opinion, the most compelling reason to turn off the Office personalization is that it isn't advantageous to allow Office to hide powerful features that you might need to use in the future. In this section we'll show you how to customize all of the menu bars, toolbars, and most of the Office 2003 shortcut menus to convert the personalized Office interface to a business interface.

Changing Toolbar Options

In Office 2003, you can click the drop-down Toolbar Options arrow at the end of any toolbar and see a menu of buttons that aren't currently displayed on the toolbar:

The menu also includes the Show Buttons On Two Rows command, which gives the Standard and Formatting toolbars each a row of its own. (When two toolbars are displayed the menu includes the Show Buttons On One Row command). Each toolbar has its own set of built-in buttons, some of which are only displayed if you explicitly select them. (For example, Word's Standard toolbar includes an Envelopes and Labels button that is hidden by default.) To quickly display or hide built-in buttons on a toolbar, choose Add Or Remove Buttons from the menu. If more than one toolbar is displayed, choose the toolbar from the menu to open the menu of built-in buttons. Buttons currently displayed on the toolbar have a check mark. Click the button name to display or hide the button.

For additional settings, with the Toolbar Options menu open choose Add or Remove Buttons and then Customize, or right-click any toolbar or menu bar and choose Customize from the shortcut menu. The Customize dialog box opens. Choose the Options tab to view the options for menus and toolbars (see Figure 18.1).

FIGURE 18.1

Change toolbar options in the Customize dialog box.

Two options in this dialog box are specific to the current application: Show Standard And Formatting Toolbars On Two Rows and Reset My Usage Data. All the other options affect all of the Office applications, regardless of which application you set them in. Here are the options:

Show Standard And Formatting Toolbars On Two Rows   This option is turned on by default, but you can clear the check box in every Office application to stack the toolbars one above the other and provide enough room for all the buttons.

Always Show Full Menus   With this option turned off, each application shows you a personalized menu with the commands you use frequently. Turn this option on in any Office app and you'll see full menus in all applications without clicking again or waiting for the rest of the menu to unfold.

Show Full Menus After A Short Delay   If you turn the Always Show Full Menus option off, you should probably leave this option turned on. If you don't, then you must click the Expand icon at the bottom of a collapsed menu—as opposed to pausing a moment—to see the items you don't select often.

Reset My Usage Data   For menus to be personalized, each app needs to track how often you use different menu options and toolbar buttons. This button resets the buttons and the menu commands shown in the personalized menus and toolbars to the default settings.

Large Icons   Intended for users with impaired vision, these buttons are truly large. Just turn them on for a moment, and you'll either love them or rush to return them to their normal size.

List Font Names In Their Fonts   This option affects only the Font drop-down list on the Formatting toolbar. It makes it easier to choose a font, but you'll take a slight performance hit, particularly if you have a large number of fonts installed on your computer.

Show ScreenTips On Toolbars   Formerly called ToolTips, these are enabled by default; remember that turning them off in any application turns them off throughout Office.

Show Shortcut Keys In ScreenTips   Heads up keyboarders! Here's your opportunity to learn the keyboard shortcuts for toolbar buttons. Enable this setting and you'll see the shortcuts in the ScreenTips when you point to a button. Look at them enough and you'll have them memorized in no time.

Menu Animations   Although interesting initially, these effects (Unfold, Slide, Fade, and Random) can become boring rather quickly. Cheap entertainment for sure.

In Word, you can modify the toolbars in each document. Choose Normal (the default) to modify the toolbars in Word's default template. Choose another open document to modify the toolbars and menus for that document only. After you've changed the options, click Close to close the Customize dialog box and apply the options you chose.

TIP   *To make toolbars appear and behave as they did in Office 97, enable two check boxes on the Options tab: Show Standard And Formatting Toolbars On Two Rows and Always Show Full Menus.*

Adding Commands to Toolbars and Menus

Whenever the Customize dialog box is open, all displayed toolbars are open for editing; before opening the Customize dialog box, display all the toolbars you want to edit. You can drag menu or button commands to new locations to rearrange them, or drop commands in the document window to delete them. To add a toolbar button or menu command, click the Commands tab of the Customize dialog box. The Commands tab from Word is shown in Figure 18.2.

FIGURE 18.2

Drag commands
from the Commands
tab to a toolbar
or menu

Commands are grouped into categories. Choose a category in the Categories tab, and then locate the command you want to add in the Commands tab. To add a command to a toolbar, drag it from the Customize dialog box and drop it in place on the toolbar. To add a command to an existing menu, click on the menu. Drop the command where you want it to appear on the open menu.

The commands in the Macros category let you add macros to toolbars and menus. Creating macros and adding them to the user interface—and there are great reasons you might want to do this—is covered in Chapter 19, "Using Macros to Do More with Office."

REARRANGING TOOLBARS AND MENUS

New!

To rearrange toolbar buttons, just drag and drop the buttons while the Customize dialog box is open. You can also do this with menus, but it's tedious. Office 2003 includes a new Rearrange Commands dialog box to help with this process.

Rearrange Commands...

To open the dialog box, shown in Figure 18.3, click the Rearrange Commands button on the Commands tab of the Customize dialog box. Choose the Menu or Toolbar option and then select the menu (or submenu) or toolbar you want to rearrange. Select a command then use the Move Up and Move Down buttons to move the command into place relative to the other commands. Click Add to open the Commands page as a dialog box and add more commands to the toolbar or menu. Select a button and click Delete to remove the button from the toolbar.

FIGURE 18.3

The Rearrange Commands dialog box comes in handy when you want to rearrange menus.

The Modify Selection button opens a menu you can use to change the command's ScreenTip, caption, image, and other options. This doesn't make a lot of sense for the built-in commands, but is very useful for buttons and menu items that run commands you create (like macros). The Modify Selection options are discussed in the next chapter, "Using Macros To Do More With Office."

MASTERING THE OPPORTUNITIES: FAST ACCESS TO FREQUENTLY USED WORD DOCUMENTS

One of our favorite "hidden" commands is a menu in Word called the Work menu. Follow these steps to add the Work menu to the Word menu:

1. Right-click any toolbar or the menu and choose Customize from the shortcut menu.

2. On the Command tab, choose the Built-In Menus category.

Continued on next page

MASTERING THE OPPORTUNITIES: FAST ACCESS TO FREQUENTLY USED WORD DOCUMENTS *(continued)*

3. Drag the Work command from the Commands list and drop it on the menu between the Table and Window commands:

4. Close the Customize dialog box.

The Work menu is a place to list and quickly open frequently used documents. To add a document to the Work menu, open the document and then choose Work ➤ Add To Work Menu. Word adds the document to the menu. The next time you need to open the document, just open the Work menu and select the document. To delete a document from the Work menu, don't open the Customize dialog box. Instead, in any document, hold Ctrl-Alt and press the - (minus or hyphen key). The mouse pointer looks like a bold minus symbol. Choose Work, then click on the document you want to remove. (You can use this shortcut to remove any submenu from a menu).

You can rearrange, delete, or display toolbar buttons and menus without opening the Customize dialog box: Simply hold the Alt key while you drag the command.

RESTORING THE DEFAULT TOOLBARS AND MENUS

The default settings for an application's built-in menu and toolbars are retained even after you customize the menu or toolbar. To return a toolbar to its original settings, switch to the Toolbars tab of the Customize dialog box, select the toolbar, and then click Reset.

CREATING TOOLBARS FOR SPECIFIC TASKS

You aren't limited to the built-in toolbars. Creating a new toolbar gives you the opportunity to gather all the toolbar buttons you frequently use in one place, or build special-use toolbars for specific tasks. For example, I have an Excel toolbar that I use when I work with databases. My database toolbar includes several commands from the Data menu, as well as the Conditional Formatting command and other commands from the Format menu. When I work with databases in Excel, I right-click any toolbar and turn on my database toolbar.

To create an entirely new toolbar, right-click any toolbar and choose Customize to open the Customize dialog box. On the Toolbar tab, click the New button. Enter a name for your toolbar when prompted. (You can't use the names of any of the built-in toolbars, so if you want to create a replacement toolbar, give it a unique name like MyFormatting.) The new toolbar is a little stub of a toolbar because it doesn't have any buttons yet. Drag buttons onto the toolbar from the Commands list. To copy a button from an existing toolbar, hold down the Ctrl key while dragging the button. When you're finished creating your toolbar, close the Customize dialog box.

MASTERING THE OPPORTUNITIES: CREATING DOCUMENT-SPECIFIC TOOLBARS IN WORD

Creating and displaying toolbars for a specific document used to require Visual Basic code. With Word 2003, you can easily create customized menus, shortcuts, and toolbars for individual documents.

You can save a customized toolbar or set of shortcut keys in the Normal template (`Normal.dot`), any other active template, or the active document. The Normal template is loaded each time Word is launched, so customizations saved in Normal become the new default toolbars. When you save in another template, the toolbars and shortcuts are loaded when the template is loaded. If you save changes in the current document, the customized items are displayed only when the document is opened. Use the Save In drop-down list on the Commands tab of the Customize dialog box (refer back to Figure 18.2) to choose where to save your customized toolbars before clicking Close to close the dialog box. For keyboard shortcuts (discussed in the next section), use the Save Changes In list in the Customize Keyboard dialog box.

When you right-click a toolbar button when the Customize dialog box is open, the Assign Hyperlink command opens up some creative opportunities for presentation of online Word documents. You can create a Supporting Documents toolbar that contains links to other documents and web pages that your reader might be interested in. Save the customization in the document, and the Supporting Documents toolbar is loaded each time the document is opened.

CREATING YOUR OWN SHORTCUT KEYS

Keyboard... If you like to use shortcut keys, here's how to assign shortcut keys to the commands that you use frequently in Word. Click the Keyboard button in the Customize dialog box to open the Customize Keyboard dialog box, shown in Figure 18.4.

Use the Categories and Commands list to choose the command you wish to add shortcut keys for. A description of the command appears in the Description section of the dialog box. Existing shortcut combinations for the command are displayed in the Current Keys list—in Figure 18.4 you can see the three preset combinations for File ➤ Open. If there's already a combination, you may just want to memorize it, or you can add a different shortcut combination that makes sense for you—for example, the shortcut keys you use in another application that you're more familiar with.

FIGURE 18.4

Change or add shortcut keystrokes in the Customize Keyboard dialog box.

To add a shortcut combination for the selected command, click in the Press New Shortcut Key text box and execute the keystroke combination. If the combination is already assigned to another command, that information appears just below the text box. In Figure 18.4, the keystroke combination entered is already used for the Double Underline command. Click Assign to assign the shortcut to the command, which overwrites the current assignment, or select the information (in the Press New Shortcut Key text box) and try a different shortcut key combination.

You can continue creating keyboard shortcuts. Just select another command, enter another set of keys, and click Assign. When you have finished creating keyboard shortcuts, close the dialog box.

WARNING *Beware of using Alt+key combinations for keyboard shortcuts. Nearly all are used, but they aren't always reported in the Current Keys list. For example, if you enter Alt+F as a shortcut it is shown as unassigned even though it's the keyboard shortcut used to open the File menu in every Windows program, including the Office applications.*

You can quickly create a printable list of all the shortcut keys in Word (with the exception of the Alt + shortcut keys used for the menu). Follow these steps:

1. Choose Tools ➢ Macro ➢ Macros to open the Macros dialog box.

2. Choose Word Commands from the Macros In drop-down list.

3. In the Macro Name box, choose the ListCommands macro.

4. Click Run to open the List Commands dialog box.

5. Choose the Current Menu and Keyboard Settings option.

6. Click OK to paste a table of all Word commands and shortcut keys into a new document.

Adding More Options to Shortcut Menus

Office power users tend to right-click on anything and everything that appears on the screen. Microsoft has populated the shortcut menus with great commands, but you can improve on them. Starting with Office 2000, you've had the ability to customize the Word, PowerPoint, and Access shortcut menus. You can't create or delete shortcut menus in these applications, but you can customize most of the shortcut menus as you would other toolbars. On the Toolbars tab of the Customize dialog box in Word, PowerPoint, or Access, enable the Shortcut Menus check box in the Toolbars list. A toolbar with the three categories of shortcut menus, the Text, Table, and Draw, opens

This doesn't look like much (unless you look at Access) until you click a category to open its list of shortcut menus. In Figure 18.5, we've opened Word's Table menu. With the menu open, add commands by dragging them from the Commands tab of the Customize dialog box. Delete commands by dragging them from the menu.

FIGURE 18.5

Even shortcut menus can be customized in Office 2003.

For example, assume you would like to be able to easily access the Sort command when you have a table selected (what a good idea!). The shortcut menu that opens when an entire table is selected is the Whole Tables menu. Select the Whole Tables menu, then click the Commands tab of the Customize dialog box. From the Table category, drag the Sort Ascending command and position it on the menu as shown in Figure 18.6. Close the Customize dialog box. The next time you select an entire table and right-click, Sort Ascending is on the shortcut menu.

FIGURE 18.6

Drag commands from the Customize dialog box and drop them on the shortcut menu.

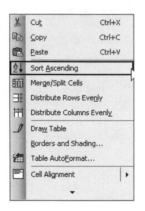

Setting Application Options

Each Office 2003 application has other user-customizable option settings. Outlook has the widest range of option settings (although not the most tabs in the Options dialog box) because of the number of modules and the large number of options related to electronic mail.

Options control how the application looks and acts. In Excel, for example, option settings determine whether you see sheet tabs, where the cell pointer goes when you press Enter, and how zero values are treated in bar, column, and line charts. In Outlook, a mail option determines whether the text of an original message is included in a reply. Word's scroll bars appear or disappear based on an option setting. If an Office program behaves differently than you think it should or remember it did, it's a good idea to check the option settings. To open the Options dialog box in any Office 2003 application, choose Tools ➢ Options from the menu bar. The Options dialog box for Word is shown in Figure 18.7.

FIGURE 18.7

Option settings control application appearance and behavior.

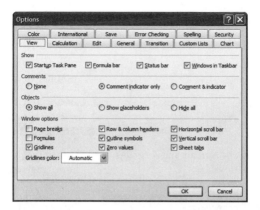

Each application's Options dialog box has different tabs, but there are some general rules about tabs used in most of the applications. The settings on the General tab include global settings that are required when the application launches, such as the number of recently opened files to display on the File menu and the default file location. The View options display or hide features like scroll bars and the application status bar. Edit options determine how the application should respond to your actions (like selecting and dragging text or cells). Other options differ between applications. Table 18.1 lists the types of option settings available in each Office 2003 application.

TABLE 18.1: OFFICE 2003 OPTIONS

APPLICATION	TYPES OF OPTIONS
Access	Advanced, Datasheet, Edit/Find, Forms/Reports, General, Keyboard, Tables/Queries, View, Pages, International, Spelling, Error Checking
Excel	Calculation, Chart, Color, Custom Lists, Edit, General, View, Transition, International, Save, Error Checking, Spelling, Security
FrontPage	Configure Editor, General, Reports View
Outlook	Preferences, Mail Setup, Mail Format, Spelling, Security, Other
PowerPoint	Edit, General, Print, Save, Spelling And Style, View, Security
Word	Compatibility, Edit, File Locations, General, Print, Save, Spelling & Grammar, Track Changes, User Information, View, Security

To change options, choose Tools ➢ Options to open the dialog box. After changing option settings, click OK to close the dialog box and apply the changes.

We won't attempt to describe each of the options for all the Office applications. There are, however, some options that we'd like to highlight because they are frequently used or solve a specific problem that Office users encounter.

Outlook options are described in Chapters 2, 3, and 4. Tables 18.2, 18.3, and 18.4 list frequently accessed options for Excel, Word, and PowerPoint.

TABLE 18.2: EXCEL OPTIONS

PAGE	OPTION	DESCRIPTION
View	Gridlines	Turn this off for workbooks viewed onscreen without gridlines, or when using the Camera command.
Calculation	Accept Labels in Formulas	Turn this on if you are working with an Excel 2000 workbook that uses column and row labels rather than names in formulas.
Edit	Extend List Formats and Formulas	Turn this off if you do not want Excel to automatically format and copy formulas for rows added to the bottom of databases.
Edit	Fixed Decimal Places	Turn this on and set the number of decimal places to force fixed decimal formatting in this workbook.
General	Recently Used Files List	Set the number of recently used workbooks that should appear at the bottom of the File menu.
General	Prompt for Workbook Properties	Turn this on to be reminded to fill in the Properties.
General	Standard Font	Change the default font (Arial) and size (10) here.
General	Default File Locations	Default location for files you save and open in Excel.
General	User Name	Name that will appear in comments, tracking, and the workbook properties.
Color	Standard Colors	Click the Modify button to change the default palette for font and fill colors.
Color	Chart Fills/Chart Lines	Click the Modify button to change the default palettes for chart data series and points.
Save	Save AutoRecover Info Every X Minutes	Determines how frequently Excel saves the info required to restore a workbook if you lose power or Excel crashes.
Error Checking	Reset Ignored Errors	Click this button to have Excel check all cells for errors, even those errors you previously (and perhaps erroneously) ignored.
Error Checking	Rules	Enable/disable the rules that Excel uses to identify errors. You may choose, for example, to have Excel ignore numbers stored as text.
Security	Password to Open	Enter a password required to open this workbook.
Security	Password to Modify	Enter a password required to make and save changes to this workbook. Can be the same as the Password to Open.

Continued on next page

TABLE 18.2: EXCEL OPTIONS *(continued)*

PAGE	OPTION	DESCRIPTION
Chart	Plot Empty Cells As	Options for the active chart only; choose Interpolated to have Excel "create" data points where values are missing.
Chart	Plot Visible Cells Only	Options for the active chart only. Turn this on to have Excel ignore hidden rows and columns within the chart's source range.
Chart	Chart Tips—Show Values	For charts displayed within Excel; turn check boxes off if you do not want users to be able to see precise numeric values behind the chart when they hover over a data point.

Excel includes other options that aren't in the Options dialog box. One of the most difficult options to find is the default chart type. Out of the box, the default chart type is a two-dimensional column chart. To set the default chart type, select a chart. Right-click and choose Chart Type from the shortcut menu. Select a chart type and click the Set As Default Chart button at the bottom of the dialog box.

TABLE 18.3: WORD OPTIONS

PAGE	OPTION	DESCRIPTION
View	Formatting Marks	Enable check boxes to display (but not print) tabs, spaces, paragraph marks, and hidden text.
General	Recently Used Files List	Set the number of recently used Word documents that should appear at the bottom of the File menu.
General	Automatically Create Drawing Canvas	Turn this off to get rid of the frame that appears when you use a drawing tool.
Edit	Insert/Paste Pictures As	Set the default wrap for pictures.
Edit	Cut and Paste Options	Click the Settings button to change how Word formats pasted text, lists, and Excel and PowerPoint objects
Edit	When Selecting, Automatically Select Entire Word	Turn this option off if you frequently need to select characters rather than words.
Print	Reverse Print Order	Turn this option on if your printer prints and stacks pages in reverse order.
Save	Always Create Backup Copy	Turn this option on if you're concerned about overwriting existing files (or if you wish to always create a backup copy, which can be good practice.) You will, of course, periodically need to delete unneeded backups.

Continued on next page

TABLE 18.3: WORD OPTIONS *(continued)*

PAGE	OPTION	DESCRIPTION
Save	Prompt for Document Properties	If you want to use document properties, but often forget, turn this on.
Save	Prompt to Save Normal Template	Turn this on and you will be asked to confirm changes to Word's default template. Basic macro virus protection.
Save	Save AutoRecover Info Every X Minutes	Determines how frequently Word saves the info required to restore a document if you lose power or Word crashes.
User Information	Name	Some companies put the company name here. Edit this so your name appears as document author, editor, etc.
File Locations	Documents	The default folder for documents you save and open.
File Locations	User Templates	Files with the DOT extension in this folder and its subfolders appear when you click the Templates link in Word.
File Locations	Workgroup Templates	Secondary templates location for templates shared with others. Save templates you create for your workgroup in this folder and give other users permission to the folder.
Track Changes	Insertions	Change this to Color Only if you want to be able to easily view inserted text.
Spelling & Grammar	Show Readability Statistics	Enable this check box to have Grammar check include an analysis of how easy it is to read your document.
Spelling & Grammar	Check Grammar As You Type	Turn this off to suppress Grammar checking on-the-fly.
Security	Warn Before Printing or Sending…	If you track changes, turn this on to prevent accidentally printing or e-mailing a document that includes unaccepted changes. (This assumes you send directly from Word rather than an e-mail client.)
Security	Macro Security	Click the Macro Security button to set Word's security level at High, Medium, or Low. Medium requires your confirmation to run unsigned macros.
Security	Password to Open	Enter a password required to open this document.
Security	Password to Modify	Enter a password required to make and save changes to this workbook. Can be the same as the Password to Open.

TABLE 18.4: POWERPOINT OPTIONS

PAGE	OPTION	DESCRIPTION
Security	Password to Modify	Enter a password required to make and save changes to this presentation. Can be the same as the Password to Open.
View	Slide Layout Task Pane When Inserting New Slides	Turn this off to have PowerPoint insert slides using the Title and Text layout rather than prompting you with each insertion.
View	Show Popup menu button	Turn this off to suppress the arrow button that appears during a slideshow.
View	Default view	Set the view for each presentation you open.
General	Recently Used File List	Set the number of recently used presentations that should appear at the bottom of the File menu.
General	Link Sounds with File Size Greater Than	Sets the upper limit for sound files that are saved within this presentation. You can choose to increase the size if you use large sound files and save your presentations to CD or on a network rather than on floppy disk.
Edit	New Charts Take On PowerPoint Font	Turn this off to retain the original formatting on charts.
Edit	Maximum Number of Undos	Increase this number if you're really into experimenting in PowerPoint.
Edit	Disable New Features	If you share work with Office XP or 2000 users, consider turning off features they can't use.
Save	Embed TrueType Fonts	For the current presentation only; embed fonts if you need to collaborate with others or show the presentation on a different computer.
Save	Save PowerPoint Files As	In a mixed environment, choose the option that will allow other users to open, edit, and show presentation.
Spelling and Style	Check Style	Enable style checking and set options to have the Office Assistant offer design and style suggestions.
Security	Password to Open	Enter a password required to open this presentation.
Security	Password to Modify	Password required to modify this presentation. This can be the same as the Password to Open.
Security	Macro Security	Change the macro security setting to allow macros in presentations.

If you have a question about a specific option in any Office application, click the Help button in the title bar of the Options dialog box, then click the option you want to learn about to view a short description of the option.

In the next chapter, we'll discuss the ultimate in customization: creating macros to program the Office applications.

Chapter 19

Using Macros to Do More with Office

THIS CHAPTER LOOKS AT the most powerful Office tool of all: the *programmability* of the Office applications. Using the tools you'll explore in this chapter, you can create instructions—macros—to automate tasks ranging from simple-but-repetitive to highly complex. Excel, Word, PowerPoint, and Access share a common programming language, Visual Basic for Applications (VBA). VBA is like Visual Basic, but can't be used to create stand-alone programs; VBA code is Visual Basic code that requires an Office application to run. (Outlook is programmed with two related languages: VBScript and Visual Basic.)

There are two ways to create macros. If you're already familiar with Visual Basic, you can program Excel, PowerPoint, or Word macros by opening the Visual Basic interface and typing code. You'll learn about Visual Basic and Visual Basic for Applications later in this chapter, but you don't have to know anything about Visual Basic to create macros in Office 2003. The simplest way to create VB code in Word, Excel, and PowerPoint is to use the Macro Recorder, which automatically writes VB code as you step through a task.

This chapter presents its topics in roughly the same order in which you'll do the operations. In the first half of the chapter, we'll create, play, and edit macros. In the second half of the chapter, we'll make it easy for users to play the macros with command buttons, toolbar buttons, hyperlinks, and menu commands.

- ◆ Recording a macro using the Macro Recorder

- ◆ Storing and naming macros

- ◆ Running macros from the Macro dialog box

- ◆ Viewing and modifying your Visual Basic code

- ◆ Creating custom menus and toolbars

- ◆ Creating custom menu items and buttons to run macros

- ◆ Assigning macros to commands

◆ Assigning hyperlinks to commands

◆ Using form buttons to run macros

Creating Macros Using the Macro Recorder

In Excel, Word, and PowerPoint, you can use the Macro Recorder to create macros. You turn on the recorder, complete the steps you want to repeat, and save the macro. The next time you need to complete the steps, you "play back" the steps by running the macro.

NOTE *There are two main limitations to macros created with the Macro Recorder: you can only duplicate user actions, and not all user actions can be recorded.*

Before recording a macro, practice the steps you want to record, because once you begin recording, *all* your actions are recorded, mistakes included. Take note of the conditions your macro will operate under and set up those conditions. Will you always use the macro in a specific document? If so, open the document. Will the macro always be used to change or format a selection? Then have something selected before you begin recording the macro, just as you will when you run the macro later.

Recording a Macro in PowerPoint

We'll begin by walking through the steps required to record two macros in PowerPoint. The steps are similar in Word and Excel, so PowerPoint is a fine place to start. Later in this chapter, we'll modify the template to include two buttons that run the macros.

Before we begin, here's an explanation of what we are going to accomplish with the macros. In Chapter 16, "Constructing Forms for User Input," we created an ABC Theater template with two color schemes: a blue background and a white background. Now, we want to make it easy for users to switch between the light background color scheme for printed materials like overheads and handouts and the blue scheme used for electronic presentations. To accomplish this we need two macros: one that switches to each color scheme.

We'll begin by opening the file that we want to put the macros into: the `ABC Theater.pot` template. Choose File ➤ Open and find the template to open a template directly.

TIP *If you choose the template in the New task pane, you open a new presentation based on the template, not the template itself.*

Follow these steps to record a macro in PowerPoint. If you're playing along, Table 19.1 lists the commands to create the macro that applies the blue color scheme.

1. Select Tools ➤ Macro ➤ Record New Macro to open the Record New Macro dialog box, shown in Figure 19.1.

FIGURE 19.1

The Record Macro dialog box in PowerPoint

2. The suggested name is Macro1, just as the name of a new presentation is Presentation1. Enter a more descriptive name for the macro (see the "Naming Macros" sidebar below).

Unlike Word and Excel, there's no default template in PowerPoint. You can store a macro in the current presentation or template or another open presentation/template.

3. Choose a location for the macro. This macro will be used in the template, so leave the default: the current template.

4. Edit the description so that it briefly describes the macro's actions; include your name and contact information (extension or e-mail address) so other users will know who to contact if there are questions or problems with the macro (see Figure 19.1).

5. Click the OK button to begin macro recording. You'll then step through the commands you'd like to record (described in detail after step 6).

6. When you have executed all the steps that you want to record, click the Stop Recording button to stop recording and hide the toolbar.

Be sure to note that when you start recording, the Stop Recording toolbar opens. It's easy to miss: it has only one button. The Macro Recorder records the actions you take, but not the delay between actions, so there's no rush.

To include menu commands in the macro, just make menu selections as you normally would. When you format text in a macro, choose the formatting options from a Format dialog box rather than clicking toolbar buttons to select font style and alignment. If you use the toggle buttons, the results when you run the macro are unpredictable: if selected cells are already italicized, clicking the Italics button turns italics off.

Table 19.1 describes the actions we recorded for our mcrApplyBlueScheme macro.

TABLE 19.1: ACTIONS FOR MCRAPPLYBLUESCHEME MACRO

ACTION	RESULT
Choose Format ➢ Slide Design from the menu	Opens the Slide Design pane if it is not already open
Click the Color Schemes link in Slide Design pane	Opens the Color Schemes pane if it is not already open
Click the dark blue color scheme	Applies the selected color scheme to the presentation

We also recorded another macro, mcrApplyWhiteScheme, following the same steps but choosing the other color scheme in the template. Table 19.2 lists the actions we took to create it. Note that the first action is to open the task pane. If you just recorded the first macro, the pane is already open, but it might not be the next time the macro runs.

TABLE 19.2: ACTIONS FOR MCRAPPLYWHITESCHEME MACRO

ACTION	RESULT
Choose Format ➤ Slide Design from the menu	Opens the Slide Design pane if it is not already open
Click the Color Schemes link in Slide Design pane	Opens the Color Schemes pane if it is not already open
Click the white color scheme	Applies the selected color scheme to the presentation
Click the Stop Recording button	Ends macro recording

Macros are saved when the document that contains the macros is saved. Save and close the presentation template to save the macros.

NAMING MACROS

Here are rules to bear in mind when naming a macro:

◆ Visual Basic names, including macro names, can be up to 255 characters long, and they can contain numbers, letters, and underscores but not spaces or other punctuation.

◆ Names must begin with a letter.

◆ Names can include both uppercase and lowercase letters.

Visual Basic will preserve your capitalization style, but it is not case sensitive: it won't recognize MyMacro and mymacro as different names.

If your organization uses a naming convention, you'll probably prefix the macro name with mcr for a macro created with the recorder or bas for a macro written in the Visual Basic editor. Some companies use only the bas prefix, whether or not you create the macro with a macro recorder. Check the standards for your organization to determine the appropriate prefix.

Recording a Macro in Excel

Macro recording is similar in Excel; we'll point out the differences between Excel and PowerPoint in our example. Like the PowerPoint macros, our Excel macro example is a variation of macros created to solve real business problems for our clients. Here is the situation: our client has two groups of users who aren't sophisticated about Excel. The two groups use a common worksheet but need to have different things highlighted in the worksheet. Conditional formatting solves this problem for either group of users, but the users don't want to learn how to switch the conditional formatting. And they shouldn't have to. Both groups would be happy if there were an easy way to show the worksheet with **THEIR** formatting. Two macros that apply different conditional formats are the answer. Here's the worksheet with conditional formatting applied:

	A	B	C	D	E	F	G	H	I	J
1	User Support Call Log		Total Calls	12						
2			Total Time	2:57						
3										
4										
5	Start Date		6/1/2003	End Date	6/30/2003					
6										
7	User	Department	Date	Start Time	End Time	Length	Application	Type	Platform	Charge
8	Benth	Training	6/1/03	8:15 AM	8:18 AM	0:03	Outlook	App Error	Desk/Laptop	2.78
9	Keener	Administration	6/1/03	9:20 AM	9:30 AM	0:10	Excel	Code	Desk/Laptop	9.25
10	Lieberman	Web - IT	6/1/03	11:40 AM	12:00 PM	0:20	Word	Beginning	Desk/Laptop	18.50
11	Hing	Training	6/1/03	1:35 PM	1:55 PM	0:20	Data Analyzer	Intermediate	Desk/Laptop	18.50
12	Benson	Accounting	6/1/03	1:55 PM	2:10 PM	0:15	Excel	Advanced	Desk/Laptop	13.88
13	Turik	Info Tech	6/1/03	2:14 PM	2:30 PM	0:16	Connectivity	Beginning	PDA	14.80
14	Laramie	Manufacturing	6/1/03	3:00 PM	3:40 PM	0:40	Data Analyzer	Advanced	Desk/Laptop	37.00
15	Smith	Communications	6/1/03	3:45 PM	3:50 PM	0:05	Excel	Intermediate	Desk/Laptop	4.62
16	Keener	Administration	6/1/03	4:10 PM	4:13 PM	0:03	Excel	Code	Desk/Laptop	2.77
17	Fitzgerald	Training	6/2/03	8:32 AM	8:50 AM	0:18	FrontPage	Intermediate	Desk/Laptop	16.65
18	Song	Manufacturing	6/2/03	9:02 AM	9:18 AM	0:16	Excel	Intermediate	Desk/Laptop	14.80
19	Wilson	Maintenance	6/2/03	9:22 AM	9:33 AM	0:11	Outlook	Intermediate	PDA	10.18

Follow these steps to record a macro in Excel. Tables 19.3 and 19.4 show the steps we recorded for our two macros, mcrMgmtConditionalFormat and mcrTrainingConditionalFormat.

1. Select Tools ➤ Macro ➤ Record New Macro to open the Record New Macro dialog box, shown in Figure 19.2.

FIGURE 19.2

The Record Macro dialog box in Excel

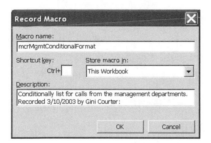

2. Enter a name for the macro.

3. Edit the description so it includes the macro's purpose and your name and contact information (extension or e-mail address) so other users will know who to contact if there are questions or problems with the macro.

4. In the Store Macro In drop-down list, select the workbook you want to store the macro in.

5. If you wish, assign a shortcut key combination for the macro. But before you do, check out the sidebar below.

6. Click the OK button to begin macro recording. The message *Recording* is displayed at the left end of the status bar and the Stop Recording toolbar (with two buttons) opens. The Macro Recorder records the actions you take, but not the delay between actions, so there's no rush. If you want the macro to enter text, enter the text now. Type carefully—if you make a mistake, then reverse it later, the mistake and correction will be included when you replay the macro unless you edit the macro (see "Viewing and Modifying Your VB Code" later in this chapter).

7. When you are finished entering all the steps you want the macro to execute, click the Stop Recording button on the Stop Recording toolbar. You don't need to do anything special to save the macro now. Local macros are saved when you save the workbook. Excel saves global macros when you close Excel.

STORING A MACRO IN EXCEL

The storage location determines how you'll be able to access and run the macro later:

◆ If you select the current workbook (or another workbook), the macro will be directly available in that workbook only. If you want to use the same macro somewhere else, you'll have to copy or re-create it, or insert Visual Basic code that loads the workbook before the macro can be run. Macros that are stored in a workbook or template are called *local macros*.

◆ Storing an Excel macro in the Personal Macro Workbook creates a *global macro*, which is available to all workbooks created in Excel.

If you're not sure where to store a macro, err on the conservative side and store it locally. While global macros are convenient, all global macros are loaded each time you launch Excel, consuming valuable resources. And macro names you use globally can't be reused in individual workbooks. Unless a macro is going to be widely used, it's best to store it locally.

The macros in Tables 19.3 and 19.4 were recorded in the UserSupportCallLog workbook used in previous chapters. You can download the workbook from www.sybex.com or www.triadconsulting .com/resources.html if you want to practice by creating these macros.

TABLE 19.3: ACTIONS FOR MCRACCTCONDITIONALFORMAT MACRO

ACTION	RESULT
Click in cell A7. Hold Ctrl and Shift then press → followed by ➤	Selects the list
Choose Format ➤ Conditional Formatting from the menu	Opens the Conditional Format dialog box
In the first drop-down list, choose Format Is	Determines the formatting for the results
Enter the formula =**$J8>15** in the text box	Creates criteria to determine whether the chargeback is more than $15
Click the Format button	Opens the Format dialog box
On the Patterns page, choose a light blue fill	Adds a fill color to the conditional format
On the Font page, choose Bold	Adds bold text to the conditional format
Click OK	Closes the Format dialog box
Click OK	Closes the Conditional Format dialog box and applies the format
Click the Stop Recording button	Ends macro recording

TABLE 19.4: ACTIONS FOR mcrMGMTCONDITIONALFORMAT MACRO

ACTION	RESULT
Click in cell A7. Hold Ctrl and Shift then press → followed by ➤	Selects the list
Choose Format ➤ Conditional Formatting from the menu	Opens the Conditional Format dialog box
In the first drop-down, choose Format Is	Determines the formatting styles for the results
Enter the formula **=OR($B8="Administration",$B8= "Communications",$B8="Accounting")** in the text box	Uses the OR function to create a criterion that is True if a call came from one of the three management areas: Administration, Communications, or Accounting (see Figure 19.3)
Click the Format button	Opens the Format dialog box
On the Patterns page, choose a light yellow fill	Adds a different fill color to the conditional format
On the Font page, choose Bold	Adds bold text to the conditional format
Click OK	Closes the Format dialog box
Click OK	Closes the Conditional Format dialog box and applies the format
Click the Stop Recording button	Ends macro recording

FIGURE 19.3

Setting up a
conditional format
for management calls
in the mcrMgmt-
ConditionalFormat
macro

TIP   The OR function (see Figure 19.3) and its companion the AND function, are indispensable for conditional for-matting. The arguments for these functions consist of a list of conditions, separated by commas. AND returns the result TRUE if every argument is true; OR returns TRUE if any of the arguments is true.

ASSIGNING SHORTCUT KEYS TO MACROS

In the Record Macro dialog box, you can assign a shortcut keystroke combination to a macro. In practice, this is not a very good idea; most of the Ctrl combinations and many of the Ctrl+Shift combinations are already in use. It is better practice to assign frequently used macros to a menu or a toolbar button; you have more control over menus and toolbars, which can be turned on and off programmatically.

Continued on next page

ASSIGNING SHORTCUT KEYS TO MACROS (*continued*)

There's another reason to hold off on shortcut key assignments: if you add the macro to a menu and add a keyboard shortcut, you must choose a shortcut that isn't already used on the menu. If you like keyboard shortcuts, create the shortcut later as part a plan to make it easy for users to run the macro. See "Designing the User Interface" later in this chapter for more information.

ABSOLUTE AND RELATIVE CELL REFERENCES IN EXCEL MACROS

In Excel macros, all cell references are absolute by default. If you click in a cell during macro recording, the macro will select that cell each time you play it back. This is not always useful. For example, you might want a macro to format selected cells and move to the cell below the selection. When you record the macro, the cell below the selection is J22. But each time you play the macro, you don't want Excel to select J22; you want to select the cell below the cells you just formatted.

To use relative cell references, click the Relative References button on the Stop Recording toolbar. The macro will record references relative to the current cell until you click the button again to turn relative references off. Then you can record other actions using absolute references.

Recording a Macro in Word

The steps to record a Word macro are similar to those for recording Excel macros. Choose Tools ➢ Macro ➢ Record New Macro to open the Record Macro dialog box shown in Figure 19.4.

FIGURE 19.4

The Record Macro dialog box in Word

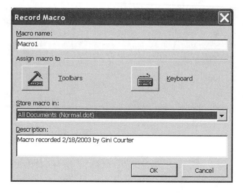

Word macro recording differs from recording in Excel in two ways:

♦ Storage options include `Normal.dot` (for global macros), the current document, or another open document (for local macros).

♦ You can assign a macro to a toolbar and a keyboard combination.

There's an advantage to assigning the macro to a toolbar in this dialog box. Word automatically displays the toolbars for the storage location you selected, so if you're recording the toolbar in a template, you'll only see the toolbars that are displayed in the template. After entering the macro name and description and selecting a storage location, follow these steps if you want to assign the macro to a toolbar:

1. Click the Toolbar button in the Record New Macro dialog box to open the Customize dialog box, shown in Figure 19.5.

FIGURE 19.5

Assign a macro to a toolbar button using the Customize dialog box.

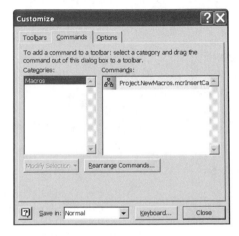

2. There is one item in the Commands list: a button for the macro you're going to record. Drag the item from the Commands list and drop it on a toolbar or menu.

3. Click the Modify Selection button in the dialog box to open the shortcut menu so you can change the button text, add an image, or modify the button in some other way. (See Chapter 18, "Tweaking Office to Fit the Way You Work" for more information on customizing buttons.)

4. When you're finished customizing the button, click the Close button in the Customize dialog box to begin recording the macro.

Word's Stop Recording toolbar has two buttons: the Stop Recording button and a Pause Recording button so you can pause recording, take actions that aren't recorded, then resume recording the macro. Click the Stop Recording button when you are finished recording.

TIP   You can't use the mouse to select text while recording a macro. Here are some useful shortcuts: Use the right and left arrow keys to move the insertion point character-by-character. Hold Ctrl and arrow to move word-by-word. Home and End move to the beginning and end of the line. Hold Shift while moving the insertion point to select text. You can use Ctrl-Home to move to the beginning of the document, and Ctrl-End to move to the end of the document, too.

A perennial favorite Word macro applies a custom header and/or footer. The macro actions for this type of macro are listed in Table 19.5. A macro like this will be used with various documents, so it should be stored in the Normal template.

TABLE 19.5: ACTIONS FOR MCRMYHEADERFOOTER

ACTION	RESULT
Choose View ➢ Header and Footer	Opens the Header and Footer dialog box.
Enter and format header text	This is optional. (Note that you can't select text using the mouse while recording a macro. Use Ctrl, the arrow keys, Home, and End to move the insertion point. Hold Shift and move the insertion point to select text.)
Click the Switch Between Header And Footer button	Switches to the footer.
From the Insert AutoText menu, choose Filename And Path	Inserts a placeholder for the filename and path.
Select the filename and path. Choose a small font size (6 or 8) from the menu	Changes the placeholder font to small print.
Tab twice	Moves to the right margin.
Type the word **Page**	
Click the Insert Page Number button	Inserts a placeholder for the page number.
Select and format the text and page number	Format to match document text or the filename/path text—your choice.
Click the Close Header And Footer button	Closes the Header And Footer toolbar.
Click the Stop Recording button	Ends macro recording.

The macro is saved when you save your Word document.

DELETING MACROS

There are two ways to delete a macro: by overwriting, or by deleting. If you need to drastically change the way a macro executes, record the macro again using the same name. You will be prompted to overwrite the existing macro with the new one. If you no longer need a macro, choose Tools ➤ Macro ➤ Macros, select the macro from the macro list, and click the Delete button.

Deleting Excel Global Macros

The global macro workbook PERSONAL.XLS is open but hidden when Excel is running. You can't delete macros from hidden workbooks using the Macro dialog box. To delete a macro from the global workbook, choose Window ➤ Unhide to open the Unhide dialog box:

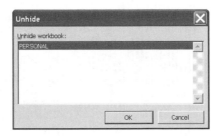

Choose the PERSONAL workbook, then click OK to unhide the workbook. With the workbook unhidden, you can open the Macro dialog box and delete the macro. If you're feeling adventurous or are VB experienced, you might prefer to select the macro in the Macro dialog box and click Edit to open the Visual Basic Editor. Select all the lines of code in the macro and delete them to delete the macro.

NOTE   *If the Unhide command is disabled, there are no global macros.*

Running Macros

You might need to change an application's security settings before you can run macros. It's also good to review your settings to make sure that security is set at an appropriate level.

Changing Macro Security Settings

Virus security has been beefed up in Office 2003. This is a good thing. Millions of people use Office, which makes Office applications a great target for individuals who write viruses. Over two-thirds of viruses "in the wild" were written to target Word or Outlook. If *YOU* can add code to an Office document, so can the people who write viruses. Viruses are self-replicating programs. When you open a workbook that contains a virus, the virus copies its code into the default template, effectively becoming a global virus. From that point forward, every document you create using the template will be infected, which means that every file you give to someone else on a disk or attached to an e-mail will contain the virus.

Office does not include virus detection software; you're responsible for installing and updating anti-virus software on your computer. Your computer is at risk unless you never receive files from another computer via disk, CD, network, or Internet connection. (And if that were the case, why would you even own a PC?) However, Word, Excel, and PowerPoint scan documents to see if they contain macros. Based on your security settings, the application disables the macros, notifies you that the document has macros and asks whether they should be enabled, or does nothing.

By default, macro security is set at a very high level. Most macros are automatically disabled without any input from the user. There are exceptions: see the "Digitally Signing Your Macros" sidebar for a discussion of signed macros and trusted sources. Until (and unless) you sign your macros, choose a slightly lower level of security so you can test and use your macros.

Follow these steps to change macro security in the current application:

1. Choose Tools ➤ Macro ➤ Security from the menu to open the Security dialog box shown in Figure 19.6.

FIGURE 19.6

Change the Macro Security level for an application in the Security dialog box.

2. Choose the Medium security setting so you'll be prompted to enable macros in documents that contain code.

3. Click OK to close the dialog box and save the settings.

OPENING A DOCUMENT THAT CONTAINS MACROS

With the medium level of security, you'll see this message when you open a document with macros:

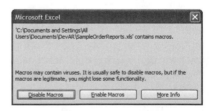

If you know that the document contains macros that you or a trustworthy person created, choose Enable. If you're not sure the document should contain macros, choose Disable. Disabling the macros gives you an opportunity to look at them in the Visual Basic Editor without endangering your computer, software, or relationships with coworkers. If you decide the macros are legitimate, close the Visual Basic Editor, then close and reopen the workbook and choose Enable Macros. (The Visual Basic Editor is discussed later in this chapter.)

NOTE *Clicking the More Information button doesn't give you more information about the macros in the document; it opens the help topic on macros and security.*

Running Macros from the Macro Dialog Box

To run a macro, choose Tools ➤ Macro ➤ Macros to open the Macro dialog box, shown in Figure 19.7. Select the macro from the list and click the Run button. The macro will execute. You can't enter text or choose menu options while the macro is executing. When the macro is done playing, the application will return control to you. It's a good idea to save any open documents before you run a new macro. If you've made a mistake during recording, the playback results may not be what you expected.

FIGURE 19.7

Run macros directly from the Macro dialog box

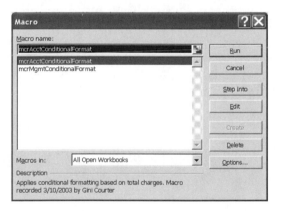

TROUBLESHOOTING TERMINATING A MACRO DURING EXECUTION

You can accidentally create a macro that gets caught in a loop; you'll know it's caught because the mouse pointer turns into an hourglass and stays there. If a macro doesn't end on its own, press Ctrl+Break to stop macro execution and open the Visual Basic dialog box so you can halt or pause and debug the macro (see "Viewing and Modifying Your VB Code").

Continued on next page

TROUBLESHOOTING TERMINATING A MACRO DURING EXECUTION *(continued)*

If Ctrl+Break doesn't stop macro execution, launch Microsoft Office Application Recovery (Start ➤ Programs ➤ Microsoft Office Tools) and choose Recover Application to display the window shown here. If the application cannot be recovered, choose End Application. If you can't open Application Recovery, press Ctrl+Alt+Del to open the Windows Task Manager. Select the application that contains the macro and click the End Task button, then reopen the application.

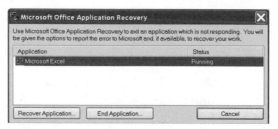

Viewing and Modifying Your VB Code

The Macro Recorder turns the actions you take into Visual Basic code. You can edit this code to modify the macro in the Visual Basic Integrated Development Environment, also called the VB IDE or the VB Editor. To examine or edit a macro, choose Tools ➤ Macro ➤ Macros to open the Macros dialog box, select the macro you want to examine, then click the Edit button to open the VB Editor (see Figure 19.8). You can also open the VB Editor (Tools ➤ Macro ➤ Visual Basic Editor) then select the macro you want to work with in the Editor.

FIGURE 19.8

Macros are displayed in the Visual Basic Editor's window.

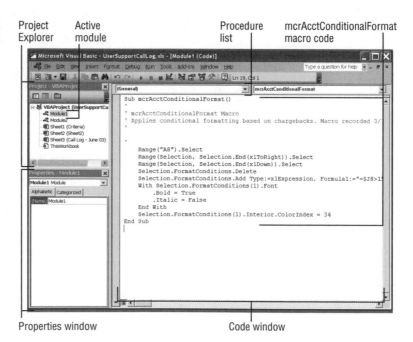

NOTE While Office's Macro features are included in a typical installation, the Office 2003 Administration Kit allows installers to omit Visual Basic and all the VB tools when they install Office. If the Macro commands don't appear on the Tools menu or are disabled, talk to your network administrator.

Finding Your Way Around the VB Editor

Macros aren't stored in documents; they're stored in a VBA project attached to the document. Within the VBA project, macros are stored in modules; each macro you record is placed in a new module. Think of the modules as folders: you can rename modules, create new modules, and delete empty modules. The Project Explorer (see Figure 19.9) shows all open VBA projects; if, for example, you have three workbooks open that contain macros, all three workbooks' VBA projects are displayed in the Explorer.

The project in Figure 19.9 has two types of components: *application objects* (worksheets and a workbook) and modules. Projects can include other types of objects, including user forms and references to templates or other documents.

TIP If you have lots of macros, the Project Explorer will quickly fill up with modules. Use Cut & Paste to move the macros to one module window, or use two or three modules to organize your macros by functionality, and then delete the empty modules. To delete a module, right-click it in the Project Explorer and choose Remove Module N from the shortcut menu.

The Properties window displays the properties for the object selected in the Project Explorer; it will be familiar if you've designed tables or other objects in Microsoft Access.

The Code window shows the code that's in the active module. Double-click a module or select the module and click the View Code button in the Project Explorer to display the module's code. If there are a number of macros in a module, scroll to the macro you want to see or select the macro name from the Procedure list at the top of the Code window.

The green lines of code that begin with apostrophes (') are *remarks* that explain the code. The code itself is displayed in the default text color, black. Programming commands and other reserved words are in navy blue.

Earlier in this chapter we created the Accounting department's conditional formatting macro using the Macro Recorder. The Macro Recorder generated the Visual Basic code shown in Figure 19.9.

Unpacking the Code

You need to be slightly familiar with the VB IDE if you want to edit macros created with the Macro Recorder, or if you want to create macros that can't be recorded. The Macro Recorder is limited to elements that are visible in the interface. There are other objects (for example, the Document Properties dialog box that you open from the File menu) that are best manipulated or can only be manipulated by writing code.

FIGURE 19.9

In the code window, comments are preceded by a postrophes; code is in navy blue and black.

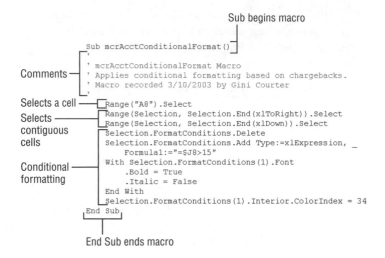

OPENING AND COMMENTS

The code begins with the word Sub (for *subroutine*), the macro name we entered in the Record Macro dialog box, and a set of parentheses that enclose arguments just like in an Excel function. The username, the date recorded, and other remarks are from the Description in the Record Macro dialog box.

```
Sub mcrAcctConditionalFormat()
' mcrAcctConditionalFormat Macro
' Applies conditional formatting based on chargebacks.
' Macro recorded 3/10/2003 by Gini Courter
```

SELECTING THE LIST

The next three lines select cell A8 and then extend the selection to the right and down to select the entire list. If you recorded this macro, you probably remember the keystrokes that you used and can see them reflected in these three lines:

```
Range("A8").Select
Range(Selection, Selection.End(xlToRight)).Select
Range(Selection, Selection.End(xlDown)).Select
```

SETTING UP THE CONDITIONAL FORMAT

You didn't do anything to explicitly record the next command. When you change conditional formatting, Excel deletes the old formatting. That's what this line does: deletes any conditions for the current selection:

```
Selection.FormatConditions.Delete
```

The next line sets up the condition. The underscore character is a line continuation code. In the VB Editor we typed the _ and then pressed Enter to break the line so we could see all the code without scrolling left to right. You can do this almost anywhere in VB except within text that is in quotes:

```
Selection.FormatConditions.Add Type:=xlExpression,_
    Formula1:="=$J8>15"
```

The next four lines are a block. The first line indicates that the block is about font choices for the conditional formatting of the selection. The next two lines are the Bold and Italic settings on the Font tab of the Format Cells dialog box. The fourth line marks the end of the block.

```
With Selection.FormatConditions(1).Font
    .Bold = True
    .Italic = False
End With
```

The Office color palette has 56 colors. The next line chooses color 34 (light yellow on the default palette) as the shading color, which VB refers to as the `Interior.ColorIndex`.

```
Selection.FormatConditions(1).Interior.ColorIndex = 34
```

End Sub marks the end of the macro.

```
End Sub
```

EDITING A MACRO

You don't need to know much about programming to do some simple editing here. For example, you can include italics in the conditional format simply by changing `.Italic = False` to `.Italic = True`. You could change the condition by changing the value that `Formula1` refers to. You could change the fill color by entering a different `ColorIndex` number.

TURNING OFF THE LIST SELECTION

There's one change we want to make in this macro and the related macro, mcrMgmtConditionalFormat. In both macros, when we stopped the Macro Recorder the entire list was still selected. It would be better for users if only A8 were selected when Excel returned control to the user. Both macros include the command to select this cell: Range("A8").Select. We copied this line and pasted it immediately above the last line in the macro End Sub. Now, when we run the macro, A8 is the only cell selected when the macro ends.

When you're finished editing, choose File ➤ Close and Return to Microsoft Excel to close the VB Editor.

Now that you know how to create and edit macros in PowerPoint, Excel, and Word, we'll turn to ways to make macros accessible to people who use your documents and templates.

Making Macros Easy to Use

If you're like many Office power users, you create documents and templates for others to use. If you create a macro that saves three steps, but requires the user to complete three steps to run the macro, you've wasted your time. Business users who would get the most benefit from macros that automate relatively simple tasks also require a low level of complexity. Running a macro from the Macros dialog box always takes at least four steps (Tools ➢ Macro ➢ Macros, double-click the macro name). More importantly, you don't want inexperienced users kicking around in the Macro dialog box, checking to see what exciting functionality lurks behind the Delete and Edit buttons.

There are three other, better ways to have users run macros: from a menu, a toolbar, or command button. We'll examine all three methods in this section. In this section, we'll show you how to develop suites of macros and add an interface to make the macros easy for your colleagues to use.

TIP   Are you creating navigational macros—Excel macros that move to a particular sheet and select a specific cell, Word macros that move to a specific place in a document? If you are, this is a good time to stop. Office applications support hyperlinks, which your web users already know how to use. See Chapter 10, "Taming Complex Publications," and the section "Mastering the Opportunities: Assigning a Hyperlink to a Command" in this chapter for more information on hyperlinks.

Designing the User Interface

When you record a macro, you decide whether it should be stored locally (in the document) or globally (in the Excel Personal Macros workbook or `Normal.dot` in Word). The decision about where to place buttons or menu items that let users run the macros is related. Users should *always* be able to find the commands for available macros. And they should *only* be able to see commands if the macros are available.

For example, let's say you're creating macros to automate an Excel workbook that will be distributed to customers, colleagues, or suppliers at a variety of locations. In this case, you should store the macros locally in the workbook you'll distribute. The buttons or menu commands that users click to run the macros should be displayed in the workbook and should not be visible if your client switches from your workbook to another open workbook. To achieve this, you can create a custom toolbar that will be turned on when the workbook opens and off when it closes, or add command buttons that run the macro. In either case, commands that run macros should be available only when the macros are available.

On the other hand, you might create macros that everyone in your department uses in a variety of documents. For example, you could create a macro that adds a custom footer to Word documents with the date, file name, and the text "© All rights reserved" with the year and your company and department name. This is a good candidate for a global macro. Store the macro in `Normal.dot` and place a button or menu command that runs the macro on one of the command bars that are displayed by default: the Word menu, Standard toolbar, or Formatting toolbar.

Adding Macros to Command Bars

From Office user's point of view, there are few differences between menus and toolbars. Menus and toolbars are both members of the command bar family. Menu items and toolbar buttons are generically called *commands* or *command items*. There is one major difference between the menu bar and toolbars: you can hide toolbars, but you can't hide the menu bar in Excel, Word, and PowerPoint.

NOTE   *Adding existing items to menus and toolbars and creating custom toolbars are discussed in Chapter 18.*

Menus and toolbars are functionally interchangeable: a toolbar can include a menu, and a menu can include toolbar buttons . For example, let's look at the Hyperlink command that appears on the Insert menu in Excel, PowerPoint, and Word:

The Hyperlink menu item includes the following:

The command name   Hyperlink, which the user can click on to choose this command. The name is followed by ellipses because choosing this command opens a dialog box.

A keyboard accelerator   The key combination Alt+I (the underlined letter in the command name), used to select the menu item if the Insert menu is open.

The shortcut key   Ctrl+K, listed with the menu item, used to insert a hyperlink without opening the menu.

A button image   To help the user find this command when it appears on a toolbar.

Here are some general rules to consider when adding commands to menus and toolbars:

◆ If you want to use text to describe the command, it belongs on a menu.

◆ If you want to use an icon without text, put the command on a toolbar.

◆ All menu commands should have keyboard accelerators—the underlined letter like *F* for *File* and *E* for *Edit* on the menu.

◆ Assign shortcut keys (for example, Ctrl + C to copy) to frequently used commands only.

◆ If the same command appears on a menu and a toolbar, add the button image to the menu command for consistency.

While you can add commands to the Standard and Formatting toolbars, you can't guarantee that the commands will be displayed. The personalized toolbars feature moves less frequently used buttons off the toolbars. To really ensure that choices are available for users, either place them on the menu or create and display a custom toolbar.

CREATING A CUSTOM MENU ITEM OR TOOLBAR BUTTON

You'll create a custom menu item or toolbar button to accomplish the following:

◆ add a command that runs a global macro to the application's menu bar—for example, add a command to run mcrMyHeaderFooter to the Word menu bar

◆ add a command to run a local macro to a custom toolbar that you'll turn on/off with the document—for example, add commands that run mcrAcctConditionalFormat and mcrMgmtConditionalFormat to a custom toolbar (MyReports) that opens with the UserSupportCallLog workbook

Whether you're adding a command to run a macro to a toolbar or the menu bar, you'll work in the Customize dialog box. The process is different in Word and PowerPoint than in Excel, which we'll examine first.

Adding Custom Commands in Excel

In Excel, you add a generic custom command to a toolbar or menu and then assign a macro to the command. Follow these steps to add a command:

1. Right-click any menu or toolbar and choose Customize, or choose View ➤ Toolbars ➤ Customize, or choose Tools ➤Customize to open the dialog box and then click the tab for the Commands page.

2. In the Categories list, select Macros to see the two choices in the Commands list: Custom Menu Item or Custom Button, as shown in Figure 19.10.

FIGURE 19.10

Use the Customize dialog box to create custom menu items and toolbar buttons.

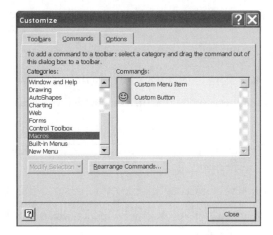

3. To create a custom menu item, drag the Custom Menu Item button from the Customize dialog box. Point to the menu that you want to add the item to and wait for the menu to open; for example, to add a macro to the Tools menu, point to Tools. After the menu opens, point to the position where the custom menu item should appear and release the mouse button. To create a custom toolbar button, display the toolbar you want to customize. Drag the Custom Toolbar button from the Customize dialog box and drop it on a toolbar.

4. With the Customize dialog box open, click the Modify Selection button in the Customize dialog box or right-click the custom command to open the Modify Selection shortcut menu, shown in Figure 19.11.

FIGURE 19.11

Open the Modify Selection menu to set the name and assign a macro to the command.

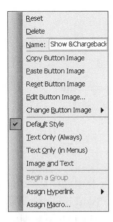

The shortcut menu is used for customizing both menu commands and toolbar buttons. Table 19.6 describes the commands on the Modify Selection menu in Excel, PowerPoint, and Word.

TABLE 19.6: MENU ITEM OPTIONS

OPTION	DESCRIPTION
Reset	Restores the original menu command text or button image
Delete	Removes the menu item or button
Interface Options	
Name	Command name, displayed on menus
Copy Button Image	Copies the button image to the Clipboard
Paste Button Image	Pastes the button image from the Clipboard
Reset Button Image	Restores the item's original button image
Edit Button Image	Opens the Button Editor so you can modify or customize the current button image
Change Button Image	Opens a palette of 42 compelling, well designed images that you can use (or not) on your custom buttons
Default Style	Applies the default style: for buttons, the button image is displayed; for menu items, the menu text and the button image are both displayed
Text Only (Always)	Uses the Name text as the caption in both menus and toolbars; omits the image in both settings
Text Only (In Menus)	Uses the Name text as the command caption on menus only
Image and Text	Uses the button image and text on both menus and toolbars
Begin a Group	Adds a separator to group commands on a menu or toolbar

Continued on next page

Table 19.6: Menu Item Options *(continued)*

Option	Description
Action Options	
Assign Hyperlink	Inserts an image or opens a document
Assign Macro	Chooses a macro for this button (Excel only)

5. Choose Assign Macro from the Modify Selection menu to open the Assign Macro dialog box, shown in Figure 19.12. In the Macros In drop-down list in Excel, choose This Workbook for a local macro or Personal Macro Workbook to assign a global macro. Select the macro from the list and click OK to assign the macro to the command.

FIGURE 19.12

Select the appropriate workbook in the Assign Macro dialog box and then select the macro to assign to the menu item.

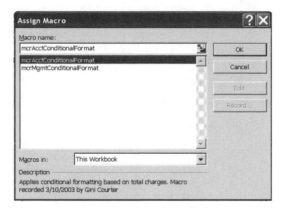

If you rename a macro that's assigned to a menu item or toolbar button, you must return to the Assign Macro dialog box and assign the macro using its new name.

Don't close the Customize dialog box yet. See "Modifying a Custom Command" (following the next section) to finish the command.

Adding Custom Commands in Word

There's one Word feature that we really hope will be added to Excel at some point: toolbars and menus are automatically customized for each document, which makes it very easy to create local menus and toolbars. When you add a local macro to a toolbar or menu, it is added to the document's command bars. Global macros are added to the default toolbars.

Follow these steps to add a custom command in Word:

1. Right-click any menu or toolbar and choose Customize, or choose View ➢ Toolbars ➢ Customize, or choose Tools ➢ Customize to open the dialog box.

2. On the Commands tab, choose Macros in the Categories list to display macros, as shown in Figure 19.13.

FIGURE 19.13

The Word Customize dialog box lists specific macros.

3. In the Save In drop-down list, choose the current workbook to see all local and global macros, or Normal to see global macros only. Global macros have the Normal prefix; local macros are prefixed with Project.

4. To create a custom menu item, drag the Macro from the Customize dialog box. Point to the menu that you want to add the item to and wait for the menu to open. After the menu opens, drop the Macro in place on the menu.

See the section "Modifying a Custom Command" to finish the button or menu item.

Adding a Custom Command in PowerPoint

There's only one difference between adding commands in PowerPoint and Word: PowerPoint has no default template, so all the macros are local macros. On the other hand, the built-in toolbars and menus are opened with every presentation, so they are global. If you add macros to the default toolbars and menu, users will click buttons that don't do anything.

Here's the PowerPoint strategy: put buttons on custom toolbars that you can turn on with a template or presentation, or use ActiveX command buttons, discussed later in this chapter. Don't add anything to the menus unless you want to create an alternative menu system and turn it on and off with VB code.

To add a command to a custom toolbar, drag the command from the Customize dialog box and drop it on the toolbar. Here's our custom toolbar for the ABC Theater template:

MODIFYING A CUSTOM COMMAND

Whether you added your macro to a toolbar or menu, you'll want to change some of its properties.

Changing the Command Name

When you assign a macro to a command, the macro's name is used as the menu and ScreenTip text (except in Excel, which uses Custom Menu Item or Custom Button as the names). To modify the name, open the Customize dialog box if it is not open. Select the button or menu item, then click the Modify Selection button or right-click and open the shortcut menu. In the Name text box, enter or edit the text to appear when the command is placed on a menu (see Figure 19.11). Within a menu, each command must use a different letter as an accelerator, and the letters are not case sensitive. To designate a letter as the keyboard accelerator, precede it with the ampersand symbol (&). When the menu is displayed, the accelerator letter is underlined. Enter a name even if you're only creating a toolbar button. For macro buttons, the Name is used as the button's ScreenTip.

Choosing a Button Image

Choose Change Button Image from the shortcut menu to open a palette of button images. Select an image to assign it to the command:

Editing a Button Image

Select an image and then choose Edit Button Image from the shortcut menu to Edit the image.

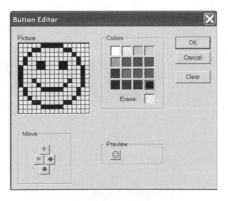

When you are finished customizing the command, the command text, and command image, close the Customize dialog box. Test the button or menu item.

Hyperlinks are used to navigate within and between documents. You can also assign a hyperlink to a menu item or toolbar button to do the following:

◆ open any document that has an assigned application installed on the computer

◆ launch the default browser and open an HTML document

◆ create a new document

◆ send an e-mail

◆ insert an image

When you assign a hyperlink to a button, the hyperlink address (URL or file path) is displayed as the ScreenTip.

To assign a hyperlink that opens a file, creates a new document, or opens an e-mail message, choose Assign Hyperlink ➢ Open from the shortcut menu to display the Assign Hyperlink: Open dialog box.

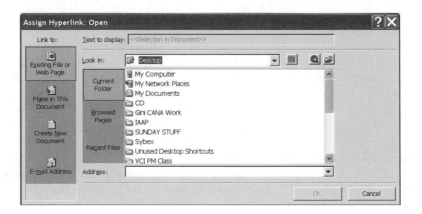

In the Link To bar, choose Existing File or Web Page, Create New Document, or E-mail Address. Or, you can assign a hyperlink to a command to make it easy for users to insert frequently used images like logos. On the shortcut menu, choose Assign Hyperlink ➢ Insert Picture to open the Assign Hyperlink: Insert Picture dialog. Browse to select the image file and then click OK to create the assignment.

See Chapter 11 for more information on hyperlinks.

CREATING A NEW MENU

Windows users like menus. If a user can't remember where to find a command, they often start with File and open each menu in turn, hoping to locate the lost command. If you're adding a number of macros to a worksheet, for example, take advantage of this frequently observed user behavior: create a new menu and add the macros to the menu.

In Windows applications, if the menu bar includes Window and Help menus, those appear at the right end of the menu bar. Your new menu should be added directly to the left of the Window menu. Follow these steps to add a new menu, which you can then populate with macros:

1. Right-click any toolbar or menu and choose Customize to open the Customize dialog box.

2. On the Commands page, choose New Menu in the Categories list.

3. Drag the New Menu command from the Commands window and drop it before the Window command on the menu bar.

4. Click the Modify Selection button in the Customize dialog box or right-click the command and open the shortcut menu.

5. In the Name text box, enter a name for the menu. Type the ampersand symbol in front of the letter that will be used with the Alt key to open the menu. The letter does not have to be the first letter of the word, and cannot duplicate those already used: F for File, E for Edit, and so on.

Add commands to the custom menu as you would to the built-in menus.

Running a Macro from a Button

In the interest of full disclosure, we'll start by noting that some developers believe that all commands belong on a toolbar or menu, and discourage the use of form-style buttons in the user interface. And not many people will argue passionately for the other side in this argument. However, there are reasons you might choose to use form buttons or ActiveX buttons, particularly with local macros.

Developers who are using ActiveX command buttons in Excel might choose to use form buttons on a chart sheet because chart sheets don't support ActiveX controls.

Users who don't want to deal with Visual Basic code to hide and display custom toolbars in Excel might choose form buttons because they are easy to create and modify.

In PowerPoint, commands added to a menu or toolbar appear in all presentations, even presentations the macros aren't stored in. The ActiveX buttons used to automate PowerPoint appear in the active presentation only.

NOTE *You'll find a comparison of ActiveX and Form controls in Chapter 16.*

ADDING FORM BUTTONS IN EXCEL

To access the form controls, open the Form toolbar (View ➤ Toolbars ➤ Forms). Click the Button control, then click or drag in the worksheet to create the form button. When you release the mouse button, the Assign Macro dialog box automatically opens. Choose a macro from the Macros list and click OK to assign the macro, or click the Record button to begin recording a macro to assign to the form button.

To edit the button name, drag the button text to select it and begin typing. If you have moved away from the button, you might need to right-click, select Edit Text and then drag the button text to insert or delete text. Move and resize the button as you would any object. You might need to select the Edit Text mode here again. If you do so, be sure to select Exit Edit Text when you're finished. To change other button properties, right-click the button and choose Format Control from the shortcut menu to open the Format Control dialog box shown in Figure 19.14.

FIGURE 19.14

Set button options in the Format Control dialog box.

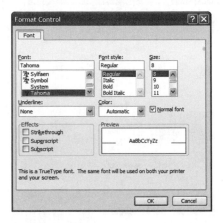

Pay particular attention to the Properties page. These settings determine whether the button will print as part of the worksheet and how the button behaves when a user resizes or hides the column or row that the button is positioned in. When you have finished formatting the button control, close the dialog box and click somewhere else in the worksheet to deselect the form button.

When the button isn't selected, clicking the button fires up the macro. To edit the button control's properties, select the button by right-clicking. To change the button text, right-click the button and then press Esc to close the menu but leave the button selected.

ADDING CONTROL BUTTONS IN POWERPOINT

In some previous versions of PowerPoint, custom commands included the path to open the presentation that contained the item's macro. When a user clicked the button or chose the menu item, PowerPoint fired up the presentation in the background and ran the macro. New concerns about security make this a bad idea. In Office 2003, PowerPoint will find and run macros from any open presentation, but won't open a presentation when a user executes a command. The easiest way to make sure commands are available always and only when a particular presentation or template is open is to add command buttons to the presentation. There's one disadvantage: command buttons are only enabled in Slide Show view. Users must run the presentation to use the buttons.

In this example, we'll add the buttons for mcrAcctConditionalFormat and mcrMgmtConditionalFormat to the first slide in the ABC Theater template. The buttons and macros will appear in every presentation based on the template.

To add a command button to a presentation:

1. Open the presentation or template. In Normal view, switch to the slide that will hold the buttons. Most developers put buttons that affect the entire presentation on either the first or last slide of the presentation and hide the slide.

2. Right-click any toolbar and choose Control Toolbox to open the toolbar, shown in Figure 19.15.

FIGURE 19.15

Use the command button from the ActiveX Control Toolbox to automate PowerPoint.

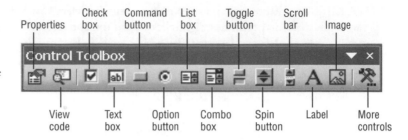

3. Click the Command Button icon.

4. Click in the slide to drop a default button, or drag to size the button.

5. Right-click the button to open the shortcut menu.

6. Choose Properties to open the button's Properties list.

7. Double-click the Name property and change the default name to a name prefixed with cmd (for command button) that describes what the button will do.

8. Right-click the button again and choose View Code to open the presentation's VBA project in the VB Editor.

Two stubs—the start and end of the code that will run when the button is clicked—appear in the code window.

```
Private Sub cmdBlueBackground_Click()

End Sub
```

9. In the Project Explorer, double-click the module that contains your macro(s).

10. Select the code that you want the button to run. Do not select the Sub and End Sub lines of the macro.

11. Copy the selection.

12. In the Project Explorer, double-click the slide with the button.

13. Click between the Private Sub and End Sub lines and paste the code lines.

14. Choose File ➢ Close and return to Microsoft PowerPoint.

15. Right-click the button and choose CommandButton Object ➢ Edit from the menu to change the text that appears on the button.

16. Edit the text.

Other formatting is done in the button's Properties, including font color and font, button color (back color), and button style.

17. When you're finished formatting the button, close the Properties window.

To test the button, press F5 to start the slide show. Click the button to run the macro code.

The lack of a default template makes PowerPoint the most challenging application for macros. Global menus and toolbars require you to think globally. See the sidebar below for another way we could add our macros to the interface.

TURNING A PRESENTATION INTO AN ADD-IN

If you have macros that should be available to all PowerPoint presentations, there's an elegant way to do it: create a PowerPoint add-in (like the Solver add-in in Excel) that holds the macros. Once installed, add-ins load whenever PowerPoint is launched.

For more information, visit the Microsoft Developer's Network site: `http://msdn.microsoft.com` and search for **PowerPoint add-in**.

Appendix: Speech and Handwriting Recognition Tools

In the dawning years of the twenty-first century, computers are not quite as advanced as Arthur C. Clarke dreamed in *2001: A Space Odyssey*. We can't yet interact with them as if they were human. Don't let that discourage you, however. With Office 2003's speech and handwriting recognition tools, you can issue verbal commands to your software and dictate documents to your own personal electronic transcriptionist. The Speech Recognition System works in Word, Excel, PowerPoint, Outlook, Access, and even FrontPage. While it may still be a far cry from Clarke's vision of Hal, a computer with a little too much personality for most people's taste, these tools add an entirely new dimension to office productivity.

In this appendix, we'll show you how to set up the speech and handwriting recognition tools and how to use them most effectively. We'll point out their strengths and weaknesses and give you some tips for avoiding their pitfalls. We'll also let you know what hardware you'll need to make this new software worthwhile.

Preparing to Use Office 2003's Speech Recognition Tools

Speech recognition has come a long way in the last five years. Certainly, software developments have played a part in speech recognition's move into the mainstream. But it's hardware advancements that have really tipped the scales. The availability of more memory, faster processors, better microphones, and larger hard drives are all players in the speech recognition equation. Before deciding whether you want to delve into this new technology, take a look at the following hardware and software requirements recommended by Microsoft:

- A high-quality close-talk (headset) microphone with gain adjustment support (USB preferred)
- A 400MHz or faster computer
- 128MB or more of memory
- Windows 2000 with Service Pack 3 or Windows XP or later
- Microsoft Internet Explorer 5.01 or later

NOTE   *Gain adjustment support is a feature in microphones that filters out background noises to clarify your input for use by the speech recognition software.*

You also need a good-quality sound card—read the sidebar "Can a Different Microphone Help Me Improve Recognition Accuracy" for suggestions. Most sound cards are designed primarily for quality output. Only recently have sound cards and soundboards been designed to handle input to complement speech and voice recognition software.

NOTE   *Speech recognition software is software that translates spoken words into typed text. Voice recognition hardware and software identifies individual voice patterns and is primarily designed for security purposes.*

Be aware that the hardware requirements for processor speed and RAM are minimum requirements. Although we have used speech recognition on 128MB of RAM and a slower processor, it is less than ideal. In fact, you may even find it interfering with speed and responsiveness when you run other software. If you can afford to upgrade to 196MB of RAM, you'll find it makes a drastic difference.

After you've selected and installed the sound card and microphone (if you didn't have one or both of these already installed), you're just two short steps away from speaking your text and commands:

1. Set up your microphone with the Microphone Wizard (less than 5 minutes).

2. Create speech files with the Voice Training Wizard (less than 20 minutes).

CAN A DIFFERENT MICROPHONE HELP ME IMPROVE RECOGNITION ACCURACY?

When selecting a microphone, USB microphones with gain adjustment support are clearly the best choice. You can choose from desktop, headset, collar, and digital microphones. If you go with a headset or collar, choose one that fits you well and is comfortable so that the microphone stays positioned near your mouth at all times—off to the side of your mouth is usually best. A microphone with a swivel arm makes it easy to move it out of the way and return it to the same position when you are ready to dictate. If you choose a desktop model, be sure you can maintain a completely quiet background and can keep it in the same place each time you dictate. Moving it around could affect accuracy, especially if the distance changes. Finding quality microphones for under $50 that are especially designed for speech recognition is becoming easier. The key is to not just settle for the microphone that came with your computer; chances are it will not do the job for you. Invest a few dollars and you'll have a lot more fun with Speech.

Setting Up Your Microphone

Locate the microphone and headphone jacks on your computer and plug in your microphone. If you have a USB microphone, plug it into the USB port. You can run the Microphone Wizard from any Office application. Choose Tools ➢ Speech from the menu bar. If Speech is not already installed, Office prompts you to install it and then prompts you to configure it and begin training.

If Speech is already installed, the Language bar appears, floating somewhere over the application window.

NOTE   Options on the Language bar may vary depending on the options you've installed and what is currently active. For more about Language bar options, see "Working with the Language Bar" later in this appendix.

If the microphone has not been previously set up, you are prompted to run the Microphone Wizard. The wizard adjusts the volume from your microphone so that it works well with the Office applications. Even if the microphone has been set up before, we recommend running it again to adjust its settings to your preferences. If you are not prompted for the Microphone Wizard, choose Tools ➤ Options from the Language bar to open the Speech Input Settings. Select Advanced Speech to open the Speech Properties dialog box.

Click the Configure Microphone button in the Speech Properties dialog box to start the Microphone Wizard. Follow the instructions in the wizard to configure your microphone for optimal use with Microsoft Office 2003.

NOTE   If you're using your headset microphone and laptop in an airport rather than your office, or anytime you go from a noisier or quieter environment to another, it's a good idea to invest a few minutes and run the wizard again to ensure the best recognition.

Training the Speech Recognition System

After the microphone is configured, you will use the microphone to train the Speech Recognition System. Train the system in the environment where you intend to use it: If you're going to use it in your office, train the system in your office with the normal level of office noise. The first time you set up your microphone, the voice training process starts automatically as soon as your microphone is configured. If you need to start it manually, choose Tools ➤ Training on the Language bar to create a user profile and begin training the system to recognize the way you pronounce words. You read the text that's displayed in the dialog box, and the Speech Recognition System highlights each word as it recognizes it, as shown in Figure A.1. Your first training session will probably take around 20 minutes. You can pause at any point and continue later, but we don't recommend it. If you stop prior to the end of the session, you need to start at the beginning the next time you wish to train.

FIGURE A.1

As you read the session text, each recognized word is highlighted by the Speech Recognition System.

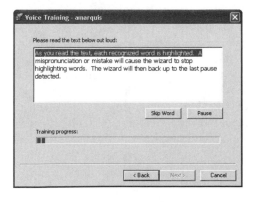

When you've completed the introductory training session, your speech settings are saved in a speech profile. The system keeps a separate profile for each user. After you've worked with the Speech Recognition System in Office 2003 applications for a little while, we suggest going back for more training using other materials to increase recognition. Just choose Tools ➤ Training on the Language bar and choose one of the sessions from the list.

NOTE *When you complete the initial training, Office plays a short training video to help you get started. It's worth seeing just to hear how Microsoft suggests using the tools.*

Using the Speech Recognition System

You can use the Speech Recognition System in Office 2003 in three ways:

◆ Dictate or correct text

◆ Issue voice commands to activate buttons, menu commands, and dialog boxes

◆ Play back printed text from a document

Dictating in Office 2003

To use the dictation or voice command features of Office 2003, open the Tools menu on any application and choose Speech. This activates the Language bar.

NOTE *If you've never used speech recognition software before, we suggest you start dictating in the application in which you feel most comfortable. For most people, that is Word.*

Click the Microphone button on the Language bar to turn the microphone on, if it is not already active. When the microphone is active, you can see additional options on the Language bar for Dictation and Voice Command. To the right of Voice Command is a message box that displays messages as you dictate. Some messages, such as Too Soft, let you know to speak up. When you are in Voice Command mode, this message box displays the last recognized command or suggests more appropriate voice commands.

To begin dictating text, make sure the Dictation button is dark blue. If it is not, click it and then begin speaking to enter text in your document. Speak each word clearly, and speak the names of the punctuation marks (comma, period, question mark). When you want a new paragraph, say **New Paragraph**. When you first begin, don't worry about making corrections. Just keep dictating and get comfortable with developing an appropriate speed and rhythm. If you are getting good recognition, keep going and worry about editing later. Don't forget to speak punctuation marks.

In addition to punctuation marks, you can also use the commands listed in Table A.1 in Dictation mode.

TABLE A.1: COMMANDS YOU CAN SAY IN DICTATION MODE

YOU SAY	TO
New Line	Start text on the next line.
New Paragraph	Start a new paragraph.
Microphone Off	Turn the microphone off.
Tab	Press the Tab key once.
Shift Tab	Backspace a Tab.
Enter	Press the Enter key once.
Spelling Mode	Spell out the next word. You have to pause for a second after spelling out the word to switch back to normal Dictation mode.
Forcenum	Enter a number or symbol instead of spelling it out, such as 2 instead of *two*. Pause for a second after using this command so the system can revert to normal Dictation mode.

TIP   If you want to enter several numbers, dictate the numbers without the Forcenum command. Speech recognizes strings of numbers and enters them as numbers rather than text. It even formats phone numbers for you automatically.

You can dictate in any Office 2003 application. In Outlook, select the text box in an open form before you begin speaking. In Excel, cell navigation is part of dictation: precede the direction with the words **Go To, Go Up, Go Down, Go Left,** or **Go Right** and then indicate how many cells—**One Cell, Two Cells,** and so on.

When you are finished dictating or need to take a break, click the Microsoft button again to turn Speech off or say **Microphone Off**.

MAKING CORRECTIONS AND ENHANCING RECOGNITION

If the speech recognition system does not accurately recognize a word or string of words, select the words and click the Correction button on the Language toolbar to hear a recording of your dictation of the word or phrase (the Correction button is not displayed by default). Choose the correct words from the list of suggestions, or select and respeak the words. Remember, you can always use the mouse and keyboard to make corrections if the words you want are not in the list.

If you would like to add words to the speech dictionary to aid in recognition, you can add them individually or you can use the Speech tools to review a document and identify any words it does not know. This second option is particularly valuable if you have a document that contains a lot of words that are unique to your business. To add words individually, follow these steps:

1. Click Tools on the Language bar.
2. Click Add/Delete Words to open the Add/Delete Words dialog box.

3. Select a word from the list or enter your own word.

4. Click Record Pronunciation and say the word correctly.

5. Repeat steps 3 and 4 until you have added all the words you want to add.

6. You may also want to delete a word that was automatically added to the list from your documents. Select the word and click Delete.

7. Click Close when you are finished adding and deleting words.

To review an entire Word document for words that are not in the speech dictionary, choose Tools ➤ Learn From Document. When the document has been reviewed, a Learn From Document dialog box appears with the list of words it identified. Select and delete words you don't want to add. Click Add All to add the rest of the words. If you'd like to add pronunciation, follow the steps listed above to access the Add/Delete Words dialog box.

After you've done all you can to enhance recognition using these tools and you are still having recognition problems, return to the training tool (choose Tools ➤ Options on the Language bar). The more you train, the better recognition should become.

Giving Voice Commands in Office 2003

You can switch from dictating text that you want recognized to giving voice commands to operate the application by activating the microphone and clicking the Voice Command button on the Language bar. You can use voice commands to move the insertion point within a document, to activate a toolbar button or a menu, and to input responses in a dialog box.

For example, suppose you want to designate specific page setup options for a document. You want your document to have landscape orientation with 1-inch left and right margins on 11.5-inch × 8.5-inch paper with a different first page header.

NOTE   *If you use the metric system, you might choose 2.54-centimeter left and right margins on 29.7-centimeter by 21-centimeter paper.*

Use your voice to make these setting changes:

1. Activate the microphone if it is not already on. Say **Voice Command** to switch to Voice Command mode.

2. Say **File** to open the File menu.

3. Say **Page Setup** to open the Page Setup dialog box.

4. Say **Margins** to select the Margins tab.

5. Say **Left** to set the left margin—the insertion point should move into the Left Margin text box.

6. Say **Down Arrow, Down Arrow, Down Arrow** to reduce the left margin to 1 inch (or, if using metric, make your own adjustments).

7. Say **Tab** to move the insertion point to the Right Margin text box.

8. Say **Down Arrow, Down Arrow, Down Arrow** to reduce the margin to 1 inch.

9. Say **Paper** to switch to the Paper tab.

10. Say **Paper Size** to open the Paper Size drop-down list.

11. Say **Legal** to select Legal from the drop-down list.

12. Say **Layout** to switch to the Layout tab.

13. Say **Different First Page** to select the Different First Page check box.

14. Say **OK** to accept the changes and close the dialog box.

When you are dictating or entering text, you can use voice commands to move the insertion point around your document. Tables A.2, A.3, and A.4 show voice commands that are available in Word 2003. For a list of more voice commands, look up Commands in Language Bar Help.

TABLE A.2: WORD 2003 BASIC FORMATTING COMMANDS

SAY	TO
New line	Start text on the next line
New paragraph	Start a new paragraph
Microphone	Turn the microphone off
Tab	Press the TAB key once
Enter	Press the ENTER key once
Delete	Delete the selected text or the last recognized phrase
Undo	Undo the last action
Cut	Delete and copy the selected text to the Clipboard
Copy	Copy the selected text to the Clipboard
Paste	Paste the text into the Clipboard at the insertion point
Space	Insert a space at the insertion point
Backspace	Delete the character to the left of the insertion point
Next cell	Move the insertion point one cell to the right

TABLE A.3: WORD 2003 SELECTION COMMANDS

SAY	TO
Select word or Select phrase	Select the word or phrase given
Select word	Select the last recognized word
Unselect that	Unselect the currently selected text

TABLE A.4: WORD 2003 CORRECTION COMMANDS

SAY	TO
Correct word or Correct phrase	Delete the word or phrase given
Correction	Delete the selected text or the last recognized phrase
Correct that	Delete the last recognized word or phrase
Insert after word or Insert after phrase	Move the insertion point to right of the word or phrase given
Insert before word or Insert before phrase	Move the insertion point to left of the word or phrase given
Scratch that	Delete the last recognized phrase
Delete that	Delete the last recognized phrase

NOTE   If you are having trouble using a particular voice command, minimize the application you are working in or switch to another application and then switch back to the application and try it again. Chances are it will work better after this little kick.

Some people think that speech and handwriting recognition tools are ways to avoid learning how to use applications. However, to use these tools effectively in Office, you must first know how to use the application you want to work in or you will not know how to use the voice commands. Speech and handwriting will help people who don't know how or are unable to type, but those users still have to learn how an application works before they can use it.

Tweaking the Speech Recognition System

Speech recognition is a trade-off between recognition speed and accuracy. Words are recognized in context; the more surrounding words the system has to examine, the more likely it is to determine which word you actually spoke. The more words the system examines, the longer it takes to display your dictated text on screen.

If the lag between dictation and display is too long, or if the percentage of incorrectly recognized words is too high, you can change the recognition/accuracy settings to improve recognition or speed. You can also adjust the Rejection Rate setting if the system frequently ignores menu commands in Voice Command mode.

To access the Speech Recognition System settings, choose Tools ➢ Options from the Language bar menu and click the Advanced Speech button. In the Speech Properties dialog box (see Figure A.2), select your profile, and then click the Settings button to open the Recognition Profile Settings dialog box, shown in Figure A.3. Here you can adjust Pronunciation Sensitivity and the Accuracy vs. Recognition Response Time. If you set the sensitivity too high, you may find that it's trying to translate all of your *ums* and mumbles, so keep this setting toward the center. If you have a fast processor and lots of memory, increase the accuracy levels for the best recognition. To have the system automatically adjust and learn from your speech patterns as you are dictating, make sure the Background Adaptation check box is selected.

FIGURE A.2

In the Speech Properties dialog box, you can create new profiles and augment your speech training.

FIGURE A.3

Use the settings in the Recognition Profile Settings dialog box to tweak the performance of the Speech Recognition System.

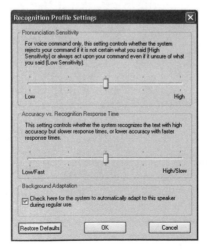

Creating a New Profile on Your Computer

Speech recognition files are specific to each person's voice and should not be shared. Another user who wants to use speech on the same computer needs to set up an additional speech profile. You may also find it useful to have a different profile at work and at home if the noise level is drastically different. To set up a user profile, choose Tools ➤ Options on the Language bar, click Advanced Speech to open the Speech Properties dialog box (see Figure A.2). Click the New button on the Speech Recognition tab of the Speech Properties dialog box. The Profile Wizard guides you through the steps to create another user profile.

After you create a user profile, you can select the profile you want to use from the Speech Properties dialog box or from the Tools button on the Language bar. Choose Current User from the Tools menu on the Language bar to verify the current user or select a different one.

Removing Speech Recognition Services

If you've given Speech a fair trial and you decide that it just isn't for you (or for your computer), you can remove Speech Recognition from Office 2003 without uninstalling the entire feature from your computer. To remove the service, right-click the Language bar and choose Settings to open the Text Services and Input Languages dialog box shown in Figure A.4. Select Speech Recognition in the Installed Services list and click Remove. After it is removed, it no longer loads with your software and as a result frees up any memory it was using. If you decide you want the speech service back, just reverse the process, clicking Add in the Installed Services list.

To completely uninstall the speech recognition service from your computer, use Add/Remove Programs in the Control Panel.

NOTE   If you have text services installed for more than one language, select the language first from the Default Input Language drop-down list and then remove the speech text service.

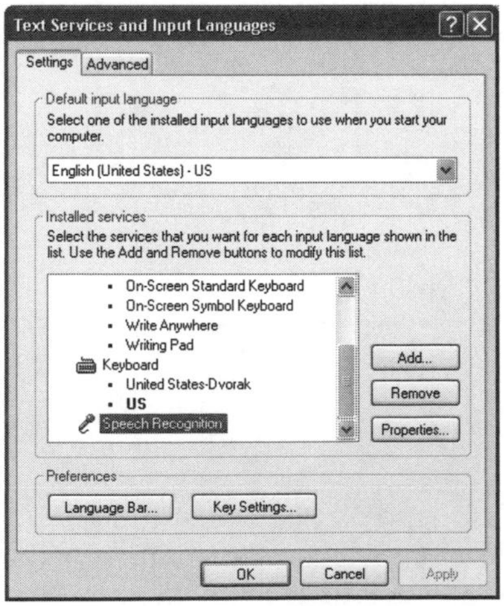

FIGURE A.4

Temporarily remove Speech Recognition from Office 2003 with the Text Services dialog box.

Working with the Language Bar

The Language bar is a different kind of Office toolbar. Rather than docking in the application window, the Language bar floats above it. You can move the Language bar around the application window by pointing to the left edge—the pointer becomes a four-header arrow so you can drag it where you want it.

To control the Language bar, right-click anywhere on it for a shortcut menu of options. These are:

Minimize Positions the Language bar as a series of icons to the left of the system tray on the Windows task bar. You can activate Microphone, change Speech Tools, and activate and use Handwriting Tools from the buttons on the task bar. Click the Restore button to make the Language bar visible again.

Transparency Makes the Language bar turn clear when not in use so as not to obscure whatever is beneath it. Can be toggled on and off.

Text Labels Toggles between showing text and icons on the Language bar buttons.

Additional Icons In Taskbar Adds a microphone, handwriting, and other icons to the Taskbar when the Language bar is minimized.

Settings Takes you to the Text Services dialog box.

Close The Language bar Shuts down the Language bar. To reactivate, choose Tools ➤ Speech.

You can also control which buttons appear on the Language bar by clicking the Options button (the small downward-pointing arrow on the right end of the bar). Select the buttons you would like to have available on the Language bar from the list that appears.

MASTERING THE OPPORTUNITIES: USING TEXT TO SPEECH WITH EXCEL

Text To Speech is a feature that reads back to you text you have entered into a document. Designed as one of Microsoft's Accessibility features, Text To Speech is only available in Excel. Microsoft is working hard to develop software that is accessible to people with disabilities, so we expect that this feature will be expanded in future releases.

Before using the Text To Speech feature, you first want to visit the Speech Engine settings in the Windows Control Panel, available by clicking the Speech icon. On the Text To Speech tab, you can choose from the Voice Selection drop-down list whether you'd like to have LH Michael, LH Michelle, or Microsoft Sam reading to you. Be sure to have your headset or speakers on so you can preview both of the voices before making this momentous choice. You can also adjust the speed at which your choice speaks to you, so if you are from New York you can have it read faster and if you're from New Orleans you can slow it down. You are now ready to activate Text To Speech. To use the feature, start Excel and choose Tools ➤ Speech ➤ Show Text To Speech Toolbar.

Continued on next page

> **MASTERING THE OPPORTUNITIES: USING TEXT TO SPEECH WITH EXCEL** *(continued)*
>
> To start reading from a particular position on the worksheet, click that cell and then click the Speak Cells button on the Text To Speech toolbar. By default, the selected voice (Michael, Michelle, or Sam) reads across the rows until she comes to the last cell of the worksheet and then returns to column A. Click the Stop Speaking button to stop the operation. To change directions and have her read down the column rather than across the row, click the By Columns button. If you'd like Michelle to speak entries as you enter them, click the Speak On Enter button. Just close the toolbar when you are finished with the Text To Speech tools.

Handwriting Recognition

Handwriting recognition offers a wealth of opportunity for new types of computers. No longer tying us to a keyboard, new computing devices will offer the same freedom that legal pads and steno books have given us for years. Already, personal digital assistants (PDAs) and handheld computers such as Palms and Pocket PCs offer handwriting recognition as the primary input method. Tablet computers, offering pen and keyboard data entry, are becoming as common as traditional laptop computers. Handwriting recognition in Office 2003 brings us one step closer to throwing out our keyboards and giving laptop and desktop users more natural and flexible computing options.

The handwriting tools in Office 2003 include soft keyboards, on-screen drawing, and actual handwriting recognition.

NOTE   Tablet PCs comes with their own handwriting recognition engine and don't rely on the handwriting recognition in Office 2003.

Using On-Screen Keyboards

As part of the set of Handwriting tools, Office 2003 offers two on-screen keyboards: Standard and Symbol. The Standard keyboard, shown in Figure A.5, is a traditional QWERTY keyboard that floats on the screen. The Symbol keyboard, shown in Figure A.6, is a collection of language symbols for written languages other than English. The Standard keyboard option offers little advantage to the desktop or laptop user—it is designed primarily for installations where a keyboard isn't available. The Symbol keyboard, however, used in conjunction with a traditional keyboard, can be an effective shortcut for users who have to enter text in languages that require keys not readily available on the QWERTY keyboard.

FIGURE A.5

The Standard keyboard offers handheld computer users a familiar input method.

FIGURE A.6

The Symbol keyboard gives ready access to characters that are not available on the QWERTY keyboard.

To activate either the Standard or Symbol soft keyboards, click the Handwriting button on the Language bar to select the keyboard you want to use.

If you would like to add the keyboard to the Language bar so you can easily turn it on and off, click the Options button at the right end of the Language bar (the small black arrow) and choose On Screen Keyboard from the menu. With this option turned on, whatever handwriting item you select in the Handwriting menu appears on the toolbar.

To enter text on the screen, either click the keys on the on-screen keyboard with a mouse pointer or touch them with a pen/stylus. When you want to turn the keyboard off, click the Close button on the keyboard (or the Handwriting button on the Language bar).

Drawing On-Screen

The Drawing Pad is designed to make it easy to insert a quick drawing into a document. Although you have many more tools available to you using the Drawing toolbar, the Drawing Pad offers simplicity and flexibility for alternative computer devices. To activate the Drawing Pad, click Handwriting on the Language bar and choose Drawing Pad. This opens the Drawing Pad shown in Figure A.7.

FIGURE A.7

Use the Drawing Pad to create and insert simple drawings into a document.

NOTE   *If the Drawing Pad button doesn't appear on the Language bar, click the Language bar's Option button and select Microsoft Handwriting Item from the list of button choices.*

To use the Drawing Pad, just point and draw. You don't have any pen or brush choices, but you can change the width and color of the lines you draw. Click the Options button in the title bar of the Drawing Pad to open the Draw Options dialog box, shown in Figure A.8. You must return to the Draw Options dialog box every time you want to change pen color or width.

FIGURE A.8

Change the pen color and width and also the toolbar layout of the Drawing Pad in the Draw Options dialog box.

a　　　　b　　　　c　　　　d

To clear the Drawing Pad window, click the Clear button (*a* above) on the Drawing Pad toolbar. To erase your last stroke, click the Remove Last Stroke button (*b*).

When you are ready to insert your masterpiece into your document, click the Insert Drawing button (*c*).

If you decide it needs a little more work in another application, click the Copy To Clipboard button (*d*). You can then paste your drawing into Microsoft Paint or a drawing application to apply the finishing touches.

Using Handwriting to Input Text

Handwriting recognition in Office 2003 is amazingly accurate even if all you have available to you is your trustworthy mouse. Obviously, handwriting tablets will become more common as more people experience the ease with which Office converts even the most illegible scrawl into typed text. Figure A.9 shows an example of writing in Office 2003.

To activate handwriting, click Handwriting on the Language bar and then choose Writing Pad. This opens the Writing Pad shown in Figure A.9.

FIGURE A.9

Office 2003 can accurately convert even this scrawl into typed text—it truly is amazing!

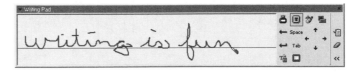

You have the option of writing so that it is automatically converted into text. You can also leave it as handwriting if, for example, you want to sign a letter.

To use automatic handwriting recognition, click the Text button on the Writing Pad. You can choose to print or use cursive on the Writing Pad. In either case, your writing is automatically transcribed when you pause for more than a second or two (a much more common occurrence when you print, so be prepared).

To write using the mouse, hold the mouse button down to write; release it to move to the next word. It definitely takes a little work to get used to writing this way, but with a little practice, you'll do fine.

NOTE *If you have access to a graphics tablet (as you might use with 3-D or Computer-Aided Drafting software), you will find handwriting a much more pleasant experience. You will also find new tablet-PCs and handwriting tablets available in your local or online computer store. If you have a laptop with a touchpad, you can purchase a pack of PDA styluses or a stylus pen and use the touchpad as your writing surface—depress the left touchpad button as you write. As far as tablets go, we've been impressed with the WACOM Graphire (*<www.wacom.com>*). The tablet comes with a cordless pen and mouse—you must use the mouse on the tablet—and a bunch of bundled software. Some of the software is unnecessary with the handwriting and drawing features in Office 2003, but they still give you some cool toys to play with and a solid well-made tablet all for under $100.*

 If you would prefer to transfer your handwriting without having it transcribed, click the Ink button on the Writing Pad. Be sure to write directly above the line on the Writing Pad to have your writing appear inline with the text. Use this option to add a real signature to an e-mail or letter.

The text you write appears in whatever size font you have selected. If you're working in a 10-point font, then the handwriting appears very small. If you would like to format the handwriting, select it just as you would any other text and change the text size, color, and alignment or even add bold, italics, and underline.

CORRECTING YOUR HANDWRITING

Whether you are using the Ink or Text tools to enter handwriting, you can correct mistakes that Office makes or that you make in the text. To correct transcribed text, right-click any word and select the correct word from the list of choices just as you would if the word were misspelled.

You can also select the erroneous word and click the Correction button on the Writing Pad to see a list of word alternatives.

If you want to correct handwriting itself, right-click the word and choose Ink Object and then choose either Alternate List or Recognize. If you choose Alternate List, Office displays a list of possible word choices. You can select a word from the list or click outside the list to retain the handwriting. If you choose Recognize or select an option from the list, Office converts the handwriting into typed text. If you want to make a correction and keep the handwriting, the only option is to rewrite it.

WRITING ANYWHERE ON THE SCREEN

If the lined page of the Writing Pad restricts your style, you can choose Write Anywhere from the Handwriting menu on the Speech toolbar. With Write Anywhere, you are free to enter handwriting anywhere on the screen using Ink or Text mode. The Writing Anywhere toolbar, shown in Figure A.10, gives you control over your handwriting entries, even providing access to other writing tools.

FIGURE A.10

Activate the Write Anywhere toolbar to have easy access to handwriting tools anytime you need them.

The most important thing to get used to when Write Anywhere is activated is that the mouse pointer acts differently. You can drag the mouse pointer to select text that you input using Handwriting—it first draws a line through the text and then selects it—but you must use other selection methods such as double-clicking and keyboard commands to select text you type.

If you need to use the mouse pointer without drawing, click the Write Anywhere button on the Speech toolbar or click the Close button on the Write Anywhere toolbar. This deactivates Write Anywhere and gives back keyboard control. Click Write Anywhere on the Speech toolbar, if available, or click Handwriting ➤ Write Anywhere if it is not.

Finding Help for Speech and Handwriting Recognition

Although you'll find some help files in each application, the general help files on speech and handwriting recognition are available on the Language bar. Click the yellow question mark Help button on the Language bar and choose Language bar Help (If the Help button does not appear on the Language bar, click the down-arrow on the right of the Language bar and select Help). Double-click Language Bar in the Contents tab and make your selection for the help you'd like.

Speech and Handwriting tools may have a way to go before they are perfect, but we think you'll be amazed at the level of accuracy and the ease of use you'll find with these tools.

Index

Note to the Reader: Throughout this index, **boldfaced** page numbers indicate primary discussions of a topic. *Italicized* page numbers indicate illustrations.

X

Z